Dodge Aries Plymouth Reliant Automotive Repair Manual

D1608435

by Larry Warren
and John H Haynes Member of the Guild of Motoring Writers

Models covered

2-door, 4-door and Station Wagon
2.2L (135 cu in), 2.5L (153 cu in) and 2.6L (156 cu in)
engines with 4-speed, 5-speed and automatic transaxles

ISBN 1 85010 702 5

Haynes Publishing Group
Sparkford Nr Yeovil
Somerset BA22 7JJ England

Haynes North America, Inc
861 Lawrence Drive
Newbury Park
California 91320 USA

Acknowledgements

We are grateful for the help and cooperation of Chrysler Motors Corporation, USA, who supplied technical information, certain illustrations and vehicle photos, the Champion Spark Plug Company, who supplied the illustrations showing the various spark plug conditions and Holt Lloyd Ltd, suppliers of 'Turtle Wax', 'Dupli-color Holts' and other Holts products, who prepared the bodywork repair photographs used in this manual.

About this manual

Its purpose

The purpose of this manual is to help you get the best value from your vehicle. It can do so in several ways. It can help you decide what work must be done even if you choose to get it done by a dealer service department or a repair shop; it provides information and procedures for routine maintenance and servicing; and it offers diagnostic and repair procedures to follow when trouble occurs.

It is hoped that you will use the manual to tackle the work yourself. For many simpler jobs, doing it yourself may be quicker than arranging an appointment to get the vehicle into a shop and making the trips to leave it and pick it up. More importantly, a lot of money can be saved by avoiding the expense the shop must pass on to you to cover its labor and overhead costs. An added benefit is the sense of satisfaction and accomplishment that you feel after having done the job yourself.

Using the manual

The manual is divided into Chapters. Each Chapter is divided into numbered Sections, which are headed in bold type between horizontal lines. Each Section consists of consecutively numbered paragraphs.

The two types of illustrations used (figures and photographs), are referenced by a number preceding their captions. Figure reference numbers denote Chapter and numerical sequence in the Chapter; i.e. Fig. 12.4 means Chapter 12, figure number 4. Figure captions are followed by a Section number which ties the figure to a specific portion of the text. All photographs apply to the Chapter in which they appear, and the reference number pinpoints the pertinent Section and paragraph; i.e. 3.2 means Section 3, paragraph 2.

Procedures, once described in the text, are not normally repeated. When it is necessary to refer to another Chapter, the reference will be given as Chapter and Section number; i.e. Chapter 1/16. Cross references given without use of the word 'Chapter' apply to Sections and/or paragraphs in the same Chapter. For example, 'see Section 8' means in the same Chapter.

Reference to the left or right side of the vehicle is based on the assumption that one is sitting in the driver's seat facing forward.

Even though extreme care has been taken during the preparation of this manual, neither the publisher nor the author can accept responsibility for any errors in, or omissions from, the information given.

Introduction to the Dodge Aries and Plymouth Reliant

These vehicles, which make up the Chrysler Corporation K Car line, were introduced in the 1981 model year.

The cross mounted, four cylinder, overhead cam engine is available in 2.2 liter (135 cu in), 2.5 liter (153 cu in) or 2.6 liter (156 cu in) displacement. Power is transmitted through a four-speed or five-speed manual or a three-speed automatic transaxle to the front wheels by drive axles which feature constant velocity joints.

Steering is rack and pinion with power assist as an option. The braking system is vacuum assisted and features disc brakes at the front with self-adjusting drums at the rear.

The front suspension consists of a spring and strut assembly which connects to the steering knuckle and lower A-frame. Rear suspension is trailing link with a beam type axle, which is supported by springs and shock absorbers.

Two-door, four-door and station wagon body styles are available in a wide variety of trim levels.

Contents

Plymouth Reliant 4-door sedan

Dodge Aries station wagon

General dimensions and weights

Overall length
2-door and 4-door .... 176.0 in
Station Wagon .... 175.2 in

Overall height
2-door .... 52.4 in
4-door .... 52.7 in
Station wagon .... 52.8 in

Overall width .... 68.6 in

Wheelbase
1981 .... 99.6 in
1982 .... 99.9 in
1983 .... 100.1 in

Curb weight (base model)
2-door .... 2317 lbs
4-door .... 2323 lbs
Station wagon .... 2432 lbs

Buying parts

Replacement parts are available from many sources, which generally fall into one of two categories – authorized dealer parts departments and independent retail auto parts stores. Our advice concerning these parts is as follows:

Retail auto parts stores: Good auto parts stores will stock frequently needed components which wear out relatively fast, such as clutch components, exhaust systems, brake parts, tune-up parts, etc. These stores often supply new or reconditioned parts on an exchange basis, which can save a considerable amount of money. Discount auto parts stores are often very good places to buy materials and parts needed for general vehicle maintenance such as oil, grease, filters, spark plugs, belts, touch-up paint, bulbs, etc. They also usually sell tools and general accessories, have convenient hours, charge lower prices and can often be found not far from home.

Authorized dealer parts department: This is the best source for parts which are unique to the vehicle and not generally available elsewhere (such as major engine parts, transmission parts, trim pieces, etc.).

Warranty information: If the vehicle is still covered under warranty, be sure that any replacement parts purchased – regardless of the source – do not invalidate the warranty!

To be sure of obtaining the correct parts, have engine and chassis numbers available and, if possible, take the old parts along for positive identification.

Vehicle identification numbers

Modifications are a continuing and unpublicized process in vehicle manufacture. Since spare parts manuals and lists are compiled on a numerical basis, the individual vehicle numbers are essential to identify correctly the component required.

Vehicle identification number (VIN)

This very important identification number is located on a plate attached to the left top of the dashboard and can be easily seen while looking through the windshield from the outside of the vehicle. The VIN also appears on the vehicle safety certification label. It gives such valuable information as where and when the vehicle was manufactured, the year of manufacture and the body style.

Vehicle safety certification label

The vehicle safety certification label is located on the rear face of the driver's door. This label contains the VIN, gross vehicle weight and gross axle weight ratings and date of manufacture.

Engine identification number (EIN)

On 2.2L engines, the EIN is located at the rear of the block, just above the bellhousing. On 2.6L engines the EIN is found on the radiator side of the block, between the rear face and the core plug.

Engine serial number

The engine serial number is located directly below the engine identification number. On 2.6L engines the number is found on the rear (firewall) side of the block, next to the exhaust manifold stud.

Transaxle identification number (TIN)

The transaxle identification number is stamped on a boss located near the top of the transaxle housing.

Transaxle assembly part number

On automatic transaxles, the part number is stamped on the rear lower edge of the housing, just above the oil pan. The assembly part number on manual transaxles is found on a metal tag affixed to the front of the housing.

Production changes

Information reflecting the running changes made on these models during production is found on a stamped metal tag located on the radiator brace. Always include these numbers when ordering parts.

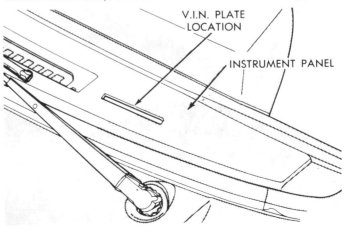

V.I.N. PLATE LOCATION

INSTRUMENT PANEL

The vehicle identification number is visible through the driver's side of the windshield

8

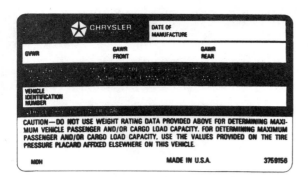

The vehicle safety certificate label is located on the rear edge of the driver's door

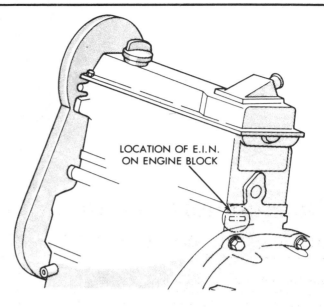

2.2L engine identification number (EIN) location

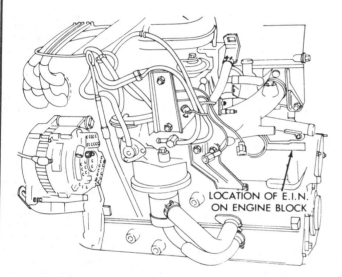

Engine identification number (EIN) location on 2.6L engine

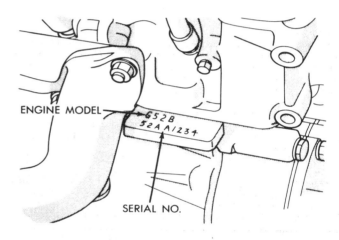

2.6L engine model and serial number location

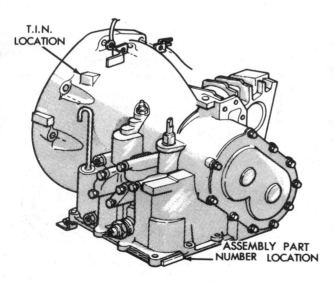

Automatic transaxle identification number (TIN) and assembly part number locations

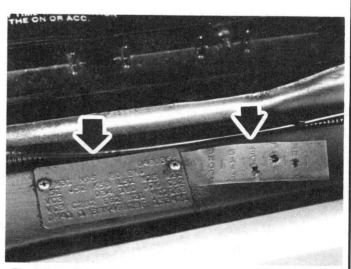

The information on these tags (arrows) reflects running changes made during production

Maintenance techniques, tools and working facilities

Maintenance techniques

There are a number of techniques involved in maintenance and repair that will be referred to throughout this manual. Application of these techniques will enable the home mechanic to be more efficient, better organized and capable of performing the various tasks properly, which will ensure that the repair job is thorough and complete.

Fasteners

Fasteners, are nuts, bolts, studs and screws used to hold two or more parts together. There are a few things to keep in mind when working with fasteners. Almost all of them use a locking device of some type; either a lock washer, locknut, locking tab or thread adhesive. All threaded fasteners should be clean and straight, with undamaged threads and undamaged corners on the hex head where the wrench fits. Develop the habit of replacing damaged nuts and bolts with new ones. Special locknuts with nylon or fiber inserts can only be used once. If they are removed, they lose their locking ability and must be replaced with new ones.

Rusted nuts and bolts should be treated with a penetrating fluid to ease removal and prevent breakage. Some mechanics use turpentine in a spout-type oil can, which works quite well. After applying the rust penetrant, let it "work" for a few minutes before trying to loosen the nut or bolt. Badly rusted fasteners may have to be chiseled or sawed off or removed with a special nut breaker, available at tool stores.

If a bolt or stud breaks off in an assembly, it can be drilled and removed with a special tool commonly available for this purpose. Most automotive machine shops can perform this task, as well as other repair procedures (such as repair of threaded holes that have been stripped out).

Flat washers and lock washers, when removed from an assembly should always be replaced exactly as removed. Replace damaged washers with new ones. Always use a flat washer between a lock washer and any soft metal surface (such as aluminum), thin sheet metal or plastic.

Fastener sizes

For a number of reasons, automobile manufacturers are making wider and wider use of metric fasteners. Therefore, it is important to be able to tell the difference between standard (sometimes called U.S., English or SAE) and metric hardware, since they cannot be interchanged.

All bolts, whether standard or metric, are sized according to diameter, thread pitch and length. For example, a standard $\frac{1}{2}$ – 13 x 1 bolt is $\frac{1}{2}$ inch in diameter, has 13 threads per inch and is 1 inch long. An M12 – 1.75 x 25 metric bolt is 12 mm in diameter, has a thread pitch of 1.75 mm (the distance between threads) and is 25 mm long. The 2 bolts are nearly identical, and easily confused, but they are not interchangeable.

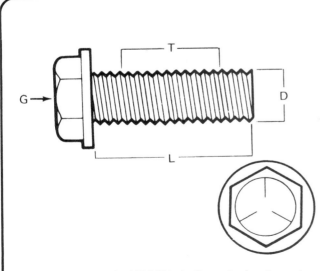

Standard (SAE) bolt dimension/grade marks

G	=	Grade marks (bolt strength)
L	=	Length (inches)
T	=	Thread pitch (number of threads per inch)
D	=	Diameter (inches)

Metric bolt dimensions/grade marks

P	=	Property class (bolt strength)
L	=	Length (millimeters)
T	=	Thread pitch (distance between threads in millimeters)
D	=	Nominal diameter (millimeters)

In addition to the differences in diameter, thread pitch and length, metric and standard bolts can also be distinguished by examining the bolt heads. To begin with, the distance across the flats on a standard bolt head is measured in inches, while the same dimension on a metric bolt is measured in millimeters (the same is true for nuts). As a result, a standard wrench should not be used on a metric bolt and a metric wrench should not be used on a standard bolt. Also, standard bolts have slashes radiating out from the center of the head to denote the grade or strength of the bolt (which is an indication of the amount of torque that can be supplied to it). The greater the number of slashes, the greater the strength of the bolt (grades 0 through 5 are commonly used on automobiles). Metric bolts have a property class (grade) number, rather than a slash, molded into their heads to indicate bolt strength. In this case, the higher the number the stronger the bolt (property class numbers 8.8, 9.8 and 10.9 are commonly used on automobiles).

Strength markings can also be used to distinguish standard hex nuts from metric hex nuts. Standard nuts have dots stamped into one side, while metric nuts are marked with a number. The greater the number of dots, or the higher the number, the greater the strength of the nut.

Metric studs are also marked on their ends according to property class (grade). Larger studs are numbered (the same as metric bolts), while smaller studs carry a geometric code to denote grade.

It should be noted that many fasteners, especially Grades 0 through 2, have no distinguishing marks on them. When such is the case, the only way to determine whether it is standard or metric is to measure the thread pitch or compare it to a known fastener of the same size.

Since fasteners of the same size (both standard and metric) may have different strength ratings, be sure to reinstall any bolts, studs or nuts removed from your vehicle in their original locations. Also, when replacing a fastener with a new one, make sure that the new one has a strength rating equal to or greater than the original.

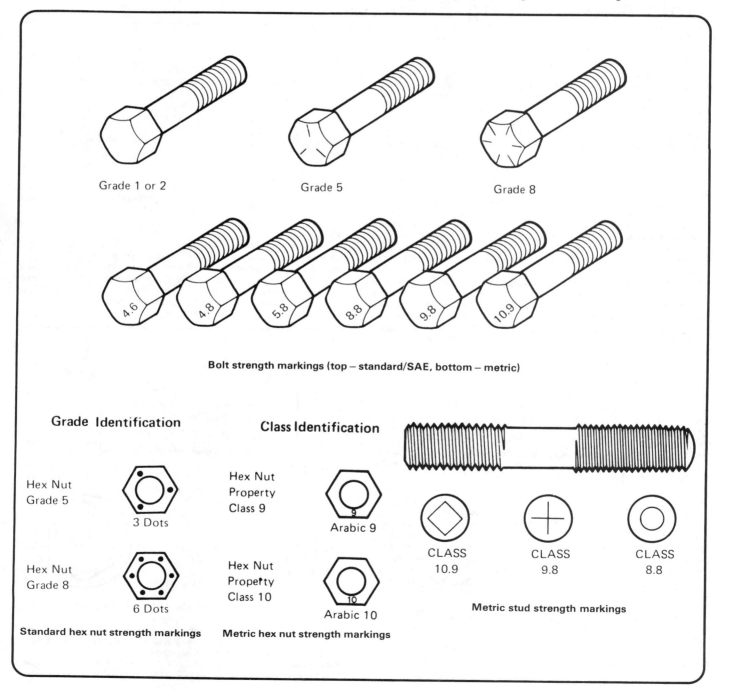

Grade 1 or 2   Grade 5   Grade 8

4.6   4.8   5.8   8.8   9.8   10.9

Bolt strength markings (top – standard/SAE, bottom – metric)

Grade Identification

Hex Nut
Grade 5

3 Dots

Hex Nut
Grade 8

6 Dots

Standard hex nut strength markings

Class Identification

Hex Nut
Property
Class 9

Arabic 9

Hex Nut
Property
Class 10

Arabic 10

Metric hex nut strength markings

CLASS
10.9

CLASS
9.8

CLASS
8.8

Metric stud strength markings

	ft-lb	Nm
Metric thread sizes		
M-6	6 to 9	9 to 12
M-8	14 to 21	19 to 28
M-10	28 to 40	38 to 54
M-12	50 to 71	68 to 96
M-14	80 to 140	109 to 154
Pipe thread sizes		
1/8	5 to 8	7 to 10
1/4	12 to 18	17 to 24
3/8	22 to 33	30 to 44
1/2	25 to 35	34 to 47
U.S. thread sizes		
1/4 - 20	6 to 9	9 to 12
5/16 - 18	12 to 18	17 to 24
5/16 - 24	14 to 20	19 to 27
3/8 - 16	22 to 32	30 to 43
3/8 - 24	27 to 38	37 to 51
7/16 - 14	40 to 55	55 to 74
7/16 - 20	40 to 60	55 to 81
1/2 - 13	55 to 80	75 to 108

Tightening sequences and procedures

Most threaded fasteners should be tightened to a specific torque value (torque is basically a twisting force). Over-tightening the fastener can weaken it and lead to eventual breakage, while under-tightening can cause it to eventually come loose. Bolts, screws and studs, depending on the materials they are made of and their thread diameters, have specific torque values (many of which are noted in the Specifications at the beginning of each Chapter). Be sure to follow the torque recommendations closely. For fasteners not assigned a specific torque, a general torque value chart is presented here as a guide. As was previously mentioned, the sizes and grade of a fastener determine the amount of torque that can safely be applied to it. The figures listed here are approximate for Grade 2 and Grade 3 fasteners (higher grades can tolerate higher torque values).

Fasteners laid out in a pattern (i.e. cylinder head bolts, oil pan bolts, differential cover bolts, etc.) must be loosened and tightened in a definite sequence to avoid warping the component. This sequence will normally be shown in the appropriate Chapter. If a specific pattern is not given, the following procedures can be used to prevent warping. Initially, the bolts or nuts should be assembled finger-tight only. Next, they should be tightened one full turn each, in a criss-cross or diagonal pattern. After each one has been tightened one full turn, return to the first one and tighten them all one half turn, following the same pattern. Finally, tighten each of them one-quarter turn at a time until they all have been tightened to the proper torque value. To loosen and remove them the procedure would be reversed.

Component disassembly

Component disassembly should be done with care and purpose to help ensure that the parts go back together properly. Always keep track of the sequence in which parts are removed. Make note of special characteristics or marks on parts that can be installed more than one way (such as a grooved thrust washer on a shaft). It is a good idea to lay the disassembled parts out on a clean surface in the order that they were removed. It may also be helpful to make simple sketches or take instant photos of components before removal.

When removing fasteners from an assembly, keep track of their locations. Sometimes threading a bolt back in a part or putting the washers and nut back on a stud can prevent mixups later. If nuts and bolts cannot be returned to their original locations, they should be kept in a compartmented box or a series of small boxes. A cupcake or muffin tin is ideal for this purpose, since each cavity can hold the bolts and nuts from a particular area (i.e. oil pan bolts, valve cover bolts, engine mount bolts, etc.). A pan of this type is especially helpful when working on assemblies with very small parts such as the carburetor, alternator, valve train or interior dash and trim pieces. The cavities can be marked with paint or tape to identify the contents.

Whenever wiring looms, harnesses or connectors are separated, it's a good idea to identify them with numbered pieces of masking tape so that they can be easily reconnected.

Gasket sealing surfaces

Throughout any vehicle, gaskets are used to seal the mating surfaces between two parts and keep lubricants, fluids, vacuum or pressure contained in an assembly.

Many times these gaskets are coated with a liquid or paste-type gasket sealing compound before assembly. Age, heat and pressure can sometimes cause the two parts to stick together so tightly that they are very difficult to separate. Often, the assembly can be loosened by striking it with a soft-faced hammer near the mating surfaces. A regular hammer can be used if a block of wood is placed between the hammer and the part. Do not hammer on cast parts or parts that could be easily damaged. With any particularly stubborn part, always recheck to see that every fastener has been removed.

Avoid using a screwdriver or bar to pry apart an assembly, as they can easily mar the gasket sealing surfaces of the parts (which must remain smooth). If prying is absolutely necessary, use an old broom handle, but keep in mind that extra clean-up will be necessary if the wood splinters.

After the parts are separated, the old gasket must be carefully scraped off and the gasket surfaces cleaned. Stubborn gasket material can be soaked with rust penetrant or treated with a special chemical to soften it so that it can be easily scraped off. A scraper can be fashioned from a piece of copper tubing by flattening and sharpening one end. Copper is recommended because it is usually softer than the surfaces to be scraped, which reduces the chance of gouging the part. Some gaskets can be removed with a wire brush, but regardless of the method used, the mating surfaces must be left clean and smooth. If, for some reason the gasket surface is gouged, then a gasket sealer thick enough to fill scratches will have to be used upon reassembly of the components. For most applications, a non-drying (or semi-drying) gasket sealer should be used.

Hose removal tips

Caution: *If the vehicle is equipped with air conditioning, do not disconnect any of the a/c hoses without first having the system depressurized by a dealer service department or air conditioning specialist.*

Hose removal precautions closely parallel gasket removal precautions. Avoid scratching or gouging the surface that the hose mates against or the connection may leak. This is especially true for radiator hoses. Because of various chemical reactions, the rubber in hoses can bond itself to the metal spigot that the hose fits over. To remove a hose, first loosen the hose clamps that secure it to the spigot. Then, with slip-joint pliers, grab the hose at the clamp and rotate it around the spigot. Work it back-and-forth until it is completely free, then pull it off. Silicone or other lubricants will ease removal if they can be applied between the hose and the spigot. Apply the same lubricant to the inside of the hose and the outside of the spigot to simplify installation.

As the last resort (and if the hose is to be replaced with a new one anyway), the rubber can be slit with a knife and the hose peeled from its spigot. If this must be done, be careful that the metal connection is not damaged.

If a hose clamp is broken or damaged, do not re-use it. Wire-type clamps usually weaken with age, so it is a good idea to replace them with screw-type clamps whenever a hose is removed.

Tools

A selection of good tools is a basic requirement for anyone who plans to maintain and repair his or her own vehicle. For the owner who has few tools, if any, the initial investment might seem high, but when compared to the spiraling costs of professional auto maintenance and repair, it is a wise one.

To help the owner decide which tools are needed to perform the tasks detailed in this manual, the following tool lists are offered: *Maintenance and minor repair, Repair and overhaul* and *Special*. The newcomer to practical mechanics should start off with the *Maintenance and minor repair* tool kit, which is adequate for the simpler jobs performed on a vehicle. Then, as his confidence and experience grow, he can tackle more difficult tasks, buying additional tools as they are needed. Eventually the basic kit will be expanded into the *Repair and overhaul* tool set. Over a period of time, the experienced do-it-yourselfer will assemble a tool set complete enough for most repair and overhaul procedures and will add tools from the *Special* category when he feels the expense is justified by the frequency of use.

Maintenance and minor repair tool kit

The tools in this list should be considered the minimum for performance of routine maintenance, servicing and minor repair work. We recommend the purchase of combination wrenches (box end and open end combined in one wrench); while more expensive than open-ended ones, they offer the advantages of both types of wrench.

> Combination wrench set ($\frac{1}{4}$ in to 1 in or 6 mm to 19 mm)
> Adjustable wrench – 8 in
> Spark plug wrench (with rubber insert)
> Spark plug gap adjusting tool
> Feeler gauge set
> Brake bleeder wrench
> Standard screwdriver ($\frac{5}{16}$ in x 6 in)
> Phillips screwdriver (No.2 x 6 in)
> Combination pliers – 6 in
> Hacksaw and assortment of blades
> Tire pressure gauge
> Grease gun
> Oil can
> Fine emery cloth
> Wire brush
> Battery post and cable cleaning tool
> Oil filter wrench
> Funnel (medium size)
> Safety goggles
> Jack stands (2)
> Drain pan

Note: *If basic tune-ups are going to be a part of routine maintenance, it will be necessary to purchase a good quality stroboscopic timing light and a combination tachometer/dwell meter.*

Although they are included in the list of *Special* tools, they are mentioned here because they are absolutely necessary for tuning most vehicles properly.

Repair and overhaul tool set

These tools are essential for anyone who plans to perform major repairs and are in addition to those in the *Maintenance and minor repair tool kit*. Included is a comprehensive set of sockets which, though expensive, are invaluable because of their versatility (especially when various extensions and drives are available). We recommend the $\frac{1}{2}$ in drive over the $\frac{3}{8}$ in drive. Although the larger drive is bulky and more expensive, it has the capability of accepting a very wide range of large sockets (ideally, the mechanic would have a $\frac{3}{8}$ in drive set and a $\frac{1}{2}$ in drive set).

> Socket set(s)
> Reversible ratchet
> Extension – 10 in
> Universal joint
> Torque wrench (same size drive as sockets)
> Ballpein hammer – 8 oz
> Soft-faced hammer (plastic/rubber)
> Standard screwdriver ($\frac{1}{4}$ in x 6 in)
> Standard screwdriver (stubby – $\frac{5}{16}$ in)
> Phillips screwdriver (No.3 x 8 in)
> Phillips screwdriver (stubby – No.2)
> Pliers – vise grip
> Pliers – lineman's
> Pliers – needle nose
> Pliers – spring clip (internal and external)
> Cold chisel – $\frac{1}{2}$ in
> Scriber
> Scraper (made from flattened copper tubing)
> Center punch
> Pin punches ($\frac{1}{16}$, $\frac{1}{8}$, $\frac{3}{16}$ in)
> Steel rule/straightedge – 12 in
> Allen wrench set ($\frac{1}{8}$ to $\frac{3}{8}$ in or 4 mm to 10 mm)
> A selection of files
> Wire brush (large)
> Jack stands (second set)
> Jack (scissor or hydraulic type)

Note: *Another tool which is often useful is an electric drill motor with a chuck capacity of $\frac{3}{8}$ in (and a set of good quality drill bits).*

Special tools

The tools in this list include those which are not used regularly, are expensive to buy, or which need to be used in accordance with their manufacturer's instructions. Unless these tools will be used frequently, it is not very economical to purchase many of them. A consideration would be to split the cost and use between yourself and a friend or

Valve spring compressor

Piston ring groove cleaning tool

Piston ring compressor

Piston ring removal/installation tool

Cylinder ridge reamer

Cylinder surfacing hone

Cylinder bore gauge

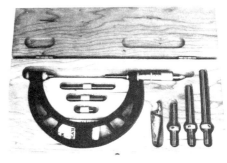

Micrometer set

Dial caliper

Hydraulic lifter removal tool

Universal-type puller

Dial indicator set

Hand-operated vacuum pump

Brake shoe spring tool

friends. In addition, most of these tools can be obtained from a tool rental shop on a temporary basis.

This list contains only those tools and instruments widely available to the public, and not those special tools produced by vehicle manufacturers for distribution to dealer service departments. Occasionally, references to the manufacturer's special tools are included in the text of this manual. Generally, an alternate method of doing the job without the special tool is offered. However, sometimes there is no alternative to their use. Where this is the case, and the tool cannot be purchased or borrowed, the work should be turned over to the dealer, a repair shop or an automotive machine shop.

> *Valve spring compressor*
> *Piston ring groove cleaning tool*
> *Piston ring compressor*
> *Piston ring installation tool*
> *Cylinder compression gauge*
> *Cylinder ridge reamer*
> *Cylinder surfacing hone*
> *Cylinder bore gauge*
> *Micrometer(s) and/or dial calipers*
> *Hydraulic lifter removal tool*
> *Balljoint separator*
> *Universal-type puller*
> *Impact screwdriver*
> *Dial indicator set*
> *Stroboscopic timing light (inductive pickup)*
> *Hand-operated vacuum/pressure pump*
> *Tachometer/dwell meter*
> *Universal electrical multimeter*
> *Cable hoist*
> *Brake spring removal and installation tools*
> *Floor jack*

Buying tools

For the do-it-yourselfer who is just starting to get involved in vehicle maintenance and repair, there are a couple of options available when purchasing tools. If maintenance and minor repair is the extent of the work to be done, the purchase of individual tools is satisfactory. If, on the other hand, extensive work is planned, it would be a good idea to purchase a modest tool set from one of the large retail chain stores. A set can usually be bought at substantial savings over the individual tool prices (and they often come with a tool box). As additional tools are needed, add-on sets, individual tools and a larger tool box can be purchased to expand the tool selection. Building a tool set gradually allows the cost of the tools to be spread over a longer period of time and gives the mechanic the freedom to choose only those tools that will actually be used.

Tool stores will often be the only source of some of the special tools that are needed, but regardless of where tools are bought, try to avoid cheap ones (especially when buying screwdrivers and sockets) because they won't last very long. The expense involved in replacing cheap tools will eventually be greater than the initial cost of quality tools.

Care and maintenance of tools

Good tools are expensive, so it makes sense to treat them with respect. Keep them in a clean and usable condition and store them properly when not in use. Always wipe off any dirt, grease or metal chips before putting them away. Never leave tools lying around in the work area. Upon completion of a job, always check closely under the hood for tools that may have been left there (so they don't get lost during a test drive).

Some tools, such as screwdrivers, pliers, wrenches and sockets, can be hung on a panel mounted on the garage or workshop wall, while others should be kept in a tool box or tray. Measuring instruments, gauges, meters, etc. must be carefully stored where they cannot be damaged by weather or impact from other tools.

When tools are used with care and stored properly, they will last a very long time. Even with the best of care, tools will wear out if used frequently. When a tool is damaged or worn out, replace it; subsequent jobs will be safer and more enjoyable if you do.

For those who desire to learn more about tools and their uses, a book entitled *How to Choose and Use Car Tools* is available from the publishers of this manual.

Working facilities

Not to be overlooked when discussing tools is the workshop. If anything more than routine maintenance is to be carried out, some sort of suitable work area is essential.

It is understood, and appreciated, that many home mechanics do not have a good workshop or garage available and end up removing an engine or doing major repairs outside. It is recommended, however, that the overhaul or repair be completed under the cover of a roof.

A clean, flat workbench or table of comfortable working height is an absolute necessity. The workbench should be equipped with a vise that has a jaw opening of at least 4 inches.

As mentioned previously, some clean, dry storage space is also required for tools, as well as the lubricants, fluids, cleaning solvents, etc. which soon become necessary.

Sometimes waste oil and fluids, drained from the engine or transmission during normal maintenance or repairs, present a disposal problem. To avoid pouring oil on the ground or into the sewage system, simply pour the used fluids into large containers, seal them with caps and deliver them to a local recycling center or disposal facility. Plastic jugs (such as old antifreeze containers) are ideal for this purpose.

Always keep a supply of old newspapers and clean rags available. Old towels are excellent for mopping up spills. Many mechanics use rolls of paper towels for most work because they are readily available and disposable. To keep the area under the vehicle clean, a large cardboard box can be cut open and flattened to protect the garage or shop floor.

Whenever working over a painted surface (such as when leaning over a fender to service something under the hood), always cover it with an old blanket or bedspread to protect the finish. Vinyl covered pads, made especially for this purpose, are available at auto parts stores.

Automotive chemicals and lubricants

A number of automotive chemicals and lubricants are available for use in vehicle maintenance and repair. They include a wide variety of products ranging from cleaning solvents and degreasers to lubricants and protective sprays for rubber, plastic and vinyl.

Contact point/spark plug cleaner is a solvent used to clean oily film and dirt from points, grime from electrical connectors and oil deposits from spark plugs. It is oil free and leaves no residue. It can also be used to remove gum and varnish from carburetor jets and other orifices.

Carburetor cleaner is similar to contact point/spark plug cleaner but it is a stronger solvent and may leave a slight oily residue. It is not recommended for cleaning electrical components or connections.

Brake system cleaner is used to remove grease or brake fluid from brake system components where clean surfaces are absolutely necessary and petroleum-based solvents cannot be used. It also leaves no residue.

Silicone-based lubricants are used to protect rubber parts such as hoses, weatherstripping and grommets and are used as lubricants for hinges and locks.

Multi-purpose grease is an all-purpose lubricant used whenever grease is more practical than a liquid lubricant such as oil. Some multi-purpose grease is white and specially formulated to be more resistant to water than ordinary grease.

Bearing grease/wheel bearing grease is a heavy grease used where increased loads and friction are encountered (i.e. wheel bearings, universal joints, etc.).

High temperature wheel bearing grease is designed to withstand the extreme temperatures encountered by wheel bearings in disc brake equipped vehicles. It usually contains molybdenum disulfide, which is a 'dry' type lubricant.

Gear oil (sometimes called gear lube) is a specially designed oil used in differentials, manual transmissions and transfer cases, as well as other areas where high friction, high temperature lubrication is required. It is available in a number of viscosities (weights) for various applications.

Motor oil, of course, is the lubricant specially formulated for use in the engine. It normally contains a wide variety of additives to prevent corrosion and reduce foaming and wear. Motor oil comes in various weights (viscosity ratings) of from 5 to 80. The recommended weight of the oil depends on the seasonal temperature and the demands on the engine. Light oil is used in cold climates and under light load conditions; heavy oil is used in hot climates and where high loads are encountered. Multi-viscosity oils are designed to have characteristics of both light and heavy oils and are available in a number of weights from 5W-20 to 20W-50.

Oil additives range from viscosity index improvers to slick chemical treatments that purportedly reduce friction. It should be noted that most oil manufacturers caution against using additives with their oils.

Gas additives perform several functions, depending on their chemical makeup. They usually contain solvents that help dissolve gum and varnish that build up on carburetor and intake parts. They also serve to break down carbon deposits that form on the inside surfaces of the combustion chambers. Some additives contain upper cylinder lubricants for valves and piston rings.

Brake fluid is a specially formulated hydraulic fluid that can withstand the heat and pressure encountered in brake systems. Care must be taken that this fluid does not come in contact with painted surfaces or plastics. An opened container should always be resealed to prevent contamination by water or dirt.

Undercoating is a petroleum-based, tar-like substance that is designed to protect metal surfaces on the underside of a vehicle from corrosion. It also acts as a sound deadening agent by insulating the bottom of the vehicle.

Weatherstrip cement is used to bond weatherstripping around doors, windows and trunk lids. It is sometimes used to attach trim pieces as well.

Degreasers are heavy-duty solvents used to remove grease and grime that accumulate on engine and chassis components. They can be sprayed or brushed on and, depending on the type, are rinsed with either water or solvent.

Solvents are used alone or in combination with degreasers to clean parts and assemblies during repair and overhaul. The home mechanic should use only solvents that are non-flammable and that do not produce irritating fumes.

Gasket sealing compounds may be used in conjunction with gaskets, to improve their sealing capabilities, or alone, to seal metal-to-metal joints. Many gaskets can withstand extreme heat, some are impervious to gasoline and lubricants, while others are capable of filling and sealing large cavities. Depending on the intended use, gasket sealers either dry hard or stay relatively soft and pliable. They are usually applied by hand, with a brush, or are sprayed on the gasket sealing surfaces.

Thread cement is an adhesive locking compound that prevents threaded fasteners from loosening because of vibration. It is available in a variety of types for different applications.

Moisture dispersants are usually sprays that can be used to dry out electrical components such as the distributor, fuse block and wiring connectors. Some types can also be used as a treatment for rubber and as a lubricant for hinges, cables and locks.

Waxes and polishes are used to help protect painted and plated surfaces from the weather. Different types of paint may require the use of different types of wax or polish. Some polishes utilize a chemical or abrasive cleaner to help remove the top layer of oxidized (dull) paint in older vehicles. In recent years, many non-wax polishes that contain a wide variety of chemicals such as polymers and silicones have been introduced. These non-wax polishes are usually easier to apply and last longer than conventional waxes and polishes.

Jacking and towing

Jacking

The jack supplied with the vehicle should only be used for raising the vehicle during a tire change or when placing jackstands under the frame. **Under no circumstances should work be performed beneath the vehicle or the engine started while this jack is being used as the only means of support.**

All vehicles are supplied with a scissors-type jack which fits into a locater pin in the vertical rocker panel flange nearest to the wheel being changed.

The vehicle should be on level ground with the wheels blocked and the transaxle in Park (automatic) or Reverse (manual). Pry off the hub cap (if equipped) using the tapered end of the lug wrench. Loosen the wheel nuts one half turn and leave them in place until the wheel is raised off the ground.

Place the jack under the side of the vehicle in the locater pin. Use the supplied wrench to turn the jackscrew clockwise until the wheel is raised off the ground. Remove the wheel nuts, pull off the wheel and replace it with the spare.

With the beveled side in, replace the wheel nuts and tighten them until snug. Lower the vehicle by turning the jackscrew counterclockwise. Remove the jack and tighten the nuts in a diagonal fashion. Replace the hubcap by placing it into position and using the heel of your hand or a rubber mallet to seat it.

Towing

Manual transaxle equipped vehicles can be towed at legal highway speeds with all four wheels on the ground and the shift lever in Neutral. Vehicles with automatic transaxles may be towed in Neutral for a distance of not more than 15 miles at a speed not to exceed 25 mph. If an automatic transaxle equipped vehicle is to be towed for more than 15 miles, or if either type of transaxle is inoperative, the vehicle should be towed with the front wheels off the ground.

Towing equipment specifically designed for this purpose should be used and should be attached to the main structural members of the vehicle and not the bumper or brackets.

Safety is a major consideration when towing a vehicle and all applicable state and local laws must be obeyed. A safety chain system must be used for all towing.

While towing, the parking brake should be fully released and the transaxle should be in Neutral. The steering must be unlocked (ignition switch in the Off position). Remember that power steering and power brakes will not work with the engine off.

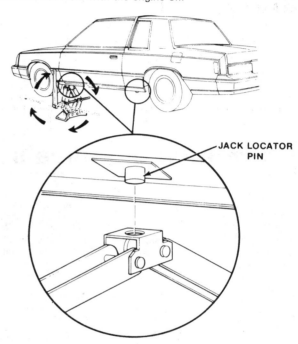

Jack lifting points

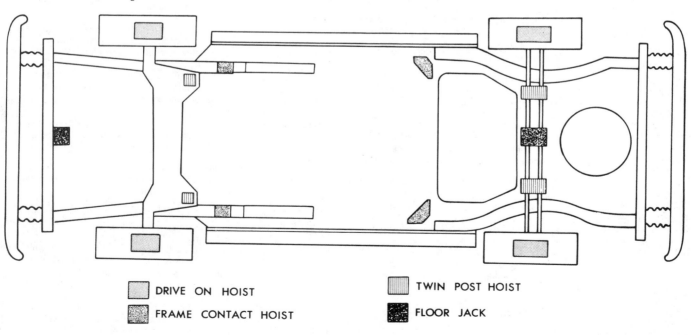

◻ DRIVE ON HOIST   ▦ TWIN POST HOIST

▨ FRAME CONTACT HOIST   ▩ FLOOR JACK

Frame lifting locations

Safety first!

Regardless of how enthusiastic you may be about getting on with the job at hand, take the time to ensure that your safety is not jeopardized. A moment's lack of attention can result in an accident, as can failure to observe certain simple safety precautions. The possibility of an accident will always exist, and the following points should not be considered a comprehensive list of all dangers. Rather, they are intended to make you aware of the risks and to encourage a safety conscious approach to all work you carry out on your vehicle.

Essential DOs and DON'Ts

DON'T rely on a jack when working under the vehicle. Always use approved jackstands to support the weight of the vehicle and place them under the recommended lift or support points.

DON'T attempt to loosen extremely tight fasteners (i.e. wheel lug nuts) while the vehicle is on a jack — it may fall.

DON'T start the engine without first making sure that the transmission is in Neutral (or Park where applicable) and the parking brake is set.

DON'T remove the radiator cap from a hot cooling system — let it cool or cover it with a cloth and release the pressure gradually.

DON'T attempt to drain the engine oil until you are sure it has cooled to the point that it will not burn you.

DON'T touch any part of the engine or exhaust system until it has cooled sufficiently to avoid burns.

DON'T siphon toxic liquids such as gasoline, antifreeze and brake fluid by mouth, or allow them to remain on your skin.

DON'T inhale brake lining dust — it is potentially hazardous (see *Asbestos* below)

DON'T allow spilled oil or grease to remain on the floor — wipe it up before someone slips on it.

DON'T use loose fitting wrenches or other tools which may slip and cause injury.

DON'T push on wrenches when loosening or tightening nuts or bolts. Always try to pull the wrench toward you. If the situation calls for pushing the wrench away, push with an open hand to avoid scraped knuckles if the wrench should slip.

DON'T attempt to lift a heavy component alone — get someone to help you.

DON'T rush or take unsafe shortcuts to finish a job.

DON'T allow children or animals in or around the vehicle while you are working on it.

DO wear eye protection when using power tools such as a drill, sander, bench grinder, etc. and when working under a vehicle.

DO keep loose clothing and long hair well out of the way of moving parts.

DO make sure that any hoist used has a safe working load rating adequate for the job.

DO get someone to check on you periodically when working alone on a vehicle.

DO carry out work in a logical sequence and make sure that everything is correctly assembled and tightened.

DO keep chemicals and fluids tightly capped and out of the reach of children and pets.

DO remember that your vehicle's safety affects that of yourself and others. If in doubt on any point, get professional advice.

Asbestos

Certain friction, insulating, sealing, and other products — such as brake linings, brake bands, clutch linings, torque converters, gaskets, etc. — contain asbestos. *Extreme care must be taken to avoid inhalation of dust from such products since it is hazardous to health.* If in doubt, assume that they *do* contain asbestos.

Fire

Remember at all times that gasoline is highly flammable. Never smoke or have any kind of open flame around when working on a vehicle. But the risk does not end there. A spark caused by an electrical short circuit, by two metal surfaces contacting each other, or even by static electricity built up in your body under certain conditions, can ignite gasoline vapors, which in a confined space are highly explosive. Do not, under any circumstances, use gasoline for cleaning parts. Use an approved safety solvent.

Always disconnect the battery ground (–) cable *at the battery* before working on any part of the fuel system or electrical system. Never risk spilling fuel on a hot engine or exhaust component.

It is strongly recommended that a fire extinguisher suitable for use on fuel and electrical fires be kept handy in the garage or workshop at all times. Never try to extinguish a fuel or electrical fire with water.

Fumes

Certain fumes are highly toxic and can quickly cause unconsciousness and even death if inhaled to any extent. Gasoline vapor falls into this category, as do the vapors from some cleaning solvents. Any draining or pouring of such volatile fluids should be done in a well ventilated area.

When using cleaning fluids and solvents, read the instructions on the container carefully. Never use materials from unmarked containers.

Never run the engine in an enclosed space, such as a garage. Exhaust fumes contain carbon monoxide, which is extremely poisonous. If you need to run the engine, always do so in the open air, or at least have the rear of the vehicle outside the work area.

If you are fortunate enough to have the use of an inspection pit, never drain or pour gasoline and never run the engine while the vehicle is over the pit. The fumes, being heavier than air, will concentrate in the pit with possibly lethal results.

The battery

Never create a spark or allow a bare light bulb near the battery. The battery normally gives off a certain amount of hydrogen gas, which is highly explosive.

Always disconnect the battery ground (–) cable *at the battery* before working on the fuel or electrical systems.

If possible, loosen the filler caps or cover when charging the battery from an external source. Do not charge at an excessive rate or the battery may burst.

Take care when adding water and when carrying a battery. The electrolyte, even when diluted, is very corrosive and should not be allowed to contact clothing or skin.

Always wear eye protection when cleaning the battery to prevent the caustic deposits from entering your eyes.

Household current

When using an electric power tool, inspection light, etc., which operates on household current, always make sure that the tool is correctly connected to its plug and that, where necessary, it is properly grounded. Do not use such items in damp conditions and, again, do not create a spark or apply excessive heat in the vicinity of fuel or fuel vapor.

Secondary ignition system voltage

A severe electric shock can result from touching certain parts of the ignition system (such as the spark plug wires) when the engine is running or being cranked, particularly if components are damp or the insulation is defective. In the case of an electronic ignition system, the secondary system voltage is much higher and could prove fatal.

Troubleshooting

Contents

This section contains an easy-reference guide to the more common problems which may occur during the operation of your vehicle. These problems and their probable causes are grouped under their respective systems (Engine, Cooling system, etc.) and also refer to the Chapter and/or Section which deals with the problem.

Remember that successful troubleshooting is not a mysterious 'black art' practiced only by professional mechanics; it's simply the result of a bit of knowledge combined with an intelligent, systematic approach to the problem. Always work by a process of elimination, starting with the simplest solution and working through to the most complex — and never overlook the obvious. Anyone can forget to fill the gas tank or leave the lights on overnight, so don't assume that you are above such oversights.

Finally, always get clear in your mind why a problem has occurred and take steps to ensure that it doesn't happen again. If the electrical system fails because of a poor connection, check all other connections in the system to make sure that they don't fail as well; if a particular fuse continues to blow, find out why — don't just go on replacing fuses. Remember, failure or incorrect functioning of a small component can often be indicative of potential failure or improper operation of a more important component or system.

Engine

1 Engine will not rotate when attempting to start

1 Battery terminal connection loose or corroded. Check the cable terminals at the battery; tighten or clean off corrosion as necessary.
2 Battery discharged or faulty. If the cable connectors are clean and

tight on the battery posts, turn the key to the On position and switch on the headlights and/or windshield wipers. If these fail to function, the battery is discharged.

3   Automatic transaxle not fully engaged in Park or manual transaxle clutch not fully depressed.

4   Broken, loose or disconnected wiring in the starting circuit. Inspect all wiring and connectors at the battery, starter solenoid (at lower right side of engine) and ignition switch (on steering column).

5   Starter motor pinion jammed on flywheel ring gear. If manual transaxle, place gearshift in gear and rock the vehicle to manually turn the engine. Remove starter (Chapter 5) and inspect pinion and flywheel (Chapter 2) at earliest convenience.

6   Starter solenoid faulty (Chapter 5).

7   Starter motor faulty (Chapter 5).

8   Ignition switch faulty (Chapter 10).

2   Engine rotates but will not start

1   Fuel tank empty.

2   Battery discharged (engine rotates slowly). Check the operation of electrical components as described in previous Section.

3   Battery terminal connections loose or corroded. See previous Section.

4   Carburetor flooded and/or fuel level in carburetor incorrect. This will usually be accompanied by a strong fuel odor from under the hood. Wait a few minutes, depress the accelerator pedal all the way to the floor and attempt to start the engine.

5   Choke control inoperative (Chapter 4).

6   Fuel not reaching carburetor. With ignition switch in Off position, open hood, remove the top plate of air cleaner assembly and observe the top of the carburetor (manually move choke plate back if necessary). Have an assistant depress accelerator pedal fully and check that fuel spurts into carburetor. If not, check fuel filter (Chapter 1), fuel lines and fuel pump (Chapter 4).

7   Excessive moisture on, or damage to, ignition components (Chapter 5).

8   Worn, faulty or incorrectly adjusted spark plugs (Chapter 1).

9   Broken, loose or disconnected wiring in the starting circuit (see previous Section).

10   Distributor loose, thus changing ignition timing. Turn the distributor as necessary to start the engine, then set ignition timing as soon as possible (Chapter 1).

11   Broken, loose or disconnected wires at the ignition coil, or faulty coil (Chapter 5).

3   Starter motor operates without rotating engine

1   Starter pinion sticking. Remove the starter (Chapter 5) and inspect.

2   Starter pinion or engine flywheel teeth worn or broken.

4   Engine hard to start when cold

1   Battery discharged or low. Check as described in Section 1.

2   Choke control inoperative or out of adjustment (Chapters 1 and 4).

3   Carburetor flooded (see Section 2).

4   Fuel supply not reaching the carburetor (see Section 2).

5   Carburetor worn and in need of overhauling (Chapter 4).

5   Engine hard to start when hot

1   Choke sticking in the closed position (Chapter 1).

2   Carburetor flooded (see Section 2).

3   Air filter in need of replacement (Chapter 1).

4   Fuel not reaching the carburetor (Section 2).

6   Starter motor noisy or excessively rough in engagement

1   Pinion or flywheel gear teeth worn or broken.

2   Starter motor retaining bolts loose or missing.

7   Engine starts but stops immediately

1   Loose or faulty electrical connections at distributor, coil or alternator.

2   Insufficient fuel reaching the carburetor. Disconnect the fuel line at the carburetor (Chapter 1). Place a container under the disconnected fuel line. Observe the flow of fuel from the line. If little or none at all, check for blockage in the lines and/or replace the fuel pump (Chapter 4).

3   Vacuum leak at the gasket surfaces of the intake manifold and/or carburetor. Check that all mounting bolts (nuts) are tightened to specifications and all vacuum hoses connected to the carburetor and manifold are positioned properly and in good condition.

8   Engine 'lopes' while idling or idles erratically

1   Vacuum leakage. Check mounting bolts (nuts) at the carburetor and intake manifold for tightness. Check that all vacuum hoses are connected and in good condition. Use a doctor's stethoscope or a length of fuel line hose held against your ear to listen for vacuum leaks while the engine is running. A hissing sound will be heard. A soapy water solution will also detect leaks. Check the carburetor and intake manifold gasket surfaces.

2   Leaking EGR valve or plugged PCV valve (Chapter 6).

3   Air filter clogged and in need of replacement (Chapter 1).

4   Fuel pump not delivering sufficient fuel to the carburetor (see Section 7).

5   Carburetor out of adjustment (Chapter 4).

6   Leaking head gasket. If this is suspected, take the vehicle to a repair shop or dealer where this can be pressure checked without the need to remove the head.

7   Timing belt/chain or gears worn and in need of replacement (Chapter 2).

8   Camshaft lobes worn, necessitating the removal of the camshaft for inspection (Chapter 2).

9   Engine misses at idle speed

1   Spark plugs faulty or not gapped properly (Chapter 1).

2   Faulty spark plug wires (Chapter 1).

3   Carburetor choke not operating properly (Chapter 1).

4   Sticking or faulty emissions systems.

5   Clogged fuel filter and/or foreign matter in fuel. Remove the fuel filter (Chapter 1) and inspect.

6   Vacuum leaks at carburetor, intake manifold or at hose connections. Check as described in Section 8.

7   Incorrect idle speed or mixture (Chapter 1).

8   Incorrect ignition timing (Chapter 1).

9   Uneven or low cylinder compression. Remove plugs and use compression tester as per manufacturer's instructions.

10   Engine misses throughout driving speed range

1   Fuel filter clogged and/or impurities in the fuel system (Chapter 1). Also check fuel output at the carburetor (see Section 4).

2   Faulty or incorrectly gapped spark plugs (Chapter 1).

3   Incorrectly set ignition timing (Chapter 1).

4   Check for a cracked distributor cap, disconnected distributor wires or damage to the distributor components (Chapter 1).

5   Leaking spark plug wires (Chapter 1).

6   Emission system components faulty (Chapter 6).

7   Low or uneven cylinder compression pressures. Remove spark plugs and test compression with gauge.

8   Weak or faulty ignition system (see Chapter 5).

9   Vacuum leaks at carburetor, intake manifold or vacuum hoses (see Section 8).

11   Engine stalls

1   Carburetor idle speed incorrectly set (Chapter 1).

2   Fuel filter clogged and/or water and impurities in the fuel system (Chapter 1).
3   Choke improperly adjusted or sticking (Chapter 1).
4   Distributor components damp or damage to distributor cap, rotor, etc. (Chapter 5).
5   Emission system components faulty (Chapter 6).
6   Faulty or incorrectly gapped spark plugs (Chapter 1). Also check spark plug wires (Chapter 1).
7   Vacuum leak at the carburetor, intake manifold or vacuum hoses. Check as described in Section 8.
8   Valve clearances incorrectly set (Chapter 1).

12 Engine lacks power

1   Incorrect ignition timing (Chapter 1).
2   Excessive play in distributor shaft. At the same time check for worn rotor, faulty distributor cap, wires, etc. (Chapter 5).
3   Faulty or incorrectly gapped spark plugs (Chapter 1).
4   Carburetor not adjusted or excessively worn (Chapter 4).
5   Weak coil (Chapter 5).
6   Brakes binding (Chapter 9).
7   Automatic transaxle fluid level incorrect, causing slippage (Chapter 7).
8   Manual transaxle clutch slipping (Chapter 8).
9   Fuel filter clogged and/or impurities in the fuel system (Chapter 1).
10 Emission control system not functioning properly (Chapter 6).
11 Use of sub-standard fuel. Fill tank with proper octane fuel.
12 Low or uneven cylinder compression pressures. Test with compression tester, which will detect leaking valves and/or blown head gasket.

13 Engine backfires

1   Emission system not functioning properly (Chapter 6).
2   Ignition timing incorrect (Chapter 1).
3   Carburetor in need of adjustment or worn excessively (Chapter 4).
4   Vacuum leak at carburetor, intake manifold or vacuum hoses. Check as described in Section 8.
5   Valve clearances incorrectly set, and/or valves sticking (Chapter 1).

14 Pinging or knocking engine sounds during acceleration or uphill

1   Incorrect grade of fuel. Fill tank with fuel of the proper octane rating.
2   Ignition timing incorrect (Chapter 1).
3   Carburetor in need of adjustment (Chapter 4).
4   Improper spark plugs. Check plug type with that specified on label located inside engine compartment. Also check plugs and wires for damage (Chapter 1).
5   Worn or damaged distributor components (Chapter 5).
6   Faulty emission system (Chapter 6).
7   Vacuum leak (check as described in Section 8).

15 Engine 'diesels' (continues to run) after switching off

1   Idle speed too fast (Chapter 1).
2   Electrical solenoid at side of carburetor not functioning properly (not all models, see Chapter 4).
3   Ignition timing incorrectly adjusted (Chapter 1).
4   Air cleaner valve not operating properly (Chapter 6).
5   Excessive engine operating temperatures. Probable causes of this are: malfunctioning thermostat, clogged radiator, faulty water pump (see Chapter 3).

Engine electrical

16 Battery will not hold a charge

1   Alternator drivebelt defective or not adjusted properly (Chapter 1).

2   Electrolyte level too low or too weak (Chapter 1).
3   Battery terminals loose or corroded (Chapter 1).
4   Alternator not charging properly (Chapter 5).
5   Loose, broken or faulty wiring in the charging circuit (Chapter 5).
6   Short in vehicle circuitry causing a continual drain on battery.
7   Battery defective internally.

17 Ignition light fails to go out

1   Fault in alternator or charging circuit (Chapter 5).
2   Alternator drivebelt defective or not properly adjusted (Chapter 1).

18 Ignition light fails to come on when key is turned on

1   Ignition light bulb faulty (Chapter 10).
2   Alternator faulty (Chapter 5).
3   Fault in the printed circuit, dash wiring or bulb holder (Chapter 10).

Engine fuel system

19 Excessive fuel consumption

1   Dirty or choked air filter element (Chapter 1).
2   Incorrectly set ignition timing (Chapter 1).
3   Choke sticking or improperly adjusted (Chapter 1).
4   Emission system not functioning properly (not all vehicles, see Chapter 6).
5   Carburetor idle speed and/or mixture not adjusted properly (Chapter 1).
6   Carburetor internal parts excessively worn or damaged (Chapter 4).
7   Low tire pressure or incorrect tire size (Chapter 11).

20 Fuel leakage and/or fuel odor

1   Leak in a fuel feed or vent line (Chapter 4).
2   Tank overfilled. Fill only to automatic shut-off.
3   Emission system filter in need of replacement (Chapter 6).
4   Vapor leaks from system lines (Chapter 4).
5   Carburetor internal parts excessively worn or out of adjustment (Chapter 4).

Engine cooling system

21 Overheating

1   Insufficient coolant in system (Chapter 1).
2   Fault in electric fan motor or wiring.
3   Radiator core blocked or radiator grille dirty and restricted (Chapter 3).
4   Thermostat faulty (Chapter 3).
5   Fan blades broken or cracked (Chapter 3).
6   Radiator cap not maintaining proper pressure. Have cap pressure tested by gas station or repair shop.
7   Ignition timing incorrect (Chapter 1).

22 Overcooling

1   Thermostat faulty (Chapter 3).
2   Inaccurate temperature gauge (Chapter 10).

23 External coolant leakage

1   Deteriorated or damaged hoses. Loose clamps at hose connections (Chapter 1).
2   Water pump seals defective. If this is the case, water will drip from the water pump body (Chapter 3).
3   Leakage from radiator core or header tank. This will require the

radiator to be professionally repaired (see Chapter 3 for removal procedures).
4   Engine drain plugs or water jacket freeze plugs leaking (see Chapters 2 and 3).

24 Internal coolant leakage

Note: *Internal coolant leaks can usually be detected by examining the oil. Check the dipstick and inside of valve cover for water deposits and an oil consistency like that of a milkshake.*
1   Faulty cylinder head gasket. Have the system pressure tested professionally or remove the cylinder head (Chapter 2) and inspect.
2   Cracked cylinder bore or cylinder head. Dismantle engine and inspect (Chapter 2).

25 Coolant loss

1   Overfilling system (Chapter 1).
2   Coolant boiling away due to overheating (see causes in Section 15).
3   Internal or external leakage (see Sections 23 and 24).
4   Faulty radiator cap. Have the cap pressure tested.

26 Poor coolant circulation

1   Inoperative water pump. A quick test is to pinch the top radiator hose closed with your hand while the engine is idling, then let it loose. You should feel the surge of water if the pump is working properly (Chapter 3).
2   Restriction in cooling system. Drain, flush and refill the system (Chapter 3). If it appears necessary, remove the radiator (Chapter 3) and have it reverse-flushed or professionally cleaned.
3   Thermostat sticking (Chapter 3).

Clutch

27 Fails to release (pedal depressed to the floor – shift lever does not move freely in and out of Reverse)

1   Improper linkage adjustment (Chapter 8).
2   Clutch linkage malfunction (Chapter 8).
3   Clutch disc warped, bent or excessively damaged (Chapter 8).

28 Clutch slips (engine speed increases with no increases in vehicle speed)

1   Linkage in need of adjustment (Chapter 8).
2   Clutch disc oil soaked or worn. Remove disc (Chapter 8) and inspect.
3   Clutch disc not seated in. It may take 30 or 40 normal starts for a new disc to seat.

29 Grabbing (chattering) as pedal is released

1   Oil on clutch disc facings. Remove disc (Chapter 8) and inspect. Repair any leakage source.
2   Worn or loose engine or transmission mounts. These units move slightly when clutch is released. Inspect mounts and bolts.
3   Worn splines on clutch gear. Remove clutch components (Chapter 8) and inspect.
4   Warped pressure plate or flywheel. Remove clutch components and inspect.

30 Squeal or rumble with clutch fully engaged (pedal released)

1   Improper adjustment; no lash (Chapter 8).
2   Release bearing binding on transmission bearing retainer. Remove

clutch components (Chapter 8) and check bearing. Remove any burrs or nicks, clean and relubricate before reinstallation.
3   Weak linkage return spring. Replace the spring.

31 Squeal or rumble with clutch fully disengaged (pedal depressed)

1   Worn, faulty or broken release bearing (Chapter 8).
2   Worn or broken pressure plate springs (or diaphragm fingers) (Chapter 8).

32 Clutch pedal stays on floor when disengaged

1   Bind in leakage or release bearing. Inspect linkage or remove clutch components as necessary.
2   Linkage springs being over-traveled. Adjust linkage for proper lash. Make sure proper pedal stop (bumper) is installed.

Manual transaxle
Note: *The following Sections are contained within Chapter 7A unless otherwise noted.*

33 Noisy in Neutral with engine running

1   Input shaft bearing worn.
2   Damaged main drive gear bearing.
3   Worn countergear bearings.
4   Worn or damaged countergear shims.

34 Noisy in all gears

Any of the above causes, and/or insufficient lubricant (see checking procedures in Chapter 1).

35 Noisy in one particular gear

1   Worn, damaged or chipped gear teeth for that particular gear.
2   Worn or damaged synchronizer for that particular gear.

36 Slips out of high gear

1   Damaged shift linkage.
2   Interference between the floor shift handle and console.
3   Broken or loose engine mounts.
4   Shift mechanism stabilizer bar loose.
5   Damaged or worn transaxle internal components.
6   Improperly installed shifter boot.

37 Difficulty in engaging gears

1   Clutch not releasing fully (see clutch adjustment, Chapter 8).
2   Loose, damaged or maladjusted shift linkage. Make a thorough inspection, replacing parts as necessary. Adjust as described in Chapter 7.

38 Lubricant leakage

1   Excessive amount of lubricant in transaxle (see Chapter 1 for correct checking procedures). Drain lubricant as required.
2   Rear oil seal or speedometer oil seal in need of replacement.

Automatic transaxle
Note: *Due to the complexity of the automatic transaxle, it is difficult for the home mechanic to properly diagnose and service this component. For problems other than the following, the vehicle should be taken to a reputable mechanic.*

39 Fluid leakage

1   Automatic transaxle fluid is a deep red color and fluid leaks should not be confused with engine oil which can easily be blown by air flow to the transaxle.

2   To pinpoint a leak, first remove all built-up dirt and grime from around the transaxle. Degreasing agents and/or steam cleaning will achieve this. With the underside clean, drive the vehicle at low speeds so that air flow will not blow the leak far from its source. Raise the vehicle and determine where the leak is coming from. Common areas of leakage are:

   a)   *Fluid pan:* tighten mounting bolts and/or replace pan gasket as necessary (see Chapter 7B)
   b)   *Rear extension:* tighten bolts and/or replace oil seal as necessary (Chapter 7B)
   c)   *Filler pipe:* replace the rubber seal where pipe enters transaxle case
   d)   *Transaxle oil lines:* tighten connectors where lines enter transaxle case and/or replace lines
   e)   *Vent pipe:* transaxle over-filled and/or water in fluid (see checking procedures, Chapter 1)
   f)   *Speedometer connector:* replace the O-ring where speedometer cable enters transaxle case

40 General shift mechanism problems

Chapter 7B deals with checking and adjusting the shift linkage on automatic transaxles. Common problems which may be attributed to out of adjustment linkage are:

   a)   Engine starting in gears other than Park or Neutral
   b)   Indicator on quandrant pointing to a gear other than the one actually being used
   c)   Vehicle will not hold firm when in Park position. Refer to Chapter 7B to adjust the manual linkage

41 Transaxle will not downshift with the accelerator pedal pressed to the floor

Chapter 7B deals with adjusting the downshift cable or downshift switch to enable the transaxle to downshift properly.

42 Engine will start in gears other than Park or Neutral

Chapter 7B deals with adjusting the Neutral start switches used with the automatic transaxle.

43 Transaxle slips, shifts rough, is noisy or has no drive in forward or reverse gears

1   There are many probable causes for the above problems, but the home mechanic should concern himself with only one possibility: fluid level.

2   Before taking the vehicle to a professional, check the level of the fluid and condition of the fluid as described in Chapter 1. Correct fluid level as necessary or change the fluid and filter if needed. If the problem persists, have a professional diagnose the probable cause.

Drive axles

44 Clicking noise in turns

Worn or damaged outboard joint. Check for cut or damaged boots. Repair as necessary (Chapter 8).

45 Knock or clunk when accelerating from a coast

Worn or damaged inboard joint. Check for cut or damaged boots. Repair as necessary (Chapter 8).

46 Shudder or vibration during acceleration

1   Excessive joint angle. Have it checked and correct as necessary (Chapter 8).

2   Worn or damaged inboard or outboard joints. Repair or replace as necessary (Chapter 8).

3   Sticking inboard joint assembly. Correct or replace as necessary (Chapter 8).

Brakes

Note: *Before assuming that a brake problem exists, make sure that the tires are in good condition and properly inflated (see Chapter 1), the front end alignment is correct (see Chapter 11), and that the vehicle is not unequally loaded.*

47 Vehicle pulls to one side during braking

1   Defective, damaged or oil-contaminated brake pad on one side. Inspect as described in Chapter 1. Refer to Chapter 9 if replacement is required.

2   Excessive wear of brake pad material or disc on one side. Inspect and correct as necessary.

3   Loose or disconnected front suspension components. Inspect and tighten all bolts to specifications (Chapter 11).

4   Defective caliper assembly. Remove caliper and inspect for stuck piston or damage (Chapter 9).

48 Noise (high-pitched squeal without the brakes applied)

Front brake pads worn out. This noise comes from the wear sensor or backing material rubbing against the disc. Replace pads with new ones immediately (Chapter 9).

49 Excessive brake pedal travel

1   Partial brake system failure. Inspect entire system (Chapter 1) and correct as required.

2   Insufficient fluid in master cylinder. Check (Chapter 1) and add fluid and bleed system if necessary (Chapter 9).

3   Rear brakes not adjusting properly. Make a series of starts and stops while the vehicle is in Reverse. If this does not correct the situation, remove drums and inspect self-adjusters (Chapter 9).

50 Brake pedal spongy when depressed

1   Air in lines. Bleed the brake system (Chapter 9).

2   Faulty flexible hoses. Inspect all system hoses and lines. Replace parts as necessary.

3   Master cylinder mount loose. Inspect master cylinder bolts (nuts) and torque tighten to specifications.

4   Master cylinder faulty (Chapter 9).

51 Excessive effort required to stop vehicle

1   Power brake booster not operating properly (Chapter 9).

2   Excessively worn linings or pads. Inspect and replace if necessary (Chapter 1).

3   One or more caliper pistons (front wheels) or wheel cylinders (rear wheels) seized. Inspect and rebuild as required (Chapter 9).

4   Brake linings or pads contaminated with oil or grease. Inspect and replace as required (Chapter 1).

5   New pads or linings installed and not yet 'bedded in'. It will take a while for the new material to seat against the drum (or rotor).

52 Pedal travels to the floor with little resistance

Little or no fluid in the master cylinder reservoir caused by leaking wheel cylinder(s), leaking caliper piston(s), loose, damaged or disconnected brake lines. Inspect entire system and correct as necessary.

53 Brake pedal pulsates during brake application

1 Wheel bearings not adjusted properly or in need of replacement (Chapter 1).
2 Caliper not sliding properly due to improper installation or obstructions. Remove and inspect (Chapter 9).
3 Rotor not within specifications. Remove the rotor (Chapter 9) and check for excessive lateral runout and parallelism. Have the rotor professionally machined or replace it with a new one.
4 Out-of-round rear brake drums. Remove the drums (Chapter 9) and have them professionally machined, or replace them.

Suspension and steering

54 Vehicle pulls to one side

1 Tire pressures uneven (Chapter 1).
2 Defective tire (Chapter 1).
3 Excessive wear in suspension or steering components (Chapter 1).
4 Front end in need of alignment (Chapter 11).
5 Front brakes dragging. Inspect braking system as described in Chapter 1.

55 Shimmy, shake or vibration

1 Tire or wheel out of balance or out of round. Have professionally balanced.
2 Loose or worn wheel bearings (Chapter 1) Replace as necessary (Chapter 11).
3 Shock absorbers and/or suspension components worn or damaged (Chapter 11).

56 Excessive pitching and/or rolling around corners or during braking

1 Defective shock absorbers. Replace as a set (Chapter 11).
2 Broken or weak coil springs and/or suspension components. Inspect as described in Chapter 11.

57 Excessively stiff steering

1 Lack of lubricant in power steering fluid reservoir (Chapter 1).
2 Incorrect tire pressures (Chapter 1).
3 Lack of lubrication at balljoints (Chapter 1).
4 Front end out of alignment.
5 See also Section 59.

58 Excessive play in steering

1 Loose wheel bearings (Chapter 1).
2 Excessive wear in suspension or steering components (Chapter 1).

59 Lack of power assistance

1 Steering pump drivebelt faulty or not adjusted properly (Chapter 1).
2 Fluid level low (Chapter 1).
3 Hoses or pipes restricting the flow. Inspect and replace parts as necessary.
4 Air in power steering system. Bleed system (Chapter 11).

60 Excessive tire wear (not specific to one area)

1 Incorrect tire pressures (Chapter 1).
2 Tires out of balance. Have professionally balanced.
3 Wheel damaged. Inspect and replace as necessary.
4 Suspension or steering components excessively worn (Chapter 1).

61 Excessive tire wear on outside edge

1 Inflation pressures not correct (Chapter 1).
2 Excessive speed on turns.
3 Front end alignment incorrect (excessive toe-in). Have professionally aligned.
4 Suspension arm bent or twisted.

62 Excessive tire wear on inside edge

1 Inflation pressures incorrect (Chapter 1).
2 Front end alignment incorrect (toe-out). Have professionally aligned (Chapter 11).
3 Loose or damaged steering components (Chapter 1).

63 Tire tread worn in one place

1 Tires out of balance. Balance tires professionally.
2 Damaged or buckled wheel. Inspect and replace if necessary.
3 Defective tire.

64 General vibration at highway speeds

1 Out of balance front wheels or tires. Have them professionally balanced.
2 Front or rear wheel bearings defective. Check (Chapter 1) and replace as necessary (Chapter 11).
3 Defective tire or wheel. Have them checked and replaced if necessary.

65 Noise (whether coasting or in drive)

1 Road noise. No corrective measures available.
2 Tire noise. Inspect tires and tire pressures (Chapter 1).
3 Front wheel bearings loose, worn or damaged. Check (Chapter 1) and replace if necessary (Chapter 11).
4 Lack of lubrication in the balljoints or tie-rod ends (Chapter 1).
5 Damaged shock absorbers or mountings (Chapter 1).
6 Loose wheel lug nuts. Check and tighten as necessary (Chapter 11).

Chapter 1 Tune-up and routine maintenance

Refer to Chapter 13 for specifications and information applicable to later models

Contents

Specifications

Note: *Additional Specifications and torque settings can be found in each individual Chapter.*

Quick reference capacities

	US	Metric
Engine oil (including filter)		
2.2L engine	4.0 qts	3.0 liters
2.6L engine	5.0 qts	5.0 liters
Fuel tank	13 gal	49.0 liters
Automatic transaxle (1981 and 1982)		
From dry, including torque converter		
2.2L engine	7.5 qts	7.1 liters
2.6L engine	8.5 qts	8.1 liters
Transaxle refill (all)	2.8 qts	3.0 liters
Differential (all)	1.2 qts	1.1 liters
Automatic transaxle (1983)		
From dry, including torque converter (all)	8.9 qts	8.4 liters
Transaxle refill (all)	3.8 qts	4.0 liters
Manual transaxle		
4-speed	2.0 qts	1.8 liters
5-speed	2.3 qts	2.1 liters
Power steering	2.5 qts	1.2 liters
Cooling system		
1981 and 1982		
2.2L engine	7.0 qts	6.6 liters
2.6L engine	8.5 qts	8.1 liters
1983 (all)	9.0 qts	8.5 liters

Recommended fluids and lubricants

Engine oil	
Type	API SE or SF classification

Recommended SAE viscosity grades
    Above 32°F (0°C) 20W20
                                                                  20W40
                                                                  20W50
                                                                  10W30
                                                                  10W40
    May be used as low as 10°F (-12°C) 10W30
                                                                    10W40
                                                                    10W50
                                                                   5W40
    Consistently below 10°F (-12°C) 5W20
                                                                    5W30
                                                                     5W40

Manual and automatic transaxle fluid .... DEXRON II automatic transmission fluid
Transaxle shift linkage .... NLGI No. 2 chassis grease
Clutch linkage .... NLGI No. 2 chassis grease
Power steering reservoir .... Mopar 4-253 power steering fluid or equivalent
Brake system and master cylinder .... DOT type 3 brake fluid
Carburetor choke shaft .... Mopar combustion chamber conditioner No. 2933500 or equivalent
Engine coolant .... 50/50 mixture of ethylene glycol base antifreeze and water
Parking brake mechanism .... White lithium base grease NLGI No. 2
Chassis lubrication .... NLGI No. 2 EP chassis grease
Steering shaft seal .... NLGI No. 2 multi-purpose lubricant
Rear wheel bearing .... NLGI No. 2 EP grease
Steering gear .... API GL-4 SAE 90 oil
Hood and door hinges .... Engine oil
Door hinge half and check spring .... NLGI No. 2 multi-purpose grease
Key lock cylinders .... Graphite spray
Hood latch assembly .... Mopar Lubriplate or equivalent
Door latch striker .... Mopar Door Ease No. 3744859 or equivalent
Differential (automatic transaxle) .... DEXRON II automatic transmission fluid

General data

Thermostat .... 195°F (91°C)
Radiator pressure cap opening pressure .... 16 psi
Idle speed adjustment .... Refer to the vehicle Emission Control Information Label in the engine compartment
Firing order 1-3-4-2
Spark plug gap
    2.2L engine .... 0.035 in (0.9 mm)
    2.6L engine .... 0.040 in (1.0 mm)
Alternator drivebelt deflection
    2.2L engine
        New .... 0.12 in (3 mm)
        Used .... 0.25 in (6 mm)
    2.6L engine
        New .... 0.18 in (4 mm)
        Used .... 0.25 in (6 mm)
Power steering pump drivebelt deflection
    2.2L engine
        New .... 0.25 in (6 mm)
        Used .... 0.44 in (11 mm)
    2.6L engine
        New .... 0.25 in (6 mm)
        Used .... 0.38 in (9 mm)
Water pump drivebelt deflection
    2.2L engine
        New .... 0.12 in (3 mm)
        Used .... 0.25 in (6 mm)
    2.6L engine
        New .... 0.31 in (8 mm)
        Used .... 0.38 in (9 mm)
Air pump drivebelt deflection (2.2L engine)
    New .... 0.20 in (5 mm)
    Used .... 0.25 in (6 mm)
Air conditioning compressor drivebelt deflection
    2.2L engine
        New .... 0.31 in (8 mm)
        Used .... 0.38 in (5 mm)
    2.6L engine
        New .... 0.25 in (6 mm)
        Used .... 0.31 in (8 mm)
2.6L engine valve clearance *(hot* engine)
    Intake .... 0.006 in (0.15 mm)
    Exhaust .... 0.010 in (0.25 mm)

1

Torque specifications

	Ft-lb	Nm
Automatic transaxle differential fill plug	24	33
Automatic transaxle pan bolts	14	19
Manual transaxle fill plug	24	33
2.2L engine air cleaner wing nut-to-carburetor stud	1.5	2.0
Oil pan drain plug		
2.2L engine	20	27
2.6L engine	19	25
Spark plug		
2.2L engine	26	35
2.6L engine	18	25
Wheel lug nuts	80	108
Carburetor nut		
2.2L engine	17	23
2.6L engine	13	17

1 General information

Caution: *The electric fan on some models can start at any time, even when the engine is turned off. Consequently, the negative battery cable should be disconnected whenever you are working in the vicinity of the fan.*

Front wheel drive vehicles incorporate several features which vary from the usual automotive practice and require special maintenance techniques. Among these are the drive axles, transaxle and cooling system. Consult this Chapter and the *General information* Sections of each Chapter to determine which components are unique to these vehicles.

2 Introduction to routine maintenance

This Chapter was designed to help the home mechanic maintain his (or her) car for peak performance, economy, safety and longevity.

On the following pages you will find a maintenance schedule along with Sections which deal specifically with each item on the schedule. Included are visual checks, adjustments and item replacements.

Servicing your car using the time/mileage maintenance schedule and the sequenced Sections will give you a planned program of maintenance. Keep in mind that it is a full plan, and maintaining only a few items at the specified intervals will not give you the same results.

You will find as you service your car that many of the procedures can, and should, be grouped together, due to the nature of the job at hand. Examples of this are as follows:

If the car is fully raised for a chassis inspection, for example, this is the ideal time for the following checks: manual transaxle fluid, exhaust system, suspension, steering and the fuel system.

If the tires and wheels are removed, as during a routine tire rotation, go ahead and check the brakes and wheel bearings at the same time.

If you must borrow or rent a torque wrench, it is a good idea to service the spark plugs and/or repack (or replace) the wheel bearings all in the same day to save time and money.

The first step of this or any maintenance plan is to prepare yourself before the actual work begins. Read through the appropriate Sections for all work that is to be performed before you begin. Gather together all necessary parts and tools. If it appears you could have a problem during a particular job, don't hesitate to ask advice from your local parts man or dealer service department.

Note: *The following maintenance intervals are recommended by the manufacturer. In the interest of vehicle longevity, we recommend shorter intervals on certain operations such as fluid and filter replacements.*

Weekly or every 250 miles (400 km)

Check the engine oil level, adding as necessary
Check windshield wiper blade condition
Check the engine coolant level, adding as necessary
Check the tires and tire pressures
Check the automatic transaxle fluid level
Check the power steering reservoir level
Check the brake fluid level
Check the battery condition

Check the windshield washer level
Check the operation of all lights
Check horn operation

Every 3000 miles (5000 km) or 3 months, whichever comes first

Change engine oil and filter (Chapter 1)
Check the suspension balljoint and steering linkage boots for damage or lubricant leakage (Chapters 1 and 11)
Check the steering gear boots for cracks or lubricant leakage (Chapter 11)
Inspect the drive axle CV joint boots for damage, wear or lubricant leakage (Chapter 8)

Every 7500 miles (12000 km) or 6 months, whichever comes first

Check the differential fluid level (1981 and 1982 automatic transaxle) (Chapter 1)
Check the manual transaxle fluid level (Chapter 1)
Check the deflection of all drivebelts (Chapter 1)
Check the engine idle speed (Chapter 4)
Check the fuel hoses, tubes and connections for leaks or damage (Chapter 4)
Check the brake hoses and lines for leaks or damage (Chapter 9)

Every 15 000 miles (24 000 km) or 12 months, whichever comes first

Check the cooling system hoses and connections for leaks or damage (Chapter 3)
Check the front disc brake pads (Chapter 1)
Check for freeplay in the steering linkage and balljoints (Chapter 11)
Check the hoses and connections in the fuel evaporative emission system (Chapter 6)
Check the exhaust pipes and hangers (Chapter 1)
Check the EGR system components for proper operation (Chapter 6)
Check the condition of the vacuum hoses and connections (Chapter 4)
Check the condition of the wiring harness connections (Chapter 10)
Adjust the rear drum brake shoes (1981 and 1982 models)
Check the condition of the ignition wiring and spark plug wires (Chapter 1)
Check the distributor cap and rotor for cracks, wear and damage (Chapter 5)
Check the choke shaft, fast idle cam and pivot pin for free movement, cleaning with solvent as necessary (Chapter 1)
Check and adjust the drivebelt tension (Chapter 1)
Check and adjust the valve clearance (2.6L engine) (Chapter 1)

Every 22 500 miles (36 000 km) or 18 months, whichever comes first

Lubricate the front suspension and steering balljoints (Chapter 1)
Check the ignition timing (Chapter 1)
Check the engine idle speed (Chapter 1)
Replace the air filter element (2.6L engine)
Check the air conditioning hoses, belts and sight glass (Chapter 3)
Replace the fuel filter (Chapter 1)

FRONT

Fig. 1.1 Typical view of engine compartment

1 Ignition coil	7 Voltage regulator, starter relay, fan relay and anti-diesel relay
2 Oil filler cap	
3 Vent module	8 Battery
4 PCV valve	9 Spark control computer
5 Air cleaner	10 Coolant reservoir
6 Brake fluid reservoir	11 Radiator cap

12 Fan shroud
13 Fan motor
14 Fan motor connector
15 Oil dipstick
16 Oil filter
17 Air conditioner compressor
18 Charcoal canister location

Fig. 1.2 Typical view of engine compartment underside (2.2L engine shown)

FRONT

1	Alternator	6	Left driveaxle
2	Fuel pump	7	Outer CV joint boot
3	Oil filter	8	Swaybar
4	Oil pan	9	Catalytic converter
5	Transaxle oil pan	10	Oil drain plug

11	Lower control arm
12	Lower balljoint grease fitting
13	Inner CV joint boot
14	Brake caliper
15	Brake hose

Check the emissions control system hoses and connections for looseness or damage (Chapter 6)

Every 30 000 miles (48 000 km) or 24 months, whichever comes first

Drain and replace the engine coolant (Chapter 3)
Replace the air filter element (2.2L engine) (Chapter 1)
Clean and lubricate the crankcase vent module (Chapter 1)
Replace the PCV valve (Chapter 1)
Change the automatic transaxle fluid (Chapter 7B)
Check the rear brake linings and drums for wear or damage (Chapter 1)
Adjust the automatic transaxle bands (Chapter 7B)
Inspect and adjust the rear wheel bearings (Chapter 11)
Check the parking brake operation (Chapter 9)
Check the steering shaft seal, lubricating as necessary (Chapter 11)
Replace the spark plugs (Chapter 1)

Severe operating conditions

Severe operating conditions are defined as:
Stop and go driving
Driving in dusty conditions
Frequent short trips
Sustained high speed driving during hot weather (over 90°F, 32°C)

Severe operating conditions maintenance intervals:
Change automatic transaxle fluid and filter and adjust the bands every 15 000 miles (24 000 km)
Change the engine oil and filter every 2000 miles (3200 km)
Inspect the disc brake linings every 6000 miles (96 000 km)
Inspect the rear brakes and drums every 12 000 miles (19 200 km)
Relubricate and adjust the rear wheel bearings every 12 000 miles (19 200 km)
Inspect the drive axle CV joint boots and front suspension boots every 2000 miles (3200 km)
Lubricate the tie-rod ends every 15 000 miles (24 000 km)

3   Fluid levels check

1   There are a number of components on a vehicle which rely on the use of fluids to perform their job. Through the normal operation of the car, these fluids are used up and must be replenished before damage occurs. See *Recommended lubricants and fluids* for the specific fluid to be used when adding is required. When checking fluid levels it is important that the car is on a level surface.

Engine oil

2   The engine oil level is checked with a dipstick which is located at the front side of the engine block. This dipstick travels through a tube and into the oil pan at the bottom of the engine.
3   The oil level should be checked preferably before the car has been

Fig. 1.3 Typical rear underside of vehicle

1	Muffler	5	Fuel tank	8	Rear spring
2	Track bar diagonal brace	6	Rear axle	9	Rear shock absorber
3	Fuel filler tube	7	Exhaust pipe	10	Track bar bracket
4	Track bar				

FRONT

1

3.6 Engine oil is added to the 2.2L engine after removing the cap in the valve cover

driven, or about 15 minutes after the engine has been shut off. If the oil is checked immediately after driving the car, some of the oil will remain in the upper engine components, giving an inaccurate reading on the dipstick.

4   Pull the dipstick from its tube and wipe all the oil from the end with a clean rag. Insert the clean dipstick all the way back into the oil pan and pull it out again. Observe the oil at the end of the dipstick. At its highest point, the level should be between the Add and Full marks.

5   It takes approximately 1 quart of oil to raise the level from the Add mark to the Full mark on the dipstick. Do not allow the level to drop below the Add mark as this may cause engine damage due to oil starvation. On the other hand, do not overfill the engine by adding oil above the Full mark, as this may result in oil-fouled spark plugs, oil leaks or oil seal failures.

6   Oil is added to the engine after removing a twist-off cap located either on the rocker arm cover or through a raised tube near the front of the engine. The cap should be marked 'Engine oil' or something similar. An oil can spout or funnel will reduce spills as the oil is poured in (photo).

7   Checking the oil level can also be a step towards preventative

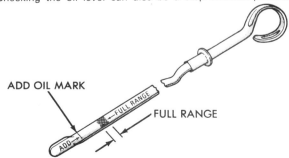

ADD OIL MARK

FULL RANGE

Fig. 1.4 Oil level check (Sec 3)

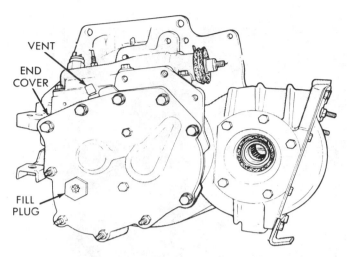

Fig. 1.5 Manual transaxle check/filler plug location (Sec 3)

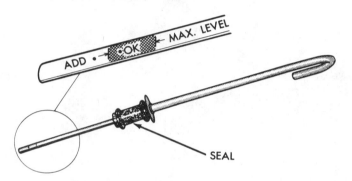

Fig. 1.7 Automatic transaxle fluid level check (Sec 3)

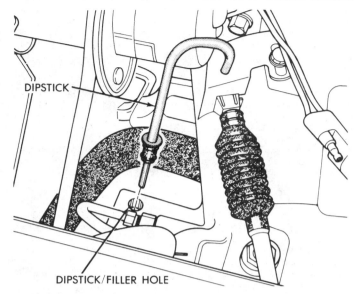

Fig. 1.6 Automatic transaxle dipstick/filler location (Sec 3)

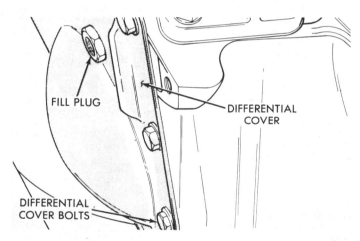

Fig. 1.8 Automatic transaxle differential filler plug location (Sec 3)

maintenance. If you find the oil level dropping abnormally, it is an indication of oil leakage or internal engine wear which should be corrected. If there are water droplets in the oil, or if it is milky looking, this also indicates component failure and the engine should be checked immediately. The condition of the oil can also be checked along with the level. With the dipstick removed from the engine, wipe your thumb and index finger up the dipstick, looking for small dirt particles or filings which will cling to the dipstick. This is an indication that the oil should be drained and fresh oil added (Section 5).

Engine coolant

8   All vehicles are equipped with a pressurized coolant recovery system which makes coolant level checks very easy. A coolant reservoir attached to the inner fender panel is connected by a hose to the radiator cap. As the engine heats up during operation, coolant is forced from the radiator, through the connecting tube and into the reservoir. As the engine cools, this coolant is automatically drawn back into the radiator to keep the correct level (photo).

9   The coolant level should be checked when the engine is cold. Merely observe the level of fluid in the reservoir, which should be at or near the Full cold mark on the side of the reservoir. If the system is completely cooled, also check the level in the radiator by removing the cap.

10 The coolant level can also be checked by removing the radiator cap. However, the cap should not under any circumstances be removed while the system is hot, as escaping steam could cause serious injury. Wait until the engine has cooled, then wrap a thick cloth around the cap and turn it to its first stop. If any steam escapes from the cap, allow the engine to cool further. Then remove the cap and check the level in the radiator.

11 If only a small amount of coolant is required to bring the system up to the proper level, regular water can be used. However, to maintain the proper antifreeze/water mixture in the system, both should be mixed together to replenish a low level. High-quality

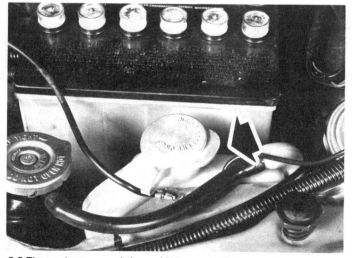

3.8 The coolant reservoir (arrow) is located adjacent to the radiator

antifreeze offering protection to -20° should be mixed with water in the proportion specified on the container. These vehicles have aluminium cylinder heads, so the use of the proper coolant is critical to avoid corrosion. Do not allow antifreeze to come into contact with your skin or painted surfaces of the car. Flush contacted areas immediately with plenty of water.

12 On systems with a recovery tank, coolant should be added to the reservoir after removing the cap at the top of the reservoir.

13 As the coolant level is checked, observe the condition of the coolant. It should be relatively clear. If the fluid is brown or rust colored, this is an indication that the system should be drained, flushed and refilled (Section 28).

14 If the cooling system requires repeated additions to keep the proper level, have the radiator pressure cap checked for proper sealing ability. Also check for leaks in the system (cracked hoses, loose hose connections, leaking gaskets, etc.).

Windshield washer fluid

15 The fluid for the windshield washer system is located in a plastic reservoir. The level inside the reservoir should be maintained at the Full mark. The washer and coolant reservoirs are combined in one container with a partition between. Be careful to put fluids in their proper container (photo).

16 An approved washer solvent should be added through the plastic cap whenever replenishing is required. Do not use plain water alone in this system, especially in cold climates where the water could freeze.

Battery electrolyte

Note: *There are certain precautions to be taken when working on or near the battery; a) never expose a battery to open flame or sparks which could ignite the hydrogen gas given off by the battery; b) wear protective clothing and eye protection to reduce the possibility of the corrosive sulfuric acid solution inside the battery harming you (if the fluid is splashed or spilled, flush the contacted area immediately with plenty of water); c) remove all metal jewelry which could contact the positive terminal and another grounded metal source, thus causing a short circuit; d) always keep battery acid out of reach of children.*

17 Vehicles equipped with maintenance-free batteries require no maintenance as the battery case is sealed and has no removable caps for adding water.

18 If a maintenance-type battery is installed, the caps on the top of the battery should be removed periodically to check for a low water level. This check will be more critical during the warm summer months.

19 Remove each of the caps and add distilled water to bring the level of each cell to the split ring in the filler opening.

20 At the same time the battery water level is checked, the overall condition of the battery and its related components should be inspected. If corrosion is found on the cable ends or battery terminals, remove the cables and clean away all corrosion using a baking soda/water solution or a wire brush cleaning tool designed for this purpose. See Section 30 for complete battery care and servicing.

Brake fluid (master cylinder)

21 The brake master cylinder is located on the left side of the engine compartment firewall and has a cap which must be removed to check the fluid level.

22 Before removing the cap, use a rag to clean all dirt, grease, etc. from around the cap area. If any foreign matter enters the master cylinder with the cap removed, blockage in the brake system lines can occur. Also make sure all painted surfaces around the master cylinder are covered, as brake fluid will ruin paint.

23 Unscrew the reservoir cap.

24 Carefully lift the cap off the cylinder and observe the fluid level (photo). It should be approximately $\frac{1}{4}$ inch below the top edge of each reservoir.

25 If additional fluid is necessary to bring the level up to the proper height, carefully pour the specified brake fluid into the master cylinder. Be careful not to spill the fluid on painted surfaces. Be sure the specified fluid is used, as mixing different types of brake fluid can cause damage to the system. See *Recommended lubricants and fluids* or your owner's manual.

26 At this time the fluid and master cylinder can be inspected for contamination. Normally, the braking system will not need periodic draining and refilling, but if rust deposits, dirt particles or water droplets are seen in the fluid, the system should be dismantled, drained and refilled with fresh fluid.

3.15 The windshield washer is located just below the left wiper arm

3.24 Checking the brake master cylinder reservoir fluid level

27 Reinstall the master cylinder cap. Make sure the lid is properly seated to prevent fluid leakage and/or system pressure loss.

28 The brake fluid in the master cylinder will drop slightly as the brake shoes or pads at each wheel wear down during normal operation. If the master cylinder requires repeated replenishing to keep it at the proper level, this is an indication of leakage in the brake system which should be corrected immediately. Check all brake lines and their connections, along with the wheel cylinders and booster (see Chapter 9 for more information).

29 If upon checking the master cylinder fluid you discover one or both reservoirs empty or nearly empty, the braking system should be bled (Chapter 9). When the fluid gets low, air can enter the system and should be removed by bleeding the brakes.

Manual transaxle lubricant

30 Manual shift transaxles do not have a dipstick. The fluid level is checked by removing a plug in the side of the transaxle case. Locate this plug and use a rag to clean the plug and the area around it.

31 With the vehicle components cold, remove the plug. if fluid immediately starts leaking out, thread the plug back into the transaxle because the fluid level is alright. If there is no fluid leakage, completely remove the plug and place your finger inside the hole. The fluid level should be just at the bottom on the plug hole. Use only the specified transmission fluid, do not use gear oil.

32 If the transaxle needs more fluid, use a syringe to squeeze the

appropriate lubricant into the plug hole to bring the fluid up to the proper level.

33 Thread the plug back into the transaxle and tighten it securely. Drive the car and check for leaks round the plug.

Automatic transaxle fluid

34 The fluid inside the transaxle must be at normal operating temperature to get an accurate reading on the dipstick. This is done by driving the car for several miles, making frequent starts and stops to allow the transaxle to shift through all gears.

35 Park the car on a level surface, place the selector lever in Park and leave the engine running at an idle.

36 Remove the transaxle dipstick and wipe all the fluid from the end of the dipstick with a clean rag.

37 Push the dipstick back into the transaxle until the cap seats firmly on the dipstick tube. Now remove the dipstick again and observe the fluid on the end. The highest point of fluid should be between the Full mark and $\frac{1}{4}$ inch below the Full mark.

38 If the fluid level is at or below the Add mark on the dipstick, add sufficient fluid to raise the level to the Max. level mark. One pint of fluid will raise the level from Add to Max. level. Fluid should be added directly into the dipstick guide tube, using a funnel to prevent spills.

39 It is important that the transaxle not be overfilled. Under no circumstances should the fluid level be above the Max. level mark on the dipstick, as this could cause internal damage to the transaxle. The best way to prevent overfilling is to add fluid a little at a time, driving the car and checking the level between additions.

40 Use only transaxle fluid specified by the manufacturer. This information can be found in the *Recommended lubricants and fluids* Section.

41 The condition of the fluid should also be checked along with the level. If the fluid at the end of the dipstick is a dark reddish-brown color, or if the fluid has a 'burnt' smell, the transaxle fluid should be changed. If you are in doubt about the condition of the fluid, purchase some new fluid and compare the two for color and smell.

42 On 1981 and 1982 models, the differential fluid must be checked separately from the transaxle fluid. Raise the vehicle, support it securely and remove the differential fill plug. The fluid level must be within $\frac{3}{8}$ inch of the filler hole bottom edge. If the level is low, add the specified fluid with a syringe and replace the plug.

Drive axle lubricant

43 The drive axle constant velocity joints are lubricated for life at the time of manufacture and it is important to inspect the protective boots for cracks, tears or splits (photo).

44 With the vehicle raised securely, inspect the area around the boots for signs of grease splattering, indicating damage to the boots or retaining clamps.

45 Inspect around the inboard joint for signs of fluid leakage from the transaxle differential seal.

Power steering fluid

46 Unlike manual steering, the power steering system relies on fluid which may, over a period of time, require replenishing.

47 The reservoir for the power steering pump is located on the rear side of the engine.

48 The power steering fluid level should be checked only after the car has been driven, with the fluid at operating temperature. The front wheels should be pointed straight ahead.

49 With the engine shut off, use a rag to clean the reservoir cap and the areas around the cap. This will help to prevent foreign material from falling into the reservoir when the cap is removed.

50 Twist off the reservoir cap (photo), which has a built-up dipstick attached to it. Pull off the cap and clean the fluid at the bottom of the dipstick with a clean rag. Now reinstall the dipstick assembly to get a fluid level reading. Remove the dipstick/cap and observe the fluid level. It should be at the Full hot mark on the dipstick.

51 If additional fluid is required, pour the specified lubricant directly into the reservoir using a funnel to prevent spills.

52 If the reservoir requires frequent fluid additions, all power steering hoses, hose connections, the power steering pump and the steering box should be carefully checked for leaks.

---

4 Tire and tire pressures

1 Periodically inspecting the tires can prevent you from being

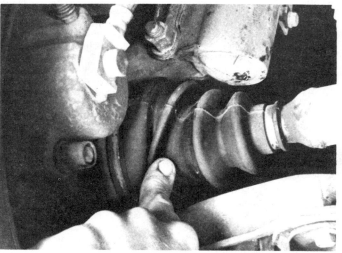

3.43 Carefully check the CV joint boots for cracks or leaks

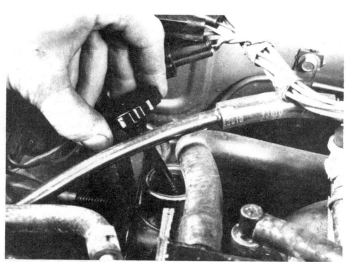

3.50 Checking the power steering fluid level

stranded with a flat tire and can also give you clues as to possible problems with the steering and suspension systems before major damage occurs.

2 Proper tire inflation adds miles to the lifespan of the tires, allows the car to achieve maximum miles per gallon figures, and contributes to overall riding comfort of the car.

3 When inspecting a tire, first check the wear on the tread. Irregularities in the tread pattern (cupping, flat spots, more wear on one side than the other) are indications of front end alignment and/or balance problems. If any of these conditions are found, take the car to a competent repair shop which can correct the problem.

4 Also check the tread area for cuts or punctures. Many times a nail or tack will embed itself into the tire tread and yet the tire will hold its air pressure for a short time. In most cases, a repair shop or gas station can repair the punctured tire.

5 It is also important to check the sidewalls of the tire, both inside and outside. Check for the rubber being deteriorated, cut or punctured. Also inspect the inboard side of the tire for signs of brake fluid leakage, indicating a thorough brake inspection is needed immediately.

6 Incorrect tire pressure cannot be determined merely by looking at the tire. This is especially true for radial tires. A tire pressure gauge must be used. If you do not already have a reliable gauge, it is a good idea to purchase one and keep it in the glove compartment. Built-in pressure gauges at gas stations are often unreliable. if you are in doubt

as to the accuracy of your gauge, many repair shops have 'master' pressure gauges which you can use for comparison purposes.

7   Always check tire inflation when the tires are cold. Cold, in this case, means the car has not been driven more than one mile after sitting for three hours or more. It is normal for the pressure to increase 4 to 8 pounds or more when the tires are hot.

8   Unscrew the valve cap protruding from the wheel or hubcap and firmly press the gauge onto the valve stem. Observe the reading on the gauge and check this figure against the recommended tire pressure listed on the tire placard.

9   Check all tires and add air as necessary to bring all tires up to the recommended pressure levels. Do not forget the spare tire. Be sure to reinstall the valve caps which will keep dirt and moisture out of the valve stem mechanism.

5   Engine oil and filter change

1   Frequent oil changes may be the best form of preventative maintenance available for the home mechanic. When engine oil ages it get diluted and contaminated which ultimately leads to premature parts wear.

2   Although some sources recommend oil filter changes every other oil change, we feel that the minimal cost of an oil filter and the relative ease with which it is installed dictates that a new filter be used whenever the oil is changed.

3   The tools necessary for a routine oil and filter change are, a wrench to fit the drain plug at the bottom of the oil pan, an oil filter wrench to remove the old filter, a container with at least a 5 quart capacity to drain the old oil into and a funnel or oil can spout to help pour fresh oil into the engine.

4   In addition, you should have plenty of clean rags and newspapers handy to mop up any spills. Access to the underside of the car is greatly improved if the car can be lifted on a hoist, driven onto ramps or supported by jackstands. **Caution:** *Do not work under a car which is supported only by a bumper, hydraulic or scissors-type jack.*

5   If this is your first oil change on the car, it is a good idea to crawl underneath and familarize yourself with the locations of the oil drain plug and the oil filter. Since the engine and exhaust components will be warm during the actual work, it is best to figure out any potential problems before the car and its accessories are hot.

6   Allow the car to warm up to normal operating temperature. If the new oil or any tools are needed, use this warm-up time to gather everything necessary for the job. The correct type of oil to buy for your application can be found in the *Recommended lubricants and fluids* Section, near the front of this Chapter.

7   With the engine oil warm (warm engine oil will drain better and more built-up sludge will be removed with the oil), raise the vehicle for access beneath. Make sure the car is firmly supported. If jackstands are used, they should be placed towards the front of the frame rails which run the length of the car.

8   Move all necessary tools, rags and newspapers under the car. Position the drain pan under the drain plug. Keep in mind that the oil will initially flow from the pan with some force, so place the pan accordingly.

9   Being careful not to touch any of the hot exhaust pipe components, use the wrench to remove the drain plug near the bottom of the oil pan. Depending on how hot the oil has become, you may want to wear gloves while unscrewing the plug the final few turns.

10   Allow the old oil to drain into the pan. It may be necessary to move the pan further under the engine as the oil flow reduces to a trickle.

11   After all the oil has drained, clean the drain plug thoroughly with a clean rag. Small metal filings may cling to this plug which could immediately contaminate your new oil.

12   Clean the area around the drain plug opening and reinstall the drain plug. Tighten the plug securely with your wrench.

13   Move the drain pan into position under the oil filter.

14   Now use the filter wrench to loosen the oil filter. Chain or metal band-type filter wrenches may distort the filter canister, but don't worry too much about this as the filter will be discarded anyway.

15   Sometimes the oil filter is on so tight it cannot be loosened, or it is positioned in an area which is inaccessible with a filter wrench. As a last resort, you can punch a metal bar or long screwdriver directly through the **bottom** of the canister and use this as a T-bar to turn the filter. If this must be done, be prepared for oil to spurt out of the canister as it is punctured.

16   Completely unscrew the old filter. Be careful, it is full of oil. Empty the old oil inside the filter into the drain pan.

17   Compare the old filter with the new one to make sure they are of the same type.

18   Use a clean rag to removal all oil, dirt and sludge from the area where the oil filter mounts to the engine. Check the old filter to make sure the rubber gasket is not stuck to the engine mounting surface. If this gasket is stuck to the engine (use a flashlight if necessary), remove it.

19   Open one of the cans of new oil and fill the new filter $\frac{1}{2}$ full with fresh oil. Also apply a light coat of this fresh oil to the rubber gasket of the new oil filter.

20   Attach the new filter to the engine following the tightening directions printed on the filter canister or packing box. Most filter manufacturers recommend against using a filter wrench due to possible overtightening or damage to the canister (photo).

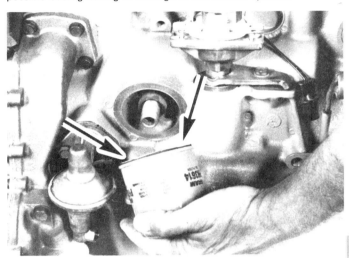

5.20 With the gasket (arrows) smeared with a coat of oil, install the filter

21   Remove all tools, rags, etc, from under the car, being careful not to spill the oil in the drain pan. Lower the car off its support devices.

22   Move to the engine compartment and locate the oil filler cap on the engine.

23   If an oil spout if used, push the spout into the top of the oil can and pour the fresh oil through the filler opening. A funnel placed into the opening may also be used.

24   Pour about three quarts of fresh oil into the engine. Wait a few minutes to allow the oil to drain to the pan, then check the level on the oil dipstick (see Section 3 if necessary). If the oil level is at or above the lower Add mark, start the engine and allow the new oil to circulate.

25   Run the engine for only about a minute and then shut it off. Immediately look under the car and check for leaks at the oil pan drain plug and around the oil filter. If either is leaking, tighten with a bit more force.

26   With the new oil circulated and the filter now completely full, recheck the level on the dipstick and add enough oil to bring the level to the Full mark on the dipstick.

27   During the first few trips after an oil change, make it a point to check for leaks and keep a close watch on the oil level.

28   The old oil drained from the engine cannot be reused in its present state and should be disposed of. Oil reclamation centers, auto repair shops and gas stations will normally accept the oil (which can be refined and used again). After the oil has cooled, it can be drained into a suitable container (capped plastic jugs, topped bottles, milk cartons, etc.) for transport to one of these disposal sites.

6   Chassis lubrication

1   A grease gun and a cartridge filled with the proper grease (see *Recommended lubricants and fluids*) are usually the only equipment necessary to lubricate the chassis components. Occasionally, on later model vehicles, plugs will be installed rather than grease fittings, in

1

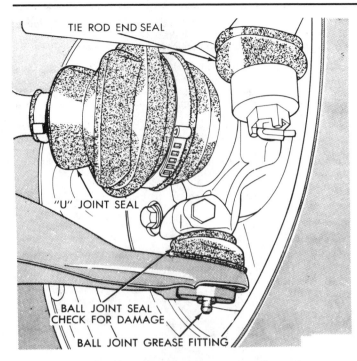

Fig. 1.9 Balljoint grease fitting location (Sec 6)

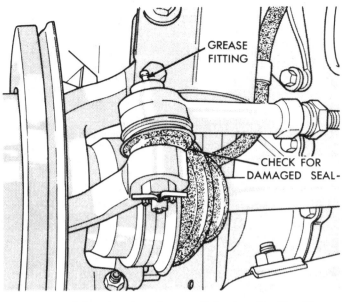

Fig. 1.10 Steering tie-rod grease fitting location (Sec 6)

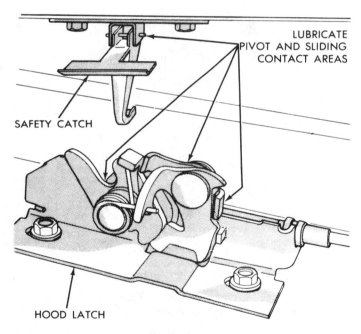

Fig. 1.11 Hood latch lubrication points (Sec 6)

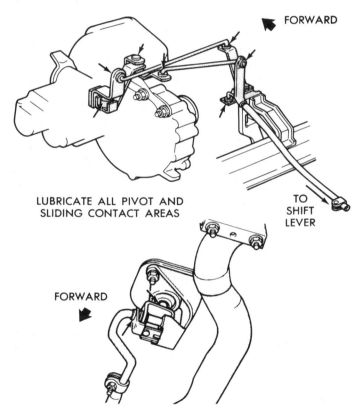

Fig. 1.12 Manual transaxle shift linkage lubrication points (Sec 6)

which case grease fittings will have to be purchased and installed.

2   Look under the vehicle and see if grease fittings or solid plugs are installed. If there are plugs, remove them with the correct wrench and buy grease fittings which will thread into the component. A Chrysler dealer or auto parts store will be able to find replacement fittings. Straight, as well as angled, fittings are available for easy greasing.

3   For easier access under the vehicle, raise the vehicle with a jack and place jackstands under the frame. Make sure it is firmly supported by the stands.

4   Before you do any greasing, force a little of the grease out of the nozzle to remove any dirt from the end of the gun. Wipe the nozzle clean with a rag.

5   With the grease gun, plenty of clean rags and the location diagram, go under the vehicle to begin lubricating the components.

6   Wipe the grease fitting nipple clean and push the nozzle firmly over the fitting nipples. Squeeze the trigger on the grease gun to force grease into the component. The balljoints should be lubricated until the rubber reservoir is firm to the touch. Do not pump too much grease into these fittings as this could rupture the reservoir. For all other suspension and steering fittings, continue pumping grease into the nipple until grease seeps out of the joint between the two components. If the grease seeps out around the grease gun nozzle, the

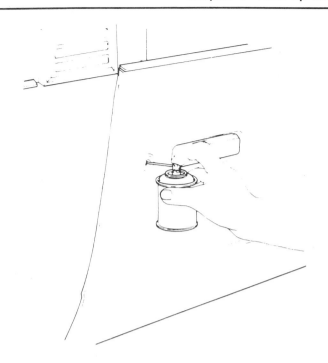

Fig. 1.13 Spraying graphite into the lock cylinder (Sec 6)

Fig. 1.14 Spraying silicone lubricant on the door weatherstripping (Sec 6)

nipple is clogged or the nozzle is not fully seated around the fitting nipple. Re-secure the gun nozzle to the fitting and try again. If necessary, replace the fitting.

7   Wipe the excess grease from the components and the grease fitting. Follow these procedures for the remaining fittings.

8   Lubricate the sliding contact and pivot points of the manual transaxle shift linkage with the specified grease. While you are under the vehicle, clean and lubricate the parking brake cable along with its cable guides and levers. This can be done by smearing some of the chassis grease onto the cable and its related parts with your fingers.

9   Lower the vehicle to the ground for the remaining body lubrication process.

10   Open the hood and smear a little chassis grease on the hood latch mechanism. If the hood has an inside release, have an assistant pull the release knob from inside the car as you lubricate the cable at the latch.

11   Lubricate all the hinges (door, hood, etc.) with a few drops of light engine oil to keep them in proper working order.

12   The key lock cylinders can be lubricated with spray-on graphite which is available at auto parts stores.

13   Lubricate the door weatherstripping with silicone spray. This will reduce chafing and retard wear.

7   Cooling system check

Caution: *The electric cooling fan on some models can activate at any time, even when the ignition switch is in the Off position. Disconnect the fan motor or the battery negative cable when working in the vicinity of the fan.*

1   Many major engine failures can be attributed to a faulty cooling system. If equipped with an automatic transaxle the cooling system also plays an integral role in transaxle longevity.

2   The cooling system should be checked with the engine cold. Do this before the car is driven for the day or after it has been shut off for one or two hours.

3   Remove the radiator cap and thoroughly clean the cap (inside and out) with clean water. Also clean the filler neck on the radiator. All traces of corrosion should be removed.

4   Carefully check the upper and lower radiator hoses along with the smaller diameter heater hoses. Inspect their entire length, replacing any hose which is cracked, swollen or shows signs of deterioration. Cracks may become more apparent if the hose is squeezed.

5   Also check that all hose connections are tight. A leak in the cooling system will usually show up as white or rust colored deposits on the areas adjoining the leak.

6   Use compressed air or a soft brush to remove bugs, leaves, etc from the front of the radiator or air conditioning condenser. Be careful not to damage the delicate cooling fins, or cut yourself on the sharp fins.

7   Finally, have the cap and system tested for proper pressure. If you do not have a pressure tester, most gas stations and repair shops will do this for a minimal charge.

8   Exhaust system check

1   With the exhaust system cold (at least three hours after being driven), check the complete exhaust system from its starting point at the engine to the end of the tailpipe. This is best done on a hoist where full access is available.

2   Check the pipes and their connections for signs of leakage and/or corrosion indicating a potential failure. Check that all brackets and hangers are in good condition and are tight.

3   At the same time, inspect the underside of the body for holes, corrosion, open seams, etc. which may allow exhaust gases to enter the trunk or passenger compartment. Seal all body openings with silicone or body putty.

4   Rattles and other driving noises can often be traced to the exhaust system, especially the mounts and hangers. Try to move the pipes, muffler and catalytic converter. If the components can come into contact with the body or driveline parts, secure the exhaust system with new mountings.

5   This is also an ideal time to check the running condition of the engine by inspecting the very end of the tailpipe. The exhaust deposits here are an indication of engine tune. If the pipe is black and sooty or bright white deposits are found here, the engine is in need of a tune-up including a thorough carburetor inspection and adjustment.

9   Suspension and steering check

1   Whenever the front of the car is raised for service it is a good idea to visually check the suspension and steering components for wear.

2   Indications of a fault in these systems are excessive play in the

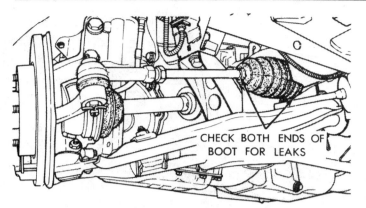

Fig. 1.15 Checking the steering gear boots (Sec 9)

steering wheel before the front wheels react, excessive sway around corners, body movement over rough roads or binding at some point as the steering wheel is turned.

3   Before the car is raised for inspection, test the shock absorbers by pushing downward to rock the car at each corner. If you push the car down and it does not come back to a level position within one or two bounces, the chocks are worn and need to be replaced. As this done, check for squeaks and strange noises from the suspension components. Information on shock absorber and suspension components can be found in Chapter 11.

4   Now raise the front end of the car and support firmly by jackstands placed under the frame rails. Because of the work to be done, make sure the car cannot fall from the stands.

5   Check the front wheel hub nut for looseness and make sure that it is properly crimped in place.

6   Crawl under the car and check for loose bolts, broken or disconnected parts and deteriorated rubber bushings on all suspension and steering components. Look for grease or fluid leaking from around the steering gear boots. Check the power steering hoses and their connections for leaks. Check the steering joints for wear.

7   Have an assistant turn the steering wheel from side to side and check the steering components for free movement, chafing or binding. If the steering does not react with the movement of the steering wheel, try to determine where the slack is located.

10 Fuel system check

1   There are certain precautions to take when inspecting or servicing the fuel system components. Work in a well ventilated area and do not allow open flames (cigarettes, appliance pilot lights, etc.) to get near the work area. Mop up spills immediately and do not store fuel-soaked rags where they could ignite.

2   The fuel system is under some amount of pressure, so if any fuel lines are disconnected for servicing, be prepared to catch the fuel as it spurts out. Plug all disconnected fuel lines immediately after disconnection to prevent the tank from emptying itself.

3   The fuel system is most easily checked with the car raised on a hoist where the components under the car are readily visible and accessible.

4   If the smell of gasoline is noticed while driving, or after the car has sat in the sun, the system should be thoroughly inspected immediately.

5   Remove the gas filler cap and check for damage, corrosion and a proper sealing imprint on the gasket. Replace the cap with a new one if necessary.

6   With the car raised, inspect the gas tank and filler neck for punctures, cracks or any damage. The connection between the filler neck and the tank is especially critical. Sometimes a rubber filler neck will leak due to loose clamps or deteriorated rubber; problems a home mechanic can usually rectify.

7   Do not under any circumstances try to repair a fuel tank yourself (except rubber components) unless you have considerable experience. A welding torch or any open flame can easily cause the fuel vapors to explode if the proper precautions are not taken.

8   Carefully check all rubber hoses and metal lines leading away from the fuel tank. Check for loose connections, deteriorated hose, crimped

lines or damage of any kind. Follow these lines up to the front of the car, carefully inspecting them all the way. Repair or replace damaged sections as necessary.

11 Engine drivebelt check and adjustment

Caution: *The electric cooling fan on some models can activate at any time. even when the ignition switch is in the Off position. Disconnect the fan motor or battery negative cable when working in the vicinity of the fan.*

1   The drivebelts, or V-belts as they are sometimes called, at the front of the engine, play an important role in the overall operation of the car and its components. Due to their function and material make-up, the belts are prone to failure after a period of time and should be inspected and adjusted periodically to prevent major damage.

2   The number of belts used on a particular car depends on the accessories installed. Drivebelts are used to turn the generator (alternator), AIR smog pump, power steering pump, water pump, fan and air conditioning compressor. Depending on the pulley arrangement, a single belt may be used for more than one of these components.

3   With the engine off, open the hood and locate the various belts at the front of the engine. Using your fingers (and flashlight if necessary), move along the belts checking for cracks or separation. Also check for fraying and for glazing which gives the belt a shiny appearance. Both sides of the belts should be inspected, which means you will have to twist the belt to check the underside.

4   The tension of each belt is checked by pushing on the belt at a distance halfway between the pulleys. Push firmly with your thumb and see how much the belt moves downward (deflects). Refer to the Specifications for the amount of deflection allowed in each belt.

5   If it is found necessary to adjust the belt tension, either to make the belt tighter or looser, this is done by moving the belt-driven accessory on its bracket.

6   For each component there will be an adjustment or strap bolt and a pivot bolt. Both bolts must be loosened slightly to enable you to move the component.

7   After the two bolts have been loosened, move the component away from the engine (to tighten the belt) or toward the engine (to loosen the belt). Hold the accessory in this position and check the belt tension. If it is correct, tighten the two bolts until snug, then recheck the tension. If it is alright, fully tighten the two bolts.

8   It will often be necessary to use some sort of pry bar to move the accessory while the belt is adjusted. If this must be done to gain the proper leverage, be very careful not to damage the component being moved, or the part being pried against.

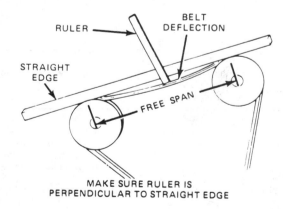

Fig. 1.16 Checking drivebelt deflection with a ruler and straightedge (Sec 11)

12 Air filter element, PCV valve and crankcase vent module maintenance

1   At the intervals specified, the air filter element and PCV valve should be replaced with new ones and the crankcase vent module cleaned and inspected. In addition, all should be inspected periodically.

Fig. 1.17 2.6L engine air cleaner element replacement (Sec 12)

2   The filter element is located inside the air cleaner housing on the top of the engine.

3   To remove the filter element on 2.6L engines, release the clips, lift off the top plate and remove the element. On 2.2L models, remove the three wing nuts and three hold-down clips, lift off the air cleaner crossover and remove the filter element.

4   To check the filter, hold it up to strong sunlight, or place a flashlight or droplight on the inside (2.6L) or behind (2.2L) the element. If you can see light coming through the paper element, the filter is alright.

5   Clean the inside of the air cleaner housing with a rag.

6   Place the old filter (if in good condition) or the new filter (if the specified interval has elapsed) back into the air cleaner housing. Make sure it seats properly in the bottom of the housing.

7   On the 2.6L engine, install the air cleaner top plate and secure the hold-down clips.

8   On the 2.2L engine, the air cleaner crossover cover must be properly installed in order to avoid air leaks. Install the filter with the

screen side up into the air cleaner housing bottom section. Place the steel top cover in place with the studs protruding and the hold-down clips aligned. Install and tighten the two plastic wing nuts securing the cover to the carburetor. Install the third wing nut which secures the air cleaner tab to the bracket and tighten it securely. Install the hold-down clips.

9   The positive crankcase ventilation (PCV) valve should be replaced with a new one at the specified interval or when the valve accumulates deposits which could cause it to stick.

10   To replace the PCV valve, simply pull it from the hose and vent module (2.2L) or valve cover (2.6L) and install a new one (photo).

11   Inspect the hose prior to installation to ensure that it isn't plugged or damaged. Compare the new valve with the old one to make sure they are the same.

12   When replacing the PCV valve on 2.2L engines, inspect the vent module for cracks or damage. Remove the vent module and wash it thoroughly with a suitable solvent for ease of inspection. Prior to installation, invert the module and fill it with engine oil. Allow the oil to drain out through the vent at the top into a suitable container. With the interior of the module now coated with oil, the module can be reinstalled (photo).

12.12 Removing the vent module

12.10 Grasp the PCV valve and pull it from the vent module (2.2L engine)

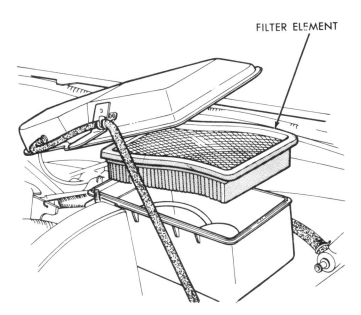

Fig. 1.18 2.2L engine air filter element (Sec 12)

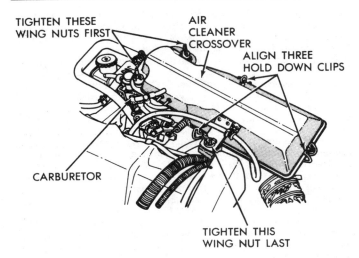

Fig. 1.19 2.2L engine air cleaner crossover installation (Sec 12)

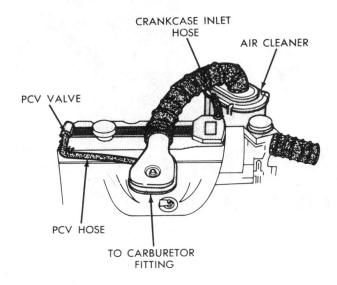

Fig. 1.20 2.6L engine PCV system layout (Sec 12)

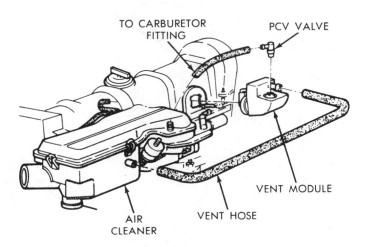

Fig. 1.21 2.2L engine PCV component layout (Sec 12)

13 Clutch pedal free travel

There is no need for checking clutch pedal travel on these models because the clutch control system incorporates a self-adjuster device. Excessive clutch pedal effort, failure of the clutch to disengage or noise from the adjuster indicates faults in this device. Refer to Chapter 8 for further information on the clutch, adjuster and linkage.

14 Tire rotation

1   The tires should be rotated at the specified intervals and whenever uneven wear is noticed. Since the car will be raised and the tires removed anyway, this is a good time to check the brakes (Section 23) and/or repack the wheel bearings. Read over these Sections if this is to be done at the same time.
2   The location for each tire in the rotation sequence depends on the type of tire used on your car. Tire type can be determined by reading the raised printing on the sidewall of the tire. The accompanying figure shows the rotation sequence of each type of tire.
3   See the information in *Jacking and Towing* at the front of this manual for the proper procedures to follow in raising the car and changing a tire; however, if the brakes are to be checked, do not apply the parking brake as stated. Make sure the tires are blocked to prevent the car from rolling.
4   Preferably, the entire car should be raised at the same time. This can be done on a hoist or by jacking up each corner of the car and then lowering the car onto jackstands placed under the frame rails. Always use four jackstands and make sure the car is firmly supported all around.
5   After rotation, check and adjust the tire pressures as necessary and be sure to check wheel lug nut tightness.

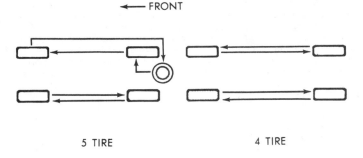

Fig. 1.22 Radial tire rotation pattern (Sec 14)

15 Heated inlet air system – general check

1   All models are equipped with a heated inlet air cleaner which draws air to the carburetor from different locations depending upon the engine temperature.
2   This is a simple visual check; however, if access is tight, a small mirror may have to be used.
3   Open the hood and find the vacuum flapper door on the air cleaner assembly. It will be located inside the long 'snorkel' of the metal air cleaner. Check that the flexible air hose(s) are securely attached and are not damaged.
4   If there is a flexible air duct attached to the end of the snorkel, leading to an area behind the grille, disconnect it at the snorkel. This will enable you to look through the end of the snorkel and see the flapper inside.
5   The testing should preferably be done when the engine and outside air are cold. Start the engine and look through the snorkel at the flapper door which should move to a closed position. With the door closed, air cannot enter through the end of the snorkel, but rather air enters the air cleaner through the flexible duct attached to the exhaust manifold.
6   As the engine warms up to operating temperature, the door should open to allow air through the snorkel end. Depending on ambient

temperature, this may take 10 to 15 minutes. To speed up this check you can reconnect the snorkel air duct, drive the car and then check that the door is fully open.
7 If the air cleaner is not operating properly, see Chapter 4 for more information.

16 Engine idle speed adjustment

1 Engine idle speed is the speed at which the engine operates when no accelerator pedal pressure is applied. This speed is critical to the performance of the engine itself, as well as many engine sub-systems.
2 A hand-held tachometer must be used when adjusting idle speed to get an accurate reading. The exact hook-up for these meters varies with the manufacturer, so follow the particular directions included.
3 Since the manufacturer used several different throttle linkages and positioners on these vehicles in the time period covered by this book, and each has its own peculiarities when setting idle speed, it would be impractical to cover all types in this Section. Chapter 4 contains information on each individual carburetor used. The carburetor used on your particular engine can be found in the Specifications Section of Chapter 4. However, all vehicles covered in this manual have an Emission Control Information label in the engine compartment. The printed instructions for setting idle speed can be found on this label, and should be followed since they are for your particular engine.
4 Basically, for most applications, the idle speed is set by turning an adjustment screw located at the side of the carburetor. This screw changes the linkage, in essence, depressing or letting up on your accelerator pedal. This screw may be on the linkage itself or may be part of the idle stop solenoid. Refer to the emissions label or Chapter 4.
5 Once you have found the idle screw, experiment with different length screwdrivers until the adjustments can be easily made, without coming into contact with hot and moving engine components.
6 Follow the instructions on the emissions label or in Chapter 4, which will probably include disconnecting certain vacuum or electrical connections. To plug a vacuum hose after disconnecting it, insert a properly-sized metal rod into the opening, or thoroughly wrap the open end with tape to prevent any vacuum loss through the hose.
7 If the air cleaner is removed, the vacuum hose to the snorkel should be plugged.

8 Make sure the parking brake is firmly set and the wheels blocked to prevent the car from rolling. This is especially true if the transaxle is to be in Drive. An assistant inside the car, pushing on the brake pedal is the safest method.
9 For all applications, the engine must be completely warmed-up to operating temperature, which will automatically render the choke fast idle inoperative.

17 Fuel filter replacement

1 The fuel filter is of the disposable paper element type and is located in the fuel line between the fuel pump and the carburetor.
2 This job should be done with the engine cold (after sitting at least three hours) and the cooling fan or battery negative cable disconnected. You will need pliers or a similar tool, to remove the fuel line clips, the correct replacement filter and some clean rags.
3 Place some rags under the fuel filter to catch any fuel as the fuel line is disconnected.
4 Disconnect the clamps, pull the hoses from the filter and remove the filter. On 2.6L engines it will also be necessary to disengage the mounting bracket.
5 Push the hoses onto the new filter and install the clamps.
6 Connect the battery and/or fan, start the engine, check for leaks and make sure the filter is securely mounted.

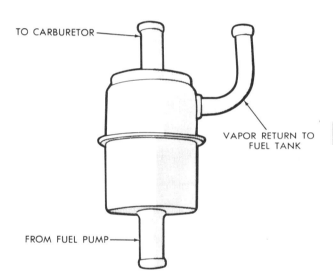

Fig. 1.24 2.2L engine fuel filter hose locations (Sec 17)

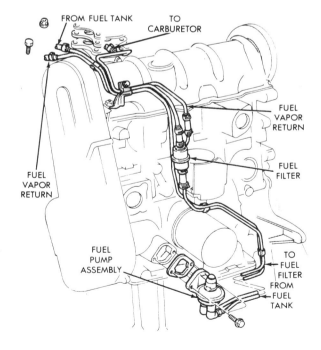

Fig. 1.23 2.2L engine fuel system layout and filter location (Sec 17)

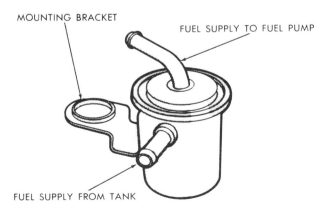

Fig. 1.25 2.6L engine fuel filter hose locations (Sec 17)

18 Ignition timing – adjustment

1   All vehicles are equipped with an emissions label inside the engine compartment. The label gives important ignition timing settings and procedures to be followed specific to that vehicle. If information on the emissions label supersedes the information given in this Section, the label should be followed.

2   At the specified intervals, or when the distributor has been removed, the ignition timing must be checked and adjusted if necessary.

3   Before attempting to check the timing, make sure the idle speed is as specified (Section 16).

4   Disconnect the vacuum hose from the distributor and plug the now-open end of the hose with a rubber plug, rod or bolt of the proper size. Make sure the idle speed remains correct; adjust as necessary.

5   Connect a timing light in accordance with the manufacturer's instructions. Generally, the light will be connected to power and ground sources and to the number 1 spark plug in some fashion. The number 1 spark plug is the first one on the left as you are facing the engine from the front. If the vehicle is equipped with a carburetor switch, connect a jumper wire between the switch and a good ground.

6   Locate the numbered timing tag on the front cover of the engine or at the timing window in the transaxle bellhousing (2.2L engine) referring to the accompanying figure. It is just behind the lower

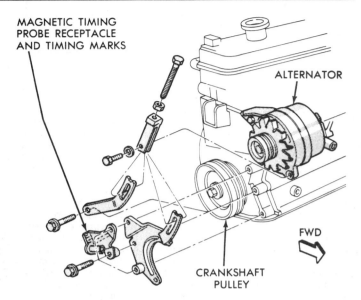

Fig. 1.27 2.6L engine timing pointer location (Sec 18)

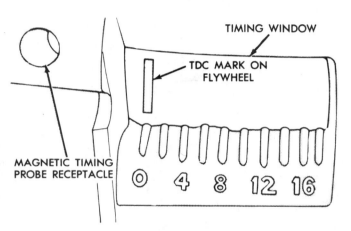

Fig. 1.26 2.2L engine timing mark location (Sec 18)

crankshaft pulley. Clean it off with solvent if necessary to read the printing and small grooves.

7   Locate the notched groove across the crankshaft pulley or flywheel. It may be necessary to have an assistant temporarily turn the ignition off and on in short bursts without starting the engine to bring this groove into a position where it can easily be cleaned and marked. Stay clear of all moving engine components if the engine is turned over in this manner.

8   Use white soap-stone, chalk or paint to mark the groove on the crankshaft pulley or flywheel. Also put a mark on the timing tab in accordance with the number of degrees called for in the Specifications (Chapter 5) or on the emissions label inside the engine compartment. Each peak or notch on the timing tab represents 2°. The word 'Before' or the letter 'A' indicates advance and the letter 'O' indicates Top Dead Centre (TDC). Thus if your vehicle specifications call for 8° BTDC (Before Top Dead Center), you will make a mark on the timing tab 4 notches 'before' the 'O'. On some models the 'O' will be a 'T'.

9   Check that the wiring for the timing light is clear of all moving engine components, then start the engine.

10   Point the flashing timing light at the timing marks, again being careful not to come into contact with moving parts. The marks you made should appear stationary. If the marks are in alignment, the timing is correct. If the marks are not aligned, turn off the engine.

11   Loosen the locknut at the base of the distributor. Loosen the locknut only slightly, just enough to turn the distributor (See Chapter 5 for further details, if necessary).

12   Now restart the engine and turn the distributor until the timing marks coincide.

13   Shut off the engine and tighten the distributor locknut, being careful not to move the distributor.

14   Start the engine and recheck the timing to make sure the marks are still in alignment.

15   Remove the ground jumper wire from the carburetor switch (if equipped). Disconnect the timing light, unplug the distributor vacuum hose and connect the hose to the distributor.

16   Drive the car and listen for 'pinging' noises. These will be most noticeable when the engine is hot and under load (climbing a hill, accelerating from a stop). If you hear pinging, the ignition timing is too far advanced (Before Top Dead Center). Reconnect the timing light and turn the distributor to move the mark 1° or 2° in the retard direction. Road test the car again for proper operation.

17   To keep the 'pinging' at a minimum, yet still allow you to operate the car at the specified timing setting, it is advisable to use gasoline of the same octane at all times. Switching fuel brands and octane levels can decrease performance and economy, and possibly damage the engine.

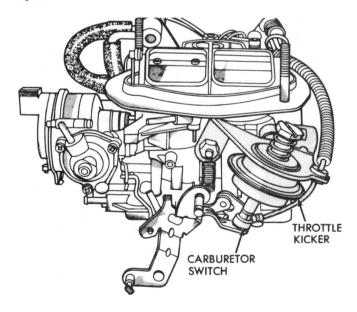

Fig. 1.28 Carburetor switch (2.2L engine) (Sec 18)

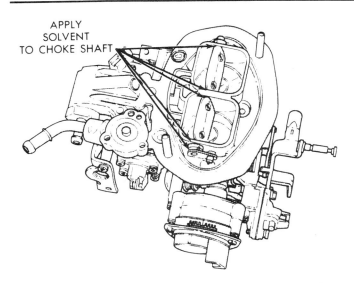

APPLY SOLVENT TO CHOKE SHAFT

Fig. 1.29 Choke shaft solvent application points (Sec 19)

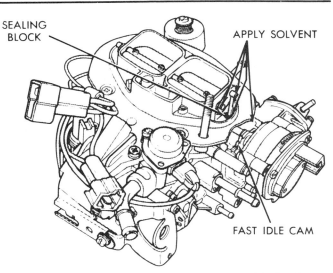

SEALING BLOCK

APPLY SOLVENT

FAST IDLE CAM

Fig. 1.30 2.2L engine choke shaft link and sealing block solvent application points (Sec 19)

19 Carburetor choke check

1 The choke only operates when the engine is cold, and thus this check can only be performed before the car has been started for the day.

2 Open the hood and remove the top plate of the air cleaner assembly as described in Section 12. If any vacuum hoses must be disconnected, make sure you tag the hoses for reinstallation to their original positions.

3 Look at the top of the carburetor at the center of the air cleaner housing. You will notice a flat plate in each of the carburetor throats.

4 Have an assistant press the accelerator pedal to the floor. The plates should close fully. Start the engine while you observe the plates at the carburetor. Do not position your face directly over the carburetor, as the engine could backfire, causing serious burns. When the engine starts, the choke plates should open slightly.

5 Allow the engine to continue running at an idle speed. As the engine warms up to operating temperature, the plates should slowly open, allowing more cold air to enter through the top of the carburetor.

6 After a few minutes, the choke plates should be fully open to the vertical position.

7 You will notice that the engine speed corresponds with the plate opening. With the plate fully closed, the engine should run at a fast idle speed. As the plate opens, the engine speed will decrease.

8 If during the above checks a fault is detected, refer to Chapter 4 for specific information on adjusting and servicing the choke components.

9 At the recommended intervals, apply the specified solvent or equivalent to the contact surfaces of the choke shaft to ensure free movement, Also, apply the solvent to the link connecting the choke shaft to the thermostat and the sealing block through which it passes.

20 Compression check

1 A compression check will tell you what mechanical condition the engine is in. Specifically, it can tell you if the compression is down due to leakage caused by worn piston rings, defective valves and seats or a blown head gasket.

2 Begin by cleaning the area around the spark plugs before you remove them. This will keep dirt from falling into the cylinders while you are performing the compression test.

3 Remove the coil high-tension lead from the distributor and ground it on the engine block. Block the throttle and choke valves wide open.

4 With the compression gauge in the number one cylinder's spark plug hole, crank the engine over at least four compression strokes and observe the gauge (the compression should build up quickly in a healthy engine). Low compression on the first stroke, followed by gradually increasing pressure on successive strokes, indicates worn

piston rings. A low compression reading on the first stroke, which does not build up during successive strokes, indicates leaking valves or a defective head gasket. Record the highest gauge reading obtained.

5 Repeat the procedure for the remaining cylinders and compare the results to the Specifications. Compression readings 10% above or below the specified amount can be considered normal.

6 Pour a couple of teaspoons of engine oil (a squirt can works great for this) into each cylinder, through the spark plug hole, and repeat the test.

7 If the compression increases after the oil is added, the piston rings are definitely worn. If the compression does not increase significantly, the leakage is occurring at the valves or head gasket.

8 If two adjacent cylinders have equally low compression, there is a strong possibility that the head gasket between them is blown. The appearance of coolant in the combustion chamber or the crankcase would verify this condition.

9 If the compression is higher than normal, the combustion chambers are probably coated with carbon deposits. If that is the case, the cylinder head (or heads) should be removed and decarbonized.

10 If compression is way down, or varies greatly between cylinders, it would be a good idea to have a 'leak-down' test performed by a reputable automotive repair shop. This test will pinpoint exactly where the leakage is occurring and how severe it is.

21 Spark plug replacement

1 The spark plugs are located on the front side of the engine, facing the radiator grille on 2.2L engines and on the back (firewall) side on 2.6L engines. Before beginning work, disconnect the battery negative cable as the electric fan could activate at any time.

2 In most cases the tools necessary for a spark plug replacement job are a plug wrench or spark plug socket which fits onto a ratchet wrench (this special socket will be insulated inside to protect the porcelain insulator) and a feeler gauge to check and adjust the spark plug gap. A special plug wire removal tool is available for separating the wire boot from the spark plug.

3 The best policy to follow when replacing the spark plugs is to purchase the new spark plugs beforehand, adjust them to the proper gap and then replace each plug one at a time. When buying the new spark plugs it is important that the correct plug is purchased for your specific engine. This information can be found on the emissions label located under the hood of your car or in the factory owner's manual. If differences exist between these sources, purchase the spark plug type specified on the label as this information was printed for your specific engine.

4 With the new spark plugs at hand, allow the engine to thoroughly cool before attempting the removal. During this cooling time, each of the new spark plugs can be inspected for defects and the gap can be checked.

1

5   The gap is checked by inserting the proper thickness gauge between the electrodes at the tip of the plug. The gap between these electrodes should be the same as that given in the Specifications or on the emissions label. The wire should touch each of the electrodes. If the gap is incorrect, use the notched adjuster on the feeler gauge body to bend the curved side electrode slightly until the proper gap is achieved. Also at this time check for cracks in the spark plug body, indicating the spark plug should be replaced with a new one. If the side electrode is not exactly over the center one, use the notched adjuster to align the two. If the spark plug is in good condition, the electrode can be cleaned and carefully filed flat with the proper file.

6   Cover the fenders of the car to prevent damage to exterior paint.

7   With the engine cool, remove the spark plug wire from one spark plug. Do this by grabbing the boot at the end of the wire, not the wire itself. Sometimes it is necessary to use a twisting motion while the boot and plug wire is pulled free. Using the plug wire removal tool is the easiest and safest method (photo).

21.7 Grasp the top of the spark plug boot firmly when removing the wire

8   If compressed air is available, use this to blow any dirt or foreign material away from the spark plug area. A common bicycle pump will also work. The idea here is to eliminate the possibility of material falling into the engine cylinder as the spark plug is replaced.

9   Now place the spark plug wrench or socket over the plug and remove it from the engine by turning in a counterclockwise direction.

10 Compare the spark plug with those shown to get an indication of the overall running condition of the engine.

11 Insert one of the new plugs into the engine, tightening it as much as possible by hand. The spark plug should screw easily into the engine. If it doesn't, change the angle of the spark plug slightly, as chances are the threads are not matched (cross-threaded). **Note:** *Be extremely careful, as these models have aluminium cylinder heads which can be easily damaged.*

12 Install the plug wire to the new spark plug, again using a twisting motion on the boot until it is firmly seated on the spark plug. Make sure the wire is routed away from the hot exhaust manifold.

13 Follow the above procedures for the remaining spark plugs, replacing them one at a time to prevent mixing up the spark plug wires.

22 Wheel bearing check and repack

1   The front wheel bearings are adjusted and lubricated at the factory and normally need only be checked for looseness indicating bearing wear or improperly tightened hub nut. Refer to Chapter 11 for checking and maintenance of the front wheel bearings.

2   Adjustment, removal and installation and repacking procedures of the rear wheel bearings are also described in Chapter 11.

23 Brake check

1   The brakes should be inspected every time the wheels are removed or whenever a fault is suspected. Indications of a potential braking system fault are: the car pulls to one side when the brake pedal is depressed; noises coming from the brakes when they are applied; excessive brake pedal travel; pulsating pedal; and leakage of fluid, usually seen on the inside of the tire or wheel.

Disc brakes

2   Disc brakes can be visually checked without the need to remove any parts except the wheels.

3   Raise the vehicle and place it securely on jackstands. Remove the front wheels (see *Jacking and towing* at the front of this manual if necessary).

4   Now visible is the disc brake caliper which contains the pads. There is an outer brake pad and an inner pad. Both should be inspected (photo).

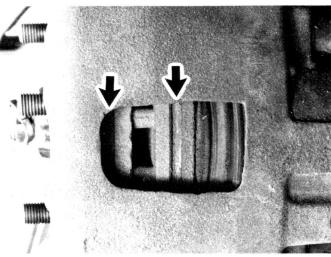

23.4 The pad linings (arrows) can be checked with the wheel removed

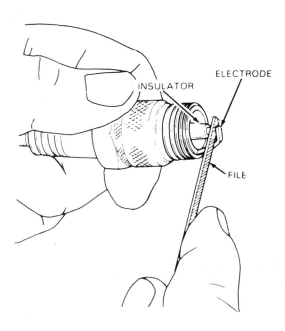

Fig. 1.31 Cleaning the spark plug electrode (Sec 21)

CARBON DEPOSITS

Symptoms: Dry sooty deposits indicate a rich mixture or weak ignition. Causes misfiring, hard starting and hesitation.

Recommendation: Check for a clogged air cleaner, high float level, sticky choke and worn ignition points. Use a spark plug with a longer core nose for greater anti-fouling protection.

OIL DEPOSITS

Symptoms: Oily coating caused by poor oil control. Oil is leaking past worn valve guides or piston rings into the combustion chamber. Causes hard starting, misfiring and hesition.

Recommendation: Correct the mechanical condition with necessary repairs and install new plugs.

TOO HOT

Symptoms: Blistered, white insulator, eroded electrode and absence of deposits. Results in shortened plug life.

Recommendation: Check for the correct plug heat range, over-advanced ignition timing, lean fuel mixture, intake manifold vacuum leaks and sticking valves. Check the coolant level and make sure the radiator is not clogged.

PREIGNITION

Symptoms: Melted electrodes. Insulators are white, but may be dirty due to misfiring or flying debris in the combustion chamber. Can lead to engine damage.

Recommendation: Check for the correct plug heat range, over-advanced ignition timing, lean fuel mixture, clogged cooling system and lack of lubrication.

HIGH SPEED GLAZING

Symptoms: Insulator has yellowish, glazed appearance. Indicates that combustion chamber temperatures have risen suddenly during hard acceleration. Normal deposits melt to form a conductive coating. Causes misfiring at high speeds.

Recommendation: Install new plugs. Consider using a colder plug if driving habits warrant.

GAP BRIDGING

Symptoms: Combustion deposits lodge between the electrodes. Heavy deposits accumulate and bridge the electrode gap. The plug ceases to fire, resulting in a dead cylinder.

Recommendation: Locate the faulty plug and remove the deposits from between the electrodes.

NORMAL

Symptoms: Brown to grayish-tan color and slight electrode wear. Correct heat range for engine and operating conditions.

Recommendation: When new spark plugs are installed, replace with plugs of the same heat range.

ASH DEPOSITS

Symptoms: Light brown deposits encrusted on the side or center electrodes or both. Derived from oil and/or fuel additives. Excessive amounts may mask the spark, causing misfiring and hesitation during acceleration.

Recommendation: If excessive deposits accumulate over a short time or low mileage, install new valve guide seals to prevent seepage of oil into the combustion chambers. Also try changing gasoline brands.

WORN

Symptoms: Rounded electrodes with a small amount of deposits on the firing end. Normal color. Causes hard starting in damp or cold weather and poor fuel economy.

Recommendation: Replace with new plugs of the same heat range.

DETONATION

Symptoms: Insulators may be cracked or chipped. Improper gap setting techniques can also result in a fractured insulator tip. Can lead to piston damage.

Recommendation: Make sure the fuel anti-knock values meet engine requirements. Use care when setting the gaps on new plugs. Avoid lugging the engine.

SPLASHED DEPOSITS

Symptoms: After long periods of misfiring, deposits can loosen when normal combustion temperature is restored by an overdue tune-up. At high speeds, deposits flake off the piston and are thrown against the hot insulator, causing misfiring.

Recommendation: Replace the plugs with new ones or clean and reinstall the originals.

MECHANICAL DAMAGE

Symptoms: May be caused by a foreign object in the combustion chamber or the piston striking an incorrect reach (too long) plug. Causes a dead cylinder and could result in piston damage.

Recommendation: Remove the foreign object from the engine and/or install the correct reach plug.

5   Inspect the pad thickness by looking at each end of the caliper and through the cut-out inspection hole in the caliper body. If the lining material is $\frac{5}{16}$ inch or less in thickness, the pads should be replaced. Keep in mind that the lining material is riveted or bonded to a metal backing shoe and the metal portion is not included in this measurement.

6   Since it will be difficult, if not impossible, to measure the exact thickness of the remaining lining material, if you are in doubt as to the pad quality, remove the pads for further inspection or replacement. See Chapter 9 for disc brake pad replacement.

7   Before installing the wheels, check for any leakage around the brake hose connections leading to the caliper or damage (cracking, splitting etc.) to the brake hose. Replace the hose or fittings as necessary, referring to Chapter 9.

8   Also check the condition of the disc for scoring, gouging or burnt spots. If these conditions exist, the hub/rotor assembly should be removed for servicing (Chapter 9).

Drum brakes (rear)

9   Raise the vehicle and support it firmly on jackstands. Block the front tires to prevent the car from rolling; however, do not apply the parking brake as this will lock the drums in place.

10   Remove the wheels, referring to *Jacking and towing* at the front of this manual if necessary.

11   Mark the hub so it can be reinstalled in the same place. Use a scribe, chalk, etc. on the drum and center hub and backing plate.

12   Remove the brake drum as described in Chapter 11.

13   With the drum removed, carefully brush away any accumulations of dirt and dust. *Do not blow this out with compressed air. Make an effort not to inhale this dust as it contains asbestos and is harmful to your health.*

14   Observe the thickness of the lining material on both front and rear brake shoes. If the material has worn away to within $\frac{1}{8}$ in of the recessed rivets or metal backing, the shoes should be replaced. If the linings look worn, but you are unable to determine their exact thickness, compare them with a new set at the auto parts store. The shoes should also be replaced if they are cracked, glazed (shiny surface), or wet with brake fluid.

15   Check that all the brake assembly springs are connected and in good condition.

16   Check the brake components for any signs of fluid leakage. With your finger, carefully pry back the rubber cups on the wheel cylinder located at the top of the brake shoes. Any leakage here is an indication that the wheel cylinders should be overhauled immediately (Chapter 9). Also check all hoses and connections for signs of leakage.

17   Wipe the inside of the drum with a clean rag, and denatured alcohol. Again, be careful not to breathe the dangerous asbestos dust.

18   Check the inside of the drum for cracks, scores, deep scratches or 'hard spots' which will appear as small discolorations. If these imperfections cannot be removed with fine emery cloth, the drum must be taken to a machine shop equipped to turn the drums.

19   If after the inspection process all parts are in good working condition, reinstall the brake drum. Install the wheel and lower the car to the ground.

Parking brake

20   The easiest way to check the operation of the parking brake is to park the car on a steep hill, with the parking brake set and the transmission in Neutral. If the parking brake cannot prevent the car from rolling, it is in need of adjustment (see Chapter 9).

24 Carburetor mounting torque check

1   The carburetor is attached to the top of the intake manifold by two or four nuts. These fasteners can sometimes work loose through normal engine operation and cause a vacuum leak.

2   To properly tighten the carburetor mounting nuts, a torque wrench is necessary. If you do not own one, they can usually be rented on a daily basis.

3   Remove the air cleaner assembly, tagging each hose to be disconnected with a piece of numbered tape to make reassembly easier.

4   Locate the mounting nuts at the base of the carburetor. Decide what special tools or adaptors will be necessary, if any, to tighten the nuts with a properly sized socket and the torque wrench.

5   Tighten the nuts to the specified torque. Do not overtighten the nuts, as this may cause the threads to strip.

6   If you suspect a vacuum leak exists at the bottom of the carburetor, get a length of spare hose about the diameter of fuel hose. Start the engine and place one end of the hose next to your ear as you probe around the base of the carburetor with the other end. You will be able to hear a hissing sound if a leak exists. A soapy water solution brushed around the suspect area can also be used to pinpoint pressure leaks.

7   If, after the nuts are properly tightened, a vacuum leak still exists, the carburetor must be removed and a new gasket installed. See Chapter 4 for more information.

8   After tightening the nuts, reinstall the air cleaner, connecting all hoses to their original positions.

25 Spark plug wire check

1   The spark plug wires should be checked at the recommended intervals or whenever new spark plugs are installed.

2   The wires should be inspected one at a time to prevent mixing up the order which is essential for proper engine operation.

3   Disconnect the plug wire from the spark plug. A removal tool can be used for this, or you can grab the rubber boot, twist slightly and then pull the wire free. Do not pull on the wire itself, only on the rubber boot.

4   Inspect inside the boot for corrosion which will look like a white, crusty powder.

5   Now push the wire and boot back onto the end of the spark plug. It should be a tight fit on the plug end. If not, remove the wire and use a pair of pliers to carefully crimp the metal connector inside the wire boot until the fit is secure.

6   Now, using a clean rag, clean the wire along its entire length. Remove all built-up dirt and grease. As this is done, inspect for burns, cracks or any other form of damage. Bend the wires in several places to ensure the conductive wire inside has not hardened.

7   Check the installation of the wires to the distributor cap and make sure they are not loose and the wires and boots are not cracked or damaged. Do not attempt to pull the wires from the cap, as they are retained on the inside by wire clips. The manufacturer does not recommend removing the wires from the cap for inspection because this could damage the integrity of the boot seal. If the wires are determined to be damaged, replace them with new ones. Remove the distributor cap (Chapter 5), release the wire clips with pliers and remove the wires. Insert the new wires into the cap while squeezing the boots to release any trapped air as you push them into place. Continue pushing until you feel the wire electrodes snap into position.

8   A visual check of the spark plug wires can also be made. In a darkened garage (make sure there is ventilation), start the engine and observe each plug wire. Be careful not to come into contact with any moving engine parts. If there is a break or fault in the wire, you will be able to see arcing or a small spark at the damaged area.

26 Windshield wiper blade element – removal and installation

1   The windshield wiper blade elements should be checked periodically for signs of cracking or deterioration. Two types of wiper blades are used, Type A and Type B.

2   To gain access to the wiper blades, turn on the ignition switch and cycle the windshield wipers to a position on the windshield where the work can be performed. Turn off the ignition.

3   On Type A wipers, the blade assembly is detached from the arm by pressing on the end bridges simultaneously so that the torsion bar is released from the pin lock groove. On Type B wipers, use a screwdriver to lift the release tab and pull the blade from the arm.

4   To remove the element from the blade assembly on Type A wipers, pinch the lock on the end and then slide the element out. On Type B blades, move the blade slightly in the opposite direction of its normal curve and remove it from the end bridge claws.

5   Installation is the reverse of removal.

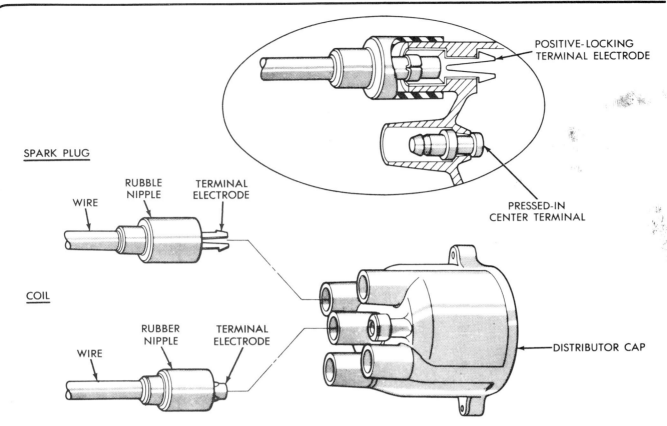

SPARK PLUG

POSITIVE-LOCKING TERMINAL ELECTRODE

WIRE — RUBBLE NIPPLE — TERMINAL ELECTRODE

COIL

WIRE — RUBBER NIPPLE — TERMINAL ELECTRODE

PRESSED-IN CENTER TERMINAL

DISTRIBUTOR CAP

Fig. 1.32 Distributor cap wire installation (Sec 25)

1

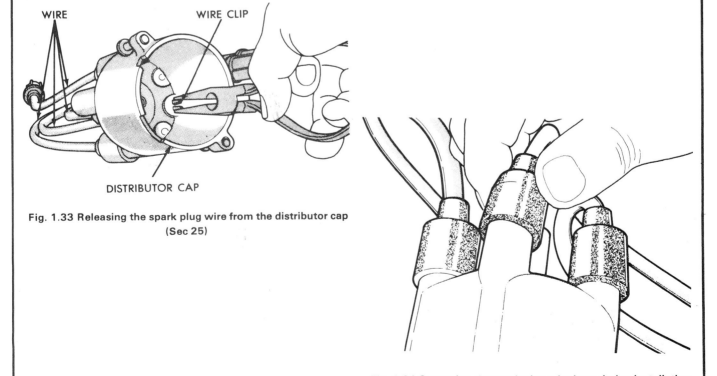

WIRE

WIRE CLIP

DISTRIBUTOR CAP

Fig. 1.33 Releasing the spark plug wire from the distributor cap (Sec 25)

Fig. 1.34 Squeezing the spark plug wire boot during installation (Sec 25)

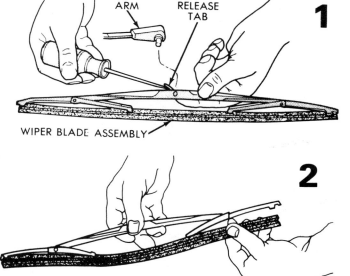

Fig. 1.35 Type A wiper blade replacement (Sec 26)

1   *Removing the assembly from the car*
2   *Disengaging the element from the bridge*

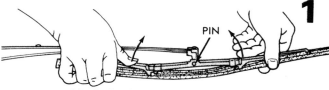

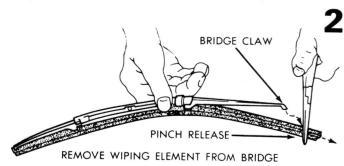

Fig. 1.36 Type B wiper blade element replacement (Sec 26)

1   *Removal from the arm*
2   *Removing the element from the bridge*

27 Rear window washer reservoir fluid – check

1   It is important that the rear window washer reservoir be checked periodically as it is easy for it to run dry because of its remote location.
2   The washer reservoir filler is located adjacent to the right hand taillight. Fill this reservoir with the proper washer solution at the same time the under-hood reservoir is checked.

28 Cooling system servicing (draining, flushing and refilling)

Caution: *Because antifreeze is highly toxic, the radiator should always be drained into a suitable container. Never allow the coolant to run onto the ground or driveway where a pet could drink it and be poisoned. The container should be capped and stored until it can be properly disposed of.*
1   Periodically, the cooling system should be drained, flushed and refilled. This is to replenish the antifreeze mixture and prevent rust and corrosion which can impair the performance of the cooling system and ultimately cause engine damage.
2   At the same time the cooling system is serviced, all hoses and the radiator cap should be inspected and replaced if faulty (see Section 7).
3   As antifreeze is a poisonous solution, take care not to spill any of the cooling mixture on the vehicle's paint or your own skin. If this happens, rinse immediately with plenty of clear water. Also, it is advisable to consult your local authorities about the dumping of antifreeze before draining the cooling system. In many areas recla-mation centers have been set up to collect automobile oil and drained antifreeze/water mixtures rather than allowing these liquids to be added to the sewage and water facilities.
4   With the engine cold, remove the radiator cap.
5   Move a large container under the radiator to catch the water/antifreeze mixture, as it is drained.
6   Drain the radiator. Most models are equipped with a drain plug at the bottom of the radiator which can be opened using a wrench to hold the fitting while the petcock is turned to the open position. If this drain has excessive corrosion and cannot be turned easily, or the radiator is not equipped with a drain, disconnect the lower radiator hose to allow the coolant to drain. Be careful that none of the solution is splashed on your skin or in your eyes.
7   Disconnect the coolant reservoir hose as shown, remove the reservoir and flush it with clean water.
8   Place a cold water hose (a common garden hose is fine) in the

radiator filler neck at the top of the radiator and flush the system until the water runs clean at all drain points.
9   In severe cases of contamination or clogging of the radiator, remove it (see Chapter 3) and reverse flush it. This involves simply inserting the cold pressure hose in the bottom radiator outlet to allow the clear water to run against the normal flow, draining through the top. A radiator repair shop should be consulted if further cleaning or repair is necessary.
10 Where the coolant is regularly drained and the system refilled with the correct antifreeze mixture there should be no need to employ chemical cleaners or descalers.
11 Install the coolant reservoir, reconnect the hoses and replace the drain plug.
12 Fill the radiator to the base of the filler neck and then add more coolant to the expansion reservoir so that it reaches the Full cold mark.
13 Run the engine until normal operating temperature is reached and with the engine idling, add coolant up to the correct level.
14 Always refill the system with a mixture of high quality antifreeze and water in the proportion called for on the antifreeze container or in your owner's manual. Chapter 3 also contains information on antifreeze mixtures.
15 Keep a close watch on the coolant level and the various cooling hoses during the first few miles of driving. Tighten the hose clamps and/or add more coolant mixture as necessary.

29 Underhood hoses – check and replacement

Caution: *Replacement of air conditioner hoses should be left to a dealer or air conditioning specialist who can depressurise the system and perform the work safely.*
1   The high temperatures present under the hood can cause de-terioration of the numerous rubber and plastic hoses.
2   Periodic inspection should be made for cracking, loose clamps and leaking because some of the hoses are part of the emissions system and can affect the engine's running and idling.
3   Remove the air cleaner if necessary and trace the entire length of each hose. Squeeze the hose to check for cracks and look for swelling, discoloration and leaks.
4   If the vehicle has considerable mileage or one or more of the hoses is suspect, it is a good idea to replace all of the hoses at one time.
5   Measure the length and inside diameter of each hose and obtain and cut the replacement to size. As original equipment hose clamps

are often good for only one or two uses, it is a good idea to replace them with screw-type clamps.

6   Replace each hose one at a time to eliminate the possibility of confusion. Hoses attached to the heater system, choke or ported vacuum switches contain coolant so newspapers or rags should be kept handy to catch the spill when they are disconnected.

7   After installation, run the engine until up to operating temperature, shut it off and check for leaks. After the engine has cooled, retighten all of the screw-type clamps.

30 Battery maintenance

1   These models are equipped with either a maintenance-free battery, which doesn't require the addition of water, or a conventional-type which should be checked periodically and topped up to the ring at the bottom of the filler cap with distilled water. Both types of batteries have built-in test indicators which exhibit different colors in accordance with battery condition. If the indicator shows green, the battery is properly charged but if it is dark colored, charging is required. A light yellow indicator means the battery needs water or possibly replacement.

2   The top of the battery should be kept clean and free from dirt and moisture so that the battery does not become partially discharged by leakage through dampness and dirt. Clean the top of the battery with a baking soda and water solution, making sure that it does not enter the battery.

3   Once every three months, remove the battery and inspect the securing bolts, battery clamp bolts and leads for corrosion (white fluffy deposits which are brittle to the touch).

4   Clean the battery posts with a battery cleaning tool or wire brush.

5   Clean the battery cable terminals with a wire brush until the corrosion is removed and the metal in the terminal contact area is bright.

6   Apply grease or petroleum jelly around the base of the battery posts and install the battery cables (positive cable first) and tighten the terminal cable nuts securely.

7   If any doubt exists about the state of charge of the battery, it should be tested by a dealer or properly equipped shop.

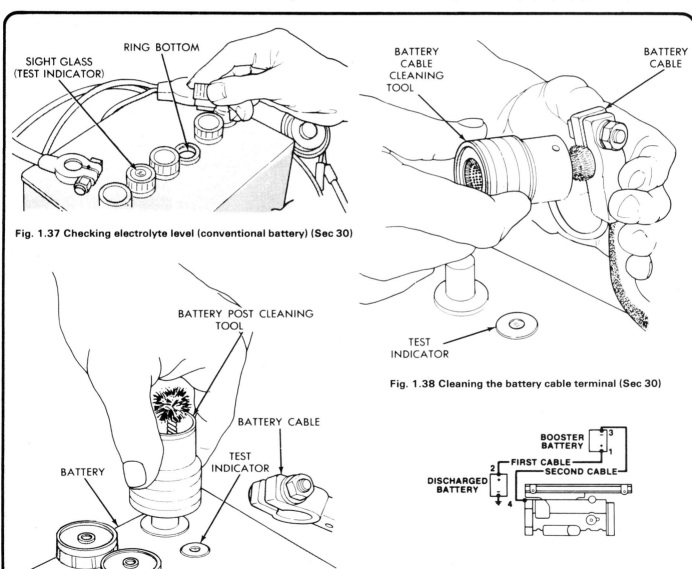

Fig. 1.37 Checking electrolyte level (conventional battery) (Sec 30)

Fig. 1.38 Cleaning the battery cable terminal (Sec 30)

Fig. 1.39 Removing corrosion from the battery post (Sec 30)

Fig. 1.40 Booster battery (jump start) connection sequence (Sec 31)

31 Booster battery (jump) starting

1   Certain precautions are necessary prior to using a booster battery to 'jump' start the vehicle.

Before connecting the booster battery, make sure that the ignition switch is in the Off position.
The eyes should be shielded; safety goggles are a good idea.
Make sure that the booster battery source is 12 volt and not 24 volt, which could damage the starter
The two vehicles must not touch each other.

2   Connect the end of one jumper cable to the positive (+) terminals of each battery.
3   Connect one end of the other jumper cable to the negative (-) terminal of the good battery. The other end of this cable should be connected to a good ground on the vehicle to be started, such as a bolt on the engine block.
4   Start the engine using the jumper battery and, with the engine running at idle speed, disconnect the jumper cables in the reverse sequence of connection.

32 Steering shaft seal – lubrication

1   The steering shaft seal protects the steering shaft at the point where it passes through the firewall. Lubricate the inner circumference of the seal with the specified lubricant if the shaft makes a noise or sticks to the seal when it is turned.
2   Raise the vehicle and support it securely.
3   Peel back the upper edge of the seal and apply a light coat of grease all of the way around the inner circumference where it contacts the steering shaft (photo).
4   Lower the vehicle.

33 Valve adjustment (2.6L engine)

1   Remove the valve cover.
2   Adjust the valve clearances using the hot engine Specifications.
3   While watching the rocker arms for the number one cylinder, rotate the engine in a clockwise direction (with a wrench on the large bolt at the front of the crankshaft) until the exhaust valve is closing and the intake valve has just started to open (the intake valve is on the carburetor side of the engine, the exhaust valve is on the exhaust manifold side of the engine). Line up the notch in the pulley on the front of the crankshaft with the T on the timing mark tab on the timing chain case. At this point, the number 4 piston will be at TDC on the compression stroke and the number 4 cylinder valve clearances can be adjusted. The jet valve clearance is always adjusted before the intake and exhaust valve clearances.
4   The intake valve and jet valve adjusting screws are located on a common rocker arm. Make sure the intake valve adjusting screw has been backed off at least two full turns, then loosen the locknut on the jet valve adjusting screw. Turn the jet valve adjusting screw counterclockwise and insert the appropriate size feeler gauge between the jet valve stem and the adjusting screw. Carefully tighten the adjusting screw until you can feel a slight drag on the feeler gauge as it is withdrawn from between the stem and adjusting screw (photo). Since the jet valve spring is relatively weak, use special care not to force the jet valve open. Be particularly careful if the adjusting screw is hard to turn. Hold the adjusting screw with a screwdriver (to keep it from turning) and tighten the locknut (photo). Recheck the clearance to make sure it hasn't changed.
5   Next, adjust the intake valve clearance. Insert the appropriate size feeler gauge between the intake valve stem and the adjusting screw. Carefully tighten the adjusting screw until you can feel a slight drag on the feeler gauge as it is withdrawn from between the stem and adjusting screw. Hold the screw with a screwdriver (to keep it from turning) and tighten the locknut, then recheck the clearance to make sure it hasn't changed.
6   Loosen the locknut on the exhaust valve adjusting screw. Turn the adjusting screw counterclockwise and insert the appropriate size feeler gauge between the valve stem and the adjusting screw. Carefully tighten the adjusting screw until you can feel a slight drag on the feeler

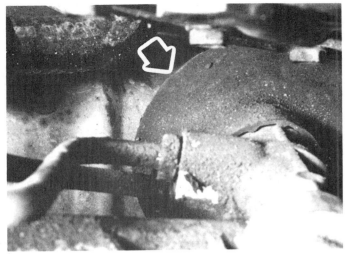

32.3 Lubricate the inside of the steering shaft seal after pulling the upper edge (arrow) away from the shaft

33.4a Using a feeler gauge and screwdriver to adjust the jet valve clearance

33.4b Hold the adjusting screw in position while tightening the jet valve locknut

gauge, as it is withdrawn from between the stem and adjusting screw. Hold the adjusting screw with a screwdriver and tighten the locknut. Recheck the clearance to make sure it hasn't changed.

7   Repeat the procedure to adjust the valve clearances for cylinders 1, 2 and 3. Use the following table for determining when the pistons are at TDC:

Exhaust valve closing – intake valve just opening:	Adjust valve clearances at:
No. 1 cylinder	No. 4 cylinder
No. 2 cylinder	No. 3 cylinder
No. 3 cylinder	No. 2 cylinder
No. 4 cylinder	No. 1 cylinder

Remember to align the notch in the crankshaft pulley with the T on the timing mark tab before making the adjustments.

8   Install the valve cover.

1

Chapter 2 Part A 2.6L engine

Contents

Specifications

General

Displacement	2.6 liters (156 cu in)
Bore and stroke	3.59 x 3.86 in (91.1 x 9.0 mm)
Firing order	1-3-4-2
Compression ratio	8.2:1
Compression pressure	149 psi at 250 rpm

Valve timing
  Intake valve
    Opens (BTDC) .... 25°
    Closes (ABDC) .... 59°
  Exhaust valve
    Opens (BBDC) .... 64°
    Closes (ATDC) .... 20°
  Jet valve
    Opens (BTDC) .... 59°
    Closes (ABDC) .... 45°

Engine block

Cylinder bore diameter	3.5866 in (91.1 mm)
Taper and out-of-round limit	0.0008 in (0.02 mm)

Silent Shaft

Front bearing journal diameter	0.906 in (23 mm)
Front bearing oil clearance	0.0008 to 0.0024 in (0.02 to 0.06 mm)
Rear bearing journal diameter	1.693 in (43 mm)
Rear bearing oil clearance	0.0020 to 0.0035 in (0.05 to 0.09 mm)

Pistons and rings

Piston diameter	3.5966 in (91.1 mm)
Piston ring-to-groove clearance	
Standard	
Top ring	0.0024 to 0.0039 in (0.06 to 0.10 mm)
Second ring	0.008 to 0.0024 in (0.02 to 0.06 mm)
Oil ring	Side rails must rotate freely after assembly
Service limit	
Top ring	0.004 in (0.1 mm)
Second ring	0.004 in (0.1 mm)
Piston ring end gap	
Standard	
Top ring	0.010 to 0.018 in (0.25 to 0.45 mm)
Second ring	0.010 to 0.018 in (0.25 to 0.45 mm)
Oil ring	0.008 to 0.055 in (0.2 to 0.4 mm)
Service limit	
Top ring	0.039 in (1 mm)
Second ring	0.039 in (1 mm)
Oil ring	0.059 in (1.5 mm)
Piston pin installation pressure	1614 to 3859 psi (7350 to 17100 Nm)

Crankshaft and flywheel

Main journal diameter	2.3622 in (60 mm)
Taper and out-of-round limit	0.004 in (0.01 mm)
Main bearing oil clearance	0.0008 to 0.0028 in (0.02 to 0.07 mm)
Connecting rod journal diameter	2.08666 in (53 mm)
Taper and out-of-round limit	0.0004 in (0.01 mm)
Connecting rod bearing oil clearance	0.0008 to 0.0028 in (0.02 to 0.07 mm)
Connecting rod side clearance	0.004 to 0.010 in (0.1 to 0.25 mm)
Crankshaft end play	0.002 to 0.007 in (0.05 to 0.18 mm)
Flywheel clutch face runout limit	0.020 in (0.51 mm)

Camshaft

Bearing oil clearance	0.002 to 0.004 in (0.05 to 0.09 mm)
Lobe height	
Intake and exhaust	
Standard	1.6614 in (42.2 mm)
Service limit	1.6414 in (41.7 mm)
End play	0.005 to 0.008 in (0.1 to 0.2 mm)

Cylinder head and valve train

Head warpage limit	0.004 in (0.1 mm)
Valve seat angle	45°
Valve seat margin width	
Intake	0.028 to 0.047 in (0.7 to 1.2 mm)
Exhaust	0.039 to 0.079 in (1 to 2 mm)
Valve stem-to-guide clearance	
Intake	
Standard	0.0012 to 0.0024 in (0.03 to 0.06 mm)
Service limit	0.004 in (0.1 mm)
Exhaust	
Standard	0.0020 to 0.0035 in (0.05 to 0.09 mm)
Service limit	0.006 in (0.15 mm)
Valve spring free length	
Standard	1.869 in (47.5 mm)
Service limit	1.479 in (46.5 mm)
Valve spring pressure (lbs at specified length)	61 lbs at 1.59 in (270 Nm at 40.4 mm)
Out-of-square service limit	3° max
Valve spring installed height	
Standard	1.590 in (40.4 mm)
Service limit	1.629 in (41.4 mm)
Jet Valve	
Stem diameter	0.1693 in (4.3000 mm)
Seat angle	45°
Spring free length	1.1654 in (29.60 mm)
Spring pressure	5.5 lbs at 0.846 in (34.3 Nm at 21.5 mm)
Valve clearance (HOT engine)	
Intake	0.006 in (0.15 mm)
Exhaust	0.010 in (0.25 mm)
Jet valve	0.006 in (0.15 mm)
Timing chain tensioner	
Spring free length	2.587 in (65.7 mm)
Spring load	4.4 lbs at 1.453 in (19.6 Nm at 36.9 mm)

Oil pump

Relief valve opening pressure	49.8 to 64.0 psi (343 to 441 kPa)

2A

Gear-to-housing clearance .... 0.0043 to 0.0059 in (0.11 to 0.15 mm)
Pump body gear-to-bearing clearance .... 0.0008 to 0.0020 in (0.02 to 0.05 mm)
Pump cover gear-to-bearing clearance .... 0.0016 to 0.0028 in (0.04 to 0.07 mm)
Gear end play .... 0.0024 to 0.0047 in (0.06 to 0.12 mm)
Relief spring free length .... 1.850 in (47 mm)
Relief spring load .... 9.5 lbs at 1.575 in (42.2 Nm at 40 mm)
Oil pressure switch minimum actuating pressure .... 4 psi (28 kPa) or less

Torque specifications

	Ft-lb	Nm
Spark plug	19	25
Intake manifold nut	13	17
Exhaust manifold nut	13	17
Water pump drive pulley	40	54
Water pump mounting bolt	17	23
Cylinder head-to-block bolt (HOT)	76	103
Cylinder head-to-block bolt (COLD)	69	54
Crankshaft sprocket bolt	87	118
Camshaft bearing cap bolt	15	18
Driveplate bolts	85	115
Valve cover bolt	4.4	6
Cylinder head-to-timing chain case bolt	15	18
Jet valve	14.1	19
Engine mount plate bolt	15	18
Engine-to-transaxle bolts	70	95
Timing chain case cover bolt	15	18
Torque converter-to-driveplate	40	54
Oil pan screw	4.4	6
Camshaft sprocket bolt	40	54
Timing chain guide screw	15	18
Silent Shaft chain guide screw	15	18
Silent Shaft chain sprocket bolt	25	34
Engine mount through-bolts	40	54
Oil pump sprocket bolt	25	34
Main bearing cap bolt	58	79
Connecting rod bearing cap bolt	34	46
Oil pump mounting screw	5.9	8

1 General information

The engine is an inline vertical four, with a chain-driven overhead camshaft and a Silent Shaft counterbalancing system which cancels the engine's power pulses and produces relatively vibration-free operation. The crankshaft rides in five renewable insert-type main bearings, with the center bearing assigned the additional task of controlling crankshaft end play.

The pistons have two compression rings and one oil control ring. The piston pins are semi-floating, press fit in the small end of the connecting rod. The connecting rod big ends are also fitted with renewable insert-type plain bearings.

The engine is equipped with a Jet valve assembly, which reduces certain exhaust emissions.

The engine is liquid-cooled, utilizing a centrifugal impeller-type pump, driven by a belt from the crankshaft, to circulate coolant around the cylinders and combustion chambers and through the intake manifold.

Lubrication is handled by a gear-type oil pump mounted on the front of the engine under the timing chain cover. It is driven by the Silent Shaft chain. The oil is filtered continuously by a cartridge-type filter mounted on the right side of the engine.

2 Repair operations possible with the engine in the vehicle

1 Many major repair operations can be accomplished without removing the engine from the vehicle.

2 It is a very good idea to clean the engine compartment and the exterior of the engine with some type of pressure washer before any work is begun. A clean engine will make the job easier and will prevent the possibility of getting dirt into internal areas of the engine.

3 Remove the hood and cover the fenders to provide as much working room as possible and to prevent damage to the painted surfaces.

4 If oil or coolant leaks develop, indicating a need for gasket or seal replacement, the repairs can generally be made with the engine in the vehicle. The oil pan gasket, the cylinder head gasket, intake and exhaust manifold gaskets, timing chain case gaskets and the front and rear crankshaft oil seals are accessible with the engine in place. In the case of the rear crankshaft oil seal, the transmission, the clutch components and the flywheel must be removed first.

5 Exterior engine components, such as the starter motor, the alternator, the distributor, the fuel pump and the carburettor, as well as the intake and exhaust manifolds, are quite easily removed for repair with the engine in place.

6 Since the cylinder head can be removed without pulling the engine, valve servicing can also be accomplished with the engine in the vehicle.

7 Repairs to or inspection of the camshaft, the timing chain assembly, the Silent Shafts and chain assembly and the oil pump are all possible with the engine in place.

8 In extreme cases caused by a lack of necessary equipment, repair or replacement of piston rings, pistons, connecting rods and rod bearings and reconditioning of the cylinder bores is possible with the engine in the vehicle. This practice is not recommended because of the cleaning and preparation work that must be done to the components involved.

3 Engine overhaul – general note

1 It is not always easy to determine when, or if, an engine should be completely overhauled, as a number of factors must be considered.

2 High mileage is not necessarily an indication that an overhaul is needed while low mileage, on the other hand, does not preclude the need for an overhaul. Frequency of servicing is probably the single most important consideration. An engine that has regular (and frequent) oil and filter changes, as well as other required maintenance, will most likely give many thousands of miles of reliable service. Conversely, a neglected engine may require an overhaul very early in its life.

3 Excessive oil consumption is an indication that piston rings and/or valve guides are in need of attention (make sure that oil leaks are not responsible before deciding that the rings and guides are bad). Have a

cylinder compression or leak-down test performed by an experienced tune-up mechanic to determine for certain the extent of the work required.

4 If the engine is making obvious 'knocking' or rumbling noises, the connecting rod and/or main bearings are probably at fault.

5 Loss of power, rough running, excessive valve train noise and high fuel consumption rates may also point to the need for an overhaul (especially if they are all present at the same time). If a complete tune-up does not remedy the situation, major mechanical work is the only solution.

6 An engine overhaul generally involves restoring the internal parts to the specifications of a new engine. During an overhaul, the piston rings are replaced and the cylinder walls are reconditioned (rebored and/or honed). If a rebore is done, then new pistons are also required. The main and connecting rod bearings are replaced with new ones and, if necessary, the crankshaft may be reground to restore the journals. Generally, the valves are serviced as well, since they are usually in less-than-perfect condition at this point. While the engine is being overhauled, other components such as the carburetor, the distributor, the starter and the alternator can be rebuilt also. The end result should be a like-new engine that will give as many trouble-free miles as the original.

7 Before beginning the engine overhaul, read through the entire procedure to familiarize yourself with the scope and requirements of the job. Overhauling an engine is not that difficult, but it is time-consuming. Plan on the vehicle being tied up for a minimum of two weeks, especially if parts must be taken to an automotive machine shop for repair or reconditioning. Check on availability of parts and make sure that any necessary special tools and equipment are obtained in advance. Most work can be done with typical shop hand tools, although a number of precision measuring tools are required for inspecting parts to determine if they must be replaced. Often a reputable automotive machine shop will handle the inspection of parts and offer advice concerning reconditioning and replacement. As a general rule, time is the primary cost of an overhaul, so it doesn't pay to install worn or sub-standard parts.

8 As a final note, to ensure maximum life and minimum trouble from a rebuilt engine, everything must be assembled with care in a spotlessly clean environment.

4 Engine removal

1 Disconnect the negative battery cable from the battery.
2 Remove the hood (Chapter 12).
3 Drain the cooling system, remove the radiator hoses and disconnect the automatic transaxle cooler lines from the radiator.
4 Remove the radiator (Chapter 3).
5 If equipped, remove the air conditioning compressor but do not disconnect any of the hoses as they are under high pressure. Unbolt the power steering pump and move it out of the way (if equipped).
6 Remove all electrical connections to the engine, one at a time, marking them with pieces of tape or tags for ease of reinstallation.
7 Remove the alternator.
8 Disconnect and tag the fuel line connections.
9 Disconnect the throttle cable from the carburetor.
10 Disconnect the exhaust pipe from the manifold.
11 Remove the starter (Chapter 5).
12 Remove the transaxle lower cover.
13 Mark the relationship of the driveplate to the torque converter.
14 Remove the torque converter-to-driveplate bolts.
15 Retain the torque converter in place with a C-clamp so it will not fall during engine removal.
16 Support the transaxle with a jack.
17 Attach a suitable lifting device to the engine and lift it sufficiently to take up the slack in the chain and remove the weight from the engine mounts.
18 Remove the engine compartment right side inner splash panel.
19 Remove the engine-to-chassis ground strap.
20 Remove the right side engine mount-to-insulator through-bolt. If the insulator is removed, mark its position as it must be reinstalled in the same position.
21 Remove the transaxle-to-engine block bolts.
22 Remove the front engine mount through-bolt.
23 Begin lifting the engine from the engine compartment, making

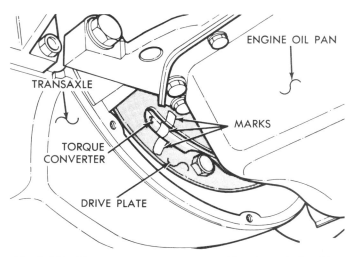

Fig. 2.1 Marking the torque converter-to-driveplate relationship (Sec 4)

sure that there are no wires, hoses or other components still connected. Lift the engine clear of the vehicle and lower it to the floor or a suitable workbench.

5 Automatic transaxle driveplate – removal and installation

1 Remove the attaching bolts and separate the driveplate from the crankshaft.
2 To install, hold the driveplate in position and install the attaching bolts.
3 While locking the crankshaft so it won't turn, tighten the bolts (using a criss-cross pattern) to the specified torque (photo).

5.3 Lock the driveplate with a screwdriver while tightening the bolts

6 Engine – disassembly and reassembly

1 To completely disassemble the engine, remove the following items in the order given:

Engine external components	(Section 7)
Oil pan	(Section 8)
Cylinder head/valve train components	(Section 9)
Timing chain case/Silent Shaft chain and sprockets	(Section 11)
Timing chain and sprockets	(Section 12)
Piston/connecting rod assemblies	(Section 15)
Crankshaft	(Section 16)
Left Silent Shaft	(Section 13)
Oil pump/right Silent Shaft	(Section 14)

2A

2 Engine reassembly is basically the reverse of disassembly. Install the following components in the order given:

---

7 External engine components – removal

Note: *When removing the external components from the engine, pay close attention to details that may be helpful or important during installation. Look for the correct positioning of gaskets, seals, spacers, pins, washers, bolts and other small items.*

1 It is much easier to dismantle and repair the engine if it is mounted on a portable-type engine stand. These stands can often be rented, for a reasonable fee, from an equipment rental yard.

2 If a stand is not available, it is possible to dismantle the engine with it blocked up on a sturdy workbench or on the floor. Be extra careful not to tip or drop the engine when working without a stand.

3 Before the engine can be mounted on a stand, the driveplate, the dust shield and the rear seal housing must be removed. Remove the flywheel and dust shield by referring to Section 5, then loosen and remove the seven bolts attaching the seal housing to the rear of the engine block and the oil pan. Carefully remove the housing (try not to let the oil separator inside the seal housing fall out of place). Note how the oil separator is installed, to prevent confusion during reassembly. You may have to tap the seal housing lightly with a soft-faced hammer to break it loose. Do not pry between the seal housing and engine block, as damage to the gasket sealing surfaces may result. At this point, the engine is ready to mount on the stand.

4 Remove the engine mounts and brackets. Store the right and left motor mount bracket components separately, to avoid confusion during reassembly. Be sure to inspect the metal parts for cracks and the rubber parts for deterioration and delamination from the metal. If any defects are found, replace the parts with new ones.

5 If your vehicle is equipped with air-conditioning, remove the upper and lower compressor brackets from the engine block. There are a total of eight bolts attaching the brackets to the engine.

6 Remove the four bolts and lift the power steering pump bracket away from the lower right side of the engine.

7 Remove the crankcase emissions control system components.

8 Remove the nine nuts and one bolt attaching the intake manifold to the engine cylinder head and lift the manifold and the carburetor, as an assembly, from the head. Note the position of the engine hoisting bracket attached to the rear intake manifold studs.

9 Remove the two nuts attaching the fuel pump to the cylinder head and slip off the fuel pump and the insulator.

10 Remove the distributor cap by depressing and turning the spring-loaded screws on the cap. Remove the distributor mounting nut and slip the distributor out of the engine by pulling straight out on it.

11 Loosen and slide back the hose clamp on the rubber hose connecting the water pump to the coolant transfer tube. Remove the seven bolts attaching the water pump to the front of the engine and pull the water pump off. You may have to tap lightly on the pump body with a soft-faced hammer to break the gasket seal.

12 Remove the coolant transfer tube. It is held in place by a bracket on the right side of the engine and a bracket at the rear of the engine.

13 Unscrew and remove the oil pressure sending unit at the right front side of the engine.

14 Remove the Pulse Air Feeder (PAF) system (Chapter 6).

15 Remove the four bolts attaching the spark plug lead brackets to the valve cover and lift the distributor cap and spark plug leads away from the engine as an assembly.

16 Unscrew and remove the oil filter and take out the oil dipstick.

---

8 Oil pan – removal and installation

---

1 Remove the bolts securing the oil pan to the engine block.

2 Tap on the pan with a soft-faced hammer, to break the gasket seal, and lift the oil pan off the engine.

3 Using a gasket scraper, scrape off all traces of the old gasket from the engine block, the timing chain cover and the oil pan. Be especially careful not to nick or gouge the gasket sealing surface of the timing chain cover (it is made of aluminum and is quite soft).

4 Clean the oil pan with solvent and dry it thoroughly. Check the gasket sealing surfaces for distortion.

5 Before installing the oil pan, apply a thin coat of RTV-type gasket sealer to the engine block gasket sealing surfaces. Lay a new oil pan gasket in place and carefully apply a coat of gasket sealer to the exposed side of the gasket.

6 Gently lay the oil pan in place (do not disturb the gasket) and install the bolts. Start with the bolts closest to the center of the pan and tighten them to the specified torque using a criss-cross pattern. Do not overtighten them or leakage may occur.

---

9 Cylinder head – removal

---

1 Remove the two bolts, washers and rubber seals attaching the valve cover to the cylinder head and lift off the cover. Remove the breather grommet from the front of the cylinder head and the circular seal from the rear of the cylinder head.

2 Rotate the engine (with a wrench on the large bolt at the front of the crankshaft) until the number one piston is at top dead center on the compression stroke. To do this, watch the rocker arms for the number one cylinder valves while slowly rotating the crankshaft in a clockwise direction (viewed from the front). When the intake valve closes, continue rotating the crankshaft until the mark on the pulley is aligned with the T on the timing tab.

3 Locate the timing mark on the camshaft sprocket and make sure the plated link of the cam chain is opposite the mark.

4 Remove the camshaft sprocket bolt and oil shield from the front of the camshaft (photo). Hold the large bolt on the end of the crankshaft (to keep the engine from turning) while loosening the bolt. Remove the distributor drive gear from the front of the camshaft by tapping it with a soft-faced hammer. Pull the camshaft sprocket (with the chain in place) off the camshaft, and allow it to rest on the sprocket holder.

9.4 Removing the bolt and oil shield from the front of the camshaft

5 Loosen the ten camshaft bearing cap bolts, $\frac{1}{2}$ turn each, in sequence, until all pressure from the valve springs has been released. Then remove the six inner bolts and lift the rocker arm shaft assembly away from the cylinder head with the four end bolts in place. Do not disassemble the components any further, unless new parts are required. Carefully lift the camshaft out of the cylinder head and store it where it will not be damaged.

6 Remove the two bolts attaching the cylinder head to the timing chain cover (at the very front of the cylinder head). Remove the ten bolts attaching the cylinder head to the engine block. Turn them $\frac{1}{4}$ of

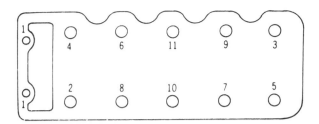

Fig. 2.2 Cylinder head bolt *loosening* sequence (Sec 9)

a turn each, in the sequence shown, until they are all loose enough to remove by hand.
7   Remove the cylinder head by lifting it straight up and off the engine block. Do not pry between the cylinder head and the engine block, as damage to the gasket sealing surfaces may result. Instead, use a soft-faced hammer to tap the cylinder head and break the gasket seal.
8   Lift off the old head gasket.

10 Cylinder head – disassembly

1   Cylinder head disassembly involves removal and disassembly of the Jet valves and removal of the intake and exhaust valves and their related components.
2   Using a six-point deep socket and a breaker bar, carefully remove the Jet valve assemblies from the cylinder head. Do not tilt the socket, as the Jet valve stems can be bent very easily by the force exerted on the valve spring retainer (which will cause defective Jet valve operation). Label each Jet valve assembly so it can be reinstalled in the same hole it was removed from.
3   Disassemble each Jet valve by carefully compressing the spring and removing the keepers, the valve spring retainer and the valve spring. Slide the valve out of the body and pull off the seal with a plier (discard the oil seals, as they should not be reused). Keep the parts for each Jet valve assembly separate (photo) so they are not accidentally interchanged with parts from other Jet valve assemblies.

10.4 Measuring the installed height of the valve spring with a dial caliper

10.5 Compressing the valve spring with a valve spring compressor

2A

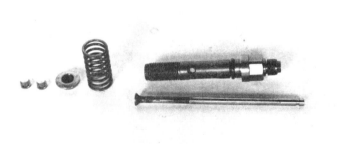

10.3 Jet valve assembly components

4   Before the valves are removed, arrange to label and store them, along with their related components, so they can be kept separate and reinstalled in the same valve guides they were removed from. Also, measure the valve spring installed height (for each valve) and compare it to the Specifications (photo). If it is greater than specified, the valve seats and valve faces need attention.
5   Compress the valve spring on the first valve with a spring compressor (photo) then remove the keepers and the retainer from the valve assembly. Carefully release the valve spring compressor and remove the spring, the spring seat and the valve from the head. If the

10.6 Intake/exhaust valve components

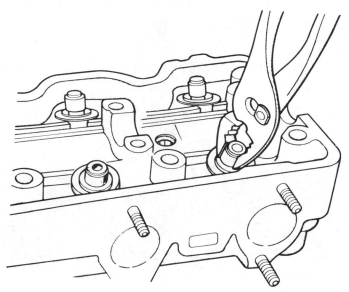

Fig. 2.3 Removing the valve stem seals with pliers (Sec 10)

valve binds in the guide (won't pull through), push it back into the head and deburr the area around the keeper groove with a fine file.
6   Repeat the procedure for the remaining valves. Remember to keep all the parts for each valve in order so they can be reinstalled in the same position (photo).
7   Once the valves have been removed and safely stored, pull off the valve stem seals with a pliers and discard them; *the old seals should never be reused.*
8   Refer to Section 22 for cylinder head cleaning and inspection procedures.

---

11 Silent Shaft chain/sprockets – removal and inspection

1   Before attempting to remove the Silent Shaft chain and sprockets, remove the cylinder head and the oil pan by referring to the appropriate Sections.
2   Remove the large bolt at the front of the crankshaft and slide the pulley off.

3   Remove the bolts attaching the timing chain case to the engine block. Draw a simple diagram showing the location of each of the bolts (so they can be returned to the same holes they were removed from).
4   Tap the timing chain case with a soft-faced hammer, to break the gasket seal, and remove the case from the engine block. Do not pry between the case and the engine block as damage to the gasket sealing surfaces will result.
5   Remove the chain guides labeled A, B and C. They are held in place with two bolts each. Again, draw a simple diagram showing the location of each of the bolts (so they can be returned to the same holes they were removed from).
6   Reinstall the large bolt in the end of the crankshaft and hold it with a wrench (to keep the engine from turning) while loosening the bolt in the end of the right (lower) Silent Shaft, the bolt attaching the right Silent Shaft drive sprocket to the oil pump shaft and the bolt in the end of the left (upper) Silent Shaft. If the bolt in the end of the right Silent Shaft is difficult to loosen, remove the oil pump and Silent Shaft as an assembly (see Section 14), then remove the bolt with the Silent Shaft securely clamped in a vise.
7   Slide the crankshaft sprocket, the Silent Shaft sprockets and the chain off the engine as an assembly. Leave the bolt in the end of the right (lower) Silent Shaft in place. *Do not lose the keys that index the sprockets to the shafts.*
8   Check the sprocket teeth for wear and damage. Check the sprocket cushion rings and ring guides (Silent Shaft sprockets only) for wear and damage. Rotate the cushion rings and check for smooth operation. Inspect the chain for cracked side plates and pitted or worn rollers. Replace any defective or worn parts with new ones.

---

12 Timing chain/sprockets – removal, inspection and installation

1   Since the Silent Shaft chain and sprockets must be dismantled to gain access to the timing chain assembly, refer to Section 11 and remove the Silent Shaft chain and sprockets.
2   Depress the timing chain tensioner plunger (on the oil pump) and slide the camshaft sprocket, the crankshaft sprocket and the timing chain off the engine as an assembly. Do not lose the key that indexes the crankshaft sprocket in the proper place. Remove the timing chain tensioner plunger and spring from the oil pump.
3   Remove the camshaft sprocket holder and the right and left timing chain guides from the front of the engine block.
4   Inspect the sprocket teeth for wear and damage. Check the chain for cracked plates and pitted or worn rollers. Check the chain tensioner rubber shoe for wear and the tensioner spring for cracks or

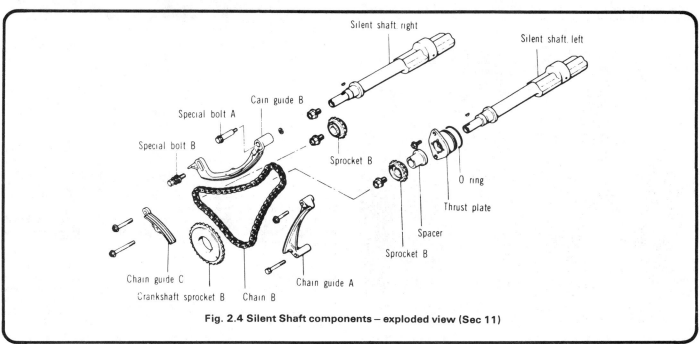

Fig. 2.4 Silent Shaft components – exploded view (Sec 11)

12.5 Installing the camshaft sprocket holder on the engine block

12.6 Installing the timing chain tensioner plunger in the oil pump bore

12.7 Installing the timing chain sprocket on the end of the crankshaft with the wide shoulder facing out

12.8 Meshing the camshaft sprocket and the timing chain with the mark on the sprocket directly opposite the plated link on the chain

2A

12.9 Installing the timing chain on the crankshaft sprocket (note that the sprocket mark and the plated link are opposite each other — arrows)

deterioration. Measure the tensioner spring free length and compare it to the Specifications. Check the chain guides for wear and damage. Replace any defective parts with new ones.

5   Install the sprocket holder (photo) and the right and left timing chain guides onto the engine block. Tighten the attaching bolts securely (the upper bolt in the left timing chain guide should be installed finger-tight only), then coat the entire length of the chain contact surfaces of the guides with clean, high-quality multi-purpose grease.

6   Turn the crankshaft, with a wrench on the large bolt at the front, until the number one piston is at top dead center (when it is flush with the top of the engine block, it is at top dead center). Apply a layer of clean multi-purpose grease (or engine assembly lube) to the timing chain tensioner plunger and install the tensioner spring and plunger loosely into the oil pump body (photo).

7   Position the timing chain sprocket on the end of the crankshaft with the wide shoulder facing out (photo). Line up the keyway in the sprocket with the key on the crankshaft.

8   Install the camshaft sprocket onto the chain, lining up the plated link on the chain with the marked tooth on the sprocket (photo).

9   Slip the chain over the crankshaft sprocket, lining up the plated link on the chain with the marked tooth on the sprocket (photo). Slide the crankshaft sprocket all the way onto the crankshaft while depressing the chain tensioner so the chain fits into place in the guides. Rest the camshaft sprocket on the sprocket holder. *Do not rotate the crankshaft for any reason until the cylinder head and camshaft have been properly installed.*

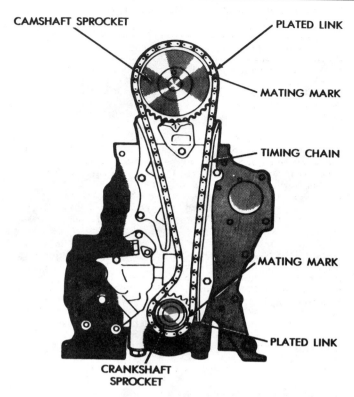

Fig. 2.5 Correct timing chain and sprocket relationship (Sec 12)

13 Silent Shafts – removal, inspection and installation

1   During engine disassembly, the Silent Shaft chain and sprockets, the timing chain and sprockets and the oil pump should be removed before the Silent Shafts.

2   Remove the left Silent Shaft chamber cover plate from the engine block. It is held in place with two bolts. You may have to tap the cover with a soft-faced hammer to break the gasket seal.

3   Remove the two bolts attaching the left Silent Shaft thrust plate to the engine block, then carefully pull out the thrust plate and the Silent Shaft as an assembly. Support the rear of the shaft (by reaching through the access hole) to prevent damage to the rear bearing as the shaft is withdrawn from the engine (photo). If the thrust plate proves

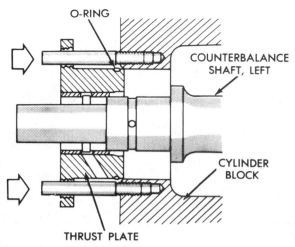

Fig. 2.6 Installing the left Silent Shaft thrust plate using bolts with the heads removed as guides (arrows) (Sec 13)

to be difficult to pull out, screw the appropriate size bolt into each of the threaded holes in the thrust plate flange until they bottom on the engine block Continue turning them with a wrench, one turn at a time, alternating between the two, until the thrust plate is backed out of the engine block. Remove the bolts from the thrust plate flange.

4   The right Silent Shaft is removed with the oil pump (refer to Section 14).

5   To disassemble the left Silent Shaft, slip off the spacer and the thrust plate/bearing assembly Do not lose the key in the end of the shaft. Remove the O-ring from the thrust plate.

6   Clean the components with solvent and dry them thoroughly. Make sure that the oil holes in the shafts and thrust plate are clean and clear.

7   Check both Silent Shafts and the thrust plate for cracks and other damage. Check the bearings in the engine block and the thrust plate (photo) for scratches, scoring and excessive wear. Check the bearing journals on the Silent Shafts for excessive wear and scoring.

13.7 Checking the bearing in the left Silent Shaft thrust plate

8   Measure the outside diameter of each bearing journal (photo) and the inside diameter of each bearing. Subtract the journal diameter from the bearing diameter to obtain the bearing oil clearance. Compare the measured clearance to the Specifications. It if is excessive, have an automative machine shop or dealer service department replace the bearings with new ones. If new bearings do not restore the oil clearance, or if the bearing journals on the shafts are damaged or worn, replace the shafts also. If the bearing in the left Silent Shaft thrust plate is bad, replace the bearing and thrust plate as an assembly.

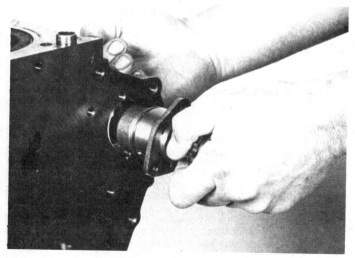

13.3 Removing the left Silent Shaft/thrust plate assembly

16 The right Silent Shaft is installed with the oil pump.

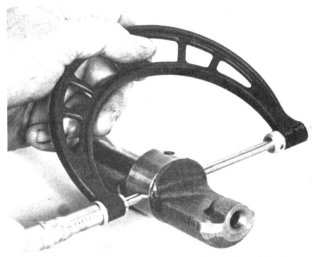

13.8 Measuring the Silent Shaft bearing journal outside diameter with a micrometer

9 Apply a thin layer of clean multi-purpose grease (or engine assembly lube) to the bearing journals on the left Silent Shaft, then carefully insert it into the engine block. Support the rear of the shaft so the rear bearing is not scratched or gouged as the shaft passes through it.

10 Install a new O-ring onto the outside of the thrust plate and lubricate it with clean multi-purpose grease. Also, apply a layer of grease to the thrust plate Silent Shaft bearing.

11 Cut the heads off two 6 x 50 mm bolts and install the bolts in the thrust plate mounting bolt holes. Using the bolts as a guide, carefully slide the thrust plate into position in the engine block. The guides are necessary to keep the bolt holes in the thrust plate aligned with the holes in the engine block. If the thrust plate is turned to align the holes, the O-ring could be twisted or damaged.

12 Remove the guide bolts, install the mounting bolts and tighten them securely.

13 Slip the spacer onto the end of the Silent Shaft (make sure that the key is in place).

14 Turn the shaft by hand and check for smooth operation.

15 Using a new rubber gasket and RTV-type gasket sealer, as well as new O-rings on the bolts, install the left Silent Shaft chamber cover plate and tighten the bolts securely.

14 Oil pump – removal, disassembly and inspection

1 The oil pump and right Silent Shaft are removed from the engine as an assembly.

2 Remove the bolt attaching the oil pump to the engine block. Some of the Silent Shaft chain guide mounting bolts also serve as oil pump mounting bolts; they have already been removed. Leave the Phillips head screw in the left side of the pump in place.

3 Carefully pull straight ahead on the oil pump and remove it, along with the right Silent Shaft, from the engine block. You may have to tap gently on the oil pump body with a soft-faced hammer to break the gasket seal. Do not pry between the oil pump and engine block, as damage to the pump body could result.

4 Remove the bolt from the end of the right Silent Shaft and pull the shaft out of the oil pump from the rear (do not lose the key in the end of the shaft). Refer to Section 13 for Silent Shaft inspection procedures.

5 Remove the plug from the upper side of the pump body and withdraw the relief spring and plunger. You may have to mount the pump body in a vise equipped with soft jaws to loosen the plug. If so, do not apply excessive pressure to the pump body.

6 Remove the Philips head screw from the left side of the pump. Separate the oil pump cover from the body and lift out the two pump gears. Do not lose the key in the lower gear shaft. Do not pry between the cover and body, as damage to the pump may result.

7 Clean the parts with solvent and dry them thoroughly. Use compressed air to blow out all of the oil hoses and passages.

8 Check the entire pump body and cover for cracks and excessive wear. Look closely for a ridge where the gears contact the body and cover.

9 Insert the relief plunger into the pump body and check to see if it slides smoothly. Look for cracks in the relief spring and measure its free length. Inspect the timing chain tensioner plunger sleeve for noticeable wear and the rubber pad for cracks and excessive wear. Measure the tensioner spring free length and compare it to the Specifications.

10 Refer to Figure 2.8. With the gears in place in the pump body, measure the top clearance (A) between the gears and the pump body with a feeler gauge. Measure the inside diameter of the bearing surfaces and the outside diameter of the gear shaft at (C) and (D). Subtract the gear shaft diameters from their matching bearing surface diameters to obtain the gear-to-bearing clearance. With the pump assembled, check the gear end play (B) using a dial indicator set. Compare the measured clearances to the Specifications.

11 If the oil pump clearances are excessive or if excessive wear is evident, replace the oil pump as a unit.

2A

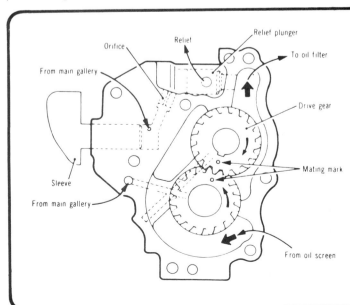

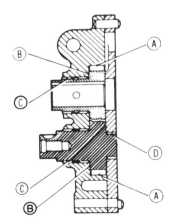

Fig. 2.8 Oil pump clearance measurement points (Sec 14)

 Fig. 2.7 Oil pump components (Sec 14)

15 Piston/connecting rod assembly – removal

1 Prior to removing the piston/connecting rod assemblies, remove the cylinder head, the oil pan, the timing chain case, the Silent Shaft chain and sprockets and the timing chain and sprockets by referring to the appropriate Sections.

2 Using a ridge reamer, completely remove the ridge at the top of each cylinder (follow the manufacturer's instructions provided with the ridge reaming tool). *Failure to remove the ridge before attempting to remove the piston/connecting rod assemblies will result in piston breakage.*

3 With the engine in the upside-down position, remove the oil pick-up tube and screen assembly from the bottom of the engine block (photo). It is held in place with two bolts.

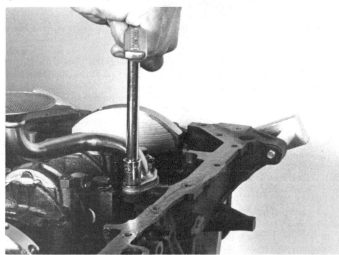

15.3 Removing the oil pickup tube mounting bolts

15.5 Short lengths of rubber hose slipped over the connecting rod cap bolts will prevent damage to the crankshaft journal during piston/connecting rod assembly removal

4 Mark each of the connecting rods and connecting rod bearing caps to ensure that they are properly mated during reassembly.

5 Loosen each of the connecting rod cap nuts approximately $\frac{1}{2}$ turn each. Remove the number one connecting rod cap and bearing insert. Do not drop the bearing insert out of the cap. Slip a short length of plastic or rubber hose over each connecting rod cap bolt (to protect the crankshaft journal when the piston is removed) (photo) and push the connecting rod/piston assembly out through the top of the engine. Use a wooden tool to push on the upper bearing insert in the connecting

rod. If resistance is felt, double-check to make sure that all of the ridge was removed from the cylinder.

6 Repeat the procedure for cylinders two, three and four. After removal, reassemble the connecting rod caps and bearing inserts to their respective connecting rods and install the cap nuts finger tight. Leaving the old bearing inserts in place until reassembly will help prevent the connecting rod bearing surfaces from being accidentally nicked or gouged.

16 Crankshaft – removal

1 Before removing the crankshaft, you must remove the flywheel, the rear oil seal housing, the cylinder head, the oil pan, the timing chain case, the Silent Shaft chain and sprockets and the timing chain and sprockets, by referring to the appropriate Sections.

2 With the engine upside-down, remove the oil pick up tube and screen assembly from the bottom of the engine block. It is held in place with two bolts.

3 Remove the piston assemblies from the engine block as described in Section 15. Be sure to mark each connecting rod and bearing cap so they will be properly mated during reassembly.

4 Loosen each of the main bearing cap bolts $\frac{1}{4}$ of a turn at a time, in sequence, starting at the center of the engine, until they can be removed by hand.

5 Gently tap the main bearing caps with a soft-faced hammer, then remove them from the engine block. If necessary, use the main bearing cap bolts as levers to remove the caps. Try not to drop the bearing shell, if it comes out with the cap. The main bearing caps are marked at the factory with a number (1 through 5, starting at the front of the engine) and an arrow (indicating the front of the engine) so you do not have to mark them.

6 Carefully lift the crankshaft out of the engine. It is a good idea to have an assistant available, as the crankshaft is quite heavy. With the bearing inserts in place in the engine block and the main bearing caps, return the caps to their respective location on the engine block and tighten the bolts finger tight.

17 Engine block – cleaning

1 Remove the ten soft plugs from the engine block. To do this, knock the plugs into the block (using a hammer and punch), then grasp them with a large pliers and pull them back through the hole.

2 Using a gasket scraper, remove all traces of gasket material from the engine block. Be very careful not to nick or gouge the gasket sealing surfaces.

3 Remove the main bearing caps and separate the bearing shells from the caps and the engine block. Tag the bearing shells according to which cylinder they were removed from (and whether they were in the cap or the block) and set them aside.

4 Using a hex wrench of the appropriate size, remove the threaded oil gallery plugs from the front and back of the block.

5 If the engine is extremely dirty, it should be taken to an automotive machine shop to be steam cleaned or hot tanked. Any bearings left in the block (such as the Silent Shaft bearings) may be damaged by the cleaning process, so plan on replacing them.

6 After the block is returned, clean all oil holes and oil galleries one more time (brushes for cleaning oil holes and galleries are available at most auto parts stores). Flushing the passages with warm water (until the water runs clear), dry the block thoroughly and wipe all machined surfaces with a light rust-preventative oil. If you have access to compressed air, use it to speed the drying process and to blow out all of the oil holes and galleries.

7 If the block is not extremely dirty or sludges up, you can do an adequate cleaning job with warm soapy water and a stiff brush. Take plenty of time and do a thorough job. Regardless of the cleaning method used, be very sure to thoroughly clean all oil holes and galleries, dry the block completely and coat all machined surfaces with light oil.

8 The threaded holes in the block must be clean to ensure accurate torque readings during reassembly. Run the proper size tap into each of the holes to remove any rust, corrosion, thread sealant or sludge and to restore any damaged threads. If possible, use compressed air or a vacuum cleaner to clear the holes of debris produced by this operation.

Now is a good time to thoroughly clean the threads on the head bolts and the main bearing cap bolts as well.

9   Reinstall the main bearing caps and tighten the bolts finger tight.

10 After coating the sealing surfaces of the new soft plugs with a good quality gasket sealer, install them in the engine block (photo). Make sure they are driven in straight and seated properly, or leakage could result. Special tools are available for this purpose, but equally good results can be obtained using a large socket (with an outside diameter slightly larger than the outside diameter of the soft plug) and a large hammer.

11 If the engine is not going to be reassembled right away, cover it with a large plastic trash bag to keep it clean.

18.7 Honing the cylinder with a surfacing hone

17.10 Installing the soft plugs in the engine block

18 Engine block – inspection

1   Thoroughly clean the engine block as described in Section 17 and double-check to make sure that the ridge at the top of the cylinders has been completely removed.

2   Visually check the block for cracks, rust and corrosion. Look for stripped threads in the threaded holes. It is also a good idea to have the block checked for hidden cracks by an automotive machine shop that has the special equipment to do this type of work. If defects are found, have the block repaired, if possible, or replaced.

3   Check the cylinder bores for scuffing and scoring.

4   Using the appropriate precision measuring tools, measure each cylinder's diameter at the top (just under the ridge), center and bottom of the cylinder bore, parallel to the crankshaft axis. Next, measure each cylinder's diameter at the same three locations across the crankshaft axis. Compare the results to the Specifications. If the cylinder walls are badly scuffed or scored, or if they are out-of-round or tapered beyond the limits given in the Specifications, have the engine block rebored and honed at an automotive machine shop. If a rebore is done, oversized pistons and rings will be required as well.

5   If the cylinders are in reasonably good condition and not worn to the outside of the limits, and if the piston-to-cylinder clearances can be maintained properly, then they do not have to be rebored; honing is all that is necessary.

6   Before honing the cylinders, install the main bearing caps (without the bearings) and tighten the bolts to the specified torque.

7   To perform the honing operation, you will need the proper size flexible hone (with fine stones), plenty of light oil or honing oil, some rags and an electric drill motor. Mount the hone in the drill motor, compress the stones and slip the hone into the first cylinder. Lubricate the cylinder thoroughly, turn on the drill and move the hone up and down in the cylinder at a pace which will produce a fine cross-hatch pattern on the cylinder walls (with the cross-hatch lines intersecting at approximately a 60° angle). Be sure to use plenty of lubricant, and do not take off any more material than is absolutely necessary to produce the desired finish. Do not withdraw the hone from the cylinder while it is running. Instead, shut off the drill and continue moving the hone

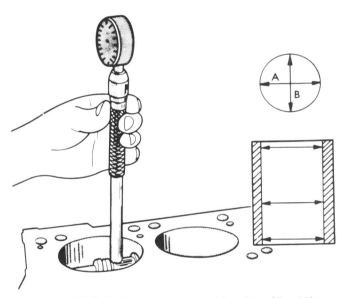

Fig. 2.9 Cylinder bore measurement locations (Sec 18)

up and down in the cylinder until it comes to a complete stop, then compress the stones and withdraw the hone. Wipe the oil out of the cylinder and repeat the procedure on the remaining cylinders. Remember, do not remove too much material from the cylinder wall. If you do not have the tools or do not desire to perform the honing operation, most automotive machine stops will do it for a reasonable fee (photo).

8   After the honing job is complete, chamfer the top edges of the cylinder bores with a small file so that the rings will not catch when the pistons are installed.

9   Next, the entire engine block must be thoroughly washed again with warm soapy water to remove all traces of the abrasive grit produced during the honing operation. Be sure to run a brush through all oil holes and galleries and flush them with running water. After rinsing, dry the block and apply a coat of light rust preventative oil to all machined surfaces. Wrap the block in a plastic trash bag to keep it clean and set it aside until reassembly.

19 Crankshaft – inspection

1   Clean the crankshaft with solvent (be sure to clean the oil holes

2A

with a stiff brush and flush them with solvent) and dry it thoroughly. Check the main and connecting rod bearing journals for uneven wear, scoring, pitting and cracks. Check the remainder of the crankshaft for cracks and damage.

2   Using an appropriate size micrometer, measure the diameter of the main and connecting rod journals (photo) and compare the results to the Specifications. By measuring the diameter at a number of points around the journal's circumference, you will be able to determine whether or not the journal is worn out-of-round. Take the measurement at each end of the journal, near the crank throw, to determine whether the journal is tapered.

3   If the crankshaft journals are damaged, tapered, out-of-round or worn beyond the limits given in the Specifications, have the crankshaft reground by a reputable automotive machine shop. Be sure to use the correct undersize bearing inserts if the crankshaft is reconditioned.

19.2 Measuring a main bearing journal diameter

20 Piston/connecting rod assembly – inspection

1   Before the inspection process can be carried out, the piston/connecting rod assemblies must be cleaned and the piston rings removed from the pistons.

2   Using a piston ring installation tool, carefully remove the rings from the pistons. Do not nick or gouge the pistons in the process.

3   Scrape all traces of carbon from the top (or crown) of the piston. A hand-held wire brush or a piece of fine emery cloth can be used once the majority of the deposits have been scraped away. *Do not, under any circumstances, use a wire brush mounted in a drill motor to remove deposits from the pistons. The piston material is soft and will be eroded away by the wire brush.*

4   Use a piston ring groove cleaning tool to remove any carbon deposits from the ring grooves (photo). If a tool is not available, a piece broken off the old ring will do the job. Be very careful to remove only the carbon deposits. Do not remove any metal and do not nick or scratch the sides of the ring grooves.

5   Once the deposits have been removed, clean the piston/rod assemblies with solvent and dry them thoroughly. Make sure that the oil hole in the big end of the connecting rod and the oil return holes in the back side of the lower ring groove are clear.

6   If the pistons are not damaged or worn excessively, and if the engine block is not rebored, new pistons will not be necessary. Normal piston wear appears as even vertical wear on the piston thrust surfaces and slight looseness of the top ring in its groove. New piston rings, on the other hand, should always be used when an engine is rebuilt.

7   Carefully inspect each piston for cracks around the skirt, at the pin bosses and at the ring lands.

8   Look for scoring and scuffing (on the thrust faces of the skirt), holes (in the piston crown) and burned areas (at the edge of the crown). If the skirt is scored or scuffed, the engine may have been suffering from overheating and/or abnormal combustion, which caused

20.4 Cleaning the piston ring grooves with a ring groove cleaning tool

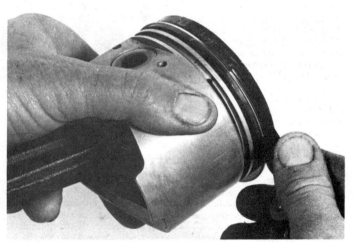

20.10 Measuring the piston ring side clearance with a feeler gauge

20.11 Measuring the piston diameter with an outside micrometer to determine the piston-to-bore clearance

excessively high operating temperatures. The cooling and lubrication systems should be checked thoroughly. A hole in the piston crown, an extreme to be sure, is an indication that abnormal combustion (preignition) was occurring. Burned areas at the edge of the piston crown are usually evidence of spark knock (detonation). If any of the above problems exist, the causes must be corrected or the damage will occur again.

9   Corrosion of the piston (evidenced by pitting) indicates that coolant is leaking into the combustion chamber and/or the crankcase. Again, the cause must be corrected or the problem may persist in the rebuilt engine.

10   Measure the piston ring side clearance by laying a new piston ring in the ring groove and slipping a feeler gauge in beside it (photo). Check the clearance at three or four locations around the groove. Be sure to use the correct ring for each groove; they are different. If the side clearance is greater than specified, new pistons will have to be used and the block rebored to accept them.

11   Check the piston-to-bore clearance by measuring the bore (see Section 18) and the piston diameter (photo). Make sure that the pistons and bores are correctly matched. Measure the piston across the skirt, on the thrust faces (at a 90° angle to the piston pin), about 0.100 in (2 mm) up from the bottom of the skirt. Subtract the piston diameter from the bore diameter to obtain the clearance. If it is greater than specified, the block will have to be rebored and new pistons and rings installed. Check the piston pin-to-rod clearance by twisting the piston and rod in opposite directions. Any noticeable play indicates that there is excessive wear, which must be corrected. The piston/connecting rod assemblies should be taken to an automotive machine shop to have new piston pins installed and the pistons and connecting rods rebored.

12   If the pistons must be removed from the connecting rods, such as when new pistons must be installed, or if the piston pins have too much play in them, they should be taken to an automotive machine shop. While they are there, it would be convenient to have the connecting rods checked for bend and twist, as automotive machine shops have special equipment for this purpose.

13   Check the connecting rods for cracks and other damage. Temporarily remove the rod cap, lift out the old bearing inserts, wipe the rod and cap bearing surfaces clean and inspect them for nicks, gouges and scratches. After checking the rods, replace the old bearings, slip the caps in place and tighten the nuts finger tight. *Unless new pistons or connecting rods must be installed, do not disassemble the pistons from the connecting rods.*

21 Main and connecting rod bearings – inspection

1   Even though the main and connecting rod bearings should be replaced with new ones during the engine overhaul, the old bearings should be retained for close examination, as they may reveal valuable information about the condition of the engine.

2   Bearing failure occurs mainly because of lack of lubrication, the presence of dirt or other foreign particles, overloading the engine and/or corrosion. Regardless of the cause of bearing failure, it must be corrected before the engine is reassembled to prevent it from happening again.

3   When examining the bearings, remove them from the engine block, the main bearing caps, the connecting rods and the rod caps and lay them out on a clean surface in the same general position as their location in the engine. This will enable you to match any noted bearing problems with the corresponding crankshaft journal.

4   Dirt and other foreign particles get into the engine in a variety of ways. It may be left in the engine during assembly, or it may pass through filters or breathers. It may get into the oil, and from there into the bearings. Metal chips from machining operations and normal engine wear are often present. Abrasives are sometimes left in engine components after reconditioning, especially when parts are not thoroughly cleaned using the proper cleaning methods. Whatever the source, these foreign objects often end up embedded in the soft bearing material and are easily recognized. Large particles will not embed in the bearing and will score or gouge the bearing and shaft. The best prevention for this cause of bearing failure is to clean all parts thoroughly and keep everything spotlessly clean during engine assembly. Frequent and regular changes of engine oil, and oil filters, is also recommended.

5   Lack of lubrication (or lubrication breakdown) has a number of interrelated causes. Excessive heat (which thins the oil), overloading (which squeezes the oil from the bearing face) and oil leakage or throw-off (from excessive bearing clearances, worn oil pump or high engine speeds) all contribute to lubrication breakdown. Blocked oil passages, which usually are the result of misaligned oil holes in a bearing shell, will also oil-starve a bearing and destroy it. When lack of lubrication is the cause of bearing failure, the bearing material is wiped or extruded from the steel backing of the bearing. Temperatures may increase to the point where the steel backing turns blue from overheating.

6   Driving habits can have a definitite effect on bearing life. Full-throttle low-speed operation (or 'lugging' the engine) puts very high loads on bearings, which tends to squeeze out the oil film. These loads cause the bearings to flex, which produces fine cracks in the bearing face (fatigue failure). Eventually the bearing material will loosen in pieces and tear away from the steel backing. Short-trip driving leads to corrosion of bearings, as insufficient engine heat is produced to drive off the condensed water and corrosive gases produced. These products collect in the engine oil, forming acid and sludge. As the oil is carried to the engine bearings the acid attacks and corrodes the bearing material.

7   Incorrect bearing installation during engine assembly will lead to bearing failure as well. Tight-fitting bearings, which leave insufficient bearing oil clearance, result in oil starvation. Dirt or foreign particles trapped behind a bearing insert result in high spots on the bearing which lead to failure.

22 Cylinder head – cleaning and inspection

1   Thorough cleaning of the cylinder head and related valve train components, followed by a detailed inspection, will enable you to decide how much valve work must be done during the engine overhaul.

Cleaning

2   Scrape away any traces of old gasket material and sealing compound from the head gasket, the intake manifold and the exhaust manifold sealing surfaces. Work slowly and do not nick or gouge the soft aluminum of the head.

3   Carefully scrape all carbon deposits out of the combustion chamber areas. A hand-held wire brush or a piece of fine emery cloth can be used once the majority of deposits have been scraped away.

4   Remove any scale that may be built up around the coolant passages.

5   Run a stiff wire brush through the oil holes, the EGR gas ports and the jet air passages to remove any deposits that may have formed in those areas (photo).

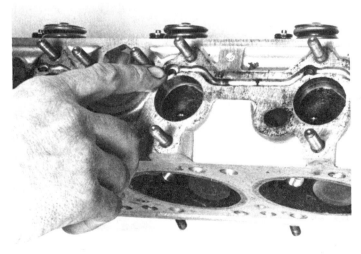

22.5 Make sure the Jet air passages, EGR gas ports and the oil holes are thoroughly cleaned

2A

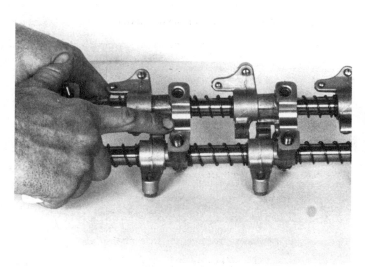

22.14 Inspecting the camshaft bearing cap bearing surfaces

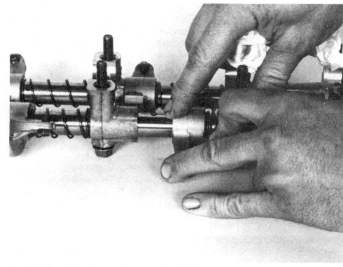

22.20 Checking the rocker arm shafts for wear

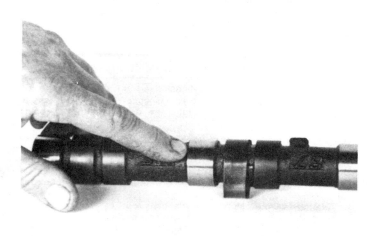

22.22 Inspecting the camshaft bearing journals for excessive wear and evidence of seizure

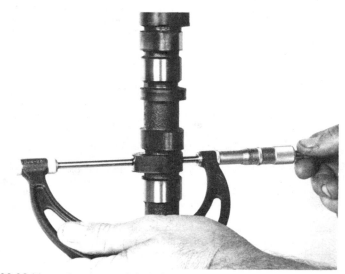

22.23 Measuring the cam lobe height

22.25 Measuring the valve margin width

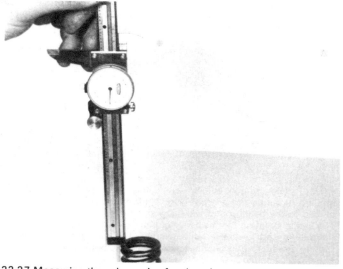

22.27 Measuring the valve spring free length

6   It is a good idea to run an appropriate size tap into each of the threaded holes to remove any corrosion or thread sealant that may be present. Be very careful when cleaning aluminum threads; they can be damaged easily with a tap. If compressed air is available, use it to clear the holes of debris produced by this operation. Clean the exhaust and intake manifold stud threads in a similar manner with an appropriate size die. Clean the camshaft bearing cap bolt threads with a wire brush.

7   Next, clean the cylinder head with solvent and dry it thoroughly. Compressed air will speed the drying process and ensure that all holes and recessed areas are clean. **Note:** *Decarbonizing chemicals are available and may prove very useful when cleaning cylinder heads and valve train components. They are very caustic and should be used with caution. Be sure to follow the directions on the container.*

8   Clean the camshaft with solvent and dry it thoroughly.

9   Without dismantling the rocker arm assembly, clean it with solvent (make sure all oil holes are clear) and dry it thoroughly. Compressed air, if it is available, will speed up the drying process and make it much easier.

10 Clean all the valve springs, keepers, retainers and spring seats with solvent and dry them thoroughly. *Do the parts from one valve at a time, so that no mixing of parts between valves occurs.*

11 Scrape off any heavy deposits that may have formed on the valves, then use a motorized wire brush to remove deposits from the valve heads and stems. Again, make sure that valves do not get mixed up.

12 Clean the jet valve components with solvent. Do one jet valve at a time so parts are not accidentally interchanged. Carefully remove any deposits from the jet valve stem and head with a fine wire brush (do not bend the valve stem in the process).

Inspection

Cylinder head

13 Inspect the head very carefully for cracks, evidence of coolant leakage and other damage. If cracks are found, a new head is in order.

14 Check the camshaft bearing surfaces in the head and the bearing caps (photo). If there is evidence of excessive wear, scoring or seizure, the cylinder head will have to be replaced with a new one to restore the camshaft bearing surfaces and proper oil clearance.

15 Using a straightedge and feeler gauge, check the head gasket mating surfaces for warpage at the points shown in Figure 2.10. If the head is warped beyond the limits given in the Specifications, it can be resurfaced at an automotive machine shop.

16 Examine the valve seats in each of the combustion chambers. If they are pitted, cracked or burned, the head will require valve service that is beyond the scope of the home mechanic.

17 Measure the inside diameters of the valve guides (at both ends and the center of the guide) with a small hole gauge and a 0-to-1 in micrometer. Record the measurements for future reference. These measurements, along with the valve stem diameter measurements, will enable you to compute the valve stem-to-guide clearance. This clearance, when compared to the Specifications, will be one factor that will determine the extent of the valve service work required. The guides are measured at the ends and at the center to determine if they are worn in a bell-mouth pattern (more wear at the ends). If they are, guide reconditioning or replacement is an absolute must.

Rocker arm assembly

18 Check the rocker arm faces (that contact the camshaft lobes) and the ends of the adjusting screws (that contact the valve stems) for pitting, excessive wear and roughness.

19 Check the adjusting screw threads for damage. Make sure they can be threaded in and out of the rocker arms.

20 Slide each rocker arm along its shaft, against the locating spring pressure, and check the rocker arm shafts for excessive wear and evidence of scoring in the areas that normally contact the rocker arms (photo).

21 Any damaged or excessively worn parts must be replaced with new ones. Refer to the exploded view of the rocker arm assembly components, which will enable you to correctly disassemble and reassemble them.

Camshaft

22 Inspect the camshaft bearing journals for excessive wear and evidence of seizure (photo). If the journals are damaged, the bearing surfaces in the head and bearing caps are probably damaged as well.

Both the camshaft and cylinder head will have to be replaced with new ones.

23 Check the cam lobes for pitting, grooves, scoring or flaking. Measure the cam lobe height and compare it to the Specifications (photo). If the lobe height is less than the minimum specified, and/or the lobes are damaged, a new camshaft must be obtained.

Valves

24 Carefully inspect each valve face for cracks, pitting and burned spots. Check the valve stem and neck for cracks. Rotate the valve and check for any obvious indication that it is bent. Check the end of the stem for pitting and excessive wear. The presence of any of the above conditions indicates a need for valve service by a professional.

25 Measure the width of the valve margin (on each valve) and compare it to the Specifications (photo). Any valve with a margin narrower than specified will have to be replaced with a new one.

26 Measure the valve stem diameter. By subtracting the stem diameter from the valve guide diameter, the valve stem-to-guide clearance is obtained. Compare the results to the Specifications. If the stem-to-guide clearance is greater than specified, the guides will have to be reconditioned or replaced and new valves may have to be installed, depending on the condition of the old ones.

Valve components

27 Check each valve spring for wear (on the ends) and pitting. Measure the free length (photo) and compare it to the Specifications. Any springs that are shorter than specified have sagged and should not be reused. Stand the spring on a flat surface and check it for squareness.

28 Check the spring retainers and keepers for obvious wear and cracks. Any questionable parts should not be reused, as extensive damage will occur in the event of failure during engine operation.

Jet valve assemblies

29 Make sure the Jet valve slides freely in the Jet valve body. It should have no detectable side play. Check the valve head and seat for cracks and pitting. Check the spring for wear (on the ends) and cracks. Measure the valve spring free length and the diameter of the valve stem (photo). Compare the results to the Specifications.

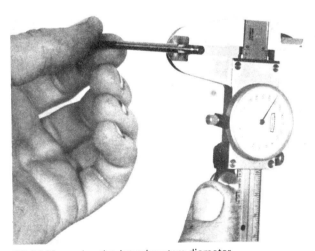

22.29 Measuring the Jet valve stem diameter

30 If defects are found in any of the Jet valve components, the entire valve assembly should be replaced with a new one.

31 Be sure to check the remaining Jet valve assemblies.

32 If the inspection process indicates that the valve components are in generally poor condition and worn beyond the limits specified, which is usually the case in an engine that is being overhauled, reassemble the valves in the cylinder head and refer to Section 23 for valve servicing recommendations.

33 If the inspection process turns up no excessively worn parts, and if the valve faces and seats are in good condition, the valve train

2A

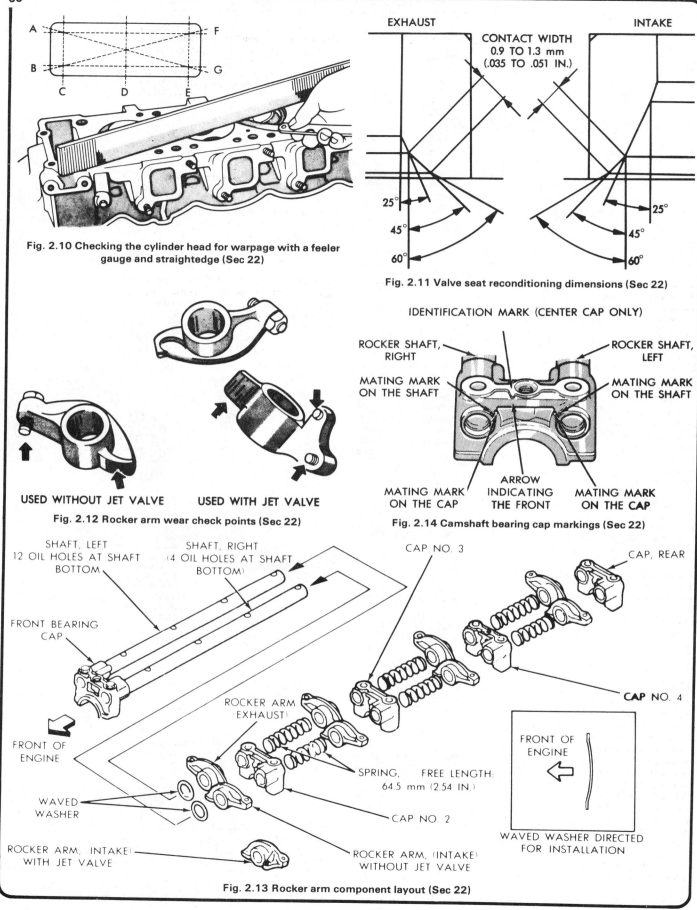

Fig. 2.10 Checking the cylinder head for warpage with a feeler gauge and straightedge (Sec 22)

EXHAUST   INTAKE

CONTACT WIDTH
0.9 TO 1.3 mm
(.035 TO .051 IN.)

25°   25°
45°   45°
60°   60°

Fig. 2.11 Valve seat reconditioning dimensions (Sec 22)

USED WITHOUT JET VALVE   USED WITH JET VALVE

Fig. 2.12 Rocker arm wear check points (Sec 22)

IDENTIFICATION MARK (CENTER CAP ONLY)

ROCKER SHAFT,
RIGHT

ROCKER SHAFT,
LEFT

MATING MARK
ON THE SHAFT

MATING MARK
ON THE SHAFT

MATING MARK
ON THE CAP

ARROW
INDICATING
THE FRONT

MATING MARK
ON THE CAP

Fig. 2.14 Camshaft bearing cap markings (Sec 22)

SHAFT, LEFT
12 OIL HOLES AT SHAFT
BOTTOM

SHAFT, RIGHT
(4 OIL HOLES AT SHAFT
BOTTOM)

CAP NO. 3

CAP, REAR

FRONT BEARING
CAP

CAP NO. 4

ROCKER ARM
(EXHAUST)

FRONT OF
ENGINE

FRONT OF
ENGINE

WAVED
WASHER

SPRING,   FREE LENGTH:
64.5 mm (2.54 IN.)

CAP NO. 2

WAVED WASHER DIRECTED
FOR INSTALLATION

ROCKER ARM, (INTAKE)
WITH JET VALVE

ROCKER ARM, (INTAKE)
WITHOUT JET VALVE

Fig. 2.13 Rocker arm component layout (Sec 22)

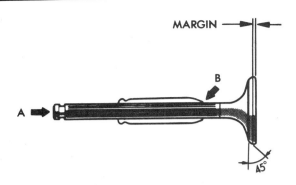

Fig. 2.15 Valve inspection points (Sec 22)

components can be reinstalled in the cylinder head without major servicing. Refer to Section 29 for cylinder head reassembly procedures.

23 Valves – servicing

1   Because of the complex nature of the job and the special tools and equipment required, servicing of the valves, the valve seats and the valve guides (commonly known as a 'valve job') is best left to a professional.

2   The home mechanic can remove and disassemble the head, do the initial cleaning and inspection, then reassemble and deliver the head to a dealer service department or a reputable automotive machine shop for the actual valve servicing.

3   The dealer service department, or automotive machine shop, will remove the valves and springs, recondition or replace the valves and valve seats, recondition or replace the valve guides, check and replace the valve springs, spring retainers and keepers (as necessary), replace the valve seals with new ones, reassemble the valve components and make sure the installed spring height is correct. The cylinder head gasket surface will also be resurfaced if it is warped.

4   After the valve job has been performed by a professional, the head will be in like-new condition. When the head is returned, be sure to clean it again, very thoroughly (before installation on the engine), to remove any metal particles and abrasive grit that may still be present from the valve service or head resurfacing operations. Use compressed air, if available, to blow out all the oil holes and passages.

24 Crankshaft – installation

1   Crankshaft installation is generally one of the first steps in engine reassembly; it is assumed at this point that the engine block and crankshaft have been cleaned and inspected and repaired or reconditioned.

2   Position the engine with the bottom facing up.

3   Remove the main bearing cap bolts and lift out the caps. Lay them out in the proper order to help ensure they are installed correctly.

4   If they are still in place, remove the old bearing inserts from the block and the main bearing caps. Wipe the main bearing surfaces of the block and caps with a clean, lint-free cloth (they must be kept spotlessly clean).

5   Clean the back side of the new main bearing inserts and lay one bearing half in each main bearing saddle (in the block) and the other bearing half from each bearing set in the corresponding main bearing cap. Make sure the tab on the bearing insert fits into the recess in the block or cap. Also, the oil holes in the block and cap must line up with the oil holes in the bearing insert. Do not hammer the bearing into place and do not nick or gouge the bearing faces. No lubrication should be used at this time.

6   The flanged thrust bearing must be installed in the number three (center) cap and saddle.

7   Clean the faces of the bearings in the block and the crankshaft main bearing journal with a clean, lint-free cloth. Check or clean the oil holes in the crankshaft, as any dirt here can only go one way – straight through the new bearings.

8   Once you are certain that the crankshaft is clean, carefully lay it in

position (an assistant would be very helpful here) in the main bearings with the counterweights lying sideways.

9   Before the crankshaft can be permanently installed, the main bearing oil clearance must be checked.

10   Trim five (5) pieces of the appropriate type of Plastigage (so they are slightly shorter than the width of the main bearings) and place one piece on each crankshaft main bearing journal, parallel with the journal axis. Do not lay them across any oil holes.

11   Clean the faces of the bearings in the caps and install the caps in their respective positions (do not mix them up) with the arrows pointing toward the front of the engine. Do not disturb the Plastigage.

12   Starting with the center main and working out toward the ends, tighten the main bearing cap bolts, in three steps, to the specified torque. *Do not rotate the crankshaft at any time during this operation.*

13   Remove the bolts and carefully lift off the main bearing caps. Keep them in order. Do not disturb the Plastigage or rotate the crankshaft. If any of the main bearing caps are difficult to remove, tap gently from side-to-side with a soft-faced hammer to loosen them.

14   Compare the width of the crushed Plastigage on each journal to the scale printed on the Plastigage container (photo) to obtain the main bearing oil clearance. Check the Specifications to make sure it is correct.

15   If the clearance is not correct, double-check to make sure that you have the right size bearing inserts. Also, recheck the crankshaft main bearing journal diameters and make sure that no dirt or oil was between the bearing inserts and the main bearing caps or the block when the clearance was measured.

16   Carefully scrape all traces of the Plastigage material off the main bearing journals and/or the bearing faces. Do not nick or scratch the bearing faces.

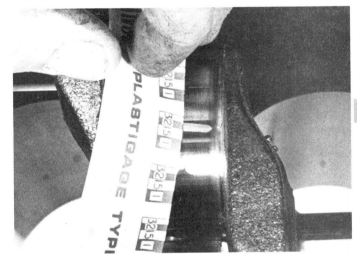

24.14 Comparing the width of the crushed Plastigage to the scale on the container to obtain the main bearing oil clearance

17   Carefully lift the crankshaft out of the engine. Clean the bearing faces in the block, then apply a thin, uniform layer of clean, high quality multi-purpose grease (or engine assembly lube) to each of the bearing faces. Be sure to coat the thrust flange faces as well as the journal face of the thrust bearing in the number three (center) main. Make sure the crankshaft journals are clean, then carefully lay it back in place in the block. Clean the faces of the bearings in the caps, then apply a thin, uniform layer of clean, high-quality multi-purpose grease to each of the bearing faces and install the caps in their respective positions with the arrows pointing toward the front of the engine. Install the bolts and tighten them to the specified torque, starting with the center main and working out toward the ends. Work up to the final torque in three steps.

18   Rotate the crankshaft a number of times by hand and check for any obvious binding.

19   The final step is to check the crankshaft end play. This can be done with a feeler gauge or a dial indicator set.

20   If a feeler gauge is used, gently pry the crankshaft all the way toward the back of the engine with a large screwdriver. Slip a feeler gauge between the crankshaft thrust face and the bearing thrust face

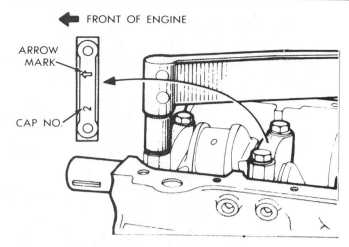

FRONT OF ENGINE

ARROW MARK

CAP NO.

Fig. 2.16 Correct main bearing cap installation (Sec 24)

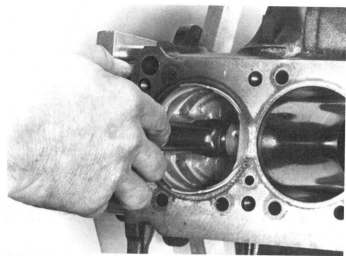

25.3a Using the piston to square up the piston ring in the cylinder prior to measuring the end gap

at the rear side of the number three (center) main bearing. Compare the measured end play to the Specifications.

21   If a dial indicator is used, mount it at the rear of the engine with the indicator stem touching the end of the flange on the crankshaft (photo). Gently pry the crankshaft all the way to the back of the engine, then zero the dial indicator. Carefully pry the crankshaft as far as possible in the opposite direction and observe the needle movement on the dial indicator, which will indicate the amount of end play. Compare it to the Specifications.

24.21 Checking the crankshaft end play with a dial indicator

25.3b Measuring the piston ring end gap with a feeler gauge

25 Piston rings – installation

1   Before installing the new piston rings, the ring end gaps must be checked.

2   Lay out the piston/connecting rod assemblies and the new ring sets so the rings will be matched with the same piston and cylinder during the end gap measurement and engine assembly.

3   Insert the top (number one) ring into the first cylinder and square it up with the cylinder walls by pushing it in with the top of the piston (photo). The ring should be at least two inches below the top edge of the cylinder. To measure the end gap, slip a feeler gauge between the ends of the ring (photo). Compare the measurement to the Specifications.

4   If the gap is larger or smaller than specified, double-check to make sure that you have the correct rings before proceeding.

5   If the gap is too small, it must be enlarged or the ring ends may come in contact with each other during engine operation, which can

25.9a Installing the spacer expander in the oil control ring groove

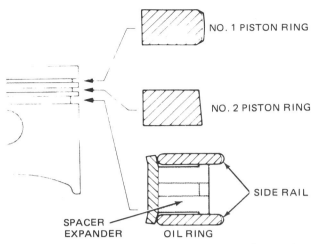

Fig. 2.17 The piston rings have different cross sections and must be installed in the correct groove (Sec 25)

25.9b Installing the upper side rail in the oil control ring groove

cause serious damage to the engine. The end gap can be increased by filing the ring ends very carefully with a fine file. Mount the ring in a vise equipped with soft jaws, holding it as close to the gap as possible. When performing this operation, file only from the outside in.

6 Excess end gap is not critical unless it is greater than 0.040 in (1 mm). Again, double-check to make sure you have the correct rings for your engine.

7 Repeat the procedure for each ring that will be installed in the first cylinder and for each ring in the remaining cylinders. Remember to keep rings, pistons and cylinders matched up.

8 Once the ring end gaps have been checked/corrected, the rings can be installed on the pistons.

9 The oil control ring (lowest one on the piston) is installed first. It is composed of three separate components. Slip the spacer expander into the groove (photo) then install the upper side rail (photo) with the size mark and manufacturer's stamp facing up (photo). *Do not use a piston ring installation tool on the oil ring side rails, as they may be damaged.* Instead, place one end of the side rail into the groove between the spacer expander and the ring land, hold it firmly in place and slide a finger around the piston while pushing the rail into the groove (photo). Next, install the lower side rail (again, the size mark and manufacturer's stamp must face up) in the same manner.

10 After the three oil ring components have been installed, check to make sure that both the upper and lower side rails can be turned smoothly in the ring groove.

11 The number two (middle) ring is installed next. It is stamped with a '2' so that it can be readily distinguished from the top ring. *Do not mix the top and middle rings up, as they have different cross sections.*

12 Use a piston ring installation tool and make sure that the identification mark is facing up, then fit the ring into the middle groove

25.9c The piston rings must be installed with the marked side (arrow) up

2A

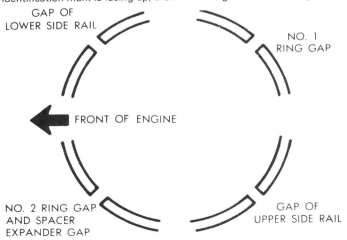

Fig. 2.18 Piston ring end gap position diagram (Sec 25)

25.12 Installing a piston ring with a piston ring installation tool on the piston (photo). Do not expand the ring any more than is necessary to slide it over the piston.

13 Finally, install the number one (top) ring in the same manner. Make sure the identifying mark is facing up.

14 Repeat the procedure for the remaining pistons and rings. Be careful not to confuse the number one and number two rings.

26 Piston/connecting rod assembly – installation

1 Before installing the piston/connecting rod assemblies, the cylinder walls must be perfectly clean, the top edge of each cylinder must be chamfered, and the crankshaft must be in place.

2 Remove the connecting rod cap from the end of the number one connecting rod. Remove the old bearing inserts and wipe the bearing surfaces of the connecting rod and cap with a clean, lint-free cloth (they must be spotlessly clean).

3 Clean the back side of the new upper bearing half, then lay it in place in the connecting rod. Make sure that the tab on the bearing fits into the recess in the rod. Also, the oil holes in the rod and bearing insert must line up. Do not hammer the bearing insert into place, and be very careful not to nick or gouge the bearing face. *Do not lubricate the bearing at this time.*

4 Clean the back side of the other bearing insert half and install it in the rod cap. Again, make sure the tab on the bearing fits into the recess in the cap and do not apply any lubricant. It is critically important to ensure that the mating surfaces of the bearing and connecting rod are perfectly clean and oil-free when they are assembled together.

5 Position the piston ring gaps as shown, then slip a section of plastic or rubber hose over the connecting rod cap bolts.

6 Lubricate the piston and rings with clean engine oil and install a piston ring compressor on the piston. Leave the skirt protruding about $\frac{1}{4}$ inch to guide the piston into the cylinder. The rings must be compressed as far as possible.

7 Rotate the crankshaft until the number one connecting rod journal is as far from the number one cylinder as possible (bottom dead center), and apply a uniform coat of engine oil to the number one cylinder walls.

8 With the arrow on top of the piston pointing to the front of the engine, gently place the piston/connecting rod assembly into the number one cylinder bore (photo) and rest the bottom edge of the ring compressor on the engine block. Tap the top edge of the ring compressor to make sure it is contacting the block around its entire circumference.

9 Clean the number one connecting rod journal on the crankshaft and the bearing faces in the rod.

10 Carefully tap on the top of the piston with the end of a wooden hammer handle while guiding the end of the connecting rod into place on the crankshaft journal. The piston rings may try to pop out of the ring compressor just before entering the cylinder bore, so keep some downward pressure on the ring compressor. Work slowly, and if any resistance is felt as the piston enters the cylinder, stop immediately, find out what is hanging up and fix it before proceeding. *Do not, for any reason, force the piston into the cylinder, as you will break a ring and/or the piston.*

11 Once the piston/connecting rod assembly is installed, the connecting rod bearing oil clearance must be checked before the rod cap is permanently bolted in place.

12 Trim a piece of the appropriate type Plastigage so it is slightly shorter than the width of the connecting rod bearing and lay it in place on the number one connecting rod journal, parallel with the journal axis (it must not cross the oil hole in the journal).

13 Clean the connecting rod cap bearing face, remove the protective hoses from the connecting rod bolts and gently install the rod cap in place. Make sure the mating mark on the cap is on the same side as the mark on the connecting rod. Install the nuts and tighten them to the specified torque, working up to it in three steps. *Do not rotate the crankshaft at any time during this operation.*

14 Remove the rod cap, being very careful not to disturb the Plastigage. Compare the width of the crushed Plastigage to the scale printed on the Plastigage container (photo) to obtain the oil clearance. Compare it to the Specifications to make sure the clearance is correct. If the clearance is not correct, double-check to make sure that you have the correct size bearing inserts. Also, recheck the crankshaft connecting rod journal diameter and make sure that no dirt or oil was

26.8 Placing the piston/connecting rod assembly (with the ring compressor installed) into the cylinder bore

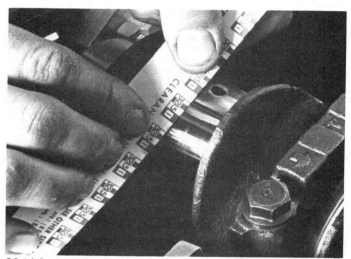

26.14 Comparing the width of the crushed Plastigage to the scale printed on the container to obtain the connecting rod bearing oil clearance

26.20 Checking the connecting rod big end side clearance with a feeler gauge

between the bearing inserts and the connecting rod or cap when the clearance was measured.

15 Carefully scrape all traces of the Plastigage material off the rod journal and/or bearing face (be very carefully not to stratch the bearing). Make sure the bearing faces are perfectly clean, then apply a uniform layer of clean, high quality multi-purpose grease (or engine assembly lube) to both of them. You will have to push the piston into the cylinder to expose the face of the bearing insert in the connecting rod; be sure to slip the protective hoses over the rod bolts first.

16 Slide the connecting rod back into place on the journal, remove the protective hoses from the rod cap bolts, install the rod cap and tighten the nuts to the specified torque. Again, work up to the torque in three steps.

17 Without turning the crankshaft, repeat the entire procedure for the number four piston/connecting rod assembly. Keep the back sides of the bearing inserts and the inside of the connecting rod and cap perfectly clean when assembling them. Make sure you have the correct piston for the cylinder and that the arrow on the piston points to the front of the engine when the piston is installed. Remember, use plenty of oil to lubricate the piston before installing the ring compressor and be sure to match up the mating marks on the connecting rod and rod cap. Also, when installing the rod caps for the final time, be sure to lubricate the bearing faces adequately.

18 After completing the procedure for piston number four, turn the crankshaft 180° and repeat the entire operation for pistons number two and three.

19 After all the piston/connecting rod assemblies have been properly installed, rotate the crankshaft a number of times by hand and check for obvious binding.

20 As a final step, the connecting rod big end side clearances must be checked. Slide the number one connecting rod all the way to one end of its journal and slip a feeler gauge between the side of the connecting rod and the crankshaft throw (photo). Be sure to compare the measured clearance to the Specifications to make sure it is correct. Repeat the procedure for the other three connecting rods.

27.3 Lining up the mating marks on the oil pump gears

27 Oil pump – reassembly and installation

1   The oil pump and right Silent Shaft are installed as a unit.

2   Coat the oil pump relief plunger with clean multi-purpose grease and insert the plunger and spring into the oil pump body. Install the cap and tighten it securely.

3   Apply a layer of multi-purpose grease to the gear teeth, the sides of the gears and the bearing surfaces in the pump body and cover. Lay the gears in place in the body with the mating marks lined up as shown (photo). If the mating marks are not properly aligned, the right Silent Shaft will be out of phase and engine vibration will result.

4   Lay the cover in place using the dowel pins to align it properly. Install the Phillips head screw in the left side of the pump, but do not tighten it completely at this time. Make sure the gears rotate smoothly without binding.

5   Lay a new gasket in place on the cover (no sealer required). The dowel pins should align it properly and hold it in place.

6   Make sure the key is in place in the front of the shaft, then slip the right Silent Shaft through the oil pump driven gear as you line up the key in the shaft with the keyway in the gear. Once the shaft and gear are properly mated, clamp the counterweight end of the shaft in a vise equipped with soft jaws, install the bolt in the front end of the shaft and tighten it to the specified torque.

7   Apply a thin layer of clean multi-purpose grease (or engine assembly lube) to the rear bearing journal of the right Silent Shaft.

8   Hold the pump upright and fill it with a minimum of 10 cubic centimeters of engine oil (photo). Insert the Silent Shaft into the engine block and through the rear bearing. Be careful not to scratch or gouge the bearing as the shaft is installed.

9   Make sure the pump is seated on the engine block, then install the mounting bolts and tighten them evenly and securely. Do not forget to tighten the Phillips head screw. The remaining pump mounting bolts will be installed with the chain guides.

10 Temporarily slip the Silent Shaft drive sprocket onto the lower pump gear shaft and use it to rotate the pump gears/Silent Shaft. Check for any obvious binding.

27.8 Filling the oil pump prior to installation on the engine

28 Silent Shaft chain/sprockets – installation

1   Before installing the Silent Shaft chain and sprockets, the timing chain must be properly installed and the number one piston must be at TDC on the compression stroke. It is assumed that both Silent Shafts and the oil pump are also in place.

2   Slide the crankshaft sprocket part way onto the front of the crankshaft (by lining up the keyway in the sprocket with the key on the shaft).

3   Install the Silent Shaft chain onto the crankshaft sprocket and the left Silent Shaft sprocket. The dished or recessed side of the left Silent Shaft sprocket must face out. Line up the plated links on the chain with the mating marks stamped into the sprockets (see Figure 2.19).

4   With the dished or recessed side facing in, install the right Silent Shaft sprocket onto the chain. Line up the plated link on the chain with the mating mark on the sprocket. Slide the Silent Shaft sprockets onto their respective shafts, lining up the keyways in the sprockets with the keys on the shafts. Simultaneously, push the crankshaft sprocket back until it bottoms on the crankshaft timing chain sprocket. Recheck the position of the mating marks on the chain and sprockets, then install the Silent Shaft sprocket attaching bolts and tighten them to the specified torque.

5   Install the chain guides labeled A, B and C (photo) and tighten the mounting bolts for chain guides A and C securely (leave the mounting bolts for chain guide B finger tight). Note the difference between the upper and lower chain guide B mounting bolts. Make sure they are installed in the proper location.

6   Adjust the chain slack as follows: rotate the right Silent Shaft clockwise and the left Silent Shaft counterclockwise so the chain slack is collected at point P (refer to Fig. 2.19). Pull the chain with your

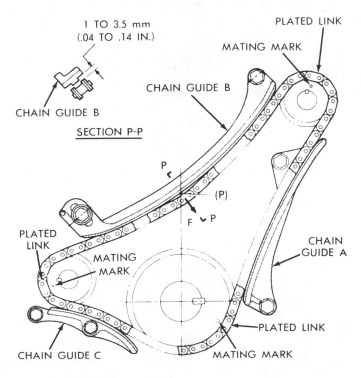

Fig. 2.19 Silent shafts and chain installation and adjustment details (Sec 28)

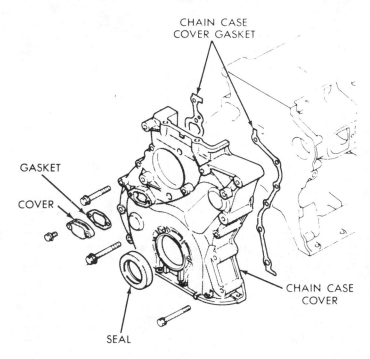

Fig. 2.20 Timing chain cover components — exploded view (Sec 28)

28.5 Installing the Silent Shaft chain guides

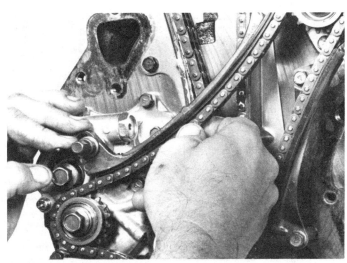

28.6 Adjusting the Silent Shaft chain slack

28.8 Driving the old oil seal out of the timing chain case

28.11 Applying grease to the seal contact surface of the crankshaft pulley

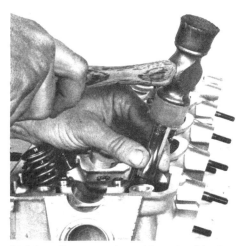

29.3 Installing new valve guide seals with a hammer and deep socket

finger tips in the direction of arrow F, then move the lower end of the chain guide B up or down, as required, until the clearance between the chain and the guide (chain slack) is as specified (photo). Tighten the chain guide B mounting bolts securely, then recheck the slack to make sure it has not changed. If the chain is not tensioned properly, engine noise will result.

7   Apply a coat of clean multi-purpose grease to the chain and chain guides.

8   Using a hammer and punch, drive the oil seal out of the timing chain case (photo).

9   Lay a new seal in place (with the lip facing in) and tap around its entire circumference, with a block of wood and a hammer, until it is properly seated.

10   Using a new gasket and RTV-type gasket sealer, fit the timing chain case onto the front of the engine. Install the bolts and tighten them securely, using a criss-cross pattern. If the gasket protrudes beyond the top or bottom of the case and engine block, trim off the excess with a razor blade.

11   Apply a thin layer of clean multi-purpose grease to the seal contact surface of the crankshaft pulley (photo), then slide it onto the crankshaft. Install the bolt and tighten it finger-tight only. The bolt should be tightened to the specified torque only after the cylinder head and camshaft have been installed.

29 Cylinder head – reassembly

1   Regardless of whether or not the head was sent to an automotive machine shop for valve servicing, make sure it is clean before beginning reassembly.

2   If the head was sent out for valve servicing, the valves and related components will already be in place. Begin the reassembly procedure with step 6.

3   Lay all the spring seats in position, then install new seals on each of the valve guides. Using a hammer and an appropriate size deep socket, gently tap each seal into place until it is properly seated on its guide (photo). Do not twist or cock the seals during installation, as they will not seal properly on the valve stems.

4   Next, install the valves (taking care not to damage the new seals), the springs, the retainers and the keepers. Coat the valve stems with clean multi-purpose grease (or engine assembly lube) before slipping them into the guides and install the springs with the painted side next to the retainer. When compressing the spring with the valve spring compressor, do not let the retainers contact the valve guide seals. Make certain that the keepers are securely locked in their retaining grooves.

5   Double check the installed valve spring height. If it was correct before disassembly, it should still be within the specified limits.

6   Install new seals on each of the Jet valve bodies. Gently tap them

into place with a hammer and the appropriate size deep socket. Lubricate and install the valves and make sure the stems slide smoothly in the valve bodies. Install the springs, the retainers and the keepers. When compressing the springs, be careful not to damage the valve stems or the new seals.

7   Install a new O-ring on each Jet valve body and apply a thin coat of clean engine oil or multi-purpose grease to each O-ring, the Jet valve threads and the Jet valve seating surfaces.

8   Carefully thread the Jet valve assemblies into the cylinder head and tighten them to the specified torque. Be careful not to tilt the socket, as the valve stems can be bent very easily.

30 Cylinder head – installation

2A

1   Before installing the cylinder head, the timing chain and sprockets, the Silent Shaft chain and sprockets and the timing chain case must be in place on the engine.

2   Make sure the gasket sealing surfaces of the engine block and cylinder head are clean and oil-free, then lay the new head gasket in place on the block (do not use any sealant) with the manufacturer's stamped mark facing up (photo). Use the dowel pins in the top of the block to properly locate the gasket.

3   Carefully set the cylinder head in place on the block. Use the dowel pins to properly align it.

4   Install the ten head bolts and tighten them, in the sequence shown, to 1/3 of the specified torque. Repeat the procedure, using the same sequence, tightening them to 2/3 of the specified torque. Repeat the procedure one last time, tightening them to the final specified torque.

5   Install the two small head bolts (with washers) in the very front of the head and tighten them to the specified torque.

6   Wipe the camshaft bearing surfaces in the cylinder head clean and apply a coat of clean multi-purpose grease (or engine assembly lube) to each of them.

7   Make sure the bearing journals on the camshaft are clean, then carefully lay it in place in the head. Do not lubricate the camshaft lobes at this time. Rotate the camshaft until the dowel pin on the front is positioned at the top.

8   Loosen the jam nuts on the valve clearance adjusting bolts and back the adjusting bolts out a minimum of two full turns.

9   Wipe the camshaft bearing cap bearing surfaces clean and apply a coat of clean multi-purpose grease (or engine assembly lube) to each of them. Also, apply a very small amount of grease to the end of each valve stem. Lay the rocker arm shaft assembly in place with the number one bearing cap at the front of the engine. Install the camshaft bearing cap bolts and tighten them to 7.5 ft-lb in the following order; center, number two, number four, front, rear. Repeat the procedure, tightening them to the final specified torque.

10 Next, lift up on the camshaft sprocket (with the chain attached) and slip it into place on the end of the camshaft. The dowel pin on the cam should slip into the hole in the sprocket.

11 Install the distributor drive gear (again, line up the dowel pin and hole) the oil shield and the bolt. Tighten the bolt to the specified torque (photo). To keep the camshaft and crankshaft from turning, install two of the flywheel mounting bolts in the rear flange of the crankshaft (180° apart), then wedge a large screwdriver between the bolts. Also, tighten the large bolt on the front of the crankshaft to the specified torque at this time.

12 The camshaft end play can be checked with a dial indicator set or a feeler gauge.

13 If a feeler gauge is used, gently pry the camshaft all the way toward the front of the engine. Slip a feeler gauge between the flange at the front of the camshaft and the number one (front) cam bearing cap. Compare the measured end play to the Specifications.

14 If a dial indicator is used, mount it at the front of the engine with the indicator stem touching the head of the bolt that attaches the sprocket to the camshaft. Carefully pry the camshaft all the way toward the front of the engine, then zero the dial indicator. Gently pry the camshaft as far as possible in the opposite direction and observe the needle movement on the dial indicator, which will indicate the amount of end play. Compare it to the Specifications.

15 Adjust the valve clearances as described in Chapter 1.

16 Temporarily install the valve cover to keep dirt and other foreign objects out of the valve gear.

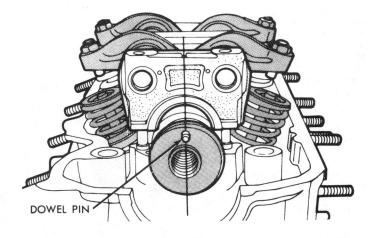

Fig. 2.23 Position the camshaft with the dowel pin at the top (Sec 30)

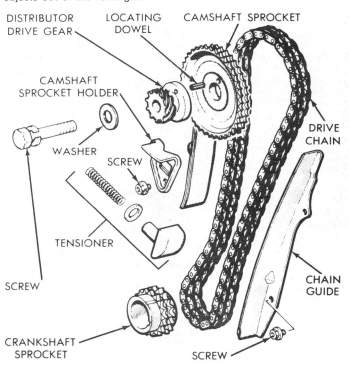

Fig. 2.21 Camshaft drive chain components — exploded view (Sec 30)

30.2 Installing the new head gasket

30.11 Tightening the camshaft sprocket mounting bolt

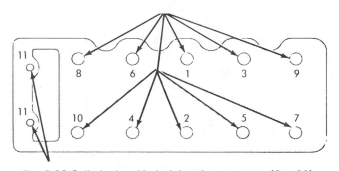

Fig. 2.22 Cylinder head bolt tightening sequence (Sec 30)

31 External engine components – installation

1 Once the engine has been assembled to the point where all internal parts, the timing chain cover, the oil pan and the cylinder head are in place, the exterior components can be installed. At this point, if the engine is mounted on a stand, it should be removed from the stand so the rear oil seal housing can be installed.

2 Lubricate the seal contact surface of the flange at the rear of the crankshaft with multi-purpose grease.

3 After noting which side is facing out, use a hammer and punch to drive the oil seal out of the housing. Lay a new seal in place (with correct side out) and seat it in the housing with a hammer and a block of wood. Tap the seal around its entire circumference to seat it squarely in the housing.

4 Place the oil separator into the housing with the oil hole facing down (toward the bottom of the case) and the tabs pointing out. One or two strategically placed dabs of heavy grease will help keep the separator positioned properly.

5 Apply a thin, even coat of RTV-type gasket sealer to both sides of the new gasket and to the exposed portion of the oil pan gasket, then install the oil seal housing. Make sure the oil separator does not fall out of place. Tap the seal housing very gently with a soft-faced hammer (photo) to seat it properly. Install and tighten the attaching bolts.

6 Install the flywheel by referring to Section 5 and slip the oil dipstick into its tube.

7 After coating its threads with a thread sealant, or sealing tape, screw the oil pressure sending unit into the block and tighten it securely (photo).

8 Lubricate the rubber gasket on the new oil filter and install it on the engine.

9 Install the motor mount brackets. Tighten the bolts/nuts to the specified torque.

10 Attach the air conditioner compressor brackets to the block and tighten the bolts securely (if so equipped).

11 Install the water pump and tighten the mounting bolts securely. Be sure to coat both sides of the gasket with RTV-type gasket sealer. Install the rubber hose and the coolant transfer tube.

12 Install the hose clamps and tighten the transfer tube mounting bolts.

13 Install the air conditioner idler pulley and the power steering pump bracket (if so equipped).

31.5 Tapping the rear oil seal housing with a soft-faced hammer to seat it on the engine block and oil pan

31.7 Installing the oil pressure sending unit

2A

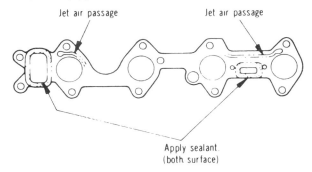

Fig. 2.24 Before installing the intake manifold, coat the areas around the gasket coolant passages with RTV-type sealer (Sec 31)

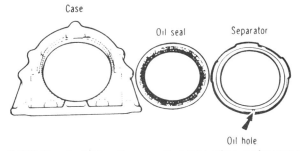

Fig. 2.25 When installing the rear oil seal housing, make sure the separator oil hole is at the bottom (Sec 31)

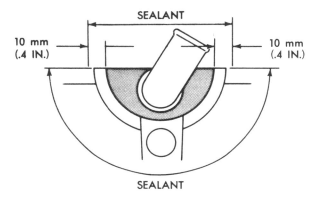

Fig. 2.26 To guard against oil leakage, apply a thin coat of RTV-type gasket sealer to the semi-circular seal and the breather before installation (Sec 31)

14 Next, install the fuel pump. Use a new gasket and coat both sides with RTV-type gasket sealer. Tighten the mounting nuts securely.

15 Coat both sides of the areas immediately around the coolant passages in the intake manifold gasket with RTV-type gasket sealer, then install the intake manifold/carburetor assembly in place on the engine. Do not allow any gasket sealer to get in the jet air passages in the manifold and head.

16 Slip the engine hoisting bracket into place on the rear studs then install the nuts (and the one bolt) and tighten them to the specified torque. When tightening, start at the center of the manifold and work out toward the ends. Tighten each fastener in sequence, a little at a time, until they are all at the specified torque.

17 Slip the rubber coolant hose onto the intake manifold spigot and tighten the hose clamps securely.

18 Using a new gasket, install the exhaust manifold and tighten the nuts to the specified torque. Be sure to install the engine hoist bracket at the front. When tightening, start at the center of the manifold and work out toward the ends. Tighten each nut in sequence, a little at a time, until they are all at the specified torque.

19 Attach the heat cowl to the exhaust manifold.

20 Install the Pulse Air Feeder (PAF) system (Chapter 6).

21 Make sure the number one piston is at top dead center on the compression stroke, then install the distributor. Line up the mating marks on the distributor housing (a line) and the driven gear (a punch mark). Slide the distributor into place in the cylinder head while lining up the mark on the distributor hold-down flange with the center of the stud. Make sure the distributor is completely seated, then install the mounting nut and tighten it securely.

22 Remove the valve cover. Coat the sealing surfaces of the cylinder head with RTV-type gasket sealer, then install the breather at the front and the semi-circular seal at the rear of the head.

23 Add the specified amount of the recommended type of oil to the engine. Pour it directly over the camshaft so the lobes are thoroughly lubricated.

24 Coat the valve cover gasket sealing surface of the breather at the front of the head with RTV-type gasket sealer. Lay a new rubber seal in place in the valve cover and install the cover in place on the engine. Install the attaching bolts, using new rubber seals and tighten them securely.

25 Install the starter.

26 Install the carburetor air heater and tubes.

32 Engine – installation

1 Attach the lifting hook to the chain and raise the engine until it clears the front of the vehicle. *Do not let the engine swing freely.*

2 Lower the engine carefully into place. Work slowly and direct the engine into place in its proper location on the motor mounts.

3 If the engine mounts have been removed, make sure they are installed in their original positions exactly, otherwise the drive axle alignment could be affected.

4 Install all of the engine mount through-bolts and nuts and then tighten them to the specified torque.

5 Install the transaxle-to-engine bolts and tighten them to the specified torque.

6 Remove the lifting chain.

7 Connect the ground strap and install the right engine splash shield.

8 Connect the starter cable.

9 Connect the exhaust system and tighten the nuts.

10 Remove the C-clamp retaining the torque converter, align the driveplate with the marks made during removal, install the bolts and tighten them to the specified torque.

11 Install the alternator.

12 Connect the fuel and heater hoses.

13 Connect the throttle cable to the carburetor.

14 Connect all of the electrical connectors to the engine and components.

15 Install the power steering pump (if equipped) and fill it with the specified fluid.

16 Install the air conditioning compressor (if equipped).

17 Install the air cleaner assembly.

18 Install the radiator and shroud, connect the hoses and fill the cooling system with the specified coolant.

19 Install the hood and connect the negative battery cable.

20 Double-check all nuts and bolts for tightness and make sure all hoses, electrical wiring and other connections are properly installed.

33 Initial start-up and break-in after overhaul

1 Once the engine has been properly installed in the vehicle, double-check the engine oil and coolant levels.

2 With the spark plugs out of the engine and the coil high-tension lead grounded to the engine block, crank the engine over until oil pressure registers on the gauge (if equipped).

3 Install the spark plugs, hook up the plug wires and the coil high-tension lead.

4 Make sure the carburetor choke plate is closed, then start the engine. It may take a few moments for gasoline to reach the carburetor, but the engine should start without a great deal of effort.

5 As soon as the engine starts, it should be set at a fast idle (to ensure proper oil circulation) and allowed to warm up to normal operating temperature. While the engine is warming up, make a thorough check for oil and coolant leaks.

6 After the engine reaches normal operating temperature, shut it off, remove the valve cover, retorque the head bolts and recheck the valve clearances (using the hot engine specifications).

7 Install the valve cover and recheck the engine oil and coolant levels. Also, check the ignition timing and the engine idle speed (refer to Chapter 1) and make any necessary adjustment.

8 Drive the vehicle to an area with minimum traffic, accelerate at full throttle from 30 to 50 mph, then allow the vehicle to slow to 30 mph with the throttle closed. Repeat the procedure 10 or 12 times. This will load the piston rings and cause them to seal properly against the cylinder walls. Check again for oil and coolant leaks.

9 Drive the vehicle gently for the first 500 miles (no sustained high speeds) and keep a constant check on the oil level. It is not unusual for an engine to use oil during the break-in period.

10 At approximately 500 to 600 miles, change the oil and filter, retorque the cylinder head bolts and recheck the valve clearances.

11 For the next few hundred miles, drive the vehicle normally. Do not pamper it or abuse it.

12 After 2000 miles, change the oil and filter again and consider the engine fully broken in.

Chapter 2 Part B 2.2L engine

Refer to Chapter 13 for specifications and information applicable to later models and the 2.5L engine

Contents

Specifications

General

Displacement	135 cu in (2.2 liters)
Bore and stroke	3.44 x 3.62 in (87.5 x 92.00 mm)
Firing order	1-3-4-2
Compression ratio	8.5:1
Compression pressure	130 to 150 psi
Max. variation between cylinders	20 psi

Valve timing
  Intake valve

Opens	12° BTDC
Closes	52° ABDC

  Exhaust valve

Opens	48° BBDC
Closes	16° ATDC

Engine block

Cylinder bore diameter	3.44 in (87.5 mm)
Taper limit	0.010 in (0.25 mm)
Out-of-round limit	0.005 in (0.12 mm)

Pistons and rings

Piston diameter	3.443 to 3.445 in (87.442 to 87.507 mm)

Piston ring-to-groove clearance
  Standard

Top ring	0.0015 to 0.0031 in (0.038 to 0.078 mm)
2nd ring	0.0015 to 0.0031 in (0.038 to 0.078 mm)
Oil ring	0.008 in (0.2 mm)

  Service limit

Top ring	0.004 in (0.10 mm)
2nd ring	0.004 in (0.10 mm)

Piston ring end gap
  Standard

Top ring	0.011 to 0.021 in (0.28 to 0.53 mm)
2nd ring	0.011 to 0.021 in (0.28 to 0.53 mm)
Oil ring	0.015 to 0.055 in (0.38 to 1.40 mm)

  Service limit

Top ring	0.039 in (1.0 mm)
2nd ring	0.039 in (1.0 mm)
Oil ring	0.074 in (1.88 mm)

Crankshaft and flywheel

Main journal	
Diameter	2.362 to 2.363 in (59.987 to 60.013 mm)
Taper	0.0003 in (0.008 mm)
Service limit	0.0004 in (0.01 mm)
Out-of-round	0.0005 in (0.013 mm)
Service limit	0.012 in (0.03 mm)
Main bearing oil clearance	
Standard	0.0003 to 0.0031 in (0.007 to 0.080 mm)
Service limit	0.004 in (0.10 mm)
Connecting rod journal diameter	1.968 to 1.969 in (49.979 to 50.005 mm)
Connecting rod bearing oil clearance	
Standard	0.0004 to 0.0025 in (0.010 to 0.064 mm)
Service limit	0.0047 in (0.12 mm)
Connecting rod side clearance	0.015 in (0.37 mm)
Crankshaft endplay	0.002 to 0.007 in (0.05 to 0.18 mm)
Endplay service limit	0.014 in (0.35 mm)

Camshaft

Endplay	0.005 to 0.013 in (0.13 to 0.33 mm)

Cylinder head and valve train

Head warpage limit	0.004 in (0.1 mm)
Valve seat angle	45°
Valve seat width	
Intake	0.069 to 0.088 in (1.75 to 2.25 mm)
Exhaust	0.059 to 0.078 in (1.50 to 2.00 mm)
Valve face angle	45°
Valve face runout limit	
Intake	0.020 in (0.5 mm)
Exhaust	0.027 in (0.7 mm)
Valve margin width	0.06 in (1.5 mm)
Valve stem diameter	
Intake	0.3124 in (7.935 mm)
Exhaust	0.3103 in (7.881 mm)
Valve head diameter	
Intake	1.60 in (40.6 mm)
Exhaust	1.39 in (35.4 mm)
Valve stem-to-guide clearance	
Intake	
Standard	0.0009 to 0.0026 in (0.022 to 0.065 mm)
Service limit	0.03 in (.793 mm)
Exhaust	
1981 and 1982	0.0028 to 0.0044 in (0.070 to 0.113 mm)
1983	0.0030 to 0.0047 (0.76 to 0.119 mm)
Valve spring free length	
Intake	2.28 in (57.9 mm)
Exhaust	2.28 in (57.9 mm)
Valve spring installed height	
Intake	1.62 to 1.68 in (41.2 to 42.7 mm)
Exhaust	1.62 to 1.68 in (41.2 to 42.7 mm)
Valve lash adjustment	Hydraulic
Collapsed tappet gap	0.024 to 0.060 in (0.62 to 1.52 mm)

Oil pump

Relief valve opening pressure	80 psi (550 kPa)
Outer rotor outside diameter-to-bore clearance	
Standard	0.010 in (0.25 mm)
Service limit	0.014 in (0.35 mm)
Outer rotor thickness	
Standard	0.826 to 0.827 in (20.98 to 21.00 mm)
Service limit	0.825 in (20.96 mm)
Inner rotor-to-outer rotor tip clearance	
Standard	0.010 in (0.25 mm)
Service limit	0.010 in (0.25 mm)
Inner and outer rotor-to-housing clearance	
Standard	0.001 to 0.003 in (0.03 to 0.08 mm)
Service limit	0.004 in (0.10 mm)
Pump cover flatness	
Standard	0.010 in (0.025 mm)
Service limit	0.015 in (0.038 mm)
Relief spring free length	
Standard	1.95 in (49.5 mm)
Service limit	1.95 in (49.5 mm)
Relief spring load	15 to 25 lbs @ 1.34 in (67 to 89 Nm @ 34 mm)
Oil pressure switch minimum actuating pressure	2 psi (14 Kpa)

Torque specifications

	Ft-lb	Nm
Cylinder head bolts		
1981 through 1985		
Step 1	30	
Step 2	45	
Step 3	45	
Step 4	Tighten an additional 1/4-turn	
1986 on		
Step 1	45	
Step 2	65	
Step 3	65	
Step 4	Tighten an additional 1/4-turn	
Camshaft sprocket bolt	65	88
Camshaft bearing cap nut	14	19
Air pump pulley bolt	20	28
Crankshaft sprocket bolt	50	68
Main bearing cap bolt	30	41
Connecting rod bearing cap nut	40	54
Front crankshaft oil seal housing bolt	9	12
Rear crankshaft oil seal housing bolt	9	12
Intermediate shaft oil seal retainer bolt	9	12
Intermediate shaft sprocket bolt	65	88
Upper timing belt cover screw	9	12
Lower timing belt cover screw	3	4
Water crossover mounting bolt	9	12
Exhaust manifold nut	17	23
Intake manifold bolt	17	23
Thermostat housing bolt	21	28
Water pump housing bolt		
Upper	21	28
Lower	40	54
Oil pan bolt	17	23
Oil pump mounting bolt	17	23
Oil pump cover bolt	9	12
Oil pump brace mounting bolt	9	12
Oil pan drain plug	20	27
Spark plug	26	35
Engine mount insulator through-bolt	40	54
Front engine mount-to-engine bolt	70	95
Front engine mount-to-chassis nut	40	54
Right engine mount-to-engine nut		
Upper	21	28
Lower	70	95
Right engine mount insulator-to-chassis bolt	21	28
Right engine mount stud	11	15
Left engine mount-to-transaxle bolt	40	54
Main bearing cap bolt	30 plus 1/4 turn	41 plus 1/4 turn
Connecting rod bolt	40 plus 1/4 turn	54 plus 1/4 turn
Engine-to-transaxle bolts	40	54
Valve cover bolt	9	12
Flywheel-to-crankshaft bolts	60	81
Torque converter-to-flywheel	40	54

2B

34 General information

The engine is an inline vertical four, with a belt-driven overhead camshaft. The drivebelt turns an intermediate shaft, mounted low in the block, which drives the fuel pump, oil pump and distributor.

The crankshaft rides in five replaceable insert-type bearings. No vibration damper is used and a sintered iron timing belt sprocket is mounted on the front of the crankshaft.

The pistons have two compression rings and one oil control ring. The piston pins are semi-floating and press fit into the small end of the connecting rod. The big ends of the connecting rods also are equipped with insert-type bearings.

The engine is liquid-cooled and coolant is circulated around the cylinders and combustion chambers and through the intake manifold by a centrifugal impeller-type pump which is driven by a belt from the crankshaft.

Lubrication is handled by a gear-type oil pump mounted in the oil pan and driven by the intermediate shaft. The oil is filtered continuously by a spin-on type filter mounted on the front side of the engine.

35 Repair operations possible with the engine in the vehicle

Refer to Section 2, Part A.

36 Engine overhaul – general note

Refer to Section 3, Part A.

37 Engine – removal

1   Remove the hood.
2   Drain the cooling system.
3   Disconnect the battery and remove the air cleaner assembly.
4   Remove the radiator hoses, disconnect the automatic transaxle cooler lines and remove the radiator.
5   On air conditioned models, have the air conditioning system discharged by a suitably equipped shop. **Caution:** *Do not attempt to do this job yourself as it is dangerous.* Remove the air conditioner compressor and set it out of the way.

37.8 Use tape to plug the fuel lines

37.18 Retain the clamps on the heater hoses so they won't be lost during removal

37.26 The diverter valve and hoses are removed as an assembly

6   Remove the alternator and bracket.
7   Disconnect the coil wire and ground strap at the right side of the engine.
8   Disconnect and plug the fuel supply and return lines at the right rear corner of the engine compartment (photo).
9   Disconnect the ground strap from the chassis at the right rear corner of the engine compartment.
10   Unplug the electrical connector from the carburetor and disconnect the throttle linkage.
11   Disconnect the carburetor vent hose.
12   Disconnect the PCV valve hose.
13   Remove the brake booster vacuum hose from the carburetor.
14   Disconnect the charcoal canister hoses from the carburetor.
15   Disconnect the heater hose from the engine.
16   Disconnect the vacuum lines from the brake booster.
17   Remove the water hose fitting from the intake manifold.
18   Disconnect the heater hoses at the firewall (photo).
19   Remove the black plastic panel cover on the left shock tower and unplug and mark any connectors which are attached to the engine.
20   Disconnect the air pump check valve hose.
21   Disconnect the check valve and diverter hoses.
22   Disconnect the ground lead.
23   Disconnect the transaxle shift linkage.
24   Disconnect the exhaust pipe at the manifold.
25   Remove the battery and tray.
26   Remove the diverter valve and bracket (photo).
27   Loosen the pivot bolt and the power steering pump and remove the drivebelt.
28   Attach a suitable chain and lifting apparatus and support the engine.
29   Remove the power steering pump and use a piece of wire to hold it out of the way.
30   Unbolt and remove the front engine mount.
31   Remove the bolts from the right side engine mount and raise the engine.
32   Unbolt and remove the left side engine and transaxle mount.
33   Lift the engine and transaxle assembly slowly and carefully straight up from the engine compartment. Guide the transaxle carefully past the left engine support mount which projects from the chassis and then remove the assembly from the vehicle.

38   Separating the engine and transaxle

1   On automatic transaxle models, remove the dust cover and mark the relationship of the driveplate and torque converter so they can be reinstalled in the same position.
2   Remove the retaining bolts and carefully separate the engine and transaxle. On automatic transaxles, make sure the torque converter remains on the input shaft.
3   With the help of an assistant, move the transaxle out of the way and cover it with a plastic bag or clean, dry tarpaulin.

39   Automatic transaxle driveplate – removal and installation

Refer to Section 5, Part A.

40   Clutch and flywheel – removal and installation

1   Remove the clutch disc and clutch cover assembly by referring to Chapter 8.
2   Remove the retaining bolts and separate the flywheel from the crankshaft.
3   Hold the flywheel in position and install the retaining bolts into the end of the crankshaft.
4   While holding the flywheel so that it doesn't turn, tighten the bolts (using a criss-cross pattern) to the specified torque.
5   Install the clutch disc and clutch cover assembly as described in Chapter 8.

41   Engine – disassembly and reassembly

1   To completely disassemble the engine, remove the following items in the order given:
   Engine external components   *(Section 42)*

2 Engine reassembly is basically the reverse of disassembly. Install the following components in the order given:

42 External engine components – removal

Note: *When removing the external components from the engine, pay close attention to details that may be helpful or important during installation. Look for the correct positioning of gaskets, seals, spacers, pins, washers, bolts and other small parts.*

1 It is much easier to dismantle and repair the engine if it is mounted on a portable-type engine stand. These stands can often be rented, for a reasonable fee, from an equipment rental yard.
2 If a stand is not available, it is possible to dismantle the engine with it blocked up on a sturdy workbench or on the floor. *Be extra careful not to tip or drop the engine when working without a stand.*
3 Remove the oxygen sensor from the exhaust manifold.
4 Disconnect the choke electrical connector.
5 Disconnect the electrical connector from the oil pressure sender located by the dipstick.
6 Disconnect the electrical connector from the distributor.
7 Unplug the TVS connectors on the thermostat housing.
8 Remove the oil pressure sender, followed by the dipstick and tube.
9 Disconnect the water hose from the thermostat housing and unscrew the adapter and coolant switch.
10 Remove the thermostat and water inlet.
11 Remove the two temperature vacuum switches (TVS) from the thermostat housing, marking them for installation in the same locations.
12 Remove the distributor cap shield.
13 Disconnect the spark plug leads and coil wire from the retainer on the valve cover.
14 Remove the distributor cap and distributor.
15 Remove the coolant temperature sender from the cylinder head.
16 Disconnect the fuel supply hoses from the carburetor.
17 Disconnect the fuel pipes from the fuel pump and remove them.
18 Remove the fuel pump.
19 Remove the spark plugs.
20 Remove the water pump.
21 Remove the crankshaft pulley (photo).
22 Remove the upper and lower timing belt covers.
23 Remove the right side engine mount.
24 Remove the ground strap from the intake manifold.
25 Disconnect the throttle cable linkage and spring from the carburetor. On automatic transaxle models it will also be necessary to remove the shift cable.
26 Remove the PCV valve, vent module and hose from the valve cover.
27 Remove the carburetor and wiring harness.
28 Remove the carburetor and water hose from the intake manifold.
29 Remove the air cleaner heat tube from the exhaust manifold.
30 Disconnect the EGR tube from the intake manifold.
31 Unbolt and remove the EGR valve and tube assembly.
32 Remove the exhaust manifold heat collector.
33 Loosen the exhaust manifold bolts, working from the middle and loosening them a little at a time.

42.21 A special Torx-type socket is required to remove the crankshaft pulley bolts

34 Remove the exhaust manifold.
35 Remove the intake manifold, loosening the bolts in the same manner as for the exhaust manifold.
36 Remove the two engine mount brackets (if equipped) at the bottom edge of the block.
37 Remove the air injection pump.

43 Oil pan – removal and installation

1 Remove the bolts securing the oil pan to the engine block.
2 Tap on the pan with a soft-faced hammer, to break the gasket seal, and lift the oil pan off the engine (photo).
3 Using a gasket scraper, scrape off all traces of the old gasket from the engine block and oil pan. Remove the end seals from the oil seal retainers.
4 Clean the oil pan with solvent and dry it thoroughly. Check the gasket sealing surfaces for distortion.
5 Before installing the oil pan, install new end seals in the oil seal retainers. Apply a $\frac{3}{16}$ inch bead of RTV sealant completely around the oil pan gasket surface of the engine block, including the end seals.
6 Gently lay the oil pan in place (photo).
7 Install the bolts and tighten them to the specified torque, starting with the bolts closest to the center of the pan and working in a criss-cross pattern. Do not overtighten or leakage may occur.

2B

43.2 Removing the oil pan. Note the RTV gasket material (arrow) which must be completely removed before installation

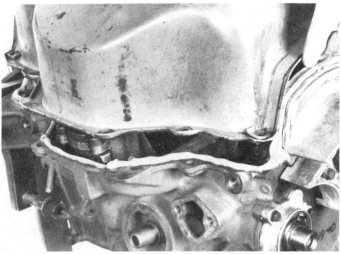

43.6 Lowering the oil pan into place over the continuous bead of RTV sealant

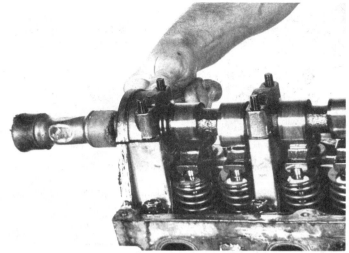

44.6 Tapping lightly on the camshaft bearing cap will dislodge it

44 Cylinder head – removal

1   Remove the timing belt (Section 46).
2   Lock the air pump pulley sprocket and remove the camshaft pulley bolt and pulley.
3   Remove the air pump bolt and pulley.
4   Remove the valve cover bolts and work carefully around the cover with a scraper or putty knife to release it from the sealant. Lift the cover off.
5   Loosen the camshaft tower nuts, working from the outside in, in $\frac{1}{4}$ turn increments until they can be removed with the fingers.
6   Lift off the cam bearing caps. It may be necessary to tap lightly with a soft-faced hammer to loosen the cap (photo).
7   Remove the camshaft (photo).
8   Reinstall the caps temporarily to protect the studs and bearing surfaces.
9   Lift off the rocker arms and either mark them or place them in a marked container so they will be reinstalled in the original locations (photo).
10   Starting from the outside, loosen the head retaining bolts, $\frac{1}{8}$ turn at a time in the sequence shown in the accompanying illustration. Remove the bolts and washers.

44.7 Lift the camshaft carefully from the cylinder head, making sure not to contact the lobes or bearings

44.9 Remove the rocker arms, noting their locations

44.11 Grasp the cylinder head securely and lift it straight up after rocking it from side-to-side to break the gasket seal

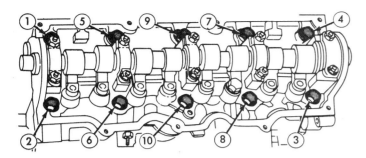

Fig. 2.27 Cylinder head bolt *loosening* **sequence (Sec 44)**

11 Use a soft-faced hammer, if necessary, to tap the cylinder head and break the gasket seal. Do not pry between the cylinder head and the engine block. Remove the cylinder head (photo).
12 Remove the gasket.

45 Cylinder head – disassembly

1 Cylinder head disassembly involves removal of the intake and exhaust valves and their related components.
2 Before the valves are removed, arrange to label and store them, along with their components, so they can be kept separate and reinstalled in the valve guides from which they were removed. Also, measure the installed height of the valve spring on each valve and compare this to the Specifications. If the measurement is greater than specified, the valve seats and valve faces need attention.
3 Compress the valve spring on the first valve with a spring compressor and then remove the keepers and the retainer from the valve assembly. Carefully release the valve spring compressor, then remove the spring, the spring seat and the valve from the head. If the valve binds in the guide (won't pull through), push it back into the head and deburr the area around the keeper groove with a fine file.
4 Repeat the procedure for the remaining valves. Remember to keep all the parts for each valve in order so they can be reinstalled in the same position.
5 Lift out the valve lash adjusters.
6 Gently pry the valve stem seals loose and remove them.

46 Timing belt and sprockets – removal, inspection and installation

1 Locate the number one piston at top dead center by removing the spark plug, placing your finger over the hole and turning the crankshaft until pressure is felt. The marks on the crankshaft and auxiliary pulley will be aligned and the arrows on the camshaft pulley will line up with the bearing cap as shown in the accompanying illustrations.
2 Use one wrench to hold the offset tensioner pulley bolt while using another wrench or socket to loosen the center bolt and release the tension from the timing belt. Remove the belt.
3 Remove the tensioner pulley assembly.
4 Remove the intermediate shaft sprocket (Section 47).
5 Remove the retaining bolt and use a suitable puller to remove the crankshaft sprocket (photo).
6 Inspect the timing belt for wear, signs of stretching or damaged teeth. Check for signs of contamination by oil, gasoline, coolant or other liquids which could cause the belt to break down and stretch.
Note: *Unless the vehicle has very low mileage, it is a good idea to change the timing belt any time it is removed.*
7 Inspect the tensioner pulley for damage, distortion and nicks or bends of the flanges. Replace the tensioner with a new one as necessary.
8 Inspect the camshaft, crankshaft and intermediate shaft sprockets for wear, damage, cracks, corrosion or rounding of the teeth. Replace with new ones as necessary as damaged or worn sprockets could cause the belt to slip and alter camshaft timing.
9 Inspect the crankshaft and intermediate shaft seals for signs of oil leakage and replace them with new ones as necessary (Sections 47 and 51).
10 When installing the sprockets, the keys on all shafts must be at the 12 o'clock position.

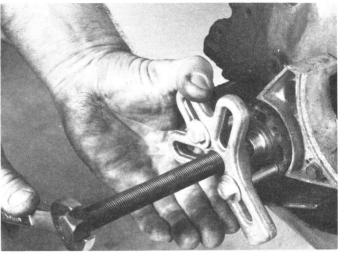

46.5 Removing the crankshaft sprocket with a puller

46.11 Use a straightedge to make sure the marks line up with the center of the sprocket bolt holes

2B

46.12 A long screwdriver inserted through the crankshaft bolts will keep it from turning while the sprocket bolt is tightened

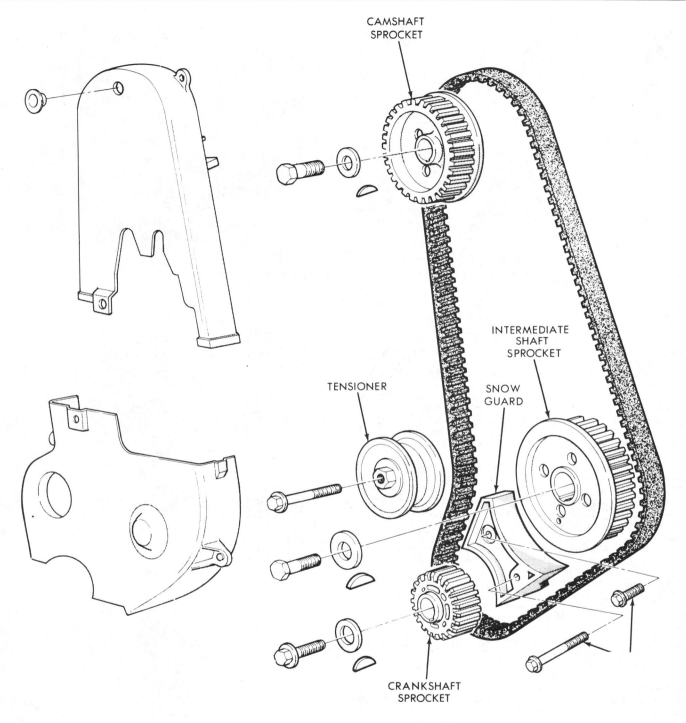

Fig. 2.28 Timing belt component layout (Sec 46)

11 Install the crankshaft and intermediate shaft sprockets with the marks aligned (photo).
12 Install the crankshaft sprocket bolt, lock the crankshaft to keep it from rotating and tighten the bolt to the specified torque (photo).
13 Install the intermediate shaft sprocket bolt and tighten it to the specified torque (Section 47).
14 Install the camshaft sprocket and bolt, tightening it to the specified torque. The arrows on the sprocket hub must align with the camshaft bearing cap surfaces as shown in Fig. 2.30 (page 86).

15 Install the timing belt.
16 Install the tensioner pulley with the bolt finger tight.
17 With the help of an assistant, apply tension to the timing belt and temporarily tighten the tensioner sprocket bolt. Measure the deflection of the belt between the camshaft and tensioner pulley. Adjust the tensioner until belt deflection is approximately $\frac{5}{16}$ inch (photo).
18 Rotate the crankshaft two complete revolutions. This will align the belt on the pulleys. Recheck the belt deflection and fully tighten the tensioner pulley.

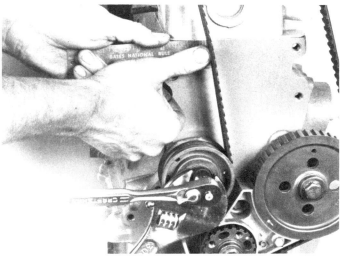

46.17 Using a straightedge to measure timing belt deflection

47.2 The intermediate shaft sprocket must be locked in place so that it doesn't rotate during bolt removal or installation

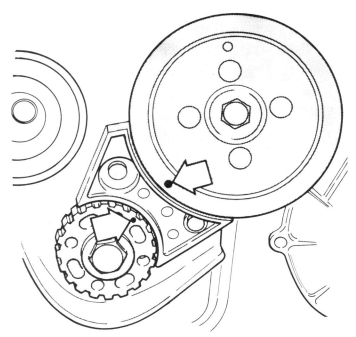

Fig. 2.29 The crankshaft and intermediate shaft sprocket marks (arrows) properly aligned (Secs 46 and 47)

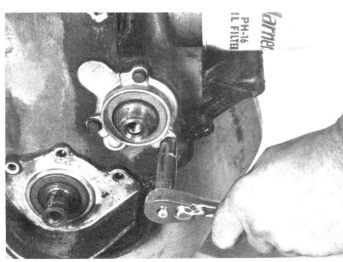

47.4 Removing the intermediate shaft retainer

47.5 Be careful not to contact the intermediate shaft bearing bores during removal of the shaft

2B

47 Intermediate shaft, sprocket and seal — removal, inspection and installation

1 Remove the timing belt (Section 46).
2 Remove the sprocket and bolt (photo).
3 Inspect the sprocket as described in Section 46.
4 Unbolt and remove the shaft retainer (photo).
5 Grasp the intermediate shaft securely and carefully withdraw it from the engine (photo).
6 Clean the shaft thoroughly with a suitable solvent and inspect the gear, bearing surfaces and lobes for wear or damage.
7 Use a suitable punch to drive the old oil seal out of the retainer. Apply a thin coat of RTV sealant to the inner surface of the retainer and tap the new seal into place (photo).
8 Lightly lubricate the gear, lobes and bearing surfaces with engine assembly lubricant and carefully insert the shaft into place. After insertion, make sure the shaft is securely in place in the oil pump. The

oil pump slot must be parallel to the crankshaft centerline and the intermediate shaft keyway must be at the 12 o'clock position.

9 Apply a thin coat of RTV sealant to the contact surface of the retainer and place it in position over the end of the shaft. Install the retaining bolts and tighten them to the specified torque.

10 Install the sprocket, making sure the mark aligns with the crankshaft sprocket mark as described in Section 46. Install the retaining bolt and tighten it to the specified torque.

11 Install the timing belt (Section 46).

48.2 Grasp the oil pump securely and lift it from the engine

47.7 With the retainer on a flat surface, carefully tap the seal securely into place with a soft-faced hammer

9 Measure the oil pressure relief spring to ensure that it is the specified length.

10 If any components are worn beyond the Specifications, the oil pump will have to be replaced with a new one.

48 Oil pump – removal, disassembly and inspection

1 Unbolt and remove the oil pickup (photo).
2 Unbolt and remove the oil pump (photo).
3 Remove the retaining bolts and lift off the oil pump cover.
4 Check the endplay of the rotors, using a feeler gauge and a straightedge, and compare the measurement to the Specifications.
5 Remove the outer rotor and measure its thickness. *Be sure to install the rotor with the large chamfered edge facing the pump body.*
6 Check the clearance between the rotors with a feeler gauge and compare the results to the Specifications.
7 Measure the outer rotor-to-body clearance and compare it to the Specifications.
8 Check the oil pump cover flatness with a feeler gauge and a straightedge to make sure it is within specification.

49 Piston/connecting rod assembly – removal

1 Prior to removing the piston/connecting rod assemblies, remove the cylinder head, oil pan, timing belt cover, timing belt and sprockets by referring to the appropriate Sections.
2 Using a ridge reamer, completely remove the ridge at the top of each cylinder (follow the manufacturer's instructions provided with the ridge reaming tool). Failure to remove the ridge before attempting to remove the piston connecting rod assemblies will result in piston breakage.
3 With the engine in the upside-down position, remove the oil pickup tube assembly from the bottom of the engine block (Section 48).

48.1 Lift the oil pickup assembly from the pump

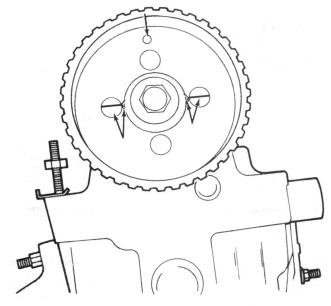

Fig. 2.30 The camshaft sprocket arrows properly aligned with the bearing cap parting line (Secs 46 and 65)

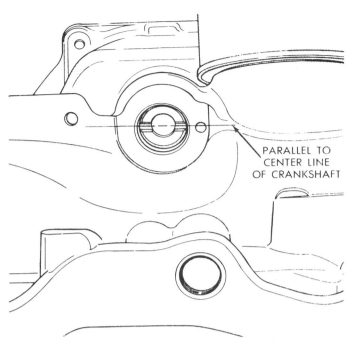

Fig. 2.31 When viewed through the distributor installation hole, the oil pump shaft slot must be parallel to the crankshaft centerline (Secs 46, 47, 63 and 66)

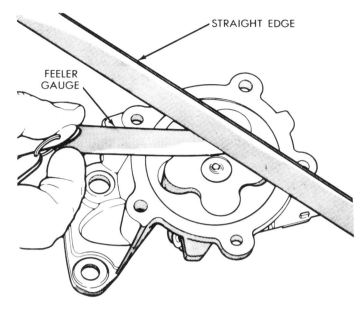

Fig. 2.32 Checking the oil pump end play (Sec 48)

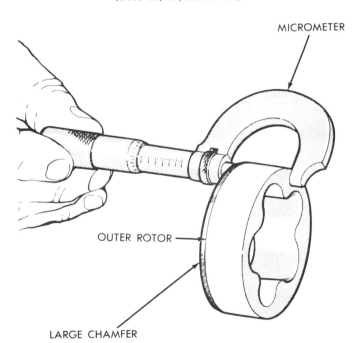

Fig. 2.33 Measuring the oil pump rotor thickness (Sec 48)

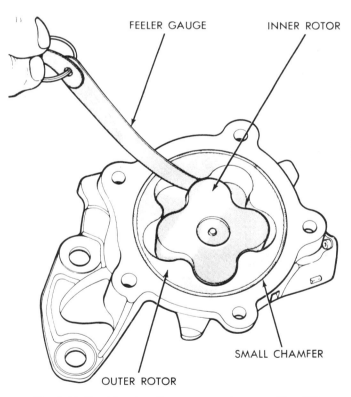

Fig. 2.34 Checking the oil pump rotor clearance (Sec 48)

2B

4   Mark each of the connecting rods and connecting rod bearing caps to ensure that they are properly mated during reassembly.

5   Loosen each of the connecting rod cap nuts approximately $\frac{1}{2}$ turn each. Remove the number one connecting rod cap and bearing insert. Do not drop the bearing insert out of the cap. Slip a short length of plastic or rubber hose over each connecting rod cap bolt (to protect the crankshaft journal when the piston is removed) and push the connecting rod/piston assembly out through the top of the engine. Use

a wooden tool to push on the upper bearing insert in the connecting rod. If resistance is felt, double-check to make sure that all of the ridge was removed from the cylinder.

6   Repeat the procedure for cylinders two, three and four. After removal, reassemble the connecting rods and install the cap nuts finger tight. Leaving the old bearing inserts in place until reassembly will help prevent the connecting rod bearing surfaces from being accidentally nicked or gouged.

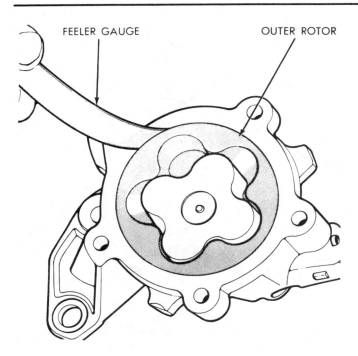

Fig. 2.35 Checking oil pump outer rotor clearance (Sec 48)

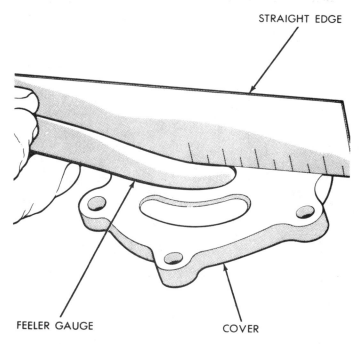

Fig. 2.36 Checking the flatness of the oil pump cover (Sec 48)

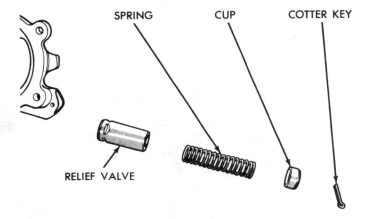

Fig. 2.37 Oil pressure relief valve components (Sec 48)

bearing inserts in place in the engine block and the main bearing caps, return the caps to their respective location on the engine block and tighten the bolts finger tight.

51 Front oil seal and housing – removal and installation

1   With the timing belt and sprockets, the oil pan and the intermediate shaft sprocket removed for access, unbolt and remove the oil seal housing (photo).
2   Use a punch and hammer to drive the old oil seal from the housing.
3   Apply a thin coat of RTV sealant to the inner surface of the housing, place the new seal in place and carefully tap it into position (photo).
4   Lubricate the inner circumference of the seal with white lithium base grease and place the housing in position. Install the retaining bolts and tighten them to the specified torque.

50 Crankshaft – removal

1   Before removing the crankshaft, you must remove the flywheel, the rear oil seal housing, the front oil seal housing, the cylinder head, the oil pan, the timing belt cover and the timing belt and sprockets by referring to the appropriate Sections.
2   With the engine inverted, remove the oil pump pickup assembly from the bottom of the engine block. It is held in place with three bolts.
3   Remove the piston assemblies from the engine block, as described in Section 49. Be sure to mark each connecting rod and bearing cap so they will be properly mated during reassembly.
4   Loosen each of the main bearing cap bolts $\frac{1}{4}$ of a turn at a time, in sequence, starting at the center of the engine, until they can be removed by hand.
5   Gently tap the main bearing caps with a soft-faced hammer, then remove them from the engine block. If necessary, use the main bearing cap bolts as levers to remove the caps. Try not to drop the bearing shell if it comes out with the cap. The main bearing caps are marked at the factory with a number (1 through 5, starting at the front of the engine).
6   Carefully lift the crankshaft out of the engine. It is a good idea to have an assistant available, as the crankshaft is quite heavy. With the

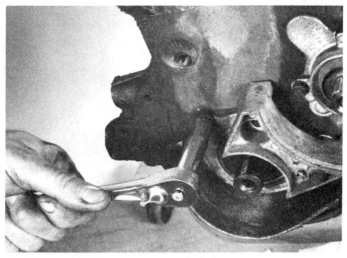

51.1 Removing the front oil seal housing bolts

51.3 Tap the new front seal securely into place with a soft-faced hammer

52.1 Pull the housing to the rear and lift it from the engine

52.4 Tap the new rear seal securely and evenly into place using a soft-faced hammer

52 Rear oil seal and housing – removal and installation

1   Remove the four retaining bolts and lift the housing and seal from the rear of the engine block (photo).
2   Drive the old seal from the housing.
3   Clean the seal surface thoroughly with a suitable solvent and inspect it for nicks or gouges.
4   Apply a thin coat of RTV sealant to the inner circumference of the housing, lay the new seal in place and tap it securely into position (photo).
5   Lubricate the seal inner surface with white lithium base grease.
6   Place the assembly into position, install the retaining bolts and tighten them to the specified torque.

53 Engine block – cleaning

Refer to Section 17, Part A.

54 Engine block – inspection

Refer to Section 18, Part A.

55 Crankshaft – inspection

Refer to Section 19, Part A.

56 Piston/connecting rod assembly – inspection

Refer to Section 20, Part A.

57 Main and connecting rod bearings – inspection

Refer to Section 21, Part A.

58 Cylinder head – cleaning and inspection

2B

1   Refer to Section 22, Part A, Steps 1 through 17 and 22 through 28.
2   The rocker arms on the 2.2L engine ride below the camshaft and contact the valve stem at one end and the hydraulic lash adjusters at the other.
3   Inspect the rocker arm for wear, galling or pitting of the contact surfaces, replacing them with new parts as necessary.
4   Inspect the contact surface of the lash adjuster for pitting or wear and replace them as necessary.
5   If the inspection process turns up no excessively worn parts, and if the valve faces and seats are in good condition, the valve train components can be reinstalled in the cylinder head without major servicing.

59 Valves – servicing

Refer to Section 23, Part A.

60 Crankshaft – installation

Refer to Section 24, Part A.

61 Piston rings – installation

Refer to Section 25, Part A.

62 Piston/connecting rod assembly – installation

Refer to Section 26, Part A. On 2.2L engines, the indentation on

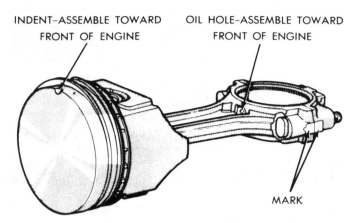

INDENT—ASSEMBLE TOWARD FRONT OF ENGINE

OIL HOLE—ASSEMBLE TOWARD FRONT OF ENGINE

MARK

Fig. 2.38 Piston/connecting rod assembly marks (Sec 62)

the piston and oil hole of the connecting rod big end must face the front (timing belt) end of the engine as shown in the accompanying illustration.

63 Oil pump – reassembly and installation

1   Install the rotor (large chamfered edge toward the pump body) and oil pressure relief valve and spring assembly.
2   Install the pump cover and tighten the bolts to the specified torque.
3   Apply a thin coat of RTV sealant to the contact surface of the pump and lower it into position. Coat the threads of the retaining bolts with sealant and install and tighten them to the specified torque. The slot in the oil pump shaft must be parallel to the crankshaft centerline when viewed through the distributor opening.
4   Install a new O-ring into the oil pump pickup opening (photo).
5   Carefully work the pickup into the pump, install the retaining bolts and tighten them to the specified torque.
6   Install the brace bolt and tighten it securely (photo).

63.4 Lightly lubricate the O-ring with engine oil and press it into place

64 Cylinder head – reassembly

1   Regardless of whether or not the head was sent to an automotive machine shop for valve servicing, make sure it is clean before beginning reassembly.

63.6 Installing the brace bolt

2   If the head was sent out for valve servicing, the valves and related components will already be in place.
3   Coat the valve stems with engine oil or assembly lube and insert them into the cylinder head.
4   Install the new valve stem seals, pushing them firmly and evenly over each valve guide so the center bead locks in the guide groove. After installation, the lower seal edge should rest on the valve guide boss.
5   Install the valve spring seats, springs and retainers. Compress the springs with the tool just enough to install the keepers. Make sure the keepers are securely locked in their grooves.
6   Double-check the installed valve spring height, measuring from the lower edge of the valve spring to its upper edge. If the height was correct before disassembly, it should still be within the specified limits.

65 Cylinder head – installation

1   Before installing the cylinder head, check to make sure the number one (front) piston is at top dead center, the timing belt sprockets are properly aligned (Section 46) and the oil pump shaft slot (viewed through the distributor installation hole) is parallel to the crankshaft centerline.
2   Place the head gasket in position on the cylinder block and press it into place over the alignment dowels.
3   Place the cylinder head in position.
4   Apply a thin coat of sealant to the threads of the head bolts and install the bolts finger tight (photo).
5   Tighten the head bolts to the specified torque, following the sequence shown in the accompanying illustration.
6   Lubricate the valve lash adjusters with engine oil and insert them into their respective bores.
7   Lightly lubricate the contact points of the valve stems and lash adjusters with assembly lube (photo).
8   Install the valve rocker arms in their respective locations (photo).
9   Lubricate the contact surfaces on the top side of the rocker arms with assembly lube.
10 Lubricate the camshaft bearing surfaces with assembly lube. Wipe the camshaft carefully with a clean, dry lint-free cloth.
11 Lubricate the contact surfaces of the camshaft with assembly lubricant and lower it into position with the sprocket keyway pointed up.
12 Apply a thin coat of assembly lubricant to the camshaft bearing caps and install them on their respective pedestals. Apply sealant to the contact surfaces of the two end bearing caps.
13 Install the bearing cap retaining bolts and tighten them with your fingers until they are snug. Tighten the bolts evenly, in $\frac{1}{4}$ turn increments, to the specified torque.
14 Remove any excess sealant from the two end bearing caps (photo).

65.4 Apply a bead of sealant to the ends of the head bolts prior to installation

65.7 Place a dab of assembly lubricant on the lash adjusters and valve stem contact surfaces

65.8 Lower the rocker arm into position and press down to securely seat it

65.14 Use a small screwdriver to remove excess sealant from the end caps

2B

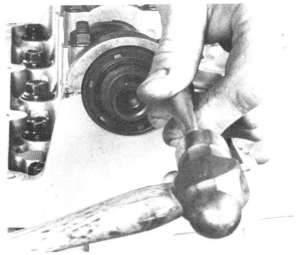

65.15 Work around the circumference of the seal and tap it securely into place

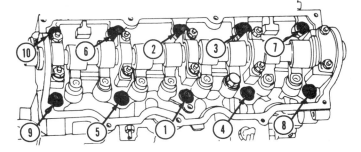

Fig. 2.39 Cylinder head bolt *tightening* sequence (Sec 65)

15 Press the camshaft seals into the end bearing caps and seat them in place with a hammer and the large end of a suitable punch (photo).
16 The camshaft endplay can be checked with a dial indicator set or a feeler gauge.
17 If a feeler gauge is used, gently pry the camshaft all the way toward the front of the engine. Slip a feeler gauge between the flange at the front of the camshaft and the front bearing cap. Compare the measured endplay to the Specifications.

66.2 Lock the air pump pulley with a breaker bar so it won't turn

66.5 Pull the tabs through the installation holes with pliers to seat the seal

66.13 Installing the oxygen sensor in the exhaust manifold

66.17 Retaining the kickdown throttle linkage with the clip

66.20 Installing the engine mount

66.25 Use sealant on both sides of the gasket when installing the water outlet and thermostat

66.26 Use teflon tape on the heater water outlet threads

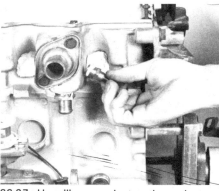

66.27a Use silicone sealant on the coolant temperature switch threads

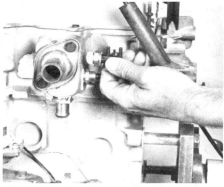

66.27b Installing the temperature vacuum switch with teflon tape on the threads

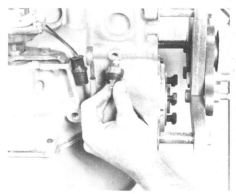

66.28 Installing the oil pressure switch with teflon tape on the threads

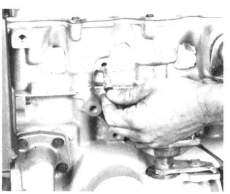

66.29 Installing the water temperature sensor, using teflon tape on the threads

67.1 Seating the alignment dowels with a plastic hammer

18 If a dial indicator is used, mount it at the front of the engine with the indicator stem touching the end of the camshaft. Carefully pry the camshaft all the way toward the front of the engine, then zero the indicator. Gently pry the camshaft as far as possible in the opposite direction and observe the needle movement on the dial indicator, which will indicate the amount of endplay. Compare this reading to the Specifications.

66 External engine components – installation

1   Install the camshaft drivebelt sprocket, making sure it is properly aligned (Section 46). Install the retaining bolt finger tight.
2   Install the air injection pump pulley and bolt. Lock the pulley to keep it from turning and tighten the bolt to the specified torque (photo).
3   Lock the air pump pulley to keep it from turning and tighten the camshaft timing belt sprocket bolt to the specified torque.
4   Install and adjust the timing belt (Section 46).
5   Attach new seals to the valve cover (photo).
6   Apply a $\frac{1}{8}$ inch bead of RTV sealant around the sealing surface of the valve cover, place the cover in place and press down to seat it. Install the retaining bolts and tighten them to the specified torque.
7   Install the air pump mount.
8   Place the PCV valve vent mount in place, work it into the valve cover and retain it with the clip.
9   Place the exhaust manifold and gasket in position, lubricate the mounting stud threads with white lithium base grease and install the nuts. Tighten them to the specific torque in a criss-cross pattern.
10 Attach the carburetor heat manifold to the exhaust manifold.
11 Install the intake manifold and bolts. Tighten the bolts to the specified torque in increments, working from the center to the ends.
12 Apply anti-seize compound to the EGR valve flare nut and mounting studs. Place the valve and gasket assembly in position and install the nuts finger tight. Thread the tube into the manifold, place the flange into position on the valve and install the bolts. Tighten the bolts and flare nut evenly and securely.
13 Apply anti-seize compound to the threads of the oxygen sensor and install it in the exhaust manifold (photo).
14 Apply RTV sealant to the contact surfaces on both sides of the carburetor spacer. Place the spacer in position, install the nuts and tighten them to the specified torque.
15 Install the throttle kickdown linkage mount (automatic transaxle).
16 Place the carburetor in position on the spacer and install the retaining nuts, tightening them to the specified torque.
17 Connect the kickdown linkage to the carburetor (photo).
18 Install the throttle return spring.
19 Connect the PCV valve and hose assembly between the carburetor and the vent module.
20 Attach the engine mount to the front of the engine (photo).
21 Install the lower timing belt cover, followed by the upper cover.
22 Using a new O-ring, install the water pump.
23 Install the fuel pump.
24 Lubricate the O-ring on the shaft with white lithium base grease and install the distributor (Chapter 5).
25 Install the water outlet and the thermostat (photo).
26 Install the heater water outlet (photo).
27 Install the coolant temperature switch and the temperature vacuum switch (TVS) in the water outlet housing (photos).
28 Install the oil pressure switch (photo).
29 Install the water temperature sensor in the cylinder head (photo).
30 Install the oil filter.

67 Connecting the engine and transaxle

1   Install the alignment dowels by tapping them into place with a hammer (photo).
2   Install the dust shield over the alignment dowels (photo).
3   Install the flywheel and clutch or automatic transaxle driveplate by referring to the appropriate Section.
4   Lift the transaxle into position and mate it to the engine over the alignment dowels. Install the mounting bolts and tighten them to the specified torque.
5   On automatic transaxles, install the torque converter-to-driveplate

67.2 Installing the dust shield

retaining bolts through the access hole adjacent to the starter. Rotate the crankshaft with a wrench to install each bolt finger tight in turn. Repeat the procedure and tighten the bolts to the specified torque.
6   Install the torque converter cover plate.
7   Install the starter.
8   Install the air injection pump.

68 Engine – installation

1   Attach a suitable lifting device and raise the engine and transaxle over the engine compartment.
2   Slowly and carefully lower the engine into place and guide the rear of the transaxle past the left hand engine mount.
3   With the engine/transaxle assembly lowered into position, install the left engine mount and through-bolt.
4   Install the right side engine mount with the bolts and nuts snug.
5   Remove the bolts from the bellhousing and attach the front engine mount to the engine and transaxle.
6   Pull the engine forward and attach the mount to the front crossmember.
7   Tighten the bolts retaining the left engine mount to the transaxle to the specified torque.
8   Tighten the bolts retaining the front engine mount to the engine and transaxle to the specified torque.
9   Check all of the engine mounts to make sure they are properly aligned, with no twisting. Tap each mount with a soft-faced hammer and ensure that the bolts turn easily.
10 Tighten the front mount-to-chassis crossmember bolts to the specified torque.
11 Tighten the right and left hand engine mount through-bolts to the specified torque.
12 Align the right and left hand mounts so that an equal amount of the rubber insulator is visible on either side of the center portion (photo).
13 Tighten the engine mount-to-chassis bolts to the specified torque.
14 Remove the lifting device.
15 Install the air injection pump.
16 Connect the exhaust manifold and pipe using new springs and tighten the nuts to the specified torque.
17 Attach the brackets to the power steering pump and install the assembly on the engine.
18 Install the drivebelt and adjust it to the specified tension (Chapter 1).
19 Install and adjust the automatic transaxle kickdown cable (Chapter 7).
20 Place the automatic transaxle in Park, push the shift lever fully forward, connect the linkage and tighten the bracket.
21 Install the battery tray.
22 Install the air cleaner bracket.
23 Install the diverter valve and hose assembly.

2B

68.12 The left engine mount, properly aligned with equal distance between the insulators (arrows)

24 Connect the throttle cable.
25 Connect the water hose from the intake manifold to the water outlet.
26 Attach the heater hoses to the heater block and the manifold.
27 On air conditioned models, install the compressor mounting plate on the engine.
28 Install the alternator and drivebelt.
29 Install the air conditioner compressor, ground strap and drivebelt.
30 Connect the compressor hoses. If the system has been discharged, take the vehicle to your dealer or a properly equipped shop to have it recharged. **Do not attempt this job yourself.**
31 Attach the fuel pipes to the fuel pump, carburetor and inlet line.
32 Connect the PCV valve and hose to the vent module.
33 Connect the carburetor float vent line.
34 Connect the brake booster valve line.
35 Install the radiator (Chapter 3) and connect the hoses.
36 Connect the cooling fan plug.
37 Attach the vacuum hoses, referring to the tags and the diagram located in the engine compartment.
38 Install the wiring harness and plug in the connectors.

69 Initial start-up and break-in after overhaul

Refer to Section 33, Part A.

Chapter 3 Cooling, heating and air conditioning systems

Contents

Specifications

3

General

Radiator pressure cap rating	14 psi (97 kpa)
Electric fan operating temperature	200°F (93°C)

Thermostat

Rating	
2.2L engine	195°F (90°C)
2.6L engine	190°F (88°C)
Initial opening temperature	
2.2L engine	195°F (90°C)
2.6L engine	190°F (88°C)
Fully open temperature	
2.2L engine	219°F (104°C)
2.6L engine	215°F (102°C)

Torque specifications

	Ft-lb	Nm
Air conditioner 'H' valve bolts	2.2	3
Air conditioner 'H' valve sealing plate retaining bolt	2.2	3
Fan motor mounting nuts	5	7
Fan shroud retaining bolts	10	12
Radiator hose clamp	4	5
Radiator upper mounting bracket nuts	10	12
Thermostat housing bolts	15	20
2.2L engine water pump cover-to-housing bolts	10	12
2.6L engine water pump-to-body screws	7	9
Water pump mounting bolts (2.2L engine)		
Upper three bolts	21	28
Lower bolt	50	68
Water pump mounting bolts (2.6L engine - all)	17	23
Water pump pulley bolts	11	15

1 General information

Caution: *Whenever working in the vicinity of the fan, always make sure the ignition is turned off or the battery negative cable is disconnected.*

The cooling system on all models consists of a radiator, an electrically-driven fan mounted in the radiator shroud, a thermostat, a water pump and a coolant reserve tank.

Coolant is circulated through the radiator tubes and is cooled by air passing through the cooling fins. The coolant is circulated by a pump mounted on the front of the engine and driven by a belt.

A thermostat allows the engine to warm up by remaining closed until the coolant in the radiator, heater and cylinder head is at operating temperature. The thermostat then opens, allowing full circulation of the coolant throughout the cooling system.

A thermal switch actuates the electric fan when a certain temperature is reached or when the air conditioner is turned on. This aids in cooling by drawing air through the radiator.

The radiator cap contains a vent valve which allows coolant to escape through a tube to the reserve tank. When the engine cools, vacuum in the radiator draws the coolant back from the tank so the coolant level remains constant.

The heating system operates by directing air through the heater core mounted in the dash and then to the interior of the vehicle by a system of ducts. Temperature is controlled by mixing heated air with fresh air, using a system of flapper doors in the ducts, and a heater motor.

Some models are equipped with an air conditioner/heater system consisting of an evaporator core and ducts in the dash and a compressor in the engine compartment.

2 Antifreeze

1   It is recommended that the cooling system be filled with a water/ethylene glycol based antifreeze solution which will give protection down to at least -20°F at all times. This provides protection against corrosion and increases the coolant boiling point. When handling antifreeze, do not spill it on the vehicle paint, since it will cause damage if not removed immediately.

2   The cooling system should be drained, flushed and refilled at least every other year. The use of antifreeze solutions for periods of longer than two years is likely to cause damage and encourage the formation of rust and scale in the system.

3   Before adding antifreeze to the system, check all hose connections and check the tightness of the cylinder head bolts as antifreeze tends to search out and leak through the minutest openings.

4   The exact mixture of antifreeze-to-water which you should use depends upon the relative weather conditions. The mixture should contain at least 50 percent antifreeze offering protection to -34°F. The mixture should never contain more than 70 percent antifreeze.

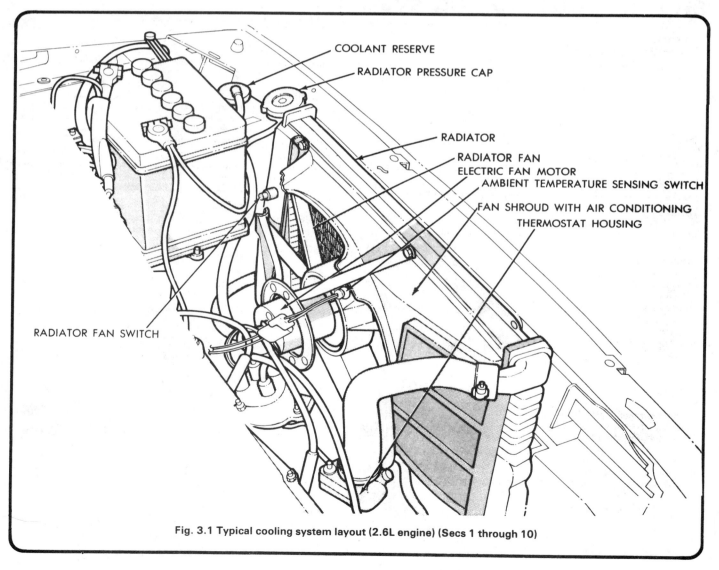

Fig. 3.1 Typical cooling system layout (2.6L engine) (Secs 1 through 10)

3   Thermostat – removal and installation

1   A faulty thermostat is indicated by a failure of the engine to reach operating temperature or taking a longer than normal time to do so.
2   Disconnect the negative battery cable.
3   Drain the coolant into a suitable container.
4   Remove the upper radiator hose.
5   Remove the thermostat housing inlet (photo).
6   Grasp the thermostat by the bridge and remove it from the housing.
7   Clean all traces of the gasket from the housing and inlet mating surfaces with a suitable scraper, taking care not to gouge or nick the metal.
8   Coat both sides of the new gasket with sealant, using the sealant to retain the gasket to the housing.
9   Install the new thermostat in the housing (photo).
10   Install the housing inlet and bolts, tightening the bolts to the specified torque.
11   Install the hose, refill the radiator with the specified coolant and connect the negative battery cable.
12   Start the engine and check for coolant leaks around the thermostat housing.

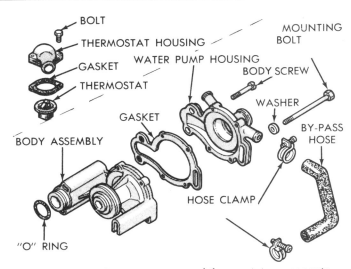

Fig. 3.2 2.6L engine water pump and thermostat components – exploded view (Sec 3)

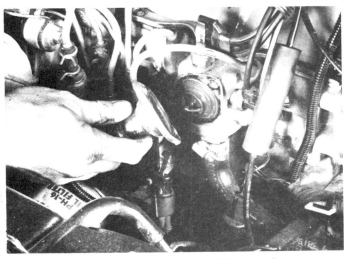

3.5 Removing the thermostat housing inlet (2.2L engine)

4   Water pump (2.2L engine) – removal and installation

1   Disconnect the negative battery cable from the battery.
2   Drain the coolant into a suitable container.
3   On air conditioner equipped models, loosen the idler pulley bolt and release the drivebelt tension. Unplug the air conditioner electrical connector, unbolt the compresser and secure it out of the way. Do not disconnect or kink the hoses, as they are under high pressure and serious injury could result.
4   Remove the ground cable and electrical connectors from the alternator.
5   Raise the front of the vehicle and support it securely. Remove the right side under engine cover (if equipped).
6   Loosen the alternator tension adjuster and remove the drivebelt.
7   Remove the alternator through-bolt and remove the alternator.
8   Unbolt and remove the air conditioner bracket (if equipped).
9   Disconnect the lower radiator hose, remove the water pump and housing assembly retaining bolts and lift the assembly from the engine.
10   Remove the retaining bolts and separate the water pump from the housing (photo).
11   Clean the mating surfaces of the water pump and housing to remove the old sealant material. Remove the O-ring from the housing (photo).

3

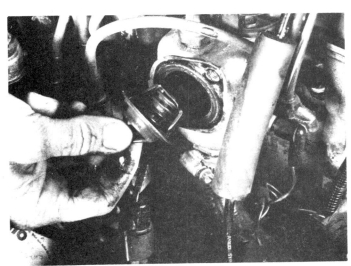

3.9 Install the thermostat with the bridge side out

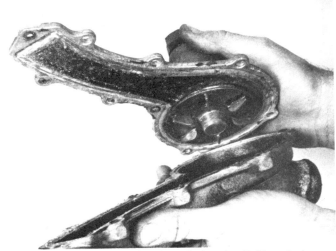

4.10 Separating the water pump from the housing (2.2L engine)

4.11 Pulling the O-ring from the groove (2.2L engine)

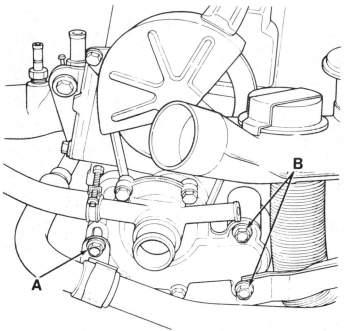

Fig. 3.4 2.6L engine water pump locking (A) and pivot (B) bolts (Sec 5)

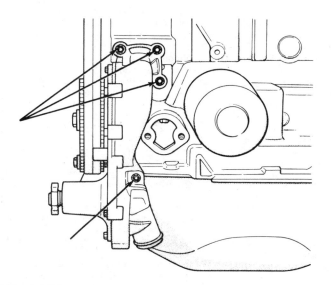

Fig. 3.3 2.2L engine water pump retaining nuts (arrows) (Sec 4)

3   Disconnect the radiator, by-pass and heater hoses from the water pump.
4   Remove the drivebelt pulley shield.
5   Remove the water pump locking and pivot bolts, remove the drivebelt and lift the water pump and housing assembly from the engine.
6   Remove the retaining screws and separate the water pump from the housing.
7   Discard the gasket and clean the mating surfaces to remove any remaining gasket material.
8   Remove the O-ring and carefully clean out the groove.
9   Coat both sides of the new gasket with RTV sealant and attach the gasket to the water pump body. Attach the pump body to the housing, tightening the screws to the specified torque.
10   Press the new O-ring into the groove.
11   Install the water pump assembly on the engine with the bolts finger tight.
12   Install the drivebelt, adjust it to the proper deflection (Chapter 1) and tighten the water pump retaining and pivot bolts to the specified torque.
13   Install the drivebelt pulley shield.
14   Attach the radiator, by-pass and heater hoses to the water pump.
15   Refill the cooling system with the specified coolant.
16   Connect the negative battery cable.
17   Start the engine and check for coolant leaks at the water pump.

12   If a new water pump is to be installed, transfer the pulley to the new pump.
13   Clean the groove in the housing and press the new O-ring into place.
14   Apply a bead of RTV sealant to the housing mating surface and install the pump. Install the bolts and tighten them to the specified torque.
15   Attach the pump and housing assembly to the engine, tightening the bolts to the specified torque. Install the radiator hose.
16   Install the air conditioner bracket and alternator and adjust the drivebelt.
17   Lower the vehicle.
18   Connect the ground cable and wiring to the alternator.
19   Install the air conditioner compressor (if removed).
20   Refill the cooling system with the specified coolant.
21   Connect the negative battery cable.
22   Start the engine and check for coolant leaks at the water pump.

6   Radiator – removal and installation

1   Disconnect the negative battery cable from the battery.
2   Drain the cooling system, making sure the heater control is in the full heat position.
3   Remove the fan motor and shroud assembly (Section 9).
4   Remove the radiator hoses.
5   Disconnect and plug the automatic transaxle-to-radiator cooler lines at the radiator. If the hose cannot be pulled from the radiator, it may be necessary to cut it at the end of the fitting. Slit the remaining hose and peel it from the fitting.
6   Remove the heater return hose.
7   Remove the radiator overflow hose (photo).
8   Remove the two bracket nuts.
9   Lift the radiator carefully up and out of the engine compartment.
10   Inspect the radiator for leaks, bent fins, damaged tubes, cracks around the tanks and signs of clogging or corrosion.

5   Water pump (2.6L engine) – removal and installation

1   Disconnect the negative battery cable from the battery.
2   Drain the cooling system.

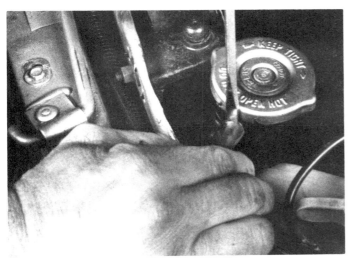

6.7 Use a screwdriver to push the overflow tube off the fitting

6.12 The radiator must seat firmly in the rubber grommet (arrow)

11 Lubricate all of the hose connections lightly with white lithium grease to ease installation.
12 Lower the radiator into place and push down to seat the tabs in the rubber grommets (photo).
13 Install the bracket nuts and tighten them securely.

14 Install the radiator, heater and automatic transaxle hoses.
15 Install the fan motor and shroud assembly.
16 Refill the cooling system with the specified coolant.
17 Connect the negative battery cable.
18 Start the engine and check for coolant leaks at the hose fittings.

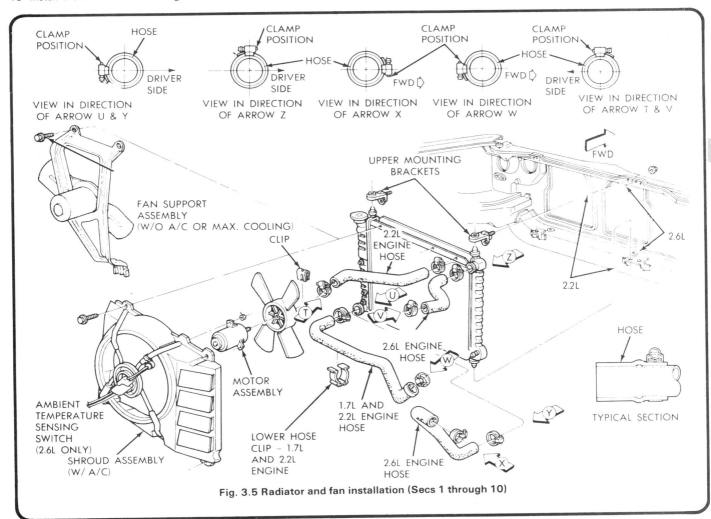

Fig. 3.5 Radiator and fan installation (Secs 1 through 10)

7   Radiator – inspection

1   The radiator should be kept free of obstructions such as leaves, paper, insects or other debris which could affect the cooling efficiency.
2   Periodically inspect the radiator for bent cooling fins or tubes, signs of coolant leakage and cracks around the upper and lower tanks.
3   Check the filler neck sealing surface for dents which could affect the radiator cap sealing effectiveness.

8   Drivebelts – inspection, replacement and tensioning

1   The drivebelts should be inspected periodically for wear, cuts and contamination by oil, gasoline or coolant as well as for signs of glazing, indicating improper tensioning.
2   To replace a drivebelt, loosen the adjustment bolts and push the pivoting components away from the belt until it can be removed. Do not pry on the pulley surface itself as this could cause nicks or gouges which will damage the new belt.
3   Install the new belt and maintain pressure on it by using a suitable lever while the adjustment bolts are tightened.
4   Check the drivebelt tension by measuring the belt deflection, referring to Chapter 1.

9   Fan motor and shroud assembly – removal and installation

1   Disconnect the negative battery cable from the battery.
2   Unplug the fan motor connector.
3   Remove the upper shroud bolts.
4   Release the clips at the bottom of the shroud, pull the assembly up and lift it from the engine compartment (photo).
5   To install it, position the motor and shroud assembly and push down to seat it in the clips.
6   Install the retaining bolts and tighten them securely.
7   Plug in the fan motor connector and connect the negative battery cable.

10 Fan motor and shroud assembly – disassembly, inspection and reassembly

1   Remove the assembly from the vehicle and place it on a workbench.
2   Remove the clip and slide the fan off the motor shaft (photo).
3   Remove the retaining nuts and withdraw the motor from the shroud (photo).
4   Inspect the motor for a bent shaft, damage and worn wiring insulation. Check the motor by inserting two 14 gauge wires into the connector and connecting them to the battery. Replace the motor with a new one if it does not run and the wiring and connector are not faulty. Inspect the fan for warping, cracks or damage, replacing it with a new one of the same design if necessary.
5   Place the motor in position on the shroud, install the nuts and tighten them securely.
6   Slide the fan onto the shaft and retain it with the clip.
7   Install the assembly.

11 Heater and air conditioner control – removal and installation

1   Disconnect the negative battery cable from the battery.
2   Remove the bezel (two screws) and the ash tray (Chapter 12).
3   Remove the retaining screws (photo).
4   Withdraw the assembly from the dash and disengage the control connectors. Be sure to mark the electrical connectors so they are not reversed during installation.
5   Remove the control assembly from the vehicle.
6   To install, place the assembly in position and connect the vacuum and electrical connectors.
7   Install the retaining screws and bezel and connect the negative battery cable.

9.4 Lift the fan and shroud assembly straight up to disengage it from the clips

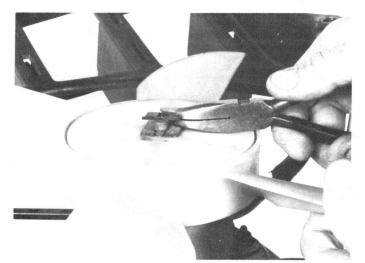

10.2 Pull the fan retaining clip off with a needle-nose pliers

10.3 Removing the fan motor retaining nuts

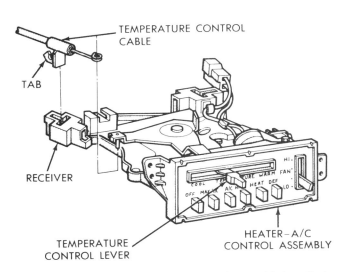

Fig. 3.6 Heater and air conditioner control assembly installation details (Sec 11)

11.3 Removing the heater/air conditioner control retaining screws

12 Heater and air conditioner evaporator assembly – removal and installation

Caution: *On air conditioner equipped vehicles, it will be necessary to have the system depressurized by your dealer or a properly equipped shop. Do not attempt this job yourself as the high pressure in the system could cause serious injury.*

1   Drain the cooling system.
2   Disconnect the negative battery cable from the battery.
3   Remove the air cleaner assembly.
4   Disconnect the heater hoses at the firewall (photo).
5   Remove the air cleaner assembly.
6   On air conditioned models, disconnect the vacuum hoses at the intake manifold and water control valve and the wiring harness from the low pressure cut-off switch at the 'H' valve.
7   Remove the air conditioning cycling switch from the sealing plate and remove the plate from the 'H' valve (photo).
8   Remove the cut-off switch from the 'H' valve and discard the O-ring.
9   Remove the 'H' valve (two Allen head screws) and discard the gasket.
10 Remove the condensate tube from the firewall.
11 Remove the right side scuff plate and trim panel.
12 Remove the glove box (Chapter 12) and center console (if equipped).
13 Remove the heater and air conditioner control (Section 11).
14 Roll down the instrument panel (Chapter 12).
15 Disconnect the control cables from the heater assembly.
16 Remove the center distribution duct on air conditioner equipped models.
17 Remove the retaining nuts, disconnect any remaining electrical wires or controls and pull the assembly down and to the rear to remove it.
18 To install the assembly, place it in position and insert the mounting studs through the firewall. Install the retaining nuts.
19 Install the center distribution duct, connect the control cables and install the instrument panel.
20 Install the heater and air conditioner control, glove box, center console (if equipped), scuff plate and trim panel.
21 In the engine compartment, install the condensate tube. Install the 'H' valve, using a new gasket, and the cut-off switch, using a new O-ring.
22 Attach the air conditioning cycling switch and sealing plate to the 'H' valve.
23 Connect the coolant and vacuum hoses and wiring harness.
24 Install the air cleaner, refill the cooling system with the specified coolant and connect the negative battery cable.
25 Have the air conditioner recharged before operating the system.

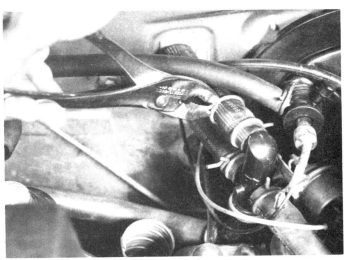

12.4 Slide the heater hose clamps away from the firewall

3

12.7 Removing the sealing plate retaining bolt (arrow) located on the 'H' valve

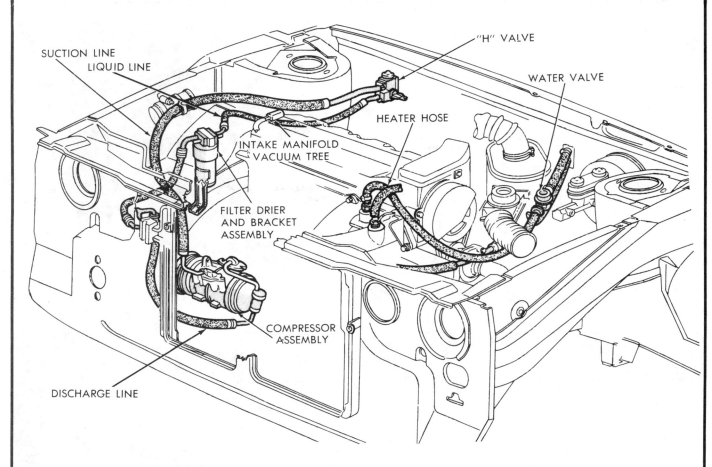

SUCTION LINE
LIQUID LINE

"H" VALVE

WATER VALVE

HEATER HOSE

INTAKE MANIFOLD
VACUUM TREE

FILTER DRIER
AND BRACKET
ASSEMBLY

COMPRESSOR
ASSEMBLY

DISCHARGE LINE

Fig. 3.7 Typical heater and air conditioner hose installation (Sec 12)

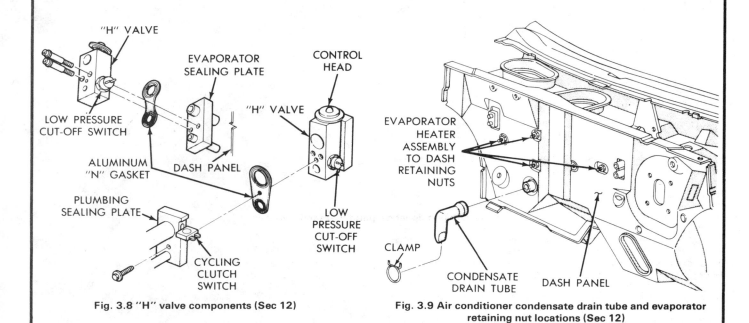

"H" VALVE

EVAPORATOR
SEALING PLATE

CONTROL
HEAD

"H" VALVE

LOW PRESSURE
CUT-OFF SWITCH

ALUMINUM
"N" GASKET

DASH PANEL

PLUMBING
SEALING PLATE

LOW
PRESSURE
CUT-OFF
SWITCH

CYCLING
CLUTCH
SWITCH

EVAPORATOR
HEATER
ASSEMBLY
TO DASH
RETAINING
NUTS

CLAMP

CONDENSATE
DRAIN TUBE

DASH PANEL

Fig. 3.8 "H" valve components (Sec 12)

Fig. 3.9 Air conditioner condensate drain tube and evaporator
retaining nut locations (Sec 12)

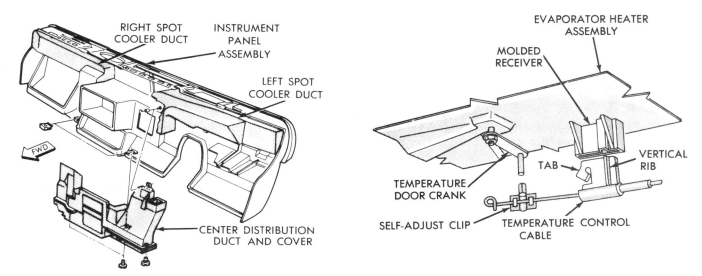

Fig. 3.10 Air conditioner center distribution duct installation details (Sec 12)

Fig. 3.11 Control cable installation (Sec 12)

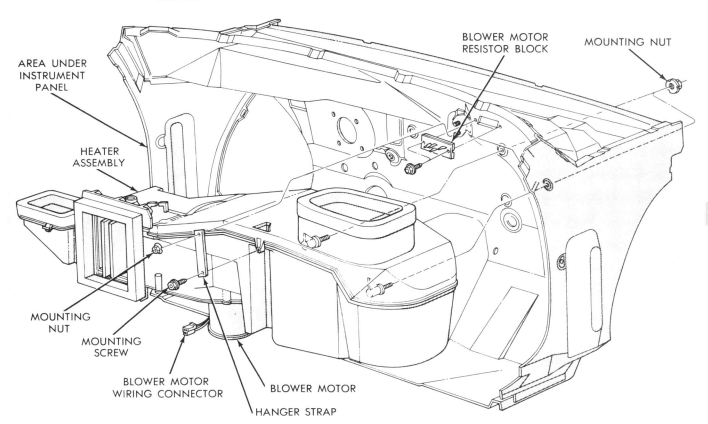

Fig. 3.12 Heater and air conditioner evaporator assembly installation (Sec 12)

---

13 Heater core and blower motor – removal and installation

1   Remove the assembly from the vehicle (Section 12).
2   Remove the mounting screw, use a screwdriver to pry the retaining clamps loose and lift off the housing cover on non-air conditioned vehicles. On air conditioned vehicles, remove the mode door retaining nut and the actuating arm, followed by the two clips, from the front edge of the cover. Remove the retaining screws and lift the cover from the assembly.

3   Remove the heater core retaining screw and lift the core from the assembly.
4   Remove the retaining nuts and remove the motor. On air conditioned models it will be necessary to also remove the recirculation door housing.
5   Remove the retaining clip and slide the fan off the motor shaft (photo).
6   Install the fan and clip, place the motor in place and install the retaining nuts. Install the door housing (if applicable).

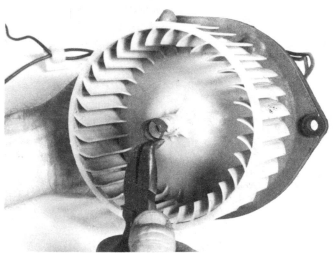

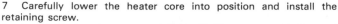

13.5 Squeeze the tabs together and lift the clip from the shaft

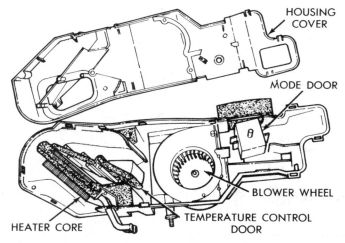

Fig. 3.13 Heater housing assembly (non-air conditioned models)
(Sec 13)

7   Carefully lower the heater core into position and install the retaining screw.
8   Install the housing cover, retain it with the screws and clips and install the actuating arm on air conditioned models.
9   Install the assembly.

14 Air conditioning system – description and testing

Caution: *The air conditioning system is pressurized at the factory and requires special equipment to repair. Any work should be left to your dealer or a properly equipped shop. Do not, under any circumstances, disconnect the air conditioning hoses while the system is under pressure.*

1   The air conditioning system consists of a condenser mounted in front of the radiator, an evaporator mounted under the dash, a belt-driven compressor incorporating a clutch, a filter-drier which contains a high pressure relief valve and associated hoses.
2   The temperature in the passenger compartment is lowered by transferring the heat in the air to the refrigerant in the evaporator and then passing the refrigerant through the filter-drier to the condenser.
3   Maintenance is confined to keeping the system properly charged with refrigerant, the compressor drivebelt tensioned properly and making sure the condenser is free of leaves and other debris.
4   The sight glass located in the top of the filter-drier can give some indication of the refrigerant level.
5   With the control on A/C, the fan switch on High and the temperature lever on Cool, run the system for several minutes. The temperature in the vehicle should be approximately 70°F (21°C).
6   The system has a full refrigerant charge if the sight glass is clear, the air conditioner compressor clutch is engaged, the inlet line to the compressor is cool and the discharge line is warm.
7   If the glass is clear, the clutch is engaged but there is no difference in temperature between the inlet and discharge lines, the refrigerant charge is very low.
8   Continuous foam or bubbles at the sight glass is another symptom of low refrigerant. Occasional foam or bubbles under certain conditions, such as very high or low temperatures in the vehicle interior, is acceptable.

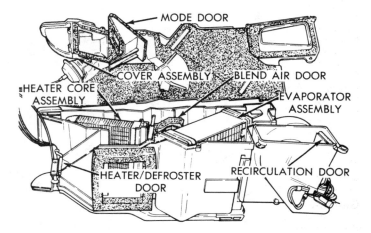

Fig. 3.14 Heater/air conditioner assembly (Sec 13)

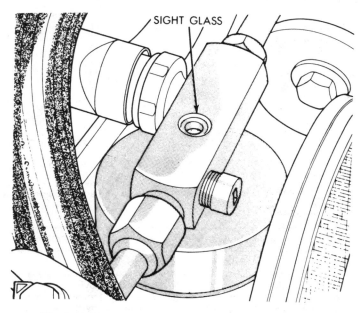

Fig. 3.15 Air conditioner filter-drier sight glass (Sec 14)

Chapter 4 Fuel and exhaust systems

Refer to Chapter 13 for specifications and information applicable to later models

Contents

Specifications

General

Fuel tank capacity .... 13.0 US gal (49 liters)
Fuel filter type .... Replaceable paper element

Carburetor adjustments

Curb idle speed .... Refer to Emissions Control Information label
Fast idle speed .... Refer to Emissions Control Information label
2.2L engine choke vacuum kick adjustment

Carburetor number	Gauge size
1981	
R9060A	0.030 in (0.76 mm)
R9065A	0.030 in (0.76 mm)
R9123A	0.030 in (0.76 mm)
R9126A	0.030 in (0.76 mm)
R9602A	0.065 in (1.65 mm)
R9603A	0.065 in (1.65 mm)
R9604A	0.065 in (1.65 mm)
R9605A	0.065 in (1.65 mm)
R9054A	0.040 in (1.0 mm)
9055A	0.040 in (1.0 mm)
R9052A	0.070 in (1.8 mm)
R9053A	0.070 in (1.8 mm)
1982	
R9824A	0.065 in (1.65 mm)
R9503A	0.085 in (2.15 mm)
R9504A	0.085 in (2.15 mm)
R9750A	0.085 in (2.15 mm)
R9751A	0.085 in (2.15 mm)
R9822A	0.080 in (2.05 mm)
R9823A	0.080 in (2.05 mm)
R9505A	0.100 in (2.55 mm)
R9506A	0.100 in (2.55 mm)
R9752A	0.100 in (2.55 mm)
R9753A	0.100 in (2.55 mm)

4

1983

R40003A	0.070 in (1.80 mm)
R40007A	0.070 in (1.80 mm)
R40008A	0.070 in (1.80 mm)
R40012A	0.070 in (1.80 mm)
R40004A	0.080 in (2.00 mm)
R40005A	0.080 in (2.00 mm)
R40006A	0.080 in (2.00 mm)
R40010A	0.080 in (2.00 mm)
R40014A	0.080 in (2.00 mm)
R40080A	0.045 in (1.20 mm)
R40081A	0.045 in (1.20 mm)
2.2L engine float drop	$1\frac{7}{8}$ in (47.6 mm)
2.2L engine dry float level	0.480 in (12.2 mm)
2.6L engine dry float level	0.799 in (19.8 mm)
2.6L engine air conditioning idle speed	900 rpm

Torque specifications

	Ft-lb	Nm
Carburetor-to-manifold (all)	17	23
2.2L carburetor air horn screws	2.5	3.4

1 General information

The fuel system consists of a rear-mounted fuel tank, a fuel pump which draws the fuel to the carburetor and associated lines and filters.

The exhaust system is made up of pipes, heat shields, muffler and catalytic converters. The catalytic converters require that only unleaded fuel be used in the vehicle.

2 Fuel system check

The fuel system should be inspected periodically for leaks, malfunctions and faulty components. This check is described in Chapter 1.

3 Air filter replacement

Replace the air cleaner filter element periodically in accordance with the maintenance schedule in Chapter 1, or when it is dirty or clogged. The replacement procedure is located in Chapter 1.

4 Thermostatically controlled air cleaner check

A malfunction of the thermostatically controlled air cleaner can affect the engine's running during warmup. Check the operation of the air cleaner flapper door and mechanism periodically as described in Chapter 1.

5 Fuel filter replacement

Replace the fuel filter according to the maintenance schedule and procedures found in Chapter 1.

6 Air conditioning idle speed (2.2L engine) – checking and adjustment

1   Air conditioned models are equipped with solenoids or kickers to increase idle speed when the air conditioning compressor engages, putting a greater load on the engine. Prior to checking the air conditioning idle speed, check the curb idle and timing to make sure they are correct. The checks should be made with the engine at normal operating temperature.

1981 and 1982 models
2   Pull the PCV valve from the vent module (plug the module opening) so the valve draws air from the engine compartment.
3   Disconnect the vacuum hose from the EGR valve and plug it.
4   Disconnect the cooling fan and connect a jumper wire so the fan will run continuously.

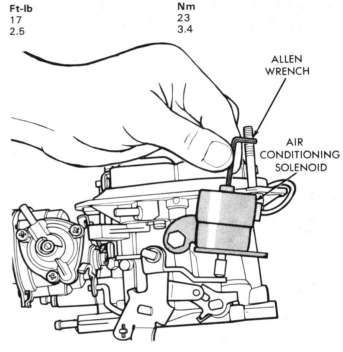

Fig. 4.1 Air conditioning idle speed adjustment (1981 and 1982 models) (Sec 6)

5   Connect a tachometer and start the engine.
6   Turn the air conditioner on with the blower control on the Low position.
7   Open the throttle sufficiently to cause the solenoid to engage.
8   Remove the adjusting screw and spring from the top of the solenoid, insert a $\frac{1}{8}$ in Allen wrench into the solenoid and adjust the idle speed to the specification on the Emissions Control Information label.
9   Check the adjustment, making sure the air conditioner clutch is engaged and the solenoid is activated.
10 Shut off the engine and the air conditioner. Install the adjusting screw and spring to the solenoid. Connect the EGR vacuum hose, fan motor and PCV valve and remove the tachometer.

1983 models
11 When the air conditioner is engaged, the idle speed on these models is increased by either a vacuum or solenoid-type kicker.
12 Kicker operation can be checked by running the engine (at normal operating temperature) and moving the temperature control to the coldest setting and then turning the air conditioning on. The kicker plunger should move in and out as the compressor clutch engages and disengages. Remove the air cleaner for better visual access to the kicker, if necessary.

13 No adjustment of the kicker is possible, although the adjusting screw on the top is used for normal curb idle adjustment. Check the kicker and vacuum hose for leaks.

14 Replace the kicker with a new one if it does not operate properly and no vacuum leaks are present.

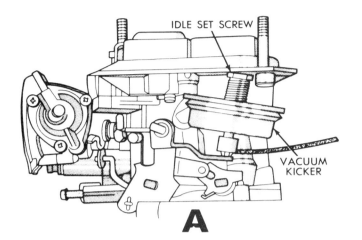

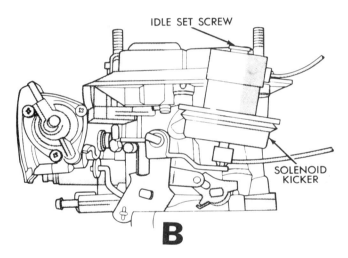

Fig. 4.2 Vacuum (A) and solenoid (B) air conditioner kickers (1983 models) (Sec 6)

7 Throttle cable – removal and installation

1   Inside the vehicle, remove the retaining plug and remove the cable end from the throttle pedal shaft.

2   In the engine compartment, remove the cable clevis from the carburetor lever stud and then separate the cable from the mounting bracket.

3   Remove the retainer clip, pull the cable assembly into the engine compartment and remove it from the vehicle.

4   To install, insert the cable through the dash panel grommet and install the retainer clip.

5   Connect the cable to the carburetor and the throttle pedal.

8 Throttle pedal – removal and installation

1   Remove the retaining plug and disengage the throttle cable from the pedal shaft and bracket.

2   In the engine compartment, remove the pedal assembly retaining studs.

3   Inside the vehicle, pull the pedal assembly from the dash panel and remove it.

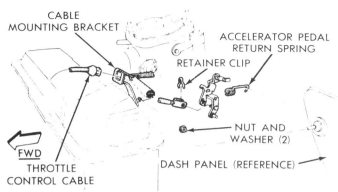

Fig. 4.3 Typical 2.2L engine throttle cable installation (Sec 7)

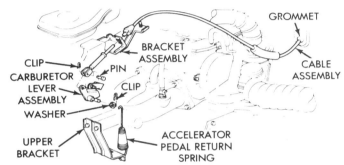

Fig. 4.4 Typical 2.6L engine throttle cable installation (Sec 7)

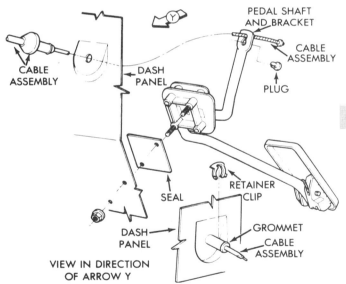

Fig. 4.5 Throttle pedal installation (Secs 7 and 8)

4   To install, place the pedal assembly in position, install the retaining nuts and connect the throttle cable.

9 Fuel pump – testing

1   A simple test of the fuel pump is to disconnect the outlet hose and route it into a suitable container.

2   Disconnect the ignition coil wire and turn the engine over with the starter while observing the fuel pump outlet hose. The pump should discharge definite spurts of fuel. If it does not or if very little fuel is seen, replace the pump with a new one.

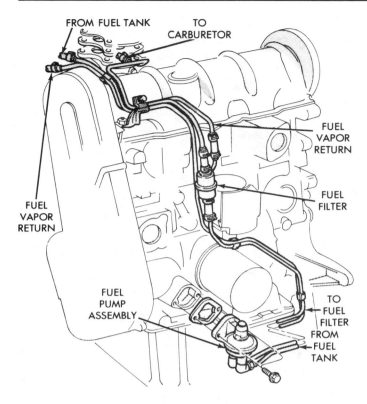

Fig. 4.6 2.2L engine fuel pump and fuel line layout (Sec 9)

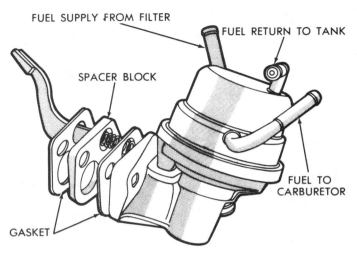

Fig. 4.8 2.6L fuel pump components (Sec 10)

10 Fuel pump (2.2L engine) – removal and installation

1   The fuel pump is bolted to the cylinder block adjacent to the oil filter.

2   Place clean rags or newspaper under the fuel pump to catch any gasoline which is spilled during removal.

3   Release the clips and remove the fuel hoses from the pump. Plug the hose ends to prevent leakage.

4   Unbolt and remove the fuel pump.

5   To install, coat both sides of the spacer block with sealant, position the fuel pump and spacer in place and install the retaining bolts.

6   Attach the hoses to the pump and secure them with new clamps.

7   Run the engine and check for leaks.

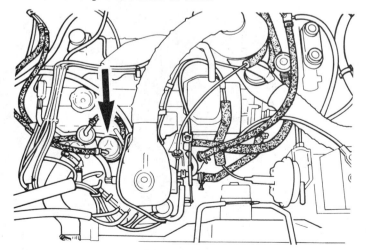

Fig. 4.7 2.6L engine fuel pump location (arrow) (Sec 10)

11 Fuel pump (2.6L engine) – removal and installation

1   The fuel pump is mounted on the cylinder head immediately in front of the carburetor. It is held in place with two nuts.

2   Pull the coil high-tension lead out of the distributor and ground it on the engine block. Remove the spark plugs and place your thumb over the number one cylinder spark plug hole.

3   Rotate the crankshaft in a clockwise direction (with a wrench on the large bolt attaching the pulley to the front of the crankshaft) until you can feel the compression pressure rising in the number one cylinder.

4   Continue rotating the crankshaft until the notch on the crankshaft pulley lines up with the T on the timing mark tab on the timing chain case. At this point, the lift of the fuel pump drive cam is reduced to a minimum, which will make the pump easier to remove.

5   Install the spark plugs and hook up the wires. Do not forget the coil high-tension lead.

6   Loosen the hose clamps and remove the fuel hoses from the pump fittings. Plug the ends of the hoses.

7   Remove the fuel pump mounting nuts and pull the pump off the engine. You may have to tap the pump body with a soft-faced hammer to break the gasket seal.

8   If the pump is difficult to remove, take off the valve cover (see Chapter 1, *Valve clearance adjustment*) and guide the pump rocker arm out of the head from the inside.

9   Remove the spacer block and scrape off all traces of the old gaskets and sealer.

10   Before installing the new pump, make sure that the rocker arm moves up and down without binding or sticking.

11   Coat both sides of the new gaskets with RTV-type gasket sealer before installation.

12   Slip the first gasket, the spacer block and the second gasket (in that order) onto the fuel pump mounting studs.

13   Install the fuel pump. It may be necessary to guide the rocker arm into place from inside the head. Work slowly; there is not much clearance between the rocker arm and the valve gear.

14   Once the fuel pump is properly seated, install the mounting nuts and tighten them evenly. Do not overtighten them or the spacer block may be cracked.

15   Install the valve cover if it was removed.

16   Install the hoses (after inspecting them for cracks) and new hose clamps.

17   Start the engine and check for fuel leaks at the hose fittings. Check for oil leaks where the fuel pump mounts on the cylinder head.

12 Carburetor – servicing

1   A thorough road test and check of carburetor adjustments should be done before any major carburetor service. Specifications for some

adjustments are listed on the vehicle Emission Control Information label found in the engine compartment.

2   Some performance complaints directed at the carburetor are actually a result of loose, misadjusted or malfunctioning engine or electrical components. Others develop when vacuum hoses leak, are disconnected or are incorrectly routed. The proper approach to analyzing carburetor problems should include a routine check of the following areas:

3   Inspect all vacuum hoses and actuators for leaks and proper installation (see Chapter 6, *Emission control systems*).

4   Tighten the intake manifold nuts and carburetor mounting nuts evenly and securely.

5   Perform a cylinder compression test.

6   Clean or replace the spark plugs as necessary.

7   Test the resistance of the spark plug wires (refer to Chapter 5).

8   Inspect the ignition primary wires and check the vacuum advance operation. Replace any defective parts.

9   Check the ignition timing as described in Chapter 1.

10 Inspect the heat control valve in the air cleaner for proper operation (refer to Chapter 1).

11 Remove the carburetor air filter element and blow out any dirt with compressed air. If the filter is extremely dirty, replace it with a new one.

12 Inspect the crankcase ventilation system (see Chapter 1).

13 Carburetor problems usually show up as flooding, hard starting, stalling, severe backfiring, poor acceleration and lack of response to idle mixture screw adjustments. A carburetor that is leaking fuel and/or covered with wet-looking deposits definitely needs attention.

14 Diagnosing carburetor problems may require that the engine be started and run with the air cleaner removed. While running the engine without the air cleaner it is possible that it could backfire. A backfiring situation is likely to occur if the carburetor is malfunctioning, but removal of the air cleaner alone can lean the air/fuel mixture enough to produce an engine backfire.

15 Once it is determined that the carburetor is indeed at fault, it should be disassembled, cleaned and reassembled using new parts where necessary. Before dismantling the carburetor, make sure you have a carburetor rebuild kit, which will include all necessary gaskets and internal parts, carburetor cleaning solvent and some means of blowing out all the internal passages of the carburetor. To do the job properly, you will also need a clean place to work and plenty of time and patience.

13 Carburetor (2.2L engine) – removal and installation

Removal

1   Disconnect the negative battery cable from the battery.

2   Remove the air cleaner assembly.

3   Remove the fuel tank filler cap as the tank could be under some pressure.

4   Place a suitable container under the fuel inlet fitting and disconnect the fitting.

5   Disconnect the wiring harness from the carburetor.

6   Disconnect the throttle linkage.

7   Tag and remove all hoses from the carburetor.

8   Remove the retaining nuts and carefully lift the carburetor from the engine compartment, taking care to hold it level.

Installation

9   Inspect the mating surfaces of the carburetor and the isolator for nicks, burrs or debris that could cause air leaks.

10 Place the carburetor in position and install the retaining nuts, taking care not to damage the fast idle lever.

11 Tighten the nuts to the specified torque.

12 Check all of the vacuum hoses and connections for wear or damage, replacing as necessary and install them.

13 Connect the throttle linkage and the fuel inlet line.

14 Check the operation of the throttle linkage and the choke plate to make sure they operate through their full travel.

15 Connect the wiring harness and install the air cleaner.

16 Connect the negative battery cable.

17 Start the engine and check for fuel leaks.

18 Check the engine idle speed.

14 Carburetor (2.6L engine) – removal and installation

Removal

1   Disconnect the negative battery cable from the battery.

2   Remove the intake housing from the carburetor air horn.

3   Release any pressure which may exist in the fuel tank by removing the filler cap.

4   Drain the radiator into a suitable container.

5   Remove the carburetor protector, tag the locations of the vacuum and coolant hoses and remove them from the carburetor.

6   Unplug the carburetor wiring harness connectors.

7   Place a suitable container under the carburetor fuel inlet to catch any residual fuel and disconnect the fuel hose from the inlet nipple.

8   Disconnect the throttle linkage.

9   Remove the retaining bolts and nut and carefully lift the carburetor from the engine. Keep the carburetor level to avoid spilling fuel.

Installation

10 Check the mating surfaces of the carburetor and intake manifold for nicks, burrs or old gasket material which could cause air leaks.

11 Using a new gasket, place the carburetor in position and install the retaining nuts and bolt, tightening them to the specified torque.

12 Connect the throttle linkage and the fuel line.

13 Connect the coolant and vacuum hoses and install the carburetor protector.

14 Refill the radiator with the specified coolant.

15 Check the operation of the throttle linkage and choke plate to make sure they operate smoothly through their entire range, with no binding.

16 Install the air intake housing and the fuel tank cap.

17 Connect the negative battery cable.

18 Check the carburetor idle speed.

15 Carburetor (2.2L engine) – disassembly

With the carburetor removed from the vehicle (Section 10) and a rebuild kit in hand, disassembly can begin. Carburetor disassembly is illustrated in a step-by-step fashion with photos. Follow the photos in the proper sequence.

Have a large and clean work area on which to lay out the parts as they are removed from the carburetor. Many of the parts are very small and can be easily lost if the area is cluttered.

Take your time during disassembly. Sketch the relationship of the various components of any assembly which appears complicated or tag the various parts for ease of reassembly. Care taken during disassembly will pay off with an easier job at the time of assembly. Begin disassembly by following the photo sequence starting with photo 15.1.

15.1 Remove the fuel inlet

15.2 Disconnect the choke rod

15.3 Remove the feedback solenoid retaining screws

15.4 Remove the feedback solenoid

15.5 Disconnect the air conditioner solenoid anti-rattle spring

15.6 Remove the air conditioner solenoid

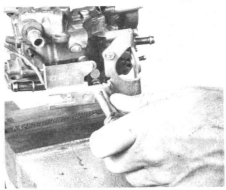

15.7 Remove the Wide Open Throttle cut-out switch

15.8 Remove the air horn retaining screws

15.9 Carefully pry the air horn free from the body

15.10 Disconnect the choke lever and lift the air horn off

15.11 Remove the float lever pin and the float

15.12 Remove the fuel inlet needle and seat

15.13 Remove the secondary (S) and primary (P) main metering jets, noting their sizes for reinstallation in the same locations

15.14 Remove the primary (P) and secondary (S) bleeds and main well tubes, noting their sizes for reinstallation in the same locations

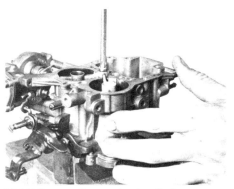

15.15 Remove the accelerator discharge pump assembly

15.16 Invert the carburetor and catch the accelerator pump discharge weight and check balls

15.17 Remove the accelerator pump cover

15.18 Remove the pump diaphragm and spring

15.19 File the head off the choke diaphragm cover retaining rivet

15.20 Remove the screws and lift the cover off

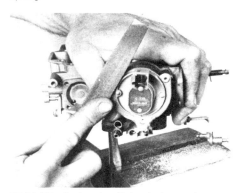

15.21 File the heads off the choke retainer ring and remove the ring

15.22 Remove the choke housing

4

16 Carburetor (2.6L engine) – disassembly

1   With the carburetor removed from the vehicle (Section 14) and a rebuild kit in hand, disassembly can begin. Have a large and clean work area on which to lay out parts as they are removed. It is a good idea to place clean newspaper on the work surface. Many of the parts are very small and can be easily lost if the work area is cluttered. Take your time during disassembly and sketch the relationship of the various parts for ease of reassembly. Also, refer to the accompanying illustrations.

2   Remove the coolant hoses from the choke and throttle valve assemblies.

3   Remove the choke cover by grinding or filing off the heads of the lock screws.

4   Remove the throttle opener link E-clip, followed by the two retaining screws. Lift the opener assembly off.

5   Disconnect the ground wire, remove the retaining screw and remove the fuel cut-off solenoid.

6   Remove the throttle return spring and damper springs.

7   Remove the choke unloader link and clips, followed by the vacuum chamber (two screws).

8   Disconnect the accelerator rod link from the throttle lever.

9   Remove the vacuum hose connector and hoses from the air horn (two screws).

10   Remove the six retaining screws and detach the air horn from the carburetor body.

11   Slide the retaining pin out and remove the float and needle assembly. Discard the air horn gasket.

12   Unscrew and remove the needle seat and screen assembly, taking care not to lose the shim located under the seat.

13   Remove the venturis and retainers, discarding the O-rings. Mark the primary and secondary venturis so they can be reinstalled in the same positions. The primary venturis are the larger of the two.

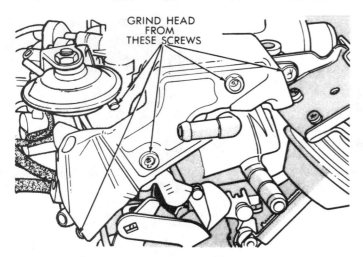

Fig. 4.9 Carburetor choke cover retaining screw locations
(2.6L engine) (Sec 16)

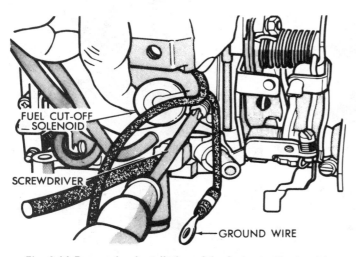

Fig. 4.11 Removal or installation of the fuel cut-off solenoid
(2.6L engine) (Secs 16 and 20)

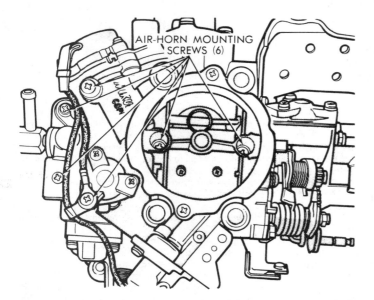

Fig. 4.13 Air horn mounting screws (2.6L engine) (Secs 16 and 20)

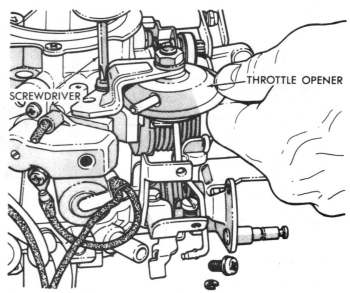

Fig. 4.10 Removal or installation of the throttle opener assembly
(2.6L engine) (Secs 16 and 20)

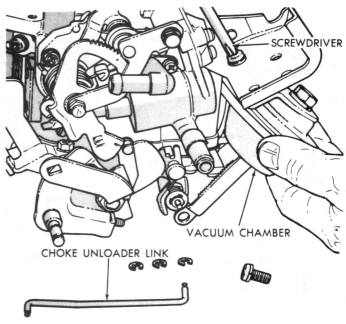

Fig. 4.12 Removing or installing the choke link and vacuum
chamber (2.6L engine) (Secs 16 and 20)

14 Unscrew the primary and secondary jets with a suitable screwdriver. Be sure to note the numbers on the jets for ease of reassembly.

15 Remove the retaining screws and the primary and secondary jet pedestals, discarding the gaskets.

16 Remove the bowl vent valve solenoid and spring (three screws), followed by the remaining screw and the bowl vent assembly. Discard the O-ring.

17 Remove the Coasting Air Valve (CAV) assembly (three screws).

18 Remove the enrichment valve assembly and jet.

19 Remove the Air Switching Valve (ASV) assembly.

20 Remove the primary pilot screw, lock and jet set.

21 Remove the secondary pilot screw, lock and jet set.

22 Remove the primary and secondary air bleed jets from the top of the air horn. Be sure to note their sizes as they must be reinstalled in the same locations.

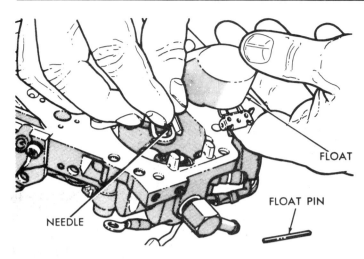

Fig. 4.14 Float and needle assembly removal or installation (2.6L engine) (Secs 16 and 20)

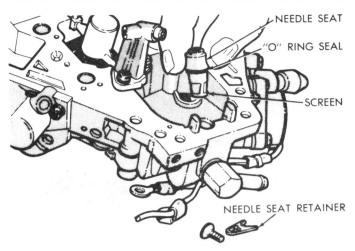

Fig. 4.15 Needle and seat assembly removal or installation (2.6L engine) (Secs 16 and 20)

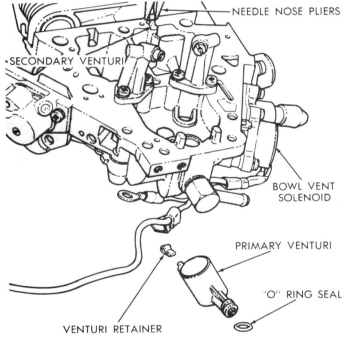

Fig. 4.16 Venturi removal or installation (2.6L engine) (Secs 16 and 20)

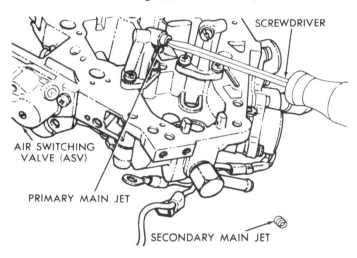

Fig. 4.17 Primary and secondary main jet removal or installation (2.6L engine) (Secs 16 and 20)

23 Turn the carburetor body over carefully and catch the check ball, weight and hex nut.
24 Remove the accelerator pump assembly.
25 Remove the Jet Air Control Valve (JACV) assembly.
26 Remove the E-clip and carefully slide the sub EGR valve pin from the lever, taking care not to lose the steel ball and spring which maintain tension on the lever. Remove the sub EGR valve assembly.

17 Carburetor (2.2L engine) – cleaning and inspection

1 After disassembly, clean the carburetor components in a suitable commercial solvent. Make sure you keep track of primary and secondary main metering jet and bleed assemblies as they must be reinstalled in their original locations.
2 The choke, vacuum diaphragms, O-rings, feedback solenoid, floats and seals should not be placed in the solvent as they could be damaged.

3 Clean the external surfaces of the carburetor with a soft brush and wash all of the parts thoroughly in the solvent. If the instructions on the solvent or cleaner recommend the use of water for rinsing, hot water will produce the best results. After rinsing, all traces of water must be blown from the passages using compressed air. *Never clean jets with a wire, drill bit or other objects. The orifices may be enlarged, making the mixture too rich for proper performance.*
4 When checking parts removed from the carburetor, it is often difficult to be sure if they are serviceable. It is therefore recommended that new parts be installed, if available, when the carburetor is disassembled. The required parts should be included in the rebuild kit.
5 After the parts have been cleaned and dried, check the throttle shaft for excessive wear. Inspect the idle mixture screw for a ridge or groove on the tapered portion.
6 Check the jets for damage or clogging. Replace them if damage is evident.
7 Check for freeness of movement of the choke mechanism in the air horn. It should move freely for proper operation.
8 Replace any worn or damaged components with new ones.

18 Carburetor (2.6L engine) – cleaning and inspection

1 Once the carburetor has been completely disassembled, clean the parts in a suitable commercial solvent.
2 The choke, vacuum diaphragms, O-rings, electric solenoids, floats

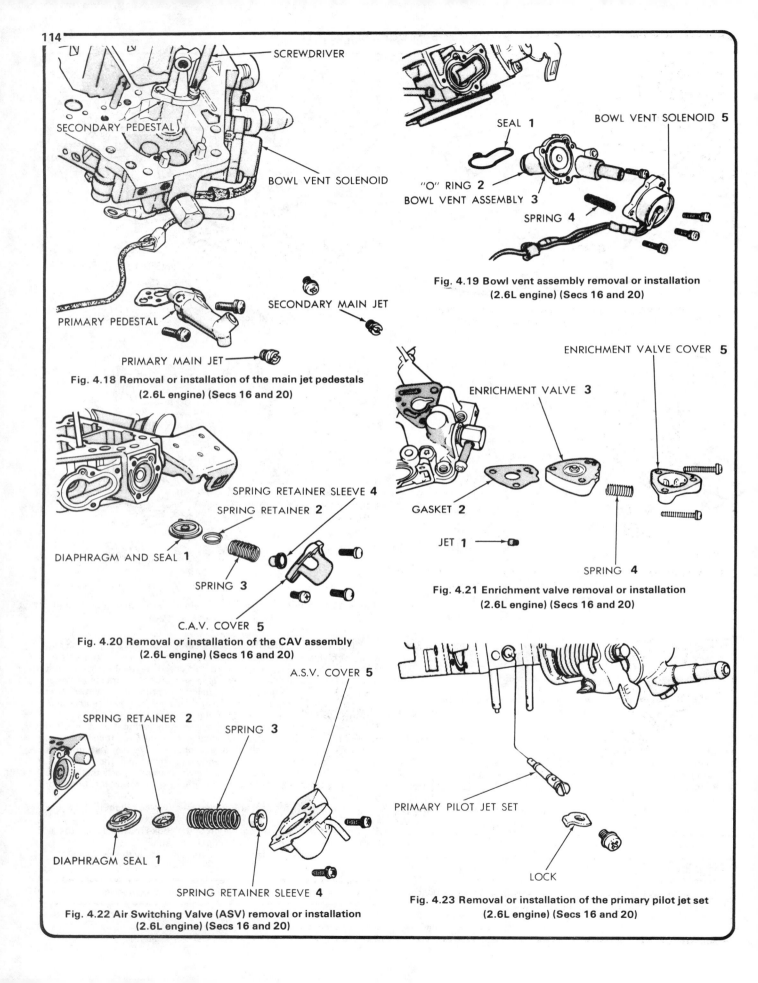

SCREWDRIVER

SECONDARY PEDESTAL

BOWL VENT SOLENOID

SEAL **1**

BOWL VENT SOLENOID **5**

"O" RING **2**

BOWL VENT ASSEMBLY **3**

SPRING **4**

Fig. 4.19 Bowl vent assembly removal or installation
(2.6L engine) (Secs 16 and 20)

PRIMARY PEDESTAL

SECONDARY MAIN JET

PRIMARY MAIN JET

Fig. 4.18 Removal or installation of the main jet pedestals
(2.6L engine) (Secs 16 and 20)

ENRICHMENT VALVE COVER **5**

ENRICHMENT VALVE **3**

GASKET **2**

JET **1**

SPRING **4**

Fig. 4.21 Enrichment valve removal or installation
(2.6L engine) (Secs 16 and 20)

SPRING RETAINER SLEEVE **4**

SPRING RETAINER **2**

SPRING **3**

DIAPHRAGM AND SEAL **1**

C.A.V. COVER **5**

Fig. 4.20 Removal or installation of the CAV assembly
(2.6L engine) (Secs 16 and 20)

A.S.V. COVER **5**

SPRING RETAINER **2**

SPRING **3**

DIAPHRAGM SEAL **1**

SPRING RETAINER SLEEVE **4**

PRIMARY PILOT JET SET

LOCK

Fig. 4.23 Removal or installation of the primary pilot jet set
(2.6L engine) (Secs 16 and 20)

Fig. 4.22 Air Switching Valve (ASV) removal or installation
(2.6L engine) (Secs 16 and 20)

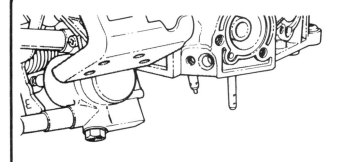

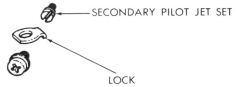

SECONDARY PILOT JET SET

LOCK

Fig. 4.24 Secondary jet set removal or installation (2.6L engine) (Secs 16 and 20)

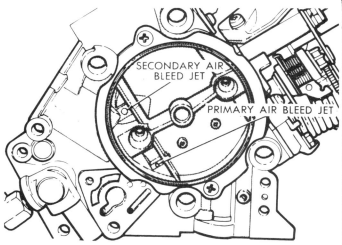

SECONDARY AIR BLEED JET

PRIMARY AIR BLEED JET

Fig. 4.25 Removal or installation of the air bleed jets (2.6L engine) (Secs 16 and 20)

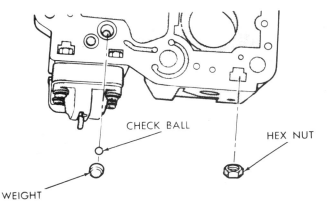

CHECK BALL

HEX NUT

WEIGHT

Fig. 4.26 Removal or installation of the weight, check ball and hex nut (2.6L engine) (Secs 16 and 20)

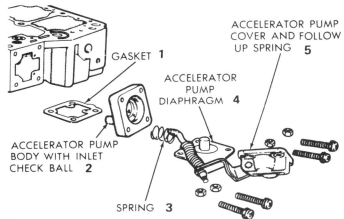

GASKET **1**

ACCELERATOR PUMP COVER AND FOLLOW UP SPRING **5**

ACCELERATOR PUMP DIAPHRAGM **4**

ACCELERATOR PUMP BODY WITH INLET CHECK BALL **2**

SPRING **3**

Fig. 4.27 Accelerator pump assembly removal or installation (2.6L engine) (Secs 16 and 20)

4

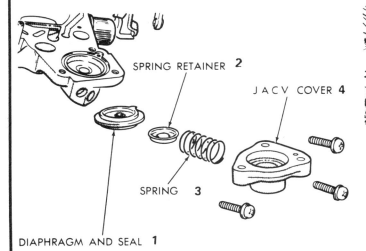

SPRING RETAINER **2**

JACV COVER **4**

SPRING **3**

DIAPHRAGM AND SEAL **1**

Fig. 4.28 Jet Air Control Valve (JACV) removal or installation (2.6L engine) (Secs 16 and 20)

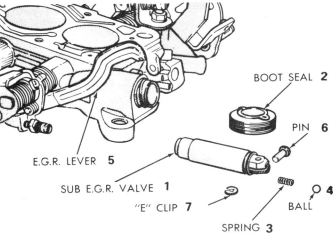

BOOT SEAL **2**

PIN **6**

E.G.R. LEVER **5**

SUB E.G.R. VALVE **1**

"E" CLIP **7**

SPRING **3**

BALL **4**

Fig. 4.29 Sub EGR valve assembly removal or installation (2.6L engine) (Secs 16 and 20)

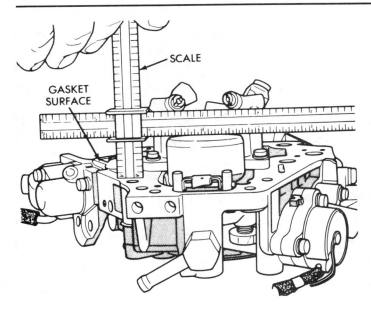

Fig. 4.30 Checking dry float level (2.6L engine) (Sec 20)

and seals should not be placed in the solvent as they could be damaged.

3 Clean the external surfaces of the carburetor with a soft brush and wash all of the parts thoroughly in the solvent. If the instructions on the solvent or cleaner recommend the use of water for rinsing, hot water will produce the best results. After rinsing, all traces of water must be blown from the passages using compressed air. *Never clean jets with a wire, drill bit or other objects. The orifices may be enlarged, making the mixture too rich for proper performance.*

4 When checking parts removed from the carburetor, it is often difficult to be sure if they are serviceable. It is therefore recommended that new parts be installed, if available, when the carburetor is disassembled. The required parts should be included in the carburetor rebuild kit.

5 After the parts have been cleaned and dried, check the throttle valve shaft for proper operation. If sticking or binding occurs, clean the shafts with solvent and lubricate them with engine oil.

6 Check the jets for damage or clogging. Replace them if damage is evident.

7 Inspect the idle mixture screw. The tapered portion of the screw must be straight and smooth. If the tapered portion is grooved or ridged, replace the screw with a new one.

8 Check the strainer screen for clogging and damage.

9 Check the vacuum chamber. Push the chamber rod in, seal off the nipple and release the rod. If the rod does not return, the vacuum chamber is most likely in good condition. If the rod returns when released the diaphragm is defective. The vacuum chamber should be replaced with a new one if this condition exists.

10 To check the fuel cut-off solenoid, connect a jumper lead to the positive (+) terminal of a 12 volt battery and the wire lead of the solenoid. Connect a second jumper lead to the negative (-) terminal of the battery and the solenoid ground wire. The needle should move in (toward the solenoid) when the battery is connected and out when the battery is disconnected. If it does, the fuel cut-off solenoid is good.

19 Carburetor (2.2L engine) – reassembly

1 Press down on the choke lever, insert the choke diaphragm and rotate it into position (photo).

2 Position the spring and place the cover in place. Install the two top screws snugly, followed by the breakaway screw in the bottom hole (photo).

3 Tighten the breakaway screw until the head breaks off. Tighten the top screws evenly and securely.

4 Install the accelerator pump, spring (small end first), cover and screws (photo).

5 Fill the float bowl with fuel to a depth of one inch and drop the check ball into the accelerator pump discharge passage (photo).

6 Use a small brass dowel to hold the check ball in place and push the throttle lever to make sure there is resistance felt and consequently no leakage. If there is leakage, drain the fuel and stake the ball in place with one or two taps of the dowel. Remove the old ball and install the new one from the rebuild kit. Install the weight ball and repeat the test.

7 Install the accelerator pump discharge nozzle assembly.

8 Install the primary main well tube and high speed bleed.

9 Install the secondary main well tube and high speed bleed.

10 Install the primary main metering jets.

11 Install the secondary main metering jets.

12 Install the fuel inlet needle and seat assembly.

13 Hook the new needle onto the float tang and lower the assembly into place. Install the float retaining pin.

14 Measure the dry float level (photo).

15 Invert the air horn and measure the float drop (photo).

16 Adjust the dry float level by carefully bending the inner adjustment tang until the level is within the specified range (photo).

17 Bend the outer adjustment tang to bring the float drop within the specified range (photo).

18 Install the choke seal and link and squeeze the link retainer bushing into place (photo).

19 Position the gasket, engage the choke link and lower the air horn assembly into place (photo).

20 Install the retaining screws and tighten them securely (photo).

21 Install the wide open throttle cutout switch with the two screws and one bolt snug.

22 Adjust the solenoid switch by loosening the retaining bolt and using a screwdriver to rotate the switch until a click is felt (photo).

23 Tighten the bolt and screws and install the anti-rattle spring.

24 Install the idle speed solenoid.

25 Lubricate the feedback solenoid tip lightly with petroleum jelly and install a new O-ring (photo).

26 Install a new gasket and insert the solenoid into position (photo).

27 Install the solenoid screws and tighten them securely and evenly.

28 Wrap a piece of teflon tape around the threads and install the fuel inlet.

29 Install the choke inner housing lever bushing, followed by the spacer and outer housing with the spring end loop over the lever (photos).

30 Install the choke housing rivets with a suitable tool. The shorter rivet goes in the bottom hole.

31 Install the air cleaner gasket (photo).

19.1 Rotate the choke diaphragm in a clockwise direction when installing it

19.2 Install the breakaway screw in the bottom hole

19.4 Hold the screws in place when installing the accelerator pump cover

19.5 Accelerator pump discharge passage

19.14 Measuring the distance between the bottom of the float and the air horn to determine dry float level

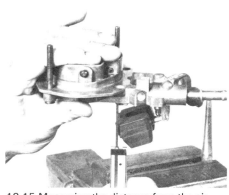
19.15 Measuring the distance from the air horn surface to the top of the float to determine float drop

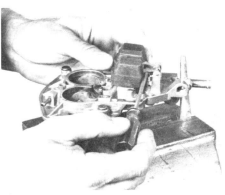
19.16 Bend the tang carefully up or down to adjust the dry float level

19.17 Be sure to support the pivot when bending the float drop adjusting tang

19.18 Installing the choke link retainer bushing

19.19 Be careful not to bend the float tangs when lowering the air horn

19.20 Tighten the screws evenly in a criss-cross pattern

19.22 Adjusting the solenoid switch

19.25 Place the O-ring in the groove and work it over the end of the solenoid

4

19.26 Rock the solenoid gently from side-to-side to seat the O-ring

19.29a Installing the choke lever bushing

19.29b Rotate the housing approximately $\frac{1}{8}$ turn clockwise to align the rivet holes

19.31 Slide the air cleaner gasket over the studs and seat it securely on the carburetor

20 Carburetor (2.6L engine) – reassembly

1   Install the sub EGR valve components in the numerical order shown in the accompanying illustration, attach the assembly to the carburetor body and secure it with the E-clip (Fig. 4.9).

2   Attach the JACV components to the throttle body in the numerical order shown in Fig. 4.28.

3   Install the accelerator pump assembly components in the numerical order shown in Fig. 4.27.

4   Install the primary and secondary air jet bleeds in the air horn, noting that the secondary bleed has the highest number (Fig. 4.25).

5   Install a new O-ring onto the secondary pilot jet set, insert the assembly and install the retaining screw.

6   Install a new O-ring onto the primary pilot jet set and install the assembly.

7   Attach the ASV components to the carburetor in the numerical order shown in Fig. 4.22.

8   Install the jet followed by the rest of the enrichment valve components in the numerical order shown in Fig. 4.21.

9   Assemble the CAV components (Fig. 4.20), attach the assembly to the air horn and retain it with the three mounting screws.

10   Assemble the bowl vent valve in the numerical order shown in Fig. 4.19, install the valve and solenoid and install the mounting screws.

11   Using new gaskets, install the primary and secondary pedestals and mounting screws, followed by the main primary and secondary jets. Remember that the secondary jet has the largest number.

12   Attach new O-rings to the primary and secondary venturis and install the venturis and retainers.

13   Install a new O-ring and screen on the needle seat and install the shim into the air horn. Install the needle seat retainer and screw and tighten it securely.

14   Place the needle and float assembly in position and retain it to the air horn with the float pin.

15   Invert the air horn and measure the distance from the gasket surface (gasket removed) to the bottom surface of the float to determine the dry float level. Compare this to the Specifications.

16   If the dry float level is more or less than it was during disassembly, remove the float, unscrew the inlet needle seat and add or remove shims (as necessary) to change the float height. Repeat the procedure as required until the distance is as specified.

17   Using a new gasket, install the mixing body to the throttle body and install the nut, check ball and weight.

18   Install the air horn, using a new gasket, to the mixing body and secure it with the six mounting screws.

19   Install the two vacuum hoses and the wiring connector to the throttle body and engage the accelerator rod link to the throttle lever.

20 Place the vacuum chamber in position on the bracket, install the retaining screws and connect the vacuum hose and link to the secondary throttle lever.Connect the choke unloader link and retain it with the E-clips.

21 Install a new O-ring on the fuel cut-off solenoid, place the solenoid onto the mixing body and install the retaining screw. Place the ground wire in position and retain it with the screw.

22 Install the throttle positioner to the air horn and connect the link with the E-clip.

23 Install the choke cover, using the special break-away screws.

24 Install the coolant hose to the carburetor and retain it with the clamps.

21 Carburetor (2.2L engine) – idle speed adjustment

Note: *Refer to Section 6 for air conditioning equipped vehicle idle speed adjustment.*

1 Start the engine and run it until normal operating temperature is reached.

2 Check the ignition timing and adjust as necessary (Chapter 1), then shut off the engine.

3 Disconnect and plug the vacuum hose at the EGR valve.

4 Unplug the fan wire connector and install a jumper wire so the fan will run continuously.

5 Remove the PCV valve from the vent module so the valve will draw air from the engine compartment. Plug the control hose at the module.

6 Leave the air cleaner in place and connect a tachometer. On 1983 models, ground the carburetor switch with a jumper wire.

7 Start the engine.

8 Check the idle speed reading on the tachometer and compare it to the Emissions Control Information label. Turn the idle speed adjusting screw as necessary to achieve the specified idle speed.

9 Shut off the engine and remove the tachometer.

10 Remove the carburetor switch jumper wire, plug in the fan connector, install the PCV valve and reinstall any vacuum hoses which were disconnected.

red and tan wires at the carburetor. On 1983 models, unplug the oxygen sensor test connector located at the left shock tower.

3 Start the engine, open the throttle slightly and set the fast idle screw on the slowest speed step of the fast idle cam.

4 With the choke valve fully open, adjust the fast idle speed to the specification on the Emissions Control Information label by turning the adjustment screw.

5 Return the engine to idle and place the fast idle screw onto the slowest speed step of the fast idle cam to verify the fast idle speed, adjusting as necessary.

6 Turn off the engine, remove the tachometer and reconnect all components removed for the adjustment procedure.

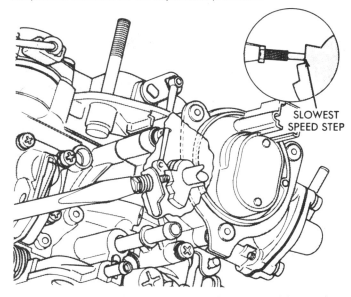

Fig. 4.32 Fast idle speed adjustment (2.2L engine) (Sec 22)

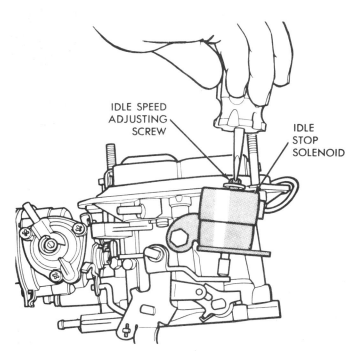

Fig. 4.31 Adjusting idle speed (2.2L engine) (Sec 21)

22 Carburetor (2.2L engine) – fast idle adjustment

1 Perform Steps 1 through 6 in Section 21.

2 On 1981 and 1982 models, unplug the wiring connector with the

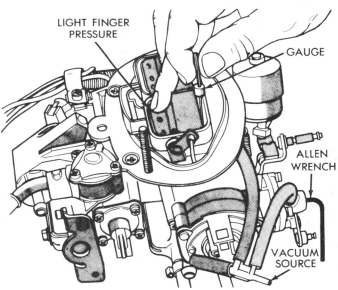

Fig. 4.33 Choke vacuum kick adjustment (2.2L engine) (Sec 23)

23 Carburetor (2.2L engine) – choke vacuum kick adjustment

1 Remove the air cleaner.

2 Open the throttle, close the choke and then the throttle so the fast idle system is trapped at the closed choke position.

3 Disconnect the carburetor vacuum hose, connect a vacuum pump and apply 15 inches of vacuum.

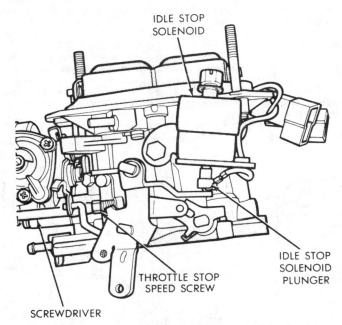

Fig. 4.34 Anti-diesel adjustment (2.2L engine) (Sec 24)

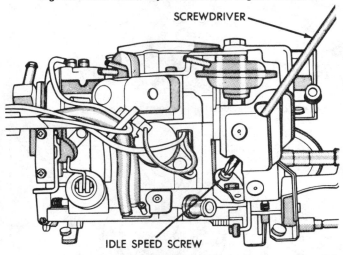

Fig. 4.35 2.6L engine carburetor idle speed adjustment (Sec 25)

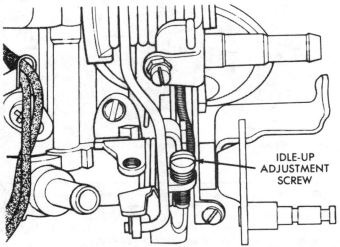

Fig. 4.36 Air conditioner idle-up adjustment screw (2.6L engine) (Sec 25)

4   Push the choke lightly closed so the plates are at their smallest opening. The choke system internal spring will now be compressed.
5   Insert a suitable sized drill bit or gauge between the plate and the air horn wall at the primary throttle end of the carburetor. Check the clearance against the Specifications and adjust as necessary using an Allen wrench inserted into the diaphragm.
6   After adjustment, replace the vacuum hose and the air cleaner assembly.

24 Carburetor (2.2L engine) – anti-diesel adjustment

1   Warm up the engine to operating temperature, then shut it off.
2   Connect a tachometer.
3   With the transaxle in Neutral, the parking brake set securely, the carburetor idle stop switch grounded with a jumper wire, the idle stop carburetor switch unplugged and the headlights off, start the engine.
4   Adjust the throttle stop screw to achieve an idle speed of 700 rpm.
5   Shut off the engine, remove the tachometer, remove the jumper wire and connect the carburetor idle stop switch.

25 Carburetor (2.6L engine) — idle speed adjustment

1   With the transaxle in Neutral, the parking brake set, the lights and accessories off and the cooling fan disconnected, connect a tachometer to the engine. Start the engine and allow it to warm up to normal operating temperature so the choke is fully open.
2   Return the engine to curb idle and check the timing with a timing light to make sure it is within the Specifications (Chapter 1).
3   After waiting one minute with the curb idle stabilized, check the rpm indicated on the tachometer and make sure this is the same as specified on the Emissions Control Information label.
4   If it is not, turn the idle speed adjusting screw to bring the rpm to the proper curb idle setting.
5   On air conditioned models, turn on the air conditioner and, with the compressor running, adjust the idle speed to the specified rpm by turning the idle-up adjustment screw (Fig. 4.36).
6   Shut off the engine, reconnect the cooling fan and remove the tachometer.

26 Fuel tank – removal and installation

Caution: *This operation is potentially hazardous. Follow all precautions listed in 'Safety first' near the front of this manual.*

Removal
1   Disconnect the negative battery cable from the battery.
2   Raise the rear of the vehicle and support it securely.
3   Remove the fuel tank filler cap.
4   Disconnect the fuel tank line located adjacent to the right front shock tower in the engine compartment, connect a hose and drain or siphon the tank into a suitable container. **Caution:** *Do not use your mouth to start the siphoning action.*
5   Remove the screws retaining the filler tube to the body.
6   Disconnect all wires and hoses from the tank (label them first to avoid problems during installation).
7   Remove the mounting strap retaining nuts, lower the tank slightly and remove the filler tube.
8   Lower the tank further and support it while disconnecting the rollover/vapor separator valve hose.
9   Remove the tank and insulator pad.

Installation
10 To install, raise the tank into position with a jack, connect the rollover/vapor separator valve hose and place the insulator pad on the top. Connect the filler tube.
11 Raise the tank with the jack, connect the retaining strap and install the retaining nut, tightening them securely.
12 Connect the fuel lines and wiring and install the filler tube retaining screws.
13 Fill the fuel tank, install the cap, connect the negative battery cable and check for leaks.

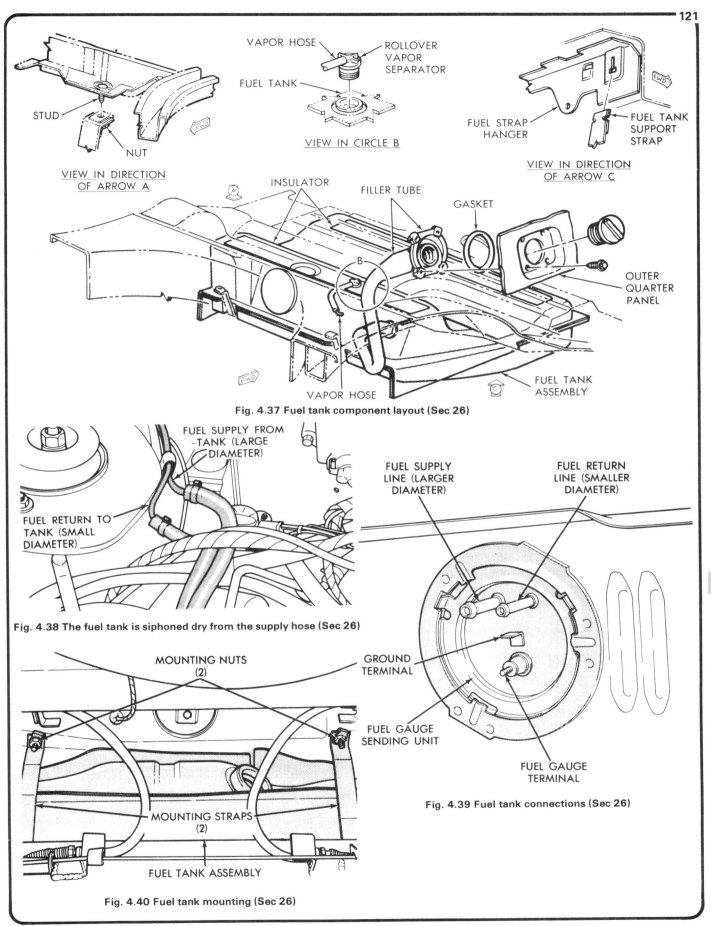

STUD

NUT

VIEW IN DIRECTION
OF ARROW A

VAPOR HOSE

ROLLOVER
VAPOR
SEPARATOR

FUEL TANK

VIEW IN CIRCLE B

FUEL STRAP
HANGER

FUEL TANK
SUPPORT
STRAP

VIEW IN DIRECTION
OF ARROW C

INSULATOR

FILLER TUBE

GASKET

OUTER
QUARTER
PANEL

VAPOR HOSE

FUEL TANK
ASSEMBLY

Fig. 4.37 Fuel tank component layout (Sec 26)

FUEL SUPPLY FROM
TANK (LARGE
DIAMETER)

FUEL RETURN TO
TANK (SMALL
DIAMETER)

Fig. 4.38 The fuel tank is siphoned dry from the supply hose (Sec 26)

FUEL SUPPLY
LINE (LARGER
DIAMETER)

FUEL RETURN
LINE (SMALLER
DIAMETER)

GROUND
TERMINAL

FUEL GAUGE
SENDING UNIT

FUEL GAUGE
TERMINAL

Fig. 4.39 Fuel tank connections (Sec 26)

4

MOUNTING NUTS
(2)

MOUNTING STRAPS
(2)

FUEL TANK ASSEMBLY

Fig. 4.40 Fuel tank mounting (Sec 26)

27 Exhaust system – removal and installation

1   The exhaust system should be inspected periodically for leaks, cracks and damaged or worn components (Chapter 1).

2   Allow the exhaust system to cool for at least one hour prior to inspecting or beginning work on it.

3   Raise the vehicle and support it securely on jackstands.

4   Exhaust system components can be removed by removing the heat shields, unbolting and/or disengaging them from the hangers and removing them from the vehicle. Pipes on either side of the muffler must be removed by cutting with a hacksaw. Install the new muffler using U-bolts. If parts are rusted together, apply a rust dissolving fluid (available in automotive supply stores) and allow it to penetrate prior to attempting removal.

5   After replacing any part of the exhaust system, check carefully for leaks before driving the vehicle.

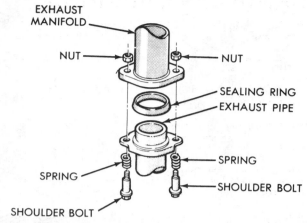

Fig. 4.41 Exhaust manifold-to-front pipe connection (Sec 27)

Chapter 5 Engine electrical systems

Refer to Chapter 13 for specifications and information applicable to later models

Contents

Specifications

Ignition system

Spark plugs
   Type .... Champion RN12YC
      Motorcraft AGR42
      Autolite 65PR

   Gap
      2.2L engine .... 0.035 in (0.9 mm)
      2.6L engine .... 0.040 in (1.0 mm)
Ignition timing .... Refer to Emission Control Information label
Firing order 1-3-4-2
Distributor
   Direction of rotation .... Clockwise
   Shaft side play (maximum)
      2.2L engine .... 0.004 in (0.1 mm)
      2.6L engine .... 0.002 in (0.05 mm)
Ignition coil resistance @ 70° to 80°F (21° to 27°C)
   Primary resistance
      2.2L engine, Echlin or Essex .... 1.41 to 1.62 ohms
      2.2L engine, Prestolite .... 1.60 to 1.74 ohms
      2.6L engine .... 0.7 to 0.85 ohms
   Secondary resistance
      2.2L engine, Echlin or Essex .... 9 K to 12.2 K ohms
      2.2L engine, Prestolite .... 9.4 to 11.4 K ohms
      2.6L engine .... 9 to 11 K ohms
Coil wire resistance
   2.2L engine .... Less than 15 K ohms
   2.6L engine .... Less than 22 K ohms
Spark plug wire resistance
   2.2L engine .... Less than 40 K ohms
   2.6L engine .... Less than 22 K ohms

Charging system

Alternator output
   2.2L engine
      Yellow tag .... 60 amps
      Brown tag .... 78 amps
   2.6L engine .... 75 amps
Brush length service limit
   2.2L engine .... 0.1969 in (5 mm)
   2.6L engine .... 0.709 in (18 mm)
2.6L engine alternator-to-timing case clearance .... 0.008 in (0.2 mm)

Torque specifications

	Ft-lb	Nm
2.2L alternator locking screw	30	41
2.2L alternator pivot bolt nut	40	54
2.6L alternator support bolt nut	15 to 18	20 to 24
2.2L alternator brush screw	1 to 1.5	2 to 4
Spark plugs		
2.2L engine	26	35
2.6L engine	18	25

5

Fig. 5.1 Engine electrical system component layout (2.2L engine) (Secs 1 through 25)

1 Battery
2 Spark plug locations
3 Coil
4 Distributor
5 Starter location (under engine)
6 Voltage regulator location (under cover)
7 Spark Control Computer

1 General information

The engine electrical system is made up of the battery, charging system, starter and ignition system.

The charging system consists of the alternator, integral voltage regulator and battery. The starting system is operated by the battery's electrical power through the starter relay which activates the starter motor. The ignition system includes the distributor, Spark Control Computer (SCC) on 2.2L engines, ignition coil, spark plugs and associated wires.

The electrical system is a 12-volt, negative ground type.

Caution: *Whenever the system is to be worked on, the negative battery cable should be disconnected from the battery.*

Information on the routine maintenance of the ignition, starting and charging systems and battery can be found in Chapter 1.

2 Battery – removal and installation

Caution: *Hydrogen gas is produced by the battery and open flames or lighted cigarettes should be kept away from the battery at all times. Battery acid is very corrosive. Avoid contact with skin or eyes.*

1 The battery is located at the left front corner of the engine compartment and is held in place by a clamp at its base.

2 Always disconnect the negative (-) battery cable first, followed by the positive (+) cable.

3 After the cables are disconnected, remove the nut and retaining clamp.

4 Remove the battery. **Note**: *When lifting the battery from the engine compartment, be careful not to twist the case as this could cause acid to spurt out of the filler openings.*

5 Installation is the reverse of removal. Be careful not to overtighten the retaining nut as this could damage the battery case.

3 Alternator – general information

The alternator is operated by a drivebelt turned by the crankshaft pulley. The rotor turns inside the stator to produce an alternating current, which is then converted to direct current by diodes. The current is adjusted to battery charging needs by an electronic voltage regulator which is incorporated into the alternator.

4 Alternator – maintenance

1 The alternator requires very little maintenance because the only components subject to wear are the brushes and bearings. The bearings are sealed for life. The brushes should be inspected for wear after about 75 000 miles (120 000 km) and the length compared to the Specifications.

2 Regular maintenance consists of cleaning to remove grease and dirt, checking the electrical connections for tightness and adjusting the drivebelt for proper tension.

5 Alternator – special precautions

Whenever the electrical system is being worked on or a booster battery is used to start the engine, certain precautions must be observed to avoid damaging the alternator. They are as follows;

a) Make sure that the battery cables are never reversed as this will damage the alternator diodes. The negative (-) cable must always be grounded.

b) The output (B) cable must never be grounded; it should always be connected to the positive battery terminal.

c) Never use a high voltage tester on the alternator.

d) Do not operate the engine with the voltage regulator plug disconnected.

e) When the alternator is to be removed or its wiring disconnected, always disconnect the battery negative cable first.

f) The alternator must never be operated with the battery-to-alternator cable disconnected.

g) Disconnect the battery cables before charging the battery with an external charger.

h) If a booster charger or battery is to be used, always double check that the battery cables are not reversed.

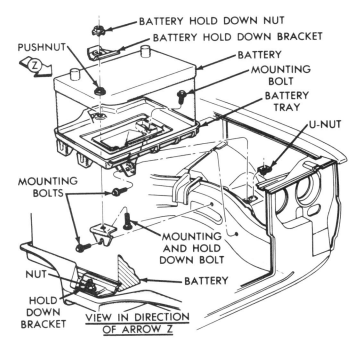

Fig. 5.2 Battery and tray installation (Sec 2)

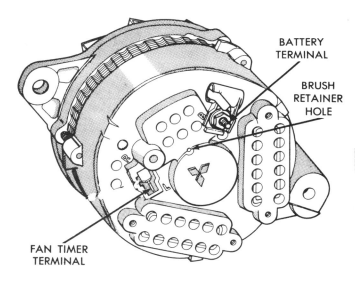

Fig. 5.3 2.6L engine alternator terminals (Secs 5 through 9)

6 Alternator – troubleshooting and repair

1 Due to the special training and equipment necessary to test or service the alternator, it is recommended that the vehicle be taken to a dealer or other repair shop with the proper equipment if a problem is suspected.

2 The most obvious sign of a problem is the alternator warning lamp on the instrument panel lighting, particularly at low speeds. This indicates that the alternator is not charging. Other symptoms are a low battery charge, evidenced by dim headlights and the starter motor turning the engine over slowly.

3 The first check should always be of the drivebelt tension (Chapter

1) followed by making sure that all electrical connections are secure and free of dirt and corrosion.

4   If the drivebelt tension, electrical connections and battery conditions are good, an internal fault in the alternator or internal voltage regulator is indicated.

5   Due to the complexity of this model and special tools and techniques required to work on the alternator, repair should be left to a properly-equipped shop. If the alternator has considerable miles on it, a good alternative is to replace it with a rebuilt unit.

7   Alternator (2.2L engine) – removal and installation

1   With the ignition switch in the Off position, disconnect the negative battery cable from the battery.
2   Disconnect the alternator wiring harness and ground strap.
3   Loosen the adjusting and locking screws and remove the drivebelt.
4   Remove the adjusting screw assembly.
5   Remove the pivot bolt and nut and separate the alternator from the engine.
6   To install, place the alternator in position and install the pivot bolt and nut finger tight.
7   Install the drivebelt.
8   Install the locking screw and adjuster assembly and adjust the drivebelt tension. Tighten the locking screw to the specified torque.
9   Tighten the pivot bolt and nut to the specified torque.

8   Alternator (2.6L engine) – removal and installation

1   With the ignition switch in the Off position, disconnect the negative battery cable from the battery.
2   Disconnect the wiring harness and the ground strap.
3   Remove the adjusting strap mounting bolt and alternator-to-engine block support bolt nut. Remove the drivebelt(s).
4   Withdraw the support bolt and remove the alternator.
5   To install, place the alternator in position and insert the support bolt from the front of the bracket.
6   Install the drivebelt(s) and push the alternator forward. Measure the clearance between the alternator leg and the timing chain case and compare it to the Specifications. If the measurement is too large, install spacers.
7   Adjust the drivebelt tension and tighten the support bolt nut and the brace bolt.
8   Connect the wiring harness and ground strap to the alternator.
9   Connect the negative battery cable.

9   Alternator brushes (2.2L engine) – removal, inspection and installation

1   Remove the alternator.
2   The brushes are mounted in plastic holders which locate the brushes in the proper position.
3   Disconnect the wires from the brushes.
4   Remove the brush screws and separate the brush assemblies from the alternator end shield.
5   Measure the distance the brushes extend from the holders and compare it to the Specifications. If the brushes are worn beyond the specified limit or are oil soaked or damaged, replace them with new ones.
6   Make sure that the brushes move smoothly in their holders with no binding.
7   Insert the brush assemblies into the alternator end shield and install the screws, tightening them securely.
8   Install the alternator.

10   Alternator brushes (2.6L engines) – removal, inspection and installation

1   Remove the alternator from the vehicle.
2   Mount the alternator in a vise, using blocks of wood to protect it.
3   Remove the through-bolts retaining the drive end shield to the stator and rectifier end shield assembly.

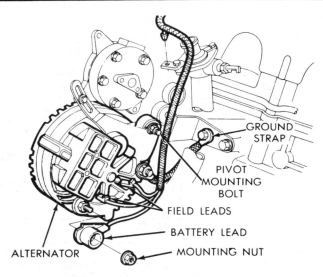

Fig. 5.4 2.2L engine alternator leads (Secs 6 through 8)

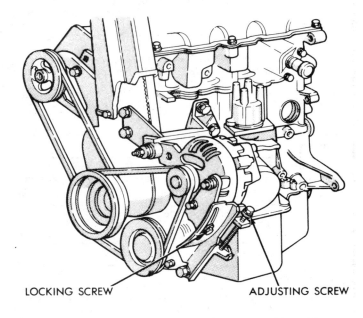

Fig. 5.5 Alternator installation (2.2L engine) (Sec 7)

4   Use a screwdriver or similar tool to separate the two halves of the alternator assembly and remove the rectifier end.
5   Remove the brushes and springs from the rectifier end shield assembly. Measure the length of the brushes. If they are shorter than specified, replace them with new ones.
6   Push the brushes into the brush holder and insert a piece of wire to hold them in place.
7   Carefully slide the drive end shield and the rotor assembly into the rectifier end assembly. Line up the bolt holes and install the three through-bolts, tightening them evenly and securely.
8   Remove the wire retaining the brushes.
9   Install the alternator.

11   Voltage regulator – general information

The voltage regulator governs the charging system voltage by limiting the alternator output voltage. The regulator is a sealed unit and is not adjustable.

If the ammeter fails to register a charge rate or the red warning

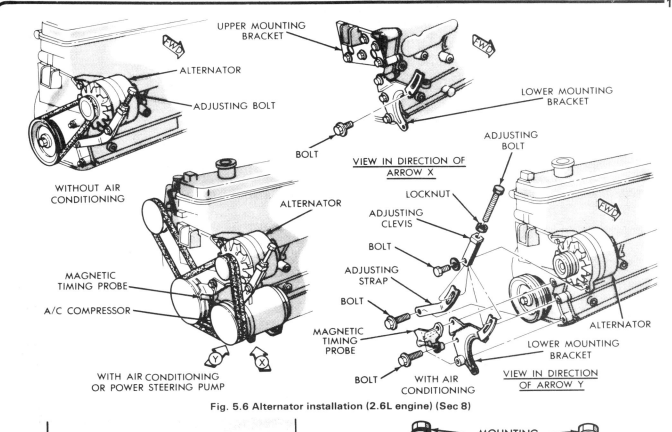

UPPER MOUNTING BRACKET

ALTERNATOR

ADJUSTING BOLT

LOWER MOUNTING BRACKET

BOLT

WITHOUT AIR CONDITIONING

ALTERNATOR

VIEW IN DIRECTION OF ARROW X

ADJUSTING BOLT

LOCKNUT

ADJUSTING CLEVIS

BOLT

ADJUSTING STRAP

BOLT

MAGNETIC TIMING PROBE

BOLT

MAGNETIC TIMING PROBE

A/C COMPRESSOR

WITH AIR CONDITIONING OR POWER STEERING PUMP

WITH AIR CONDITIONING

ALTERNATOR

LOWER MOUNTING BRACKET

VIEW IN DIRECTION OF ARROW Y

Fig. 5.6 Alternator installation (2.6L engine) (Sec 8)

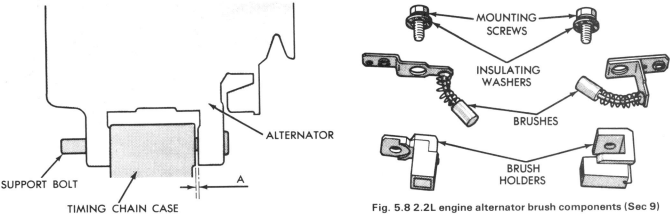

Fig. 5.8 2.2L engine alternator brush components (Sec 9)

MOUNTING SCREWS

INSULATING WASHERS

BRUSHES

BRUSH HOLDERS

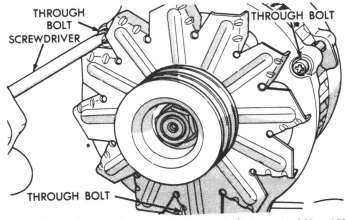

ALTERNATOR

SUPPORT BOLT

TIMING CHAIN CASE

A

Fig. 5.7 Measuring the 2.6L engine alternator-to-timing case clearance (A) (Sec 8)

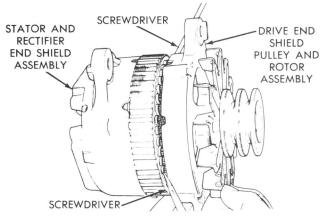

THROUGH BOLT SCREWDRIVER

THROUGH BOLT

THROUGH BOLT

Fig. 5.9 Removing the alternator through-bolt (2.6L engine) (Sec 10)

STATOR AND RECTIFIER END SHIELD ASSEMBLY

SCREWDRIVER

DRIVE END SHIELD PULLEY AND ROTOR ASSEMBLY

SCREWDRIVER

Fig. 5.10 Separating the alternator components (2.6L engine) (Sec 10)

5

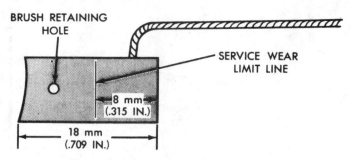

Fig. 5.11 2.6L engine alternator brush wear limits (Sec 10)

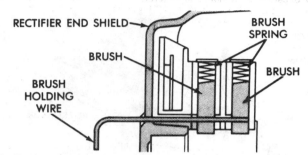

Fig. 5.12 Use a wire to retain the brushes (2.6L engine) (Sec 10)

light on the dash goes on and the alternator, battery, drivebelt tension and electrical connections seem to be in good order, have the regulator checked by your dealer or a suitably equipped shop.

The voltage regulator on 2.2L engine equipped vehicles is located on the left-hand inner fender panel in the engine compartment, under a removable cover. To replace the regulator, unplug the wiring connector, remove the retaining screws and lift it away. Installation is the reverse of removal.

The voltage regulator on 2.6L engines is of the integral type. In the event of regulator failure, the alternator will have to be replaced with a new or rebuilt unit.

12 Starting system – general information

The starting system is made up of a motor, battery, starter switch, starter relay and associated wiring.

When the ignition switch is turned to the Start position, the relay is energized through the control circuit. The relay then connects the battery to the starter motor.

13 Starter motor – testing on engine

1   If the starter motor fails to operate, then check the condition of the battery by turning on the headlights. If they glow brightly for several seconds and then gradually dim, the battery is in an uncharged condition.
2   If the headlights continue to glow brightly and it is obvious that the battery is in good condition, then check the tightness of the battery cables and other battery wiring. Check the tightness of the connections at the rear of the solenoid. Check the wiring with a voltmeter for breaks or short circuits.
3   If the wiring is in order, check the starter motor for continuity using a voltmeter.
4   If the battery is fully charged, the wiring is in order and the motor electrical circuit continuous and it still fails to operate, then it will have to be removed from the engine for examination. Before this is done, however, make sure that the pinion gear has not jammed in mesh with the ring gear due either to a broken solenoid spring or dirty pinion gear splines. To release the pinion, engage a low gear (manual transaxle) and with the ignition switched off, rock the vehicle backwards and forwards which should release the pinion from mesh with the ring gear; if the pinion still remains jammed the starter motor must be removed.

14 Starter motor (2.2L engine) – removal and installation

1   Disconnect the negative battery cable from the battery.
2   Remove the heatshield (if equipped).
3   On some models it may be necessary to disconnect the air pump tube from the exhaust manifold bracket and swivel the tube out of the way.
4   Disconnect the battery cable and solenoid wire from the starter.
5   Remove the retaining bolts and separate the starter from the bellhousing (photo).
6   To install, place the starter in position on the studs, install the retaining nuts and tighten them securely.
7   Connect the starter cable and solenoid wire.
8   Attach the air pump tube to the bracket (if equipped).
9   Install the heatshield (if equipped).
10   Connect the negative battery cable.

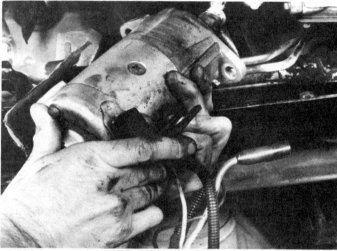

14.5 Support the starter when withdrawing it as it is heavy

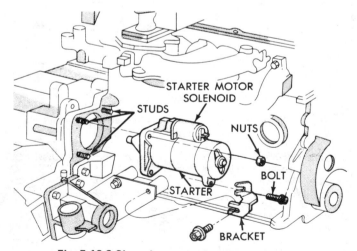

Fig. 5.13 2.2L engine starter installation (Sec 14)

15 Starter motor (2.6L engine) – removal and installation

1   Disconnect the negative battery cable from the battery.
2   Remove the starter cable and solenoid wire from the motor.
3   Remove the retaining nuts and bolts and remove the starter motor.
4   To install, hold the starter motor in place, install the retaining nuts and bolts and tighten them securely.
5   Connect the battery cable and solenoid wire.
6   Connect the negative battery cable.

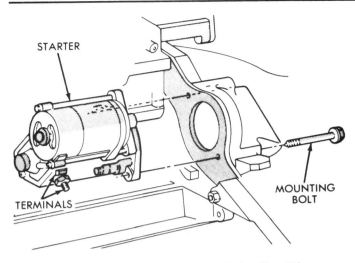

Fig. 5.14 2.6L engine starter installation (Sec 15)

16 Ignition system – general information

The ignition system is designed to ignite the fuel/air charge entering the cylinder at just the right moment. It does this by producing a high-voltage electrical spark between the electrodes of the spark plug.

On vehicles equipped with 2.2L engines the ignition system consists of a switch, the ignition coil, the distributor and a Spark Control Computer (SCC). The spark timing is constantly adjusted by the computer and distributor in response to inputs from the various sensors located on the engine.

On 2.6L engines the ignition system is made up of the switch, coil, distributor and an electronic control unit. Ignition advance is adjusted to driving conditions by centrifugal and vacuum advance mechanisms which are integral with the distributor.

Both of these electronic ignition systems are very troublefree and maintenance consists of · the checks of the ignition system components, wires and spark plugs described in the following Sections.

17 Spark control computer (SCC) (2.2L engine) – removal and installation

1   Disconnect the negative battery cable, followed by the positive cable. Remove the battery.
2   Disconnect the vacuum hose and unplug the electrical connectors. Disengage the assembly from the outside air duct.
3   Remove the three retaining screws and lift the SCC assembly from the vehicle.
4   To install, place the SCC assembly in position, engage it to the air duct and install the retaining screws. Connect the vacuum hose and plug in the connectors. Do not remove the grease from the connector or cavity. There should be at least $\frac{1}{4}$ inch of grease in the cavity to prevent the intrusion of moisture. If there is not, apply a suitable amount of multi-purpose grease to the cavity.
5   Install the battery.

18 Spark control computer (SCC) – testing

1   Prior to testing the spark control computer (SCC), check the coil and battery to make sure they are in good operating condition. Inspect the electrical harness and wires for shorts, broken or worn insulation and all connectors for security. Check the vacuum hose for kinks, damage and secure connection.
2   Connect the special jumper wires shown in Fig. 5.17 to the negative terminal of the coil and ground the other end. Pull the coil wire from the distributor and place it $\frac{1}{4}$ inch from a good ground and have an assistant turn the ignition switch on. A spark should be seen arcing from the coil wire to ground.

3   If there is a spark, proceed to Step 8.
4   If there is no spark, turn off the ignition switch, disconnect the ten wire harness connector and repeat the test. If a spark is now obtained, the computer output is shorted and the spark control computer assembly must be replaced with a new one.
5   If there was no spark, check the voltage at the battery negative terminal to make sure it is within one volt of battery output.
6   If there was no voltage reading, check the wiring between the battery and the positive terminal of the coil.
7   If there was a proper voltage reading, check the voltage at the coil negative terminal. This reading should also be within one volt of the battery voltage. If there is no voltage or there is voltage but no spark was obtained when performing the test in Step 2, replace the coil with a new one.
8   If there is a voltage reading but the engine will not start, use a thin piece of cardboard to hold the carburetor switch open and measure the voltage at the switch. The reading should be at least five volts.
9   If the voltage reading is correct, go on to Step 16.
10   If there is no voltage, turn off the ignition switch and unplug the SCC ten pin connector.
11   Turn the switch on and check the voltage at cavity 2 of the connector, which should be within one volt of the battery.
12   If there is no voltage reading, check for continuity between cavity 2 and the battery. Correct any fault and repeat the test in Step 11.
13   If there is voltage present, turn off the ignition switch and check for continuity between cavity 7 and the carburetor switch. If no continuity is present, check for an open wire between cavity 7 and the carburetor switch and correct the fault.
14   If there is continuity present, check for continuity between cavity 10 and a good ground. If there is continuity, it will be necessary to replace the computer with a new one as power is going into it but not out. Repeat the test in Step 8.
15   If continuity is not present, check for an open wire.
16   If the wiring is alright and the engine will not start, plug the connector into the computer and turn on the ignition switch. Hold the coil secondary wire near a good ground, unplug the distributor harness connector and connect a jumper wire between cavities 2 and 3. A spark should now jump between the coil wire and ground.
17   If the spark is present but the engine still does not start, replace the distributor pickup assembly, making sure the shutter blades are grounded. With the ignition switched off, check for a good ground on the distributor shaft with an ohmmeter. It may be necessary to seat the rotor securely on the shaft to achieve proper grounding. Connect one lead of the ohmmeter to the shutter blade and the other to a good ground and make sure there is continuity. If there is none, push the rotor down on the shaft until continuity is achieved. Replacement rotors should always have E.S.A. stamped on the top.
18   Repeat the test in Step 16 and if there is no spark present, measure the voltage at cavity 1 of the distributor connector. This should be within one volt of the battery voltage.

5

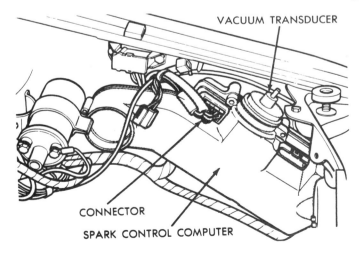

Fig. 5.15 Spark Control Computer component layout (Sec 18)

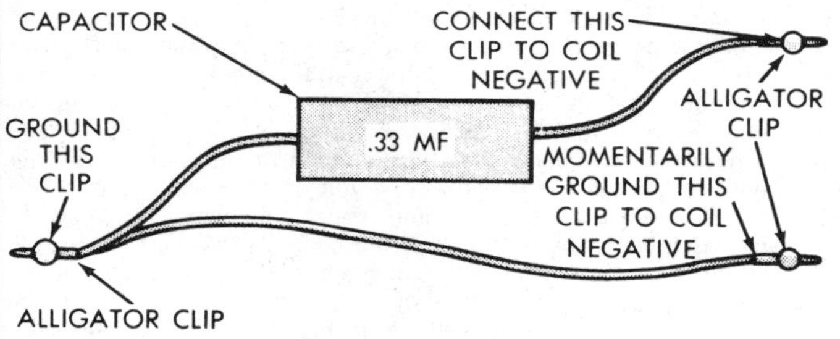

CAPACITOR

CONNECT THIS
CLIP TO COIL
NEGATIVE

GROUND
THIS
CLIP

.33 MF

ALLIGATOR
CLIP

MOMENTARILY
GROUND THIS
CLIP TO COIL
NEGATIVE

ALLIGATOR CLIP

Fig. 5.16 Test jumper wire (Sec 18)

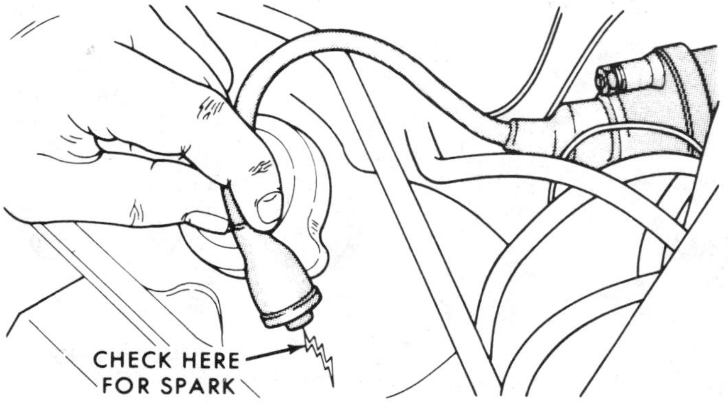

CHECK HERE
FOR SPARK

Fig. 5.17 Checking for spark (Sec 18)

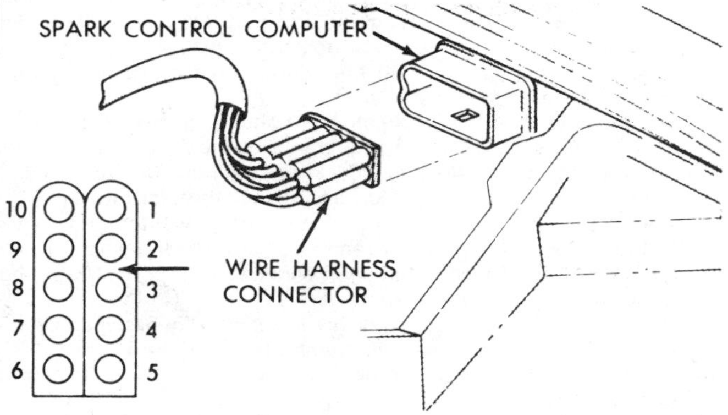

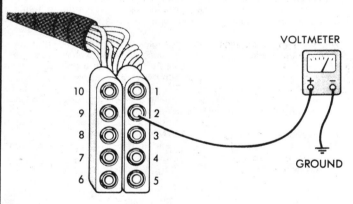

SPARK CONTROL COMPUTER

WIRE HARNESS
CONNECTOR

10 1
9 2
8 3
7 4
6 5

Fig. 5.18 Disconnecting the ten-wire harness connector (Sec 18)

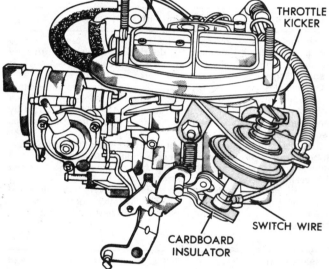

THROTTLE
KICKER

SWITCH WIRE

CARDBOARD
INSULATOR

Fig. 5.19 Use a piece of thin cardboard to hold the carburetor switch open (Sec 18)

VOLTMETER

10 1
9 2
8 3
7 4
6 5

GROUND

Fig. 5.20 Checking the connector cavity 2 voltage (Sec 18)

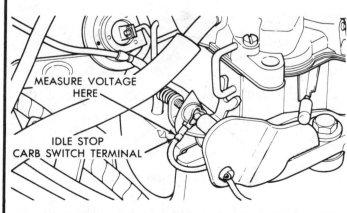

MEASURE VOLTAGE
HERE

IDLE STOP
CARB SWITCH TERMINAL

Fig. 5.21 Checking for power at the carburetor switch (Sec 18)

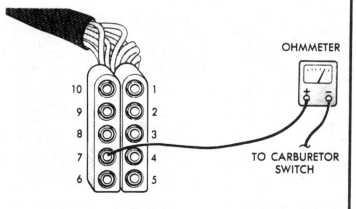

OHMMETER

10 1
9 2
8 3
7 4
6 5

TO CARBURETOR
SWITCH

Fig. 5.22 Checking for continuity between cavity 7 and the carburetor switch (Sec 18)

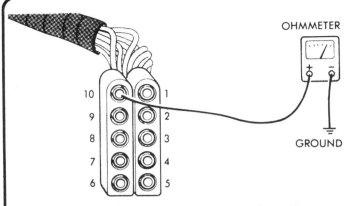

Fig. 5.23 Checking cavity 10 continuity (Sec 18)

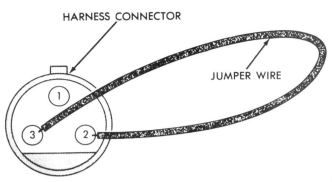

Fig. 5.24 Connecting a jumper wire between cavities 2 and 3 of the distributor harness connector (Sec 18)

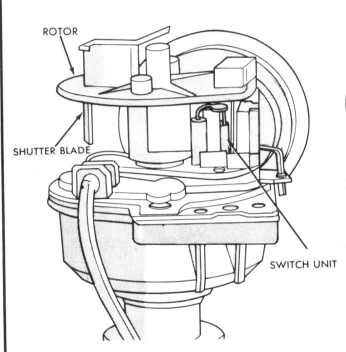

Fig. 5.25 Distributor rotor assembly installation (Sec 18)

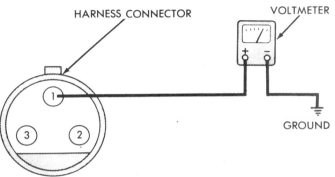

Fig. 5.26 Checking the distributor harness connector cavity 1 voltage (Sec 18)

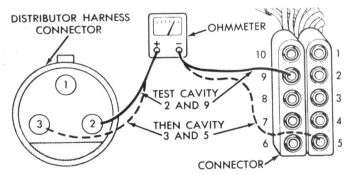

Fig. 5.27 Checking for continuity between the distributor and computer connectors (Sec 18)

5

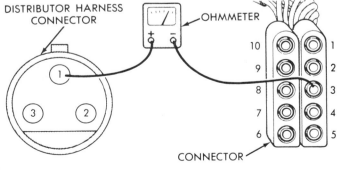

Fig. 5.28 Checking continuity between cavities 1 and 3 of the harness and computer connectors (Sec 18)

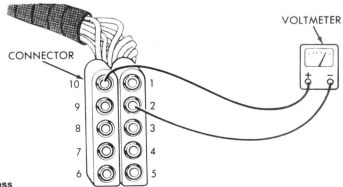

Fig. 5.29 Checking the computer connector voltage between cavities 10 and 2 (Sec 18)

19　If the voltage is correct, turn off the ignition, unplug the connector from the computer and check between cavity 2 of the distributor harness and cavity 10 of the computer connector. Follow this by checking cavity 3 of the distributor harness and cavity 5 of the computer connector. If there is no continuity, find and repair the fault in the harness. If there is continuity, replace the computer with a new one as power is going into it but not coming out.

20　Repeat the test in Step 16.

21　If no voltage is present when making the check in Step 18 turn off the ignition, unplug the computer connector and check for continuity between cavity 1 of the distributor harness connector and cavity 10 of the computer connector. If there is no continuity, repair any faults and repeat the test in Step 16.

22　If there is no voltage reading, check for continuity between cavity 1 of the distributor harness connector and cavity 10 of the computer connector. If there is no continuity between these two cavities, find and repair any harness wiring faults and repeat the Step 16 test.

23　If there is continuity, turn on the ignition switch and check for voltage between cavities 2 and 10 of the computer connector. If there is voltage, the computer is faulty and must be replaced with a new one. Repeat the test in Step 16.

24　If there is no voltage, check and repair the ground wire as the computer is not grounded. Repeat the Step 16 test.

19　Secondary ignition test (2.6L) engine

1　If ignition problems occur, perform the following test to determine whether the pickup coil and electronic ignition control unit are operating properly.

2　Check the ignition switch, wiring harness, spark plug wires and all ignition system connectors. Correct any problems found or replace any defective parts before proceeding.

3　Remove the distributor cap and lift out the rotor. Turn the ignition switch to On.

4　Disconnect the coil high tension lead from the center terminal of the distributor cap and hold it about $\frac{1}{4}$ inch away from the engine block or cylinder head.

5　Insert a flat blade screwdriver between the reluctor and stator of the distributor and see if a spark is produced between the coil lead and the engine. If a spark is not produced, a defective control unit, pickup coil, ignition coil or high-tension lead is at fault. Check all these parts thoroughly.

20　Centrifugal advance (2.6L engine) – checking

1　Refer to Chapter 1, *Ignition Timing-Adjustment,* and hook up a timing light as if you were adjusting the ignition timing.

2　With the engine running at idle speed and the timing light properly connected, remove the vacuum hose from the vacuum advance control unit on the distributor.

3　Observe the timing marks on the front of the engine and slowly accelerate the engine. The timing mark on the crankshaft pulley should appear to move smoothly in a direction away from the stationary mark on the timing tab. Then when the engine is slowed down, the mark should return to its original position.

4　If the above conditions are not met, the advance mechanism inside the distributor should be checked for broken governor springs and other problems.

21　Vacuum advance (2.6L engine) – checking

1　Refer to Chapter 1, *Ignition Timing-Adjustment,* and hook up a timing light as if you were adjusting the ignition timing.

2　Start the engine and set it at approximately 2500 rpm.

3　Observe the timing marks at the front of the engine and remove the vacuum hose from the vacuum advance control unit on the distributor. When the hose is removed, the timing mark on the crankshaft pulley should appear to move closer to the stationary mark on the timing tab. When the hose is reconnected, the mark should move away again.

4　If re-connecting the vacuum hose produces an abrupt increase in advance, or none at all, the vacuum advance control unit is probably defective.

22　Distributor (2.2L engine) – removal and installation

1　Disconnect the negative battery cable from the battery.

2　Unplug the distributor pickup coil lead wire from the harness.

3　Remove the pickup coil lead (one screw) from the coil lead retainer.

4　Remove the distributor splash shield (if equipped).

5　Loosen the two retaining screws and lift off the distributor cap.

6　Rotate the engine with a suitable wrench on the crankshaft pulley nut until the distributor rotor is pointed at the cylinder block. Scribe or paint a mark on the block so the distributor will be reinstalled with the rotor in the original position.

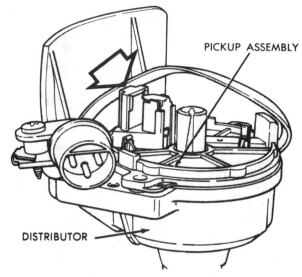

PICKUP ASSEMBLY

DISTRIBUTOR

Fig. 5.30 The distributor pickup (arrow) must point toward the cylinder block during removal and installation (2.2L engine) (Sec 22)

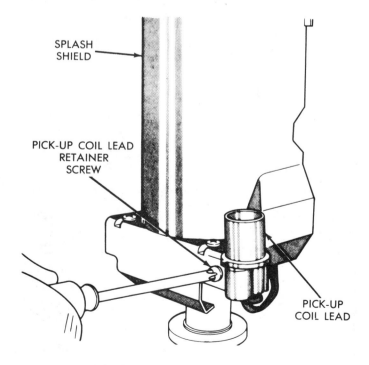

SPLASH SHIELD

PICK-UP COIL LEAD RETAINER SCREW

PICK-UP COIL LEAD

Fig. 5.31 Removing the pick-up coil lead (2.2L engine) (Sec 22)

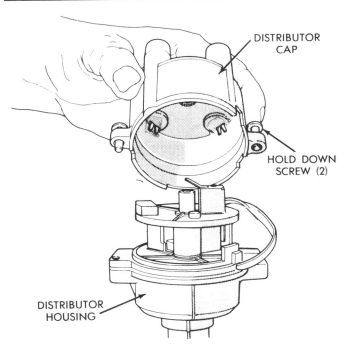

Fig. 5.32 Removing the distributor housing (2.2L engine) (Sec 22)

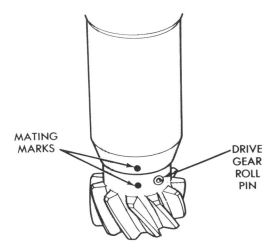

Fig. 5.34 Align the mating marks on the distributor and the gear prior to installation (2.6L engine) (Sec 23)

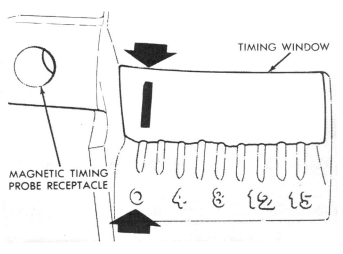

Fig. 5.33 The number 1 piston is at top dead center (TDC) when the flywheel mark aligns with the O on the bellhousing (arrows)

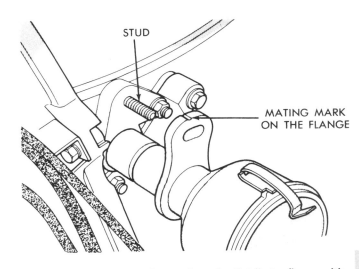

Fig. 5.35 Line up the mating mark on the distributor flange with the center of the stud during installation (2.6L engine) (Sec 23)

7   Remove the hold-down screw and carefully lift the distributor from the engine.
8   To install, lower the distributor into position, making sure the gasket is seated properly. Engage the distributor drive with the auxiliary shaft so that the rotor is aligned with the mark on the cylinder block made during removal.
9   If the engine has been rotated during the time the distributor was removed, it will be necessary to establish the proper relationship between the distributor and the number one piston position. Remove the number one cylinder spark plug, place your finger over the plug hole and rotate the crankshaft until pressure is felt, indicating that the piston is at top dead center. The pointer on the bellhousing should be aligned with the O (TDC) mark on the flywheel. If it is not, continue to turn the engine over until the mark and the O are lined up.
10 Install the distributor cap.
11 Install the hold-down screw snugly.
12 Install the splash shield.
13 Install the pickup coil lead and plug the wire into the harness.
14 Check the timing (Chapter 1) and tighten the distributor hold-down screw.
15 Connect the negative battery cable.

23 Distributor (2.6L engine) – removal and installation

1   Disconnect the negative battery cable from the battery. Unplug the wiring harness from the distributor control unit and remove the distributor cap by depressing and turning the spring-loaded screws.
2   Disconnect the vacuum hose from the vacuum advance control unit on the distributor.
3   Pull the spark plug wires off the spark plugs. Pull only on the rubber boot or damage to the spark plug wire could result.
4   Remove the spark plugs, then place your thumb over the No. 1 spark plug hole and turn the crankshaft in a clockwise direction (looking at it from the front) until you can feel the compression pressure in the No. 1 cylinder. Continue to slowly turn the crankshaft until the notch in the crankshaft pulley lines up with the T on the timing mark tab. At this point, the No. 1 piston is at TDC on the compression stroke.
5   Remove the distributor attaching nut and pull straight out on the distributor.
6   Do not allow the engine to be cranked until the distributor has been reinstalled.
7   To install the distributor, line up the mating marks on the distributor housing (line) and the distributor-driven gear (punch marks). Slide the distributor into place in the cylinder head while lining up the

mark on the distributor hold-down flange with the center of the stud. Make sure the distributor is completely seated, then install the nut and tighten it finger tight.

8   Replace the spark plugs and install the plug wires.

9   Install the distributor cap, plug in the control unit wiring harness and connect the vacuum hose to the vacuum control unit.

10   Connect the negative battery cable to the battery and check the ignition timing as described in Chapter 1. Don't forget to tighten the distributor attaching nut securely when finished.

24 Ignition coil – checking

1   Mark the wires and terminals with pieces of numbered tape, then remove the primary wires and the high-tension lead from the coil.

2   Remove the coil from its mount, clean the outer case and check it for cracks and other damage.

3   Clean the primary coil terminals and check the coil tower terminal for corrosion. Clean it with a wire brush if any corrosion is found.

4   Check the primary coil resistance by attaching the leads of an ohmmeter to the positive and negative primary terminals. Compare the measured resistance to the Specifications.

5   Check the secondary coil resistance by hooking one of the ohmmeter leads to one of the primary terminals and the other ohmmeter lead to the high-tension coil tower terminals. Compare the measured resistance to the Specifications.

6   If the measured resistances are not as specified, the coil is probably defective and should be replaced with a new one.

7   It is essential for proper ignition system operation that all coil terminals and wire leads be kept clean and dry.

8   Install the coil in the vehicle and hook up the wires.

25 Spark plug wires – checking

1   The spark plug wires should be checked at the recommended intervals and whenever new spark plugs are installed in the engine.

2   The wires should be inspected one at a time to prevent mixing up the order, which is essential for proper engine operation.

3   Disconnect the plug wire from the spark plug. A removal tool can be used for this purpose or you can grab the rubber boot, twist slightly and pull the wire free. Do not pull on the wire itself, only on the rubber boot.

4   Inspect inside the boot for corrosion, which will look like a white crusty powder. Push the wire and boot back onto the end of the spark plug. It should be a tight fit on the plug end. If it is not, remove the wire and use a pair of pliers to carefully crimp the metal connector inside the wire boot until it fits securely on the end of the spark plug.

5   Using a clean rag, wipe the entire length of the wire to remove any built up dirt and grease. Once the wire is clean, check for burns, cracks and other damage. Do not bend the wire, since the conductor might break.

6   Disconnect the wire from the distributor as described in Chapter 1. Check for corrosion.

7   Check the electrical resistance of each spark plug wire and compare it to the Specifications. If the resistance is greater than specified, the spark plug wires should be replaced.

8   Check the remaining spark plug wires, making sure they are securely fastened at the distributor and spark plug when the check is complete.

Chapter 6 Emissions control systems

Refer to Chapter 13 for specifications and information applicable to later models

Contents

Specifications

General (2.2L engine only)

Charcoal canister delay valve vacuum	10 in of vacuum
EGR valve test vacuum	10 in of vacuum
EGR valve travel	$\frac{1}{8}$ in (3 mm)

Torque specifications (2.2L engine only)

	Ft-lb	Nm
Air injection check valve injection tube-to-manifold	25 to 35	34 to 47
Air injection pump pulley bolts	6	12
Air injection relief valve-to-pump	8	14
Air pump bracket-to-transaxle	40	54
Air pump pulley shield screws	8	14
Air pump attachment bolts	29	40
Catalytic converter aspirator valve-to-tube	25	34
Aspirator valve adapter-to-tube nut	50	68
Aspirator tube bracket bolt	5	11
Oxygen sensor-to-catalytic converter	20	27
Catalytic converter clamp nut	22	30

1 General information

Since these vehicles are equipped with both 2.2L and 2.6L engines, a wide variety of emission control devices is used. Some of these devices or systems are exclusive to a particular engine, while others are applicable to all vehicles. All systems will be described in this Chapter so that all vehicles will be covered.

All engines are equipped with Fuel Evaporative Emissions Control (EVAP), Exhaust Gas Recirculation (EGR), Positive Crankcase Ventilation (PCV), heated inlet air and catalytic converter systems.

Vehicles with 2.2L engines use an air injection system and some models have an electronic feedback carburetor. The electronic feedback carburetor works in conjunction with an oxygen sensor located in the exhaust system and a spark control computer. The three work together to constantly monitor exhaust gas oxygen content and vary the spark timing and fuel mixture so that emissions are always within limits.

The 2.6L engine features a Pulse Air Feeder (PAF) air injection system which injects air into the exhaust system between the front and rear catalytic converter to promote reduced emissions. Also, a Jet valve system is used to inject a very lean fuel mixture into the combustion chamber and improve efficiency and thus emissions.

Vehicle Emission Control Information (VECI) and vacuum hose routing labels with information on your particular vehicle are located under the hood.

Before assuming that an emission control system is malfunctioning, check the fuel and ignition systems carefully. In some cases, special tools and equipment, as well as specialized training, are required to accurately diagnose the causes of a rough running or difficult to start engine. If checking and servicing becomes too difficult, or if a procedure is beyond the scope of a home mechanic, consult your dealer or a suitably equipped shop. This does not necessarily mean, however, that the emission control systems are all particularly difficult to maintain and repair. You can quickly and easily perform many checks and do most (if not all) of the regular maintenance at home with common tune-up and hand tools. **Note:** *The most frequent cause of emission system problems is simply a loose or broken vacuum hose or wiring connection. Therefore, always check hose and wiring connections first.*

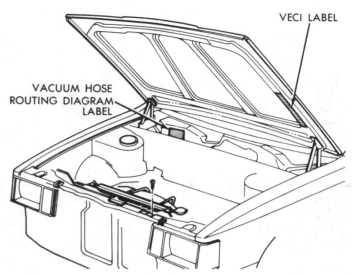

Fig. 6.1 Vacuum hose and Vehicle Emissions Control Information (VECI) label locations (Sec 1)

CATALYST	MAINTENANCE SCHEDULE	CHRYSLER CORPORATION	VEHICLE EMISSION CONTROL INFORMATION		HIGH Altitude		The carburetor idle mixture has been preset at the factory. Adjustments should not be made during routine tune-up. **See Service Manual for additional information.**
			THIS VEHICLE CONFORMS TO U.S. EPA REGULATIONS APPLICABLE TO 1982 MODEL YEAR NEW MOTOR VEHICLES.			Trans.	
					Idle Settings	Man. Auto.	
					Timing: BTC		
		CU. IN.	SPARK PLUGS	.035IN GAP	Curb Idle rpm: Fast Idle rpm:		Conversion kit not needed to meet emission standards at LOW altitude.
				Adjustments made by other than approved Service Manual procedures may violate Federal and State laws.	Under 300 miles reduce all idle speeds 75 rpm.		LOW altitude idle settings same as HIGH altitude.

Fig. 6.2 Typical Vehicle Emissions Control Information label (Sec 1)

2   Positive Crankcase Ventilation (PCV) system

General description
1   This system is designed to reduce hydrocarbon emissions (HC) by routing blow-by gases (fuel/air mixture that escapes from the combustion chamber past the piston rings into the crankcase) from the crankcase to the intake manifold and combustion chamber where they are burned during engine operation.
2   The system is very simple and consists of rubber hoses and a small, replaceable metering valve (PCV valve).

Checking and component replacement
3   With the engine at idle, disconnect the PCV valve and place your finger over the valve inlet. A strong vacuum will be felt and a hissing noise will be heard if the valve is operating properly. Replace the valve with a new one, as described in Chapter 1, if it is not operating properly.

3   Fuel Evaporative Emission Control (EVAP) system

General description
1   This system is designed to trap and store fuel that evaporates from the carburetor and fuel tank which would normally enter the atmosphere and contribute to hydrocarbon (HC) emissions.
2   The system is very simple and consists of a charcoal-filled canister, a combination rollover/separator valve, a canister check or relief valve and connecting lines and hoses.
3   When the engine is off and a high pressure begins to build up in the fuel tank (caused by fuel evaporation), the charcoal in the canister absorbs the fuel vapor. On some models, vapor from the carburetor float bowl also enters the canister. When the engine is started (cold), the charcoal continues to absorb and store fuel vapor. As the engine warms up, the stored fuel vapors are routed to the intake manifold or air cleaner and combustion chamber where they are burned during normal engine operation.

4   The canister is purged using air from the air injection pump delay or purge valve.
5   On 2.6L engines a damping canister serves as a purge control device. The fuel vapors released from the main canister pass through the damping canister and are momentarily held before passing to the intake manifold. When the engine is shut off, a bowl vent valve opens so that the carburetor is vented directly to the main canister.
6   The relief valve, which is mounted in the fuel tank filler cap, is calibrated to open when the fuel tank vacuum reaches a certain level. This allows outside air to enter the fuel tank and relieve the high vacuum.

Checking
Canister, lines, hoses, fuel filler cap and relief valve
7   Check the canister and lines for cracks or damage.
8   To check the filler cap and relief valve, remove the cap and detach the valve by unscrewing it.
9   Look for a damaged or deformed gasket and make sure the relief valve is not stuck open. If the valve or gasket is not in good condition, it will be necessary to replace the entire filter cap assembly.

Canister delay valve
10   **Note:** *A symptom of a failed delay valve is difficulty in starting the engine when it is hot.* Disconnect the top vacuum hose (photo) and connect a vacuum pump to it. If the valve cannot hold the specified vacuum, replace the canister with a new one.

Component replacement
11   The canister is located in the right corner of the engine compartment, below the headlamp.
12   Disconnect the vacuum hoses.
13   Remove the three securing bolts and lower the canister, removing it from beneath the vehicle.
14   Installation is the reverse of removal.

3.10 Connect a vacuum pump hose (arrow) to the canister delay valve and apply vacuum to check the valve

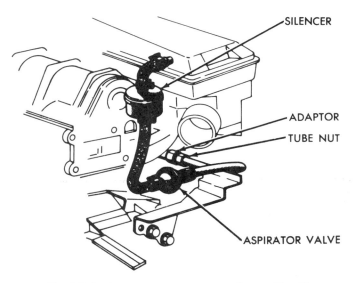

Fig. 6.3 Aspirator system component layout (Sec 4)

4 Catalytic converter

General description

1 The catalytic converter is designed to reduce hydrocarbon (HC) and carbon monoxide (CO) pollutants in the exhaust gases. The converter oxidizes these components and converts them to water and carbon dioxide.

2 The system on these vehicles consists of a mini-oxidizer converter and a main under floor converter. The mini-oxidizer converter begins the exhaust gas oxidization, which is then completed by the main converter. Later models use an aspirator air system, which uses exhaust pressure pulsation to inject air into the converter.

3 **Note:** *If large amounts of unburned gasoline enters the catalyst, it may overheat and cause a fire. Always observe the following precautions:*

> *Use only unleaded gasoline*
> *Avoid prolonged idling*
> *Do not run the engine with a nearly empty fuel tank*
> *Do not prolong engine compression checks*
> *Avoid coasting with the ignition turned Off*
> *Do not dispose of a used catalytic converter along with oily or gasoline soaked parts*

Checking

4 The catalytic converter requires little if any maintenance and servicing at regular intervals. However, the system should be inspected whenever the vehicle is raised on a lift or if the exhaust system is checked or serviced.

5 Check all connections in the exhaust pipe assembly for looseness or damage. Also check all the clamps for damage, cracks, or missing fasteners. Check the rubber hangers for cracks.

6 The converter itself should be checked for damage and for dents (maximum $\frac{3}{4}$ in deep) which could affect its performance and/or be hazardous to your health. At the same time the converter is inspected, check the heat shields under it, as well as the heat insulator above it, for damage or loose fasteners.

7 On aspirator equipped models, check the aspirator valve, rubber hose and exhaust manifold connection for leakage. Disconnect the valve and, with the engine at idle, the exhaust vacuum pulses can be felt at the aspirator inlet if the valve is working properly. If only hot exhaust is issuing from the inlet, the valve should be replaced with a new one.

Component replacement

8 Do not attempt to remove the catalytic converter until the complete exhaust system is cool. Raise the vehicle and support it securely on jackstands. Apply some penetrating oil to the clamp bolts

and allow it to soak in. Disconnect the oxygen sensor (if equipped) from the converter.

9 Remove the bolts and the rubber hangers, then separate the converter from the exhaust pipe. Remove the old gaskets if they are stuck to the pipes.

10 Installation of the converter is the reverse of removal. Use new exhaust pipe gaskets and tighten the clamp nuts to the specified torque. Replace the oxygen sensor wires (if equipped), start the engine and check carefully for exhaust leaks.

11 To remove the aspirator valve, disconnect it from the air hose and then unscrew it from the tube assembly with a suitable wrench. If the air hose is even partially hardened, replace it with a new one. Screw the valve into place, tighten it to the specified torque and connect the hose.

5 Exhaust Gas Recirculation (EGR) system

General description

1 This system recirculates a portion of the exhaust gases into the intake manifold or carburetor in order to reduce the combustion temperatures and decrease the amount of nitrogen oxide (NOx) produced.

2 The main component in the system is the EGR valve. It operates in conjunction with the coolant control EGR (CCEGR) valve on 2.2L engines and the thermo valves on 2.6L engines.

3 On 2.2L engines the control valve and the EGR valves remain shut at low engine temperatures. At higher engine temperatures the control valve opens, allowing vacuum to be applied to the EGR valve so that the exhaust gas can recirculate.

4 On 2.6L engines, the flow of recirculated exhaust gas is controlled by sub and dual EGR valves and temperature sensitive thermo valves. The sub EGR valve is operated directly by the throttle linkage, while the dual EGR valve is controlled by carburetor vacuum. The primary valve of the dual EGR valve operates during small openings of the throttle and the secondary valve takes over when the opening is larger. The vacuum which operates the dual EGR valve is supplied by a coolant temperature actuated thermo valve so that EGR function doesn't affect driveability.

Checking
2.2L engine
5 Check all hoses for cracks, kinks, broken sections and proper connection. Inspect all system connections for damage, cracks or leaks.

6 To check the EGR valve operation, bring the engine up to operating temperature and with the transmission in Neutral, allow it to idle for 70 seconds. Open the throttle abruptly so that the engine

6

speed is between 2000 and 3000 rpm and then allow it to close. The EGR valve stem should move if the system is working properly. The test should be repeated several times to make sure the stem and system are working consistently.

7   If the EGR valve stem does not move, check all of the hose connections to make sure they are not leaking or clogged. Disconnect the vacuum hose and apply the specified vacuum with a suitable hand pump (photo). If the stem still does not move, replace the EGR valve with a new one. If the valve does open, measure the valve stroke to make sure it is within the Specifications.

8   Apply vacuum with the pump and then clamp the hose shut. The valve should stay open for 30 seconds. If it does not, the diaphragm is leaking and the valve should be replaced with a new one.

9   To check the coolant control (CCEGR) valve located in the thermostat housing, bypass it with a length of $\frac{3}{16}$ inch tubing. If the EGR valve did not operate under the conditions described in Step 6, but does operate properly using the vacuum pump with the CCEGR valve bypassed, the CCEGR valve is defective and should be replaced.

10   Remove the EGR valve and inspect the poppet and seat area for deposits. If the deposits exceed more than a thin film of carbon, the valve should be cleaned and inspected. To clean the valve, apply a suitable solvent and allow it to penetrate and soften the deposits, making sure that none gets on the valve diaphragm as this could damage it. Use a vacuum pump to hold the valve open and then carefully scrape the deposits from the seat and poppet area with a suitable tool. Inspect the poppet and stem for wear and replace the valve with a new one if wear is found.

5.7 Applying vacuum to the EGR valve (arrow)

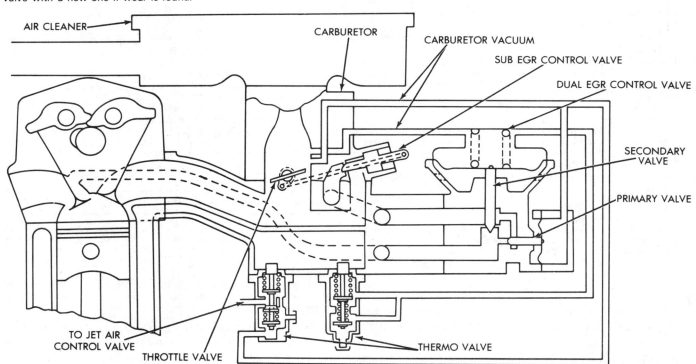

Fig. 6.4 2.6L engine EGR system (Sec 5)

2.6L engines

11   Check all hoses and connections for cracks, kinks, damage and leaks.

12   With the engine cold, start and run it at idle.

13   Check the secondary EGR valve to make sure that it does not operate when the engine is cold as this indicates the thermo valve is faulty and must be replaced with a new one.

14   Allow the engine to warm up and observe the secondary EGR valve to see that it opens as the temperature rises and the idle speed rpm increases. If it does not open, the secondary EGR valve itself or the thermo valve are faulty.

15   To check the secondary EGR valve and the thermo valve, disconnect the green striped vacuum hose from the carburetor and

connect a vacuum pump to it. Apply six inches of vacuum with the pump as you open the sub EGR valve.

16   If the engine idle becomes irregular, the secondary valve of the dual EGR is operating properly. If the idle speed is unchanged, the secondary valve and the thermo valve are faulty and must be replaced with new ones.

17   Reconnect the green striped hose and disconnect the yellow striped hose at the carburetor.

18   Connect the hand vacuum pump to the hose and, while opening the sub EGR valve, apply six inches of vacuum.

19   If the idle becomes irregular, the EGR primary valve is operating properly. If the idle is unchanged, both the EGR primary valve and the thermo valve are not operating and should be replaced with new ones.

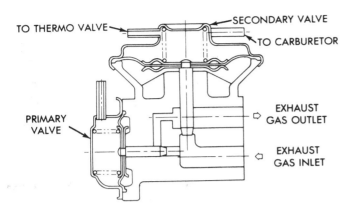

Fig. 6.5 Dual EGR control and valve layout (2.6L engine) (Sec 5)

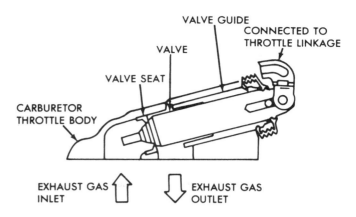

Fig. 6.6 2.6L engine sub EGR valve layout (Sec 5)

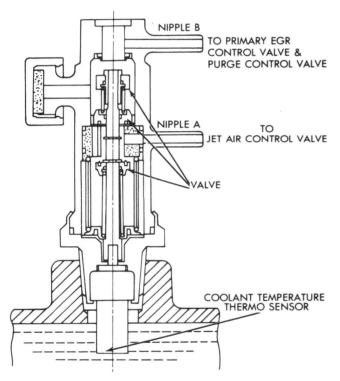

Fig. 6.7 Thermo valve A (2.6L engine EGR system) (Sec 5)

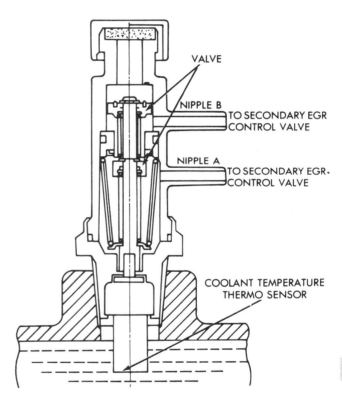

Fig. 6.8 Thermo valve B (2.6L engine EGR system) (Sec 5)

Component replacement
2.2L engine
20 The coolant controlled EGR valve can be replaced by removing the vacuum hoses and unscrewing the valve.
21 To replace the EGR valve, remove the air cleaner, air injection pump and shield. Disconnect the hose, remove the two retaining nuts and remove the valve.

2.6L engine
22 The dual EGR valve is located on the lower part of the intake manifold. It is replaced by removing the vacuum hoses and unbolting it. It may be necessary to tap the valve gently with a soft-faced hammer to break the gasket seal so it can be removed. Use a new gasket when installing and check the vacuum hoses for proper routing.
23 The sub EGR valve is located on the base of the carburetor and is connected by a linkage. Pry off the spring clip and remove the pin attaching the plunger to the linkage. Hold the end of the linkage up and remove the spring and the steel ball from the end of the plunger.
24 Slip the rubber boot off and slide the plunger out of the carburetor

throttle body. Before installing the plunger, lubricate it with a small amount of light oil. Install the steel ball and spring, hold the linkage in place and insert the pin. Carefully slide the spring clip into place, then check for smooth operation of the valve plunger.
25 The thermal valves are threaded into the intake manifold. Pull off the vacuum hose and unscrew the valve from the housing.

6   Heated inlet air system

General description
1   This system is designed to improve driveability, reduce emissions and prevent carburetor icing in cold weather by directing hot air from around the exhaust manifold to the air cleaner intake.
2   On 2.2L engines the system is made up of two circuits. When the outside air temperature is below 10°F (5°C), the carburetor intake air flows through the flexible connector , up through the snorkel into the carburetor.

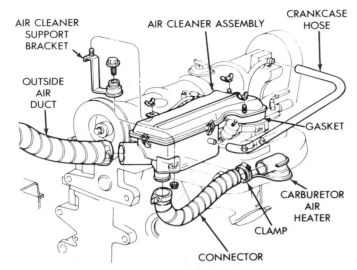

Fig. 6.9 2.2L engine heated inlet air system component layout (Sec 6)

3   When the air temperature is above 15°F (8°C), air enters the air cleaner through the outside air duct.

4   On 2.6L engines, the door in the air cleaner snorkel is controlled by a vacuum motor which is acutated by a bi-metal temperature sensor. The sensor reacts to both intake manifold vacuum and the air temperature inside the air cleaner itself.

5   When the air temperature inside the air horn is 85°F (30°C) or below, the air bleed valve in the sensor remains closed and intake manifold vacuum opens the air control door to direct heated air to the carburetor.

6   When the air temperature inside the air cleaner is 113°F (45°C) or above, the sensor air bleed valve opens the air duct door allowing outside air directly into the carburetor. At temperatures between the two extremes, the sensor provides a blend of outside and heated air to the carburetor.

Checking
General
7   Refer to Chapter 1 for the general checking procedure. If the system is not operating properly, check the individual components as follows:

8   Check all vacuum hoses for cracks, kinks, proper routing and broken sections. Make sure the shrouds and ducting are in good condition as well.

2.2L engine
9   Remove the air cleaner assembly from the engine and allow it to cool to 65°F (19°C). Apply 20 in Hg of vacuum to the sensor, using a hand vacuum pump.

10 The duct door should be in the up (heat on) position with the vacuum applied. If it is not, check the vacuum diaphragm.

11 To check the diaphragm, slowly apply vacuum with the hand pump while observing the door.

12 The duct door should not begin to open at less than 2 in Hg and should be fully open at 4 in Hg or less. With 20 in Hg applied, the diaphragm should not bleed down more than 10 in Hg in five minutes.

13 Replace the sensor and/or vacuum diaphragm with new units if they fail any of the tests. Test the new unit(s) as described before reinstalling the air cleaner assembly.

2.6L engine
14 With the engine cold and the air temperature less than 85°F (30°C), see if the air control valve is in the up (heat on) position.

15 Warm up the engine to operating temperature. With the air temperature at the entrance to the snorkel at 113°F (45°C), the door should be in the down (heat off) position.

16 Remove the air cleaner assembly from the engine and allow it to cool to 85°F (30°C). Connect a hand vacuum pump to the sensor.

17 Apply 15 in Hg of vacuum to the sensor and see if the door is now in the up (heat on) position. If it is not, check the vacuum motor.

18 Apply 10 in Hg vacuum to the motor with the vacuum pump and

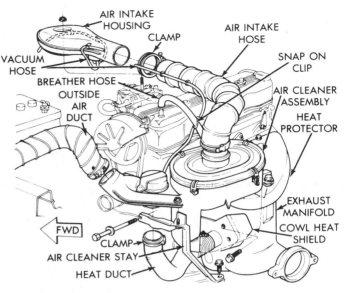

Fig. 6.10 2.6L engine heated inlet air system layout (Sec 6)

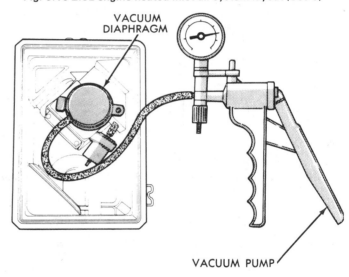

Fig. 6.11 Testing the air inlet vacuum diaphragm (2.2L engine) (Sec 6)

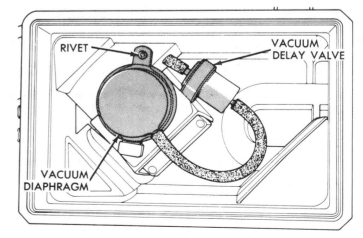

Fig. 6.12 Air inlet vacuum diaphragm and valve installation (2.2L engine) (Sec 6)

see if the valve is in the up position. If it is not, replace the motor with a new one. On these vehicles the vacuum motor is an integral part of the air cleaner body and the entire assembly must be replaced.

Component replacement
Vacuum diaphragm
19 With the air cleaner removed, disconnect the vacuum hose and use a suitable size bit to drill out the retaining rivet.
20 Disengage the diaphragm by tipping it forward slightly while turning it slightly counterclockwise. Once disengaged, the unit can be removed by moving it to one side, disconnecting the rod from the control door and then lifting it from the air cleaner assembly.
21 Check the control door for free travel by raising it to the full up position and allowing it to fall closed. If it does not close easily, remove any obstructions or interference to movement. Check the hinge pin for free movement also, using compressed air or a suitable spray cleaner to remove any foreign matter.
22 To install, insert the rod end into the control door and position the diaphragm tangs into the slot, turning the diaphragm clockwise until it engages. Rivet the tab into place.
23 Connect the vacuum hose.

Sensor
24 Disconnect the vacuum hoses and use a screwdriver to pry the retaining clips off. Lift the sensor from the housing.
25 To install, place the gasket onto the sensor and insert the sensor into position in the housing.
26 Hold the sensor in place so that the gasket is compressed to form a good seal and install the retainer clips.
27 Connect the vacuum hoses.

7 Jet valve system

1 The jet air system utilizes an additional inlet valve (jet valve) which provides for air, or a super lean mixture, to be drawn from the air intake into the cylinder. The jet valve is operated by the same cam as the inlet valve. They use a common rocker arm so the jet valve and the inlet valve open and close simultaneously.
2 On the intake stroke of the engine, fuel/air mixture flows through the intake ports into the combustion chamber. At the same time, jet air is forced into the combustion chamber because of the pressure difference between the jet intake in the throttle bore and the jet valve in the cylinder as the piston moves down. At small throttle openings, there is a large pressure difference, giving the jet air a high velocity. This scavenges the residual gases around the spark plug and creates good ignition conditions. It also produces a strong swirl in the combustion chamber, which lasts throughout the compression stroke and improves flame propagation after ignition, assuring high combustion efficiency and lowering exhaust emissions. As the throttle opening is increased, less jet air is forced in and jet swirl diminishes, but the increased flow through the intake valve ensures satisfactory combustion.

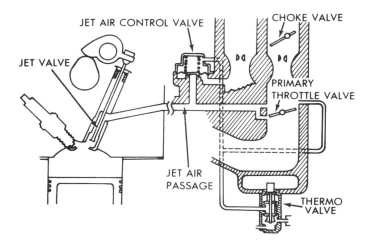

Fig. 6.13 Jet valve system component layout (2.6L engine) (Sec 7)

3 A thermo valve which works in conjunction with the EGR system controls the air flow to the Jet valve.
4 Maintenance consists of adjusting the Jet valves at the same time the engine valves are adjusted, as described in Chapter 1.

8 Air Injection (AI) system (2.2L engines)

General description
1 This system supplies air under pressure to the exhaust port to promote the combustion of unburned hydrocarbons and carbon monoxide before they are allowed to exit the exhaust system.
2 The AI system consists of an air pump driven by a belt from the rear of the camshaft, a relief valve and associated hoses and check valves, which protect the system from hot exhaust gases.

Checking
General
3 Visually check the hoses, tubes and connections for cracks, loose fittings and separated parts. Use soapy water to isolate a suspected leak.
4 Check the drivebelt condition and tension.

Air pump
5 The air pump can only be checked using special equipment. Noise from the pump can be due to improper drivebelt tension, faulty relief or check valves, loose mounting bolts and leaking hoses or connections. If these conditions have been corrected and the pump still makes excessive noise, there is a good chance that it is faulty.

Relief valve
6 If air can be heard escaping from the relief valve with the engine at idle, the valve is faulty and must be replaced with a new one.

Check valve
7 Remove the hose from the inlet tube. If the exhaust escapes past the inlet tube, the check valve is faulty and must be replaced.

Component replacement
Air pump
Caution: *Do not rotate the camshaft with the air pump removed.*
8 Remove the air hoses from the air pump and the relief valve.
9 Remove the air pump drivebelt pulley shield (photo).
10 Loosen the pump pivot and adjustment bolts and remove the drivebelt (photo).
11 Remove the bolts and lift the pump from the engine.
12 Remove the relief valve from the pump and clean any gasket material from the valve mating surface.
13 Attach the relief valve to the new air pump, using a new gasket. Transfer the pulley from the old pump to the new one.
14 With the drivebelt over the air pump pulley, place the pump in position and loosely install the attachment nuts (photo).
15 Loosen the rear air pump bracket-to-transaxle housing bolts.
16 Place the drivebelt on the camshaft pulley and use a suitable breaker bar to exert pressure on the attachment bracket (not the pump housing) and adjust the belt until deflection is $\frac{1}{4}$ in (6 mm). Tighten the locking bolt, followed by the pivot bolt (photo).
17 Tighten the air pump bracket bolt to the specified torque, install the pulley shield and reconnect the hoses to the pump and relief valve.

Relief valve
18 Disconnect the hoses from the relief valve, remove the two securing screws and lift the valve from the pump. Carefully remove any gasket material from the valve and pump mating surfaces.
19 Place a new gasket in position and install the valve, tightening the securing screws to the specified torque. Reconnect the hoses.

Check valve
20 Disconnect the hose from the valve inlet and remove the nut securing the tube to the exhaust manifold or converter. Loosen the starter motor bolt and remove the check valve from the engine.
21 Attach the new valve to the exhaust manifold or converter, tighten the starter motor bolt and connect the air hose.

6

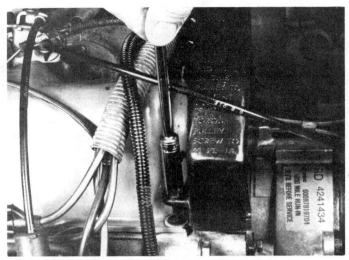

8.9 Removing the air pump drivebelt pulley shield bolts

8.10 Loosening the air pump pivot bolt

8.14 Rotate the air pump into position and place the drivebelt in the pulley groove

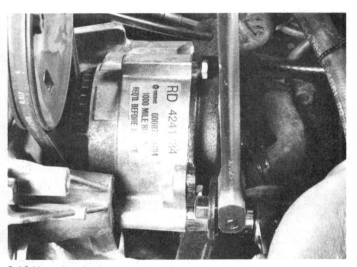

8.16 Use a breaker bar to maintain tension on the air pump bracket

9 Pulse Air Feeder (PAF) system (2.6L engine)

General description

1   The PAF system injects air into the exhaust system between the front and rear catalytic converters, using the engine power pulsations. This injected air increases the efficiency of the rear converter and reduces emissions.

2   The pulse air feeder consists of a main reed, sub reed and associated hoses. Air is drawn from the air cleaner into the main reed valve which is acutated by the power pulsations of the number 3 cylinder. The air passes to the sub reed valve, which is actuated by the exhaust system pulse, to the exhaust system and then the rear converter.

Checking

3   Disconnect the hose from the air cleaner and, with the engine running, place your hand over the end. If no vacuum is felt, check the hoses for leaks. If the hoses are alright, replace the PAF assembly with a new one.

Component replacement

4   Remove the air deflector duct from the right side of the radiator.

Remove the carburetor protector shield, the oil dipstick and the dipstick tube.

5   Raise the vehicle and support it securely.

6   Disconnect the hoses and remove the PAF assembly from the vehicle.

7   Place the new pulse air feeder assembly in position and connect the hoses.

8   Lower the vehicle and install the mounting bolts. Check the dipstick O-ring to make sure it is in good condition and install the dipstick and tube. Install the carburetor shield and radiator air deflector.

10 Electronic feedback carburetor (2.2L engine) emission system

General description

1   The electronic feedback carburetor emission system relies on an electronic signal which is generated by an exhaust gas sensor to control a variety of devices and keep emissions within limits. The system works in conjunction with a three-way catalyst to control the levels of carbon monoxide, hydrocarbons and oxides of nitrogen.

2   The system operates in two modes: open loop and closed loop. When the engine is cold, the air/fuel mixture is controlled by the

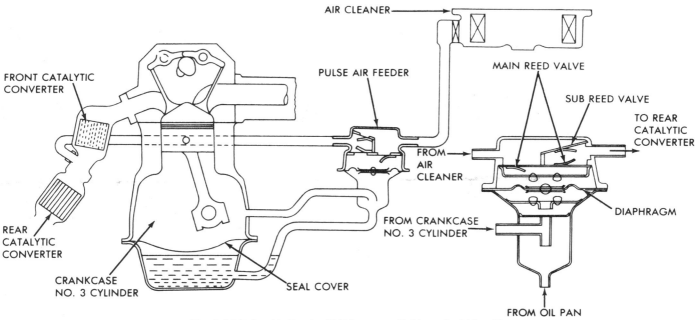

Fig. 6.14 Pulse Air Feeder (PAF) system (2.6L engine) (Sec 9)

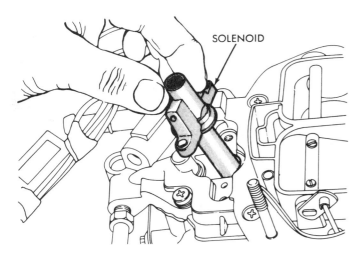

Fig. 6.15 2.2L engine carburetor feedback solenoid removal (Sec 10)

computer in accordance with a program designed in at the time of production. The air/fuel mixture during this time will be richer to allow for proper engine warm-up. When the engine is at operating temperature, the system operates at closed loop and the air/fuel mixture is varied depending on the information supplied by the exhaust gas sensor.

3   The system consists of the carburetor, computer, air switching valve, coolant control engine vacuum switch, catalytic converters and oxygen sensor.

Checking

4   Prior to checking the system, check the computer for proper operation as described in Chapter 5. Also, make sure that all vacuum hoses and electrical wires are properly routed and securely connected.

5   Apply 16 in Hg of vacuum to the computer with a vacuum pump, start the engine and allow it to warm up to operating temperature. Run the engine at approximately 2000 rpm for two minutes and make sure the carburetor switch is not grounded.

Air switching system

6   Right after starting the engine, disconnect the hose from the air switching valve and connect a vacuum gauge to the hose. There

should be a vacuum reading which will slowly drop to zero as the engine warms up (photo).

7   If there is no vacuum, check the coolant controlled engine vacuum switch (CCEVS) for continuity. If there is no continuity, correct the fault or replace the switch (photo).

8   With the engine at operating temperature, shut it off, remove the vacuum hose from the valve and then connect a hand vacuum pump to the valve. Start the engine and make sure air blows out of the side port. Apply vacuum to the valve. Air should now blow out of the bottom port of the valve.

9   Before proceeding, check the engine temperature sensor as described in Chapter 5.

Carburetor regulator

10   Remove the computer vacuum hose and plug it. Connect a vacuum pump to the carburetor and apply 14 in Hg of vacuum. With the engine at 2000 rpm, disconnect the regulator solenoid connector at the solenoid. On non air conditioned models, only the green wire need be disconnected. The engine speed should increase at least 50 rpm. Reconnect the solenoid wire(s) and make sure that the engine speed slowly returns to normal.

10.6 The reading should slowly drop on the vacuum gauge attached to the air switching valve hose

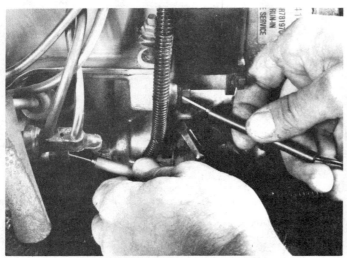

10.7 Checking the coolant controlled engine vacuum switch for continuity

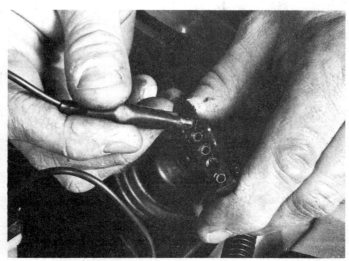

10.11 Grounding pin 15 of the six pin connector

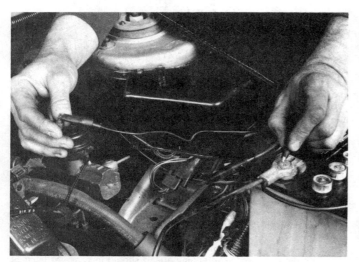

10.14 Grounding the oxygen sensor wire to the *negative* battery post

10.16 Holding the choke plates closed while testing the oxygen sensor

11 Unplug the six pin connector from the combustion control computer and momentarily connect a ground to connector pin 15 (photo).
12 Engine speed should decrease at least 50 rpm. If it does not, check the carburetor for air leaks.

Electronic fuel control computer
13 With the engine at normal operating temperature and the carburetor switch not grounded, connect a tachometer.
14 Start the engine and maintain an idle of 2000 rpm. Connect a voltmeter to the green solenoid output wire which leads to the carburetor. Disconnect the electrical harness at the oxygen sensor and connect a jumper wire between the harness connector and the negative battery terminal (photo).
15 The engine speed should increase at least 50 rpm and the voltmeter should read at least nine volts. With the wire held in one hand, touch the battery positive terminal with your other hand. The engine speed should drop by a least 50 rpm and the voltmeter reading should be three volts or less. Replace the computer with a new one if it fails both tests.

Oxygen sensor
16 Connect the voltmeter to the solenoid output wire, reconnect the oxygen sensor and make sure the carburetor switch is not grounded.

Start the engine, run it at 2000 rpm and hold the choke plates closed (photo). This simulates a full rich condition and within ten seconds the voltage should drop to three volts or less. If it does not, disconnect the PCV hose. This simulates a full lean condition and the voltage should increase to nine volts or more. Do not take more than 90 seconds to complete these tests. If the sensor fails both tests, replace it with a new one.

Component replacement
17 Replacement of the ignition computer is covered in Chapter 5.
18 Mark the hose locations on the air switching valve, remove the hoses and disconnect the valve.
19 The CCEVS is replaced by removing the vacuum hoses and unscrewing the valve. Coat the threads of the new valve with a suitable gasket sealant prior to installation.
20 To replace the carburetor solenoid switch, unplug the electrical connector and remove the two retaining screws. Lift the switch from the carburetor.
21 Disconnect the oxygen sensor wire and use a suitable wrench to unscrew the sensor. Use a tap to clean the threads in the exhaust manifold. If the sensor is to be reinstalled, apply anti-seize compound to the threads. New sensors already have the anti-seize compound on their threads.

11 Mikuni carburetor (2.6L engine) emission system

General description

1 The Mikuni carburetor on 2.6L engines is equipped with a variety of devices which reduce emissions while maintaining driveability.

2 The system consists of a coasting air valve (CAV), air switching valve (ASV), deceleration spark advance system (DSAS), high altitude compensation (HAC) (on some models) and a throttle opener.

3 The CAV, ASV and DSAS reduce hydrocarbon emissions while maintaining driveability and fuel economy by shutting off fuel flow and advancing the spark during deceleration.

4 The HAC maintains the proper fuel/air mixture during high altitude driving by means of an atmospheric pressure operated bellows.

5 The throttle opener controls the engine idle speed during operation of the air conditioner.

Checking

ASV and CAV

6 With the engine at idle, unplug the solenoid valve electrical connector. If the idle speed drops or the engine stalls, the ASV and CAV are operating properly. With the engine again at idle, check the solenoid connector with a voltmeter. If no voltage is present, the wiring or speed sensor is faulty. Check the solenoid connector with the engine at 2500 rpm to make sure there is voltage. If there is no voltage, there is a fault in the speed sensor and it must be replaced with a new one.

DSAS

7 Connect a timing light and allow the engine to run at idle. With the timing light on the timing marks, disconnect the electrical connector from the solenoid valve. If the timing does not advance, the solenoid valve and/or advance mechanism are faulty.

HAC

8 Since special equipment is required to test the HAC, checking is confined to making sure associated hoses and connections are secure.

Throttle opener

9 With the engine idling, turn on the air conditioner. If the idle speed does not increase, there is a fault in the speed sensor or wiring.

Component replacement

10 Replacement of the distributor vacuum advance unit is described in Chapter 5.

11 Locate the solenoid valve or speed sensor by tracing the wires or hoses from the component which they control. Disconnect the wires and/or hoses and install a new unit.

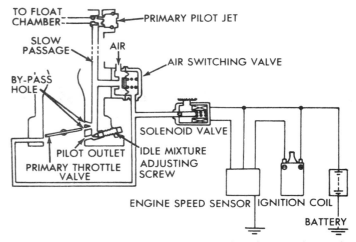

Fig. 6.16 2.6L engine Air Switching Valve (ASV) system (Sec 11)

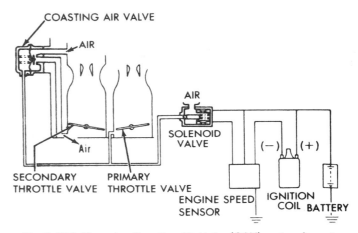

Fig. 6.17 2.6L engine Coasting Air Valve (CAV) system layout (Sec 11)

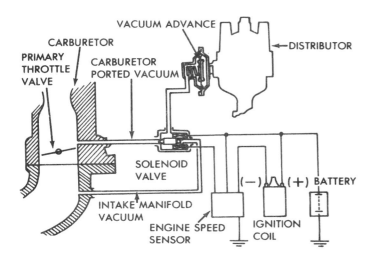

Fig. 6.18 Decelerator Spark Advance System (DSAS) (2.6L engine) (Sec 11)

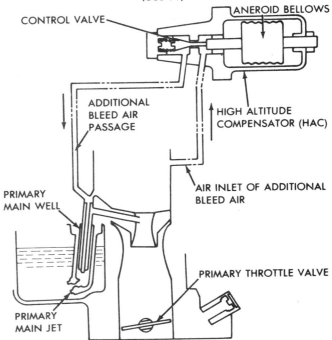

Fig. 6.19 High Altitude Compensation (HAC) system (2.6L engine) (Sec 11)

6

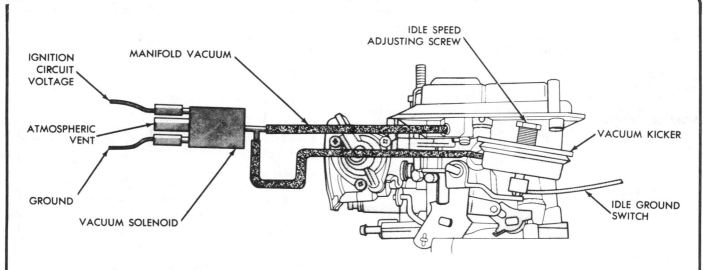

Fig. 6.20 Vacuum-type throttle kicker system (2.2L engine) (Sec 12)

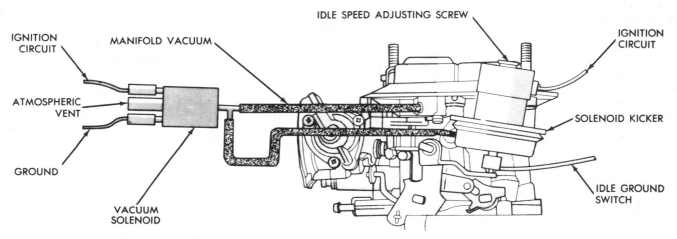

Fig. 6.21 Solenoid-type throttle kicker (2.2L engine) (Sec 12)

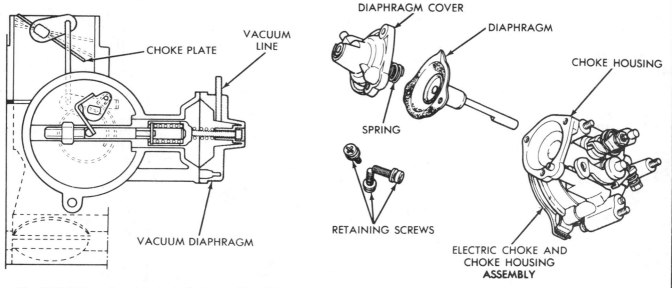

Fig. 6.22 2.2L engine electric choke layout (Sec 13)

Fig. 6.23 Electric choke components (Sec 13)

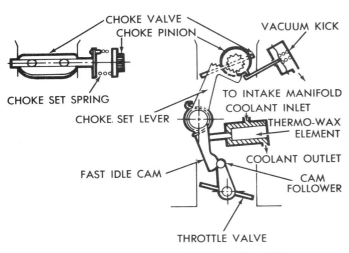

CHOKE VALVE
CHOKE PINION
VACUUM KICK
CHOKE SET SPRING
CHOKE. SET LEVER
TO INTAKE MANIFOLD
COOLANT INLET
THERMO-WAX ELEMENT
FAST IDLE CAM
COOLANT OUTLET
CAM FOLLOWER
THROTTLE VALVE

Fig. 6.24 2.6L engine choke layout (Sec 13)

12 Throttle kickers (2.2L engine)

General description

1 Solenoid and vacuum kickers are used on some models to maintain idle speed when additional loads, such as the actuation of the air conditioning, are put on the engine.

2 The vacuum kicker opens the throttle a fixed amount above idle when an electrical signal activates the kicker by supplying the necessary manifold vacuum. The idle speed is adjusted by a screw located at the top of the kicker.

3 When the engine is running, the solenoid kicker extends to hold the engine at the proper curb idle. The kicker retracts when the engine is turned off and manifold vacuum is no longer supplied. This allows the throttle to close so that fuel is cut off, reducing the possibility of the engine 'running on' or dieseling.

Checking

4 Checking consists of inspecting the kickers, wires and associated hoses for damage, wear and secure connections.

Component replacement

5 The throttle kickers can be replaced by removing the hoses and separating the electrical connectors.

13 Automatic choke system

General description

1 The automatic choke system temporarily supplies a rich fuel/air mixture to the engine by closing the choke plate(s) during cold engine starting.

2 On 2.2L engines, the choke is electrically operated, while 2.6L engines use sealed wax pellet-type choke systems.

3 On 2.2L engines, an electric signal from the oil pressure switch operates the choke control switch and activates the choke heater so that it slowly opens the choke plates as the engine warms up. This progressively leans out the mixture until the engine is warmed up.

4 On 2.6L engines, the wax pellet thermo sensing unit opens the choke as the coolant temperature increases. When started from cold, the choke valve is partially opened by a vacuum kicker actuated by manifold vacuum. This prevents an overly rich air/fuel mixture and the resultant increased emissions. The fast idle cam on the choke set lever controls the rate of throttle valve opening. If the vehicle is driven with a wide open throttle setting when cold, the choke is opened by the choke unloader so the mixture will not be overly rich.

Checking

5 The simplest test for the choke system is to warm the engine up to operating temperature (approximately five minutes running) and then remove the air cleaner to make sure the choke plates are open.

Component replacement

6 Choke component replacement is covered in Chapter 4.

6

Chapter 7 Part A Manual transaxle

Refer to Chapter 13 for specifications applicable to later models

Contents

Specifications

General

Transaxle type	4 or 5-speed, synchromesh on all forward speeds
Fluid type	DEXRON II automatic transmission fluid
Fluid capacity	
4-speed	2.0 qt (1.8L)
5-speed	2.3 qt (2.1L)

Torque specifications

	Ft-lb	Nm
Gearshift housing-to-case	21	28
Gearshift lever attaching nut	22	30
Fork stop plate-to-gearshift bolt	7	9
Anti-rotational strut bracket-to-stud nut	17	23
Fill plug	24	33
Transaxle case-to-engine mount	70	95
Rod-type gearshift linkage clamp bolt	14	19
Rod-type gearshift lockpin	9	12
Cable-type selector adjusting screw	60 In-lb	7
Cable-type crossover adjusting screw	60 In-lb	7
Cable-type lockpin	9	12
Cable-type crossover cable locknut	20	28
Cable-type selector screw-to-bracket	5.2	7
Cable-type pull-up ring retaining nut	2.2	3
Speedometer gear bolt	5.2	7

1 General information

The manual transaxle combines the transmission and differential assemblies into one compact unit.

The gearshift features a manual reverse lockout device and synchromesh is used on all forward speeds. Two types of gearshift linkage are used. On 4-speed models the shifting mechanism is operated by rods, while 5-speed models use a cable design.

2 Rod-type gearshift linkage – adjustment

1   Open the hood and cover the left front fender to protect against scratches.
2   Remove the lock pin located in the transaxle selector shaft housing.
3   Invert the lockpin so the long end is down. Insert the lockpin into the hole while pushing the selector shaft into the housing until the hole in the shaft is aligned with the pin.
4   Thread the lockpin into the housing. The selector is now locked in the 1st/2nd neutral position.
5   Raise the vehicle and support it securely.
6   From underneath the vehicle, loosen the gearshift-to-connector clamp bolt. Make sure the connector moves freely within the tube.
7   Place the shifter mechanism in position with the isolator contacting the upright flange and the isolator rib aligned with the hole

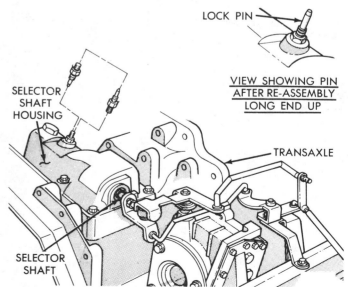

Fig. 7.1 Using the lockpin to pin the selector shaft in the 1st/2nd position (Sec 2)

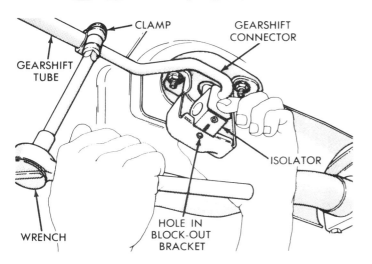

CLAMP

GEARSHIFT
CONNECTOR

GEARSHIFT
TUBE

ISOLATOR

HOLE IN
BLOCK-OUT
BRACKET

WRENCH

Fig. 7.2 Rod-type shift linkage adjustment (Sec 2)

in the lock-out bracket. With no pressure on the linkage, tighten the clamp bolt to the specified torque.
8   Lower the vehicle.
9   Remove the lockpin, reverse it so the longer end is upright, thread it into place and tighten it to the specified torque.

10 Check the gearshift action in 1st and Reverse and make sure the reverse lockout works properly.

3   Cable operated gearshift linkage – adjustment

1   Raise the hood and place a pad or blanket over the left fender to protect it.
2   Remove the lockpin from the transaxle selector shaft housing. Reverse the lockpin so the longer end is down, reinstall it into its hole and move the selector shaft in. When the lockpin aligns with the hole in the selector shaft, thread it into place so the shaft is locked in the 1st/2nd neutral position.
3   Pull off the gearshift knob, remove the pull-up ring retaining nut and lift off the pull-up ring.
4   Fabricate two five inch long adjusting pins from $\frac{5}{32}$ inch wire. Bend about one inch of each pin at right angles so the pins are easy to grasp.
5   Insert one adjusting pin into the crossover cable hole of the shift mechanism and the other into the selector cable hole as shown in the accompanying illustration.
6   Use an In-lb torque wrench to adjust the selector cable adjusting screw to the specified torque as shown in the accompanying illustration.
7   Use the In-lb torque wrench to adjust the crossover cable adjusting screw as shown in the accompanying illustration.
8   Remove the adjusting pins from the shift mechanism.
9   Install the console, pull-up ring and nut and the shift knob.
10 Unscrew the lock pin from the selector housing, reinstall it with the longer end up and tighten it to the specified torque.

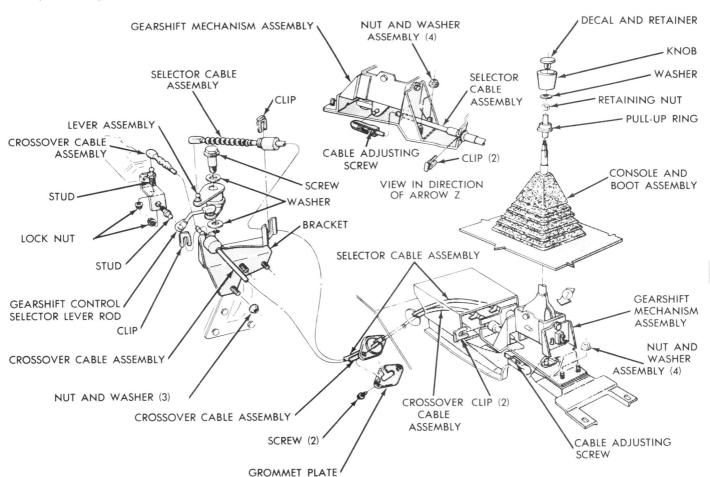

GEARSHIFT MECHANISM ASSEMBLY

NUT AND WASHER
ASSEMBLY (4)

DECAL AND RETAINER

KNOB

WASHER

SELECTOR CABLE
ASSEMBLY

SELECTOR
CABLE
ASSEMBLY

RETAINING NUT

PULL-UP RING

CLIP

LEVER ASSEMBLY

CROSSOVER CABLE
ASSEMBLY

CABLE ADJUSTING
SCREW

CLIP (2)

CONSOLE AND
BOOT ASSEMBLY

STUD

SCREW

WASHER

VIEW IN DIRECTION
OF ARROW Z

LOCK NUT

STUD

BRACKET

GEARSHIFT CONTROL
SELECTOR LEVER ROD

SELECTOR CABLE ASSEMBLY

GEARSHIFT
MECHANISM
ASSEMBLY

CLIP

NUT AND
WASHER
ASSEMBLY (4)

CROSSOVER CABLE ASSEMBLY

NUT AND WASHER (3)

CROSSOVER CABLE ASSEMBLY

CROSSOVER
CABLE
ASSEMBLY

CLIP (2)

SCREW (2)

CABLE ADJUSTING
SCREW

GROMMET PLATE

7A

Fig. 7.3 Cable type shift linkage component layout (Sec 3)

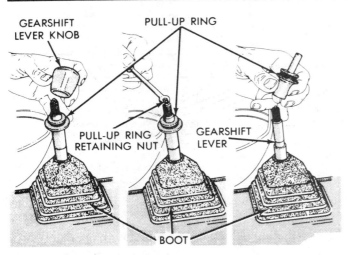

Fig. 7.4 Removal or installation of the gearshift knob and pull-up ring (cable-type) (Sec 3)

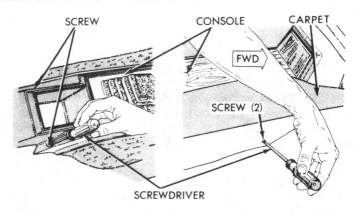

Fig. 7.5 Shift console removal or installation (Cable-type) (Sec 3)

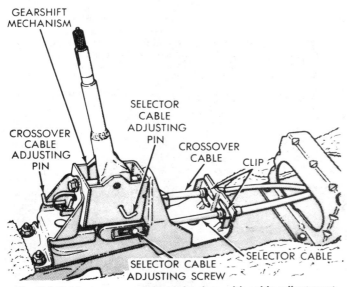

Fig. 7.6 Cable-type gearshift mechanism with cable adjustment pins installed (Sec 3)

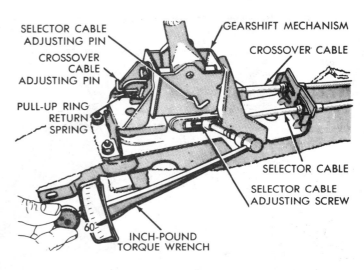

Fig. 7.7 Selector cable adjustment (Sec 3)

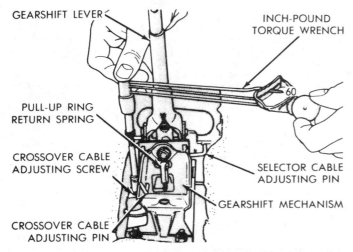

Fig. 7.8 Adjusting the crossover cable (Sec 3)

11   Check the shifter operation in 1st and Reverse and make sure the reverse lockout mechanism works properly.

4   Manual transaxle – removal and installation

1   Disconnect the negative battery cable.
2   Remove the hood (Chapter 12), raise the front end of the vehicle and support it securely.
3   Attach a suitable lifting device to the number 4 cylinder exhaust manifold bolts and support the engine weight. Alternatively, a jack can be used to support the engine.
4   Disconnect the gearshift linkage, clutch cable and speedometer drive gear.
5   Remove the front wheels and the left splash shield.
6   Place a suitable size (at least three quarts capacity) pan under the transaxle and drain the fluid by removing the rear end cover.
7   Place a jack under the transaxle to support its weight.
8   Remove the clutch housing bolts.
9   Remove the left engine mount.
10 Unbolt the anti-rotational link.
11 Remove the driveaxles as described in Chapter 8.
12 Pull the transaxle carefully away from the engine and lower it to the floor with the jack, taking care not to let the clutch plate fall.

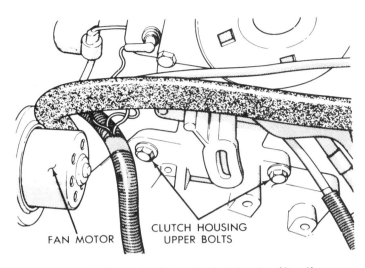

Fig. 7.9 Upper clutch housing bolt location (Sec 4)

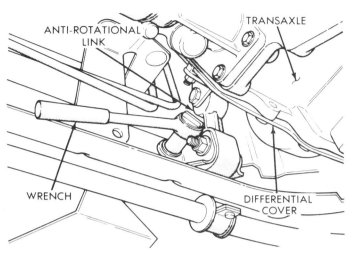

Fig. 7.10 Anti-rotational link removal or installation (Sec 4)

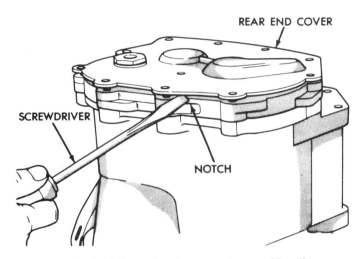

Fig. 7.11 Removing the transaxle cover (Sec 4)

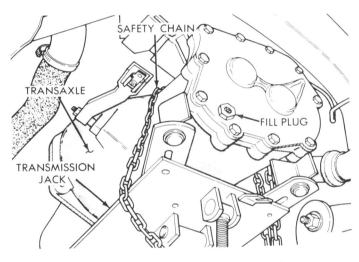

Fig. 7.12 Lowering the transaxle with a jack (Sec 4)

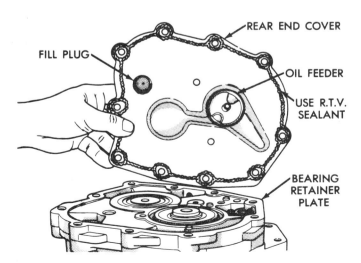

Fig. 7.13 Installing the transaxle cover (Sec 4)

7A

13 When installing the transaxle, locating pins can be fabricated and used in place of the top two bolts. Cut the heads off two suitable bolts with a hacksaw and remove any burrs from the ends with a file or grinder. Use a hacksaw to cut slots in the ends of the locating pins so they can be unscrewed with a screwdriver and replaced with bolts.

14 Install the driveaxles (Chapter 8).

15 Install the anti-rotational link, tightening the nut to the specified torque.

16 Install the left engine mount, tightening the bolts to the specified torque.

17 If the transaxle rear cover has not been installed during removal, clean the cover and mating surface thoroughly. Apply a $\frac{1}{8}$ inch bead of RTV sealant to the cover and install the cover and bolts.

18 Fill the transaxle to the bottom of the fill plug hole with the specified lubricant.

19 Install the splash shield and the front wheels.

20 Remove the support from the engine and connect the battery cable.

21 Lower the front of the vehicle.

22 Check the gearshift linkage operation to make sure all gears engage smoothly and easily. If they do not, adjust the linkage as described in the appropriate Section.

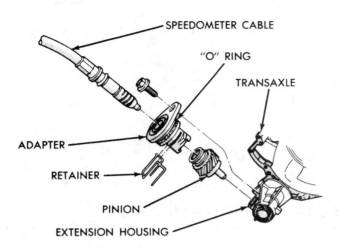

Fig. 7.14 Speedometer gear assembly (Secs 6 and 13)

Labels on figure: SPEEDOMETER CABLE, "O" RING, TRANSAXLE, ADAPTER, RETAINER, PINION, EXTENSION HOUSING

5   Manual transaxle speedometer gear assembly – removal and installation

1   The speedometer gear assembly is located in the differential extension housing.

2   Remove the retaining bolt and carefully work the speedometer assembly up and out of the extension housing.

3   Remove the retainer and separate the pinion from the adapter.

4   Check the speedometer cable to make sure that transaxle fluid has not leaked into it. If there is fluid in the cable, remove the adapter and replace the small O-ring with a new one. Reconnect the cable to the adapter.

5   Install a new O-ring and connect the adapter to the gear, making sure the assemblies are securely seated.

6   Make sure the mating surfaces of the adapter and the extension mating surfaces are clean, as any debris could cause misalignment of the gear.

7   Attach the assembly to the transaxle extension, install the retaining bolt and tighten it to the specified torque.

6   Manual transaxle service

Because of the special tools and procedures required for disassembly and overhaul of the transaxle, it is recommended that it be left to a dealer or a properly equipped shop.

Chapter 7 Part B Automatic transaxle

Contents

Specifications

General
Transaxle type .... 3-speed, fully automatic
Fluid type .... DEXRON II or equivalent
Fluid capacity
    1981 and 1982
        Transaxle .... 7.5 US qts
        Differential .... 1.2 US qts
    1983 (transaxle only) .... 8.9 US qts

Band adjustment (number of turns from the specified torque)
Kickdown .... Back off $2\frac{3}{4}$ turns from 72 In-lb (8 Nm)
Low-Reverse (rear) .... Back off $3\frac{1}{2}$ turns from 41 In-lb (5 Nm)
Low-Reverse band end gap .... 0.080 in (2 mm)

Torque specifications

	Ft-lb	Nm
Oil pan bolts	14	19
Filter-to-transaxle valve body	3	5
Kickdown band adjusting screw	72 In-lb	8
Kickdown band locknut	35	47
Low-Reverse band locknut	20	27
Low-Reverse band adjusting screw	50 In-lb	5
Neutral start and back-up light switch	24	33
Speedometer gear bolt	5.2	7
Torque converter-to-driveplate bolt	40	54

7   General information

The automatic transaxle combines a 3-speed automatic transmission and differential assembly into one unit. Power from the engine passes through the torque converter and the transmission to the differential assembly and then to the driveaxles.

The differential assemblies on 1981 and 1982 models have a fluid reservoir separate from the transaxle. It is important that the differential fluid levels be checked and maintained at the proper level (Chapter 1). On 1983 models the differential and transaxle share the same fluid and only one check is necessary to determine the level.

All models feature a transaxle oil cooler with the cooler element located in the radiator side tank.

Due to the complexity of the automatic transaxle, it is recommended that any major troubleshooting or repair be left to a dealer or properly equipped shop. This Chapter will cover information useful to the owner during routine maintenance procedures.

8   Gearshift linkage – adjustment

1   From inside the vehicle, place the gearshift lever in Park.
2   In the engine compartment, loosen the gearshift cable clamp adjustment bolt on the bellhousing.
3   Place approximately ten pounds of pressure on the transaxle shift lever located in the engine compartment and hold it against the front detent of the Park position.
4   Hold the pressure on the shift lever and tighten the cable clamp bolt (photo).
5   Check the shift lever in the Neutral and Drive positions to make sure it is within the confines of the lever stops. The engine must start only when the lever is in the Park or Neutral positions.

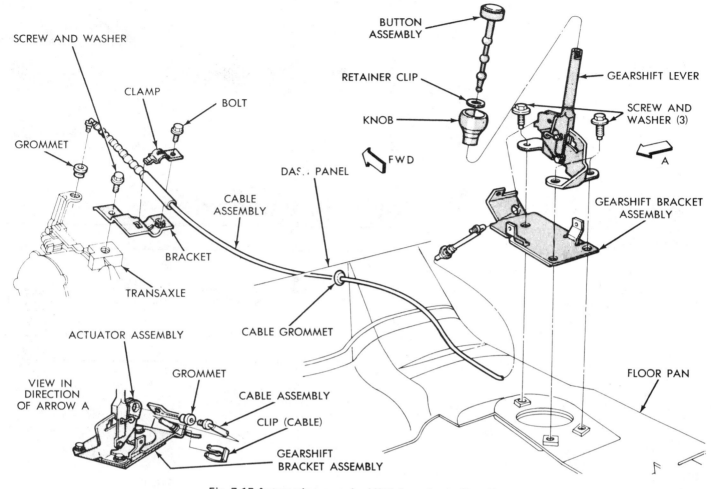

Fig. 7.15 Automatic transaxle shift linkage layout (Sec 8)

8.4 Tightening the shift cable clamp bolt

9 Throttle cable – adjustment

1   The throttle cable controls a valve in the transaxle which governs shift quality and speed. If shifting is harsh or erratic, the throttle cable should be adjusted.
2   The adjustment should be made with the engine at normal operating temperature or the choke disconnected to ensure the carburetor is not on the fast idle cam.
3   Loosen the cable adjustment bracket lock screw and check to make sure the bracket slides freely along its slot. If it does not, disassemble the bracket and clean and lubricate it and the case sliding surface.
4   With free action assured, slide the bracket toward the engine until it stops. Release the bracket and then slide it to the rear against its internal stop. Hold it firmly in place and tighten the lock screw. This adjusts the throttle cable by removing the cable backlash.
5   Connect the choke (if disconnected) and check the cable action. Move the transaxle throttle cable all the way forward, release it slowly and make sure that it returns completely.

10 Fluid and filter change

1   The automatic transaxle fluid and filter should be changed and the bands adjusted (Section 11) at the recommended intervals.
2   Raise the vehicle and support it securely.
3   Place a suitable container under the oil pan. Remove the pan bolts, tap the corner of the pan (photo) to break the sealant material loose and allow the fluid to drain into the container. Remove the oil pan.

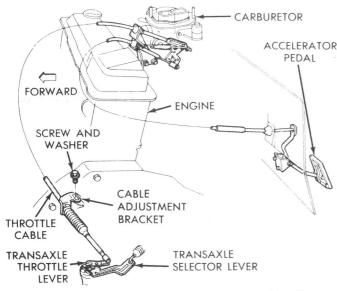

Fig. 7.16 Throttle control component layout (Sec 9)

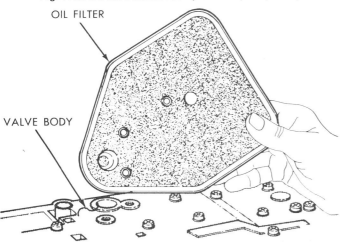

Fig. 7.17 Removing the filter (Sec 10)

10.3 Use a soft-faced hammer to break the corner of the oil pan loose

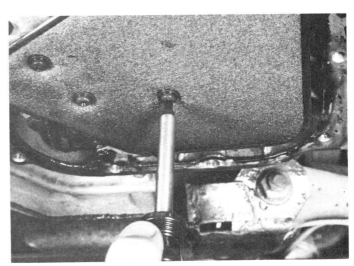

10.4 Removing the fluid filter screws

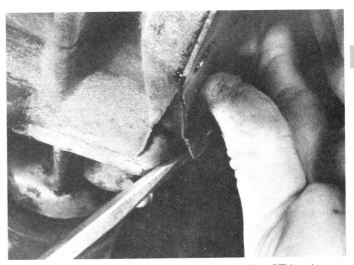

10.12 Pry the differential cover bottom edge free of the RTV sealant

4   Remove the filter screws using a screwdriver and a suitable TORX screwdriver and lower the filter from the transaxle (photo).
5   Adjust the transaxle bands at this time (Section 11).
6   Install the new filter and tighten the screws securely.
7   Carefully clean the mating surfaces of the pan and the transaxle case, removing all traces of sealant and taking care not to nick or gouge the surfaces.
8   Apply a $\frac{1}{8}$ inch bead of RTV sealant to the oil pan, place it in position, making sure the magnet is in the recess in the corner. Install the bolts and tighten them to the specified torque.
9   Lower the vehicle.
10 Pour four quarts of the specified fluid into the transaxle, taking care that the dipstick is completely seated afterward.
11 Warm up the fluid by allowing the engine to idle for approximately two minutes. Move the shift lever through each position, ending in Park or Neutral.
12 On 1981 and 1982 models only, remove the differential cover bolts, place a suitable pan underneath the cover to catch the gush of fluid and carefully pry the cover loose at the bottom (photo).
13 Clean the mating surfaces of the transaxle case and differential cover and remove all traces of RTV sealant.
14 Apply a $\frac{1}{8}$ inch bead of RTV sealant to the clean differential cover and install it on the transaxle. Install the bolts and tighten them to the specified torque in a criss-cross fashion.
15 Fill the differential to the bottom of the filler plug hole with the specified fluid. Install the plug and tighten it to the specified torque.
16 Check the transaxle fluid level as described in Chapter 1.

7B

11.7 Tighten the kickdown band locknut while holding the adjusting screw in place

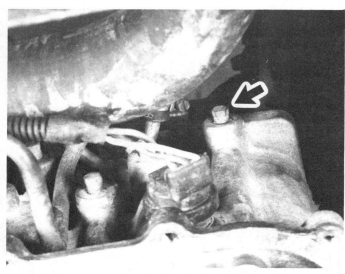

11.9 Low-Reverse pressure plug location (arrow)

11.10 Measuring the Low-Reverse band end clearance

11.11 Removing the parking rod

11.12 Tightening the Low-Reverse locknut to the specified torque

11.13 Back off the adjusting screw the specified number of turns

11.14 The shift pawl (arrow) must be pushed back before the shift rod can be inserted

11 Band adjustment

1   The transaxle bands should be adjusted when specified in the maintenance schedule or at the time of a fluid and filter change (Section 10).

Kickdown band

2   The kickdown band adjustment screw and locknut is located at the top left of the transaxle case.
3   Mark its position and then remove the throttle cable adjustment bolt. Move the cable away from the band adjustment screw.
4   Loosen the locknut approximately five turns and make sure the adjusting screw turns freely.
5   Tighten the adjusting screw to the specified torque.
6   Back the adjusting screw off the specified number of turns.
7   Hold the screw in position and tighten the locknut (photo).

Low-Reverse band

8   To gain access to the low-Reverse band, it is necessary to remove the oil pan (Section 10).
9   To determine if adjustment is necessary, remove the low-Reverse pressure plug from the transaxle case and apply 30 pounds of air pressure (photo).
10   Measure the gap between the band ends and compare this to the Specifications (photo).
11   Remove the parking rod E-clips and remove the rod (photo).
12   To adjust, loosen the locknut approximately five turns. Use an In-lb torque wrench to tighten the adjusting screw to the specified torque (photo).
13   Back the screw off the specified number of turns (photo).
14   Hold the adjusting screw in position and tighten the locknut to the specified torque.
15   Push the shift pawl in the transaxle case to the rear and reinstall the parking rod (photo).
16   Install the oil pan and refill the transaxle (Section 10).

12 Neutral start and back-up light switch – testing and replacement

1   The neutral start and back-up light switch is located at the lower front edge of the transaxle. The switch controls the back-up light and the starting of the engine in Park and Neutral. The center terminal of the switch grounds the starter solenoid circuit when the transaxle is in Park or Neutral, allowing the engine to start.
2   Prior to testing the switch, make sure the gearshift linkage is properly adjusted (Section 8).
3   Unplug the connector and use an ohmmeter to check for conti-

nuity between the center terminal and the case with the transaxle in both Park and Neutral.
4   With the transaxle in the Reverse position, check for continuity between the two outer terminals.
5   If the switch fails any of the tests, replace it with a new one.
6   Place a suitable container underneath the switch to catch the fluid released when the switch is removed. Unscrew the switch and lift it away from the transaxle.
7   Move the shift selector from Park to Neutral while checking that the switch operating fingers are centered in the opening.
8   Install the new switch, tighten it to the specified torque and plug in the connector. Repeat the described tests on the switch.
9   Check the fluid level, adding as necessary to bring it up to the proper level.

13 Speedometer gear – removal and installation

1   The speedometer gear is located at the top of the differential extension housing.
2   Remove the speedometer gear securing bolt and carefully work the assembly up and out of the differential extension housing.
3   Pull the retainer off and separate the speedometer pinion from the adaptor.
4   Check the speedometer cable for the presence of transaxle fluid. If there is fluid in the cable, separate it from the adaptor. Replace the small O-ring with a new one and reconnect the adaptor.
5   Using a new large O-ring, install the speedometer pinion onto the adaptor, taking care to seat it securely.
6   Prior to installation, make sure the speedometer pinion assembly and transaxle extension mating surfaces are clean.
7   Attach the speedometer assembly to the transaxle. Install the retaining bolt and tighten it to the specified torque.

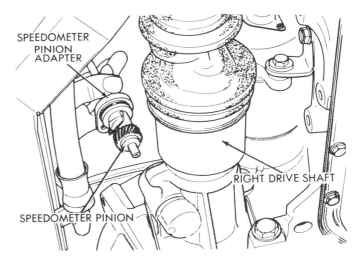

Fig. 7.18 Removing the automatic transaxle speedometer gear assembly (Sec 13)

14 Automatic transaxle – removal and installation

Removal

1   Disconnect the negative battery cable.
2   Drain the cooling system (Chapter 1).
3   On 2.2L engines, remove the air injection pump (Chapter 6).
4   Disconnect the heater hoses and move them out of the way.
5   Remove the transaxle shift and throttle position cables and fasten them out of the way.
6   Remove the air cleaner and the air injection pump support bracket.
7   Remove the axle cotter pins and nuts. Raise the vehicle and support it securely.
8   Remove the under vehicle splash shields.
9   Drain the transaxle (Section 10) and unplug all electrical connectors.

7B

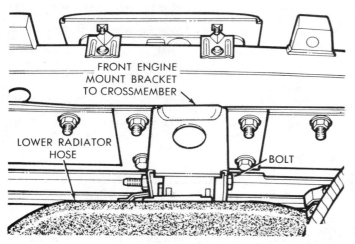

Fig. 7.19 Front transaxle mount through-bolt location (Sec 14)

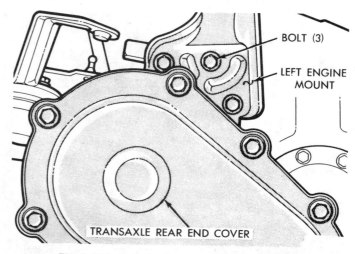

Fig. 7.20 Left transaxle mount location (Sec 14)

10 Disconnect the transaxle cooler lines from the radiator and plug them.
11 Loosen the swaybar bushing bolts, unbolt the ends from the lower control arms and pull the swaybar down out of the way.
12 Remove the driveaxles (Chapter 11).
13 Remove the three lower bellhousing bolts and loosen the engine mount-to-chassis through-bolt.
14 Remove the starter and wiring harness assembly.
15 Support the transaxle with a jack.
16 Remove the left transaxle-to-chassis mount bolts.
17 Support the engine with a jack (place a block of wood between the jack and the engine oil pan).
18 Remove the lower bellhousing cover to provide access to the torque converter.
19 Mark the torque converter-to-driveplate relationship so that they will be reinstalled in the same position. Remove the torque converter bolts.
20 Remove the front chassis-to-engine mount bolts from the engine and transaxle.
21 Remove the torque converter bolts, rotating the front pulley of the engine to expose the bolts one at a time.
22 Remove the left engine mount.
23 Remove the upper bellhousing bolts.
24 Carefully pry the transaxle away from the engine.
25 Pull the transaxle carefully away from the engine, making sure the torque converter remains on the input shaft.
26 Move the transaxle away from the engine and lower it from the engine compartment, taking care not to contact the inner end of the lower suspension arm.

Installation

27 To install, raise the transaxle into position with the torque converter in place on the input shaft.
28 Move the transaxle in place against the engine, align the bolt holes and install the upper bellhousing bolts.
29 Install the left engine mount.
30 Align the torque converter and driveplate marks made during removal, install the bolts and tighten to the specified torque.
31 Install the bellhousing cover and the front mount.

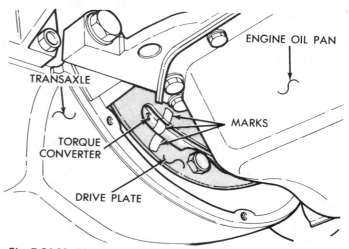

Fig. 7.21 Marking the torque converter-to-driveplate relationship
(Sec 14)

32 Install the starter and electrical harness.
33 Install the driveaxles.
34 Install the swaybar and tighten the bolts and nuts to the specified torque.
35 Plug in the transaxle electrical connectors.
36 Install the under vehicle splash shields.
37 Install the axle nuts, lower the vehicle and tighten the nuts as described in Chapter 11.
38 Install the air injection pump and bracket (2.2L engine).
39 Install the air cleaner assembly.
40 Connect the transaxle cooler lines to the radiator and tighten them securely.
41 Connect the transaxle shift and throttle cables.
42 Connect the heater hoses and refill the cooling system.
43 Refill the transaxle (Section 10).
44 Connect the negative battery cable.

Chapter 8 Clutch and driveaxles

Contents

Specifications

Clutch

Flywheel runout limit	0.003 in (0.07 mm)
Clutch lining wear limit	0.015 in (0.38 mm)
Clutch pressure plate flatness	0.020 in (0.50 mm)
Clutch cover warpage limit	0.015 in (0.38 mm)

Torque specifications

	Ft-lb	Nm
Flywheel-to-crankshaft bolts	65	88
Clutch-to-flywheel bolts	21	28
Clutch cable retainer bolt	21	28
Balljoint pinch bolt	50	68
Differential cover	14	19
Driveaxle hub nut	180	245
Wheel lug nut	80	108
Swaybar	22	30
Suspension rear bushing nut	70	94

1 General information

The clutch disc is held in place against the flywheel by the pressure plate springs. During disengagement, such as during gear shifting, the clutch pedal is depressed and operates a cable which pulls on the release lever so the release bearing pushes on the pressure plate springs, thus disengaging the clutch.

The clutch pedal incorporates a self-adjusting device which compensates for clutch disc wear. A spring in the clutch pedal arm maintains tension on the cable and the adjuster pivot grabs the positioner adjuster when the pedal is depressed and the clutch is released. Consequently the slack is always taken up in the cable, making adjustment unnecessary.

Power from the engine passes through the clutch and transaxle to the front wheels by two unequal length driveaxles. The driveaxles consist of three sections: the inner splined ends which are held in the differential by clips or springs, two constant velocity (CV) joints. The CV joints are internally splined and contain ball bearings because they operate at various lengths and angles as the driveaxles move through their full range of travel. The CV joints are lubricated with special grease and are protected by rubber boots which must be inspected periodically for cracks, tears or signs of leakage which could lead to damage of the joints and failure of the driveaxle.

2 Clutch — removal, inspection, overhaul and installation

1 Remove the transaxle (Chapter 7).
2 Mark the position of the clutch cover assembly on the flywheel so it can be installed in the same position.
3 Loosen the clutch cover bolts evenly, two turns at a time, in a criss-cross fashion so as not to warp the cover.
4 Remove the pressure plate and disc assembly.
5 Handle the disc carefully, taking care not to touch the lining surface and set it aside.
6 Remove the clutch release shaft.
7 Slide the clutch release bearing and fork assembly off the pilot. Remove the fork from the thrust plate. Inspect the bearing for damage, wear or cracks. Hold the center of the bearing and spin the outer portion. If the bearing doesn't turn smoothly or if it is noisy, replace it with a new one.
8 Clean the dust out of the clutch housing using a vacuum cleaner or clean cloth. Do not use compressed air as the dust can endanger your health if inhaled.
9 Inspect the friction surfaces of the clutch disc and flywheel for signs of uneven contact, indicating improper mounting or damaged clutch springs. Check the surfaces also for burned areas, grooves, cracks or other signs of wear. It may be necessary to remove a badly grooved flywheel and have it machined to restore the surface. Light

8

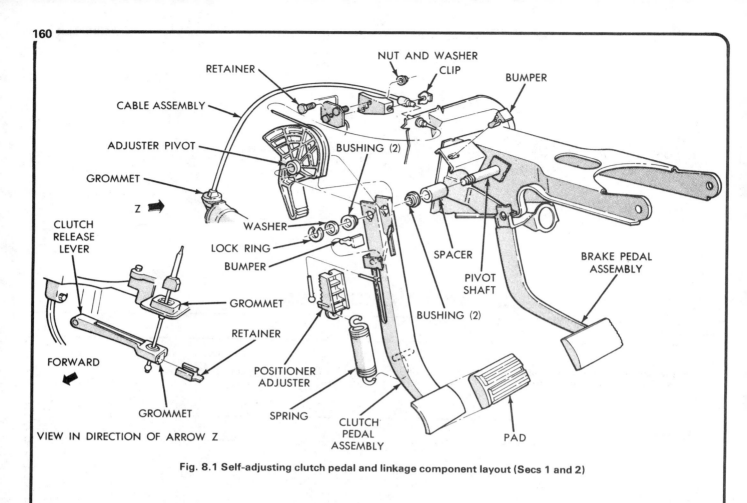

Fig. 8.1 Self-adjusting clutch pedal and linkage component layout (Secs 1 and 2)

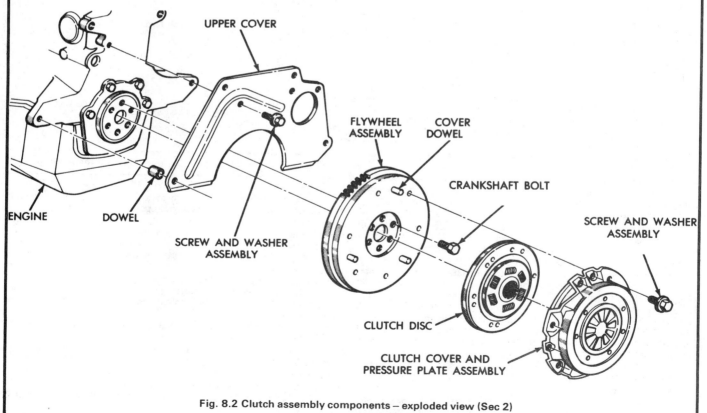

Fig. 8.2 Clutch assembly components – exploded view (Sec 2)

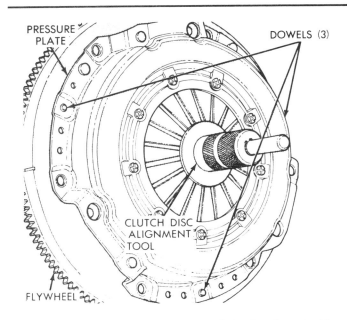

PRESSURE PLATE

DOWELS (3)

CLUTCH DISC ALIGNMENT TOOL

FLYWHEEL

Fig. 8.3 Installing the pressure plate and clutch, using a tool to align the disc (Sec 2)

glazing of the flywheel surface can be removed with fine sandpaper. Attach a dial indicator to the engine and, with the contact plunger within the wear circle of the flywheel, rotate the crankshaft 180 degrees. The flywheel runout should be within specifications. Be sure to push the crankshaft forward so its endplay won't be included in the runout measurement.

10 To determine clutch disc lining wear, measure the distance from the rivet head to the lining surface and compare this to the Specifications. Inspect the lining for contamination by oil, grease or other substances and replace the disc with a new one if any is present. Check the center of the disc to make sure it is clean and dry, shows no signs of overheating and that the springs are not broken. Slide the disc onto the input shaft temporarily to make sure the fit is snug and the splines are not burred or worn.

11 Check the flatness of the pressure plate with a straight-edge. Inspect for signs of over-heating, cracks, grooves or ridges. The inner end of the release levers should not show any signs of uneven wear. Replace the pressure plate with a new one if it is at all suspect.

12 Check the clutch cover for flatness, if possible, by using a surface plate of known accuracy. Make sure the cover fits snugly on the flywheel dowels. Replace the cover with a new one if it is warped beyond specification or fits loosely on the dowels.

13 Clean the old grease from the release bearing. Fill the cavities and coat the inner liner surfaces with multi-purpose grease.

14 Lubricate the rounded thrust pads and spring clip cavities of the fork with multi-purpose grease. Make sure the spring clips on the bearing are not distorted and then attach the fork to the bearing by sliding the thrust pads under the spring clips.

15 Position the clutch disc on the flywheel, centering it with an alignment tool.

16 With the disc held in place by the alignment tool, place the clutch cover and pressure plate assembly in position on the flywheel dowels, aligning it with the marks made at the time of removal.

17 Install the bolts and tighten them in a criss-cross manner, one or two turns at a time, until they are tightened to the specified torque.

18 Slide the fork and bearing assembly into position on the bearing pilot.

19 Install the release shaft bushings in the housing and slide the shaft into position. Retain the shaft with the clip which fits into the groove near the large bushing.

20 Install the release lever, retaining it to the shaft with the clip.

21 Install the transaxle.

3 Driveaxles, Constant velocity (CV) joints and boot – inspection

1 The driveaxles, CV joints and boot should be inspected periodically whenever the vehicle is raised, such as during chassis lubrication. The most common symptom of driveaxle or CV joint failure is a knocking or clicking noise during vehicle turns.

2 Raise the vehicle and support it securely.

3 Inspect the CV joint boots for signs of cracks, leaking lubricant or broken retaining bands. Should lubricant leak out through a hole or crack in a boot, the CV joint will wear prematurely and require replacement. Replace any damaged boots (Section 6).

4 Inspect along the length of each axle for cracks, dents or signs of twisting or bending.

5 Grasp each axle and rotate it in both directions, as well as in and out, to check for excessive movement indicating worn splines or loose CV joints.

4 Driveaxle – removal and installation

Removal

1 Remove the front hub cap, cotter key and nut lock. With the weight of the vehicle on the wheels and an assistant holding pressure on the brake pedal, loosen the axle nut.

2 Raise the vehicle, support it securely and remove the front wheel and axle nut.

3 On 1981 and 1982 automatic transaxle equipped models, it will be necessary to remove the differential cover and release the axleshaft retaining circlips. Remove the resistor plate to provide access and remove the differential cover as described in Chapter 7. Rotate the axleshafts to expose the tangs of the retaining circlips (photo).

4.3 The axleshaft retaining circlips (arrows) are located on the flat section of the inner axle ends

4 Use needle nose pliers to squeeze the tangs together and pry the tangs into the cavity in the side gear. Pull the axle out slightly.

5 On all models, remove the speedometer gear prior to removing the right hand axle.

6 Remove the steering knuckle pinch bolt.

7 Loosen the bushing bolts, unbolt the ends and lower the swaybar out of the way.

8 Remove the lower forward suspension arm through-bolt.

9 Pull the lower balljoint out of the steering knuckle.

10 Grasp the outer CV joint and pull in sharply to disengage it from the hub. Be careful not to damage the CV joint boot.

11 Grasp the CV joints so they will be supported during removal and withdraw the driveaxle from the differential (photo).

Installation

12 Prior to installation, lubricate the full circumference of the inner CV joint seal and outer wear sleeve with multi-purpose grease.

13 On 1981 and 1982 models, install new circlips in the inner CV joint grooves.

14 Apply a small amount of multi-purpose grease to the splines at both ends of the CV joints. Make sure the circlip tangs are aligned with

8

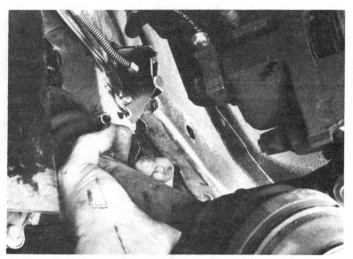

4.11 Support the CV joints so the boots are not twisted during driveaxle removal

the flat on the end of the shaft on 1981 and 1981 models (with automatic transaxles). Place the driveaxle in position and carefully insert the inner end of the shaft into the transaxle. Slide the shaft in and then thrust it in sharply, to seat the circlip in the differential. On 1981 and 1982 models with automatic transaxles, verify circlip engagement by inspecting the differential.

15 Pull the steering knuckle out and insert the outer splined shaft of the CV joint into the hub.

16 Install the balljoint stud and pinch bolt, tightening the bolt to the specified torque.

17 Install the swaybar ends, tightening all fasteners to the specified torque.

18 Install the speedometer gear.

19 On 1981 and 1982 models with automatic transaxle, install the cover and refill the differential (Chapter 7).

20 Install the wheels and the axle nut.

21 Lower the vehicle and with the weight on the suspension, tighten the lower suspension arm through-bolt to the specified torque.

22 Tighten the driveaxle hub nut to the specified torque and install the cotter key and nut lock as described in Chapter 11.

5 Constant velocity (CV) joints — removal, disassembly, inspection and installation

1 Obtain a CV joint replacement boot kit.
2 Remove the driveaxle (Section 4).

Fig. 8.4 Driveaxle and CV joint component layout (Secs 4 through 6)

1	Right outer CV joint and boot	5	Left inner CV joint and boot
2	Right inner CV joint and boot	6	Left outer CV joint and boot
3	Transaxle extension	7	Resistor plate
4	Transaxle		

8 Differential cover
9 Speedometer gear
10 Swaybar

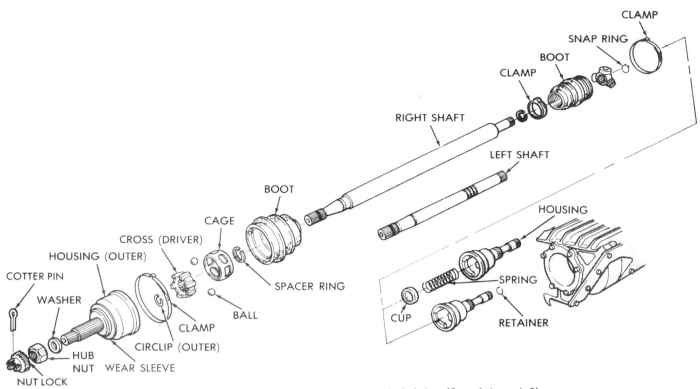

Fig. 8.5 Typical driveaxle components – exploded view (Secs 4 through 6)

3 Place the axleshaft in a vise, using wood blocks to protect its surface, so the CV joint can be easily worked on. If the CV joint has been operating properly, with no noise or vibration, replace the boot as described in Section 6. If the CV joint is badly worn or has run some time with no lubricant due to a damaged boot, it should be disassembled and inspected.

Inner CV joint
4 Remove the clamps and slide the boot back from the CV joint.
5 Clean the grease from the joint and inspect the bearings for wear, scoring or dirt contamination.
6 To remove the housing, slightly deform the retainer ring with a screwdriver at each roller (photo).
7 Rock the housing clear of one bearing, remove the outer race and lift the housing off making sure not to dislodge the needle bearings (photo).
8 Replace the outer bearing race and clean the grease from the tripod assembly. Inspect for scoring, wear, pitting or looseness and replace any damaged or worn components with new ones. Use tape to secure the bearings to the tripod assembly during removal.
9 Remove the snap-ring and use a brass drift to drive the bearing and tripod assembly from the splined shaft (photo).
10 Inspect the inner splined area of the bearing tripod for wear or damage, replacing parts as necessary.
11 Inspect the housing splines for wear, damage, nicks or rust, replacing parts as necessary.
12 Place the housing in the vise and remove the retainer ring with a pair of pliers (photo).
13 Clean out all of the old grease from the housing and inspect the wear sleeve and the housing surface for wear, nicks, dents, rust or other damage.
14 Install the new boot and retainer ring onto the axle.
15 Place the bearing tripod assembly onto the shaft with the dimpled side of the bearing body facing in (photo).
16 Use a suitable sized pipe or socket and a hammer to carefully tap the bearing assembly onto the shaft until it just clears the snap-ring groove.
17 Install a new snap-ring securely in the groove.
18 Use half of the lubricant supplied with the replacement boot kit to

carefully pack the housing evenly. Make sure to lubricate the roller bearing slots.
19 Place the housing in position on the shaft and press the retainer ring into place (photo).
20 Use a hammer and punch to stake the ring in place in the housing groove at several places around the outer circumference (photo).
21 Use the remaining grease to pack the interior of the boot and housing bearing cavity (photo).
22 Install the boot retaining strap (Section 6).
23 Install a new snap-ring at the housing splines (photo).

5.6 Carefully pry the retainer ring up at each bearing roller

5.7 Make sure the needle bearings are retained with grease while the outer race is removed

5.9 Carefully drive the bearing tripod from the shaft splines (note the tape retaining the bearings)

5.12 Pull the old retainer ring off the housing with pliers

5.15 Push the tripod assembly squarely onto the shaft splines

5.19 Seat the housing securely against the bearing tripod

5.20 Stake the ring in place in the housing groove

5.21 The housing should be packed with grease to just below the edge of the retainer ring

5.23 Carefully slide the new snap-ring onto the shaft and into the groove, taking care not to twist it

5.25A Dislodge the housing by tapping evenly around its outer circumference

5.25B Slide the housing from the splines

5.28 Mark the bearing cage and housing position with paint

5.29 With the cage tilted, the balls can be removed

5.33 Prying the wear sleeve off the housing

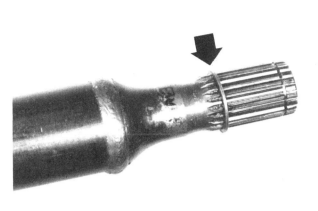

5.34 The axleshaft spacer ring (arrow) is not removed during normal inspection

5.35 The bearing cross land will slide easily into the cage at the elongated window (arrow)

5.36 Lower the cage and cross assembly into the housing with the elongated window (photo) aligned with the race

5.38 Fill the CV joint housing with grease (note that the alignment marks and bearing star counterbore all face up, indicating proper installation)

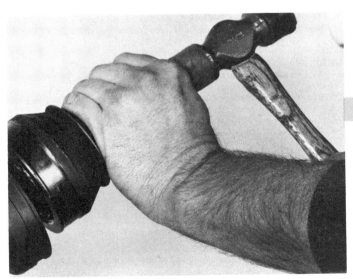

5.42 Strike the end of the CV joint housing shaft sharply with a soft-faced hammer to engage it with the axle circlip

8

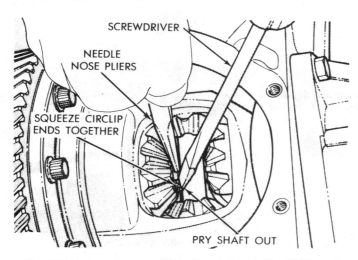

Fig. 8.6 Disengaging the axleshaft retaining circlips (1981 and 1982 automatic transaxle models) (Sec 4)

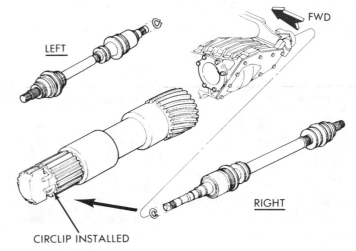

Fig. 8.7 Proper circlip installation (1981 and 1982 automatic transaxle models) (Sec 4)

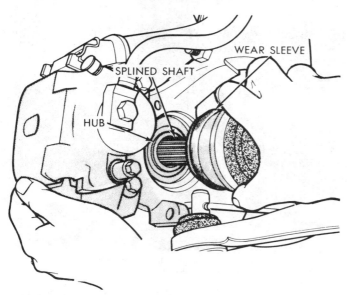

Fig. 8.8 Move the steering knuckle away, align the CV joint and hub splines and then pull the knuckle in to install the driveaxle (Sec 4)

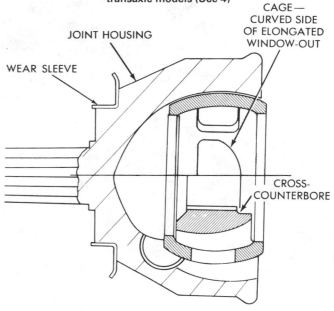

Fig. 8.9 Proper installation of the outer CV joint bearing cage (Sec 5)

Outer CV joint

24 Mount the axleshaft in a vise with wood blocks to protect it, remove the retaining straps and push the boot back.
25 Clean the grease from the joint and use a soft-faced hammer to drive the housing from the axle (photos).
26 Slide the boot off the axle.
27 Clean the axle spline area and inspect for wear, damage, corrosion and broken splines.
28 Clean the outer CV joint bearing assembly in a suitable solvent and dry it with a lint-free cloth or, preferably, with compressed air. Mark the relative positions of the bearing cage and housing (photo).
29 Place the housing securely in the wood blocks in the vise. Push down one side of the cage and remove the ball bearing from the opposite side. Repeat the procedure in a criss-cross pattern until all of the balls are removed (photo).
30 Remove the bearing race assembly from the housing.
31 Remove the bearing star from the cage.
32 Inspect the housing, splines, balls and races for damage, corrosion, pitting, wear or cracks. Check the bearing inner star for wear and scouring of the races. If any of the components are not serviceable, the entire CV joint assembly must be replaced with a new one.

33 Inspect the outer housing wear sleeve for wear, damage or dents. If it is damaged or worn, pry the sleeve from the housing and replace it with a new one (photo).
34 Inspect the axleshaft splines for damage, wear or corrosion. Remove the circlip from the groove at the end of the shaft but do not remove the spacer ring unless the shaft is to be replaced (photo).
35 Install the cross into the cage so the cross land fits into the elongated window of the cage (photo).
36 Rotate the cross into position in the cage and install the assembly into the CV joint housing, again using the elongated window for clearance (photo).
37 Rotate the cage into position so the curved side of the elongated windows and the inner cross counterbore are facing out. The marks made during disassembly should now all face up.
38 Pack the lubricant from the kit into the ball races and grooves (photo).
39 Install the balls into the elongated holes, one at a time, until they are all in position.
40 Place the axleshaft in the vise and slide the boot over it. Install a new circlip in the axle groove, taking care not to twist it.
41 If the wear sleeve has been removed, press the new one into place on the housing, making sure that it is installed squarely. This can be

achieved with a suitable size piece of pipe and a hammer if the special tool is not available.

42 Place the CV joint housing in position on the axle, align the splines and tap it sharply with a soft-faced hammer (photo).

43 Install the boot (Section 6).

44 Install the driveaxle (Section 4).

6 Constant velocity (CV) joint boot – removal and installation

1 If the boot is cut, torn or leaking, it must be replaced and the CV joint inspected as soon as possible. Even a small amount of dirt entering the joint can cause premature wear and failure. Obtain a replacement boot kit before beginning work.

2 Remove the driveaxle (Section 4).

3 Cut the retaining bands and remove the CV joint and boot (Section 5).

4 Inspect the CV joint and determine if it has been damaged by contamination of the lubricant or running with too little lubricant. If you have any doubts about the condition of the joint components, perform the inspection procedures described in Section 5.

5 Clean the old lubricant from the CV joint and repack it with the lubricant supplied with the kit.

6 Attach the new boot to the axleshaft and install the CV joint.

7 Pack the interior of the boot with the remaining lubricant.

8 Place the boot in position (photo). On tubular axleshafts, the boot lip should align with the mark on the shaft and on solid axleshafts, position the small end of the boot in the machined groove.

9 Wrap the retaining strap around the boot clamping surface and install the buckle. Bend back about $2\frac{1}{2}$ inches of the strap on the underside and secure it by pinching the strap flat with pliers. Insert the end of the strap through the buckle opening (photo).

10 Position the retaining strap on the clamping surface (photo).

11 Grasp the buckle with needle nose pliers and pull the strap until it is tight (photo).

12 Wrap the strap around the boot again, insert it through the buckle and pull it tight, using two pliers (photo).

13 Once the desired tension has been reached (deforming the boot material, but not cutting into it), bend the strap back over the buckle and cut off the excess (photo).

14 Bend the end of the strap underneath the buckle (photo).

15 Hold the strap and buckle with the pliers and then use a hammer to tap on the tip of the pliers to lock the assembly in place.

16 Repeat the operation on the other side of the CV joint boot.

17 After the boots have been replaced, install the driveaxle (Section 4).

6.8 Properly positioned outer CV joint boot

6.9 Proper retaining strap buckle installation

6.10 Placing the strap in position on the boot

6.11 Pulling the retaining strap tight

8

6.12 After inserting the strap through the buckle eye a second time, pull it tight with pliers

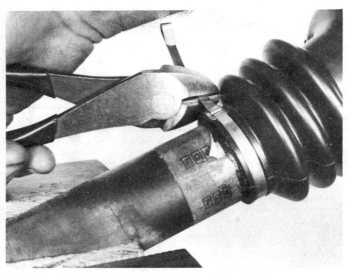

6.13 With the strap bent back over the buckle, cut off the excess, leaving about $\frac{1}{4}$ inch protruding beyond the buckle

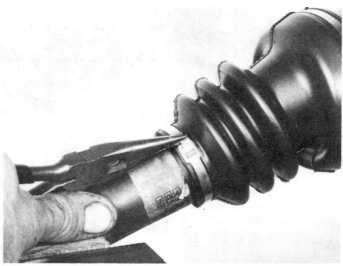

6.14 Bend the end of the strap under the buckle

Chapter 9 Braking system

Contents

Specifications

General
Brake fluid type .... DOT type 3

Drum brakes
Drum diameter
    Standard .... 7.87 in (200 mm)
    Heavy duty .... 8.6614 in (220 mm)
Wear limit .... Refer to marking on drum
Out-of-round limit .... 0.0035 in (0.8890 mm)
Runout limit .... 0.006 in (0.1524 mm)
Brake lining thickness
    Standard .... $\frac{3}{16}$ in (4.76 mm)
    Service limit .... $\frac{1}{8}$ in (3.2 mm)
Wheel cylinder bore diameter
    Standard .... $\frac{5}{8}$ in (15.9 mm)
    Heavy duty .... $\frac{9}{16}$ in (14.3 mm)

Disc brakes
Pad lining thickness
    Standard .... $\frac{11}{16}$ in (17.5 mm)
    Service limit .... $\frac{5}{16}$ in (7.9 mm)
Brake disc minimum allowable thickness .... Refer to marking on disc
Brake disc runout limit .... 0.004 in (0.1016 in)
Hub runout limit .... 0.002 in (0.04 mm)
Caliper bore diameter*
    Standard .... 2.130 in (54 mm)
    Service limit .... 0.001 in (0.0254 mm)
Piston diameter .... 2.13 in (54 mm)
Master cylinder bore diameter .... 0.8268 in (21.0 mm)
Power brake booster minimum vacuum .... 12 psi
* Measured within $\frac{1}{2}$ in of seal

Torque specifications

	Ft-lb	Nm
Brake caliper guide pin		
ATE	18 to 24	25 to 32
Kelsey Hayes	14 to 22	19 to 29
Adapter-to-steering knuckle	70 to 100	95 to 136
Bearing retainer mounting plate	14 to 22	19 to 29
Bleed screw	7 to 14	9 to 19
Brake line-to-caliper	19 to 29	26 to 40
Brake hose bracket	6 to 10	8 to 13
Splash shield bolts	17 to 25	23 to 24
Wheel cylinder-to-backing plate	6 to 10	8 to 14

Bleed screw	5 to 9	7 to 11
Bearing plate-to-rear axle bolts	35 to 55	47 to 75
Brake hose-to-wheel cylinder	10 to 15	13 to 20
Master cylinder-to-dash panel	17 to 21	23 to 29
Master cylinder-to-booster	14 to 21	19 to 29
Booster assembly-to-dash	17 to 20	23 to 28
Pedal pushrod bolt	30	41
Parking brake pedal assembly-to-side cowl	17 to 25	23 to 34
Parking brake handle-to-floor	17 to 25	23 to 24
Stoplight switch bracket	6	8
Brake pedal pivot bolt	30	41

1 General information

All models are equipped with disc-type front and drum-type rear brakes which are hydraulically operated and feature vacuum assist.

The front brakes feature a single piston, floating caliper design. The rear drum brakes are of the leading and trailing shoe type with a single anchor pivot.

The front disc brakes automatically compensate for wear during usage. The rear drum brakes on 1981 and 1982 models require adjustment at the recommended intervals. 1983 models feature automatic adjustment.

Front drive vehicles tend to wear the front brake pads at a faster rate than rear drive vehicles. Consequently it is important to inspect the pad linings frequently to make sure they have not worn to the point where the disc itself is scored or damaged.

All models are equipped with a cable-actuated parking brake which operates the rear wheels.

The system is a dual line type with a dual master cylinder and separate hydraulic systems for the front and rear brakes. In the event of a brake line or seal failure, half the brake system will still operate.

Two different types of front disc brakes are used on these models, ATE and Kelsey Hayes. 1981 and 1982 models use ATE brakes and 1983 models can be equipped with either ATE or Kelsey Hayes. The brakes differ in design and parts are not interchangeable.

2 Disc brake pads – inspection

Refer to Chapter 1 for disc brake checking procedures.

3 Disc brake pads (ATE) – removal and installation

1   Raise the front of the vehicle and support it securely. Block the rear wheels and set the parking brake. It is a good idea to disassemble only one brake at a time so the other brake can be used as a guide if difficulties are encountered during reassembly.
2   Remove the front wheels.
3   Remove the hold down spring (photo).
4   Loosen the caliper pins sufficiently to allow the caliper to be removed (photo).
5   Lift the caliper out and away from the brake disc. The inner pad will remain with the caliper (photo).
6   Unsnap the inner pad and remove it (photo).
7   Remove the outboard pad from the brake adapter (photo).
8   Support the caliper with a piece of wire so it will be out of the way and no strain is placed on the hose.
9   Measure the brake pad lining thickness and compare this to the Specifications (photo).
10 Inspect the caliper for damage, rust and leaking fluid.
11 Attach the inner pad to the caliper by pressing the retainer into the piston recess.
12 Place the outer pad into position in the caliper adapter.
13 Install the caliper over the brake disc and adapter.
14 Install the guide pins, taking care to align them as they can be easily cross threaded.
15 Install the hold down spring.
16 Install the wheels and lower the vehicle. It is a good idea to bleed the brakes.
17 Test drive the vehicle and apply the brakes smoothly and easily for the first 20 miles or so because it is easy to overheat new pads and glaze their contact surfaces.

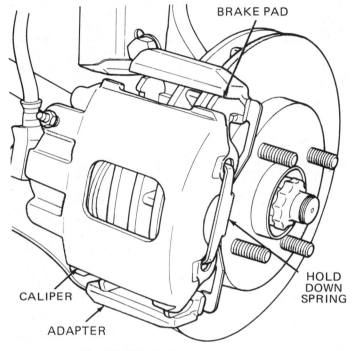

Fig. 9.1 ATE disc brake (Secs 1 and 3)

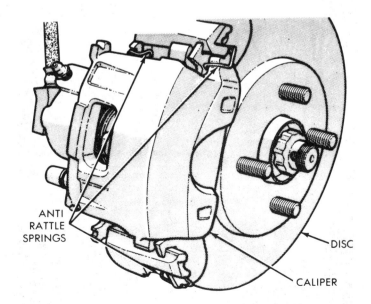

Fig. 9.2 Kelsey Hayes disc brake (Secs 1 and 3)

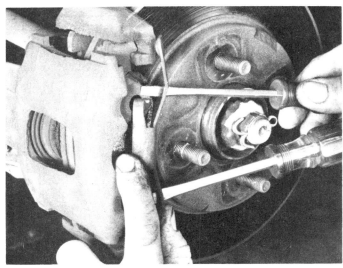

3.3 Use two screwdrivers to lift the outer ends of the hold down spring while lifting the center portion from the caliper

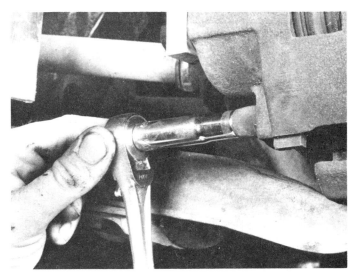

3.4 Loosen, but do not remove the caliper pins

3.5 Make sure the inner pad does not fall out when lifting the caliper off

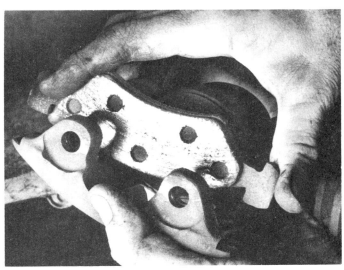

3.6 Pull the inner pad out sharply to disengage it from the piston

3.7 Lifting the outer pad from the adapter (note the wire hook retaining the caliper out of the way)

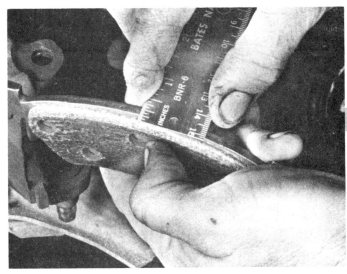

3.9 Measuring the brake pad lining thickness

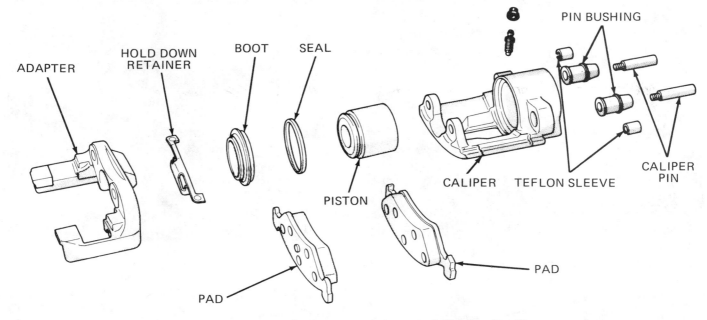

Fig. 9.3 ATE disc brake caliper components – exploded view (Sec 3)

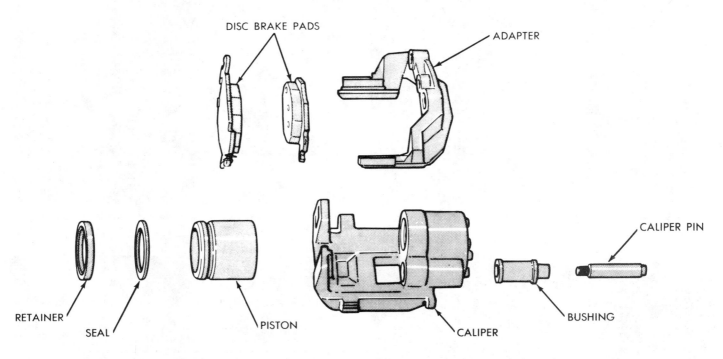

Fig. 9.4 Kelsey Hayes disc brake caliper components – exploded view (Sec 4)

4 Disc brake pads (Kelsey Hayes) – removal and installation

1 Perform Steps 1 and 2 of Section 3.
2 Remove the caliper guide pin and slide the caliper off the adapter and pads. It may be necessary to carefully pry the caliper loose with a screwdriver or similar tool.
3 Support the caliper out of the way with a wire hanger, taking care not to put a strain on the brake hose.
4 Disengage the spring and lift the outer brake pad from the adapter.
5 Remove the brake disc (Section 5).

6 Disengage the anti-rattle clip and remove the inner brake pad.
7 Measure the brake pad lining thickness and compare it to the Specifications.
8 Inspect the caliper for wear, damage, rust and fluid leaks.
9 Install the inner brake pad, making sure the anti-rattle spring is secure.
10 Install the brake disc (Section 5).
11 Place the outer pad in position in the adapter grooves.
12 Slide the caliper into position over the pad and disc assembly.
13 Install the guide pin and tighten it to the specified torque.
14 Perform Steps 15 and 16 of Section 3.

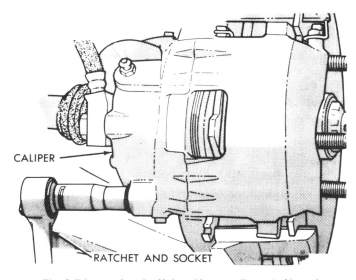

Fig. 9.5 Loosening the Kelsey Hayes caliper pin (Sec 4)

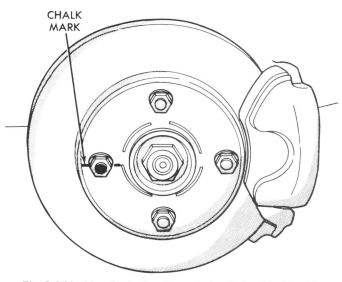

Fig. 9.6 Marking the brake disc-to-hub relationship (Sec 5)

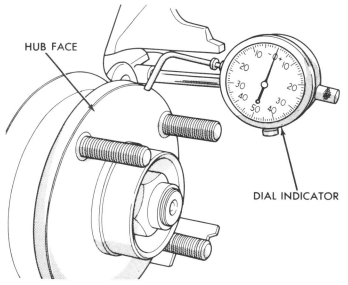

Fig. 9.7 Checking hub runout (Sec 5)

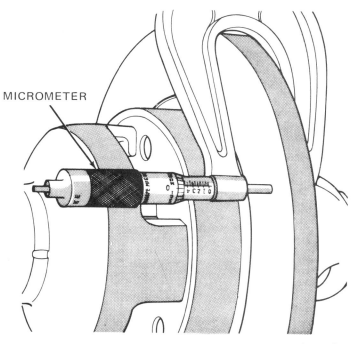

Fig. 9.8 Checking brake disc thickness with a micrometer (Sec 5)

5.4 Unscrew the disc retainer

5 Brake disc – removal, inspection and installation

1   Raise the front of the vehicle, support it securely and remove the front wheels.
2   Remove the caliper and pads (Sections 3 and 4).
3   On ATE brakes, unbolt and remove the caliper adapter.
4   Remove the disc retainer (photo).
5   Mark one wheel stud and the disc so that it can be reinstalled in the same relative position and remove the disc from the hub.
6   Use a dial indicator to check the hub runout. Replace the hub (Chapter 11) if the runout is beyond specification.
7   Inspect the disc for cracks, scoring, rust, ridges or distortion. If the damage goes so deep into the friction surface that the disc cannot be refinished and still maintain the minimum thickness, it must be replaced with a new one.
8   Reinstall the disc in the marked position and install the wheel lug nuts with the chamfered side out.
9   Check the disc for runout with a dial indicator.

9

10 If the runout is beyond the Specifications, remove the disc and reinstall it 180° from the original position. Recheck the runout and if it is still out of specification, either have the disc refaced or replace it with a new one.

11 With the disc in its original position, check the thickness at 12 places around its circumference. Replace the disc with a new one if it is out of specification or have it refinished if it can be done without reducing the thickness beyond the minimum.

12 On Kelsey Hayes brakes, reinstall the inner pad (if removed).

13 On ATE brakes, install the caliper adapter.

14 Install the caliper and pads.

15 Install the front wheels and lower the vehicle.

6   Disc brake caliper – removal, overhaul and installation

Removal

1   Raise the vehicle, support it securely and remove the front wheels.

2   Remove the caliper and brake pads as described in Sections 3 and 4.

3   Have an assistant push on the brake pedal slowly and gently until the piston is displaced from the caliper. Do not remove the piston at this time as it will be followed by a gush of brake fluid. The piston should extend from the caliper sufficiently to be easily removed but be retained by the boot. **Caution:** *Do not allow your fingers to come between the piston and the caliper, as serious injury could result (photo).*

4   Disconnect the brake hose and lift the caliper from the vehicle.

5   Place the caliper on a workbench which has been covered with several layers of newspaper to absorb the brake fluid and remove the piston.

Overhaul

6   Pry the dust boot from the bore (photos).

7   Carefully remove the piston seal from the bore using a wooden dowel.

8   Remove the caliper pin(s) (photo).

9   Remove the bushings and Teflon sleeves (if equipped) from the guide pin bore(s). Discard the bushings.

10 Clean the components with a brake cleaner and blow them dry with compressed air if possible. Inspect the cylinder bore for scratches, corrosion or signs of pitting. Light scratches or imperfections in the bore can be removed with fine crocus cloth. If deeper scratches are present, they can be removed with a honing tool if the bore measurement can be kept within specification. Replace the caliper with a new one if the bore is badly scored. Inspect the piston for grooves or pitting. Replace the piston with a new one if it is badly worn or scratched or if the cylinder bore has been honed. Remove the guide pin bushings from the caliper by pushing them out with a wooden dowel.

11 Insert the guide pin bushing(s) and install the Teflon sleeves (if equipped).

12 Lubricate the new piston seal with brake assembly lubricant or clean brake fluid and install it into the bore groove. Start the seal into the groove and carefully press it into place by working around the circumference until it is seated evenly.

13 Lubricate the inside of the new dust boot and slide it on to the piston (photo).

14 Insert the piston into the bore until it bottoms.

15 Press the new piston dust boot into the groove with a suitable tool such as Chrysler tool C4171. If this tool is not available, place the caliper in a vise, using wood blocks to protect its surface. Working around the circumference, use a suitable punch and hammer to seat the boot in place.

Installation

16 Lubricate the contact surfaces of the caliper adapter with white lithium base grease.

17 Rotate the caliper into position.

18 Taking care not to cross thread them, install the guide pin(s) and tighten them to the specified torque.

19 Attach the brake hose to the caliper, using a new sealing ring.

20 Fill the master cylinder and open the bleed screw. Allow the system to gravity bleed until no air bubbles can be seen issuing from the bleed screw. Close the bleed screw, refill the master cylinder and bleed the brakes.

6.3 When ready for removal, the piston must extend from the caliper but still be retained by the boot

6.6A Pry the boot loose from the caliper

6.6B Pull the boot from the caliper

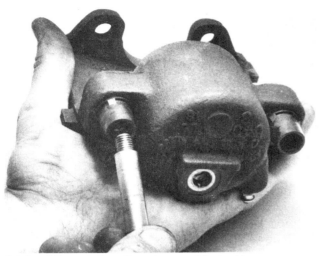

6.8 Carefully work the caliper pins out of the bushings

8.4 Pull the parking brake cable fully to the rear to disengage it from the lever

7 Rear brake shoes – inspection

Refer to Chapter 1 for rear brake checking procedures.

8 Rear brake shoes (1981 and 1982 models) – replacement

1 Raise the rear of the vehicle, support it securely and remove the wheels.
2 Remove the hub and brake drum assembly as described in Chapter 11.
3 Clean the brake assembly of dirt, dust and brake fluid by either brushing or wiping it away with a clean cloth. Do not use compressed air to remove the dust as it contains asbestos and is harmful to your health.
4 Disconnect the parking brake cable from the lever (photo).
5 Remove the two lower brake shoe-to-backing plate springs (photo).
6 Remove the shoe hold down springs (photo).
7 Back off the adjuster and remove it (photos).
8 Rotate the rear shoe forward and remove it, followed by the leading shoe (photo).
9 Inspect the shoe linings to make sure they show full contact with the drum. Measure the lining thickness and compare it to the Specifications. Replace the shoes with new ones if they are worn. Check the drum for cracks, scoring, or signs of overheating of the contact surface. Measure the internal diameter of the drum and compare this dimension with that cast into the drum. Minor imperfections in the drum surface can be removed with fine sandpaper. Deeper scoring can be removed by having the drum turned by a suitably equipped brake shop as long as the maximum diameter is maintained. Check the drum for runout. Replace the brake drum with a new one if it is beyond specification. Check the brake springs for signs of discolored paint, indicating overheating or distorted end coils, replacing with new ones if necessary. Inspect the adjuster screw assembly and threads for bent, corroded or damaged components. Replace the assembly if the screw threads are damaged or rusted. Clean the threads and lubricate them with white lithium base grease. Inspect the wheel cylinder boots for damage or signs of leakage. Rebuild or replace the wheel cylinder if there is any sign of leakage around the boots.
10 Lubricate the contact points of the backing plate and shoe pivot with multi-purpose grease (photo).
11 Insert the upper return spring into the backing plate and install the leading shoe, making sure to seat the ends securely into the wheel cylinder piston and anchor plate.
12 Install the trailing shoe upper return spring and then rotate the shoe and parking brake lever assembly to the rear, into position. Seat the shoe ends in the anchor plate and wheel cylinder (photo).

8.5 Remove the lower spring while holding the parking brake cable out of the way

8.6 Compress the hold down springs and slide them free of the pins

9

8.7A Use pliers to hold the adjuster clip out of the way while backing the screw off

8.7B Disengage the adjuster clevis from the front shoe

8.8 Remove the rear shoe and parking brake lever assembly

8.10 Lubricate all of the shoe pivot and backing plate contact points (arrows)

8.12 Rotate the trailing shoe into position

8.16 Pull back the cable housing and washer when attaching the cable to the lever

13 Insert the adjuster screw assembly into the shoe notch, making sure the forward facing clevis of the screw is pointed down. Turn the adjusting wheel until the screw is secure in the support.
14 Lightly lubricate the hold-down springs with multi-purpose grease and install them.
15 Install the shoe to anchor springs.
16 Pull the parking brake cable housing spring so the cable is exposed and attach it to the lever (photo).
17 Install the brake drum and hub assembly and adjust the wheel bearings as described in Chapter 11.
18 Adjust the brakes (Section 10), install the wheels and lower the vehicle.

9 Rear brake shoes (1983 models) – replacement

1 Perform Steps 1 through 3 of Section 8.
2 Use a pair of pliers to remove the automatic adjustment lever spring.
3 Pull the leading shoe forward and remove the adjuster lever.
4 Place the leading shoe back in position, turn the adjuster screw out and expand the shoes so that they are freed from the wheel cylinder boot.
5 Remove the hold down springs and remove the shoe assembly by pulling it down and away from the backing plate.
6 Remove the automatic adjuster screw assembly and the return spring from the shoe assembly.
7 Remove the retainer and disconnect the parking brake lever from the trailing brake shoe.

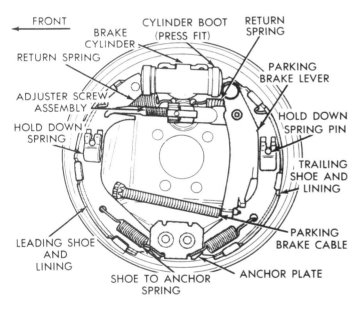

Fig. 9.9 Rear drum brake component layout (1981 and 1982 models) (Sec 8)

8 Perform the brake inspection in Step 9 of Section 8.
9 Prior to installation, lubricate the contact points on the backing plate and shoe pivot lightly with multi-purpose grease.
10 Attach the parking brake lever to the rear shoe and assemble the brake shoes and return springs. Attach the adjuster to the assembly.
11 Place the assembly in position on the backing plate with the hold down spring pins inserted through the holes in the shoes.
12 Install the hold down springs.
13 Turn the adjuster screw wheel to retract the shoes into position in the wheel cylinder boot.
14 Install the adjuster lever and connect the spring.
15 Install the drum and hub assembly as described in Chapter 11.
16 Install the wheels and lower the vehicle.
17 To adjust the brakes, drive the vehicle in Reverse and repeatedly apply the brakes. If it is necessary to adjust the brakes further, drive forward about 20 feet and repeat the operation.

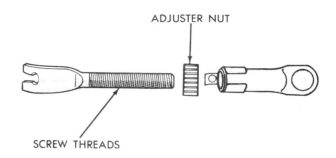

Fig. 9.10 Drum brake adjuster assembly components (Sec 8)

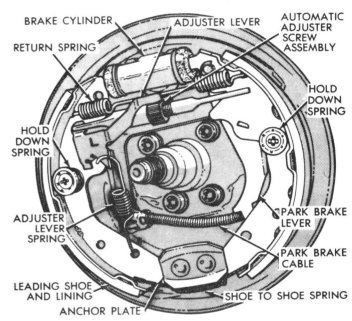

Fig. 9.11 Self adjusting drum brake component layout (1983 models) (Sec 9)

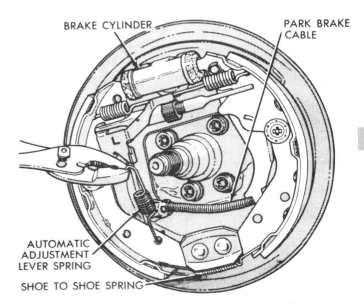

Fig. 9.12 Removing the adjustment lever spring (Sec 9)

9

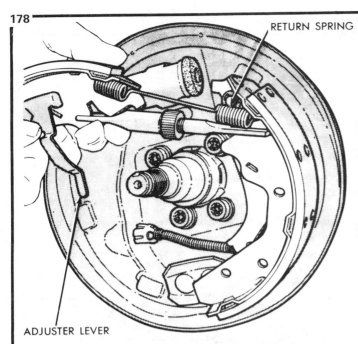

RETURN SPRING

ADJUSTER LEVER

Fig. 9.13 Removing the adjuster lever (Sec 9)

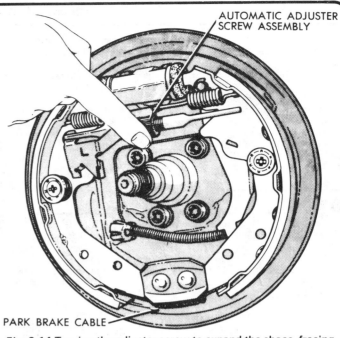

AUTOMATIC ADJUSTER SCREW ASSEMBLY

PARK BRAKE CABLE

Fig. 9.14 Turning the adjuster screw to expand the shoes, freeing them from the wheel cylinder boots (Sec 9)

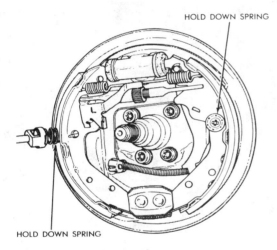

HOLD DOWN SPRING

HOLD DOWN SPRING

Fig. 9.15 Removing the hold down springs (Sec 9)

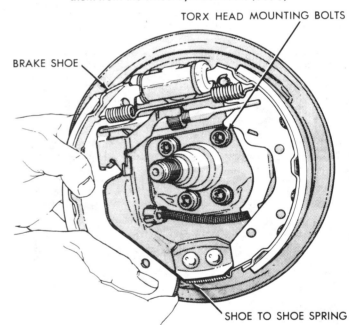

TORX HEAD MOUNTING BOLTS

BRAKE SHOE

SHOE TO SHOE SPRING

Fig. 9.16 Removing the brake shoe assembly (Sec 9)

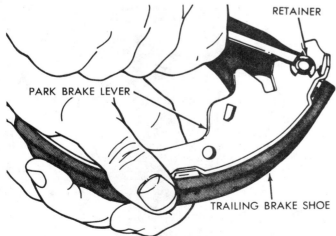

RETAINER

PARK BRAKE LEVER

TRAILING BRAKE SHOE

Fig. 9.17 Removing the parking brake lever from the brake shoe (Sec 9)

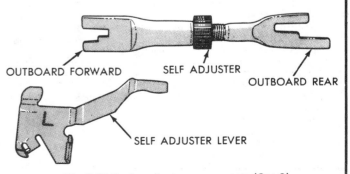

OUTBOARD FORWARD

SELF ADJUSTER

OUTBOARD REAR

SELF ADJUSTER LEVER

Fig. 9.18 Brake adjuster components (Sec 9)

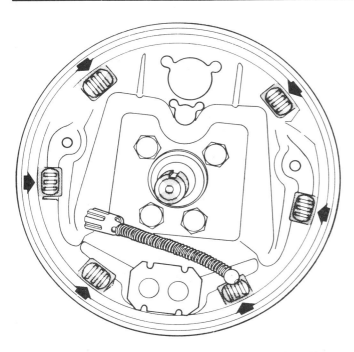

Fig. 9.19 Brake backing plate lubrication points (Sec 9)

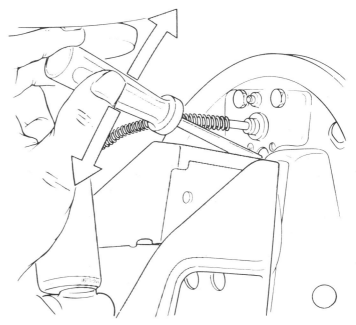

Fig. 9.20 Using a screwdriver to turn the brake adjuster wheel (Sec 10)

10 Rear brake shoes (1981 and 1982 models) – adjustment

1   The rear drum brakes on these models should be periodically adjusted to compensate for wear of the brake shoe linings.
2   Raise the rear of the vehicle, support it securely and block the front wheels.
3   Remove the rubber plug from the adjustment access hole in the backing plate.
4   Release the parking brake and if necessary back off the cable adjustment so the cable is slack.
5   Insert a narrow screwdriver through the hole in the backing plate and move the adjustment wheel down (left side) or up (right side) until the wheel will not rotate.
6   Back the adjuster off ten clicks.
7   Repeat the adjustment on the opposite wheel.
8   Install the plugs in the backing plate access holes. Apply a small amount of RTV sealant around the plugs and return spring end holes.
9   Adjust the parking brake (Section 16).
10 Lower the vehicle.

11 Rear wheel cylinder – removal and installation

1   Raise the rear of the vehicle, support it securely and remove the wheels.
2   Remove the rear hub and drum assembly (Chapter 11) and brake shoes (Sections 8 and 9).
3   Disconnect the brake line from the back of the wheel cylinder and plug it.
4   Unbolt the wheel cylinder and remove it from the vehicle.
5   To install, place the wheel cylinder in position, install the retaining bolts and tighten them to the specified torque.
6   Unplug the brake line, insert it in position in the cylinder and carefully thread the tube flare nut into plate. Once the nut is properly started, tighten it securely.
7   Install the brake shoes and the hub.
8   Bleed the brakes (Section 15).
9   Install the wheels and lower the vehicle.

12 Rear wheel cylinder – overhaul

1   You must have a clean place to work, clean rags, some

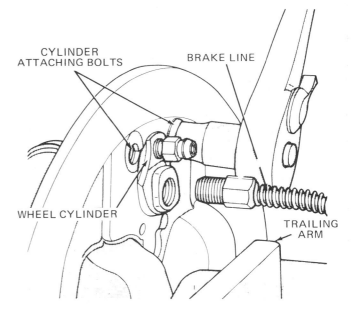

Fig. 9.21 Removing the wheel cylinder bolts (Sec 11)

newspapers, a wheel cylinder rebuild kit, a container of brake fluid and some alcohol to perform a wheel cylinder overhaul.
2   Remove the wheel cylinder as described in Section 11.
3   Remove the bleed screw and check to make sure it is not obstructed.
4   Carefully pry the boots from the wheel cylinder and remove the boots and piston.
5   Remove the boots from the piston.
6   Insert the piston fully into the cylinder and press in to remove the opposite piston, cups and spring with the cup expanders from the bore.
7   Wash the wheel cylinder, piston and spring in clean brake fluid or alcohol. Blow dry with compressed air. If this is not available, dry carefully with a clean, lint-free cloth.

9

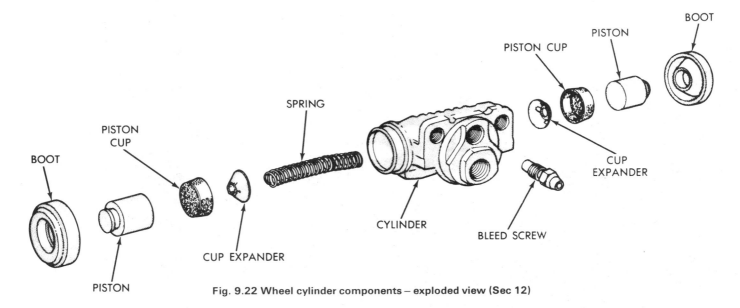

Fig. 9.22 Wheel cylinder components – exploded view (Sec 12)

8   Inspect the cylinder bore and piston for scoring and pitting. Slight imperfections of the bore can be removed with fine crocus cloth. If the piston is badly scored or pitted, replace it with a new one, making sure that the replacement unit is of the same interior dimension as different sizes are used on these models.
9   Lubricate the components with clean brake fluid or brake assembly lube prior to installation.
10   With the cylinder bore lubricated with clean brake fluid or brake assembly lube, install the expansion spring and cup expanders. Install the cups in each end of the cylinder, making sure the open ends of the cups are facing each other.
11   Engage the boot on the piston and slide the assembly into the bore. Carefully press the boot over the cylinder end until it is seated.
12   Install the bleed screw.
13   Attach the wheel cylinder to the brake backing plate.

13 Master cylinder – removal and installation

1   Place several layers of newspaper under the master cylinder to catch any spilled brake fluid.
2   Unscrew the steel line flare nuts, remove the lines and cap them. Allow the fluid in the master cylinder to drain into a suitable container.
3   Remove the retaining nuts and lift the master cylinder from the vehicle (photo).
4   To install, place the master cylinder in position and install the retaining nuts.
5   Install the lines and carefully start the flare nuts, taking care not to cross thread them.
6   Fill the master cylinder reservoir and bleed the brakes (Section 15).

14 Master cylinder – overhaul

1   Obtain a master cylinder rebuild kit prior to starting the job.
2   Remove the master cylinder (Section 13) and place it in a vise, using blocks of wood to protect the surface.
3   Grasp the reservoir, rock it back and forth to break it loose from the cylinder body and lift it away.
4   Drain the remaining fluid in the reservoir into a suitable container.
5   Remove the reservoir grommets (photo).
6   Remove the piston stop pin, using a pair of pliers (photo).
7   Remove the piston retainer snap-ring (photo).
8   Withdraw the secondary and primary pistons. It may be necessary to tap the master cylinder on a block of wood to dislodge the pistons.
9   Clean the components with clean brake fluid. Inspect the cylinder bore for pitting, scratches, scoring and flaking of the anodized surface.

13.3 Removing the retaining nuts. Note the newspaper to catch fluid spillage

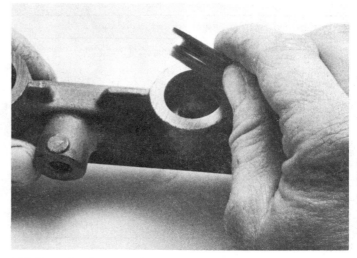

14.5 Removing the reservoir grommets

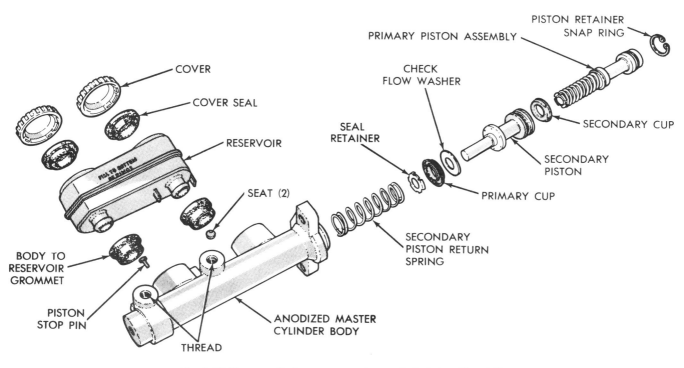

Fig. 9.23 Master cylinder components – exploded view (Sec 14)

Replace the cylinder with a new one if more than minor imperfections are present.

10 Inspect the seats of the inlet passages for nicks or damage, removing them with an EZ-out tool if necessary.

11 Lubricate the piston bore and all master cylinder components, including those supplied in the rebuild kit, with clean brake fluid or brake assembly lube.

12 Install the secondary piston with the spring end first. Carefully work the seal past the snap-ring groove.

13 Use a wood dowel to fully insert the secondary piston followed by the primary piston. Push the primary piston in sufficiently to allow installation of the snap-ring.

14 Install the piston stop pin. It may be necessary to tap the pin into place.

15 If they have been removed, install the new line seats.

16 Lubricate the reservoir grommets and install them.

17 Lubricate the reservoir mounting area, place it in position and seat it on the housing with a rocking motion. The reservoir is properly installed when the bottom edge touches the top of the grommet.

18 With the master cylinder mounted level in the vise, fill the reservoir half full while holding your fingers over the inlet ports. Use a wood dowel to slowly push the piston completely two or three times. This will fill the secondary piston cavity. Carefully remove your fingers from the ports to confirm that fluid is present. Hold a rag underneath to catch the fluid.

19 Install the master cylinder (Section 13).

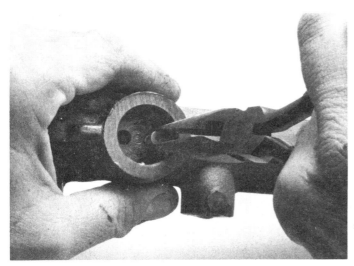

14.6 Use pliers to carefully lift the secondary stop pin out

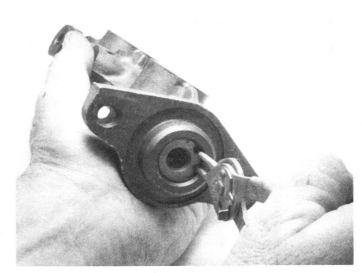

14.7 Removing piston snap-ring

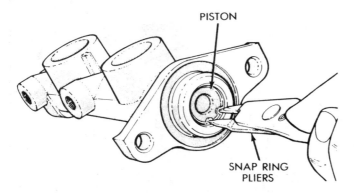

Fig. 9.24 Removing the piston retainer snap-ring (Sec 14)

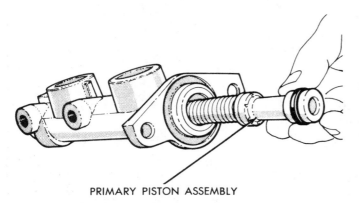

PRIMARY PISTON ASSEMBLY

Fig. 9.25 Removing the primary piston assembly (Sec 14)

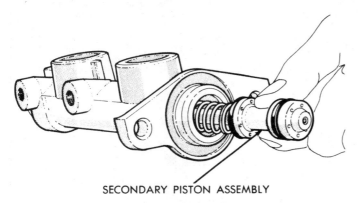

SECONDARY PISTON ASSEMBLY

Fig. 9.26 Removing the secondary piston assembly (Sec 14)

15 Brake system – bleeding

1   If the brake system has air in it, operation of the brake pedal will be spongy and imprecise. Air can enter the brake system whenever any part of the system is dismantled or if the fluid level in the master cylinder reservoir runs low. Air can also leak into the system through a hole too small to allow fluid to leak out. In this case, it indicates that a general overhaul of the brake system is required.
2   To bleed the brakes, you will need an assistant to pump the brake pedal, a supply of new brake fluid, an empty glass jar, a plastic or vinyl tube which will fit over the bleed nipple, and a wrench for the bleed screw.
3   There are five locations at which the brake system is bled; the master cylinder, the front brake caliper assemblies and the rear brake wheel cylinders.
4   Check the fluid level at the master cylinder reservoir. Add fluid, if

necessary, to bring the level up to the Full mark. Use only the recommended brake fluid, and do not mix different types. Never use fluid from a container that has been standing uncapped. You will have to check the fluid level in the master cylinder reservoir often during the bleeding procedure. If the level drops too far, air will enter the system through the master cylinder.
5   Raise the vehicle and set it securely on jackstands.
6   Remove the bleed screw cap from the wheel cylinder or caliper assembly that is being bled. If more than one wheel must be bled, start with the one farthest from the master cylinder.
7   Attach one end of the clear plastic or vinyl tube to the bleed screw nipple and place the other end in the glass or plastic jar, submerged in a small amount of clean brake fluid.
8   Loosen the bleed screw slightly, then tighten it to the point where it is snug yet easily loosened.
9   Have the assistant pump the brake pedal several times and hold it in the fully depressed position.
10 With pressure on the brake pedal, open the bleed screw approximately one-quarter turn. As the brake fluid is flowing through the tube and into the jar, tighten the bleed screw. Again, pump the brake pedal, hold it in the fully depressed position, and loosen the bleed screw momentarily. Do not allow the brake pedal to be released with the bleed screw in the open position.
11 Repeat the procedure until no air bubbles are visible in the brake fluid flowing through the tube. Be sure to check the brake fluid level in the master cylinder reservoir while performing the bleeding operation.
12 Completely tighten the bleed screw, remove the plastic or vinyl tube and install the cap.
13 Follow the same procedure to bleed the other wheel cylinder or caliper assemblies.
14 To bleed the master cylinder, have the assistant pump and hold the brake pedal. Momentarily loosen the brake line fittings, one at a time, where they attach to the master cylinder. Any air in the master cylinder will escape when the fittings are loosened. Brake fluid will damage painted surfaces, so use paper towels or rags to cover and protect the areas around the master cylinder.
15 Check the brake fluid level in the master cylinder to make sure it is adequate, then test drive the vehicle and check for proper brake operation.

16 Parking brake adjustment

1   The rear drum brakes must be properly adjusted prior to adjusting the parking brake.
2   Raise the vehicle and support it securely.
3   Underneath the vehicle, locate the cable adjuster and equalizer assembly. Clean the threads of the adjusting hook with a wire brush and lubricate them with multi-purpose grease.
4   Loosen the adjusting nut until there is slack in the cable.
5   Have an assistant rotate the rear wheels to make sure they turn easily.
6   Tighten the parking brake adjusting nut until a slight drag can be felt when the rear wheels are rotated.
7   Loosen the nut until the rear wheels turn freely and then back it off two turns.
8   Apply and release the parking brake several times to make sure it operates properly. It must lock the rear wheels when applied and the wheels must turn easily, without drag, when it is released.
9   Lower the vehicle.

17 Parking brake cable – removal and installation

1   Raise the vehicle and support it securely.

Front cable

2   Underneath the vehicle, loosen the adjusting nut (photo) and disengage the cable. It may be necessary to loosen the heat shield to gain access to the front clip.
3   Inside the vehicle, remove the brake lever assembly and roll back the carpet, giving access to the seal pan.
4   Remove the seal pan from the floor and pull the cable forward to disconnect it from the clevis.
5   Remove the cable assembly through the hole.

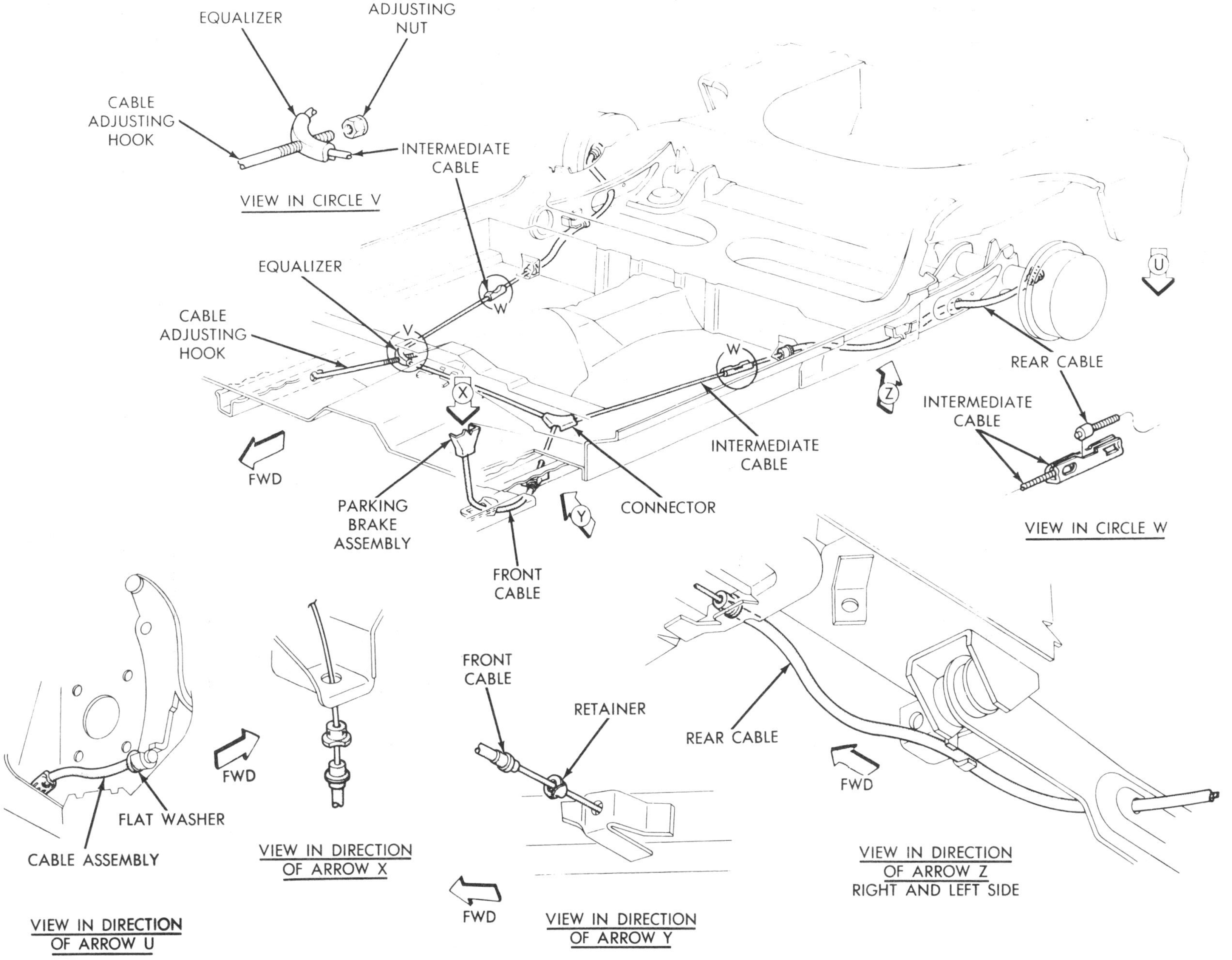

183

Fig. 9.27 Parking brake cable component layout (Secs 17 and 18)

ADJUSTING NUT

EQUALIZER

INTERMEDIATE CABLE

CABLE ADJUSTING HOOK

VIEW IN CIRCLE V

EQUALIZER

CABLE ADJUSTING HOOK

INTERMEDIATE CABLE

VIEW IN CIRCLE W

FWD

PARKING BRAKE ASSEMBLY

CONNECTOR

FRONT CABLE

INTERMEDIATE CABLE

REAR CABLE

INTERMEDIATE CABLE

VIEW IN CIRCLE W

VIEW IN DIRECTION OF ARROW Z RIGHT AND LEFT SIDE

FWD

REAR CABLE

RETAINER

FRONT CABLE

VIEW IN DIRECTION OF ARROW Y

FWD

VIEW IN DIRECTION OF ARROW X

FWD

FLAT WASHER

CABLE ASSEMBLY

VIEW IN DIRECTION OF ARROW U

9

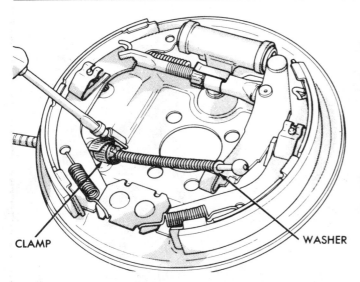

Fig. 9.28 Removing the parking brake cable from the backing plate with a hose clamp (Sec 17)

6   To install, connect the cable to the rail bracket and the parking brake assembly.
7   Feed the cable through the hole and connect it to the retainer.
8   Install the floor seal and replace the carpet.
9   Attach the cable to the equalizer bracket and install the heat shield.

Rear cables
10   Remove the rear wheels and the hub and brake drum assembly.
11   Back off the adjusting nut until the cable is slack.
12   Disengage the cable from the brake shoe lever.
13   Use a screw-type hose clamp to compress the retainers so the cable can be removed from the brake backing plate. Remove the clamp when the cable is free.
14   Remove the cable from the rear axle assembly, disengage it from the front cable assembly and remove it (photo).
15   To install, insert the cable through the trailing arms and into the backing plates.
16   Snap the cable into the chassis brackets and connect the ends to the brake shoe levers (photo).
17   Connect the cable to the front cable assembly.
18   Install the hubs and wheels and adjust the parking brake (Section 6).

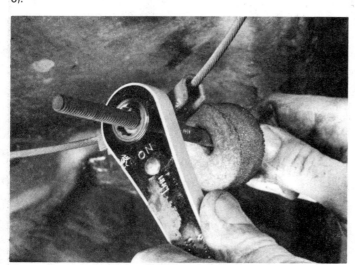

17.2 Loosening the parking brake adjuster nut

17.14 Slide the front cable to the rear to remove it from the connector

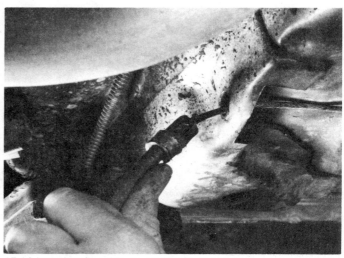

17.16 Inserting the cable prongs into the bracket

---

18 Power brake booster – removal and installation

1   Remove the master cylinder (Section 13).
2   In the engine compartment, disconnect the booster vacuum hose.
3   From underneath the dash inside the vehicle, use a small screwdriver to remove the brake pedal-to-booster retainer clip.
4   Remove the four retaining nuts.
5   Lift the brake booster from the engine compartment.
6   To install, place the brake booster in position and install the retaining nuts, tightening them to the specified torque.
7   Install the master cylinder.
8   Connect the vacuum hose to the booster.
9   Lubricate the surface of the brake pedal pin with white lithium base grease and connect the pedal pin to the pushrod, using a new retainer clip.
10   Check the operation of the stoplight switch and adjust if necessary (Section 20).
11   Check the booster for proper operation (Section 19).

---

19 Power brake booster – testing and overhaul

1   Symptoms of faults in the brake booster system are low pedal and

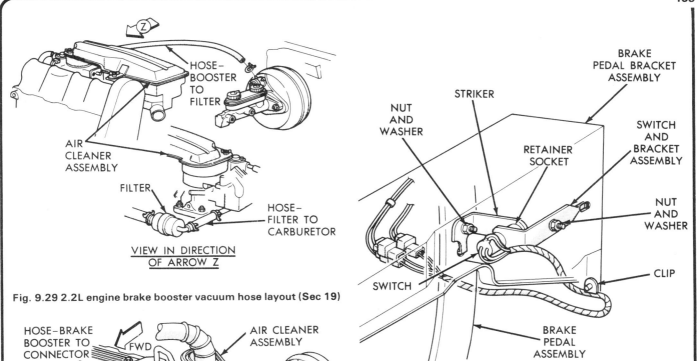

HOSE-BOOSTER TO FILTER

AIR CLEANER ASSEMBLY

FILTER

HOSE-FILTER TO CARBURETOR

VIEW IN DIRECTION OF ARROW Z

Fig. 9.29 2.2L engine brake booster vacuum hose layout (Sec 19)

HOSE-BRAKE BOOSTER TO CONNECTOR

FWD

AIR CLEANER ASSEMBLY

BRAKE BOOSTER

CONNECTOR

Fig. 9.30 2.6L engine brake booster vacuum hose layout (Sec 19)

NUT AND WASHER

STRIKER

BRAKE PEDAL BRACKET ASSEMBLY

RETAINER SOCKET

SWITCH AND BRACKET ASSEMBLY

NUT AND WASHER

CLIP

SWITCH

BRAKE PEDAL ASSEMBLY

Fig. 9.31 Stoplight switch installation (Sec 20)

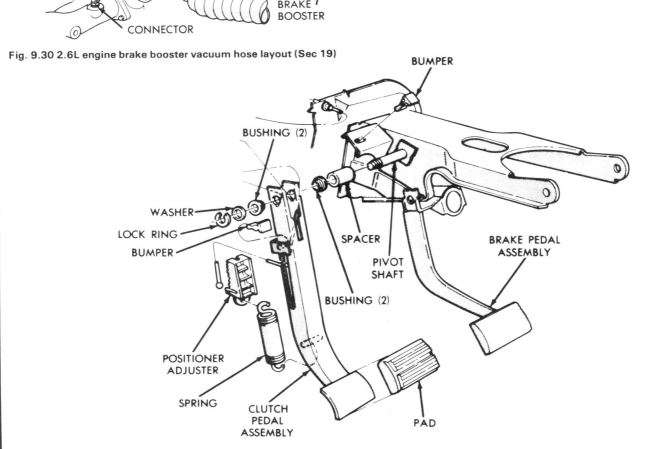

BUMPER

BUSHING (2)

WASHER

LOCK RING

BUMPER

SPACER

PIVOT SHAFT

BRAKE PEDAL ASSEMBLY

BUSHING (2)

POSITIONER ADJUSTER

SPRING

CLUTCH PEDAL ASSEMBLY

PAD

Fig. 9.32 Brake pedal components — exploded view
(manual transaxle) (Sec 21)

9

high braking effort or the brake pedal dropping after the initial application.

2   With the engine off, depress and release the brake pedal several times to bleed any vacuum from the booster.

3   Depress the pedal and hold a light (between 15 and 25 lbs) pressure. Start the engine.

4   If the system is operating properly, the pedal should drop slightly and then hold. Subsequent applications will require less pressure.

5   If the booster fails this test, or if the pedal drops after the initial application, check the vacuum supply.

6   Inspect the vacuum hose for cracks and trace it to the manifold or carburetor. Check the connections, check valve and filter (if equipped) for cracks and leaks, replacing any faulty components.

7   Disconnect the vacuum hose at the booster and connect a vacuum gauge.

8   Start the engine and make sure that at idle the vacuum gauge reads above the minimum booster vacuum. If the vacuum is above the minimum, the booster itself is faulty and should be replaced with a new unit. If the vacuum is below the minimum, there is a leak in the vacuum hose (if equipped) and/or the connection to the carburetor or manifold.

9   The brake booster must not be disassembled for any reason. If the booster is not operating properly, obtain a new or rebuilt unit and install it in the vehicle by referring to Section 18.

20 Stoplight switch – removal, installation and adjustment

1   Unplug the switch connector, grasp the switch and pull it from the retainer.

2   To install, press the switch into the bracket and plug in the connector.

3   To adjust, push the switch completely forward.This will cause the brake pedal to move slightly. Gently pull the pedal back as far as it will go, causing it to ratchet back to the correct position.

21 Brake pedal – removal and installation

1   Disconnect the power brake pushrod from the brake pedal.

2   On manual transaxle equipped models, remove the lock ring from the pivot shaft and carefully withdraw the shaft. Remove the clutch pedal assembly, followed by the brake pedal.

3   On automatic transaxle equipped vehicles, remove the pivot shaft nut, withdraw the shaft and remove the brake pedal.

4   To install, place the brake pedal in position and insert the pivot shaft.

5   On manual transaxle models, install the clutch pedal assembly and lock ring.

6   On automatic transaxle models, install the pivot shaft nut and tighten it to the specified torque.

Chapter 10 Chassis electrical system

Refer to Chapter 13 for information applicable to later models

Contents

Specifications

Bulb application

	Number
Interior	
Air conditioning control	161
Ash tray	161
Gearshift selector console	158
Heated rear window control	161
Heater control	161
Instrument cluster	194
AM radio	158
AM-FM stereo radio	53
AM-FM stereo radio (ETR)	74
AM-FM stereo cassette radio	74
Rear wiper switch	161
Speedometer	194
Switch illumination	161
Brake indicator	194
Dome light	211-2
Engine indicator	194
Fasten seat belts	194
Gate ajar	194
Glove compartment	1891
High beam indicator	194
Ignition switch	1445
Low voltage indicator	194
Oil pressure indicator	194
Oxygen sensor indicator	194
CB, AM-FM stereo radio indicator	73
Reading light	912
Trunk	1003
Turn signal indicator	194
Underhood light	1003
Vanity light	194
Exterior	
Back-up light	1156
Headlight	6052
License plate	168
Park and turn signal	2057
Side marker	168
Tail, stop and turn signal	2057

Fusible link wire code

	Gauge
Black	12
Red	14
Dark blue	16
Grey	18
Orange	20

1   General information

This Chapter covers repair and service procedures for the various lighting and electrical components not associated with the engine. Information on the battery, alternator, voltage regulator, ignition and starting systems can be found in Chapter 5.

The electrical system is of the 12 volt negative ground type. Power for the electrical system and accessories is supplied by a lead/acid-type battery which is charged by an alternator. The circuits are protected from overload by a system of fuses and fusible links.

Note: *Whenever the electrical system is worked on, the negative battery cable should be disconnected to prevent electrical shorts and/or fires.*

2   Fuses and fusible links – replacement

Caution: *Do not bypass a fuse with metal or aluminium foil as serious damage to the electrical system could result.*

1   The fuse block is located below the dash, to the left of the steering column, behind a panel. Grasp the lower edge of the panel and pull it back sharply to remove and expose the fuse block.

2   With the ignition off, remove each fuse in turn by grasping it and pulling it from the block. Replace the blown fuse with a new one of the same value by pushing it into place. Install the cover panel.

3   If the fuses in the fuse block are alright and the headlights or other components are inoperable, check the fusible links. Before replacing a fusible link, determine the reason that it burned out. Replacing the link without finding and correcting the cause for the failure could lead to serious damage to the electrical system.

4   Determine the proper gauge for the replacement link by referring to the Specifications section. Obtain the new link or link wire from your dealer.

5   Disconnect the battery negative cable and cut off all of the remaining burned out fusible link.

6   Strip off one inch of insulaton from both ends of the new fusible link and the main harness wire.

7   Install the new fusible link by twisting the ends securely around the main link wire. On multiple links, the replacement wire must be connected to the main wires beyond the connector insulators of the old link.

8   Solder the wires together with non-acid core solder. After the connection has cooled, wrap the splice with at least three layers of electrical tape.

3   Horn – testing and adjustment

1   If the horn will not sound, release the parking brake, place the transaxle selector in Park or Neutral and observe the brake lamp on the dash as you start the engine. If the lamp does not illuminate, the steering column is not properly grounded to the instrument panel so the horn switch is not grounded.

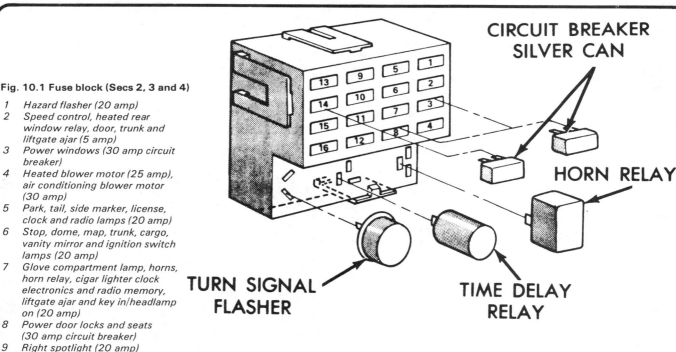

Fig. 10.1 Fuse block (Secs 2, 3 and 4)

1   *Hazard flasher (20 amp)*
2   *Speed control, heated rear window relay, door, trunk and liftgate ajar (5 amp)*
3   *Power windows (30 amp circuit breaker)*
4   *Heated blower motor (25 amp), air conditioning blower motor (30 amp)*
5   *Park, tail, side marker, license, clock and radio lamps (20 amp)*
6   *Stop, dome, map, trunk, cargo, vanity mirror and ignition switch lamps (20 amp)*
7   *Glove compartment lamp, horns, horn relay, cigar lighter clock electronics and radio memory, liftgate ajar and key in/headlamp on (20 amp)*
8   *Power door locks and seats (30 amp circuit breaker)*
9   *Right spotlight (20 amp)*
10   *Left spotlight (20 amp)*
11   *Brake warning, engine warning seat belt and electronic voltage lamps, fuel gauge and voltage limiter, low fuel relay, temperature and oil gauge (5 amp)*
12   *Radiator fan (air conditioned 2.2L engine models (20 amp)*
13   *Instrument cluster, air conditioning and heater control ash tray, console gear selector heated rear window, rear washer/wiper and radio lamps, clock display (3 amp)*
14   *Deck lid release, liftgate release, rear washer/wiper and*
   premium speaker relay (6 amp)
15   *Radio, clock display and premium speaker relay (5 amp)*
16   *Back-up and turn signal lamps, air conditioning clutch, solenoid idle stop (2.2L engine) and air conditioner radiator fan relay coil (20 amp)*

2   If the brake lamp lights but the horn still does not sound, check for a blown fuse. Should the new fuse blow out when the horn button is pushed, there is a short in the horn assembly itself or between the fuse terminal and the horn.

3   If the fuse is good and the horn still does not sound, unplug the connector at the horn and insert a test lamp lead. Ground the other lamp lead and observe whether the lamp lights. If it does, the horn is faulty or improperly grounded. Check the horn for proper grounding by connecting a wire between the battery negative cable and the horn bracket, making sure to scratch through the paint. If the horn does not sound, replace the horn relay, located on the fuse block, with a new one.

4   Should the horn sound continuously, replace the horn relay with a known good one. If the horn still sounds, pull off the horn button and make sure that the horn contact wire is not shorting out against the hub.

5   To adjust the horn loudness and tone, first determine which horn is in need of adjustment. The low-tone horn is located on the right side radiator panel and the high-tone on the right side shield. Disconnect the horn which is not being adjusted.

6   Connect the horn to the positive terminal of the battery with a remote starter switch and an ammeter in series.

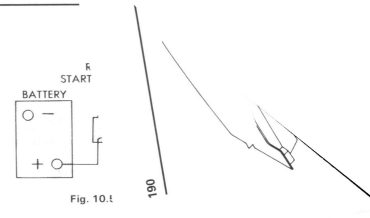

Fig. 10.5

7   With the remote st... ...e ammeter should read between 4.5 and 5... ...o adjust, turn the adjusting screw clockwise to increase or counterclockwise to decrease the current. Check the horn for satisfactory tone and current draw after each adjustment.

4   Flasher units – replacement

1   The hazard and turn signal flasher units are located in the fuse block.

2   The turn signal flasher is located on the lower left corner of the fuse block and can be replaced by removing it and plugging in a new unit.

3   The hazard flasher is located in the number one cavity of the fuse block and is replaced in the same manner as a fuse.

5   Headlight – removal and installation

1   Remove the headlight bezel (Chapter 12).

2   Remove the three retaining screws, taking care not to disturb the adjustment screws (photo).

3   Withdraw the headlight sufficiently to gain access to the connector.

4   Unplug the connector and remove the headlight (photo).

5   To install, plug in the headlight, place it in position and install the retaining screws.

6   Install the headlight bezel.

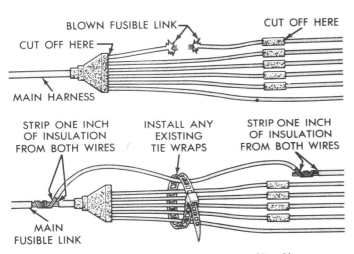

Fig. 10.2 Multiple fusible link repair (Sec 2)

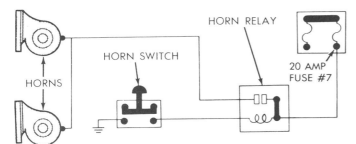

Fig. 10.3 Horn system wiring diagram (Sec 3)

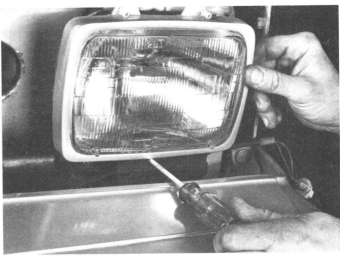

5.2 Be sure to remove the retaining screws, not the adjustment screws

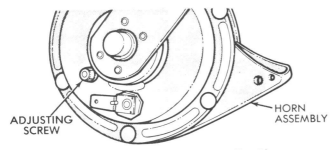

Fig. 10.4 Horn adjusting screw (Sec 3)

10

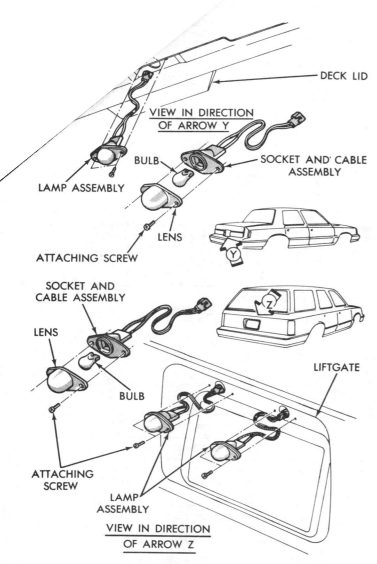

Fig. 10.6 License plate bulb removal (Sec 5)

6 Headlight – alignment

1   It is always best to have the headlights aligned on the proper equipment but if this is not available the following procedure may be used.

2   Position the vehicle on level ground 10 feet in front of a dark wall or board. The wall or board must be at right angles to the centerline of the vehicle.

3   Draw a vertical line on the wall or board in line with the centerline of the vehicle.

4   Bounce the vehicle on its suspension to ensure that it settles at the proper level and check the tires to make sure that they are at the proper pressure. Measure the height between the ground and the center of the headlights.

5   Draw a horizontal line across the board or wall at this measured height. Mark a cross on the horizontal line on either side of the vertical centerline at the distance between the center of the light and the centerline of the vehicle.

6   Turn the headlights on and switch them to high beam.

7   Use the adjusting screws to align the center of each beam onto the crosses which were marked on the horizontal line.

8   Bounce the vehicle on its suspension again to make sure the beams return to the correct position. Check the operation of the dimmer switch.

9   The headlights should be adjusted with the proper equipment at your earliest convenience.

7   Front turn signal and parking lamp bulbs – replacement

1   Remove the attaching screws and lift off the bezel.

2   Grasp the turn signal socket, push in and rotate it in a counter-clockwise direction to remove it from the bezel.

3   Push the bulb in, turn it counterclockwise and withdraw it from the socket.

4   Lubricate the contact area of the new bulb with light grease or petroleum jelly prior to installation.

5   Press the bulb in and rotate it clockwise to install it in the socket.

6   Place the socket in position with the tabs aligned with those in the bezel, press in and turn it clockwise.

7   Remove the turn signal socket from the bezel (photo).

8   Grasp the bulb firmly and rock it from side-to-side while withdrawing it.

9   Insert the new bulb securely into the socket and install the socket in the bezel.

10 Install the bezel.

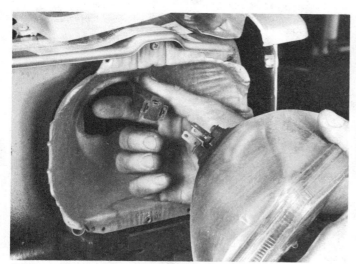

5.4 Grasp the connector securely when removing the headlight

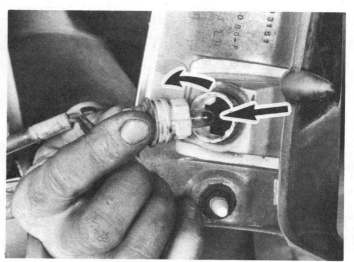

7.7 Grasp the socket securely, rotate it counterclockwise and pull it from the housing (arrows) to remove it

8   Rear exterior bulbs – replacement

Tail, stop, turn signal, running and backup lamps
Sedan
1   Open the trunk to provide access to the bulbs.
2   Remove the appropriate socket by rotating it counterclockwise and withdrawing it from the housing.
3   Remove the bulb from the socket (photo).
4   Install the new bulb by pressing in and rotating it clockwise.
5   Install the socket by aligning the tabs, pushing in and turning it clockwise.
6   To replace the running light bulb, pull the socket from the housing and then pull the bulb from the socket (photo).
7   Insert the new bulb securely into the socket and push the socket into the housing.

Station wagon
8   Remove the four tail light housing retaining nuts (photo).
9   Pull the sockets from the housing, unplug the ground terminal and set the housing aside.
10 Replace the bulb(s) with new one(s), plug the sockets into the housing and connect the ground wire terminal. Install the light housing and retaining nuts.

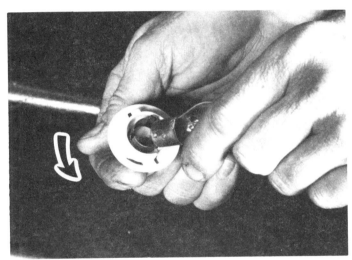

8.3 Push the bulb in, rotate it counterclockwise (arrow) and withdraw it

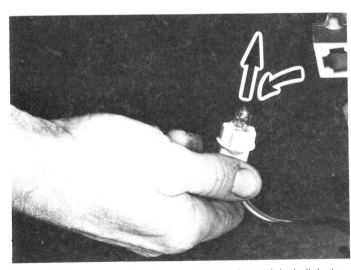

8.6 The socket is pulled directly out of the housing and the bulb is then pulled from the socket (arrows)

License plate lamp (all models)
11 Remove the lens attaching screws and lift off the lens.
12 Grasp the bulb securely and pull it from the socket.
13 Insert the new bulb and install the lens and screws.

8.8 The lower tail light nuts are located below the bumper

9   Interior bulbs – replacement

Dome lamp
1   Pry the lamp cover off with a screwdriver.
2   Grasp the bulb securely and pull it from the socket.
3   Install the new bulb and snap the lamp cover into position.

Instrument cluster
4   Remove the cluster bezel and mask (Chapter 12).
5   Replace any defective bulbs and install the bezel and mask.

Console shift indicator lamp
6   Remove the retaining screws and remove the console.
7   Place the gear shift lever in the Neutral position, then insert a small punch or pin through the hole in the bottom of the shift knob to remove the release button. Turn the lock spring counterclockwise while depressing it and remove it and the shift knob.
8   Remove the indicator housing and the lamp.
9   Replace the bulb and install the lamp and housing.
10 Install the lock spring, release button and shift knob.
11 With the shift lever in Neutral, install the console.

Liftgate ajar lamp
12 Pry the liftgate ajar lamp from the dash, replace the bulb and snap the lamp back into place.

Radio lamp
13 Remove the radio (Section 10), then snap the socket out from the bottom of the radio.
14 Replace the bulb, snap the lamp back into position and install the radio.

10   Radio – removal and installation

1   Disconnect the negative battery cable from the battery.
2   Remove the trim strip, instrument panel cover and upper right bezel (Chapter 12).
3   Remove the speaker from the top of the dash and unplug the leads.
4   Remove the retaining screws and pull the radio out sufficiently to unplug the connectors and disconnect the ground cable and antenna.
5   Remove the radio from the dash.

10

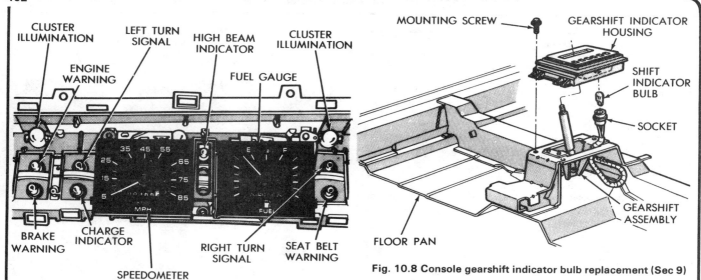

CLUSTER ILLUMINATION

ENGINE WARNING

LEFT TURN SIGNAL

HIGH BEAM INDICATOR

FUEL GAUGE

CLUSTER ILLUMINATION

BRAKE WARNING

CHARGE INDICATOR

SPEEDOMETER

RIGHT TURN SIGNAL

SEAT BELT WARNING

Fig. 10.7 Instrument cluster bulb location (Sec 9)

MOUNTING SCREW

GEARSHIFT INDICATOR HOUSING

SHIFT INDICATOR BULB

SOCKET

GEARSHIFT ASSEMBLY

FLOOR PAN

Fig. 10.8 Console gearshift indicator bulb replacement (Sec 9)

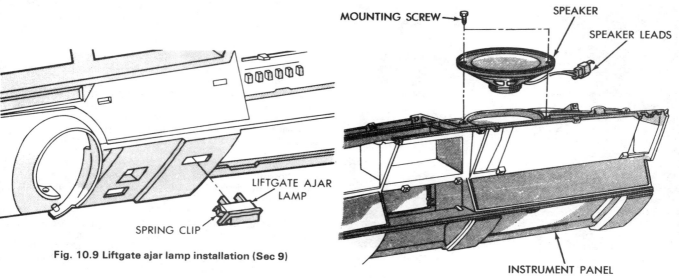

LIFTGATE AJAR LAMP

SPRING CLIP

Fig. 10.9 Liftgate ajar lamp installation (Sec 9)

MOUNTING SCREW

SPEAKER

SPEAKER LEADS

INSTRUMENT PANEL

Fig. 10.10 Radio speaker installation (Sec 10)

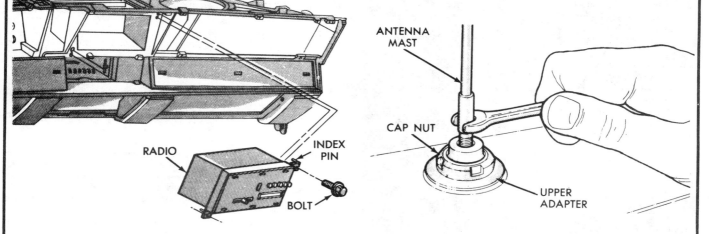

RADIO

INDEX PIN

BOLT

Fig. 10.11 Radio installation (Sec 10)

ANTENNA MAST

CAP NUT

UPPER ADAPTER

Fig. 10.12 Removing the antenna mast (Sec 11)

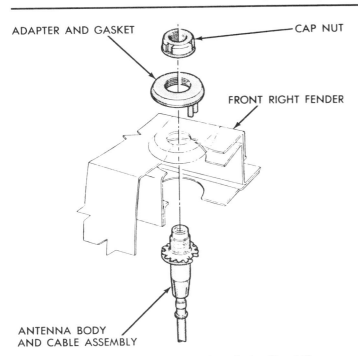

Fig. 10.13 Antenna-to-fender installation (Sec 11)

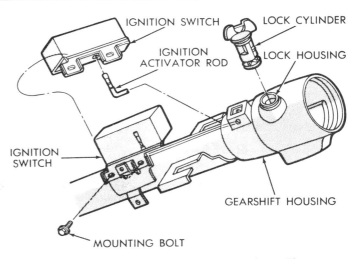

Fig. 10.14 Ignition switch installation (Sec 12)

6   To install, place the radio in position, connect the wiring harness, antenna and ground strap.
7   Install the retaining screws and the bezel.
8   Install the speaker and plug in the electrical leads.
9   Install the instrument panel cover and the trim strip.
10 Connect the negative battery cable.

11 Antenna – removal and installation

1   Disconnect the negative battery cable from the battery.
2   Remove the radio (Section 10).
3   Use a suitable wrench to unscrew the antenna mast from the cap nut.
4   Use a needle nose pliers to unscrew and remove the cap nut and adapter.
5   From under the fender, remove the three inner fender shield-to-fender screws, pull the shield back for access and remove the antenna body and cable assembly.
6   To install, insert the body and cable assembly into the fender and install the adapter, gasket and cap nut.
7   Install the antenna mast.
8   Install the fender shield screws.
9   Install the radio and connect the negative battery cable.

12 Ignition switch – removal and installation

1   Disconnect the negative battery cable from the battery.
2   Place the ignition switch in the Lock position.
3   Remove the steering column cover.
4   Remove the under panel sound deadener.
5   Remove the clutch speed control switch (manual transaxle).
6   Remove the column shift indicator wire and set screw (Chapter 12).
7   Remove the switch electrical connectors.
8   Remove the two retaining bolts, rotate the switch 90° to the right and lift it off the control rod.
9   To install, support the control rod and lower the switch into position until it snaps into place on the rod. Plug in the electrical connector.
10 Install the retaining bolts loosely and move the switch up (toward the steering wheel) to take up the slack in the control rod.
11 Tighten the retaining nuts.

12 Raise the steering column into position and install the retaining bolts (Chapter 11).
13 Install the shift indicator wire and set screw.
14 On manual transaxle vehicles, install the clutch speed control switch.
15 Install the under panel sound deadener and the steering column cover.
16 Connect the negative battery cable.

13 Ignition lock cylinder (standard column) – removal and installation

1   Disconnect the negative battery cable from the battery.
2   Remove the steering wheel.
3   Remove the turn signal switch and the key buzzer switch.
4   Remove the four retaining screws and the snap-ring and remove the upper shaft bearing.
5   Slide the spacer for the hazard switch from the column shield.
6   Remove the lockplate and spring.
7   Separate the ignition key buzzer switch wiring connector.
8   Remove the screws from the steering lock bellcrank mechanism.
9   Place the lock cylinder in the Lock position and pull the key out.
10 Release the two lock levers.
11 Insert a small screwdriver into the release while pulling out on the lock cylinder. Remove the lock cylinder.
12 To install, insert the lock cylinder into position and seat the lock

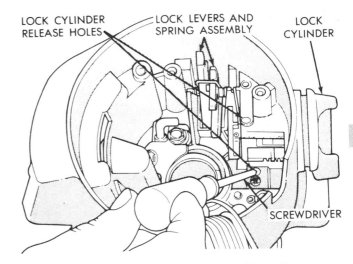

Fig. 10.15 Lock cylinder removal (Sec 13)

10

lever spring leg securely into the bottom of the notch in the lock casting.

13 Connect the actuator rod to the lock housing and attach the bellcrank. With the shift lever in Park (column shift), position the bellcrank mechanism in the lock housing while pulling down the column. Install the retaining screws.

14 Turn the key to the Lock position and remove it.

15 Push the lock cylinder housing in far enough to contact the switch actuator, insert the key, press it in and rotate the cylinder. When the inner parts of the mechanism are in alignment, the cylinder will move in, the spring loaded retainers will snap into place and the cylinder will be locked into the housing.

16 Plug in the key buzzer connector.

17 Install the lockplate and spring.

18 Install the hazard switch spacer.

19 Install the upper bearing housing, screws and snap-ring.

20 Install the turn signal and key buzzer switches.

21 Install the steering wheel.

22 Connect the negative battery cable.

14 Dimmer switch – removal, adjustment and installation

1 Disconnect the negative battery cable from the battery.

2 Remove the steering column cover.

3 Remove the retaining screws, unplug the connector and lift the switch from the steering column.

4 To install, place the switch in position, insert the control rod, install the screws finger tight and plug in the connector.

5 To adjust, fabricate an adjustment pin from a suitable piece of wire and insert the pin ends into the switch. Adjust the switch by pushing it gently to the rear to take up the slack in the control rod and tighten the retaining screws (photo).

6 Tighten the retaining screws and remove the adjustment pin.

7 Install the column cover and connect the negative battery cable.

14.5 Make sure the control rod is securely seated in the dimmer switch and pull it back gently to adjust (note the adjustment pin [arrow]) (photo)

15 Washer/wiper switch (standard column) – removal and installation

1 Disconnect the negative battery cable from the battery.

2 Remove the steering wheel (Chapter 11).

3 Remove the screw which retains the turn signal switch to the wiper/washer switch (photo).

4 Remove the switch cover and slide the foam rubber cover off the control stalk.

5 Remove the wiring trough cover and unplug the switch connector.

6 Remove the switch and carefully pull the wiring out of the steering column.

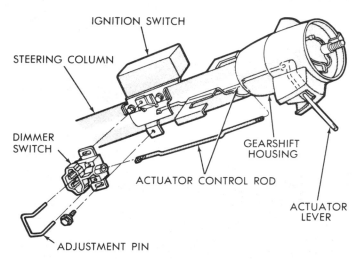

Fig. 10.16 Dimmer switch component layout and adjustment pin (Sec 14)

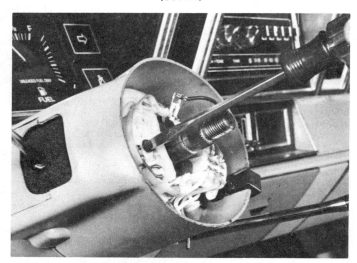

15.3 Removing the turn signal and wiper/washer pivot screw

7 To install, insert the wiring harness into the column and thread it down the column and into position. Plug in the connector.

8 Place the wipe/washer switch in position, making sure the dimmer switch actuating rod is securely seated. Install the retaining screw.

9 Install the steering wheel.

10 Slide the foam rubber cover into place and install the switch cover.

11 Install the wiring trough cover.

12 Connect the negative battery cable.

16 Turn signal/hazard warning switch (standard column) – removal and installation

1 Disconnect the negative battery cable from the battery.

2 Remove the steering wheel (Chapter 11).

3 Remove the wiring trough cover.

4 Remove the sound deadening insulation panel (if equipped) and lower instrument panel bezel from the base of the steering column.

5 Separate the wiring connector.

6 With the column shift selector in the full clockwise position, remove the screw which retains the turn signal switch and washer/wiper switch. Disengage the washer/wiper switch from the column and allow it to hang by the wires.

7 Remove the screws retaining the turn signal/hazard warning switch and the upper bearing retainer and lift the assembly from the column.

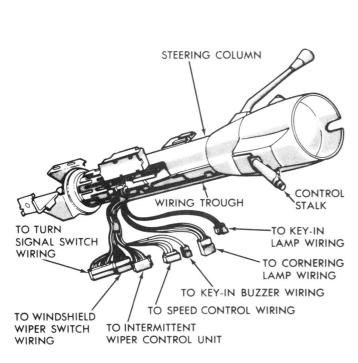

Fig. 10.17 Steering column connector layout (Secs 13, 14 and 15)

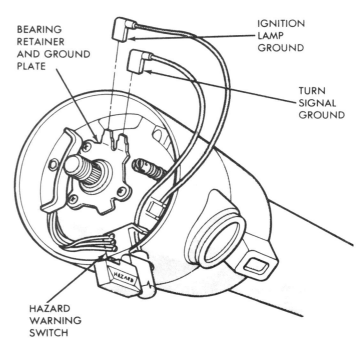

Fig. 10.18 Hazard switch components (Sec 16)

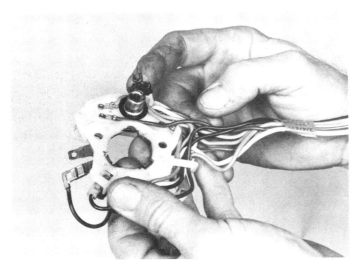

16.9 Apply a thin coat of grease to the turn signal pivot

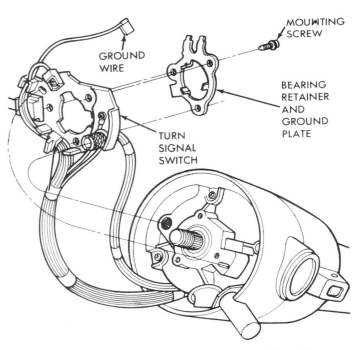

Fig. 10.19 Turn signal switch components (Sec 16)

8   Carefully pull the wiring harness up through the hub.
9   Prior to installation , lubricate the full circumference of the turn signal switch pivot with light grease (photo).
10 Insert the wiring harness through the hub and down the steering column.
11 Place the switch assembly and bearing retainer in position and install the retaining screws.
12 With the washer/wiper switch in position, install the turn signal retaining screw.
13 Plug in the connector and install the wiring trough cover.
14 Install the lower instrument panel bezel and sound deadening panel.
15 Install the steering wheel.
16 Connect the negative battery cable.

17 Key buzzer/chime switch (conventional column) – removal and installation

1   Disconnect the negative battery cable from the battery.
2   Remove the steering wheel (Chapter 11).
3   Remove the turn signal/hazard switch, the upper bearing housing and the lock plate and spring.
4   Remove the cable trough cover and disconnect the switch connector.
5   Remove the retaining screw and remove the switch and wire from the steering column.

6   To install, insert the wire down through the hub and column, place
the switch in position and install the retaining screw.
7   Install the lock plate and spring, upper bearing housing and the
turn signal/hazard switch.
8   Plug in the connector and install the wiring trough cover.
9   Install the steering wheel.
10 Connect the negative battery cable.

---

18 Headlight switch – removal and installation

1   Disconnect the negative battery cable from the battery.
2   Remove the lower left instrument panel bezel (Chapter 12).
3   Remove the switch retaining screws (photo).
4   Pull the switch away from the instrument panel and unplug the
wiring connectors (photo).
5   Remove the knob and stem from the switch (photo).
6   Remove the escutcheon from the switch (photo).
7   Install the knob, stem and escutcheon on the new switch.
8   Plug in the connectors, place the switch in position and install the
retaining screws.
9   Install the instrument panel bezel.
10 Connect the negative battery cable.

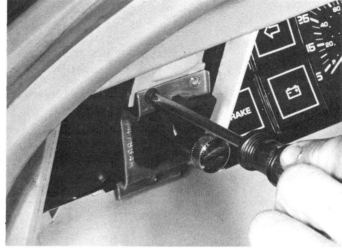

18.3 Removing the headlight switch retaining screws

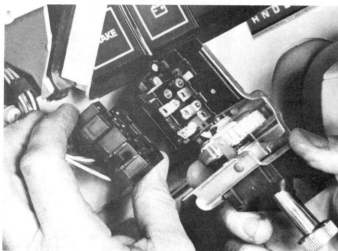

18.4 Hold the switch securely in one hand while removing the
connector with a rocking motion

18.5 Withdraw the knob and stem while depressing the release button
(arrow)

18.6 Removing the escutcheon retaining screw

19.3 Removing the speedometer retaining screw

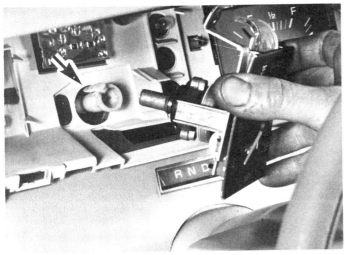

19.4 Press the release lever (arrow) to disconnect the cable from the speedometer

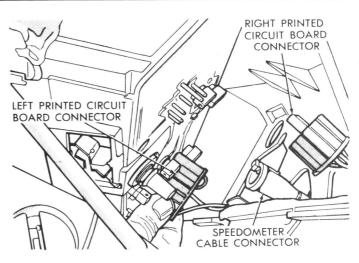

Fig. 10.20 Disconnecting the instrument cluster (Sec 21)

19 Speedometer – removal and installation

1   Disconnect the negative battery cable from the battery.
2   Remove the instrument cluster bezel and mask (Chapter 12).
3   Remove the speedometer retaining screws (photo).
4   Disconnect the cable and remove the speedometer (photo).
5   On speed control equipped vehicles, it will also be necessary to disconnect the speedometer cable from the servo unit located in the engine compartment.
6   To install, place the speedometer in position and press it into the cable assembly until it locks in place.
7   Install the retaining screws and the cluster and bezel assembly.
8   Connect the speed control servo to the cable (if equipped).
9   Connect the negative battery cable.

20 Fuel gauge – removal and installation

1   Disconnect the negative battery cable from the battery.
2   Remove the instrument cluster bezel and mask (Chapter 12).
3   Remove the retaining screws. The lower screw also retains the speedometer.
4   Remove the gauge by sliding it out from under the speedometer.
5   To install, slide the gauge into position with the lower mounting tab under the speedometer assembly and install the retaining screws.
6   Install the cluster bezel and mask.
7   Connect the negative battery cable.

21 Instrument cluster – removal and installation

1   Disconnect the negative battery cable from the battery.
2   Remove the instrument cluster bezel and mask (Chapter 12).
3   Remove the instrument panel top cover and right upper trim bezel (Chapter 12).
4   Remove the cluster retaining screws and slide the cluster assembly to the rear.
5   Reach up under the cluster assembly and disconnect the right printed circuit board connector, followed by the speedometer cable and the left circuit board connector.
6   Lift the circuit board from the instrument panel.
7   To install, place the cluster in position, connect the left circuit board connector, the speedometer and the right connector.
8   Install the right trim bezel and the panel top cover.
9   Install the bezel and mask.
10   Connect the negative battery cable.

22 Instrument cluster printed circuit board – removal and installation

1   Disconnect the negative battery cable from the battery.
2   Remove the cluster bezel and mask (Chapter 12).
3   Remove the cluster from the instrument panel (Section 21).
4   Remove the five retaining screws and lift the circuit board from the cluster.
5   To install, place the circuit board in position and install the retaining screws.
6   Install the cluster, bezel and mask.
7   Connect the negative battery cable.

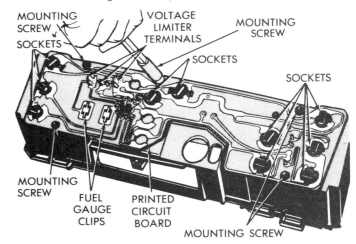

Fig. 10.21 Removing the printed circuit board from the cluster (Sec 22)

10

23 Front door electric window motor – removal and installation

1   Raise the window to the full up position.
2   Disconnect the negative battery cable from the battery.
3   Remove the door trim panel (Chapter 12).
4   Brace the window glass to ensure that it remains in the full up position.
5   Unplug the wiring connector.
6   Remove the retaining screws and disengage the motor from the regulator using a rocking motion during removal. Be careful not to get your fingers in the area of the sector gear where they could get caught in the linkage.

7   To install, place the motor in position and engage the gearbox with the regulator teeth. With the gearbox center post inserted into the pilot hole in the plate, use a rocking motion to align the retaining screw holes.
8   Install the screws and tighten them securely.
9   Plug in the wiring harness connector.
10   Remove the brace, connect the negative battery cable and check the motor for proper operation by raising and lowering the glass.
11   Install the door trim panel.

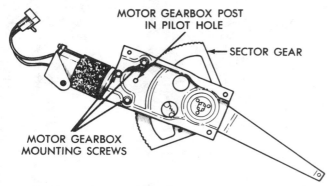

Fig. 10.22 Typical front door electric window motor (Sec 23)

---

24   Rear door electric window motor – removal and installation

1   Remove the door trim panel (Chapter 12).
2   Raise the window so that it is four inches from the full up position.
3   Disconnect the negative battery cable from the battery.

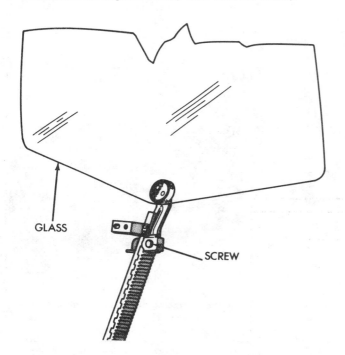

Fig. 10.23 Flex drive arm-to-rack connection (Sec 24)

4   Remove the screw retaining the flex drive arm to the rack.
5   Remove the regulator attachment rivets by knocking out the center of the rivets with a suitable punch and hammer and drilling out the remainder.
6   Remove the regulator by maneuvering the motor end through the access hole first and then rotating the regulator out.
7   If the motor is inoperative, it will be necessary to remove the rivets and lift the assembly up until the flex drive arm can be removed from the rack.
8   Remove the two screws retaining the motor gearbox to the metal T-track.
9   Attach the new motor to the T-track and tighten the screws.
10   Insert the top of the T-track into the access hole and then turn it toward the hinge pillar so the motor is in the horizontal position. Rotate the regulator a quarter turn in the opposite direction so the bracket tab aligns with the slot in the inner panel.
11   Attach the regulator to the door with a suitable rivet tool, following the sequence shown in the accompanying illustration.
12   Connect the negative battery cable and actuate the motor so the flex rack is visible through the access hole. Install the retaining screw and tighten it securely.
13   Install the door trim panel.

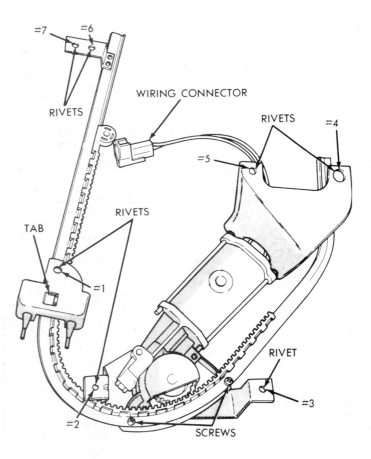

Fig. 10.24 Rear door electric window regulator numbered fastening sequence (Sec 24)

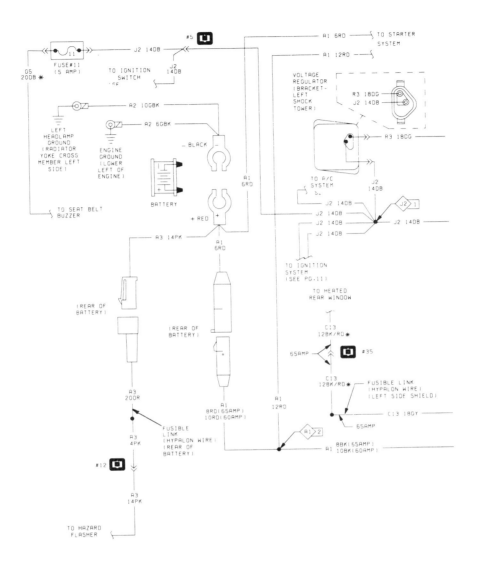

Fig. 10.25 Charging system (2.2L) wiring diagram (1981 models)

COLOR CODE					
COLOR CODE	COLOR	STANDARD TRACER COLOR	COLOR CODE	COLOR	STANDARD TRACER CODE
BK	BLACK	WH	PK	PINK	BK WH
BR	BROWN	WH	RD	RED	WH
DB	DARK BLUE	WH	TN	TAN	BK
DG	DARK GREEN	WH	VT	VIOLET	WH
GY	GRAY	BK	WT	WHITE	BK
LB	LIGHT BLUE	BK	YL	YELLOW	BK
LG	LIGHT GREEN	BK	*	WITH TRACER	
OR	ORANGE	BK			

10

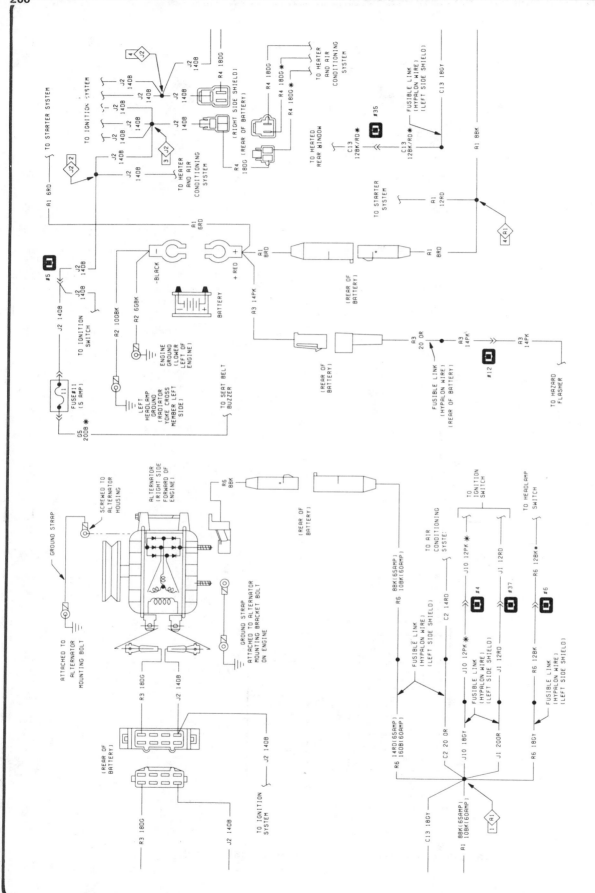

Fig. 10.27 Charging system (2.6L) wiring diagram (1981 models)

Fig. 10.26 Charging system (2.2L) wiring diagram cont. (1981 models)

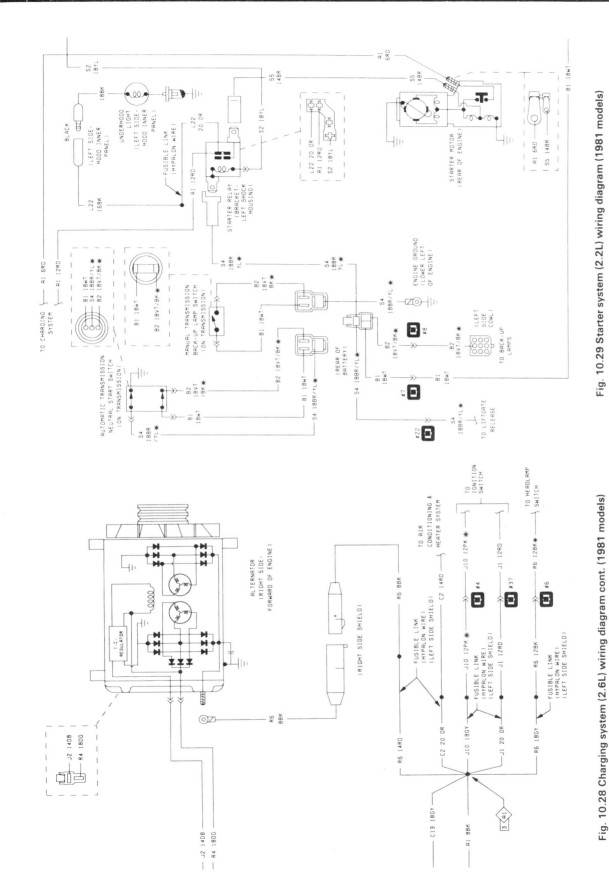

Fig. 10.29 Starter system (2.2L) wiring diagram (1981 models)

Fig. 10.28 Charging system (2.6L) wiring diagram cont. (1981 models)

10

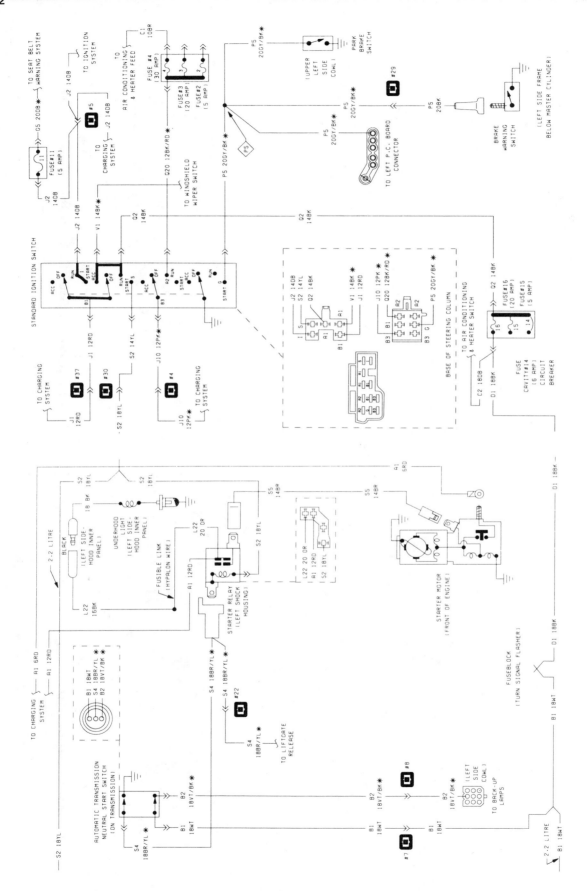

Fig. 10.31 Ignition system wiring diagram (1981 models)

Fig. 10.30 Starter system (2.6L) wiring diagram (1981 models)

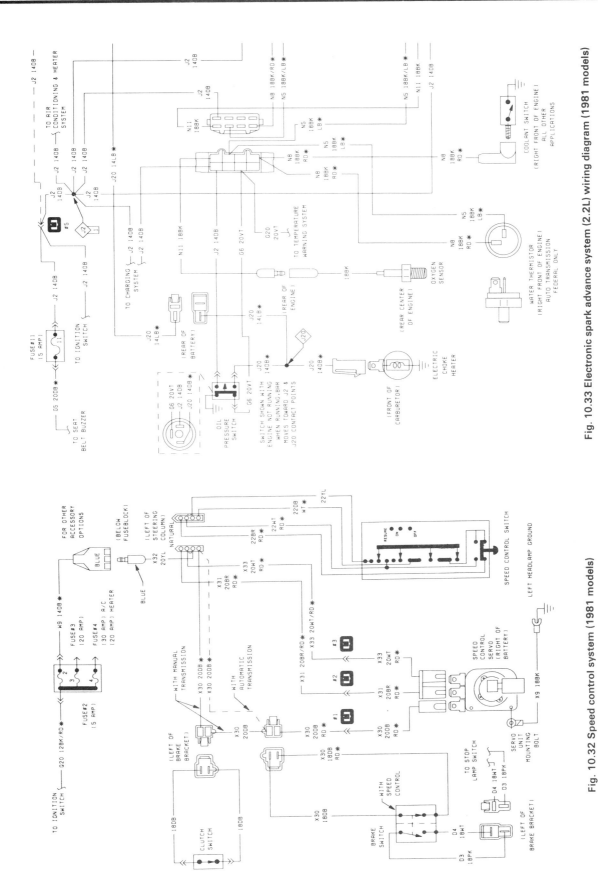

Fig. 10.33 Electronic spark advance system (2.2L) wiring diagram (1981 models)

Fig. 10.32 Speed control system (1981 models)

10

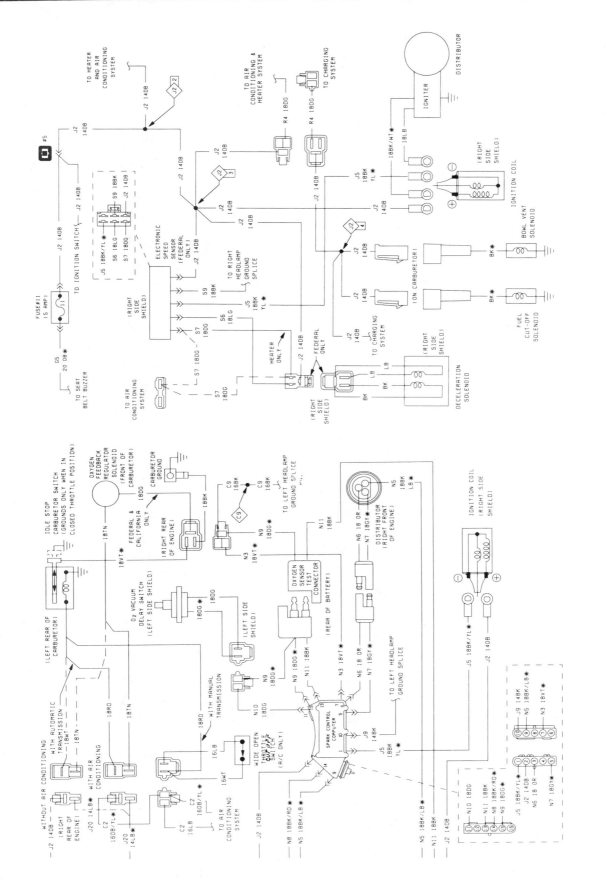

Fig. 10.35 Electronic ignition system (2.6L) wiring diagram (1981 models)

Fig. 10.34 Electronic spark advance system (2.6L) wiring diagram (1981 models)

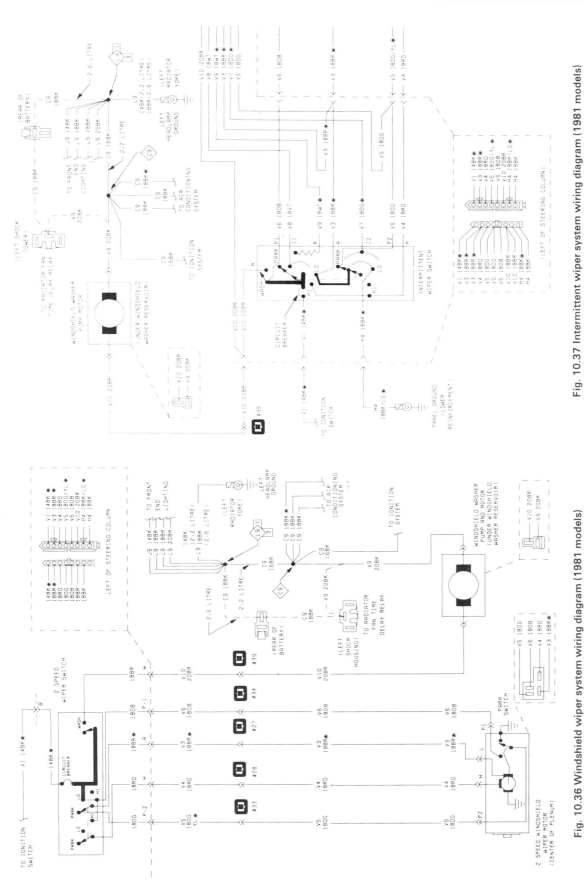

Fig. 10.37 Intermittent wiper system wiring diagram (1981 models)

Fig. 10.36 Windshield wiper system wiring diagram (1981 models)

10

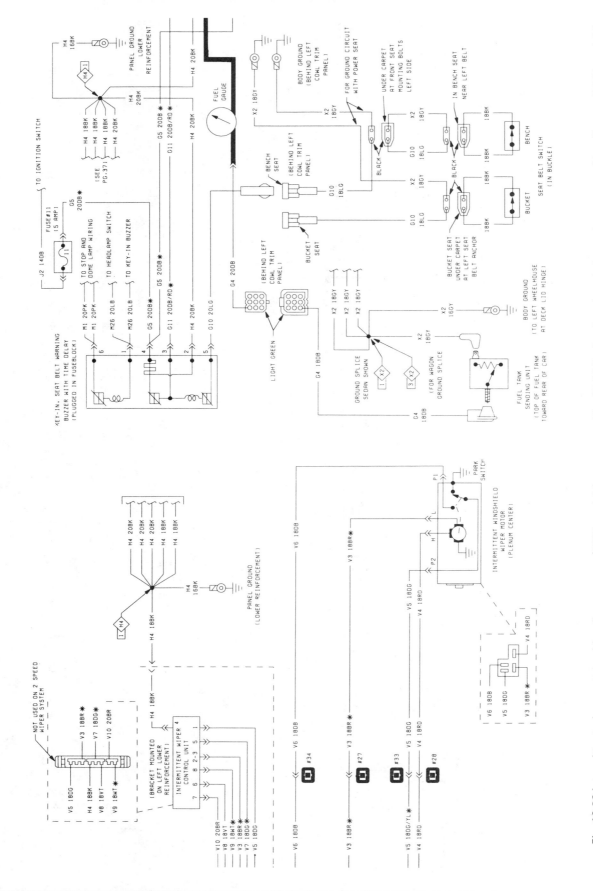

Fig. 10.39 Fuel tank and seatbelt warning system wiring diagram (1981 models)

Fig. 10.38 Intermittent wiper system wiring diagram cont. (1981 models)

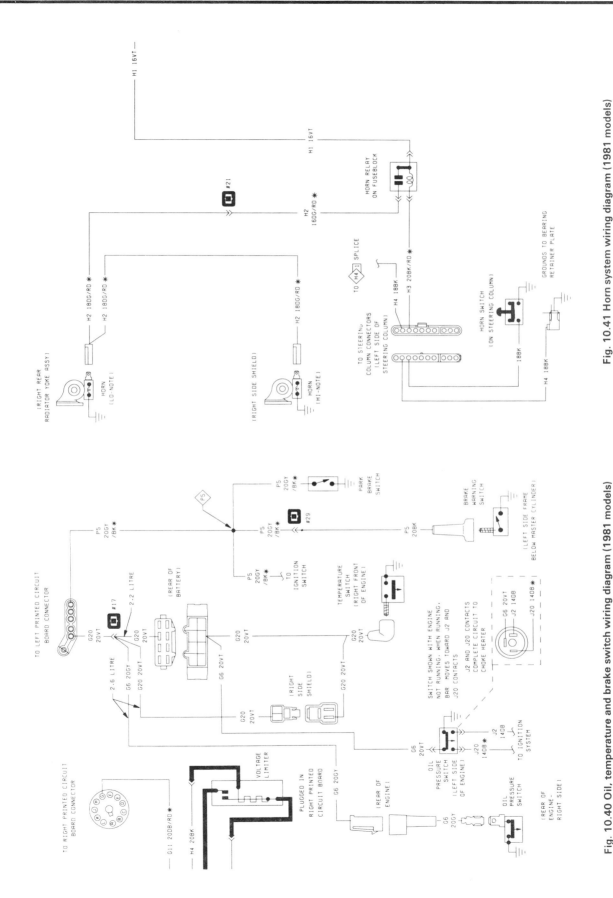

Fig. 10.41 Horn system wiring diagram (1981 models)

Fig. 10.40 Oil, temperature and brake switch wiring diagram (1981 models)

10

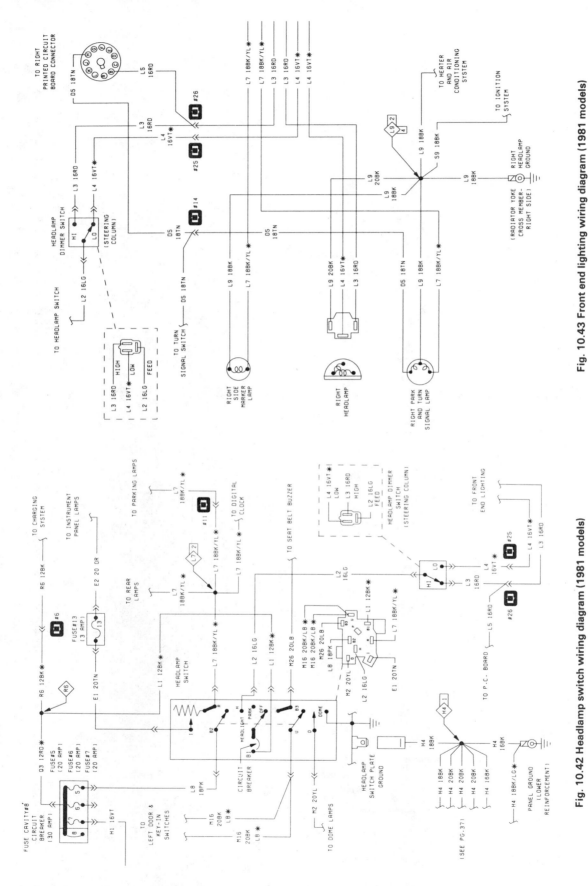

Fig. 10.43 Front end lighting wiring diagram (1981 models)

Fig. 10.42 Headlamp switch wiring diagram (1981 models)

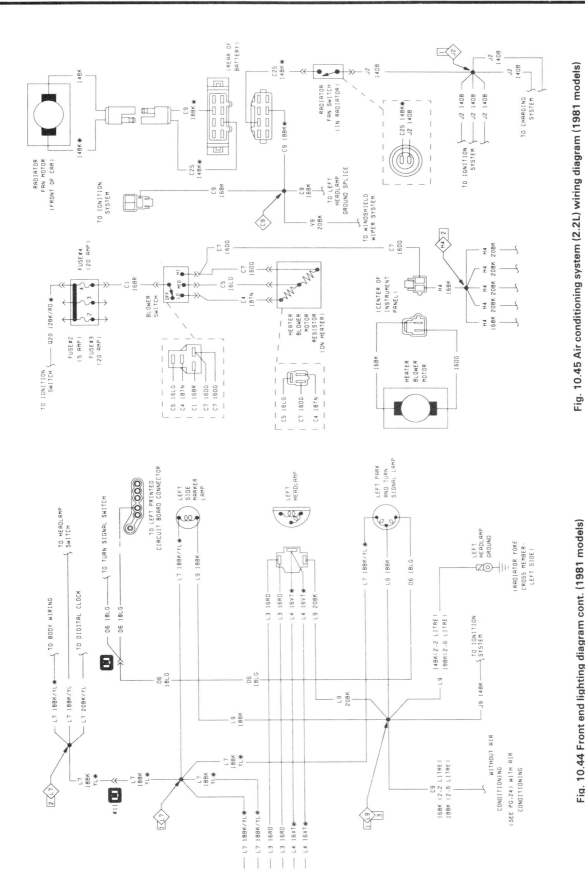

Fig. 10.45 Air conditioning system (2.2L) wiring diagram (1981 models)

Fig. 10.44 Front end lighting diagram cont. (1981 models)

10

210

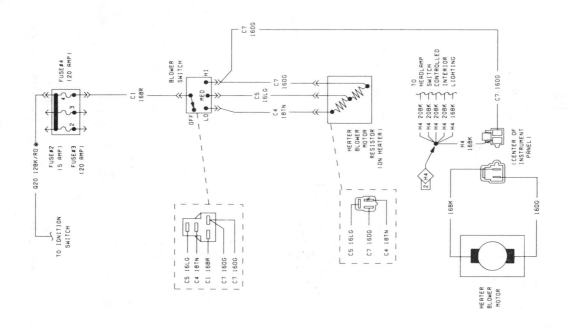

Fig. 10.47 Heater system (2.6L) wiring diagram (1981 models)

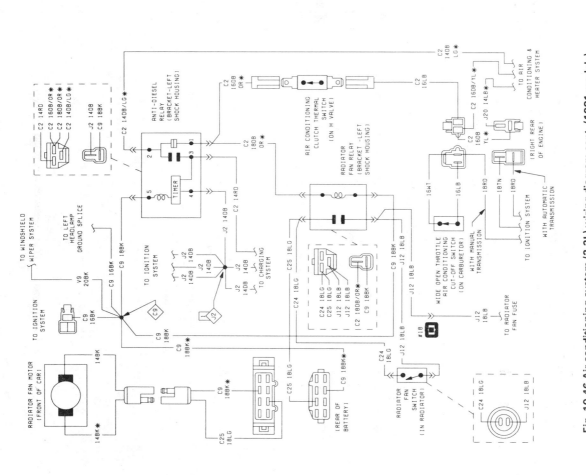

Fig. 10.46 Air conditioning system (2.2L) wiring diagram cont. (1981 models)

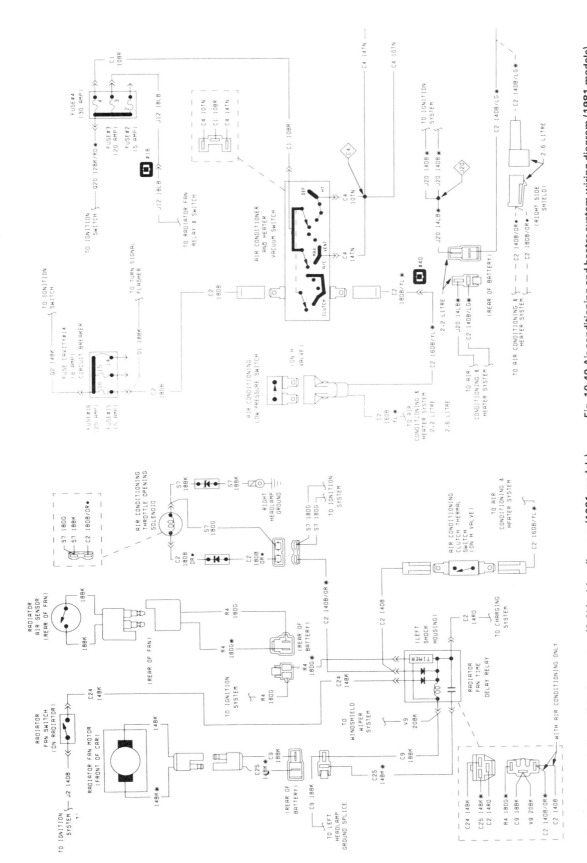

Fig. 10.49 Air conditioning and heater system wiring diagram (1981 models)

Fig. 10.48 Heater and air conditioning system (2.6L) wiring diagram (1981 models)

10

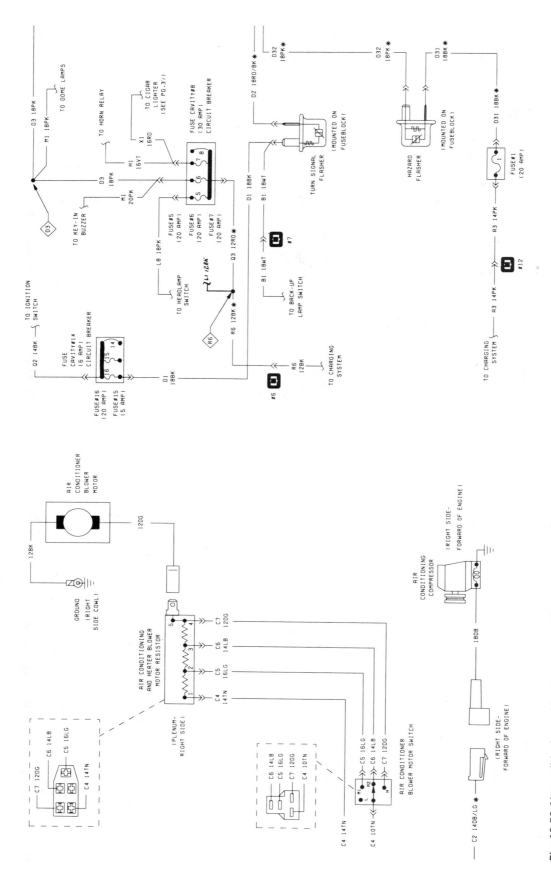

Fig. 10.51 Stop/turn and hazard flasher systems wiring diagrams (1981 models)

Fig. 10.50 Air conditioning and heater system wiring diagram cont. (1981 models)

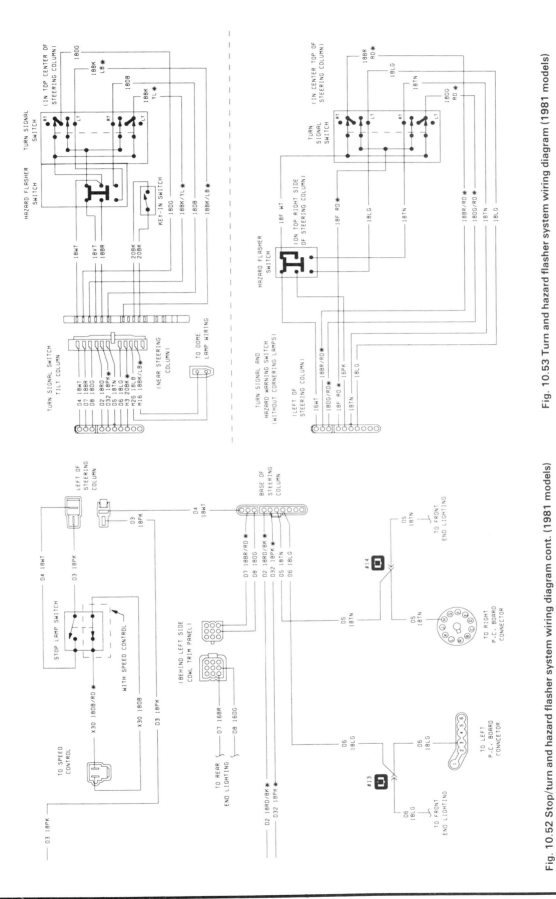

Fig. 10.53 Turn and hazard flasher system wiring diagram (1981 models)

Fig. 10.52 Stop/turn and hazard flasher system wiring diagram cont. (1981 models)

10

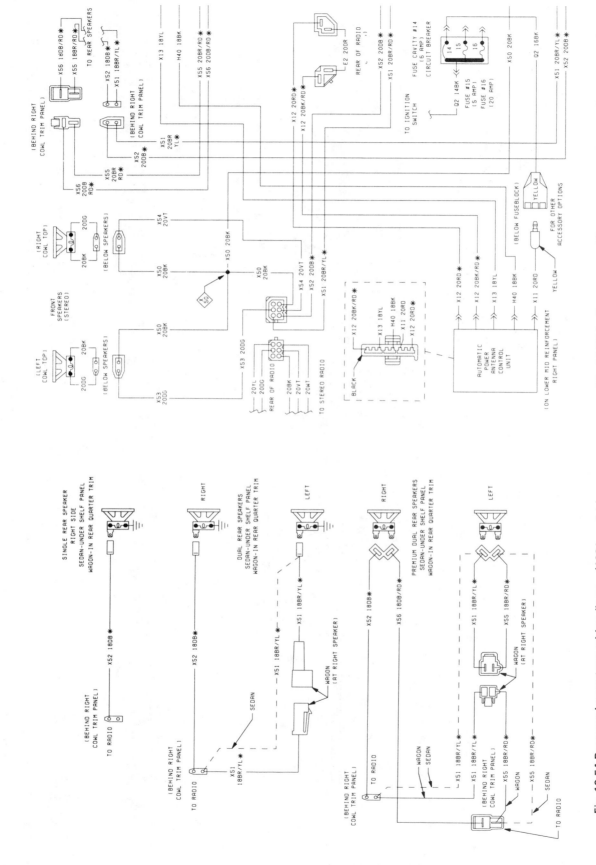

Fig. 10.55 Audio power amplifier system wiring diagram (1981 models)

Fig. 10.54 Rear speaker systems wiring diagram (1981 models)

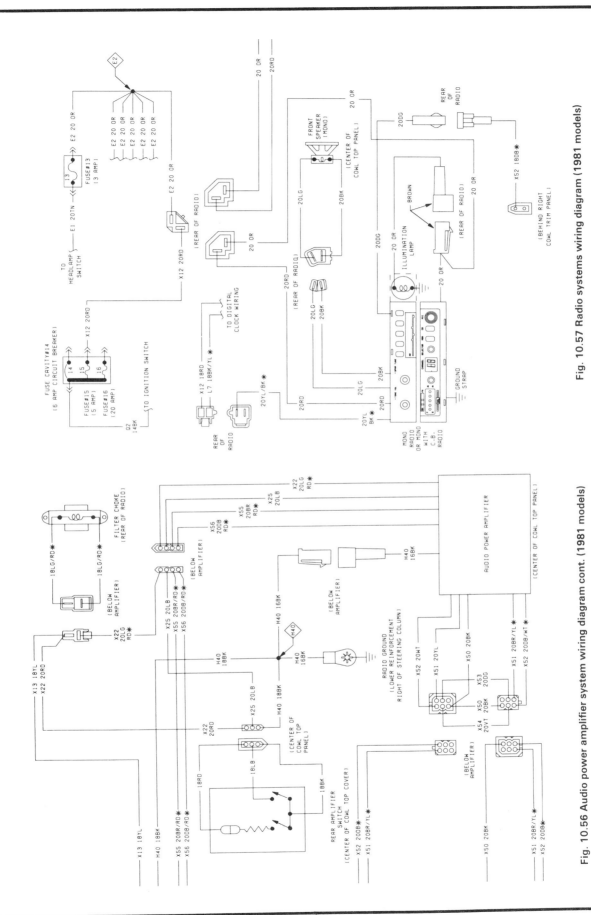

Fig. 10.57 Radio systems wiring diagram (1981 models)

Fig. 10.56 Audio power amplifier system wiring diagram cont. (1981 models)

10

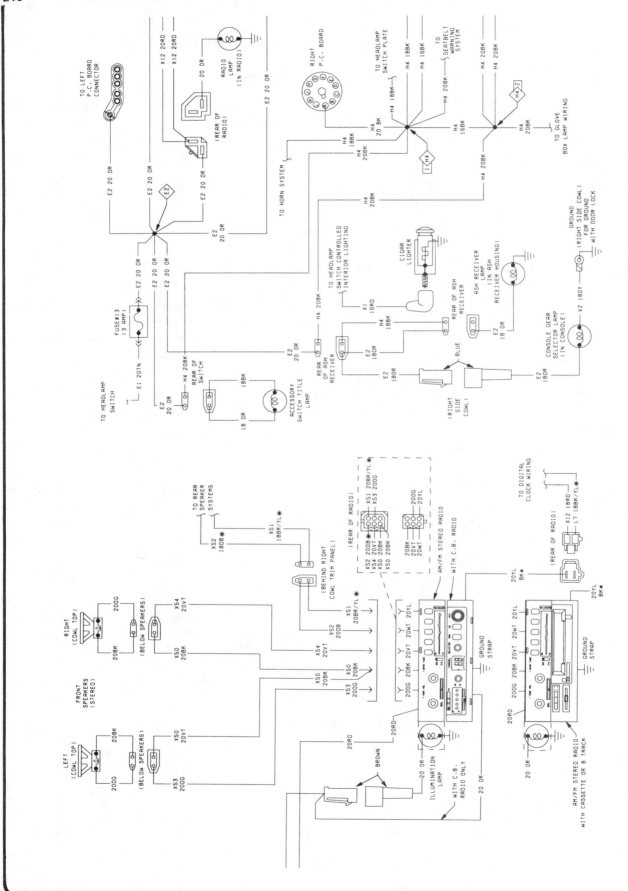

Fig. 10.59 Switch controlled interior lighting wiring diagram (1981 models)

Fig. 10.58 Radio systems wiring diagram cont. (1981 models)

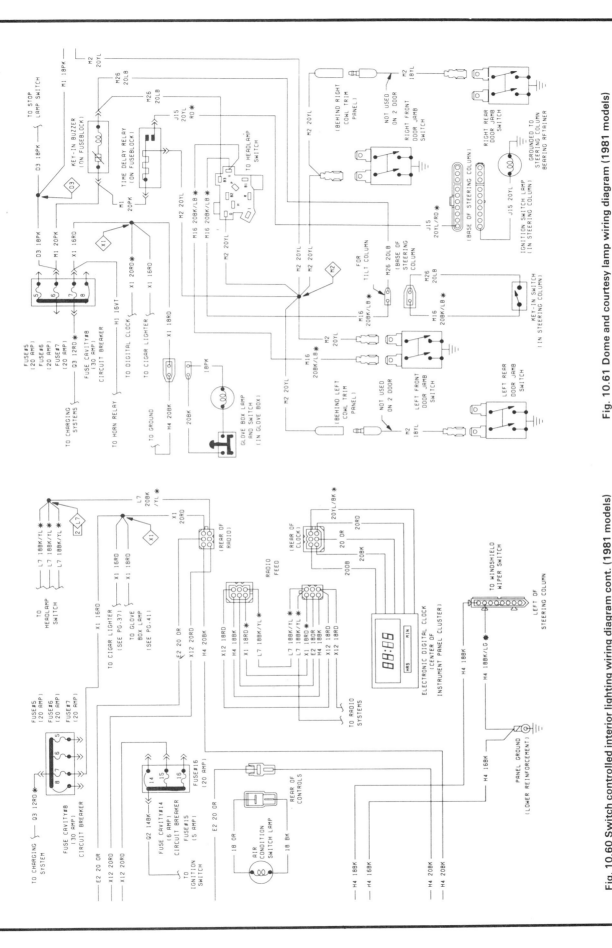

Fig. 10.61 Dome and courtesy lamp wiring diagram (1981 models)

Fig. 10.60 Switch controlled interior lighting wiring diagram cont. (1981 models)

10

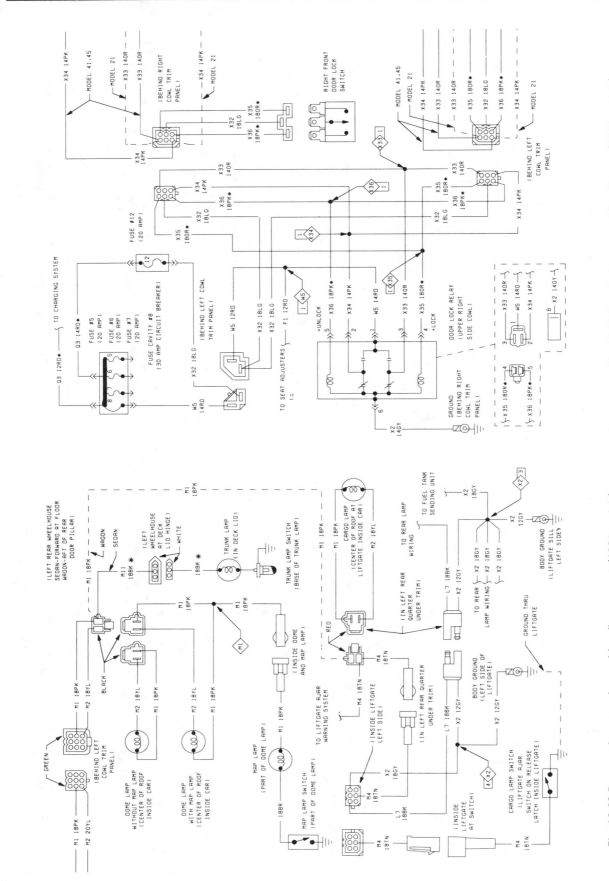

Fig. 10.63 Door lock system wiring diagram (1981 models)

Fig. 10.62 Dome and courtesy lamp wiring diagram cont. (1981 models)

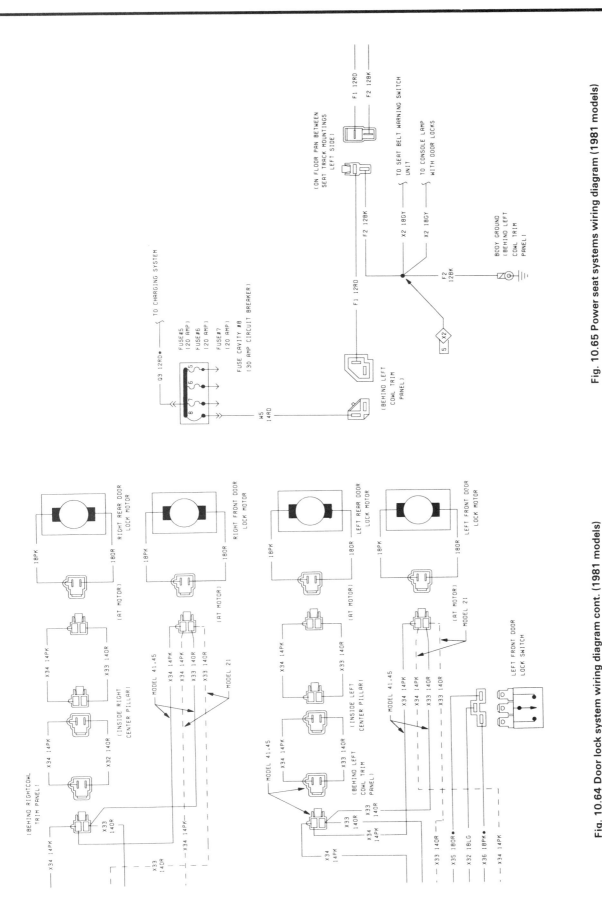

Fig. 10.65 Power seat systems wiring diagram (1981 models)

Fig. 10.64 Door lock system wiring diagram cont. (1981 models)

10

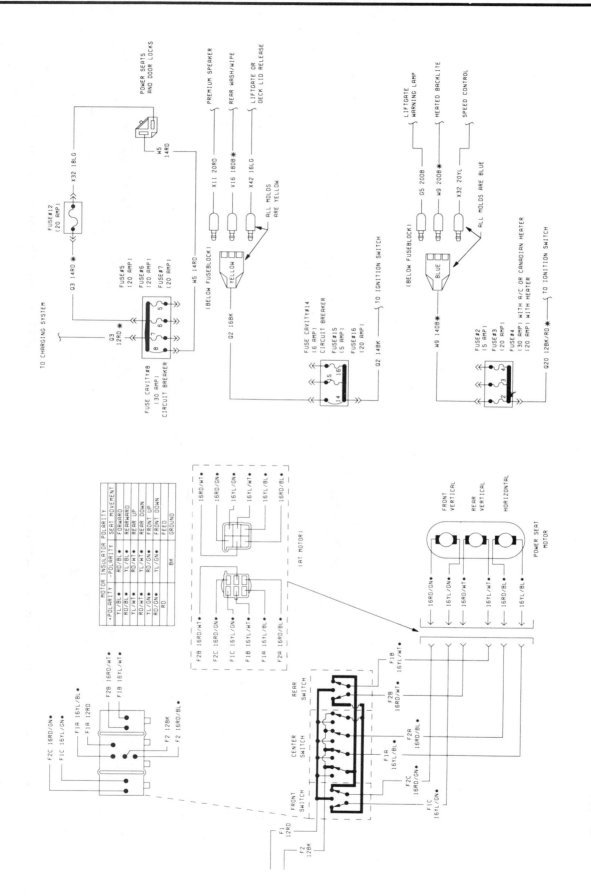

Fig. 10.67 Power assist system wiring diagram (1981 models)

Fig. 10.66 Power seat systems wiring diagram cont. (1981 models)

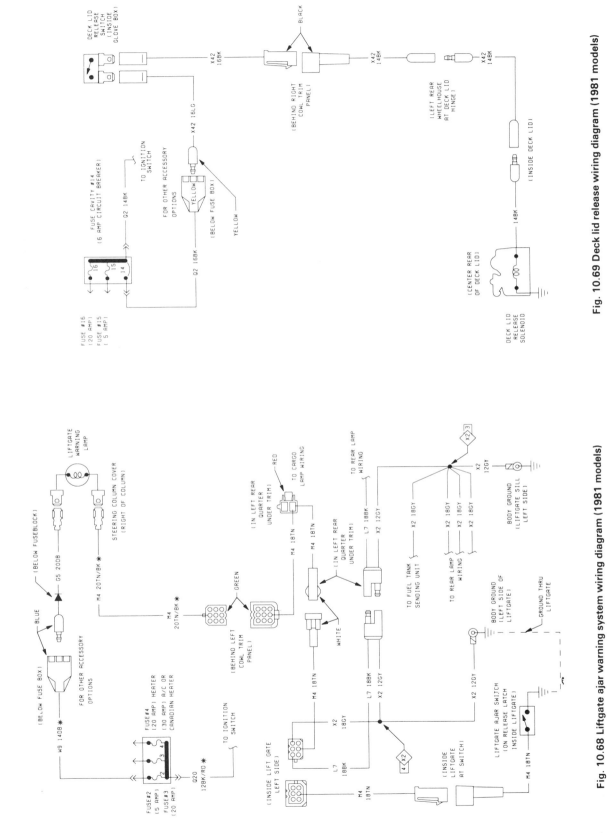

Fig. 10.69 Deck lid release wiring diagram (1981 models)

Fig. 10.68 Liftgate ajar warning system wiring diagram (1981 models)

10

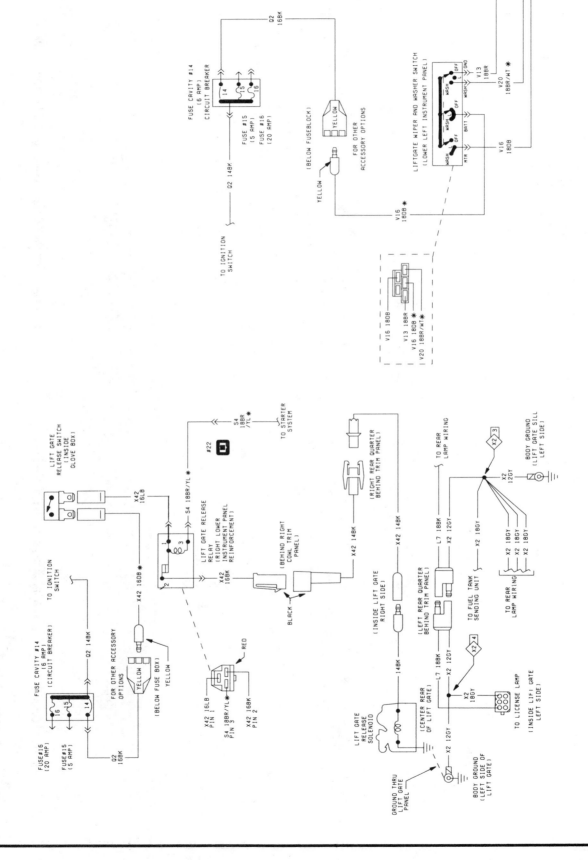

Fig. 10.71 Liftgate wiper and washer system wiring diagram (1981 models)

Fig. 10.70 Liftgate release wiring diagram (1981 models)

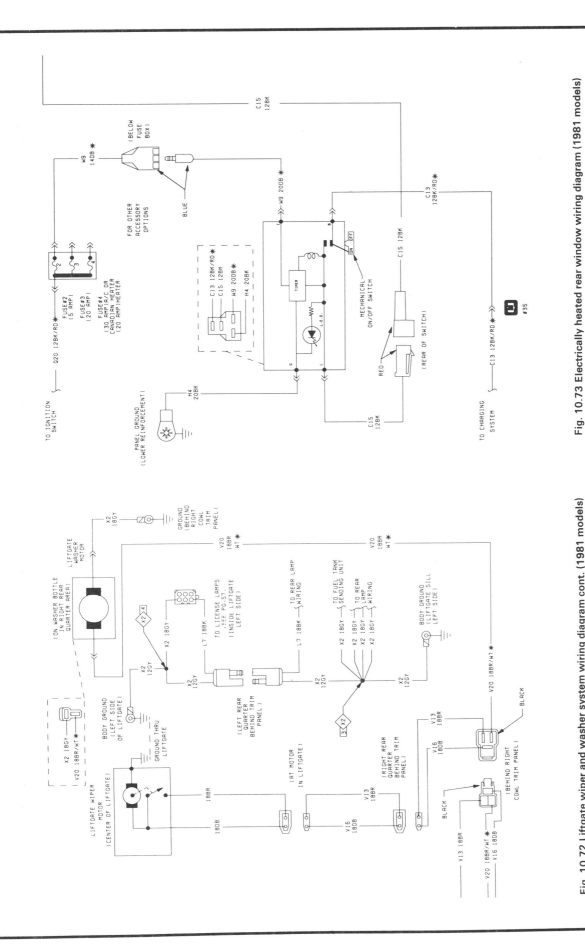

Fig. 10.73 Electrically heated rear window wiring diagram (1981 models)

Fig. 10.72 Liftgate wiper and washer system wiring diagram cont. (1981 models)

10

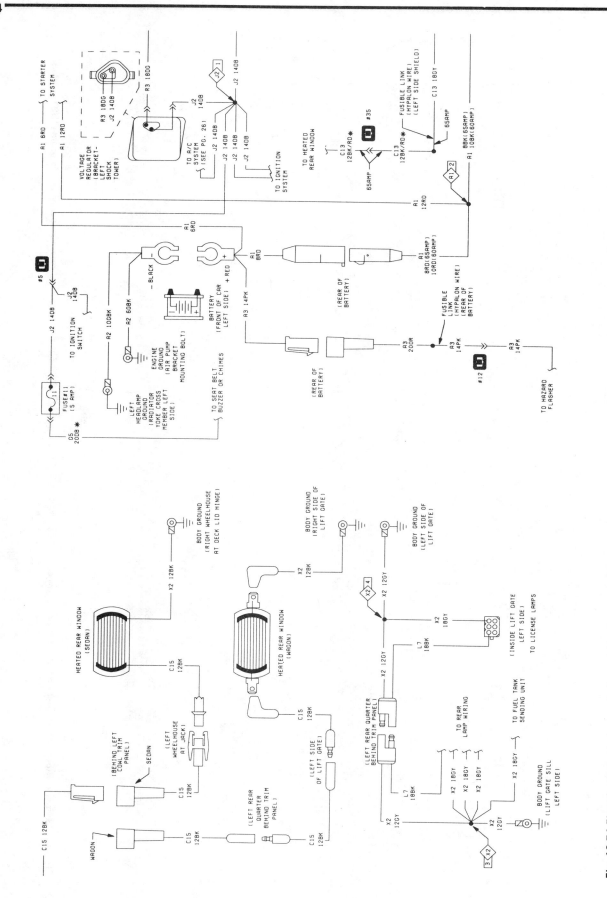

Fig. 10.75 Charging system (2.2L) wiring diagram (1982 models)

Fig. 10.74 Electrically heated rear window wiring diagram cont. (1981 models)

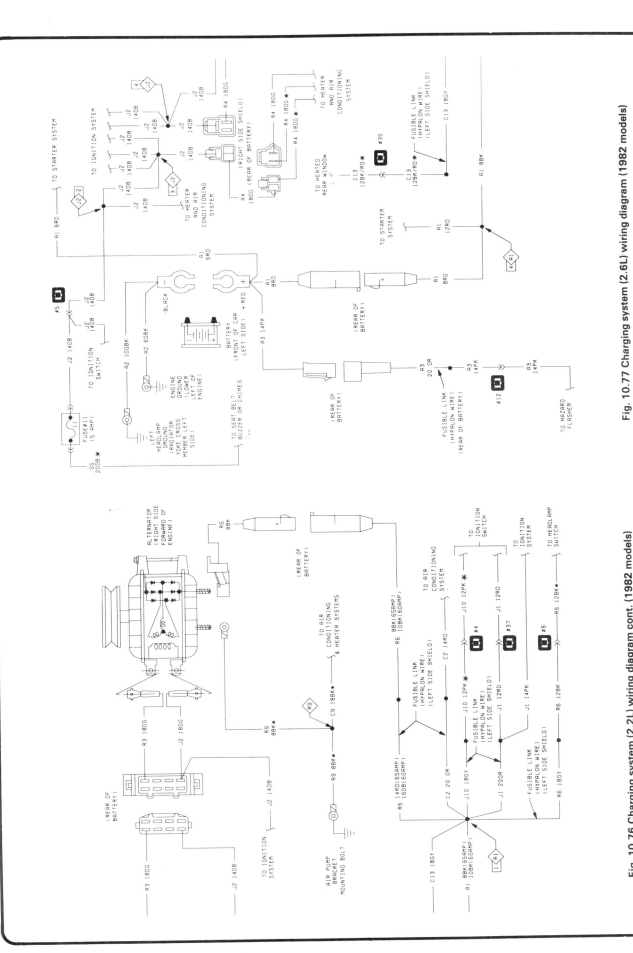

Fig. 10.77 Charging system (2.6L) wiring diagram (1982 models)

Fig. 10.76 Charging system (2.2L) wiring diagram cont. (1982 models)

10

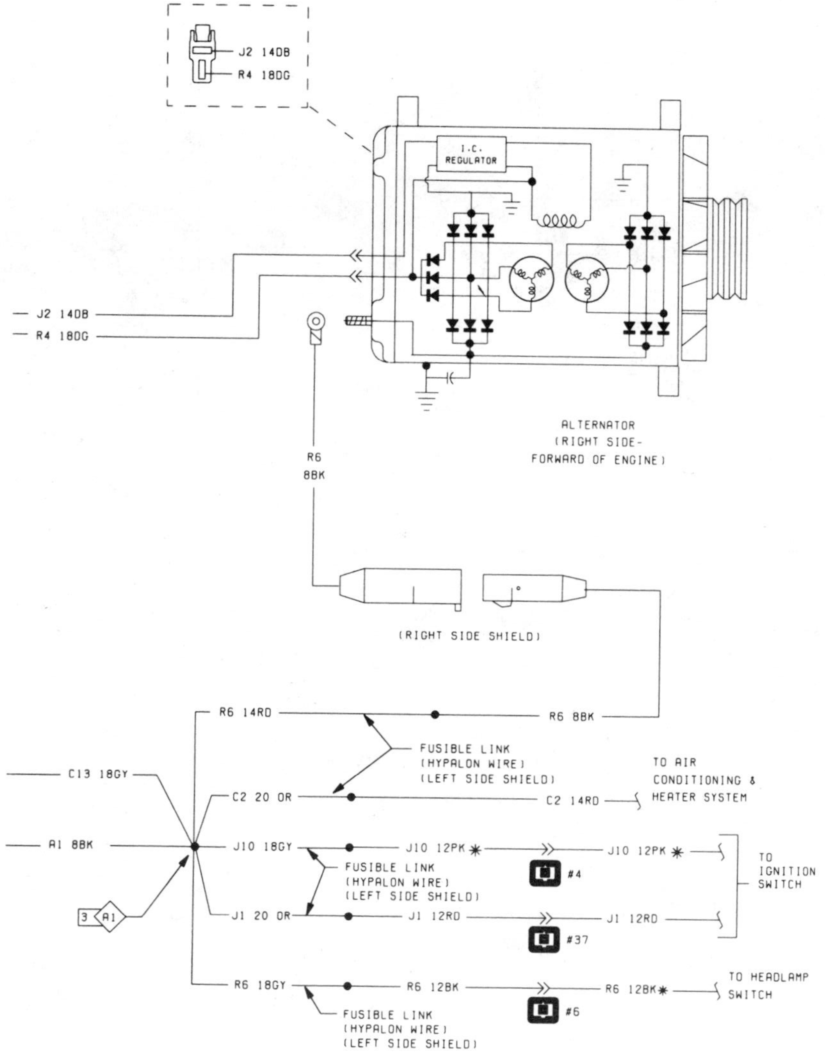

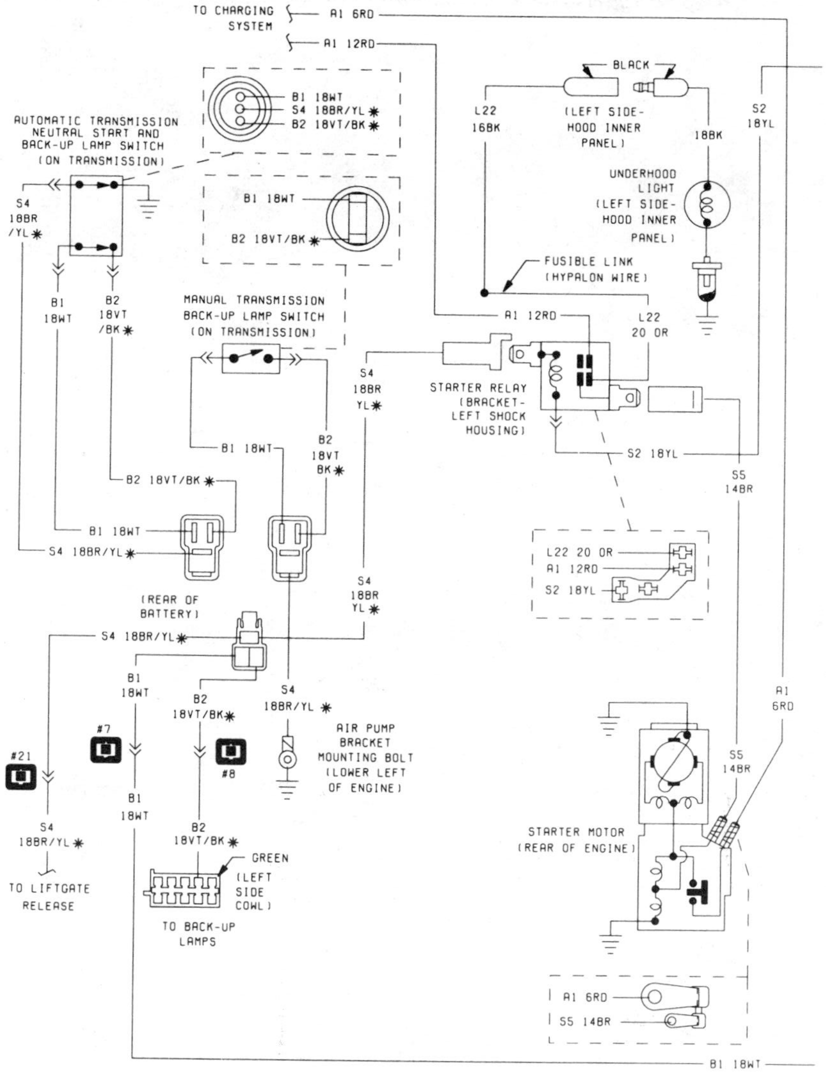

Fig. 10.79 Starter system (2.2L) wiring diagram (1982 models)

Fig. 10.78 Charging system (2.6L) wiring diagram cont. (1982 models)

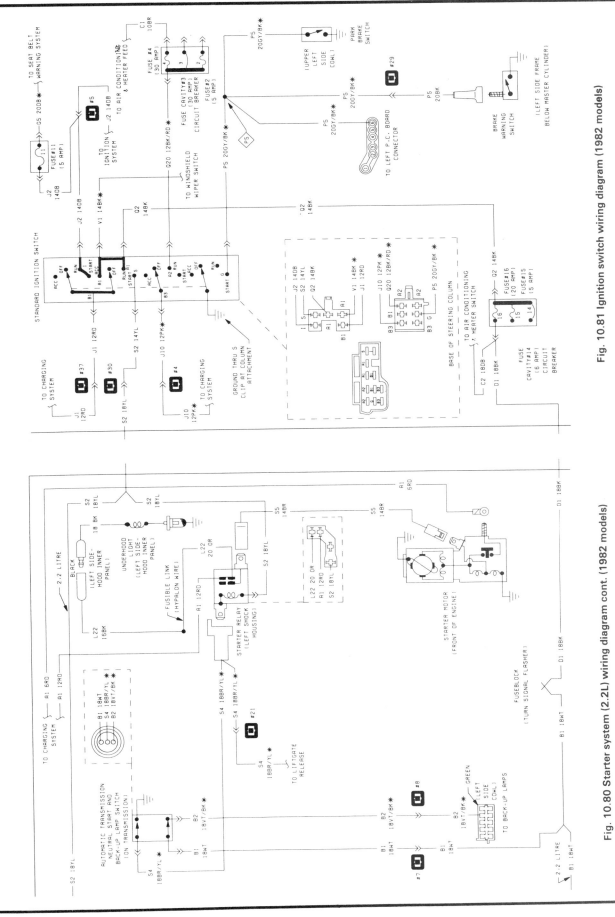

Fig. 10.81 Ignition switch wiring diagram (1982 models)

Fig. 10.80 Starter system (2.2L) wiring diagram cont. (1982 models)

10

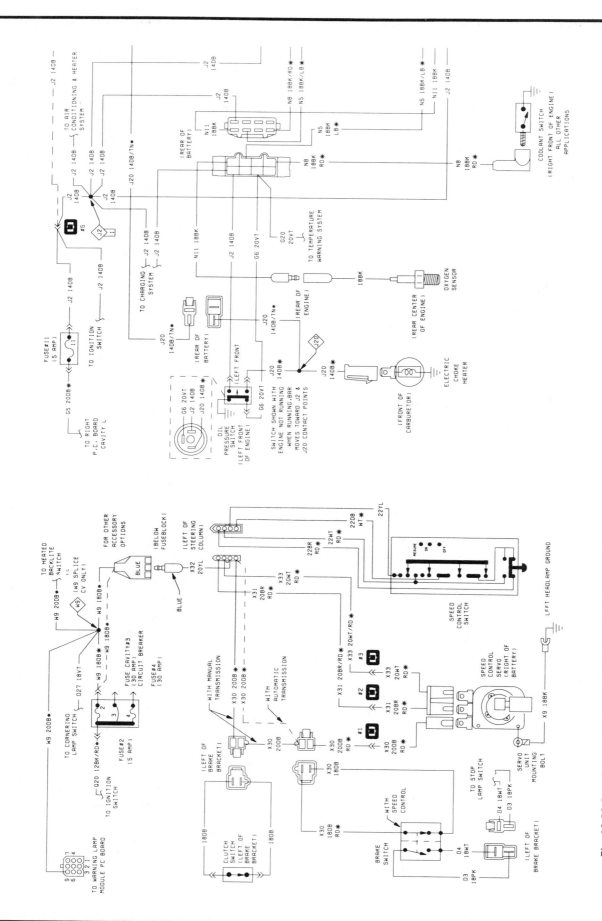

Fig. 10.83 Electronic spark advance system (2.2L) wiring diagram (1982 models)

Fig. 10.82 Speed control system wiring diagram (1982 models)

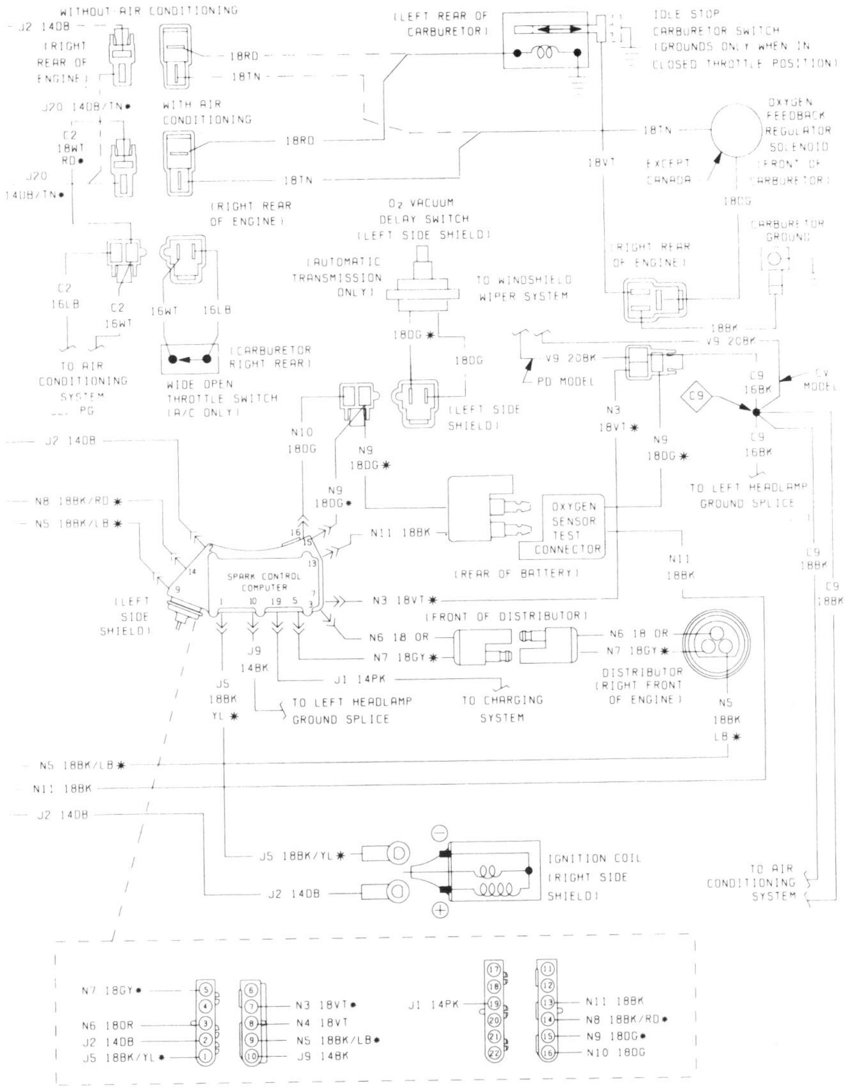

229

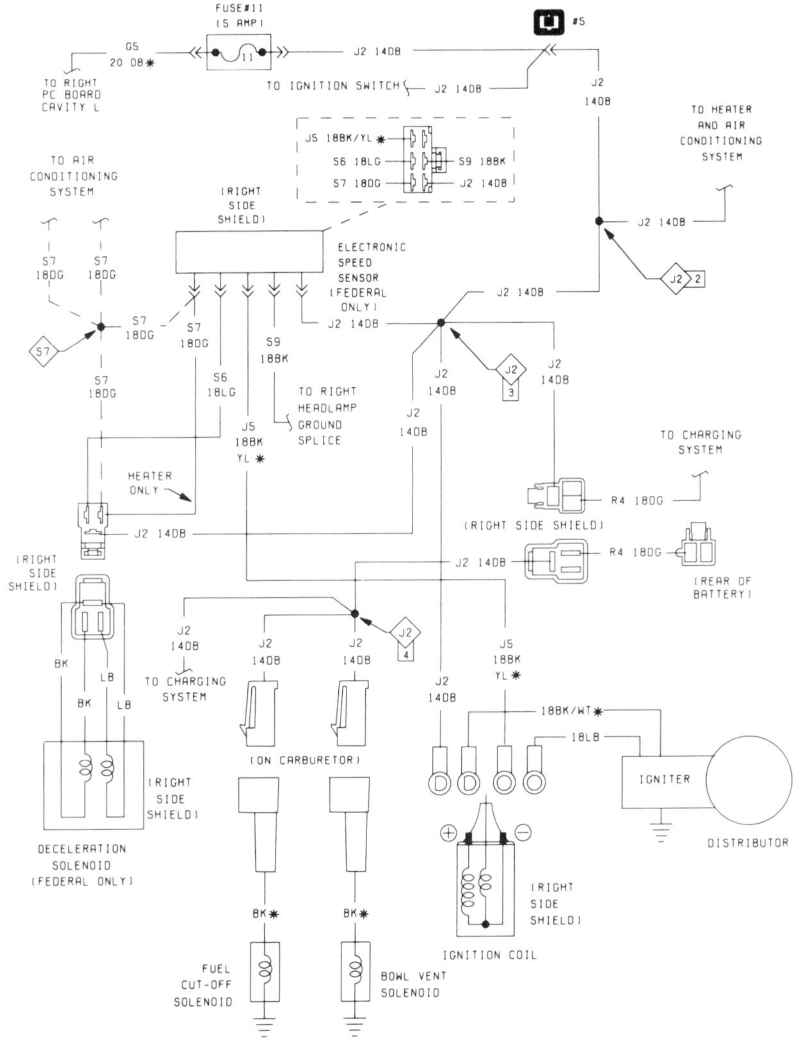

Fig. 10.85 Electronic ignition system (2.6L) wiring diagram (1982 models)

Fig. 10.84 Electronic spark advance system (2.2L) wiring diagram cont. (1982 models)

10

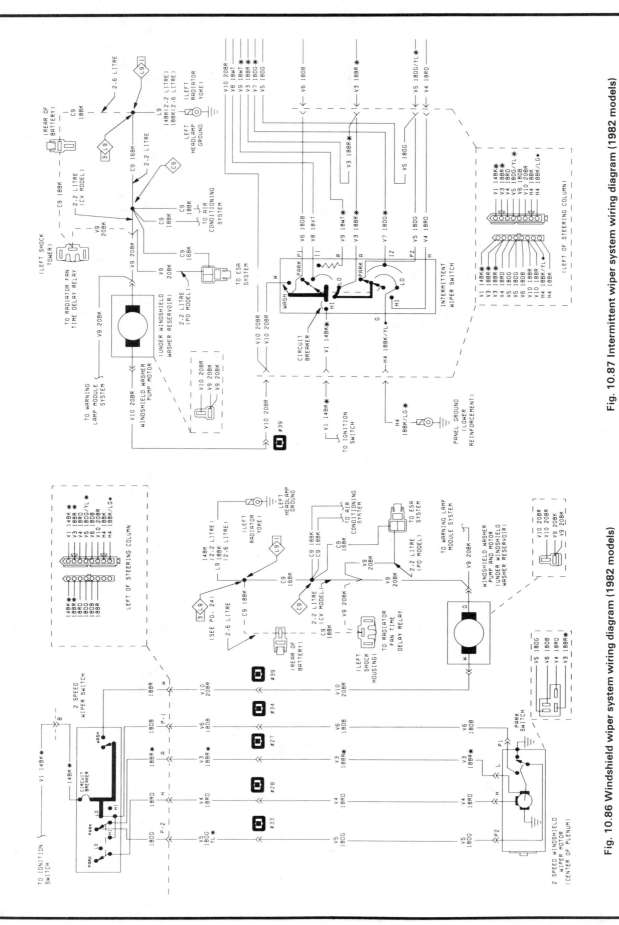

Fig. 10.87 Intermittent wiper system wiring diagram (1982 models)

Fig. 10.86 Windshield wiper system wiring diagram (1982 models)

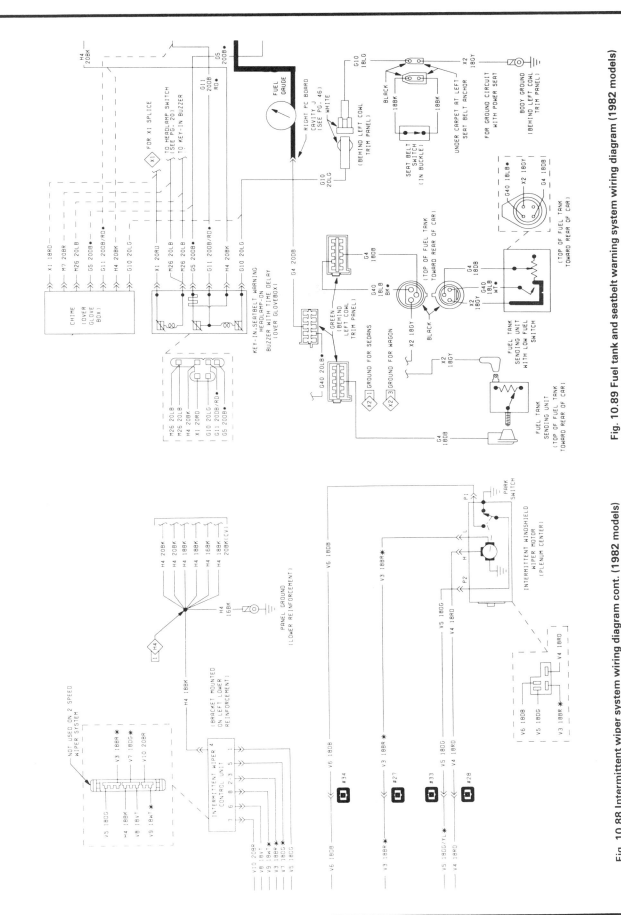

Fig. 10.89 Fuel tank and seatbelt warning system wiring diagram (1982 models)

Fig. 10.88 Intermittent wiper system wiring diagram cont. (1982 models)

10

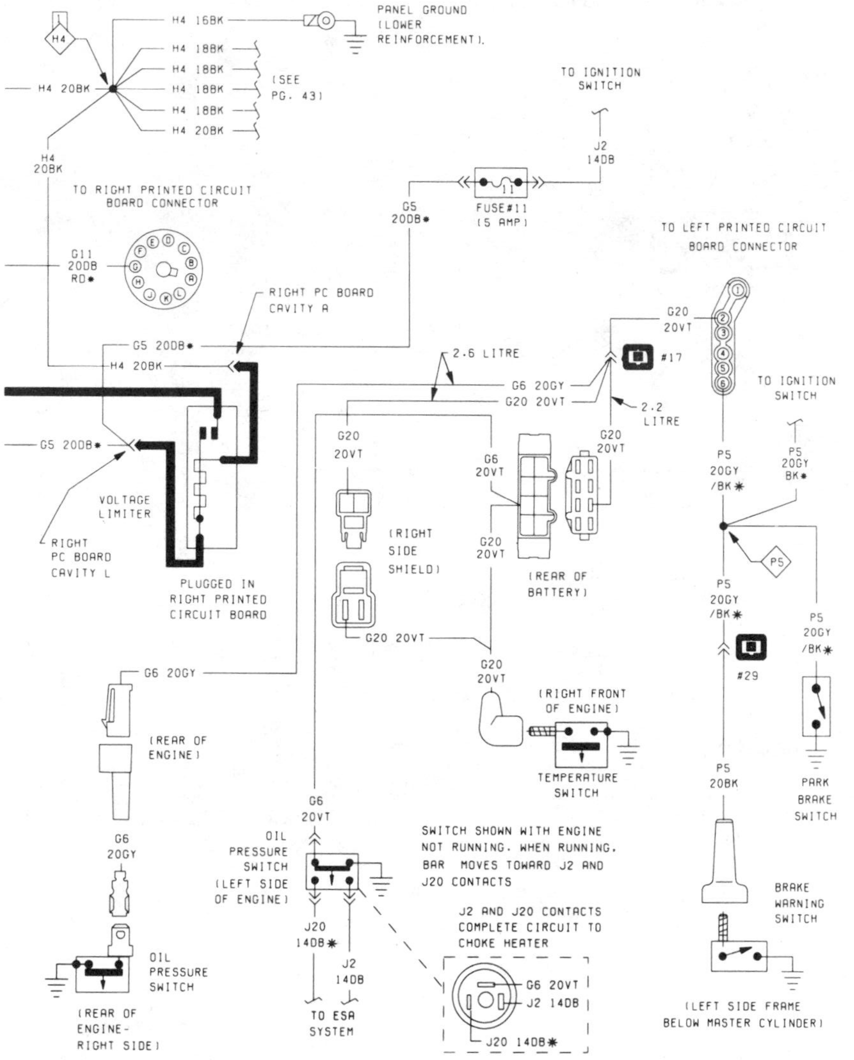

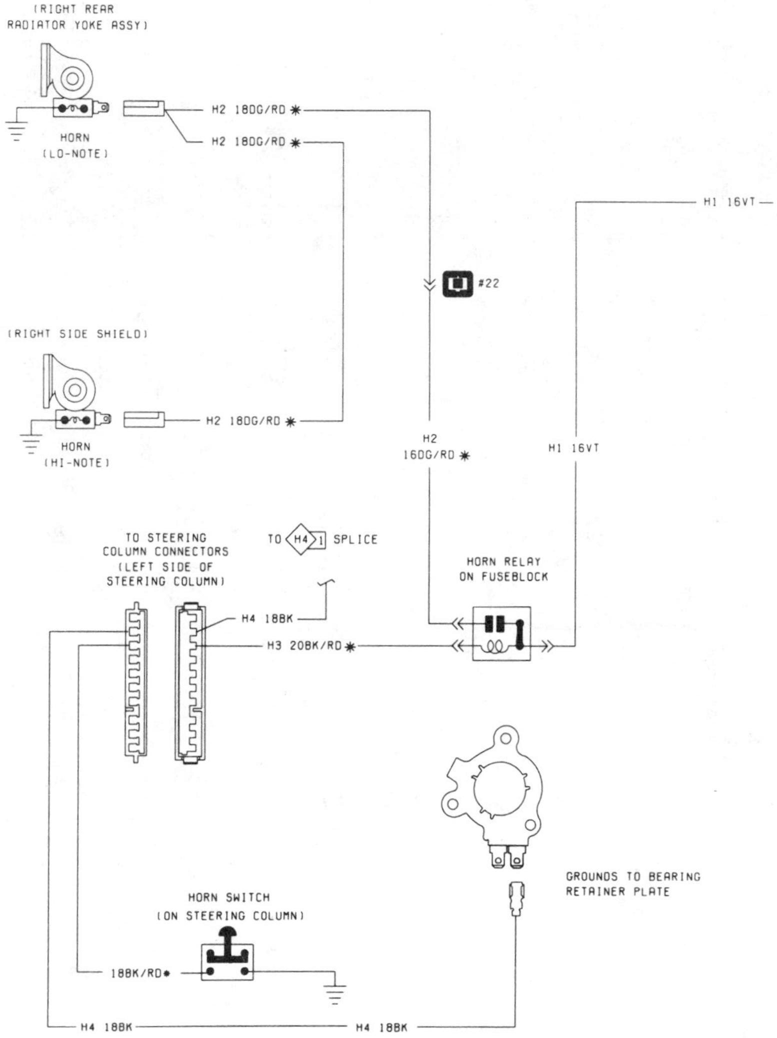

Fig. 10.91 Horn system wiring diagram (1982 models)

Fig. 10.90 Oil, temperature and brake switch wiring diagram (1982 models)

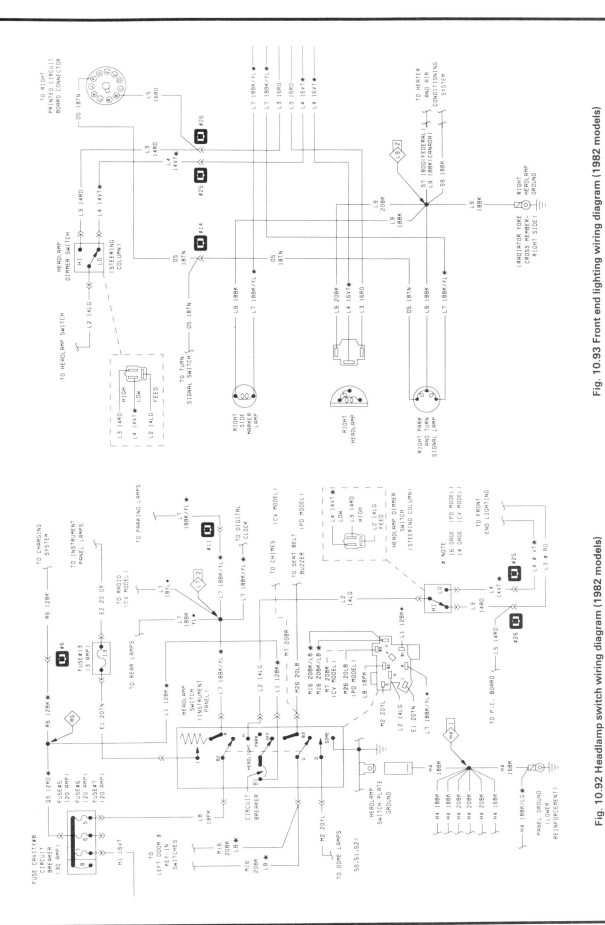

Fig. 10.93 Front end lighting wiring diagram (1982 models)

Fig. 10.92 Headlamp switch wiring diagram (1982 models)

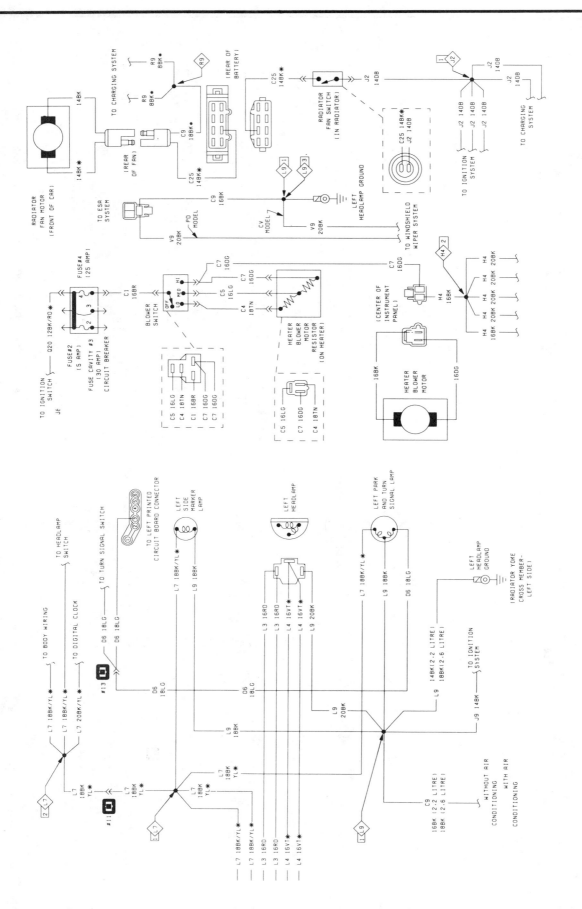

Fig. 10.95 Heater system (2.2L) wiring diagram (1982 models)

Fig. 10.94 Front end lighting wiring diagram cont. (1981 models)

235

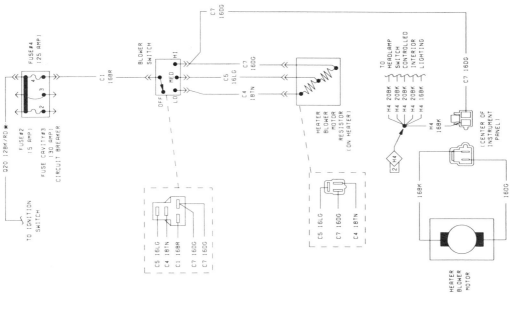

Fig. 10.97 Heater system (2.6L) wiring diagram (1981 models)

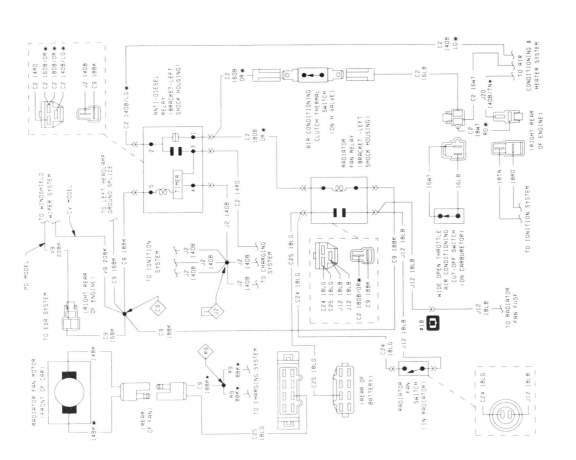

Fig. 10.96 Air conditioning system (2.2L) wiring diagram (1982 models)

10

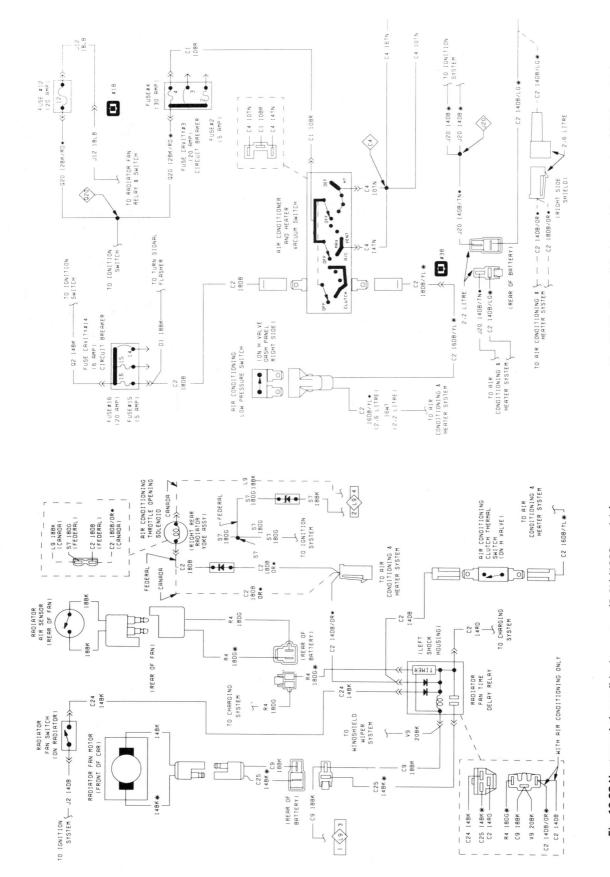

Fig. 10.99 Air conditioning and heater system (1982 models)

Fig. 10.98 Heater and air conditioning system (2.6L) (1982 models)

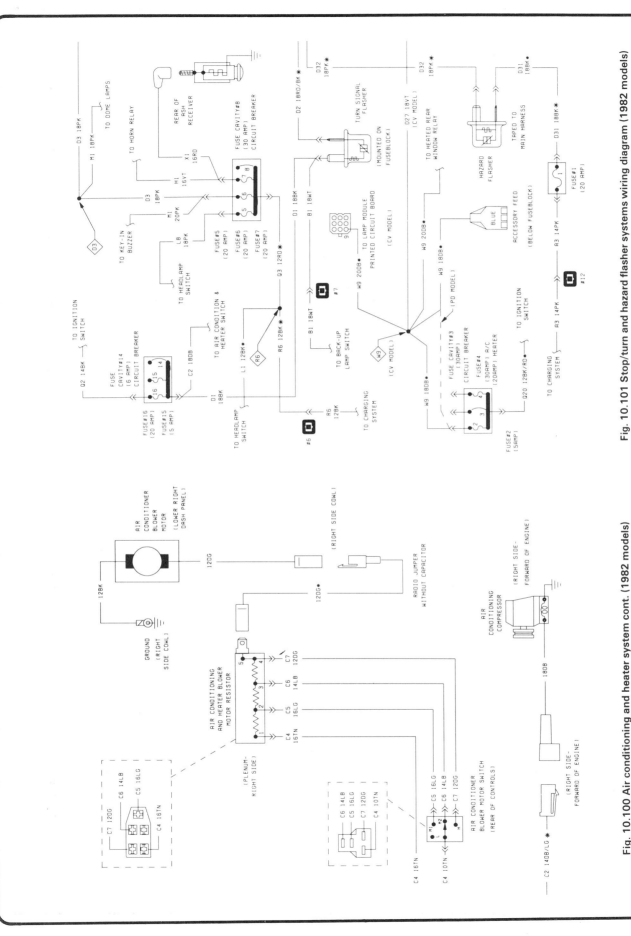

Fig. 10.101 Stop/turn and hazard flasher systems wiring diagram (1982 models)

Fig. 10.100 Air conditioning and heater system cont. (1982 models)

10

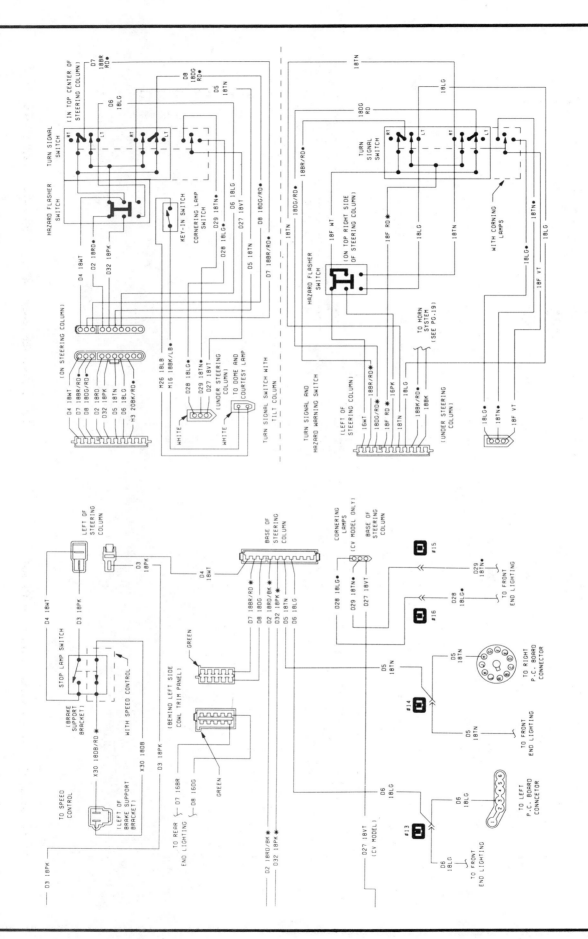

Fig. 10.103 Turn and hazard flasher systems wiring diagram (1982 models)

Fig. 10.102 Stop/turn and hazard flasher systems wiring diagram cont. (1982 models)

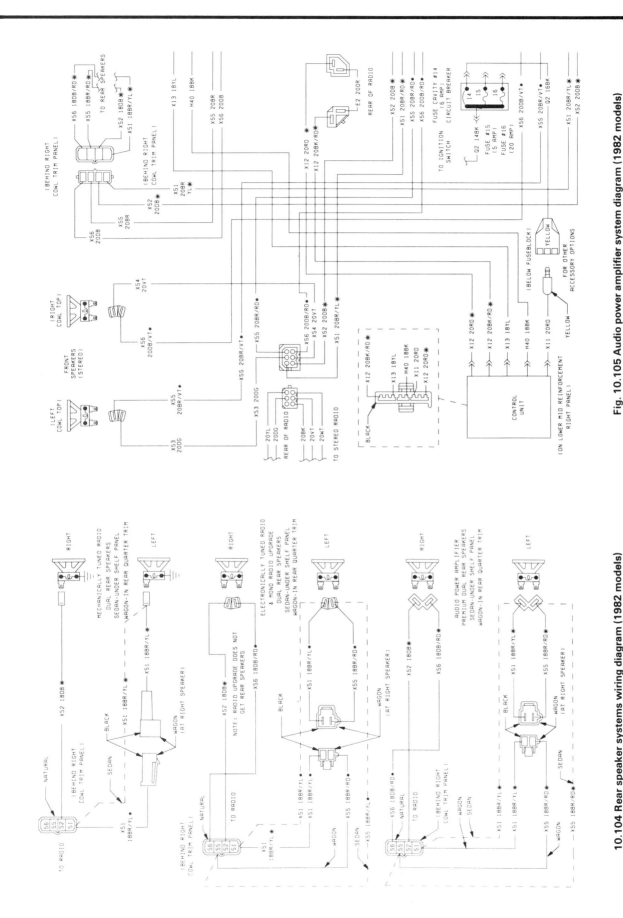

Fig. 10.105 Audio power amplifier system diagram (1982 models)

10.104 Rear speaker systems wiring diagram (1982 models)

10

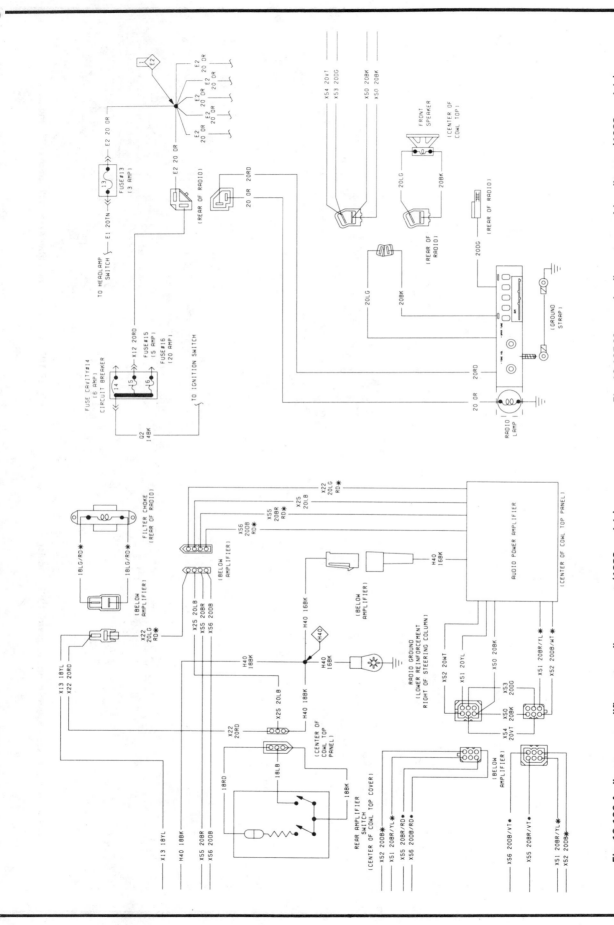

Fig. 10.107 Monaural radio systems wiring diagram (1982 models)

Fig. 10.106 Audio power amplifier system diagram cont. (1982 models)

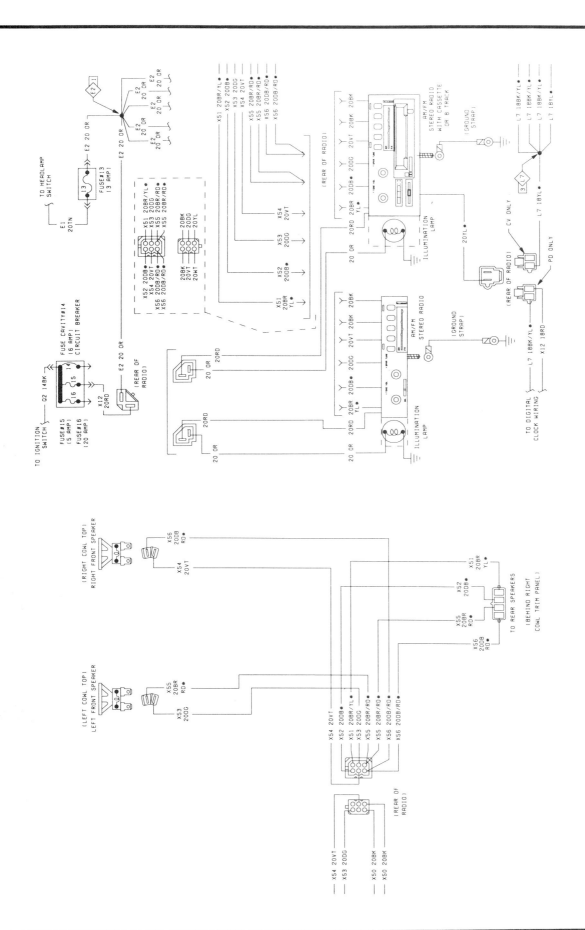

Fig. 10.109 Mechanically tuned stereo radio system wiring diagram (1982 models)

Fig. 10.108 Upgraded monaural radio system wiring diagram (1982 models)

10

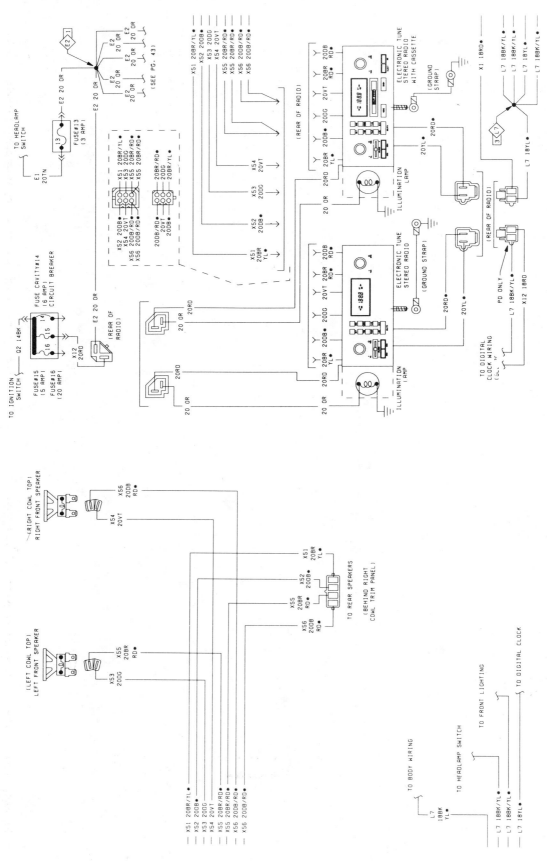

Fig. 10.111 Electronically tuned stereo radio system wiring diagram (1982 models)

Fig. 10.110 Mechanically tuned stereo radio system wiring diagram (1982 models)

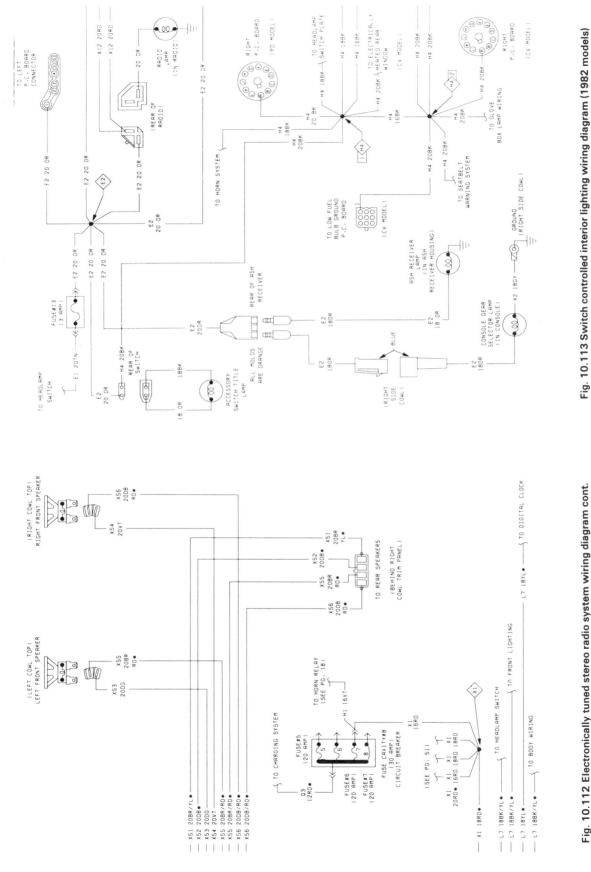

Fig. 10.113 Switch controlled interior lighting wiring diagram (1982 models)

Fig. 10.112 Electronically tuned stereo radio system wiring diagram cont. (1982 models)

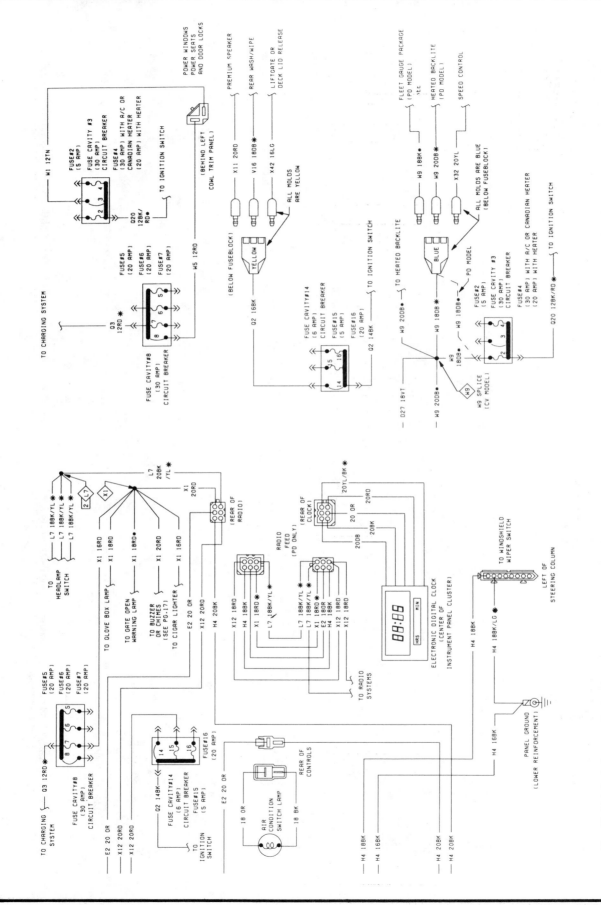

Fig. 10.115 Power assist system wiring diagram (1982 models)

Fig. 10.114 Switch controlled interior lighting system wiring diagram cont. (1982 models)

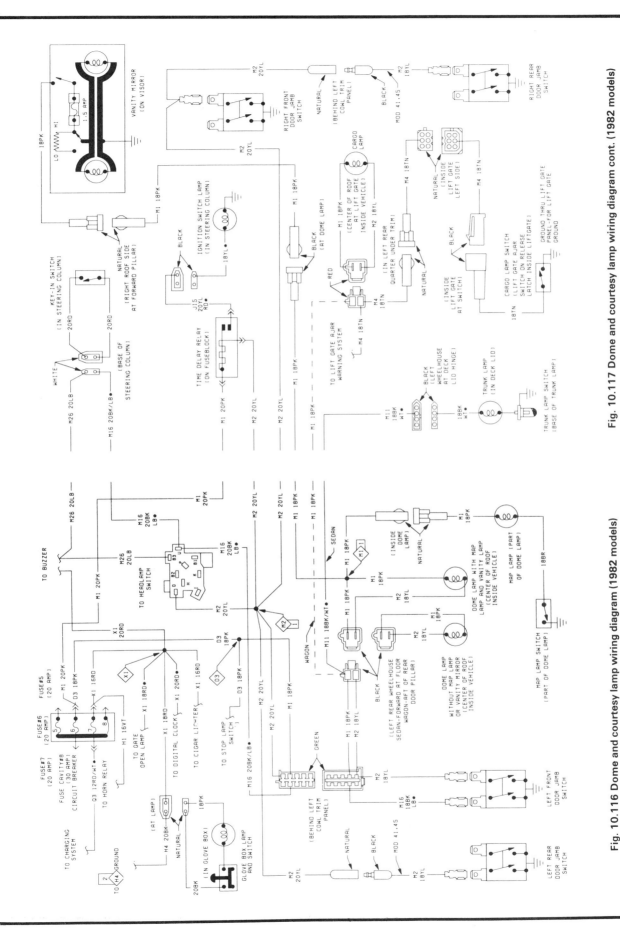

Fig. 10.117 Dome and courtesy lamp wiring diagram cont. (1982 models)

Fig. 10.116 Dome and courtesy lamp wiring diagram (1982 models)

10

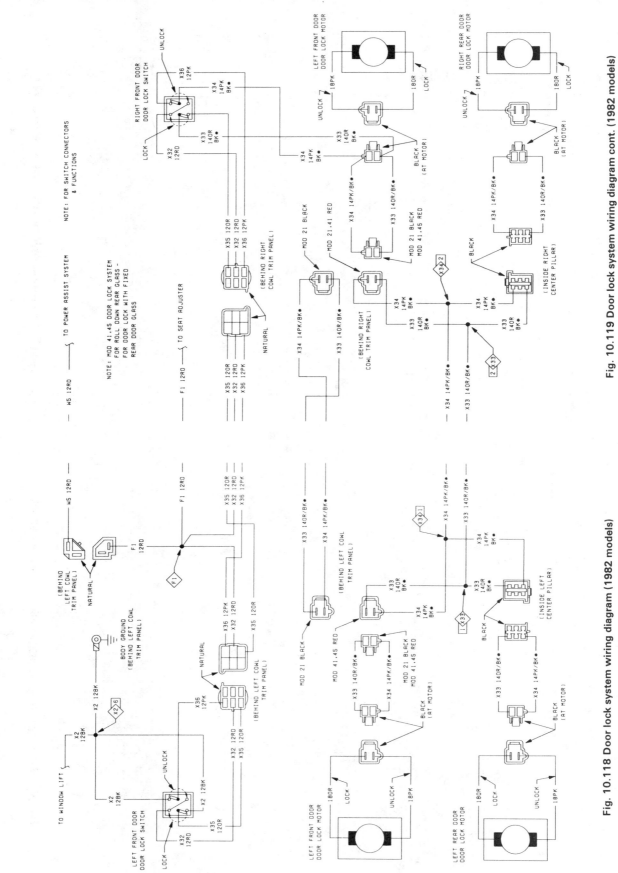

Fig. 10.119 Door lock system wiring diagram cont. (1982 models)

Fig. 10.118 Door lock system wiring diagram (1982 models)

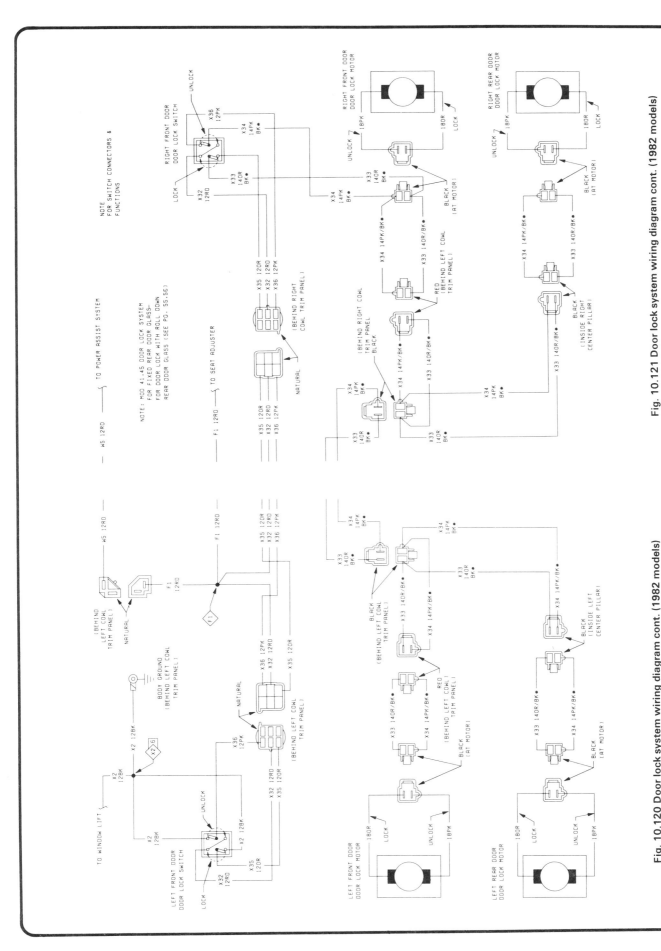

Fig. 10.121 Door lock system wiring diagram cont. (1982 models)

Fig. 10.120 Door lock system wiring diagram cont. (1982 models)

10

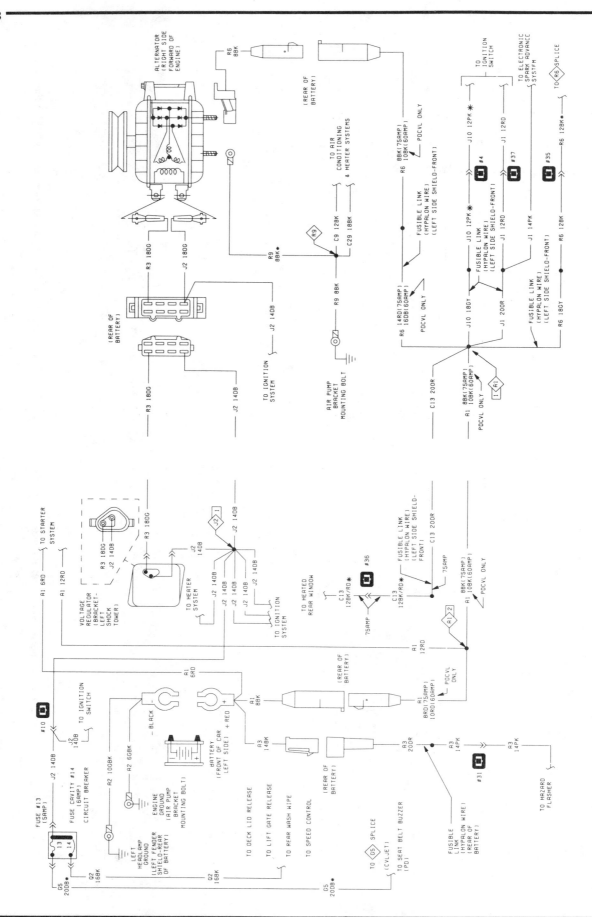

Fig. 10.123 Charging system (2.2L) wiring diagram cont. (1983 models)

Fig. 10.122 Charging system (2.2L) wiring diagram (1983 models)

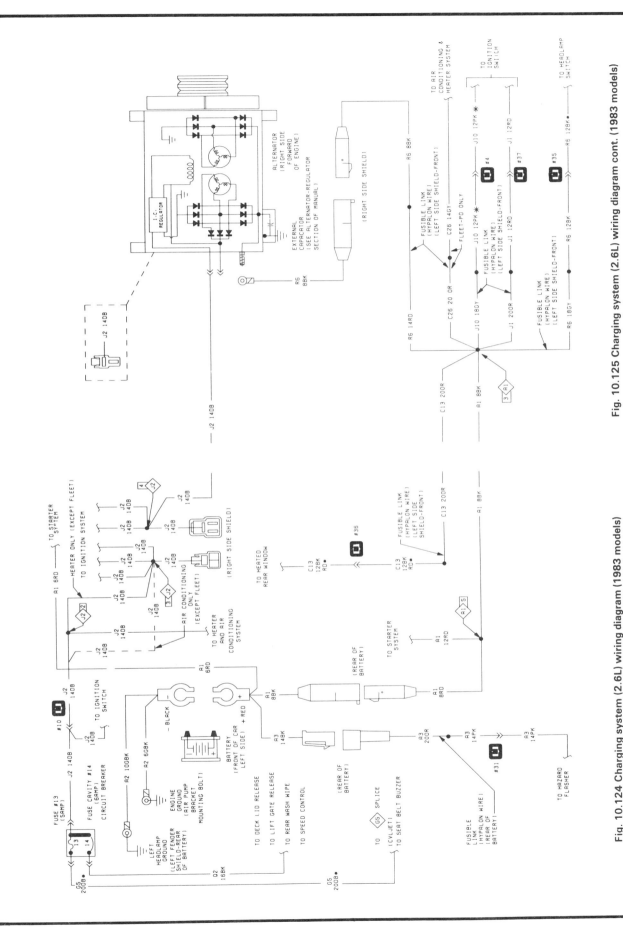

Fig. 10.125 Charging system (2.6L) wiring diagram cont. (1983 models)

Fig. 10.124 Charging system (2.6L) wiring diagram (1983 models)

10

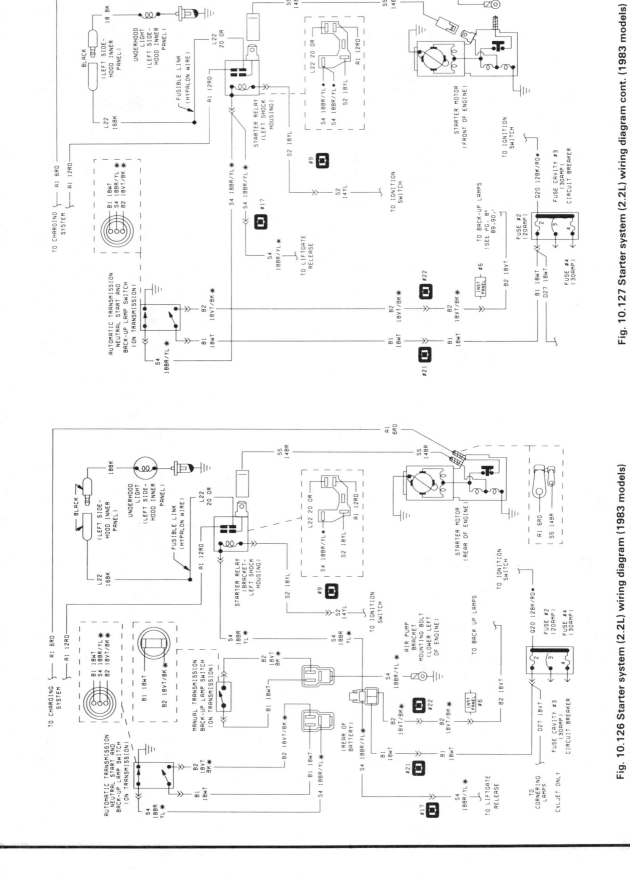

Fig. 10.127 Starter system (2.2L) wiring diagram cont. (1983 models)

Fig. 10.126 Starter system (2.2L) wiring diagram (1983 models)

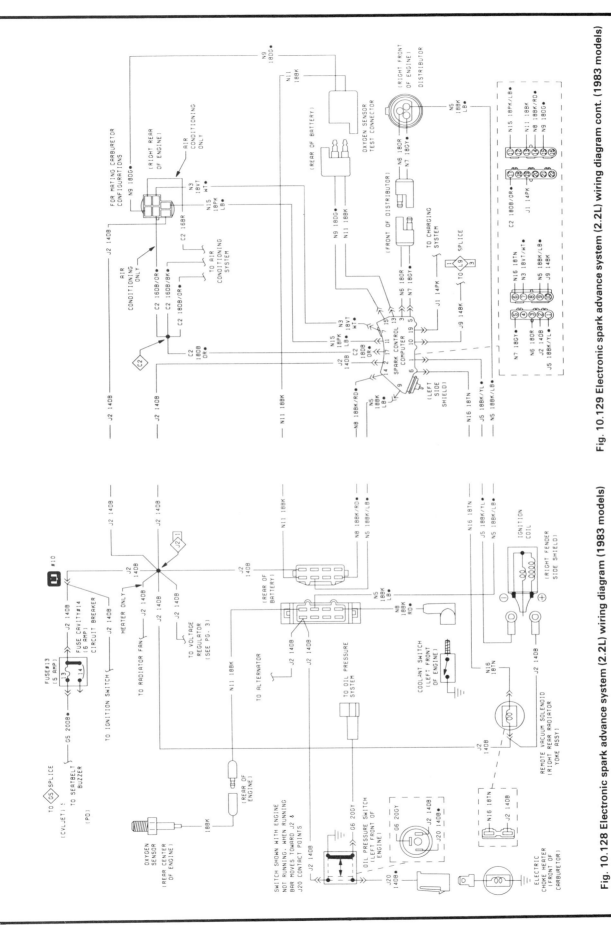

Fig. 10.129 Electronic spark advance system (2.2L) wiring diagram cont. (1983 models)

Fig. 10.128 Electronic spark advance system (2.2L) wiring diagram (1983 models)

10

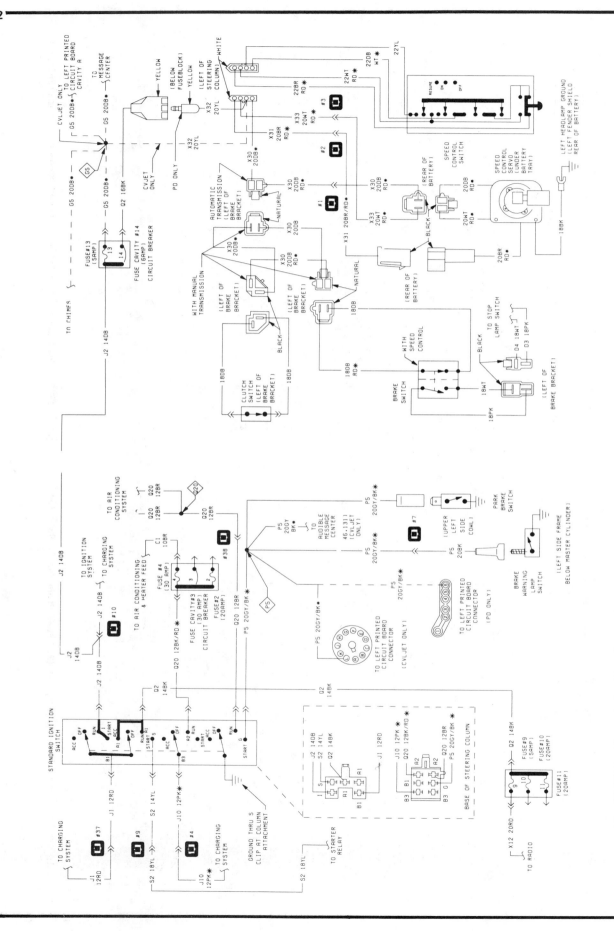

Fig. 10.131 Speed control system (1983 models)

Fig. 10.130 Ignition switch wiring diagram (1983 models)

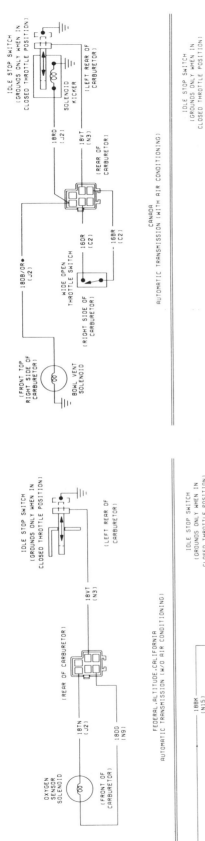

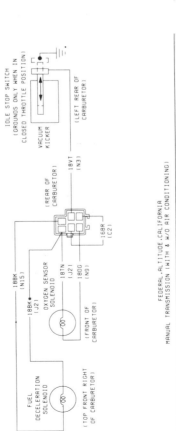

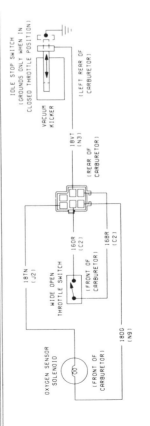

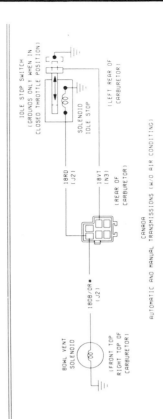

Fig. 10.132 Carburetor wiring system (2.2L) wiring diagram (1983 models)

Fig. 10.133 Carburetor wiring system (2.2L) wiring diagram cont. (1983 models)

10

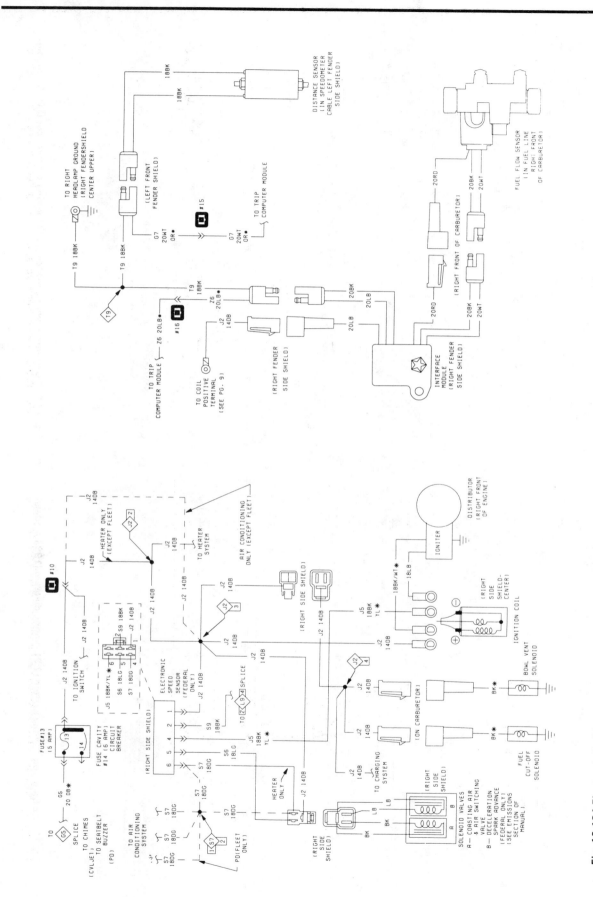

Fig. 10.135 Fuel flow and speed sensor systems wiring diagram (1983 models)

Fig. 10.134 Electronic ignition system (2.6L) wiring diagram (1983 models)

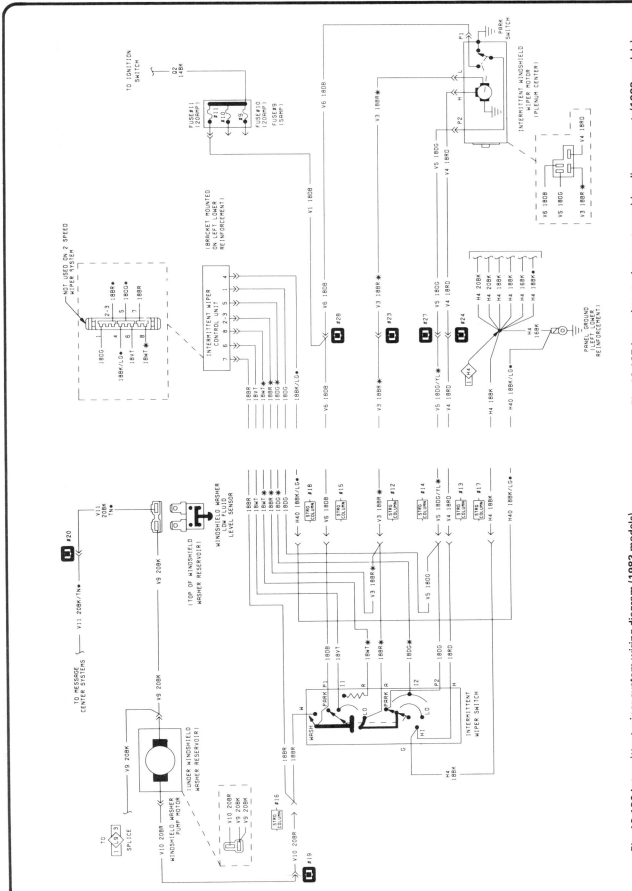

Fig. 10.137 Intermittent wiper system wiring diagram cont. (1983 models)

Fig. 10.136 Intermittent wiper system wiring diagram (1983 models)

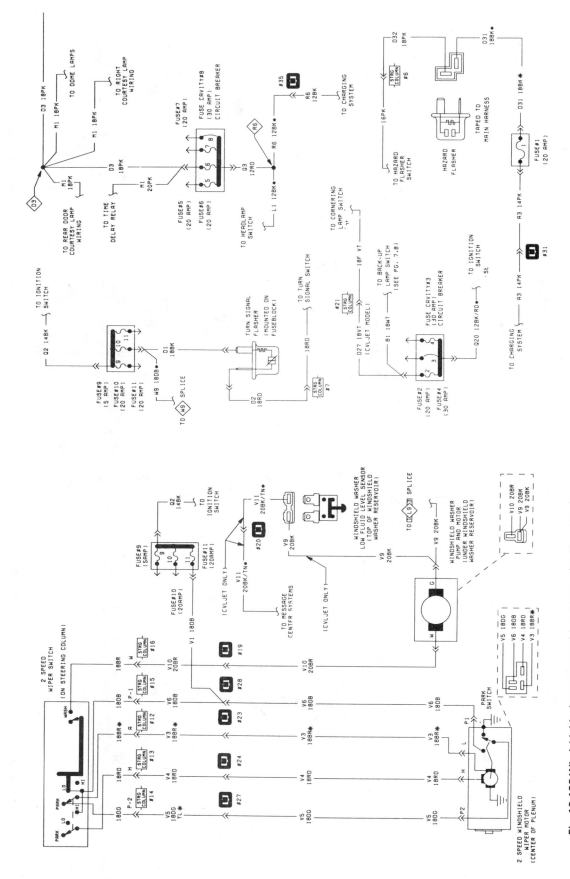

Fig. 10.139 Stop/turn and hazard flasher systems wiring diagram (1983 models)

Fig. 10.138 Windshield wiper system wiring diagram (1983 models)

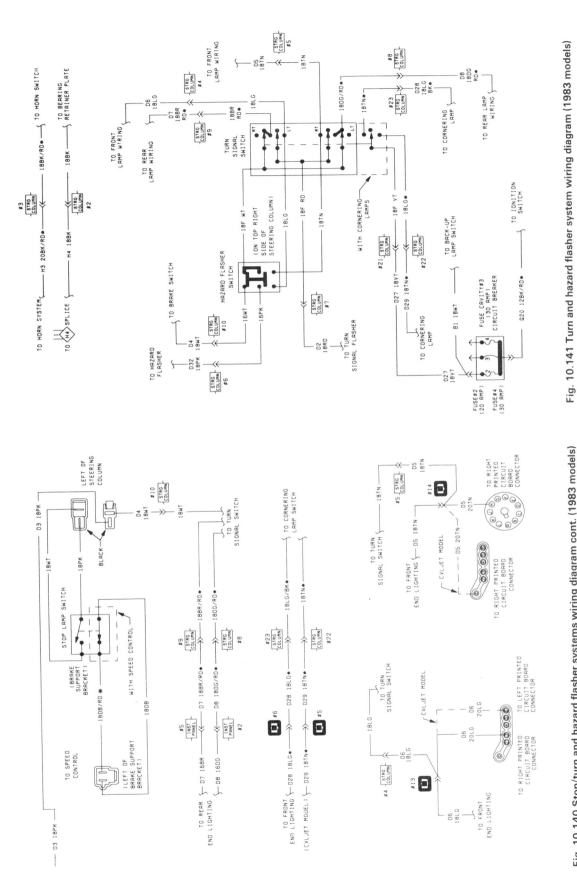

Fig. 10.141 Turn and hazard flasher system wiring diagram (1983 models)

Fig. 10.140 Stop/turn and hazard flasher systems wiring diagram cont. (1983 models)

10

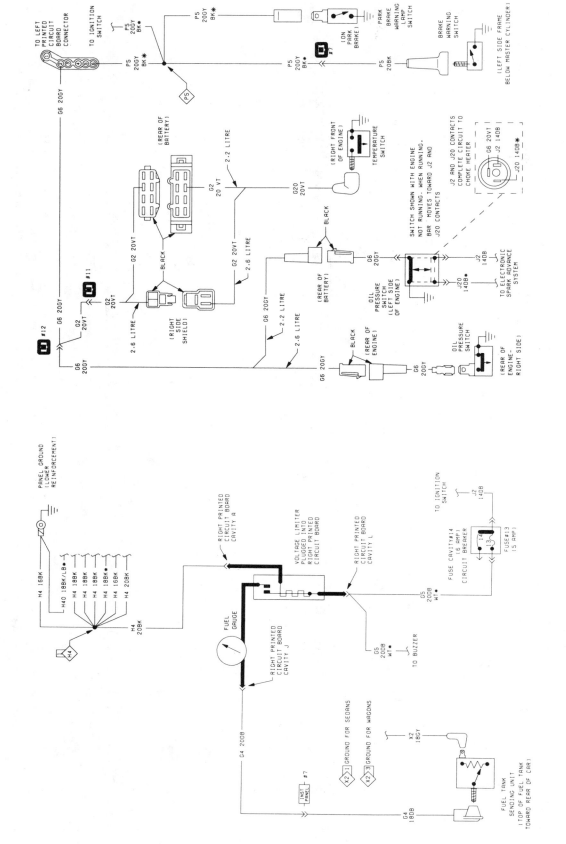

Fig. 10.143 Oil, temperature and brake switch wiring diagram (1983 models)

Fig. 10.142 Fuel tank system wiring diagram (1983 models)

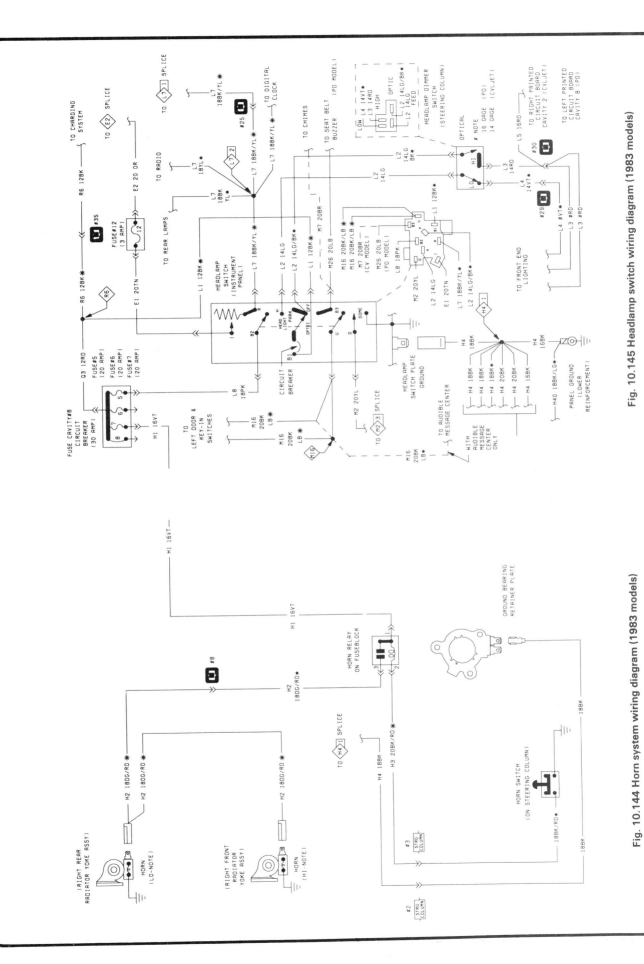

Fig. 10.145 Headlamp switch wiring diagram (1983 models)

Fig. 10.144 Horn system wiring diagram (1983 models)

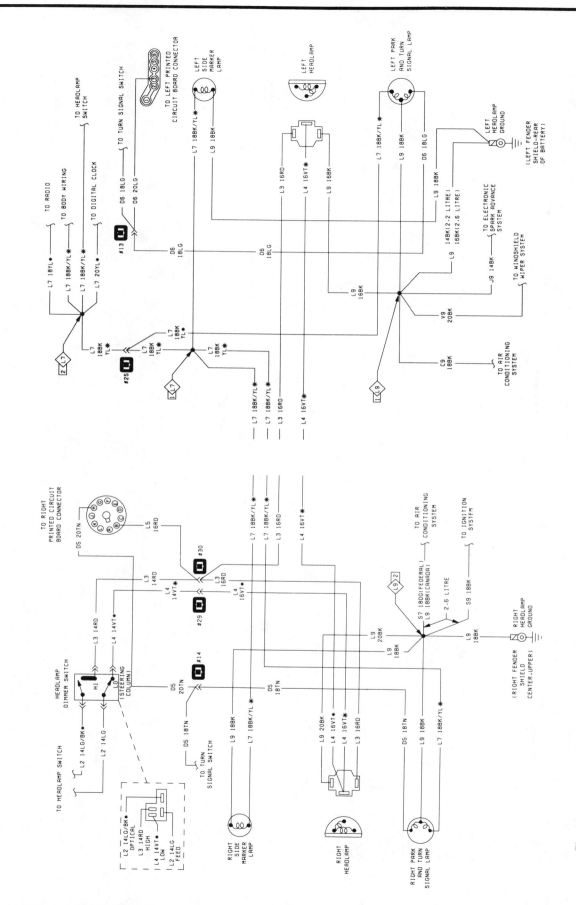

Fig. 10.147 Front end lighting system wiring diagram cont. (1983 models)

Fig. 10.146 Front end lighting system wiring diagram (1983 models)

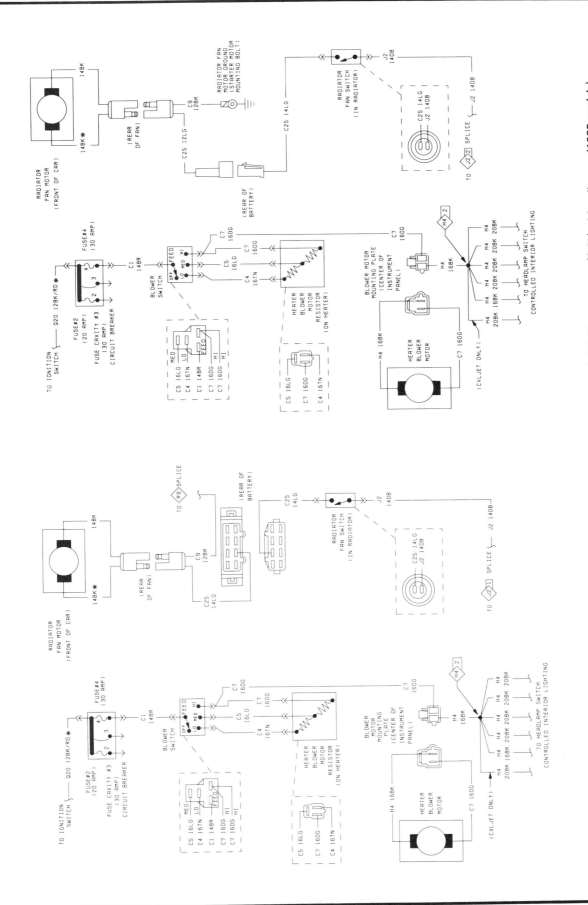

Fig. 10.149 Heater system (2.6L) wiring diagram (1983 models)

Fig. 10.148 Heater system (2.2L) wiring diagram (1983 models)

10

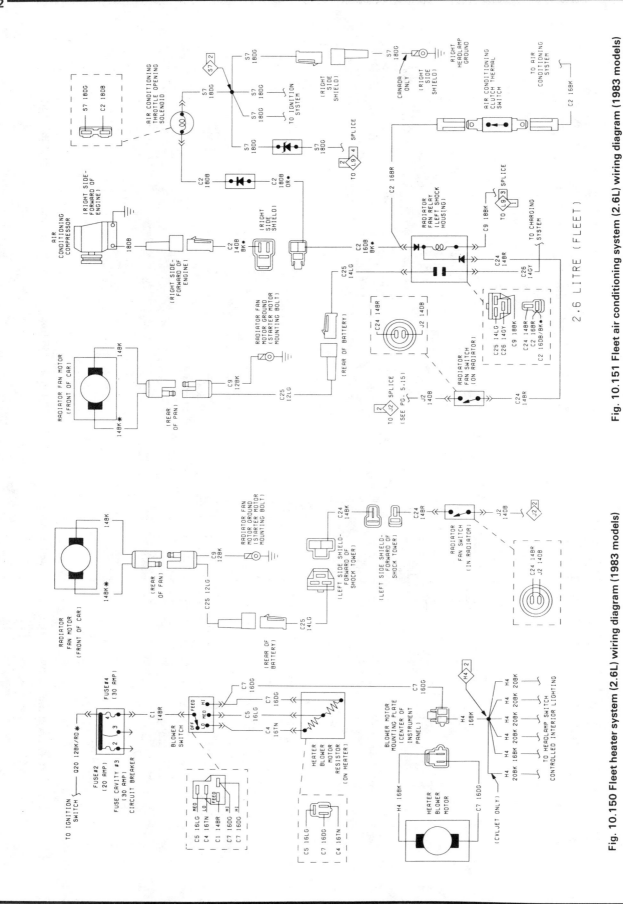

Fig. 10.151 Fleet air conditioning system (2.6L) wiring diagram (1983 models)

Fig. 10.150 Fleet heater system (2.6L) wiring diagram (1983 models)

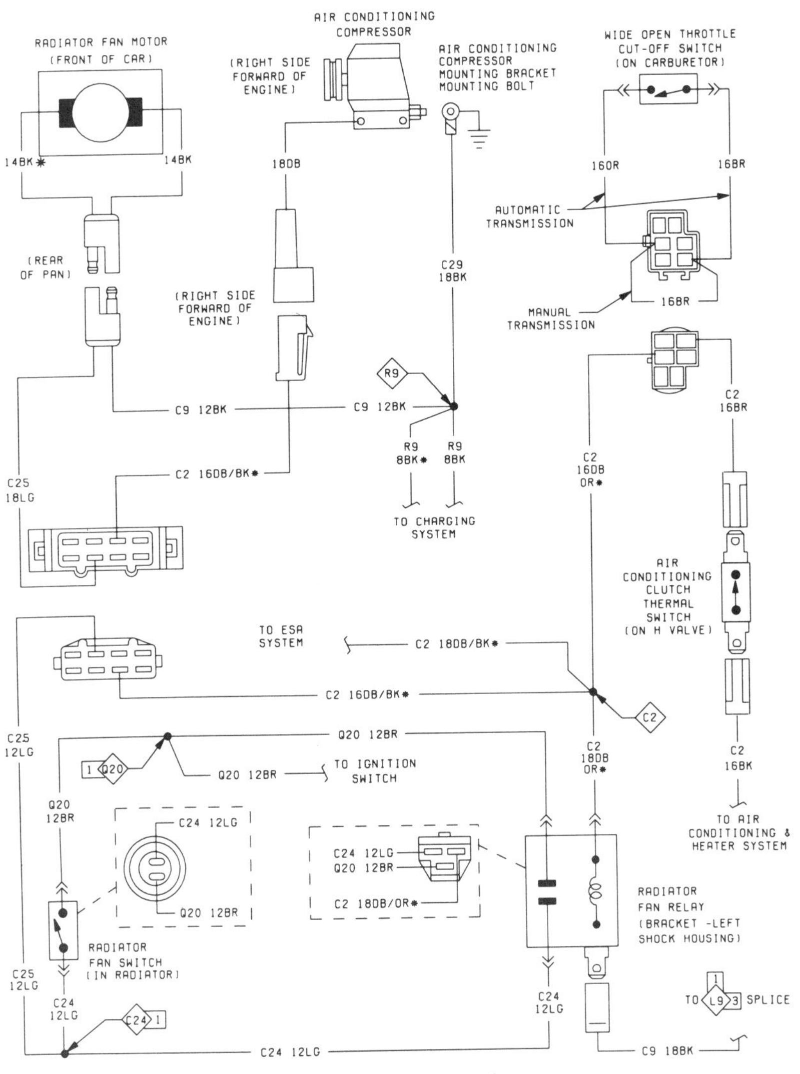

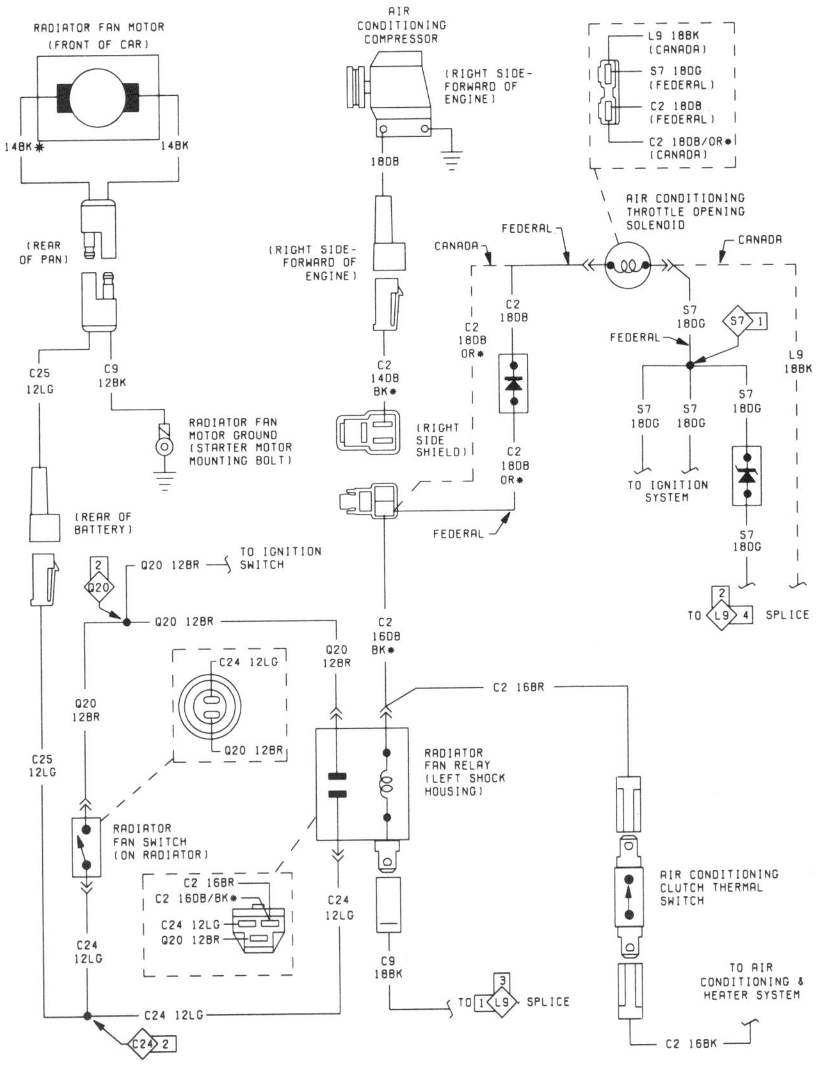

Fig. 10.153 Air conditioning system (2.6L) wiring diagram (1983 models)

Fig. 10.152 Air conditioning system (2.2L) wiring diagram (1983 models)

10

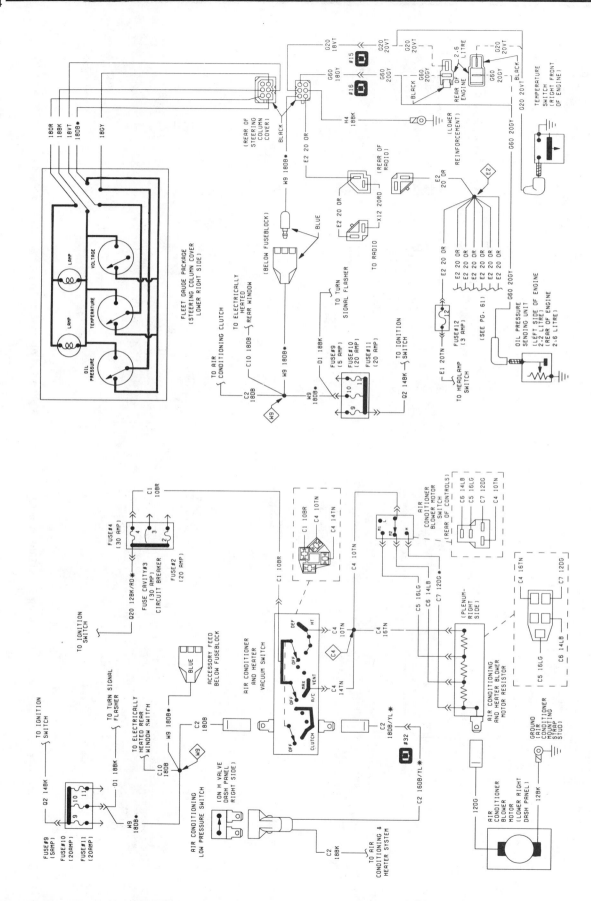

Fig. 10.155 Accessory oil pressure gauge wiring diagram (1983 models)

Fig. 10.154 Air conditioning system wiring diagram (1983 models)

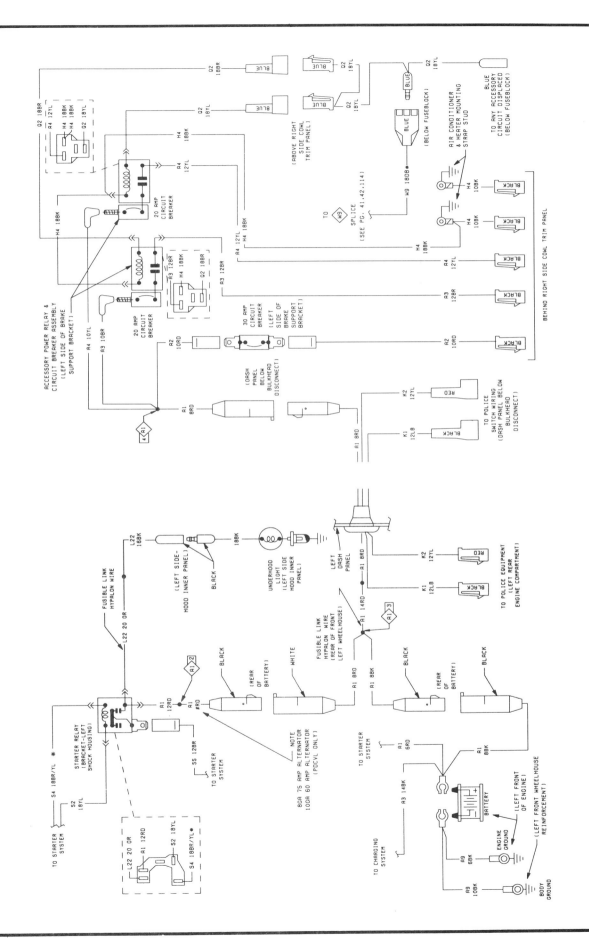

Fig. 10.157 Accessory battery wiring diagram (1983 models)

Fig. 10.156 Underhood light wiring diagram (1983 models)

10

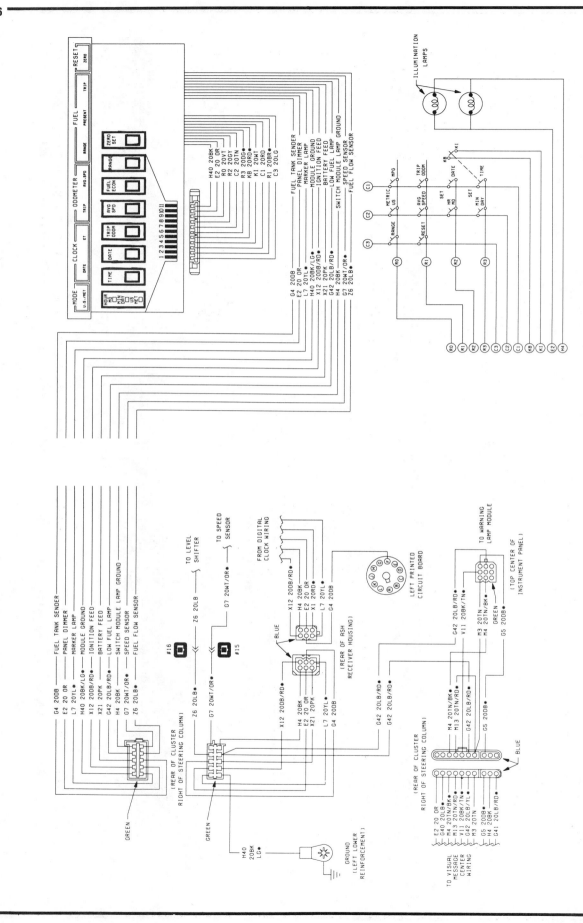

Fig. 10.159 Travel computer switch module system wiring diagram cont. (1983 models)

Fig. 10.158 Travel computer switch module system wiring diagram (1983 models)

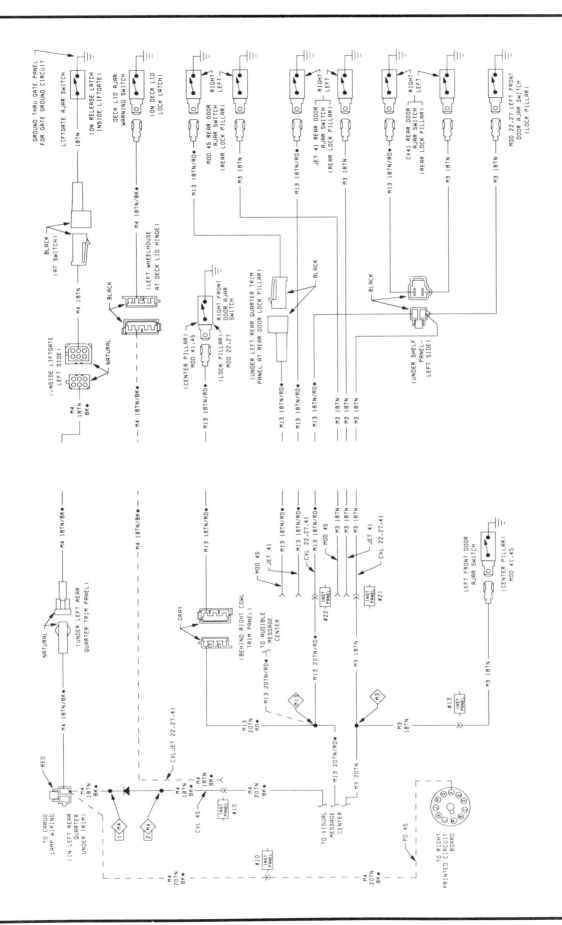

Fig. 10.161 Door deck lid and liftgate ajar warning system wiring diagram cont. (1983 models)

Fig. 10.160 Door, deck lid and liftgate warning system wiring diagram (1983 models)

10

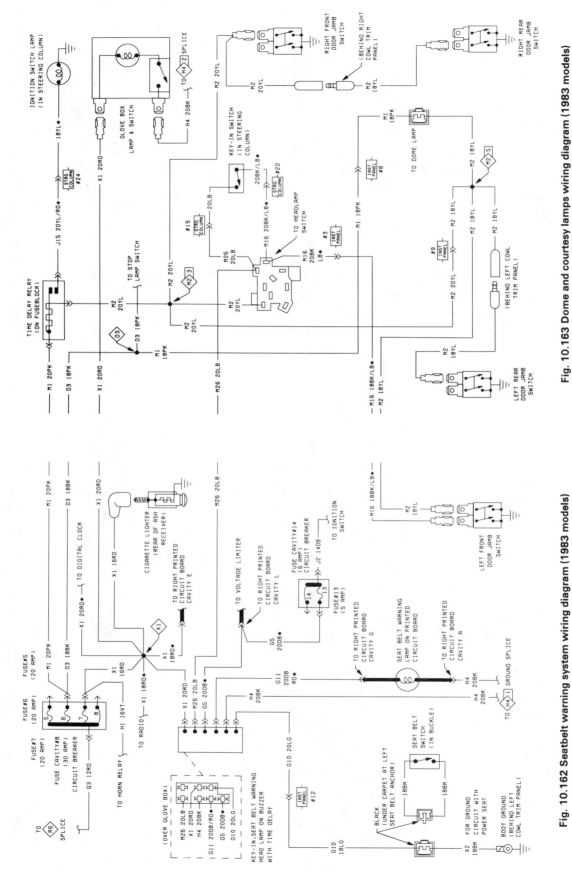

Fig. 10.163 Dome and courtesy lamps wiring diagram (1983 models)

Fig. 10.162 Seatbelt warning system wiring diagram (1983 models)

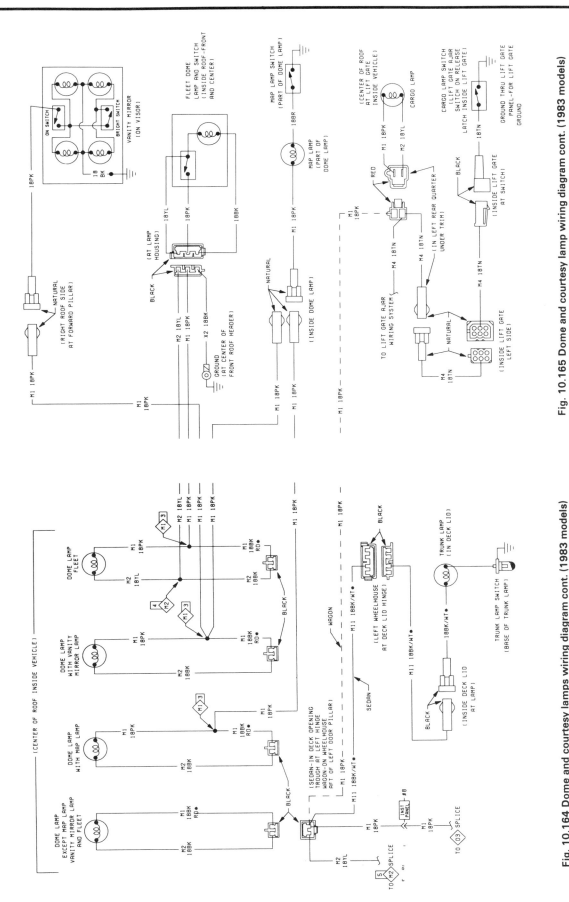

Fig. 10.165 Dome and courtesy lamp wiring diagram cont. (1983 models)

Fig. 10.164 Dome and courtesy lamps wiring diagram cont. (1983 models)

10

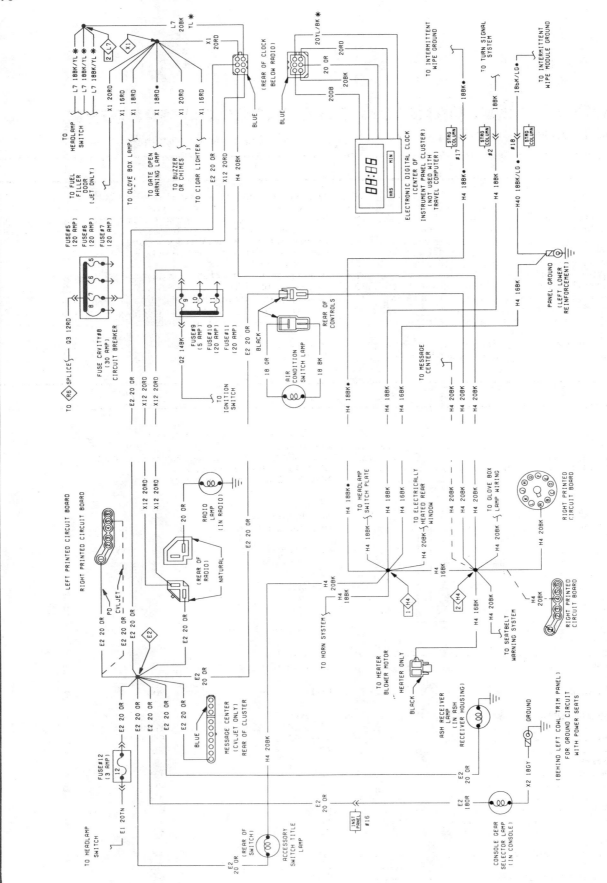

Fig. 10.167 Headlamp switch and controlled interior lighting wiring diagram cont. (1983 models)

Fig. 10.166 Headlamp switch and controlled interior lighting wiring diagram (1983 models)

Chapter 11 Suspension and steering systems

Refer to Chapter 13 for specifications and information applicable to later models

Contents

Specifications

Steering

Steering type	Rack and pinion, power assist optional
Steering gear lubricant type	API GL-4 SAE 90 oil
Power steering fluid type	Mopar 4-253 power steering fluid or equivalent
Tie-rod end lubricant type	NLGI No. 2 EP chassis grease
Steering shaft seal	NLGI No. 2 multi-purpose grease

Suspension

Front suspension type	MacPherson strut
Balljoint lubricant type	NLGI No. 2 EP grease
Front wheel camber	
Preferred	$+0.3°$ ($+\frac{5}{16}°$)
Acceptable	$-0.2°$ to $+0.8°$
Front wheel toe-in/toe-out	($-\frac{1}{4}°$ to $+\frac{3}{4}°$)
Preferred	$\frac{1}{16}$ in toe-out $\pm\frac{1}{16}$ in
Acceptable	$\frac{7}{32}$ in toe-out to 1/18 in toe-in
Rear wheel camber	
Preferred	$-.5° \pm .5°$ ($\frac{1}{2}°$)
Acceptable	$-1.0°$ to $0°$ (-1 to $0°$)
Rear wheel toe-in/toe-out	
Preferred	$0 \pm \frac{1}{8}$ in
Acceptable	$\frac{3}{16}$ in toe-out to $\frac{3}{16}$ in toe-in

Torque specifications

	Ft-lb	Nm
Steering gear		
Clamp and housing pad bolts	17 to 25	23 to 54
Tie-rod end nut	25 to 50	34 to 70
Tie-rod end jam nut	45 to 60	60 to 90
Inner tie-rod	70	95
Power steering hoses		
Pressure hose tube nut	15	20
Return tube nut	15	20
Pressure hose pump bracket	30	40
Pressure crossmember bracket	9	12
Return tube bracket	21	28
Discharge fitting	40	55
Power steering pump		
2.2L engine adjustment lock bolt	30	41
2.2L engine adjustment pivot bolt	30	41
2.2L engine lower stud nut and pivot bolt	40	54
2.6L engine adjustment and pivot bolts	40	54

Steering column

Steering wheel-to-column nut	45	61
Column clamp stud	1.5	2
Column clamp stud nut	9	12
Column clamp bolt	9	12

Front suspension

Strut-to-steering knuckle nut	45*	61*
Upper strut-to-fender shield	20	27
Brake hose retainer-to-strut	10	12
Strut rod nut	60	81
Lower control arm balljoint clamp bolt	50	68
Lower control arm inner pivot bolt	105	142
Lower control stub strut nut	70	94
Sway bar bushing retainer nuts	22	30
Brake caliper-to-steering knuckle	85	115
Hub nut	180	245

Rear suspension

Upper shock absorber pivot bolt	80	108
Lower shock absorber bolt	40	54
Axle-to-trailing arm bolt	40	54
Trailing arm bracket-to-frame bolt	40	54
Front trailing arm through-bolt	40	54
Track bar-to-axle nut	80	108
Track bar-to-brace	80	108
Track bar brace-to-frame nut	45	61
Track bar bracket-to-frame bolt	40	54
Track bar-to-axle nut	80	108
Spindle-to-axle bolt	45	61
Upper coil spring jounce bumper-to-frame nut	40	54
Jounce bumper cup-to-frame screw	6	8
Rear wheel bearing nut	20 to 25	27 to 34
Wheel nuts (all)	80	108

* Plus $\frac{1}{4}$ turn

1   General information

The front suspension is the strut type, which features a shock absorber strut and spring mounts on top of the steering knuckle. The steering knuckle is located by a lower control arm and both front control arms are connected by a sway bar.

The rear suspension features a beam-type axle which is located by rubber bushed trailing arms. It is located laterally by a track bar and diagonal brace. Springing is by coil springs mounted to seats just forward of the axle and on the chassis and damping is by vertically mounted shock absorbers located between the axle and the chassis.

The rack-and-pinion steering gear is located behind the engine and actuates the steering arms which are integral with the steering knuckles. Power assist is optional and the steering column is designed to collapse in the event of an accident.

These vehicles use a combination of standard and metric fasteners so it would be a good idea to have both types of tools available when beginning work.

2   Sway bar – removal and installation

1   Raise the front of the vehicle, support it securely and remove the front wheels.
2   Remove the sway bar nuts, bolts, and retainers at the control arms.
3   Unbolt the clamps at the crossmember and remove the sway bar from the vehicle.
4   Check the bar for damage, corrosion or signs of twisting.
5   Check the clamps, bushings and retainers for distortion, damage or wear. Replace the inner bushings by prying them open at the split and removing them. Install the new bushings with the curved surface up and the split facing toward the front of the vehicle. The outer bushing can be removed by cutting it off or hammering it from the bar. Force the new bushing onto the end of the bar so that $\frac{1}{2}$ inch of the bar is protruding.
6   Place the upper bushing retainers in position on the crossmember bushings, attach the bar to the crossmember and then install the lower clamps, bolts and nuts.
7   Install the bushing retainers, nuts and bolts at the lower control arm.

8   Raise the lower control arms to normal ride height and tighten the nuts to the specified torque.
9   Install the wheels and lower the vehicle.

3   Lower control arm – removal, inspection and installation

1   Raise the front of the vehicle, support it securely and remove the front wheels.
2   Remove the through-bolt and nut from the control arm pivot (photo).

3.2 Removing the lower control arm through-bolt nut

3   Remove the rear stub strut nut retainer and bushing.
4   Remove the balljoint clamp bolt from the steering knuckle.
5   Disconnect the balljoint stud from the steering knuckle, taking care not to separate the inner CV joint (photo).
6   Remove the sway bar nuts, separate the control arm and remove it from the vehicle.

Fig. 11.1 Front suspension layout

1	Shock and spring assembly	4	Lower suspension arm	7	Suspension arm stub strut
2	Suspension pivot bolt	5	Sway bar	8	Steering knuckle
3	Chassis crossmember	6	Steering gear		

3.5 Pull down sharply to disengage the balljoint stud

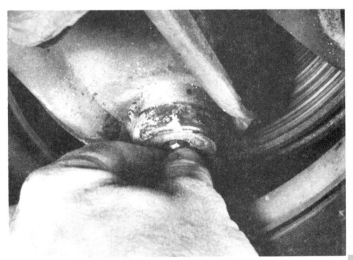

4.2 Testing the balljoint for wear by attempting to move the grease fitting with the vehicle weight resting on the front suspension

7   Remove the rear stub strut bushing and sleeve assembly.
8   Inspect the lower control arm for twisting or distortion and the bushings for wear, damage or deterioration. Replace a damaged or bent control arm with a new one. If the inner pivot bushings or the balljoint (Section 4) are worn, take the control arm assembly to a dealer or a properly equipped shop, as special tools are required to replace them. The stub strut bushings can be replaced by sliding them off the strut.

9   Assemble the retainer, bushing and sleeve onto the stub strut.
10   Place the control arm in position over the sway bar and attach the stub strut and front pivot to the crossmember.
11   Install the front pivot bolt and stub strut assembly into the crossmember, with the nuts finger tight.
12   Attach the balljoint stud to the steering knuckle and tighten the clamp bolt to the specified torque.
13   Attach the sway bar end to the control arm and tighten the clamp

11

Fig. 11.2 Rear suspension layout

1	Support bracket	3	Track bar
2	Diagonal brace	4	Shock absorber

5	Suspension trailing arm	7	Spring pocket
6	Rear axle	8	Spring

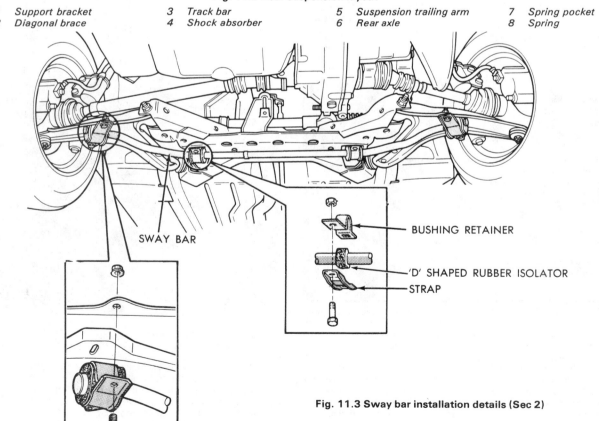

SWAY BAR

BUSHING RETAINER

'D' SHAPED RUBBER ISOLATOR

STRAP

Fig. 11.3 Sway bar installation details (Sec 2)

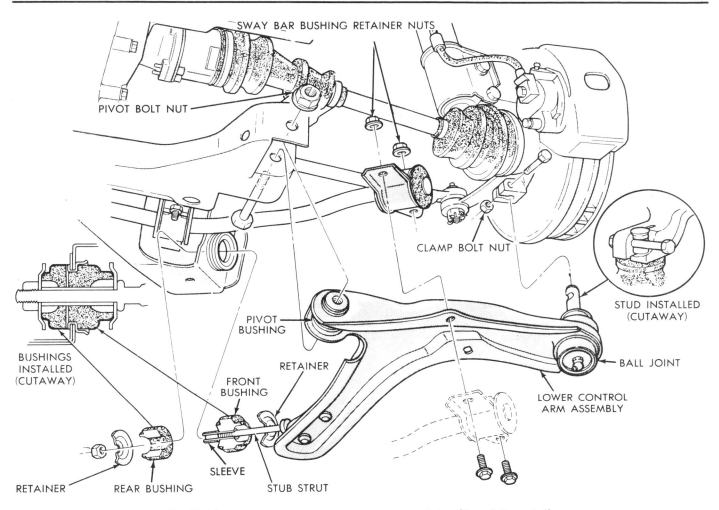

Fig. 11.4 Lower control arm components – exploded view (Secs 2 through 4)

bolt to the specified torque.

14 Install the wheels and lower the vehicle. With the vehicle weight lowered onto the suspension, tighten the front pivot bolt and stub strut nuts to the proper torque.

4 Balljoints – checking

1 The lower frame suspension balljoints are designed to operate without free play.

2 To check for wear, grasp the grease fitting and attempt to move it with the vehicle weight resting on the front suspension (photo).

3 If there is any movement, the balljoint is worn and must be replaced with a new one. Since special equipment is required to press the balljoint from the control arm, it is recommended that the job be left to a dealer or properly equipped shop.

5 Front steering knuckle and hub – removal, inspection and installation

1 With the vehicle weight resting on the front suspension, remove the hub cap, grease cup, nut lock and cotter key. Loosen, but do not remove, the front axle nut and wheel nuts.

2 Raise the front of the vehicle, support it securely and remove the front wheels.

3 Remove the axle nut and washer.

4 Push the axle in until it is free of the hub. It may be necessary to tap on the axle end with a brass drift and hammer to dislodge the axle from the hub (photo).

5 Remove the cotter key and nut and use a suitable tool to

5.4 Push the axle in until it is free of the hub

disconnect the steering tie-rod from the hub (Section 23).

6 Lift the tie-rod out of the way and secure it with a piece of wire.

7 Disconnect the brake hose from the shock strut.

8 Remove the caliper and brake pads (Chapter 9). Taking care not to twist the brake hose, hang the caliper out of the way in the wheel well with a piece of wire.

11

5.9 With the bushing bolts loose, the sway bar can be pulled down out of the way

5.13 Remove the steering knuckle nuts while holding the bolt head with a wrench

5.14 Pull the steering knuckle out and off the axle splines

9   Loosen the sway bar bushing bolts, unbolt the ends from the control arm and pull the sway bar down and out of the way (photo).
10   Remove the retainer from the wheel stud and lift the brake disc off.
11   Mark the upper cam bolt and washer location prior to removal.
12   Remove the balljoint pinch bolt and nut and disengage the balljoint from the hub.
13   Remove the steering knuckle-to-strut bolts and washers (photo).
14   With the knuckle and hub assembly in the straight-ahead position, grasp it securely and pull it directly out and off the axle splines (photo).
15   Place the assembly on a clean working surface and wipe it off with a lint-free cloth. Inspect the knuckle for rust, damage or cracks. Check the bearings by rotating them to make sure they move freely. The bearings should be packed with an adequate supply of clean grease. If there is too little grease, or if the grease is contaminated with dirt, clean the bearings and inspect them for wear, scoring or looseness. Repack the bearings with the specified lubricant. Inspect the grease seals to make sure they are not torn or leaking. Further disassembly will have to be left to your dealer or a properly equipped shop because of the special tools required.
16   Prior to installation, clean the CV joint seal and the hub grease seal with a suitable solvent. Lubricate the full circumference of the sleeve and seal contact surface with multi-purpose grease.
17   Carefully place the knuckle and hub assembly in position. Align the splines of the axle and the hub and slide the hub into place.
18   Install the knuckle retaining bolts and nuts, followed by the balljoint pinch bolt and nut. Adjust the knuckle so that the mark made during removal is aligned with the cam bolt and washer. It may be necessary to use a large C-clamp to pull the steering knuckle and strut together and line up the marks. Install the washer plate and nuts, tightening to the specified torque.
19   Install the tie-rod end, tighten the nut and install the cotter key.
20   Install the brake disc, pad and caliper assembly.
21   Connect the brake hose to the shock strut.
22   Attach the sway bar ends to the control arm and tighten the fasteners to the specified torque.
23   Push the CV joint completely into the hub to make sure it is seated and install the hub washer and nut finger tight.
24   Install the wheels and lower the vehicle.
25   With an assistant applying the brakes, tighten the hub nut to the specified torque. Install the nut lock and a new cotter key.
26   With the weight of the vehicle on the suspension, check the steering knuckle and balljoint nuts to make sure they are tightened properly.
27   Have the vehicle front end alignment checked.

6   Front shock absorber strut and spring assembly — removal, inspection and installation

1   Loosen the front wheel nuts.
2   Raise the vehicle and support it securely. Remove the wheels.
3   Open the hood and mark the outer edge of the strut bumper and the mounting tower so the strut can be installed in the same position. Loosen the two retaining nuts (photo).
4   Mark the location of the cam bolt and washer as described in Step 11 of the previous Section.
5   Remove the steering knuckle retaining nuts, bolts and washer plate.
6   Disconnect the brake hose from the strut.
7   Remove the two upper retaining nuts, disengage the strut from the steering knuckle and lift it from the vehicle.
8   Checking of the strut absorber and spring strut is limited to inspection for leaking fluid, dents, damage and corrosion. Further disassembly should be left to your dealer or a properly equipped shop because of the special tools and techniques necessary.
9   To install, place the strut assembly in position with the studs extending up through the mounting tower. Make sure the strut bumper aligns with the marks made during removal, install the nuts and tighten them to the specified torque.
10   Attach the strut to the steering knuckle, then insert the retaining bolts and washer plate.
11   Use a large C-clamp to align the knuckle and strut so the cam bolt marks line up. Install the nuts on the cam and knuckle bolts and tighten them to the specified torque, then remove the clamp.

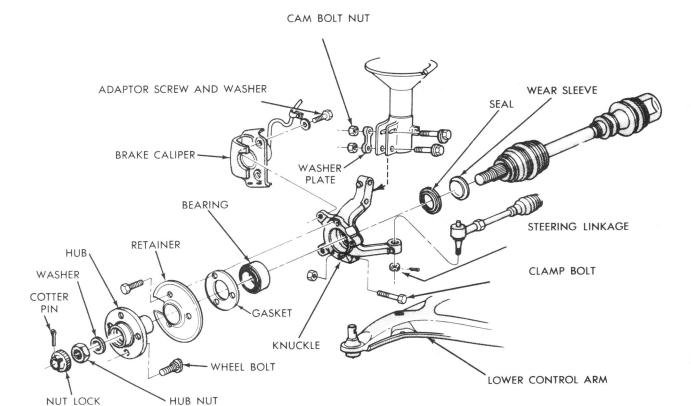

Fig. 11.5 Steering knuckle components – exploded view (Secs 4 and 5)

6.3 Loosening the upper shock strut nuts; note the strut bumper outer edge is marked (arrow) — **Caution:** *DO NOT loosen or remove the large nut in the center of the strut!*

12 Attach the brake hose to the strut.
13 Install the wheels and lower the vehicle.

---

7   Rear shock absorbers – removal, inspection and installation

1   Raise the rear of the vehicle and support it securely.
2   Support the axle and remove the rear wheels.
3   Remove the upper and lower through-bolts and nuts and remove the shock absorber (photo).
4   Grasp the shock absorber at opposite ends and pump it in and out

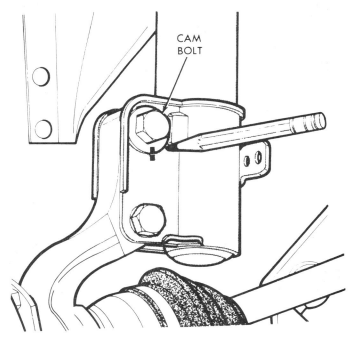

Fig. 11.6 Marking the location of the cam bolt head (Secs 5 and 6)

several times. Check to make sure the action is smooth, with no skipping or dead spots. Inspect for signs of fluid leakage. Replace the shock absorber with a new one if it is leaking or the action is not smooth. Always replace shock absorbers in axle sets.
5   Place the shock absorber in position and install the through-bolts and nuts. Tighten the upper through-bolt nut to the specified torque.

11

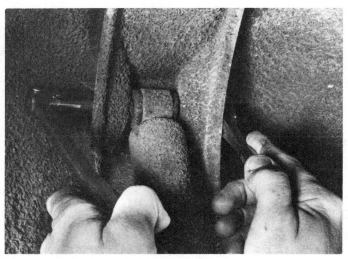

7.3 Hold the upper shock mount bolt head with a wrench while removing the nut

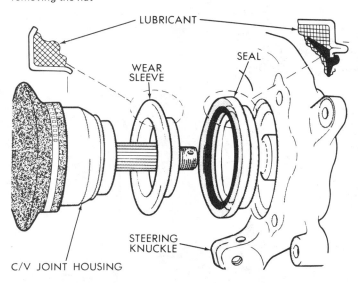

Fig. 11.7 CV joint wear sleeve and hub grease seal lubrication points (Secs 5 and 6)

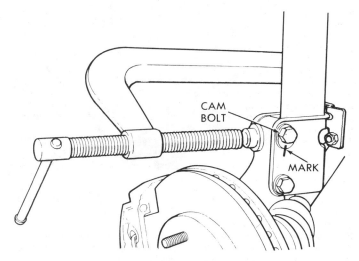

Fig. 11.8 Aligning the cam bolt head and mark with a C-clamp (Secs 5 and 6)

6   Install the wheel, remove the axle supports and lower the vehicle.
7   With the vehicle weight resting on the suspension, tighten the lower through-bolt and nut to the specified torque.

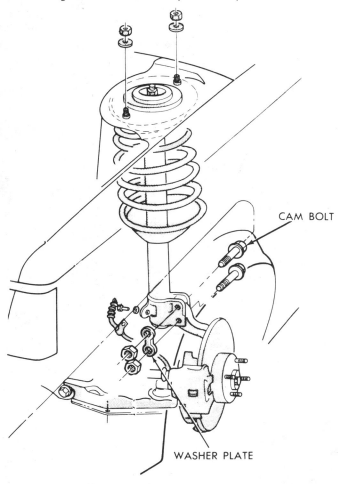

Fig. 11.9 Front shock strut and spring unit installation (Sec 6)

8   Rear coil spring and jounce bumper – removal and installation

1   Raise the vehicle, support it securely and remove the rear wheels.
2   Support the rear axle and remove the lower shock absorber through-bolt.
3   Lower the axle slowly until the spring, upper isolator and jounce bumper can be removed, taking car not to stretch the brake hose.
4   Remove the retaining screws and remove the cup from the chassis.
5   Remove the jounce bumper and isolator from the spring.
6   Replace any damaged or deteriorated bumper or isolator components.
7   Install the cup to the vehicle.
8   Install the isolator and bumper assembly to the top of the spring.
9   Place the spring in position on the lower mount and raise the axle until the isolator seats in the cup. Install the lower shock absorber through-bolt.
10   Install the wheels, lower the vehicle weight onto the suspension, and tighten the lower shock absorber nut and bolt to the specified torque.

9   Rear axle track bar, brace and bracket assembly – removal and installation

1   Raise the rear of the vehicle, support it securely and remove the wheels.

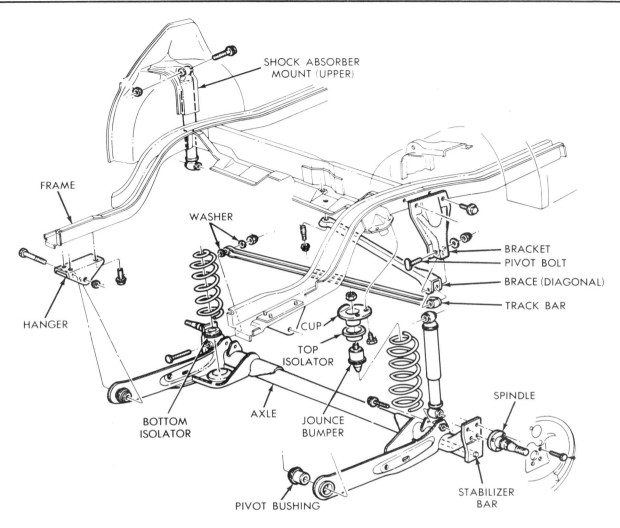

Fig. 11.10 Rear suspension components – exploded view (Secs 7 through 10)

2   Raise the axle to normal ride height and support it.
3   Remove the track bar through-bolt and pivot bolt and lift the bar from the vehicle.
4   Remove the diagonal brace and stud nut.
5   Unbolt the support bracket and remove it.
6   Inspect the bar, brake and bracket assembly for twisting or bending and the bushings for wear or deterioration. Replace any damaged components with new ones.
7   Attach the support bracket to the chassis and tighten the nuts to the specified torque.
8   Place the diagonal brace in position in the support bracket and stud. Install the nut and tighten it to the specified torque.
9   Attach the track bar to the diagonal brace, insert the through-bolt and install the nut finger tight. Place the other end of the bar over the pivot bolt, install the nut and tighten it to the specified torque. Tighten the through-bolt and nut.
10 Remove the axle support, install the wheels and lower the vehicle.

10 Rear axle – removal and installation

1   Raise the rear of the vehicle, support it securely and remove the rear wheels.
2   Support the axle with jacks.
3   Disconnect the parking brake cable at the floor pan bracket.
4   Disconnect and plug the brake lines and hoses at the trailing arm support bracket.
5   Remove the track bar-to-axle through-bolt and support the bar with a piece of wire.

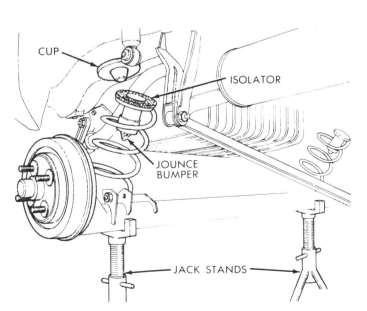

Fig. 11.11 Rear spring removal (Secs 8 through 10)

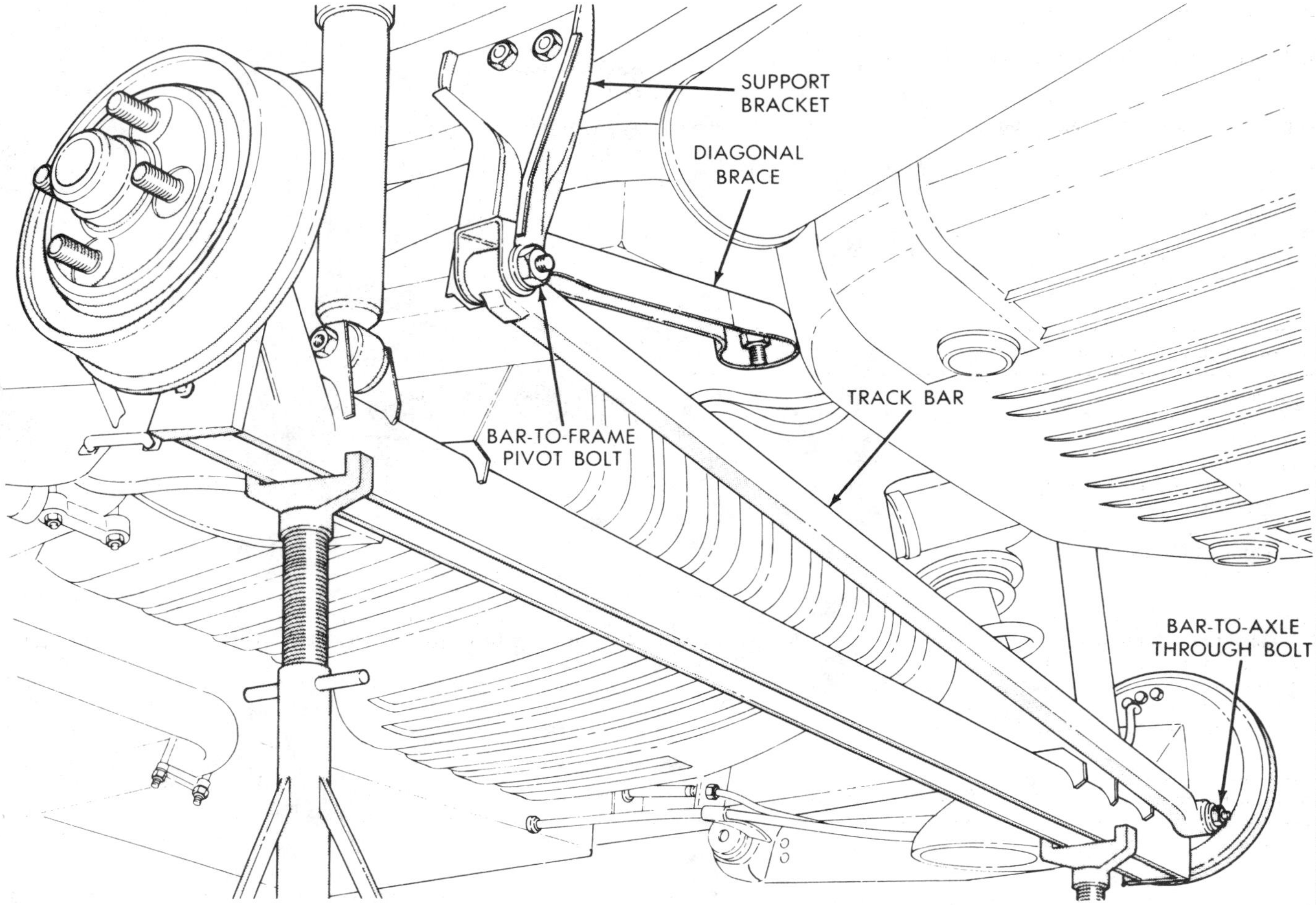

SUPPORT
BRACKET

DIAGONAL
BRACE

TRACK BAR

BAR-TO-FRAME
PIVOT BOLT

BAR-TO-AXLE
THROUGH BOLT

Fig. 11.12 Rear axle and track bar installation (Secs 8 through 10)

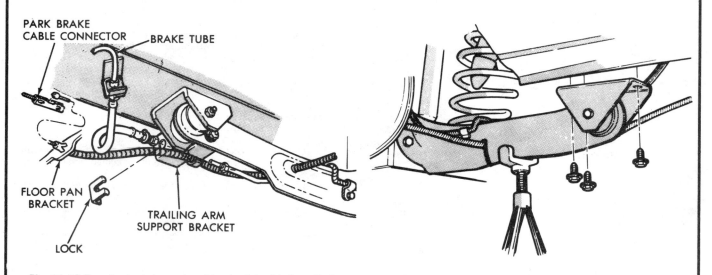

PARK BRAKE
CABLE CONNECTOR — BRAKE TUBE

FLOOR PAN
BRACKET

LOCK

TRAILING ARM
SUPPORT BRACKET

Fig. 11.13 Rear brake tube and parking brake cable installation
(Secs 10)

Fig. 11.14 Rear suspension arm hanger bracket installation
(Sec 10)

6 Remove the lower shock absorber through-bolts and lower the axle until the springs can be removed.

7 Support the front ends of the suspension trailing arms and unbolt the hanger brackets from the chassis.

8 Lower the axle assembly from the vehicle.

9 To install, raise the axle into place and attach the suspension arm hanger brackets to the chassis, tightening the bolts to the specified torque.

10 Raise the axle into position, install the springs and insert the shock absorber and track bar through-bolts. Install the nuts and tighten them to the specified torque.

11 Connect the parking brake cables and the brake hoses.

12 Bleed the rear brakes (Chapter 9).

13 Install the wheels and lower the vehicle.

11 Rear hub and bearings – removal and installation

1 Raise the rear of the vehicle, support it securely and remove the wheels. Make sure the parking brake is off and check that the hub turns freely. It may be necessary to back off on the brake adjuster (Chapter 9).

2 Remove the grease cap, cotter key, nut and washer.

3 Grasp the brake drum and pull it out sufficiently to dislodge the outer wheel bearing (photo).

4 Remove the bearing.

5 Withdraw the hub from the vehicle.

6 To install, place the hub in position on the spindle, install the outer wheel bearing and washer and push the assembly into place.

7 Install the hub nut and rotate the hub while tightening the nut to the specified torque. Back off the nut until there is no pre-load on it and then tighten it finger tight.

8 Install the nut lock, cotter key and grease cap.

9 Install the wheels and lower the vehicle.

12 Rear hub and bearing – inspection, overhaul and lubrication

1 Remove the hub from the vehicle (Section 11).

2 Inspect the bearings for proper lubrication and signs that the

11.3 Pull out on the brake drum to dislodge the outer bearing

grease has been contaminated by dirt (grease will be gritty) or water (grease will have milky white appearance) (photo).

3 Use a hammer and a $\frac{3}{4}$ inch wood dowel to drive the inner bearing and seal carefully from the hub.

4 Clean the bearings in a suitable solvent and dry them with a lint-free towel.

5 Inspect the bearings for wear, pitting or scoring of the roller or cage. Light discoloration of the bearing surfaces is normal, but if the surfaces are badly worn or damaged, replace the bearing assemblies with new ones.

6 Clean the hub with a suitable solvent and remove the old grease from the hub cavity.

7 Inspect the bearing races for wear, signs of overheating, pitting and corrosion. If the races are worn or damaged, drive them out with a hammer and a drift (photo).

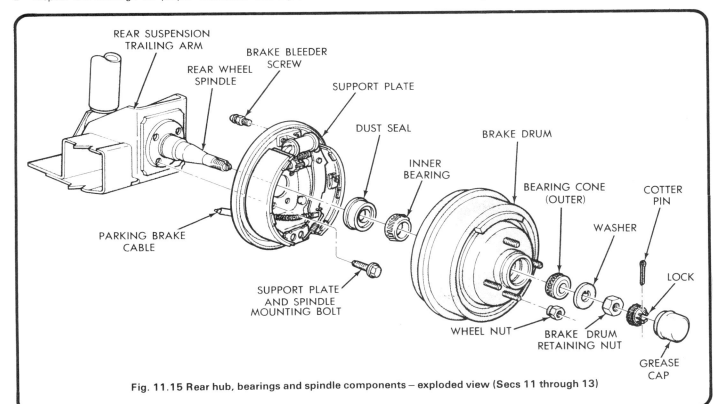

Fig. 11.15 Rear hub, bearings and spindle components – exploded view (Secs 11 through 13)

11

12.2 Check the bearing for proper lubrication; note that the bearing rollers on this vehicle (arrow) were without grease

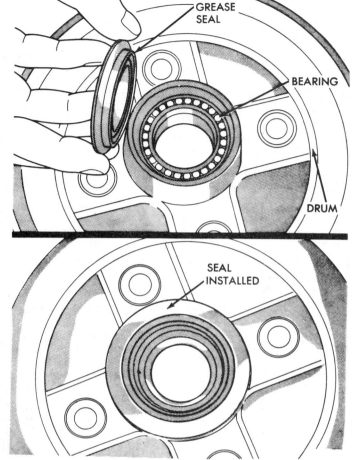

Fig. 11.16 Rotating the grease seal into position (top) and properly installed flush to the hub (bottom) (Sec 12)

12.7 Driving out the old bearing race with a punch and hammer

8   Install the new races and tap them into position with a drift and hammer, making sure they are installed squarely.
9   Use the approved grease to thoroughly pack the bearings prior to installation. Work generous amounts of grease in from the back of the cage so the grease is forced up through the rollers. Add a small amount of grease to the hub cavity.
10   Lubricate the outer lip of the new grease seal and press the seal and inner bearing into position. Make sure the seal is seated flush with the hub.
11   Install the hub, outer bearing, washer, nut, lock, cotter pin and grease cap (photo) as described in Section 11.

13 Rear spindle – inspection, removal and installation

1   Remove the rear hub.
2   Clean the spindle and inspect the bearing contact surfaces for wear or damage (photo).
3   The spindle should be replaced with a new one if it is bent, damaged or worn.
4   Disconnect the parking brake cable.
5   Disconnect and plug the rear brake line at the backing plate.
6   Remove the four torx-type retaining bolts and lift off the brake assembly and spindle. Make sure to mark the location of any spindle shims.
7   To install, place the shim(s) (if equipped), spindle and brake assembly in position, install the retaining bolts and tighten them to the specified torque.
8   Connect the brake lines and parking brake cables.
9   Install the hub (Section 11), bleed the brakes and adjust the parking brake (Chapter 9).

12.11 Use a hammer and punch to seat the grease cap at several locations around its circumference

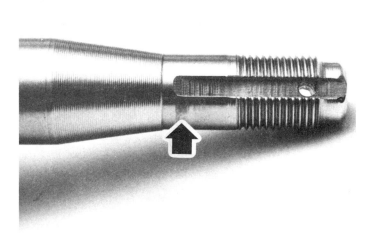

13.2 The bearing race on this vehicle has spun on the spindle causing wear (arrow)

14 Steering system – general information

All models are equipped with rack-and-pinion steering. The steering gear is bolted to the chassis directly behind the engine and operates the steering arms by way of tie-rods. The inner ends of the tie-rods are protected by rubber boots which should be inspected periodically for looseness, cuts or leaking lubricant.

As an option, some models are equipped with power assisted steering. The power assist system consists of a belt-driven pump and associated lines and hoses. The power steering pump reservoir fluid level should be checked periodically with the engine running (Chapter 1).

The steering wheel operates the steering shaft which actuates the steering gear through a universal joint. Looseness in the steering can be caused by wear in the steering shaft universal joint, the steering gear, the tie-rod ends and loose retaining bolts. Inadequate lubrication of the steering shaft seal can cause binding of the steering; the seal should be lubricated periodically (Chapter 1).

15 Steering wheel – removal and installation

1   Disconnect the negative battery cable.
2   Grasp the horn button firmly and pull it directly out to remove it (photo).

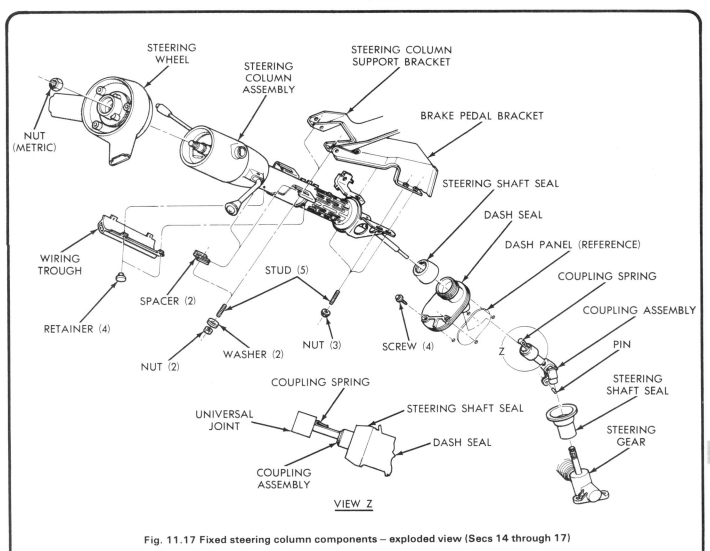

Fig. 11.17 Fixed steering column components – exploded view (Secs 14 through 17)

11

15.2 Pull out sharply to disengage the horn button

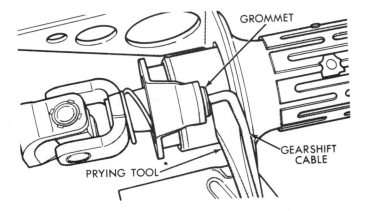

Fig. 11.18 Removing the shift cable (Sec 16)

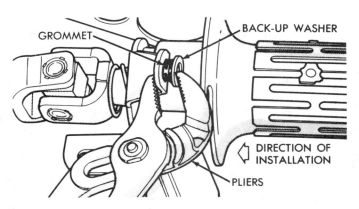

Fig. 11.19 Installing a new shift cable grommet (Sec 16)

15.5 Removing the steering wheel with a special puller

3   Unplug the connector and remove the horn switch.
4   Remove the steering wheel retaining nut and mark the relationship of the steering shaft and hub for ease of installation.
5   Use a suitable puller to remove the steering wheel, making sure not to strike the steering shaft (photo).
6   To install, align the steering wheel hub with the mark made on the shaft during removal and install the hub nut. Tighten the nut to the specified torque.
7   Install the horn switch and button.
8   Connect the negative battery cable.

16 Steering column – removal and installation

1   Disconnect the negative battery cable.
2   On column shift models, pry the gearshift cable rod from the grommet in the shift lever. Remove the cable from the lower bracket.
3   Unplug the steering column wiring connectors at the column jacket.
4   Remove the steering wheel (Section 5).
5   Remove the instrument panel column cover and the lower reinforcement and disconnect the bezel (Chapter 12).
6   Remove the shift indicator set screw and pointer (Chapter 12).

7   Remove the steering column-to-instrument panel and lower panel bracket retaining nuts. Do not remove the roll pin.
8   Grasp the steering column assembly firmly and pull it toward the rear so the lower stub shaft is disconnected from the steering gear coupling. Lift the assembly carefully from the vehicle.
9   Prior to installation, install a new grommet into the shift lever, using pliers and a back-up washer so it will snap into place. Use multi-purpose grease to lubricate the grommet.
10   Place the steering column in position with the stub shaft aligned with the lower coupling and insert the shaft into the coupling.
11   Install the retaining nuts and pull the column to the rear while tightening the nuts.
12   Using a needle nose pliers, pull the coupling spring up until it touches the flange of the universal joint.
13   Using a pair of pliers, snap the gearshift cable rod into the grommet.
14   Install the steering wheel.
15   Plug in the wiring connectors.
16   Install the shift indicator pointer.
17   Install the panel column cover, lower reinforcement and bezel.
18   Check the shift linkage adjustment (Chapter 7)
19   Move the shift lever though all positions to make sure the indicator needle aligns properly, adjusting as necessary.
20   Connect the negative battery cable and check the operation of the horn and lights.

17 Steering column (fixed) – disassembly, inspection and reassembly

1   Remove the steering column from the vehicle and place it in a vise, using blocks of wood to protect the outer surface.
2   Pry the wiring trough retainers loose and remove the trough.
3   Remove the shift lever by driving out the roll pin, using a suitable

punch and a hammer. Protect the steering column surface with masking tape and back up the opposite side of the lever base with a suitable socket while driving the pin out (photos).

4   Remove the turn signal cover and the washer/wiper and dimmer switch assemblies.

5   Remove the turn signal lever sleeve-to-wiper switch retaining screws and rotate the lever fully clockwise, then pull it directly out to remove it.

6   Remove the turn signal switch (Chapter 10).

7   Disconnect the horn and key light ground wires and remove the ignition key lamp.

8   Remove the upper bearing retaining screws and then remove the retaining snap-ring (photo).

9   Slide the bearing housing, lock plate and spring from the shaft (photos).

10 Remove the key buzzer assembly (Chapter 10).

11 Loosen the shift tube set screw and slide the tube from the lower end of the housing.

12 Inspect the steering shaft bearings for wear, looseness or signs of binding. The bearing should be replaced with a new one if there is appreciable wear or rough action. Lubricate the bearing with multi-purpose grease prior to installation (photo).

13 Check the turn signal switch for wear, damage or distortion. Inspect the wiring for worn insulation. Make sure the floor grommet is not damaged or torn.

14 Lubricate the shift tube bearing lightly with multi-purpose grease (photo), insert the tube fully into the column jacket and secure it with the set screw.

15 Lubricate the end of the shift lever, install the spring into the housing and install the lever, making sure the roll pin is securely tapped into position.

16 Install the shift lever gate to the housing and lubricate the contact surface lightly with multi-purpose grease (photo).

17 With the shift lever in the middle position, install the lock housing plate into the column jacket and install the screws. Make sure the plate is fully inserted into the slot in the jacket before tightening the screws.

18 Install the dimmer switch (Chapter 10).

19 Lubricate the lock lever assembly and install it to the lock cylinder, making sure that it is securely seated.

20 Install the ignition switch actuator rod up from the bottom of the lock housing and connect the bellcrank.

21 Install the ignition switch to the rod and rotate it 90° so the rod will lock in position.

22 Install the ignition lock, turn the key to the Lock position and remove it, which will cause the buzzer actuating lever to retract. Insert the key again, push in and turn the cylinder until the parts align and the cylinder snaps into place, Make sure the key cylinder and the ignition switch are in the Lock position and tighten the mounting screws.

23 Push the wires leading from the key buzzer switch down the column through the space between the housing and the jacket.

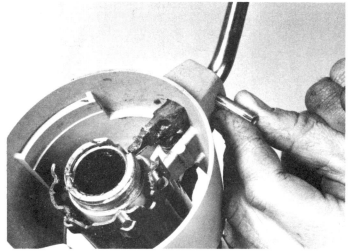

17.3a Removing the shift lever roll pin

17.3b Lifting out the lever spring

17.8 Removing the upper bearing housing snap-ring

17.9a Lifting out the bearing housing

11

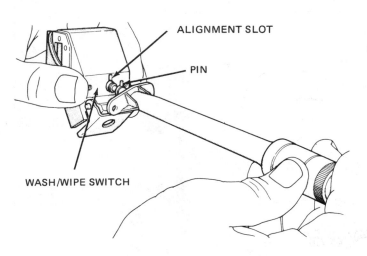

ALIGNMENT SLOT

PIN

WASH/WIPE SWITCH

**Fig. 11.20 Removing or installing the turn signal/wiper lever
(Sec 17)**

17.9b Withdrawing the lock plate

17.12 Lubricating the lower shaft bearing outer edge and contact area

17.14 Cover the shift tube bearing with a light coat of grease before
inserting the tube into the jacket

17.16 Lubricate the shift gate contact surface

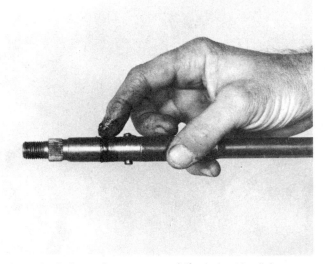

17.24 Cover the O-ring and contact area of the shaft with a light coat
of grease

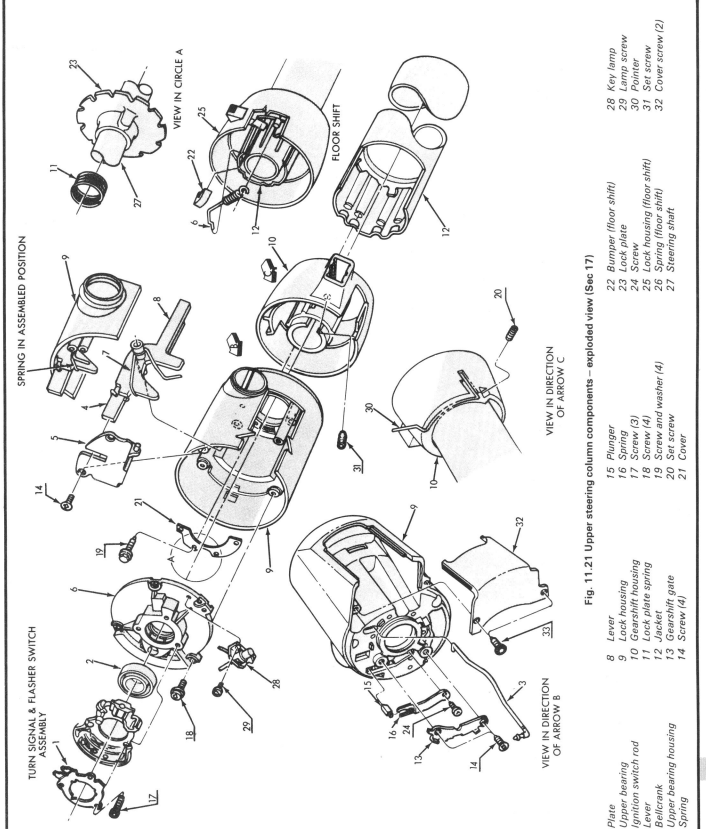

VIEW IN CIRCLE A

SPRING IN ASSEMBLED POSITION

FLOOR SHIFT

TURN SIGNAL & FLASHER SWITCH ASSEMBLY

VIEW IN DIRECTION OF ARROW C

VIEW IN DIRECTION OF ARROW B

Fig. 11.21 Upper steering column components – exploded view (Sec 17)

1	Plate	8	Lever
2	Upper bearing	9	Lock housing
3	Ignition switch rod	10	Gearshift housing
4	Lever	11	Lock plate spring
5	Bellcrank	12	Jacket
6	Upper bearing housing	13	Gearshift gate
7	Spring	14	Screw (4)

15	Plunger	22	Bumper (floor shift)
16	Spring	23	Lock plate
17	Screw (3)	24	Screw
18	Screw (4)	25	Lock housing (floor shift)
19	Screw and washer (4)	26	Spring (floor shift)
20	Set screw	27	Steering shaft
21	Cover		

28	Key lamp
29	Lamp screw
30	Pointer
31	Set screw
32	Cover screw (2)

11

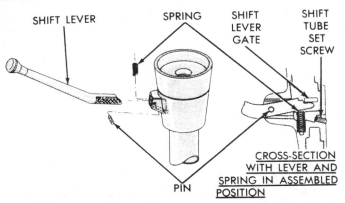

Fig. 11.22 Column shift lever installation details (Sec 17)

Tighten the buzzer switch mounting screws and remove the key.
24 Install the lower bearing support (floor shift only), bearing and spring onto the steering shaft. Install the O-ring on the shaft and lubricate it (photo).
25 Insert the steering shaft fully into the column and press the bearing into place in the housing. Push up on the steering shaft so the spring will be compressed and install the snap-ring.
26 Install the lock ring, upper bearing spring and bearing and housing assembly, retaining it with the snap-ring.
27 Install the bearing housing retaining screws.
28 Install the key lamp assembly, followed by the turn signal switch.

Insert the wires down the steering column through the opening between the bearing and lock housings.
29 Install the retainer plate and screws and connect the ground wires.
30 Insert the turn signal/wiper actuating lever into the switch assembly. Install the switch assembly to the lock housing and feed the wires through the housing.
31 Connect the wires to the turn signal switch.
32 Insert the dimmer switch actuating rod up through the housing and connect it to the wiper/washer switch.
33 Adjust the dimmer switch as described in Chapter 10.
34 Install the steering column.

18 Steering column (tilt wheel) – disassembly, inspection and reassembly

Other than removal and installation of the steering wheel and column assemblies, procedures for the tilt-wheel column vary considerably from those of the fixed column. Because of the special tools and techniques required, work on the tilt-wheel steering column assembly should be referred to your dealer or a properly equipped shop.

19 Steering gear – removal and installation

1   Raise the vehicle, support it securely and remove the front wheels.
2   Use a suitable puller to disconnect the tie-rods.
3   If equipped, remove the anti-rotational link and air diverter valve from the crossmember.

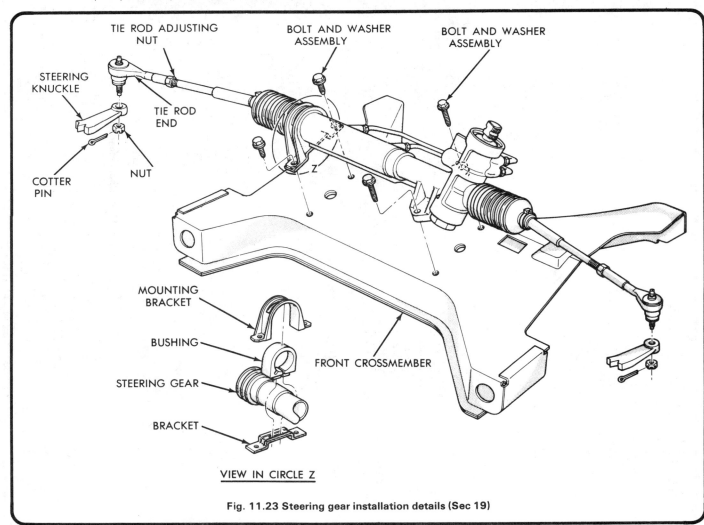

Fig. 11.23 Steering gear installation details (Sec 19)

4 Remove the four front suspension crossmember bolts.
5 Use a jack to lower the crossmember and steering gear for access.
6 Remove the boot seal and splash shields from the crossmember.
7 On power steering, disconnect the hoses and drain the fluid into a suitable container.
8 Disconnect the tie-rod ends and remove the steering gear attaching bolts. Remove the steering gear from the crossmember, lifting it from the left side of the vehicle.
9 To install, place the steering gear in position in the crossmember, install the bolts and tighten them securely.
10 Attach the tie-rod ends to the steering knuckles.
11 On power steering equipped models, reconnect the hoses, using new O-rings.
12 On manual steering equipped models, check to make sure the master serrations on the steering gear shaft are properly aligned so the steering shaft will be installed in the straight-ahead position.
13 Install the boot seal and splash shields.
14 Raise the crossmember and steering gear into position with the jack, install the four crossmember bolts and tighten them securely.
15 Install the steering column assembly (Section 16).
16 Install the front wheels and lower the vehicle.
17 On power steering equipped models, start the engine and bleed the steering system of air (Section 22). While the engine is running, check for leaks at the hose connections.
18 Have the front end alignment checked by a dealer or a properly equipped shop.

20 Power steering pump (2.2L engine) – removal and installation

1 Open the hood and disconnect the vapor separator hose at the carburetor and the two wires from the air conditioner clutch switch (if equipped).
2 Remove the drivebelt adjustment nut and bolt from the front of the pump and (if equipped) the nut from the hose end bracket.
3 Raise the vehicle and support it securely.
4 Remove the pump pressure hose locating bracket at the crossmember, disconnect the hose from the steering gear and drain the fluid through the hose into a suitable container.
5 Remove the right side splash cover to expose the drivebelts.
6 Disconnect the hoses from the pump and plug all openings so that dirt cannot enter.
7 Lower the vehicle.
8 Remove the drivebelt from the pulley, then move the pump to the rear and remove the adjustment bracket.
9 Turn the pump around so the pulley is facing toward the rear of the vehicle and lift it up and out of the engine compartment.
10 Install the adjusting bracket onto the pump.
11 Lower the pump into position in the reverse of the procedure described in Step 9.
12 Raise the vehicle and support it securely.
13 Install the lower pump bolt and stud nut finger tight.
14 Using new O-rings, attach the hoses to the pump.
15 Place the drivebelt onto the pulley and then lower the vehicle.
16 Install the adjusting bolt and nut, adjust the belt to the proper tension (Chapter 1) and tighten the nut.
17 Raise the vehicle, tighten the pump lower stud nut and install the splash cover.
18 Lower the vehicle, connect the vapor separator hoses and the air conditioner switch wires.
19 Fill the pump to the top of the filler neck with the specified fluid.
20 Start the engine, bleed the air from the system (Section 22) and check the fluid level.

21 Power steering pump (2.6L engine) – removal and installation

1 Open the hood and disconnect and plug the power steering pump hoses. Plug the pump ports.
2 Remove the pump adjusting bolts and the drivebelt.
3 Lift the pump and bracket from the engine compartment.
4 Place the pump in position and install the adjustment bolts and nuts finger tight.
5 Attach the hoses to the pump and tighten the tube nut.
6 Install the drivebelt, adjust it to the proper tension (Chapter 1) and tighten the adjusting bolt.

7 Fill the pump to the top of the filler neck with the specified fluid, bleed the system and check the fluid level.

22 Power steering system – bleeding

1 It will be necessary to bleed the power steering system whenever air is introduced into it, such as when a hose or line has been disconnected.
2 Open the hood and check the fluid level in the reservoir, adding the specified fluid as necessary to bring it up to the proper level.
3 Start the engine and slowly turn the steering wheel several times from left-to-right and back again. Do not turn the wheel fully from lock-to-lock. Check the fluid level, topping it up as necessary until it remains steady and no more bubbles appear in the reservoir.

23 Tie-rod end – removal and installation

1 Raise the front of the vehicle, support it securely and remove the front wheel on the side being worked on.
2 Disconnect the tie-rod from the steering knuckle arm, using a suitable tool (photo).
3 Mark the location of the jam nut and then loosen the nut sufficiently to allow the rod end to be unscrewed and removed from the vehicle.
4 Thread the tie-rod end onto the rod to the marked position and tighten the jam nut to the specified torque.
5 Connect the tie-rod end to the steering knuckle arm, install the nut and tighten it to the specified torque. Install the cotter key.
6 If a new tie-rod end has been installed, have the front end steering geometry checked by a properly equipped shop.

23.2 Press the tie-rod end out of the steering knuckle arm

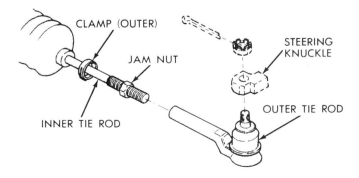

Fig. 11.24 Tie-rod end installation (Sec 23)

11

24 Steering angles and wheel alignment

1   Proper wheel alignment is essential to proper steering and even tire wear. Symptoms of alignment faults are pulling of the steering to one side or the other and uneven tire wear.

2   If these symptoms are present, check for the following before having the alignment adjusted:

> *Loose steering gear bolts*
> *Damaged or worn steering gear mounts*
> *Improperly adjusted wheel bearings*
> *Bent tie-rods*
> *Worn balljoint*
> *Insufficient steering gearbox lubricant*
> *Improper tire pressure*
> *Mixing tires of different construction*

3   Alignment faults in the rear suspension are manifest in uneven tire wear or uneven tracking of the rear wheels. This can be easily checked by driving the vehicle straight across a puddle of water onto a dry patch of pavement. If the rear wheels do not follow the front wheels almost exactly, the alignment should be adjusted.

4   Front or rear wheel alignment should be left to your dealer or a properly-equipped shop.

25 Wheels and tires

1   Check the tire pressure (cold) weekly.

2   Inspect the sidewalls and treads periodically for damage and signs of abnormal or uneven wear.

3   Make sure the wheel lug nuts are properly tightened.

4   Do not mix tires of dissimilar construction or tread pattern on the same axle.

5   Never include the temporary spare in the tire rotation pattern as it is designed for use only until a damaged tire is repaired or replaced.

6   Periodically inspect the wheels for elongated or damaged lug holes, distortion or nicks on the rim. Replace any suspect wheel.

7   Clean the wheel inside and outside and inspect for rust and corrosion which could lead to wheel failure.

8   If the wheel and tire are balanced on the car, one wheel stud and lug hole should be marked whenever the wheel is removed so that it can be reinstalled in the original position. If balanced on the vehicle, the wheel should not be moved to a different axle position.

Chapter 12 Bodywork

Contents

Specifications

Torque specifications

	Ft-lb	Nm
Door latch adjusting screw	2	3
Door latch remote control latch screw	7.4	10
Rivet replacement nut and screw	7.4	10
Window regulator-to-door	7 to 13	10 to 18
Radiator grille bezel		
Top screws	1	2
Side screws	2	3
Radiator grille screws	2	3
Bumper-to-energy absorber	20	28
Energy absorber-to-chassis	20	28
Bumper fascia retainer	9	12
Hood latch screw	9	12
Seat retaining bolts	18	25

1 General information

These models are available in 2-door and 4-door sedan and 4-door station wagon body styles.

The body is of unitized construction and certain components which are vulnerable to accident damage can be unbolted and replaced with new units. Among these are the front fenders, grille, hood, doors, trunk and bumpers.

2 Maintenance – body and frame

1   The condition of your vehicle's body is very important, as it is on this that the second hand value will mainly depend. It is much more difficult to repair a neglected or damaged body than it is to repair mechanical components. The hidden areas of the body, such as the fender walls, the frame, and the engine compartment, are equally important, although obviously not requiring as frequent attention as the rest of the body.

2   Once a year, or every 12 000 miles, it is a good idea to have the underside of the body and the frame steam cleaned. All traces of dirt and oil will be removed and the underside can then be inspected carefully for rust, damaged brake lines, frayed electrical wiring, damaged cables, and other problems. The front suspension components should be greased upon completion of this job.
3   At the same time, clean the engine and the engine compartment with a steam cleaner or a water soluble degreaser.
4   The fender wells should be carefully checked, as undercoating can peel away and stones and dirt thrown up by the tires can cause the paint to chip and flake, allowing rust to set in. If rust is found, clean down to the bare metal and apply an anti-rust paint.
5   The body should be washed once a week (or when dirty). Thoroughly wet the vehicle to soften the dirt, then wash it down with a soft sponge and plenty of clean soapy water. If the surplus dirt is not washed off very carefully, it will in time wear down the paint.
6   Spots of tar or asphalt coating thrown from the road surfaces should be removed with a cloth soaked in solvent.
7   Once every six months, give the body and chrome trim a thorough

12

wax job. If a chrome cleaner is used to remove rust on any of the vehicle's plated parts, remember that the cleaner also removes part of the chrome so use it sparingly.

3   Maintenance – upholstery and carpets

1   Every three months, remove the carpets or mats and thoroughly clean the interior of the vehicle (more frequently if necessary). Vacuum the upholstery and carpets to remove loose dirt and dust.
2   If the upholstery is soiled, apply an upholstery cleaner with a damp sponge and wipe it off with a clean, dry cloth.

4   Body repair – minor damage

Refer to the accompanying color photos which illustrate the following procedures.

Repair of minor scratches

If the scratch is very superficial and does not penetrate to the metal of the body, repair is very simple. Lightly rub the area of the scratch with a fine rubbing compound to remove loose paint from the scratch and to clear the surrounding paint of wax buildup. Rinse the area with clean water.

Apply touch-up paint to the scratch using a small brush. Continue to apply thin layers of paint until the surface of the paint in the scratch is level with the surrounding paint. Allow the new paint at least two weeks to harden, then blend it into the surrounding paint by rubbing with a very fine rubbing compound. Finally, apply a coat of wax to the scratch area.

If the scratch has penetrated the paint and exposed the metal of the body, causing the metal to rust, a different repair technique is required. Remove any loose rust from the bottom of the scratch with a pocket knife, then apply rust inhibiting paint to prevent the formation of rust in the future. Using a rubber or nylon applicator, coat the scratched area with glaze-type filler. If required, this filler can be mixed with thinner to provide a very thin paste which is ideal for filling narrow scratches. Before the glaze filler in the scratch hardens, wrap a piece of smooth cotton cloth around the top of a finger. Dip the cloth in thinner and then quickly wipe it along the surface of the scratch. This will ensure that the surface of the filler is slightly hollowed. The scratch can now be painted over as described earlier in this Section.

Repair of dents

When deep denting of the vehicle's body has taken place, the first task is to pull the dent out until the area nearly attains its original shape. There is little point in trying to restore the original shape completely as the metal in the damaged area will have stretched on impact and cannot be completely restored to its original contours. It is better to bring the level of the dent up to a point which is about $\frac{1}{8}$ inch below the level of the surrounding metal. In cases where the dent is very shallow, it is not worth trying to pull it out at all.   If the underside of the dent is accessible, it can be hammered out gently from behind using a mallet with a wooden or plastic head. While doing this, hold a block of wood firmly against the metal to absorb the hammer blows and prevent large areas of the metal from being stretched out.

If the dent is in a section of the body which has double layers, or some other factor making it inaccessible from behind, a different technique is in order. Drill several small holes through the metal inside the damaged area, particularly in the deeper sections. Screw long self-tapping screws into the holes just enough for them to get a good grip in the metal. Now the dent can be removed by pulling on the protruding heads of the screws with a pair of locking pliers.

The next stage of the repair is the removal of the paint from the damaged area and from an inch or so of the surrounding 'sound' metal. This is easily accomplished using a wire brush or sanding disc in a drill motor, although it can be done just as effectively by hand with sandpaper. To complete the preparation for filling, score the surface of the bare metal with a screwdriver or the tang of a file (or drill small holes in the affected area). This will provide a really good 'grip' for the filler material. To complete the repair, see the Section on filling and painting.

Repair of rust holes or gashes

Remove all paint from the affected area and from an inch or so of the surrounding 'sound' metal using a sanding disc or wire brush mounted in a drill motor. If these are not available, a few sheets of sandpaper will do the job just as effectively. With the paint removed, you will be able to determine the severity of the corrosion and, therefore, decide whether to replace the whole panel, if possible, or to repair the affected area. New body panels are not as expensive as most people think and it is often quicker and more desirable to install a new panel than to attempt to repair large areas of rust.

Remove all trim pieces from the affected area (except those which will act as a guide to the original shape of the damaged body ie. headlamp shells, etc.). Then, using metal snips or a hacksaw blade, remove all loose metal and any other metal that is badly affected by rust. Hammer the edges of the hole in to create a slight depression for the filler material.

Wire brush the affected area to remove the powdery rust from the surface of the metal. If the back of the rusted area is accessible, treat it with rust inhibiting paint.

Before filling can be done, it will be necessary to block the hole in some way. This can be accomplished with sheet metal riveted or screwed into place or by stuffing the hole with wire mesh.

Once the hole is blocked off, the affected area can be filled and painted (see the following Section on filling and painting).

Filling and painting

Many types of body fillers are available but generally speaking, body repair kits which contain filler paste and a tube of resin hardener are best for this type of repair work. A wide, flexible plastic or nylon applicator will be necessary for imparting a smooth contoured finish to the surface of the filler material.

Mix up a small amount of filler on a clean piece of wood or cardboard (use the hardener sparingly). Follow the maker's instructions on the package, otherwise the filler will set incorrectly.

Using the applicator, apply the filler paste to the prepared area. Draw the applicator across the surface of the filler to achieve the desired contour and to level the filler surface. As soon as a contour that approximates the correct one is achieved, stop working the paste. If you continue, the paste will begin to stick to the applicator. Continue to add thin layers of filler paste at 20-minute intervals until the level of the filler is just above the surrounding metal.

Once the filler has hardened, excess can be removed using a body file. From then on, progressively finer grades of sandpaper should be used, starting with a 180-grit paper and finishing with 600-grit wet-or-dry paper. Always wrap the sandpaper around a flat rubber or wooden block, otherwise the surface of the filler will not be completely flat. During the sanding of the filler surface, the wet-or-dry paper should be periodically rinsed in water. This will ensure that a very smooth finish is produced in the final stage.

At this point, the repair area should be surrounded by a ring of bare metal, which in turn should be encircled by the finely feathered edge of the good paint. Rinse the repair area with clean water until all of the dust produced by the sanding operation is gone.

Spray the entire area with a light coat of primer. This will reveal any imperfections in the surface of the filler. Repair these imperfections with fresh filler paste or glaze filler and once more smooth the surface with sandpaper. Repeat this spray-and-repair procedure until you are satisfied that the surface of the filler and the feathered edge of the paint are perfect. Rinse the area with clean water and allow it to dry completely.

The repair area is now ready for painting. Paint spraying must be carried out in warm, dry, windless and dustfree atmosphere. These conditions can be created if you have access to a large indoor working area but if you are forced to work in the open, you will have to pick your day very carefully. If you are working indoors, dousing the floor in the work area with water will help to settle the dust which would otherwise be in the air. If the repair area is confined to one body panel, mask off the surrounding panels. This will help to minimize the effects of a slight mismatch in paint color. Trim pieces such as chrome strips, door handles, etc., will also need to be masked off or removed. Use masking tape and several thicknesses of newspaper for the masking operations.

Before spraying, shake the paint can thoroughly, then spray a test area until the technique is mastered. Cover the repair area with a thick coat of primer. The thickness should be built up using several thin layers of primer rather than one thick one. Using 600-grit wet-or-dry sandpaper, rub down the surface of the primer until it is very smooth. While doing this, the work area should be thoroughly rinsed with water, and the wet-or-dry sandpaper periodically rinsed as well. Allow the primer to dry before spraying additional coats.

Spray on the top coat, again building up the thickness by using several thin layers of paint. Begin spraying in the center of the repair area and then, using a circular motion, work out until the whole repair area and about two inches of the surrounding original paint is covered. Remove all masking material 10 to 15 minutes after spraying on the final coat of paint. Allow the new paint at least two weeks to harden, then using a very fine rubbing compound, blend the edges of the paint into the existing paint. Finally, apply a coat of wax.

5   Body repair – major damage

1   Major damage must be repaired by an auto body/frame repair shop with the necessary welding and hydraulic straightening equipment.
2   If the damage has been serious, it is vital that the frame be checked for correct alignment as the handling of the vehicle will be affected. Other problems, such as excessive tire wear and wear in the transmission and steering may also occur.

6   Maintenance – hinges and locks

Once every 3000 miles, or every three months, the door and hood hinges and locks should be given a few drops of light oil or lock lubricant. The door striker plates can be given a thin coat of grease to reduce wear and ensure free movement.

7   Windshield, stationary quarter window and rear glass – removal and installation

The windshield, stationary quarter window and rear glass on all models are sealed in place with a special butyl compound. Removal of the existing sealant requires the use of an electric knife specially made for the operation and glass replacement is a complex operation.

In view of this, it is not recommended that stationary glass removal be attempted by the home mechanic. If replacement is necessary due to breakage or leakage, the work should be referred to your dealer or a qualified glass or body shop.

8   Weatherstripping – maintenance and replacement

1   The weatherstripping should be kept clean and free of contaminants such as gasoline or oil. Spray the weatherstripping periodically with silicone lubricant to reduce abrasion, wear and cracking.
2   The weatherstripping is retained to the doors by adhesive above the vehicle beltline and by clips below it.
3   To remove the weatherstripping, release the plastic clip at the bottom of the door. Work your way around the circumference of the door and carefully pull the weatherstripping free.
4   Clean the channel of any residual adhesive or weatherstripping which would interfere with the installation of the new weatherstripping.
5   Apply a thin coat of a suitable adhesive to the upper portion of the door and install the new weatherstripping, making sure to push it fully into the channel and secure the clips.

9   Door trim panel – removal and installation

1   Remove the armrest, door latch remote control bezel, window crank and door lock knob.
2   Insert a suitable screwdriver or pry bar between the door and the panel, adjacent to each retaining clip, and pry the panel loose. Work your way around the circumference of the panel until it can be removed (photo).
3   Lift the panel up and slide it to the rear to remove it.
4   Carefully peel the clear plastic shield and the black paper sound

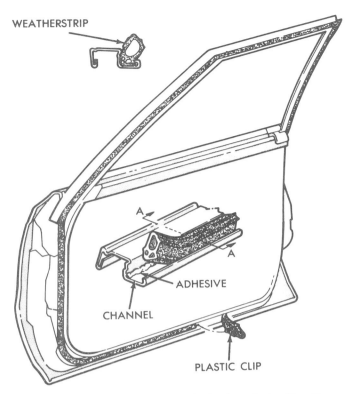

Fig. 12.1 Typical door weatherstripping installation (Sec 8)

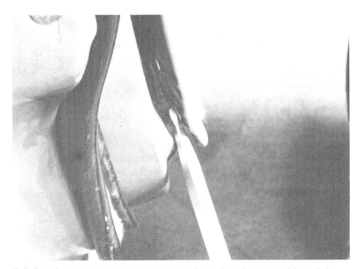

9.2 Carefully pry the trim panel loose, inserting the screwdriver right next to the clip

deadener away from the door. Be careful not to tear either of these as they will be reinstalled.
5   Prior to installation, apply a bead of silicone sealant to the door and then carefully install the plastic shield and sound deadener.
6   Place the trim panel in position and insert the upper edge into the glass opening.
7   Align the retaining clips with the holes in the door and, starting from the rear, push them into place.
8   Install the door lock knob, window crank, bezel and armrest.

10   Door latch – removal and installation

1   Raise the door glass to the full up position and remove the trim panel (Section 9).

12

These photos illustrate a method of repairing simple dents. They are intended to supplement *Body repair - minor damage* in this Chapter and should not be used as the sole instructions for body repair on these vehicles.

1 If you can't access the backside of the body panel to hammer out the dent, pull it out with a slide-hammer-type dent puller. In the deepest portion of the dent or along the crease line, drill or punch hole(s) at least one inch apart . . .

2 . . . then screw the slide-hammer into the hole and operate it. Tap with a hammer near the edge of the dent to help 'pop' the metal back to its original shape. When you're finished, the dent area should be close to its original contour and about 1/8-inch below the surface of the surrounding metal

3 Using coarse-grit sandpaper, remove the paint down to the bare metal. Hand sanding works fine, but the disc sander shown here makes the job faster. Use finer (about 320-grit) sandpaper to feather-edge the paint at least one inch around the dent area

4 When the paint is removed, touch will probably be more helpful than sight for telling if the metal is straight. Hammer down the high spots or raise the low spots as necessary. Clean the repair area with wax/silicone remover

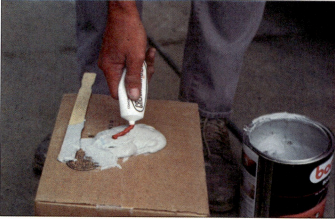

5 Following label instructions, mix up a batch of plastic filler and hardener. The ratio of filler to hardener is critical, and, if you mix it incorrectly, it will either not cure properly or cure too quickly (you won't have time to file and sand it into shape)

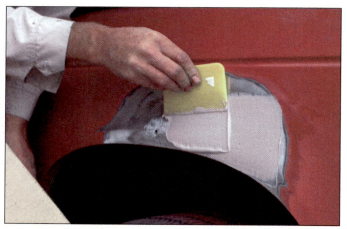

6 Working quickly so the filler doesn't harden, use a plastic applicator to press the body filler firmly into the metal, assuring it bonds completely. Work the filler until it matches the original contour and is slightly above the surrounding metal

7   Let the filler harden until you can just dent it with your fingernail. Use a body file or Surform tool (shown here) to rough-shape the filler

8   Use coarse-grit sandpaper and a sanding board or block to work the filler down until it's smooth and even. Work down to finer grits of sandpaper - always using a board or block - ending up with 360 or 400 grit

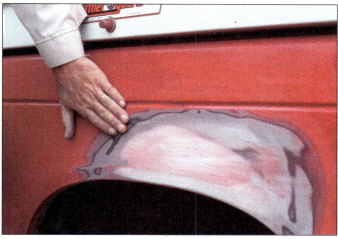

9   You shouldn't be able to feel any ridge at the transition from the filler to the bare metal or from the bare metal to the old paint. As soon as the repair is flat and uniform, remove the dust and mask off the adjacent panels or trim pieces

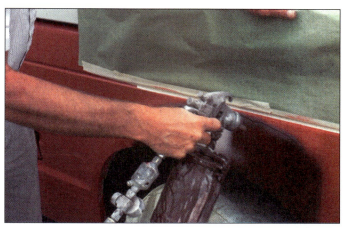

10   Apply several layers of primer to the area. Don't spray the primer on too heavy, so it sags or runs, and make sure each coat is dry before you spray on the next one. A professional-type spray gun is being used here, but aerosol spray primer is available inexpensively from auto parts stores

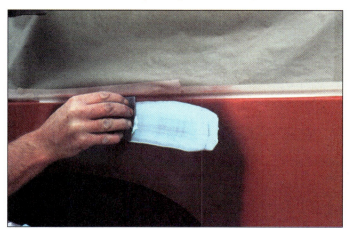

11   The primer will help reveal imperfections or scratches. Fill these with glazing compound. Follow the label instructions and sand it with 360 or 400-grit sandpaper until it's smooth. Repeat the glazing, sanding and respraying until the primer reveals a perfectly smooth surface

12   Finish sand the primer with very fine sandpaper (400 or 600-grit) to remove the primer overspray. Clean the area with water and allow it to dry. Use a tack rag to remove any dust, then apply the finish coat. Don't attempt to rub out or wax the repair area until the paint has dried completely (at least two weeks)

2   Disconnect the links from the outside handle, key cylinder, remote control, latch lock and electric motor (if equipped).
3   Remove the three latch attachment screws. It may be necessary to use an impact-type screwdriver to loosen the screws (photo).
4   Remove the latch through the access hole in the door.
5   Lubricate all sliding surfaces of the latch assembly with lithium-base grease prior to installation.
6   Place the latch in position and install the screws loosely. Tighten the screws in a criss-cross fashion so the latch is drawn up to the desired centered position.
7   Attach the various links which were disconnected during removal and install the door panel.
8   Adjust the latch (Section 21).

10.3 Loosening the door latch screws with an impact screwdriver

11 Door outside handle – removal and installation

1   Raise the glass to the full up position and remove the door trim panel.
2   Disconnect the handle link from the latch and remove the attaching nuts.
3   Remove the handle from the door.
4   Lubricate the contact surfaces of the handle (photo).
5   To install, place the handle in position, attach the link and install the nuts.
6   Install the door trim panel.

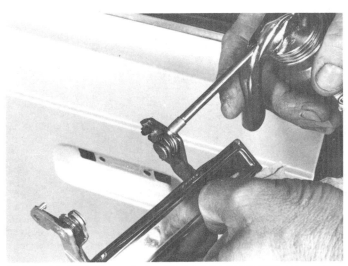

11.4 Squirt oil into the contact surfaces of the door handle mechanism

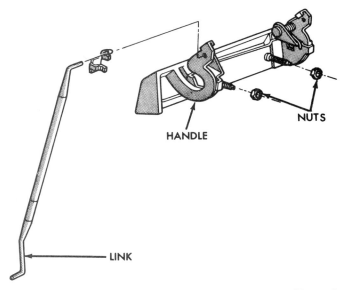

Fig. 12.2 Typical outside door handle component layout (Sec 11)

12 Door lock cylinder – removal and installation

1   Raise the glass completely and remove the door trim panel.
2   Disconnect the link from the cylinder latch and slide the cylinder retainer clip off.
3   Remove the lock cylinder and gasket.
4   To install, insert the lock cylinder and gasket into the door, slide the retainer into place and reconnect the link.
5   Install the door trim panel.

13 Door remote control assembly – removal and installation

1   Raise the window glass to the full up position and remove the door trim panel.
2   Disconnect the connecting links, remove the attaching screws and remove the control assembly and mounting plate. Squeeze the two locking tabs together and slide the assembly from the mounting plate.
3   Lubricate the assembly (photo).
4   To install, slide the control assembly into the mounting bracket, making sure the tabs lock into place. Place the assembly and mounting plate in position, install the mounting screws and connect the links.
5   Install the door trim panel.

13.3 Oiling the remote control assembly

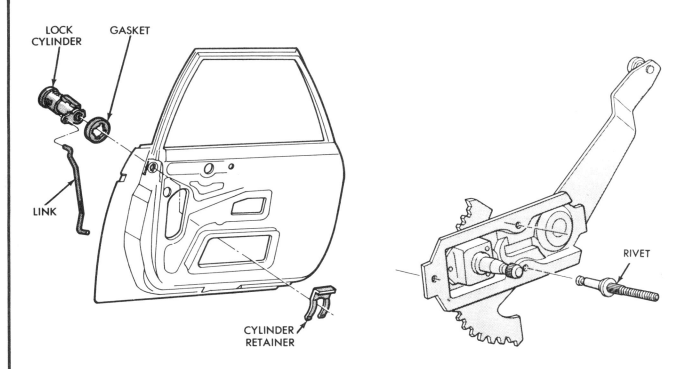

Fig. 12.3 Lock cylinder installation (Sec 12)

Fig. 12.4 Typical window regulator attachment (front door) (Sec 14)

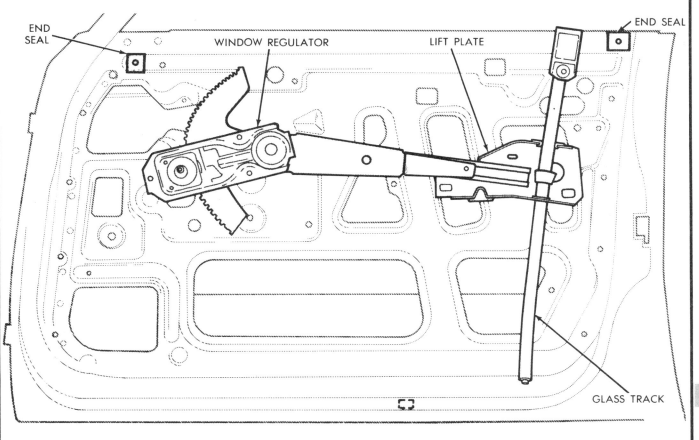

Fig. 12.5 Typical front door window regulator component layout (Secs 14 and 15)

12

14 Front door manual window glass regulator — removal and installation

1   Raise the window glass to the full up position and remove the door trim panel.
2   Brace the glass in the full up position.
3   Drive out the center of the regulator retaining rivets with a suitable punch and drill out the remainder with a $\frac{1}{4}$ inch drill.
4   Disconnect the regulator arm and remove the regulator assembly from the door.
5   To install, place the regulator in position in the door and connect the arm to the lift plate. Use $\frac{1}{4}$ x 20 nuts and screws in place of the rivets to secure the assembly to the door. Tighten them to the specified torque.
6   Install the door trim panel.

15 Flex drive-type window glass regulator — removal and installation

1   Remove the door trim panel (Section 9).
2   Move the glass to the access hole and remove the bolt attaching the glass to the flex drive arm.
3   Brace the glass securely in the up position.
4   On manual regulators, use a suitable punch to drive out the centers of the securing rivets and then drill out the rivet.
5   On electric regulators, drill out the rivets and remove the attaching screws.
6   Remove the regulator from the door by rotating it through the access hole. Unplug the wiring connector of electric regulators.
7   Carefully clean the flex drive teeth area and lubricate with silicone lubricant.
8   Plug in the electrical connector (if equipped), place the regulator in position in the door and secure it with $\frac{1}{4}$ x 20 bolts and nuts, tightened to the specified torque.
9   If the entire flex drive assembly has been removed, follow the tightening sequence in the accompanying illustrations to prevent the possibility of binding.
10   Cycle the window several times to check for proper operation.
11   Install the door trim panel.

16 Front door glass — removal and installation

1   Remove the door trim panel.
2   Lower the window sufficiently to gain access and remove the glass-to-regulator attachment nuts and bolts (photo).
3   Lower the window mechanism completely and disengage the glass.
4   Remove the outer glass weatherstrip from the door by pushing it up from underneath and disengaging the clips (photo).
5   Lift the glass up and out and carefully remove it from the door toward the outside of the window opening (photo).
6   While the glass is out, lubricate the track with white lithium-base grease (photo).
7   To install, lower the glass into the door and seat it in the mechanism.
8   Install the nuts and bolts finger tight.
9   Raise the window completely and seat the glass in the upper channel.
10   Tighten the nuts and bolts to the specified torque.
11   Lower the glass.
12   Lower the weatherstripping into position, align the clips and then press it into place.
13   Install the door trim panel.

17 Rear door fixed glass — removal and installation

1   Remove the door trim panel.
2   Remove the garnish moulding and peel back the upper portion of the clear plastic shield.
3   Remove the end seal at the rear of the door.
4   Remove the glass bracket screws.

16.2 Removing the door glass retaining nuts through the access hole

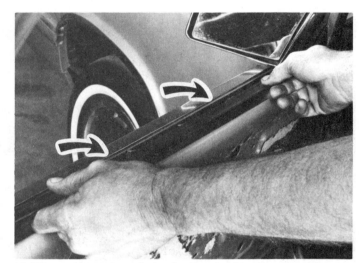

16.4 Grasp the weatherstripping firmly and pull it to the rear and up to remove it

16.5 Tilt the glass toward the outside of the door to remove it

16.6 Lubricating the glass track with white grease

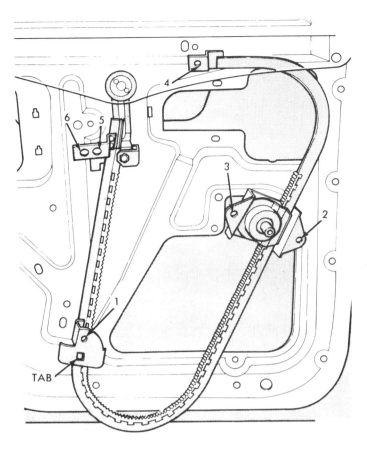

Fig. 12.6 Manual flex drive window regulator attachment points
(the retaining screws should be tightened in the sequence shown)
(Sec 15)

18.5a Remove the vent window attaching screws

5   Grasp both sides of the glass securely and push it half way down into the door.
6   Pull the top of the glass in and then lift it from the door.
7   To install, lower the glass into the door and attach it to the glass bracket.
8   Seat the glass securely into the upper channel and install and tighten the bracket screws.
9   Install the end seal, plastic shield and garnish moulding.
10   Install the door trim panel.

18 Rear door fixed glass vent window — removal and installation

1   Remove the door trim panel and peel the upper portion of the plastic shield back.
2   Remove the bolt and spacer at the base of the vent window (photo).
3   Remove the door glass bracket and nuts and disengage it from the glass. Lower the glass into the door.
4   Disconnect the vent from the latch.
5   Remove the attaching screws and tilt the vent window forward and out to remove it (photos).
6   To install, rotate the vent window into place from the outside of the door.
7   Install the center attaching screw into the rear side of the door frame first, followed by the remaining screws. Install the vent window bolt and spacer.
8   Raise the door glass into position and install the bracket and nuts.
9   Install the latch-to-vent window screws finger tight. Adjust the latch by holding the window closed and then installing the attaching screw. This will automatically center the window in the opening.
10   Install the trim panel.

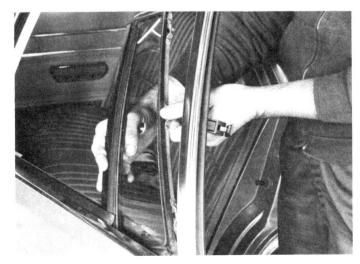

18.5b Move the window forward to remove it

12

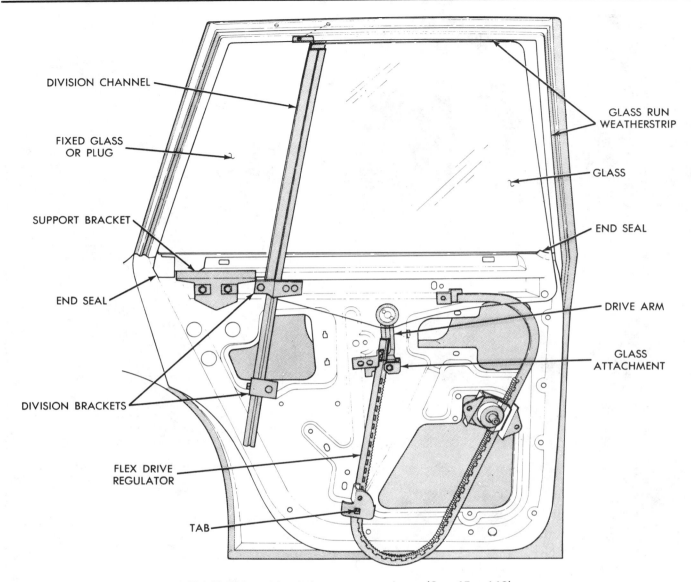

DIVISION CHANNEL

FIXED GLASS
OR PLUG

SUPPORT BRACKET

END SEAL

DIVISION BRACKETS

FLEX DRIVE
REGULATOR

TAB

GLASS RUN
WEATHERSTRIP

GLASS

END SEAL

DRIVE ARM

GLASS
ATTACHMENT

Fig. 12.7 Moveable window component layout (Secs 15 and 19)

19 Rear door moveable glass and fixed vent window — removal and installation

1   Remove the door trim panel.
2   Remove the end seals from the front and rear of the door.
3   Remove the fixed vent window support bracket and detach the division channel-to-door inner panel brackets.
4   Remove the door glass run weatherstrip.
5   Remove the screw from the top of the division channel and remove the fixed glass.
6   Detach the clips and remove the outside weatherstripping.
7   Remove the door glass-to-flex drive arm bolt.
8   Raise the division channel, door glass and drive arm assembly up, rotate it 90° and lift it out through the glass opening.
9   To install, lower the division channel, door glass and drive assembly into the window opening. Make sure the lower bracket is parallel to the opening and lower the assembly until the upper division channel is near the opening. Rotate the assembly 90° and lower the channel to the bottom of the door.
10 Lift the glass and place the drive arm in position on the flex drive arm, securing it with the shoulder bolt.
11 Install the outside weatherstripping and place the fixed glass bracket in position.

12 Use a rocking motion to position the glass in place in the door so that it rests loosely on the bracket.
13 Install the rear edge of the division channel onto the fixed glass.
14 Install the weatherstripping securely into the channel.
15 Install the upper and lower division channel brackets.
16 Push the fixed glass bracket up and secure it.
17 Install the end seals.
18 Install the door trim panel.

20 Exterior mirror — removal and installation

1   Remove the bezel mounting screw and disengage the bezel from the channel bracket. Loosen the bezel set screw to release the cable control on remote control mirrors.
2   Remove the door trim panel.
3   Remove the three screws retaining the inboard side of the channel bracket (photo).
4   Remove the two screws from the door frame and disengage the mirror and seal from the channel bracket.
5   To install, engage the mirror and seal to the bracket and install the screws.
6   Install the three screws in the inboard channel bracket.
7   Install the door trim panel.

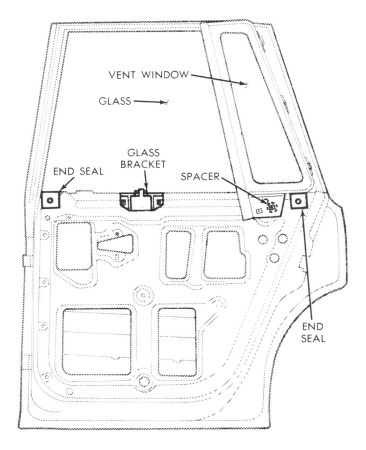

Fig. 12.8 Fixed rear glass installation (Secs 17 and 18)

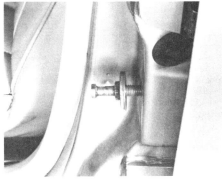

20.3 Removing the mirror retaining screws

21.1 Loosened door latch striker (for adjustment, thread the striker in until it is almost snug)

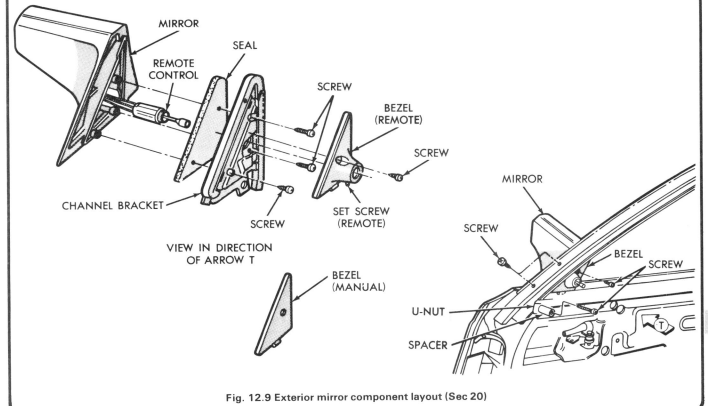

Fig. 12.9 Exterior mirror component layout (Sec 20)

12

8   On remote control mirrors, tighten the control cable set screw.
9   Install the bezel and mounting screw.

21 Door latch striker – adjustment

1   Loosen the latch striker with a suitable wrench (photo).
2   Move the striker to approximately the center of its travel and tighten it.
3   Close the door slowly and check to make sure that it does not move up or down excessively as it contacts the striker.
4   Loosen the striker, adjust it to compensate and retighten.
5   Continue adjusting until the door closes smoothly and the weatherstripping around the door compresses evenly all the way around.

22 Door latch – adjustment

1   Loosen the adjusting screw by inserting a $\frac{5}{32}$ inch Allen wrench through the hole in the door face (photo).
2   Move the Allen wrench up and tighten the screw to the specified torque.
3   Check the door handle position to make sure it is flush with the door. Readjust if necessary.
4   Check the latch and door for proper operation.
5   It may be necessary to readjust several times to obtain smooth door closing and a flush door handle condition.

22.1 The door latch adjusting screw is accessible through the access hole in the door

23 Deck lid latch, striker and lock cylinder – removal and installation

Latch
1   Open the deck lid, mark the location of the latch, remove the attaching bolts and lift the latch away.
2   To install, place the latch in the marked position and install the bolts.

Striker
3   Remove the attaching bolts and lift the striker away from the body sheet metal.
4   Installation is the reverse of removal.

Cylinder
5   Remove the retaining nut and withdraw the cylinder from the body.
6   To install, insert the cylinder into position and install the nut.

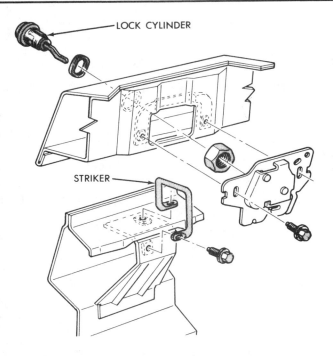

Fig. 12.10 Deck lid latch components (Sec 23)

24 Deck lid torsion bar – adjustment

1   By moving the right torsion bar in the number one slot and the left one in the number two slot, the closing tension of the deck lid can be adjusted.
2   After adjustment, close the deck lid and check that the latch action is smooth and the lid is flush with the body. Repeat the adjustment procedure until the deck lid closes easily without too much force.

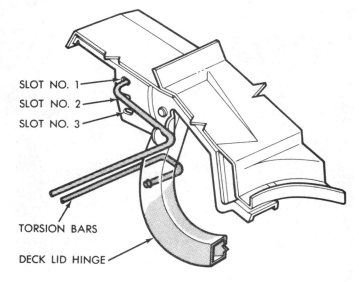

Fig. 12.11 Deck lid torsion bar adjustment (Sec 24)

25 Liftgate and deck lid weatherstripping – replacement

1   Pull the old weatherstripping from the vehicle.
2   Clean the flange area of old material and straighten any bends or distortions which could affect installation.
3   Start at the bottom of the liftgate or deck lid opening and install the new weatherstripping securely to the flange, starting at the center

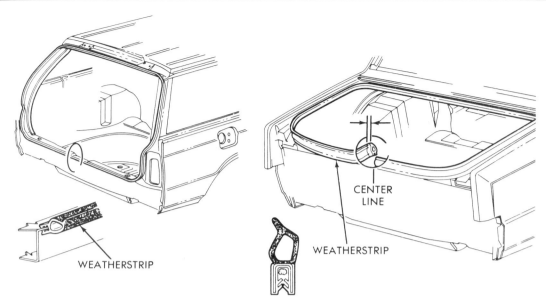

Fig. 12.12 Station wagon and sedan rear weatherstrip installation (Sec 25)

bottom of the opening. Push the weatherstripping firmly in place and, leaving an overlap of $\frac{1}{4}$ inch (6.35 mm), cut off the excess evenly. Butt the ends together to form a compression joint.

26 Radiator grille – removal and installation

1   Remove the headlight bezel (Section 27).
2   Remove the six retaining screws and lift the grille away from the vehicle.
3   To install, align the tab of the lower center support with the radiator brace support and lower the grille into position (photo).
4   Install the retaining screws finger tight.
5   Install the headlight bezels and tighten the screws.
6   Tighten the grille screws.

26.3 Radiator grille alignment tab location

27 Headlight bezel – removal and installation

1   Remove the retaining screws and pull the bezel sufficiently clear of the vehicle to gain access to the turn signal and clearance lights.
2   Disconnect the clearance and turn signal sockets.

3   Remove the bezel from the vehicle.
4   To install, insert the inner end of the bucket behind the spring-loaded tab and then push it into place.
5   Install the retaining screws and tighten them securely.

28 Hood – removal and installation

1   Mark the location of the hood retaining bolts for ease of installation.
2   Place protective padding such as old blankets on the fenders and windshield. It is also a good idea to place a block of wood between the rear of the hood and the windshield to prevent sudden rearward movement of the hood during removal.
3   Remove the retaining bolts and, with the help of an assistant, lift the hood from the vehicle (photo).
4   To install, place the hood in position and install the bolts in their previously marked positions.

28.3 Removing the hood retaining bolts (note the paint marking the bolt locations)

12

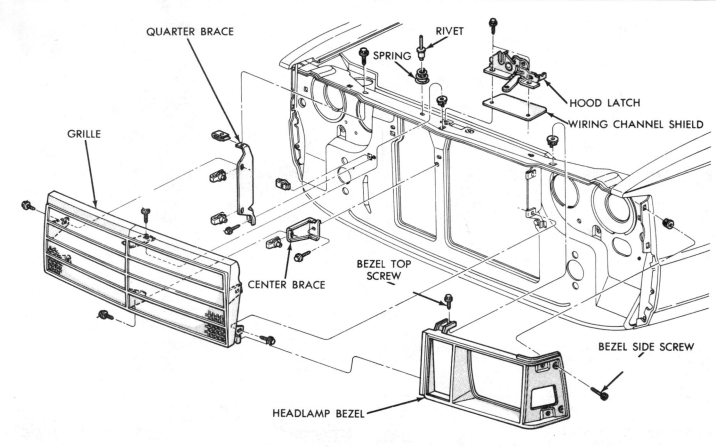

Fig. 12.13 Radiator grille and hood latch component layout (Secs 26 through 29)

29 Hood latch and cable – removal and installation

Latch
1   Disconnect the release cable from the latch, mark the retaining bolt location, remove the bolts and lift the latch away from the radiator brace.
2   To install, place the latch in position and install the bolts in the marked locations. Connect the release cable.

Release cable
3   Release the cable from the latch by pulling the cable toward the latch and lifting the ball end from the slot.
4   Release the cable clips in the engine compartment.
5   Remove the hood release control and then pull the cable through the firewall into the passenger compartment.
6   To install, insert the cable through the firewall and route it to the latch, retaining it with the clips.
7   Install the hood release control.
8   Connect the cable to the latch.

30 Bumper – removal and installation

1   Raise the vehicle and support it securely to provide access to the underside of the bumpers.
2   Remove the six bumper fascia retaining nuts.
3   Mark the location of the bumper-to-energy absorber bolts and remove them (photo).
4   Lift the bumper assembly from the vehicle.
5   To install, place the bumper in position, aligning it with the marks.
6   Make any adjustment to the bumper position prior to installing the fascia nuts. After adjustment, tighten the bumper retaining nuts followed by the fascia nuts.

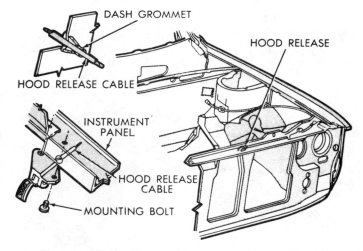

Fig. 12.14 Hood release cable component layout (Sec 29)

31 Bumper energy absorber – removal and installation

1   Remove the bumper assembly (Section 30).
2   Mark their locations and remove the energy absorber-to-chassis retaining bolts.
3   Lift the energy absorber from the vehicle (photo).
4   Installation is the reverse of removal. It is a good idea to lubricate the energy absorber bolts with chassis grease prior to installation.

30.3 After marking their locations, remove the bumper retaining nuts

31.3 Lifting the energy absorber from the vehicle (note the bolt location marking)

33.4 After removing the screw, snap the cluster bezel from the mask

33.5 Pull back sharply on the mask to unsnap it

32 Instrument panel top cover – removal and installation

1   Disconnect the battery negative cable.
2   Remove the trim strip located just beneath the rear edge of the top cover.
3   Remove the attaching screws and remove the cover.
4   To install, place the cover in position on top of the panel and install the attaching screws.
5   Install the trim strip.
6   Connect the battery negative cable.

33 Instrument panel left upper cluster bezel and mask – removal and installation

1   Disconnect the battery negative cable.
2   Remove the panel top cover (Section 32).
3   On automatic transaxle models, place the shift indicator in the l position.
4   Remove the upper and lower cluster bezel screws, snap the bezel off the five retaining clips and remove it (photo).
5   Remove the cluster mask by snapping it from the five retaining clips (photo).

6   To install, place the cluster mask in position over the four clips and press in to snap it into place.
7   Install the top cover and connect the battery negative cable.

34 Lower left trim bezel – removal and installation

1   Disconnect the battery negative cable and remove the instrument panel trim strip.
2   Remove the steering column cover by unsnapping it and pulling it to the rear.
3   Remove the gearshift indicator on automatic transaxle models (Section 35).
4   Remove the two retaining screws and snap the bezel out.
5   Unplug the wire connectors and remove the bezel.
6   To install, plug in the wire connectors, snap the bezel into position and install the retaining screws.
7   Install the gearshift indicator wire (automatic transaxle models).
8   Install the steering column cover and the instrument panel trim strip.
9   Connect the battery negative cable.

12

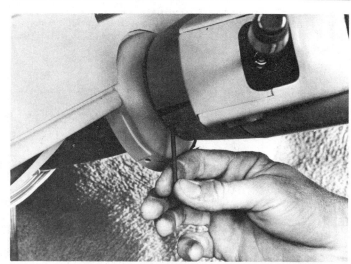

35.3 Loosen the shift indicator wire with an Allen wrench

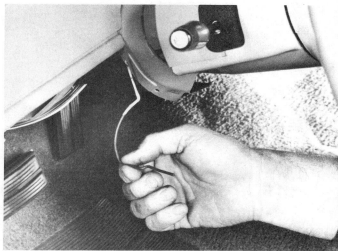

35.4 Pull the indicator wire from the column

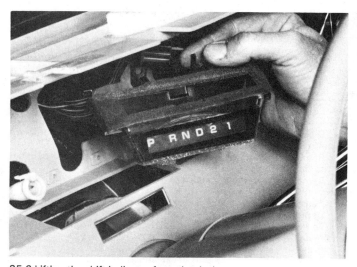

35.6 Lifting the shift indicator from the dash

35 Column gearshift indicator – removal and installation

1   Disconnect the battery negative cable.
2   Remove the steering column cover.
3   Loosen the indicator wire set screw located on the shift housing (photo).
4   Extract the indicator wire from the column (photo).
5   Remove the lower left trim bezel (Section 34).
6   Remove the two indicator-to-panel screws and lift the indicator from the dash (photo).
7   To install, place the shift indicator in position and install the retaining screws.
8   Install the trim bezel.
9   Insert the indicator wire and tighten the retaining screw.
10   Install the steering column cover.
11   Connect the battery cable.

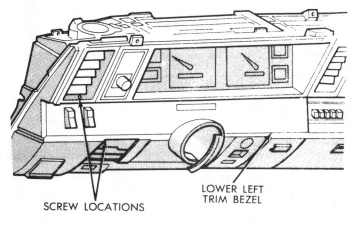

Fig. 12.15 Lower left trim bezel (Secs 34 and 35)

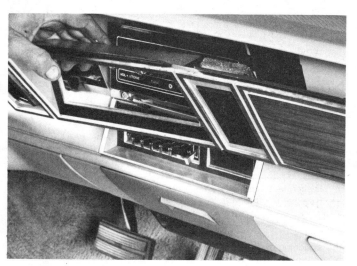

36.3 Pry the bezel loose and rotate it from the dash

36 Right upper trim bezel – removal and installation

1   Disconnect the battery negative cable.
2   Remove the trim strip.
3   Remove the retaining screws and use a screwdriver to carefully pry one edge of the bezel loose so that it can be removed (photo).
4   To install, place the bezel in position and install the retaining screws.
5   Install the trim strip and connect the battery negative cable.

37 Glove compartment – removal and installation

1   Disconnect the battery negative cable.
2   Disconnect the check strap from the glove box by pushing the center pin out of the fastener.
3   Remove the three retaining screws and lower the glove compartment from the dash.
4   To install, place the glove compartment in position, install the retaining screws and connect the check strap.
5   Connect the battery negative cable.

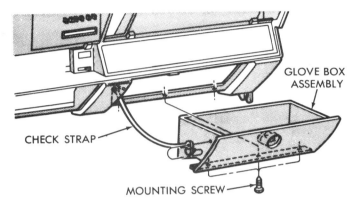

Fig. 12.16 Glove compartment installation (Sec 37)

GLOVE BOX ASSEMBLY

CHECK STRAP

MOUNTING SCREW

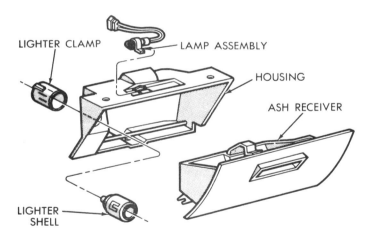

LIGHTER CLAMP   LAMP ASSEMBLY

HOUSING

ASH RECEIVER

LIGHTER SHELL

Fig. 12.17 Ash tray components (Sec 38)

38 Ash tray – removal and installation

1   Disconnect the battery negative cable.
2   Remove the cigar lighter element and pull the ash receiver out.
3   Remove the two upper and one lower housing-to-dash retaining screws.
4   Pull the housing out of the dash.
5   Disconnect the light and cigar lighter wiring harnesses and remove the housing.

6   To install, place the housing at the opening in the dash, connect the wiring harnesses and install the housing and retaining screws.
7   Install the cigar lighter element and ash receiver.
8   Connect the battery negative cable.

39 Instrument panel – removal and installation

1   In order to gain access to components behind the dash, the instrument panel can be unbolted and rolled down to the floor with the speedometer cable and wiring still attached.
2   Disconnect the battery negative cable.
3   Remove the panel top cover (Section 32).
4   Remove the A-pillar and side cowl trim covers.
5   Remove the steering column cover and the under panel sound deadener.
6   Disconnect the parking brake rod.
7   Remove the retaining screw and disengage the shift indicator wire (automatic transaxle column shift).
8   Disengage the column wiring harness from the clip on the steering column.
9   On manual shift models, remove the clutch switch.
10 Remove the three upper and two lower steering column retaining nuts and lower the column.
11 If equipped, remove the console (Section 40).
12 Loosen the panel pivot bolts, remove the four retaining screws and roll the panel down to the floor, taking care not to damage the wiring, speedometer cable and heater control rods.
13 To install, place the instrument panel in position, tighten the pivot bolts and install the attaching screws.
14 Install the console (if equipped).
15 Raise the steering column into position and install the retaining nuts.
16 Install the clutch switch (if equipped) and fasten the column wiring to the column with the clip.
17 Install the automatic transaxle column shift indicator and screw.
18 Install the under panel sound deadener and steering column cover.
19 Install the side cowl and A-pillar trim covers.
20 Install the panel top cover.

40 Console – removal and installation

1   Disconnect the battery negative cable.
2   Remove the shift knob on manual shift models.
3   Remove the fasteners and lift the console from the vehicle.
4   To install, place the console in position and install the fasteners.
5   Install the shift knob.
6   Connect the battery negative cable.

41 Seats – removal and installation

1   Whenever doing extensive work on the interior of the vehicle (such as under the instrument panel), it is a good idea to remove the seats.

Front
2   Remove the four bolts and lift the seat assembly from the vehicle.
3   To install, place the seat in position and install the bolts, tightening them to the specified torque.

Rear
4   Remove the two bolts from the base of the seat bottom and rotate the seat up and out.
5   Remove the two retaining bolts at the bottom of the seat back and disengage the back from the clip. Remove the seat back from the vehicle.
6   To install, place the seat back in position, engage it in the clip and install the retaining bolts. Slide the seat bottom into place and install the retaining bolts.

12

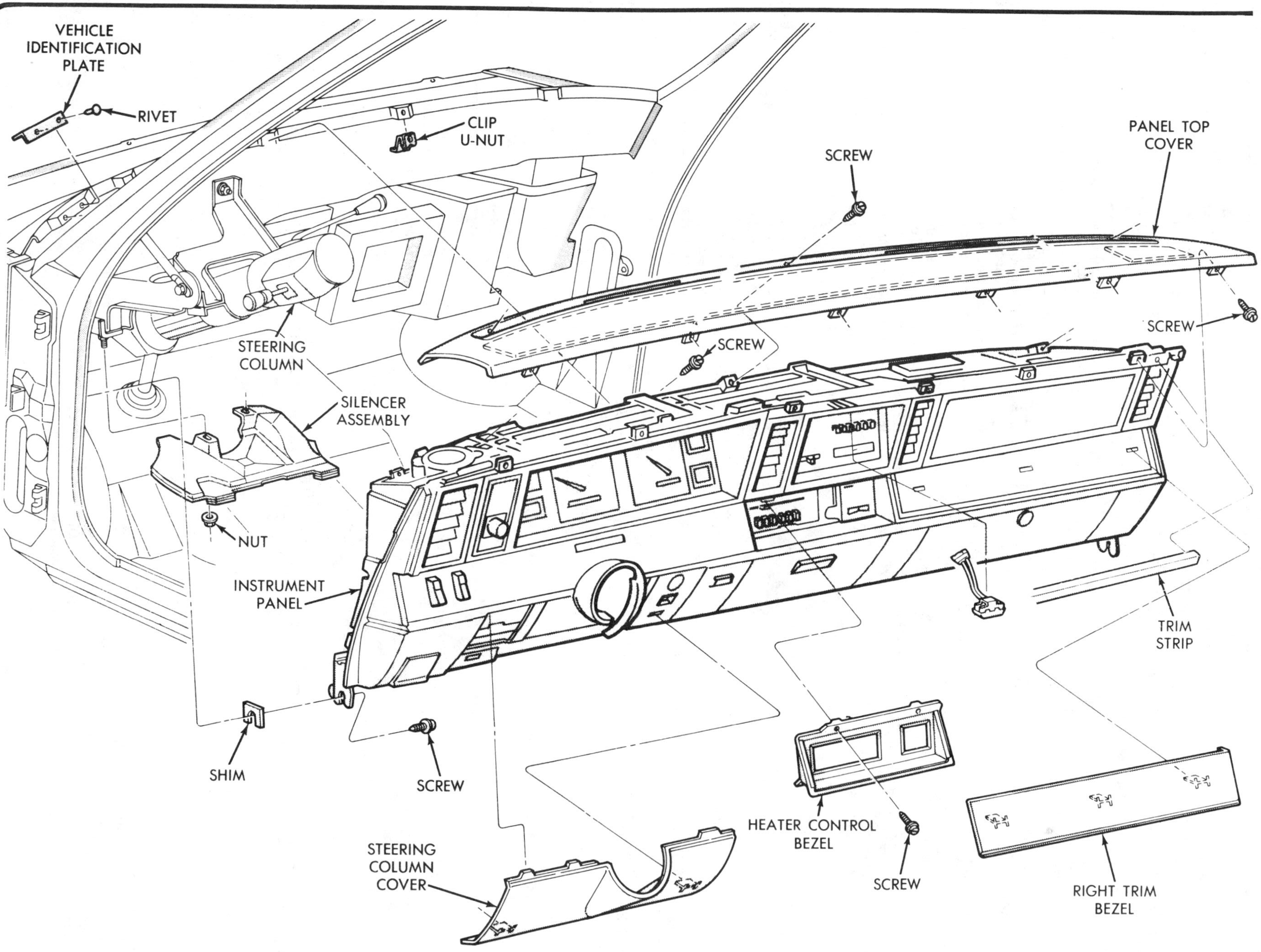

PANEL TOP COVER

SCREW

TRIM STRIP

RIGHT TRIM BEZEL

SCREW

SCREW

SCREW

HEATER CONTROL BEZEL

SCREW

CLIP U-NUT

SCREW

STEERING COLUMN COVER

SILENCER ASSEMBLY

STEERING COLUMN

NUT

INSTRUMENT PANEL

SHIM

VEHICLE IDENTIFICATION PLATE

RIVET

Fig. 12.18 Instrument panel component layout (Sec 39)

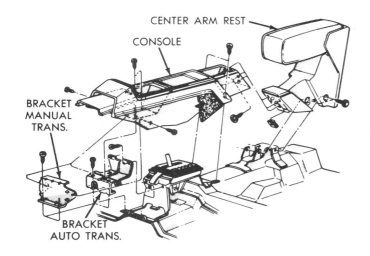

CENTER ARM REST

CONSOLE

BRACKET
MANUAL
TRANS.

BRACKET
AUTO TRANS.

Fig. 12.19 Console installation (Sec 40)

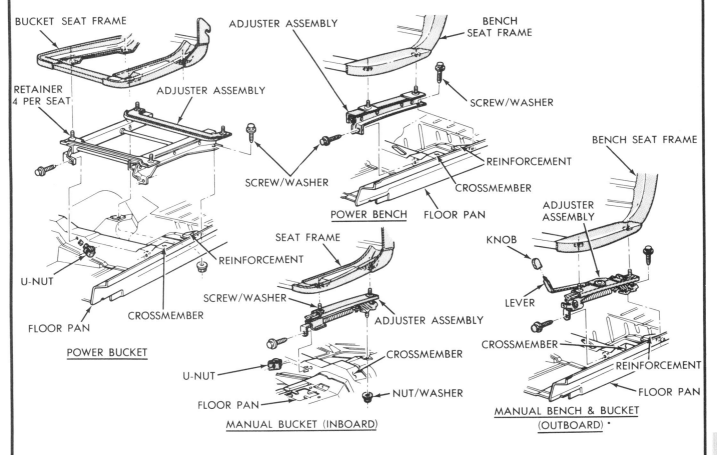

BUCKET SEAT FRAME

ADJUSTER ASSEMBLY

BENCH
SEAT FRAME

RETAINER
4 PER SEAT

ADJUSTER ASSEMBLY

SCREW/WASHER

SCREW/WASHER

BENCH SEAT FRAME

REINFORCEMENT

CROSSMEMBER

ADJUSTER
ASSEMBLY

POWER BENCH

FLOOR PAN

KNOB

U-NUT

REINFORCEMENT

SEAT FRAME

LEVER

FLOOR PAN

CROSSMEMBER

SCREW/WASHER

ADJUSTER ASSEMBLY

CROSSMEMBER

REINFORCEMENT

POWER BUCKET

U-NUT

CROSSMEMBER

NUT/WASHER

FLOOR PAN

FLOOR PAN

MANUAL BUCKET (INBOARD)

MANUAL BENCH & BUCKET
(OUTBOARD) ·

Fig. 12.20 Typical seat installation (Sec 41)

12

Chapter 13 Supplement:
Revisions and information on later models

Contents

1 Introduction

This supplement contains specifications and service procedure changes that apply to 1984 and later Dodge Aries and Plymouth Reliant models produced for sale in the US. Also included is material related to previous models which was not available at the time of the original production of this manual.

Where no differences (or very minor differences) exist between the later models and previous models, no information is given. In such instances, the original material included in Chapters 1 through 12 should be used. Therefore, owners of vehicles manufactured between the above years should refer to this Chapter before using the information in the original Chapters of the manual.

Beginning in 1986, the 2.6L Mitsubishi engine was replaced with a 2.5L engine which is very similar to the 2.2L. The main differences in the 2.5L engine are the stroke measurement (which increased the displacement) and the chain driven counter rotating shafts (to reduce vibration) mounted below the crankshaft. The majority of the engine operations are the same as those in Chapter 2 for the 2.2L engine. Specifications for the 2.2L/2.5L engine which differ from those in Chapter 2 can be found in the appropriate Sections of this supplement.

2 Specifications

The specifications listed here are revised or supplementary to those given at the beginning of each Chapter of this manual. The original specifications apply unless alternative figures are quoted here.

General (2.5L)

Displacement	153 cu in (2.5 liters)
Bore and stroke	3.44 x 4.09 in (87.5 x 104 mm)
Compression ratio	
2.2L	
1984	9:1
1985 on	9.5:1
2.5L	9:1
Compression pressure (2.5L)	100 psi
Maximum variation between cylinders	25%

Engine block
Cylinder bore diameter . . . .   3.44 in (87.5 mm)
Taper limit
  1984 . . . .   0.010 in (0.25 mm)
  1985 on . . . .   0.005 in (0.125 mm)
Out-of-round limit
  1984 . . . .   0.005 in (0.125 mm)
  1985 on . . . .   0.002 in (0.050 mm)

Crankshaft and flywheel
Connecting rod side clearance . . . .   0.005 to 0.013 in (0.13 to 0.32 mm)
Connecting rod bearing oil clearance . . . .   0.0008 to 0.0034 in (0.019 to 0.087 mm)
Service limit . . . .   0.004 in (0.10 mm)

Cylinder head and valve train
Valve spring free length . . . .   2.39 in (60.8 mm)
Valve timing

	Thru 1987	1988 only
2.2L		
Intake valve opens	16° BTDC	0° (TDC)
Intake valve closes	48° ABDC	56° ABDC
Exhaust valve opens	52° BBDC	44° BBDC
Exhaust valve closes	12° ATDC	8° ATDC
2.5L		
Intake valve opens	12° BTDC	4° BTDC
Intake valve closes	52° ABDC	60° ABDC
Exhaust valve opens	48° BBDC	40° BBDC
Exhaust valve closes	16° ATDC	12° ATDC

Oil pump (2.5L)
Outer rotor thickness . . . .   0.944 to 0.946 in (23.97 to 24.00 mm)
Inner rotor-to-outer rotor tip clearance . . . .   0.008 in (0.20 mm)

Torque specifications

	Ft-lbs	Nm
Cylinder head bolts (1986 and later 2.2L and 2.5L*)		
Step 1	45	61
Step 2	65	89
Step 3 (repeat of Step 2)	65	89
Step 4**	1/4 additional turn after reaching the torque specified in Step 3	
Main bearing cap bolt		
Step 1	30	41
Step 2	1/4 additional turn after reaching the torque specified in Step 1	
Connecting rod bearing cap		
Step 1	40	54
Step 2	1/4 additional turn after reaching the torque specified in Step 1	
Engine-to-transaxle bolts	70	95
Flywheel-to-crankshaft bolts		
1984 and 1985	65	88
1986 on	70	95
Oil pan bolt		
8 mm	17	23
6 mm	9	12
Upper and lower timing belt cover screws	3	4
2.5L oil pump strainer-to-cover screw	20	28
2.5L balance shaft carrier		
Front chain cover bolts	9	12
Chain tensioner adjustment bolt	9	12
Chain tensioner pivot bolt	9	12
Chain snubber stud and washer	9	12
Chain snubber nut	9	12
Gear cover bolts	9	12
Gear and sprocket-to-balance shaft bolt	21	28
Sprocket-to-crankshaft (Torx head bolt)	11.1	15
Rear cover bolt	9	12
Carrier-to-block bolt	40	54
Spark plugs (2.5L engine)	26	35

13

*1986 and later models use 11 mm bolts
**On 1986 and later models torque should be 90 Ft-lbs (122 Nm) after Step 4. Replace the bolt with a new one if it is not.

Fuel

2.2L engine choke vacuum adjustment

1984 Carburetor number	Gauge size
R40060-1A	0.055 in (1.35 mm)
R40085-1A	0.040 in (1.05 mm)
R40170A	0.060 in (1.55 mm)
R40171A	0.060 in (1.55 mm)
R40067A	0.070 in (1.80 mm)
R40068-1A	0.070 in (1.80 mm)
R40058-1A	0.070 in (1.80 mm)
R40107-1A	0.055 in (1.35 mm)
R40064-1A	0.080 in (2.0 mm)
R40081-1A	0.080 in (2.0 mm)
R40082-1A	0.080 in (2.0 mm)
R40071A	0.080 in (2.0 mm)
R40122A	0.080 in (2.0 mm)
1985 carburetor number	
R40058A	0.070 in (1.8 mm)
R40060A	0.055 in (1.4 mm)
R40116A	0.095 in (2.4 mm)
R40117A	0.095 in (2.4 mm)
R40134A	0.075 in (1.9 mm)
R40135A	0.075 in (1.9 mm)
R40138A	0.075 in (1.9 mm)
R40139A	0.075 in (1.9 mm)

Torque specifications	Ft-lbs	Nm
EFI Automatic Idle Speed (AIS) Torx screw	20 in-lb	2
EFI throttle body-to-manifold screws	17	23
EFI hose clamp screws	10 in-lb	1
EFI pressure regulator screw	4	5
EFI Throttle position sensor screw	20 in-lb	2
Fuel injector Torx screw	4	5
Fuel filter screw	6	8

Emission control systems

Torque specifications	Ft-lbs	Nm
Air aspirator system		
tube nut	30	40
tube bolt	50	68
bracket bolt	8	11

Manual transaxle

Fluid type (1987 on) .... SAE 5W-30 engine oil

Torque specifications	Ft-lbs	Nm
Cable-type selector adjusting screw	4.4	6
Cable-type selector crossover adjusting screw	4.4	6

Suspension and steering systems

Torque specifications	Ft-lbs	Nm
Front suspension strut-to-steering knuckle nut		
Step 1	75	100
Step 2	turn nut an additional 1/4 turn	

---

3 Routine maintenance

Maintenance schedule (EFI) equipped models

Every 52,000 miles (84,000 km)
  Replace the air cleaner filter element
  Replace the fuel filter

Air cleaner filter element replacement

1 Remove the clamp securing the connecting hose between the air cleaner and the fuel injection throttle body. Release the four air cleaner clips, pull the hose off the throttle body and lift the cover and hose from the bottom of the housing. Lift the air filter element out of the housing.
2 To install, place the element, with the screen facing up, into the air filter housing.

3 Loosely install the clamp and then push the hose onto the throttle body.
4 Align the upper and lower halves of the air cleaner and connect the clips.
5 Tighten the clamp around the hose at the throttle body securely.

Fuel filter replacement

6 Depressurize the fuel system (Section 5).
7 Remove the mounting screw and disconnect the filter from the bracket.
8 Loosen the filter inlet and outlet clamps.
9 Wrap a cloth around the fuel filter to catch the residual fuel, disconnect the hoses and remove the filter from the vehicle.
10 Place the new filter in position and install the hoses, using new clamps. Install the filter on the bracket and tighten the mounting screw securely.

4 Engine

General information

1   Most engine operations involving the 2.5L engine introduced in 1986 are the same as for the 2.2L engine described in Chapter 2. The major engine disassembly and reassembly procedural changes for the 2.5L engine are involved with the balance shaft and carrier assembly. The balance shaft assembly is designed to counterbalance vibration caused by the engine reciprocating masses. Later 2.2L and 2.5L engines use cylinder head and connecting rod bolts of a different design (see below and Specifications).

Connecting rod bolt check (2.2/2.5L)

2   The bolts used on 1984 and later models are different than earlier models and require a different tightening procedure (see the Specifications).

3   Check the bolts to make sure they are not ''necked down'' (stretched) before installation by running a 3/8 in x 24 nut all the way down the threads. If the nut does not run down the threads smoothly, replace the bolts with new ones.

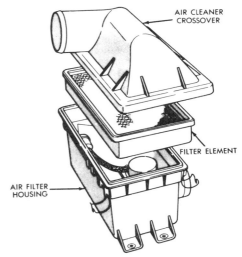

Fig. 13.1   EFI air cleaner — exploded view (Sec 3)

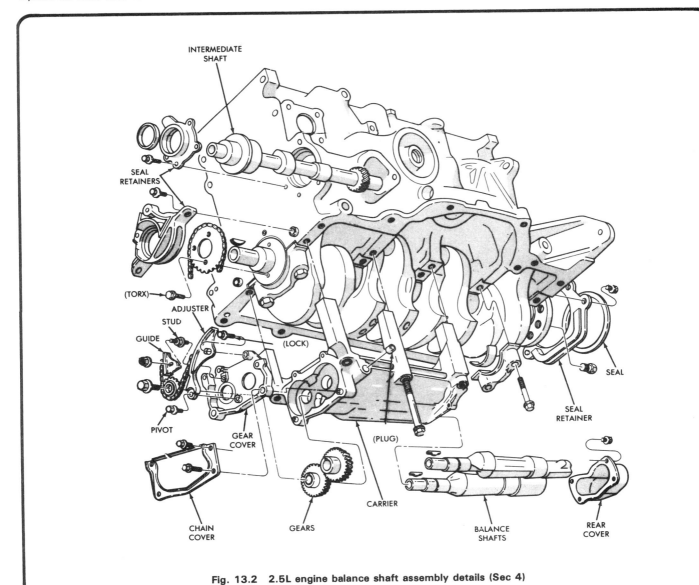

Fig. 13.2   2.5L engine balance shaft assembly details (Sec 4)

13

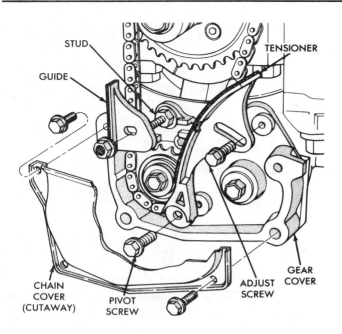

Fig. 13.3   2.5L engine balance shaft assembly chain cover, guide and tensioner component layout (Sec 4)

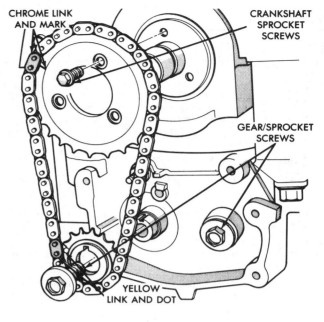

Fig. 13.4   2.5L engine balance shaft assembly drive chain and sprocket installation details (Sec 4)

Cylinder head bolts

4   1986 and later models use 11 mm cylinder head bolts (noted by "11" on the bolt head) instead of the 10 mm bolts used on earlier models. They require a different torque tightening procedure (see Specifications). The smaller bolts should not be used, as they will thread into the larger bolt hole but will strip.

Balance shaft assembly — description, removal and installation

5   The balance shaft assembly consists of two counter rotating shafts connected by gears and mounted in a carrier located below the crankshaft. The shafts are driven by a chain connected to the crankshaft at twice crankshaft speed.
6   Remove the oil pan, oil pickup, timing belt cover, crankshaft belt sprocket and front oil seal retainer as described in Chapter 2.
7   Remove the balance shaft assembly chain cover, guide and tensioner as shown in the accompanying illustration.
8   Remove the Torx head screws retaining the balance shaft gear and chain sprocket and remove the chain and sprockets as an assembly.
9   Remove the double ended balance shaft drive gear cover retaining stud and remove the cover and gears.
10 Unbolt and remove the rear cover and slide the balance shafts out of the carrier.
11 Remove the six retaining bolts and separate the carrier from the crankcase.
12 Installation is the reverse of removal.

Balance shaft carrier assembly — removal and installation

13 The carrier can be removed as an assembly with the gear cover, gears, balance shafts and rear cover intact.
14 Remove the chain cover, followed by the screw from the balance shaft driven gear.
15 Loosen the tensioner pivot and adjusting screws and push the driven balance shaft inboard and through the driven chain sprocket so the sprocket is hanging in the lower chain loop.
16 Remove the retaining bolts and lower the carrier assembly from the crankcase.
17 Installation is the reverse of removal except that the crankshaft-to-balancer shaft timing must be established as described below.

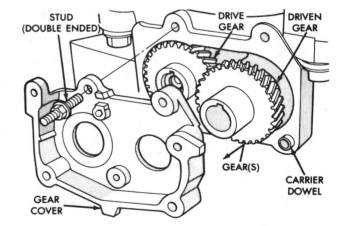

Fig. 13.5   Balance shaft cover and gear removal details (Sec 4)

Balance shaft timing

18 With the balance shafts installed in the carrier, place the carrier in position on the crankcase and install the bolts.
19 Rotate balance shafts until both keyways face up in line with the centerline of the engine block and install the gears. The short hub drive gear goes on the sprocket driven shaft and the long hub gear goes on the gear driven shaft. After installation the alignment dots must be directly opposite each other as shown in the accompanying illustration.
20 Install the gear cover and tighten the chain snubber stud to the specified torque.
21 Install the crankshaft sprocket and tighten the Torx head screws to the specified torque.
22 Rotate the crankshaft until the number one piston is at Top Dead Center (TDC). The timing marks on the chain sprocket should now be aligned with the parting line on the left side of the number one main bearing cap.
23 Place the timing chain over the crankshaft sprocket so that the

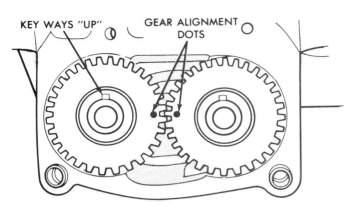

Fig. 13.6 The balance shaft gear alignment dots must be directly opposite each other when the keyways are in the up (vertical) position (Sec 4)

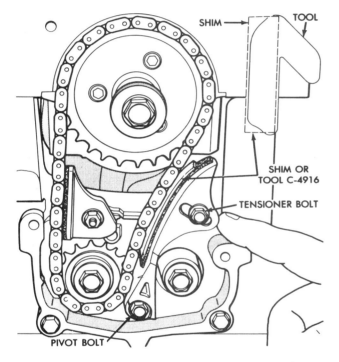

Fig. 13.8 Adjusting the balance shaft chain tension (Sec 4)

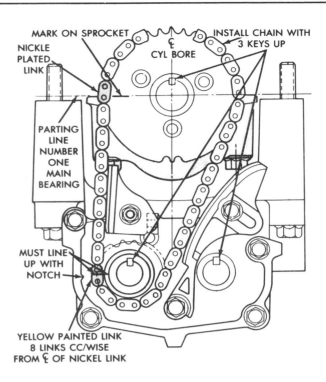

Fig. 13.7 The balance shaft chain must be installed as shown for correct crankshaft-to-balancer shaft timing (Sec 4)

2.75 in (70 mm) long or factory tool number C-4916 between the tensioner and the chain.

29 Push the tensioner and shim or tool up against the chain. Mainain pressure by pressing the tensioner directly behind the adjustment slot so that all slack is taken up as shown in the accompanying illustration.

30 With the tension maintained, tighten first the top and then the bottom tensioner bolts to the specified torque and then remove the shim.

31 Place the guide in position on the double ended stud, making sure the tab on the guide fits into the slot on the gear cover. Install the nut and washer and tighten to the specified torque.

32 Install the balance shaft assembly covers and tighen the screws to the specified torque.

5 Fuel and exhaust systems

1 Later carbureted models differ slightly from those covered in Chapter 4. Some later Mikuni carburetors used on 2.6L engines are of the feedback type, similar in operation to the feedback system used on some 2.2L engines. Starting in 1986, carburetors on all models were replaced by Electronic Fuel Injection (EFI).

Mikuni feedback carburetor (1984 and 1985) — idle speed adjustment

2 With the transaxle in Neutral, the parking brake set, the lights and accessories off, disconnect the cooling fan and connect a tachometer.

3 Start the engine, run it until normal operating temperature is reached and then turn it off.

4 Disconnect the negative battery cable for three seconds, then reconnect it.

5 Unplug the engine harness from the oxygen sensor bullet-type connector located approximately four inches from the sensor. Do not pull on the wire where it is attached to the sensor itself. **Warning:** *Be very careful working in this area as the exhaust manifold is very hot and could cause burns.*

6 Start the engine and open the throttle, allowing the engine to run at 2500 rpm for ten seconds before returning it to idle.

7 Wait two minutes with the curb idle speed stabilized, then check the rpm on the tachometer. If it is not as specified on the VECI label,

13

nickel plated (bright) link is over the timing mark on the crankshaft sprocket as shown in the accompanying illustration.

24 Place the balance shaft sprocket in position in the timing chain, making sure the yellow timing mark on the sprocket mates with the yellow painted link on the chain.

25 Make sure the balance shaft keyways are pointing straight up and slide the balance shaft sprocket onto the nose of the balance shaft. It may be necessary to push the balance shaft in slightly to obtain sufficient clearance. At this point the timing mark on the sprocket and the arrow on the side of the gear cover must be aligned if the balance shafts are timed correctly.

26 Install the balance shaft bolts. Place a wood block between the crankshaft counterbalance and the crankcase to keep the crankshaft and gear from rotating and tighten the bolts to the specified torque.

Balance shaft chain tensioning

27 Install the chain tensioner assembly with the bolts finger tight.

28 Place a piece of shim stock measuring 0.039 in (1 mm) thick and

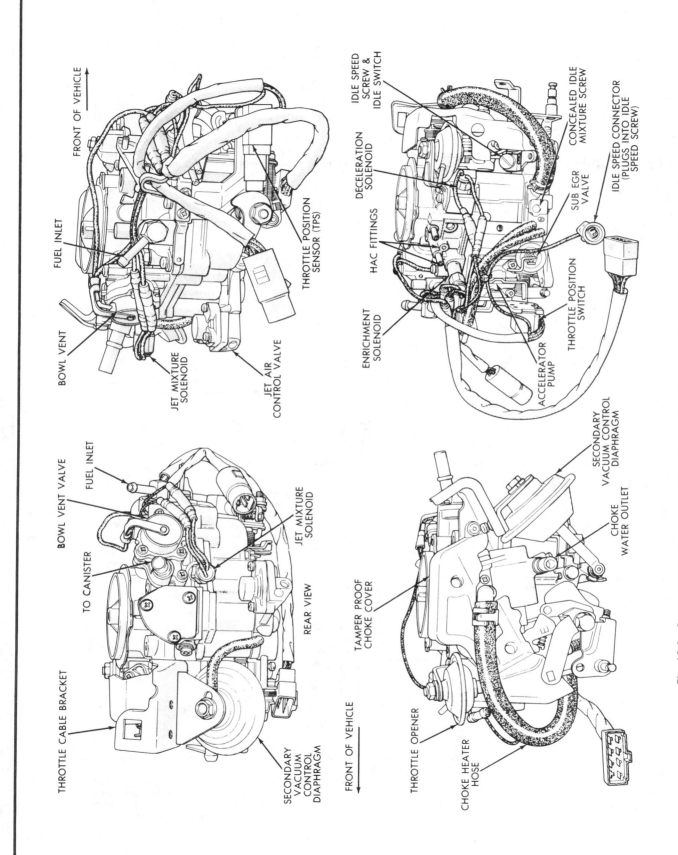

Fig. 13.9 Component locations on the Mikuni feedback carburetor used on some 1984 and 1985 models

FRONT OF VEHICLE

FUEL INLET

THROTTLE POSITION SENSOR (TPS)

BOWL VENT

JET MIXTURE SOLENOID

JET AIR CONTROL VALVE

IDLE SPEED SCREW & IDLE SWITCH

CONCEALED IDLE MIXTURE SCREW

DECELERATION SOLENOID

HAC FITTINGS

SUB EGR VALVE

IDLE SPEED CONNECTOR (PLUGS INTO IDLE SPEED SCREW)

ENRICHMENT SOLENOID

ACCELERATOR PUMP

THROTTLE POSITION SWITCH

BOWL VENT VALVE

FUEL INLET

TO CANISTER

JET MIXTURE SOLENOID

THROTTLE CABLE BRACKET

REAR VIEW

SECONDARY VACUUM CONTROL DIAPHRAGM

FRONT OF VEHICLE

SECONDARY VACUUM CONTROL DIAPHRAGM

TAMPER PROOF CHOKE COVER

CHOKE WATER OUTLET

THROTTLE OPENER

CHOKE HEATER HOSE

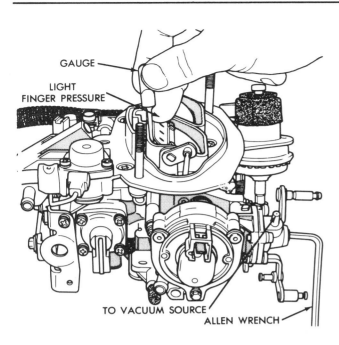

Fig. 13.10 Choke vacuum kick adjustment (2.2L engine, 1984 and later models) (Sec 5)

turn the idle speed adjusting screw to attain the proper curb idle speed setting.

8   Unplug the idle switch connector and turn off the engine.

9   Reconnect the oxygen sensor to the engine wiring harness.

10 On air conditioning equipped models, set the temperature to the coldest temperature and, with the compressor running, adjust the idle speed to the specified rpm by turning the idle-up adjustment screw.

11 Shut off the engine, connect the cooling fan, disconnect the tachometer and reconnect the idle switch connector.

Choke vacuum kick adjustment (1984 and later 2.2L engine)

12 This procedure is the same as that described in Chapter 4, except that the gauge or drill is inserted in the center of the area between the top of the choke plate and the air horn as shown in the accompanying illustration.

Electronic Fuel injection (EFI) — description and checking

Warning: *The EFI system is under considerable pressure, so always replace any clamp which is removed or released with a new one.*

13 The EFI system used through 1987 consists of a throttle body mounted on the intake manifold, which houses the fuel injector, pressure regulator, Throttle Position Sensor (TPS), Automatic Idle Speed (AIS) motor and throttle body temperature sensor, all of which interact with the power module (replacing the Spark Control Computer [SCC] used on earlier models) and the logic module. The system used on 1988 models has a single module engine controller (SMEC), which handles the functions of the power and logic modules. In addition an auto shut down relay, mounted behind the SMEC, interrupts power to the fuel pump, injector and ignition coil when there is no ignition

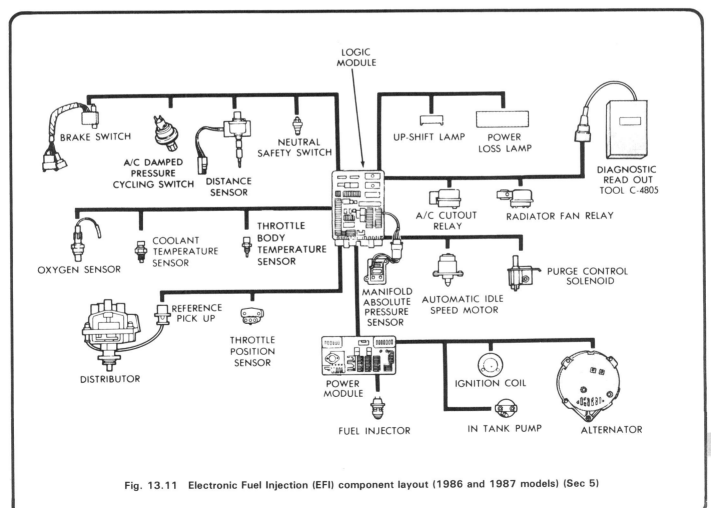

Fig. 13.11 Electronic Fuel Injection (EFI) component layout (1986 and 1987 models) (Sec 5)

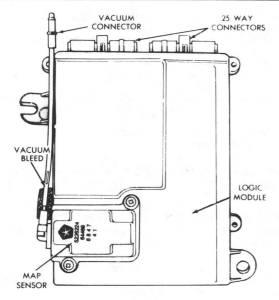

Fig. 13.12   EFI system logic module (Sec 5)

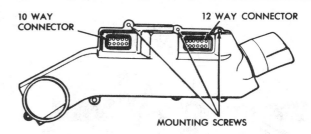

Fig. 13.13   EFI system power module (Sec 5)

module/SMEC can operate the EFI system are the Manifold Absolute Pressure (MAP) sensor, oxygen sensor and the coolant temperature sensor. The MAP sensor is located on the logic module and is connected to the throttle body by a vacuum line. It monitors the manifold vacuum. The oxygen sensor (located in the exhaust manifold) provides information on the exhaust gas makeup and the temperature sensor (threaded into the thermostat housing) monitors engine operating temperature.

16   Because the EFI system is controlled by the logic module and power module or SMEC in combination with a variety of sensors and switches, the home mechanic can do very little in the way of diagnosis without a factory Diagnosic Read Out Tool (number C-4805) or equivalent. Consequently, checking should be confined to inspection and checking of all electrical and vacuum connections to make sure they are secure and not obviously damaged.

17   The logic module/SMEC is self-testing and a problem in the system will be indicated by the power loss lamp on the dash. The power loss lamp will light when there is electrical system voltage fluctuation or a fault in the MAP, throttle position or coolant temperature sensor circuits. If the fault is severe enough to affect driveability, the logic module will go into a ''Limp-In'' mode so the vehicle can still be driven.

18   The logic module/SMEC stores trouble codes, which can be checked using the power loss lamp. Within a five second period, turn the ignition key On-Off-On-Off-On. The power loss lamp will then flash

signal present with the key in the Run position.

14   The logic module, located in the passenger compartment behind the right kick panel, is a digital computer containing a microprocessor. The module receives input signals from the sensors and switches which monitor the engine and then determines the fuel injector operation as well as the spark advance, ignition coil dwell, idle speed, canister purge solenoid, cooling fan operation and alternator charge rate. The electric fuel pump, which delivers fuel to the injectors and maintains pressure in the system, is located in the fuel tank.

15   Three components which provide basic information so the logic

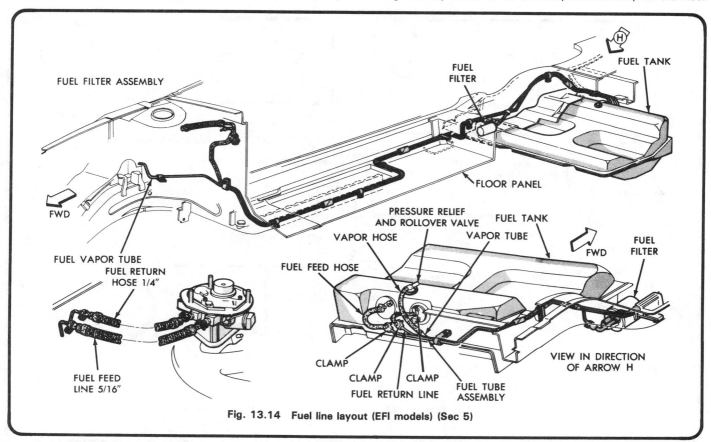

Fig. 13.14   Fuel line layout (EFI models) (Sec 5)

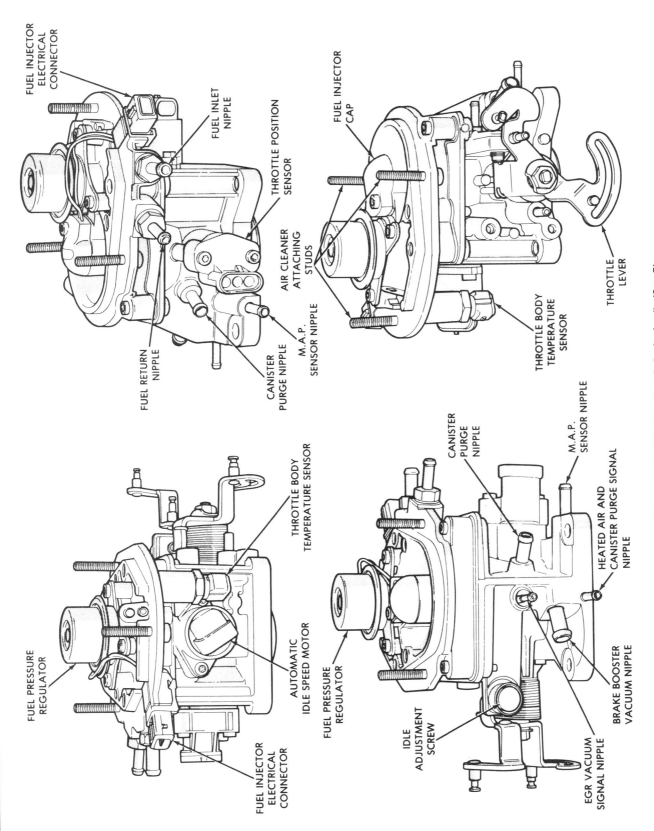

FUEL INJECTOR
ELECTRICAL
CONNECTOR

FUEL INLET NIPPLE

THROTTLE POSITION SENSOR

AIR CLEANER ATTACHING STUDS

M.A.P. SENSOR NIPPLE

CANISTER PURGE NIPPLE

FUEL RETURN NIPPLE

FUEL INJECTOR CAP

THROTTLE BODY TEMPERATURE SENSOR

THROTTLE LEVER

FUEL PRESSURE REGULATOR

THROTTLE BODY TEMPERATURE SENSOR

AUTOMATIC IDLE SPEED MOTOR

FUEL INJECTOR ELECTRICAL CONNECTOR

FUEL PRESSURE REGULATOR

IDLE ADJUSTMENT SCREW

EGR VACUUM SIGNAL NIPPLE

BRAKE BOOSTER VACUUM NIPPLE

HEATED AIR AND CANISTER PURGE SIGNAL NIPPLE

M.A.P. SENSOR NIPPLE

CANISTER PURGE NIPPLE

Fig. 13.15 Electronic Fuel Injection throttle body details (Sec 5)

13

fault codes indicating the area of the fault. The codes are two digit numbers and the Start of Test (88), for example, will be indicated by eight flashes, a pause and eight more flashes. If there is more than one code, the lamp will flash them in order, ending with the end of message (55) code. Because the fault codes indicate the location of a fault, simply checking and tightening a vacuum hose or electrical connector can often correct a problem. Any further checking of fault codes should be left to a dealer or properly equipped shop.

Fault codes

88	Start of test
11	Engine not cranked since battery disconnected
12	Memory standby power lost
13 *	MAP sensor pneumatic circuit
14 *	MAP sensor electrical circuit
15	Vehicle speed/distance sensor circuit
16 *	Loss of battery voltage sensor
17	Engine running too cold
21	Oxygen sensor circuit
22 *	Coolant sensor circuit
23	Throttle body temperature circuit
24 *	Throttle position circuit
25	Automatic Idle Speed (AIS) motor driver circuit
26	Peak injector circuit has not been reached
27	Logic Module fuel circuit internal problem
31	Purge solenoid circuit
33	Air conditioning cutout relay circuit
35	Cooling fan relay circuit
37	Shift indicator light circuit
41	Charging system excess or lack of field current
42	Automatic shutdown relay driver circuit
43	Spark interface circuit
44	Battery temperature out of range
46 *	Battery voltage too high
47	Battery voltage too low
51	Oxygen sensor stuck at lean position
52	Oxygen sensor stuck at rich position
53	Logic Module internal problem
55	End of message

* *Activates Power Loss lamp*

Fuel injection system depressurization

19 **Warning:** *The fuel system of fuel injected models is pressurized, even when the engine is off. Consequently any time the fuel system is worked on (such as when the fuel filter is replaced) the system must be depressurized to avoid the spraying of fuel when a component is disconnected.*
20 Loosen the fuel tank cap to release any pressure in the tank.
21 Unplug the harness connector at the fuel injector.
22 Ground one of the injector terminals and connect a jumper wire to the other terminal. Touch the other end of the jumper wire to the positive (+) post of the battery for no longer than five seconds to depressurize the fuel system. Do not ground the injector terminal for more than five seconds to avoid damage to the fuel injector. It is recommended that the pressure be bled in several spurts of one to two seconds to make sure the injector system is not damaged.

EFI throttle cable — removal and installation

23 Inside the vehicle, disconnect the throttle cable from the pedal shaft (Chapter 4).
24 In the engine compartment, pull the cable housing end fitting out of the firewall grommet, making sure the grommet remains in place.
25 Remove the retainer clip and disconnect the cable from the throttle body. Use pliers to compress the end fitting tabs so the cable mounting bracket can then be separated.
26 To install, insert the cable housing into the cable mounting bracket on the engine and attach the cable clevis to the throttle body with the retainer clip. Insert the cable through the firewall grommet and connect it to the throttle pedal.

EFI fuel pump replacement

27 Remove the fuel tank (Chapter 4).
28 Use a hammer and a brass punch to remove the fuel pump lock-

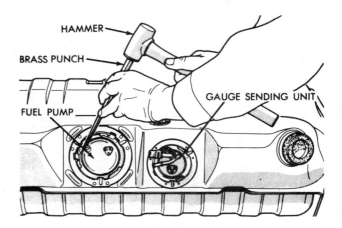

Fig. 13.16 Removing the fuel pump from the tank with a hammer and brass drift (Sec 5)

ing ring by driving it in a counterclockwise direction until it can be unscrewed.
29 Lift the fuel pump and O-ring from the fuel tank. Clean the sealing area of the fuel tank and install a new O-ring on the fuel pump. Prior to installation, inspect the sock-like filter on the fuel pump suction tube for damage or contamination, replacing it with a new one if necessary.
30 Place the fuel pump in position in the tank, install the locking ring and use the hammer and brass drift to lock the pump in place.
31 Install the fuel tank.

6 Engine electrical systems

General information

1 On 1986 and 1987 EFI engines the Spark Control Computer (SCC) is replaced by the power module, which is very similar in appearance. On 1988 SPFI engines, the logic and power modules were replaced by the single module engine controller (SMEC). Installation and removal are also very similar, but the SCC/SMEC and ignition system must, for the most part, be checked using special equipment and should be left to a dealer or properly equipped shop.

Ignition timing adjustment (EFI models)

2 Connect a timing light to the number one cylinder according to the manufacturers' instructions.
3 Connect a tachometer to the engine.
4 Start the engine and run it until normal operating temperature is reached.
5 Disconnect and then reconnect the water temperature sensor (located on the thermostat housing) connector. The Power Loss lamp should light up and stay lit and the engine speed should now be 1000 rpm.
6 Aim the timing light at the timing hole in the bellhousing to check the timing and adjust as necessary as described in Chapter 1.
7 Turn the engine off and disconnect and reconnect the positive battery cable quick disconnect. Start the vehicle and verify that the Power Loss lamp is off.
8 Shut the engine off and and check the failure codes with the Power Loss lamp as described in Section 5.

7 Emissions control systems

General information

1 The emission control systems used on 1984 and 1985 models are virtually the same as earlier models. Starting in 1986 all models are equipped with Electronic Fuel Injection (EFI) (Section 5). The operation of the EFI places the control of virtually every component having to do with the engine and to some degree the electrical system under the logic module and the power module microprocessors. Conse-

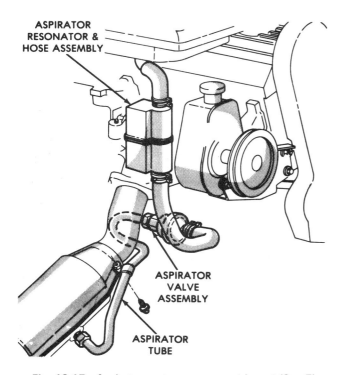

Fig. 13.17 Aspirator system component layout (Sec 7)

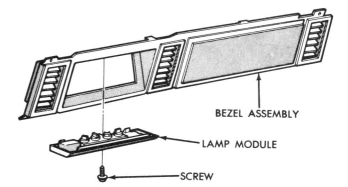

Fig. 13.18 Indicator lamp module installation details (Sec 8)

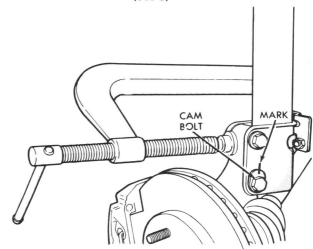

Fig. 13.19 On 1984 and later models the cam bolt is the lower steering knuckle bolt (Sec 9)

quently, checking the emission systems is limited to visual inspection for loose or damaged hoses or components. The simpler systems, such as the EGR, PCV, heated air inlet and the EFI air aspirator systems, can be checked as described in Chapter 6 and this Section.

Air aspirator system

2   This system uses exhaust pulsations to draw air from the air cleaner into the exhaust system at idle and lower engine speeds to reduce carbon monoxide and hydrocarbon emissions. The system consists of a valve, hoses and tubes between the air cleaner and the exhaust system.
3   Symptoms of a failed aspirator valve are excessive exhaust noise under the hood at idle speeds and hardening of the rubber hose between the valve and the air cleaner.
4   Check the along the length of the hose and tube assembly for loose connections. If the tube-to-exhaust manifold joint is leaking, tighten the aspirator tube connections securely. If the hose connections are leaking and the hose has not hardened, replace the clamps with new ones. If the hose has hardened, replace it with a new one as well.
5   To check the aspirator valve, disconnect the hose from the aspirator inlet. With the engine idling in Neutral, vacuum can be felt at the inlet if the valve is operating properly. If hot exhaust gas escapes from the inlet, the valve has failed and should be replaced with a new one.
6   To replace the valve, disconnect the air hose and remove the tube assembly.
7   Install the new valve and tighten the aspirator tube nut to the specified torque. Install the bracket bolt and tighten to the specified torque.
8   Connect the air hose to the valve inlet and the air cleaner.

Lock-up torque converter

9   A lock-up torque converter, used on vehicles with a 2.5L engine, was installed in 1987 and later model vehicles. The lock-up mode is activated only in direct drive and is controlled by the engine electronics. A solenoid on the transaxle valve body is activated by the SMEC to select torque converter lock-up.

---

8   Chassis electrical system

Indicator lamp module — removal and installation

1   On 1984 and later models an indicator lamp module mounted above the instrument cluster is used, making bulb replacement easier.
2   Remove the retaining screw, lower the lamp module and unplug the connector.
3   The bulbs can now be replaced.
4   Installation is the reverse of removal.

Wiring diagrams

Electrical wiring diagrams for later models are included at the end of this Chapter. If a particular circuit is not shown here, it can be assumed that the wiring has not changed from earlier models

---

9   Suspension and steering system

Front strut and spring assembly — removal and installation

1   On 1984 and later models the front suspension strut torque tightening procedure is different and the cam bolt is located in the lower steering knuckle bolt hole instead of the upper one.

13

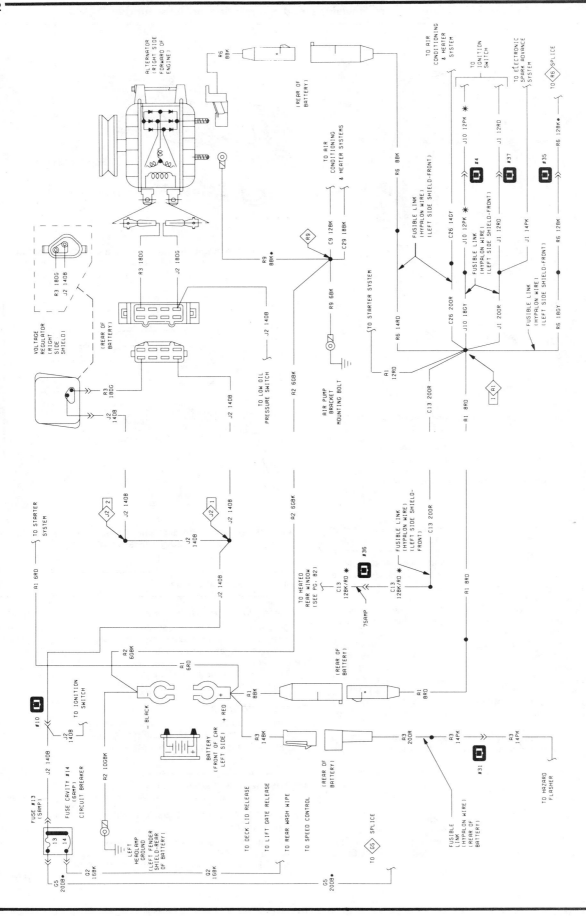

Fig. 13.21 Charging system (2.2L) wiring diagram (1984 models — 1985 similar)

Fig. 13.20 Charging system (2.2L) wiring diagram (1984 models — 1985 similar)

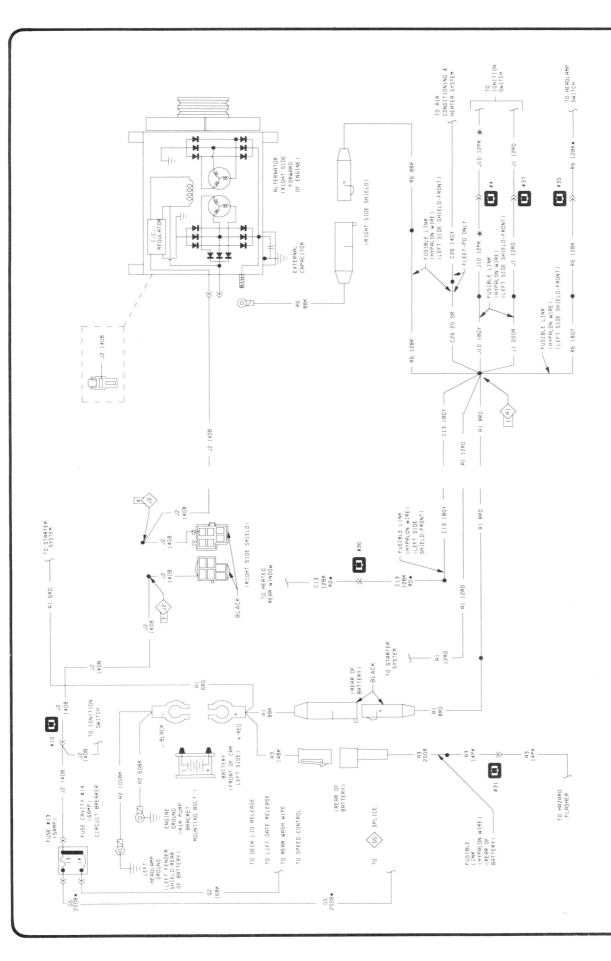

Fig. 13.22 Charging system (2.6L non-feedback) wiring diagram
(1984 models)

Fig. 13.23 Charging system (2.6L non-feedback) wiring diagram cont.
(1984 models)

13

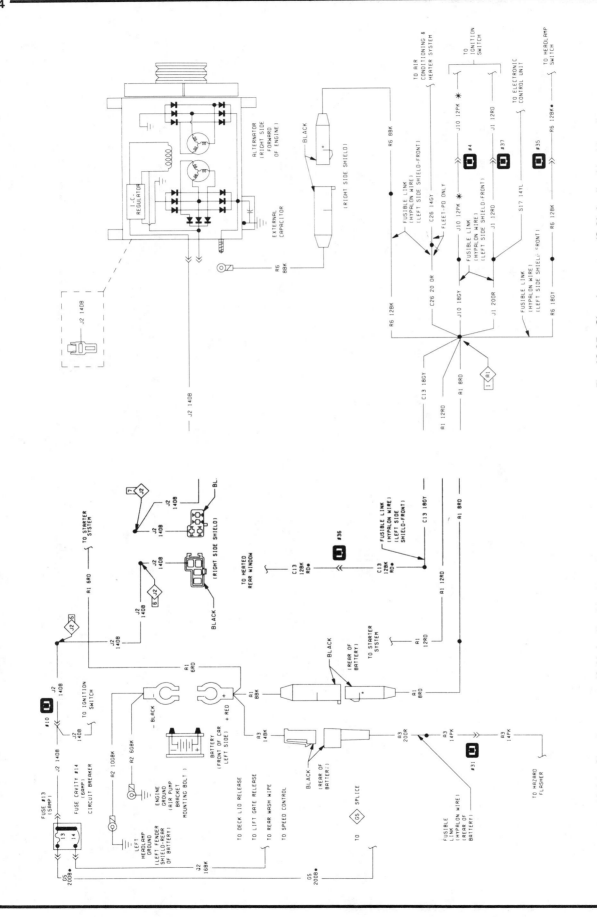

Fig. 13.25 Charging system (2.6L feedback) wiring diagram cont. (1984 models)

Fig. 13.24 Charging system (2.6L feedback) wiring diagram (1984 models — 1985 similar)

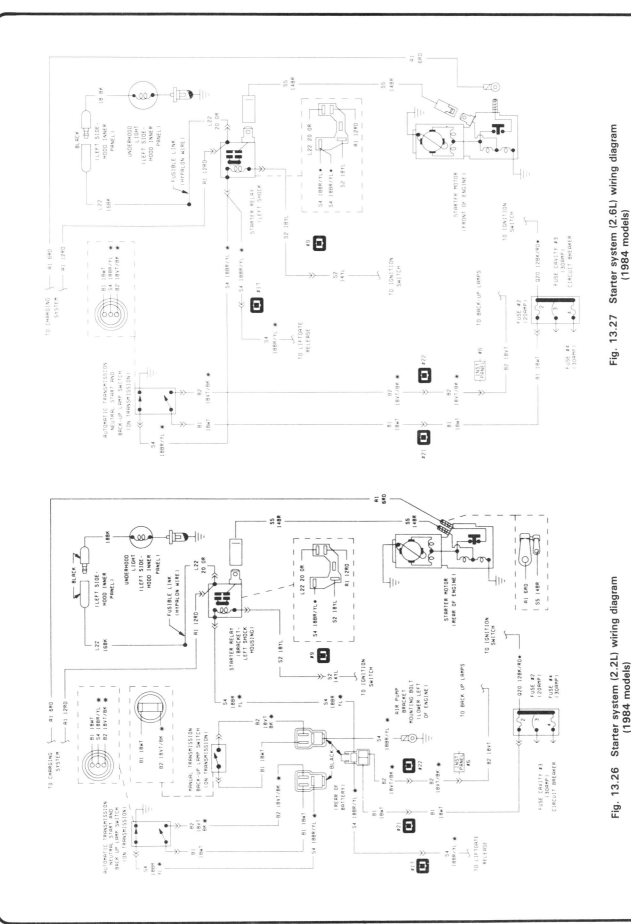

Fig. 13.27 Starter system (2.6L) wiring diagram (1984 models)

Fig. 13.26 Starter system (2.2L) wiring diagram (1984 models)

13

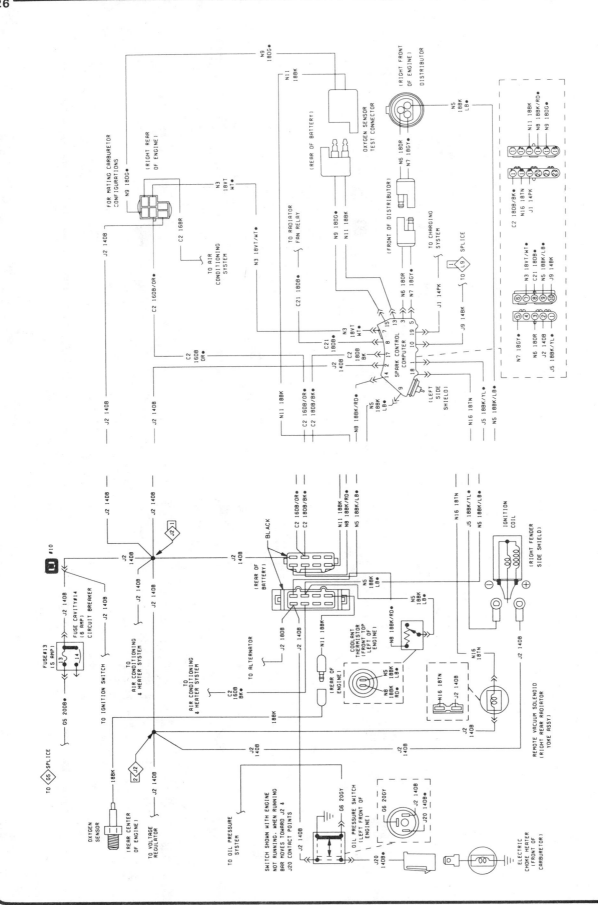

Fig. 13.29 Electronic spark advance system (2.2L) wiring diagram cont. (1984 models)

Fig. 13.28 Electronic spark advance system (2.2L) wiring diagram (1984 models)

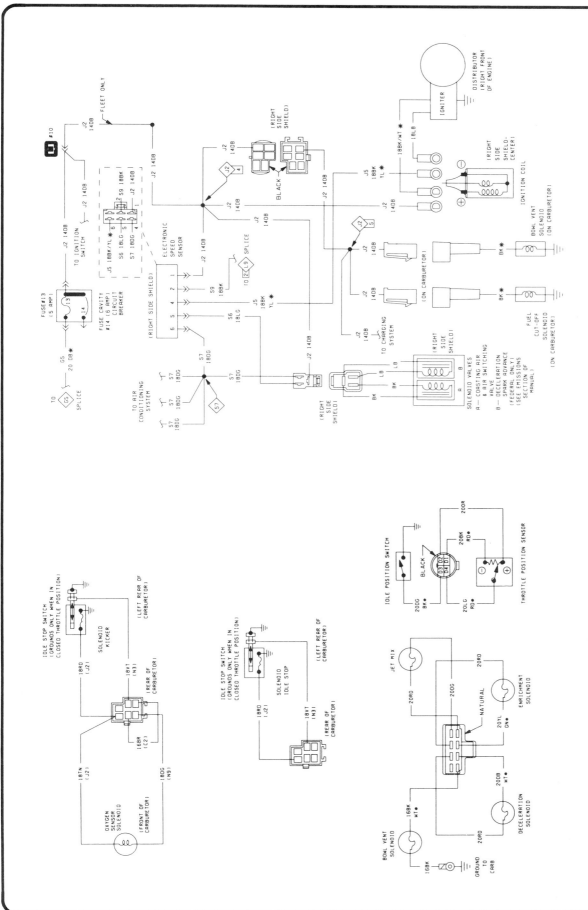

Fig. 13.31 Electronic ignition system (2.6L non-feedback) wiring diagram (1984 models)

Fig. 13.30 Carburetor wiring diagram (1984 models)

13

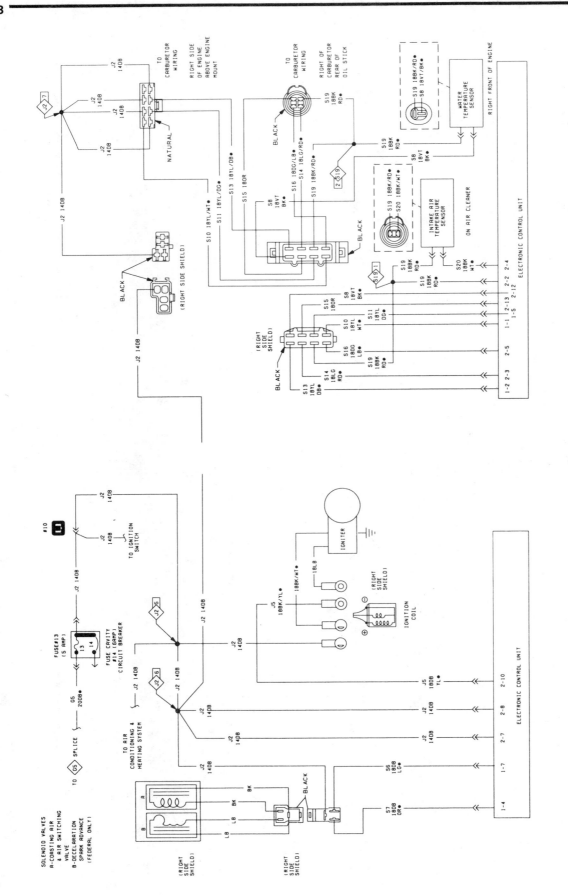

Fig. 13.33   Electronic ignition system (2.6L feedback) wiring diagram
cont. (1984 models)

Fig. 13.32   Electronic ignition system (2.6L feedback) wiring diagram
(1984 models)

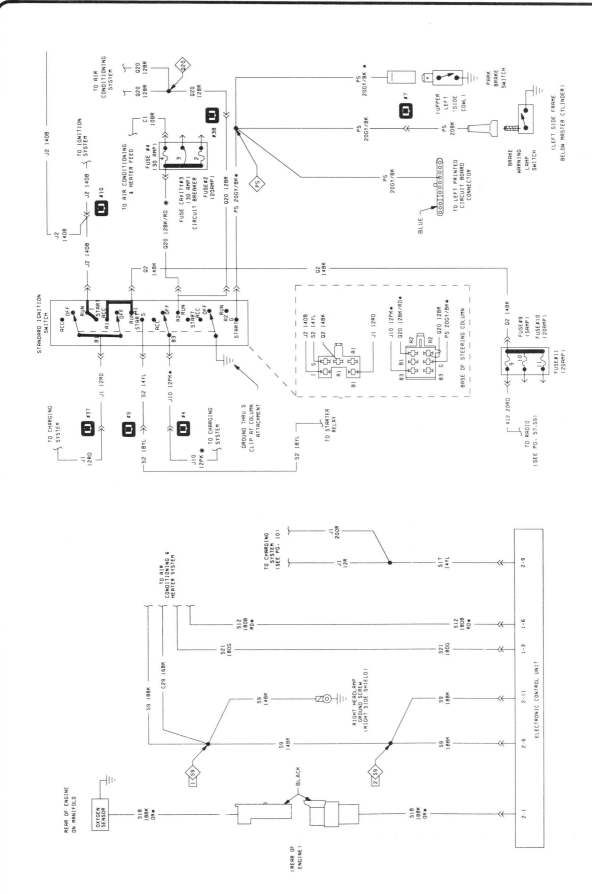

Fig. 13.35 Ignition switch wiring diagram
(1984 models — 1985, 1986 similar)

Fig. 13.34 Electronic ignition system (2.6L feedback) wiring diagram
cont. (1984 models)

13

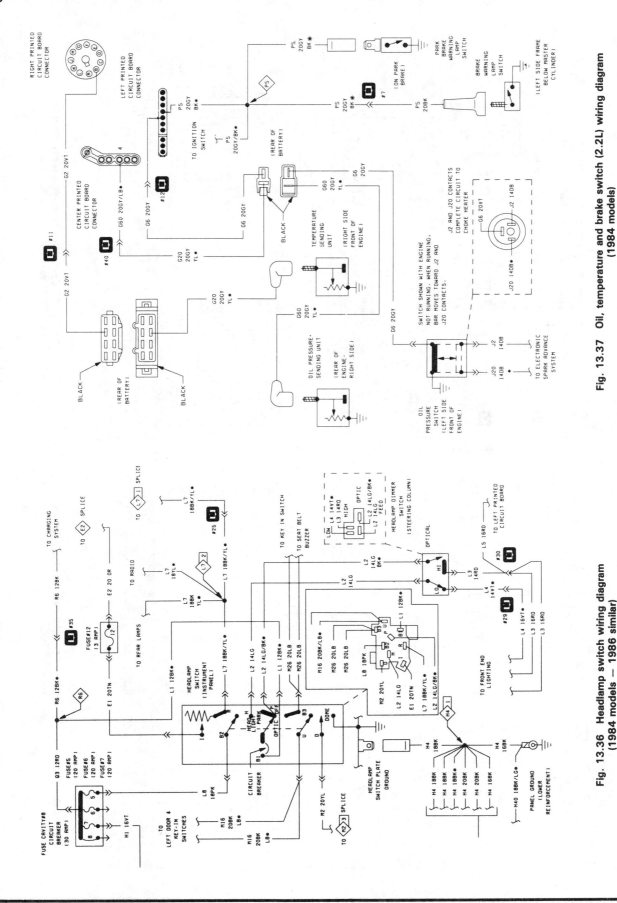

Fig. 13.37 Oil, temperature and brake switch (2.2L) wiring diagram (1984 models)

Fig. 13.36 Headlamp switch wiring diagram (1984 models — 1986 similar)

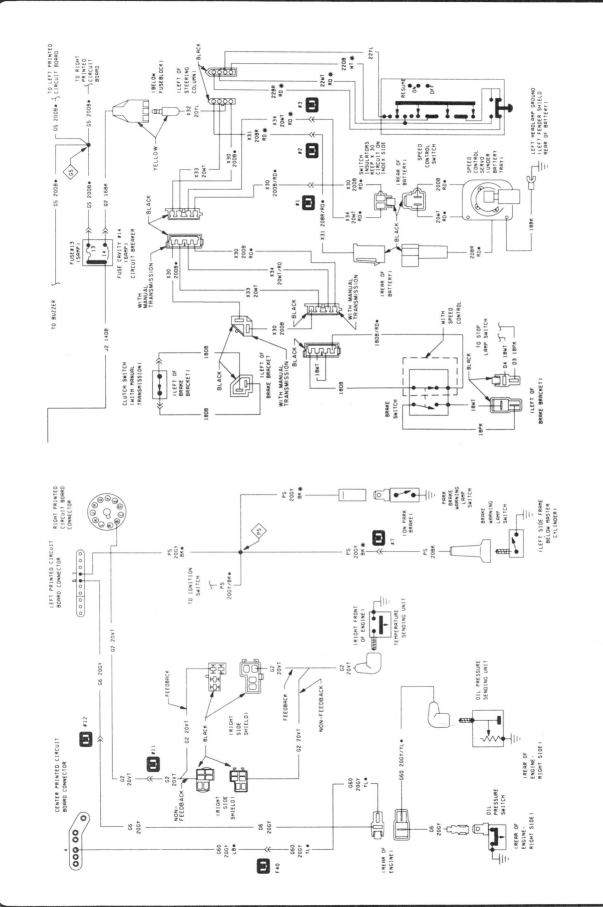

**Fig. 13.39 Speed control system wiring diagram
(1984 models)**

**Fig. 13.38 Oil, temperature and brake switch (2.6L) wiring diagram
(1984 models)**

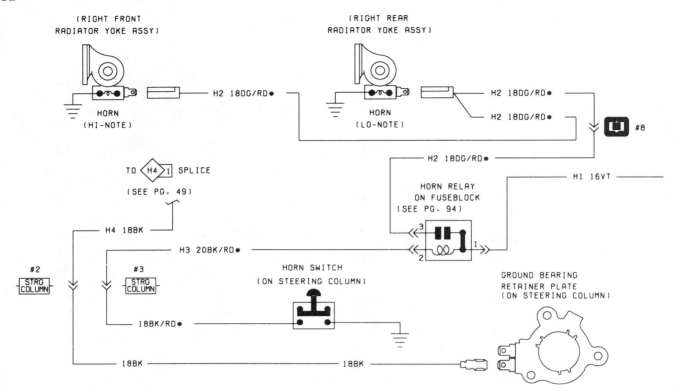

Fig. 13.40 Horn system wiring diagram (1984 through 1986 models)

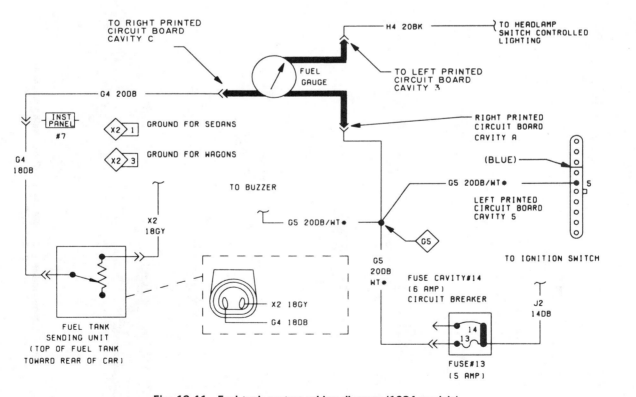

Fig. 13.41 Fuel tank system wiring diagram (1984 models)

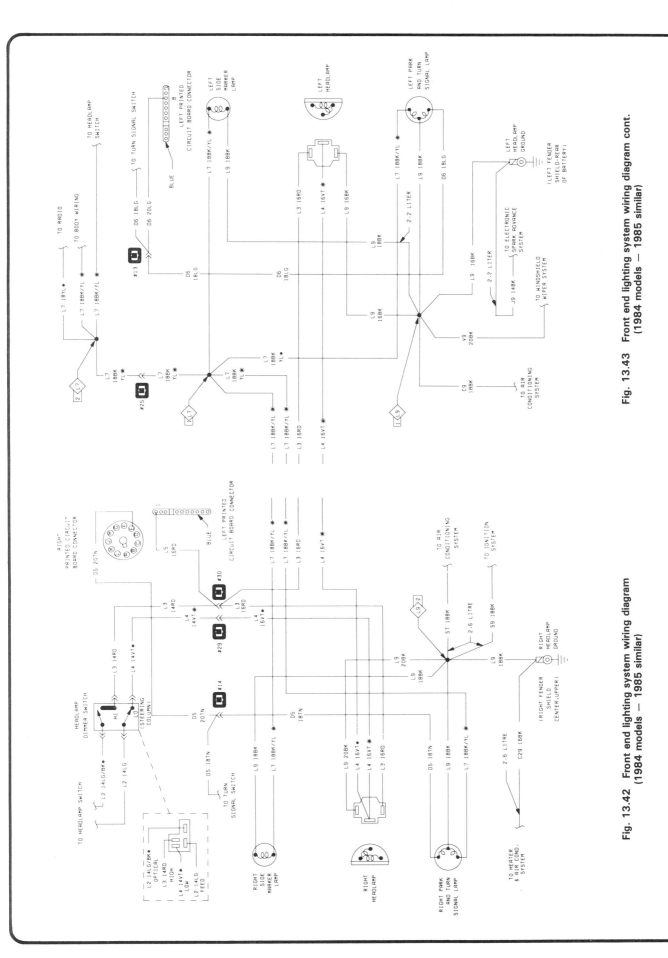

Fig. 13.43 Front end lighting system wiring diagram cont. (1984 models — 1985 similar)

Fig. 13.42 Front end lighting system wiring diagram (1984 models — 1985 similar)

13

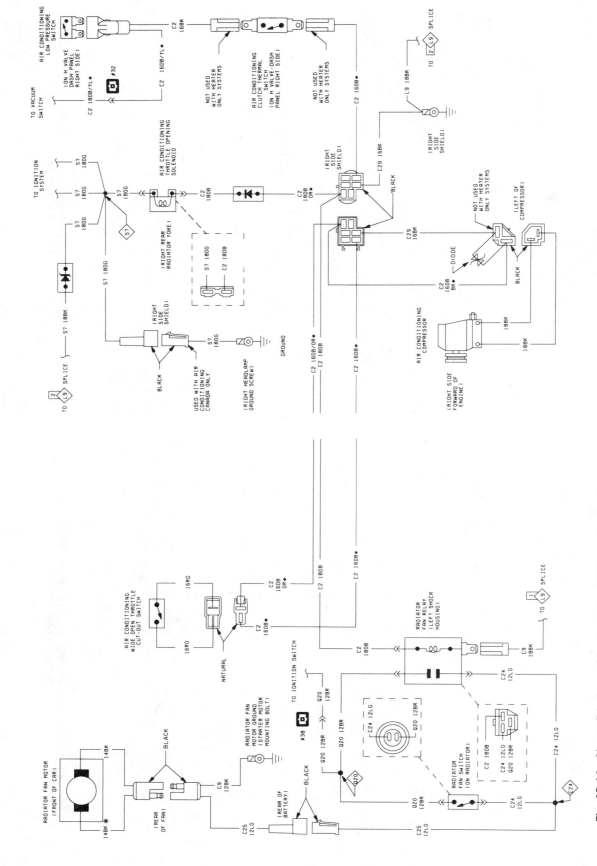

Fig. 13.45 Air conditioning and heater system (2.6L non-feedback) wiring diagram cont. (1984 models)

Fig. 13.44 Air conditioning and heater system (2.6L non-feedback) wiring diagram (1984 models)

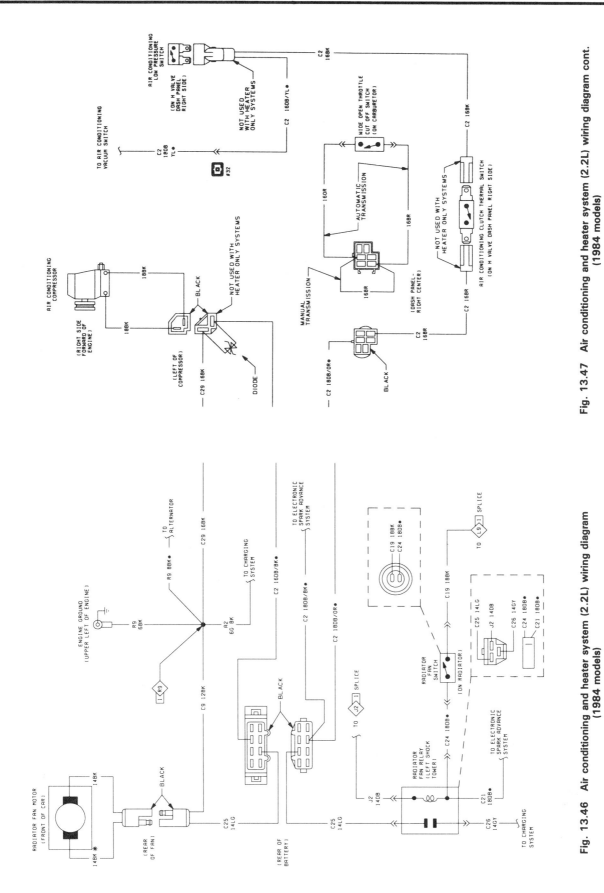

Fig. 13.47 Air conditioning and heater system (2.2L) wiring diagram cont. (1984 models)

Fig. 13.46 Air conditioning and heater system (2.2L) wiring diagram (1984 models)

13

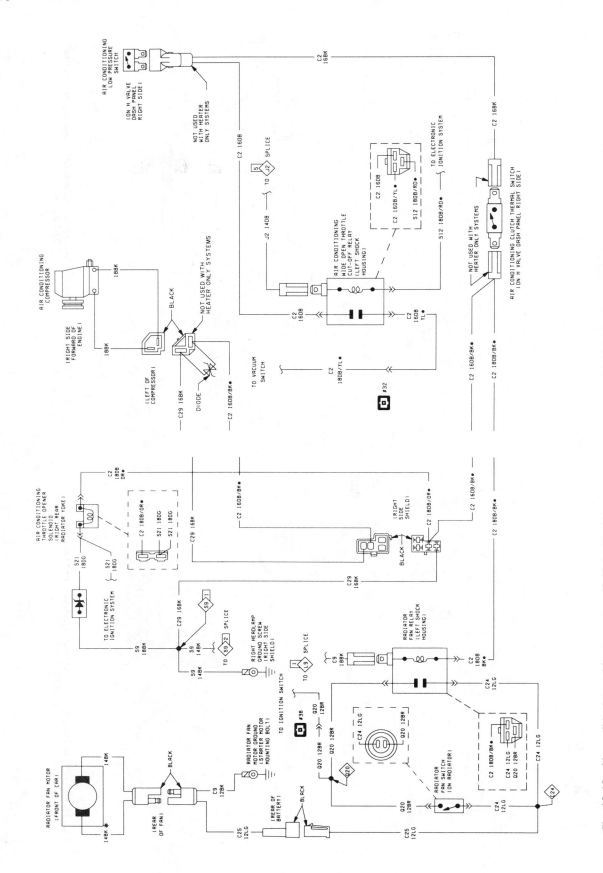

Fig. 13.49 Air conditioning and heater system (2.6L feedback) wiring diagram (1984 models — 1985 similar)

Fig. 13.48 Air conditioning and heater system (2.6L feedback) wiring diagram (1984 models)

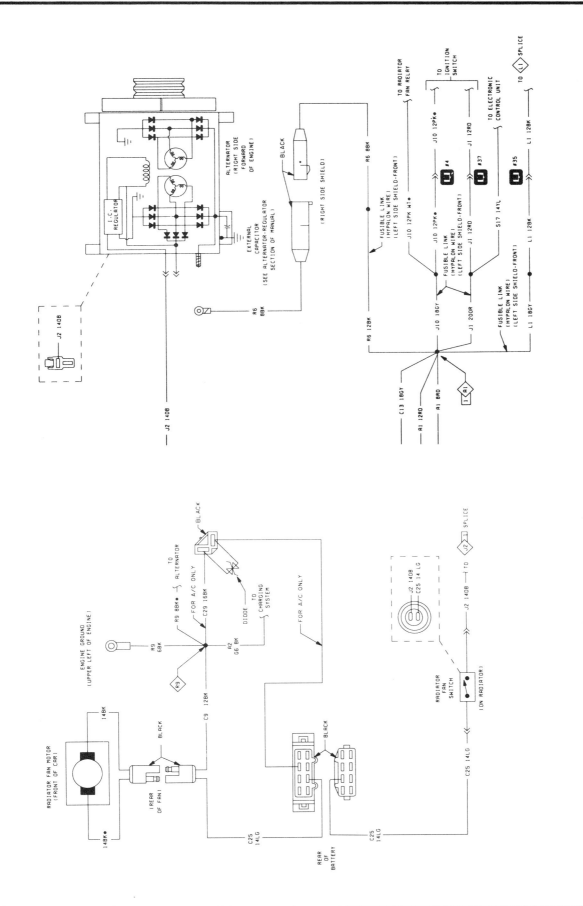

Fig. 13.51 Charging system (2.6L feedback) wiring diagram (1985 models)

Fig. 13.50 Heater system (2.2L) wiring diagram (1984 models)

13

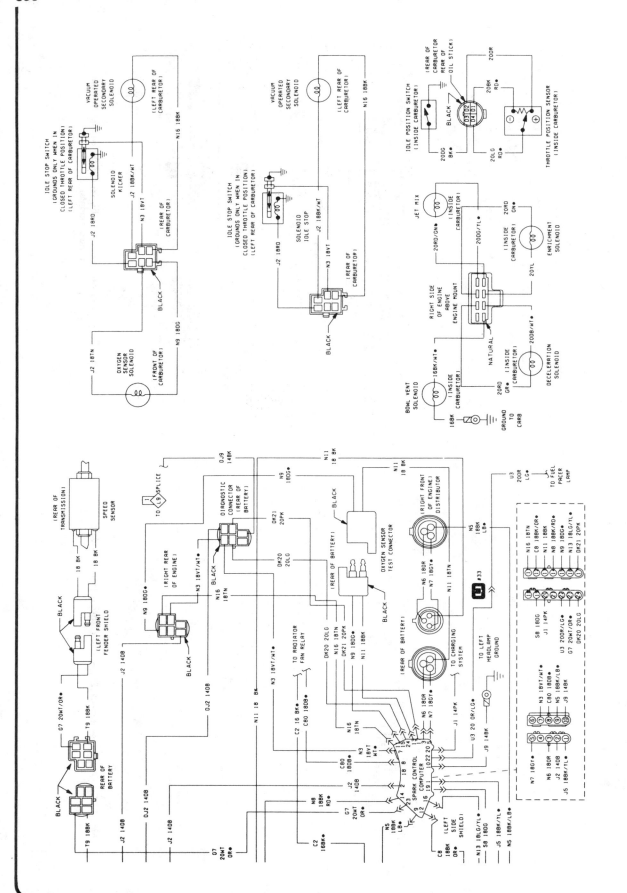

Fig. 13.53 Carburetor wiring diagram (1985 models)

Fig. 13.52 Electronic spark advance system (2.2L) wiring diagram (1985 models)

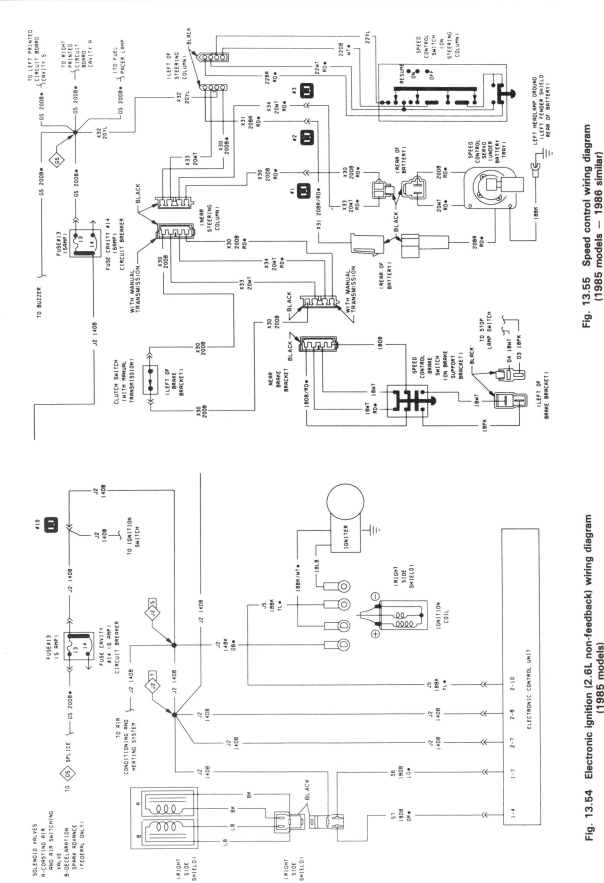

Fig. 13.55 Speed control wiring diagram
(1985 models — 1986 similar)

Fig. 13.54 Electronic ignition (2.6L non-feedback) wiring diagram
(1985 models)

13

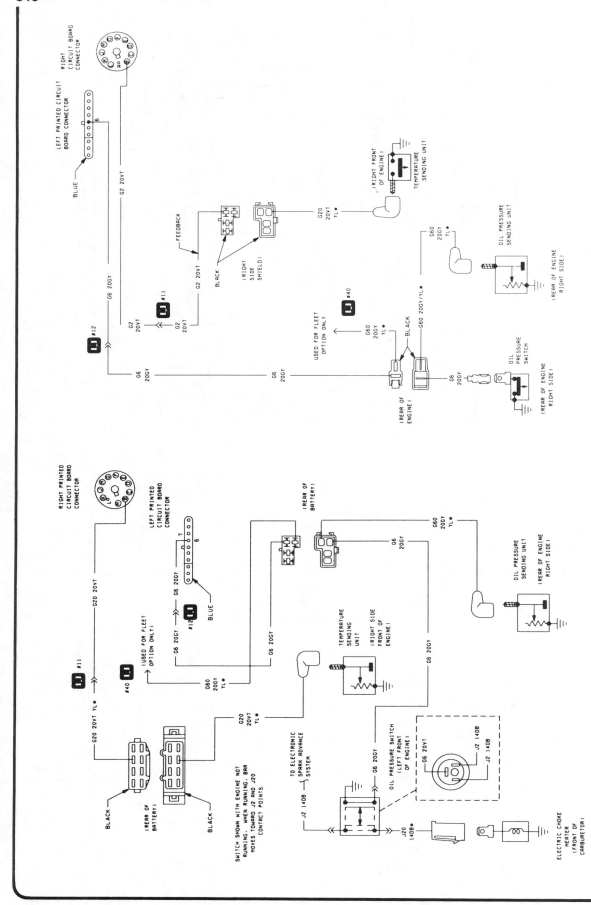

Fig. 13.57 Oil, temperature and brake switch (2.6L) wiring diagram
(1985 models)

Fig. 13.56 Oil, temperature and brake switch (2.2L) wiring diagram
(1985 models)

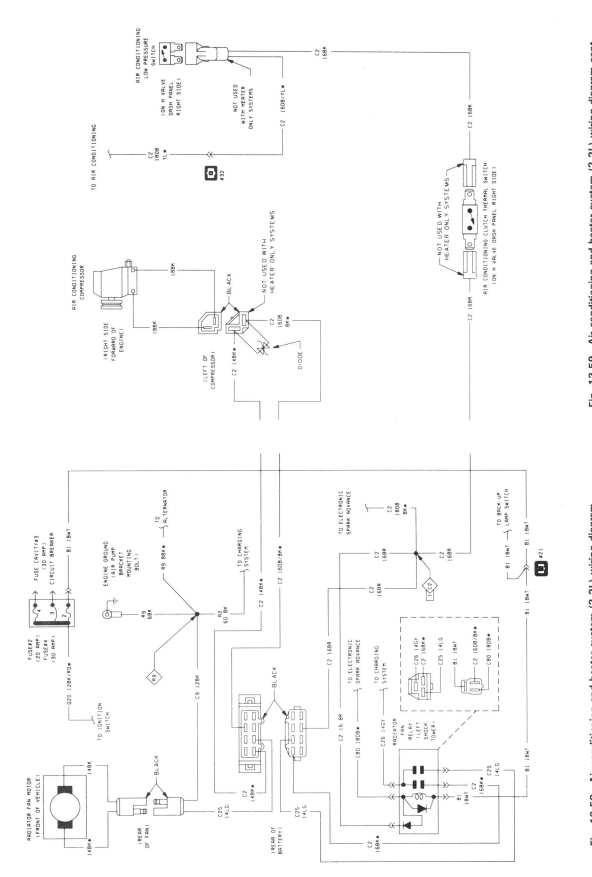

Fig. 13.59 Air conditioning and heater system (2.2L) wiring diagram cont.
(1985 models)

Fig. 13.58 Air conditioning and heater system (2.2L) wiring diagram
(1985 models)

13

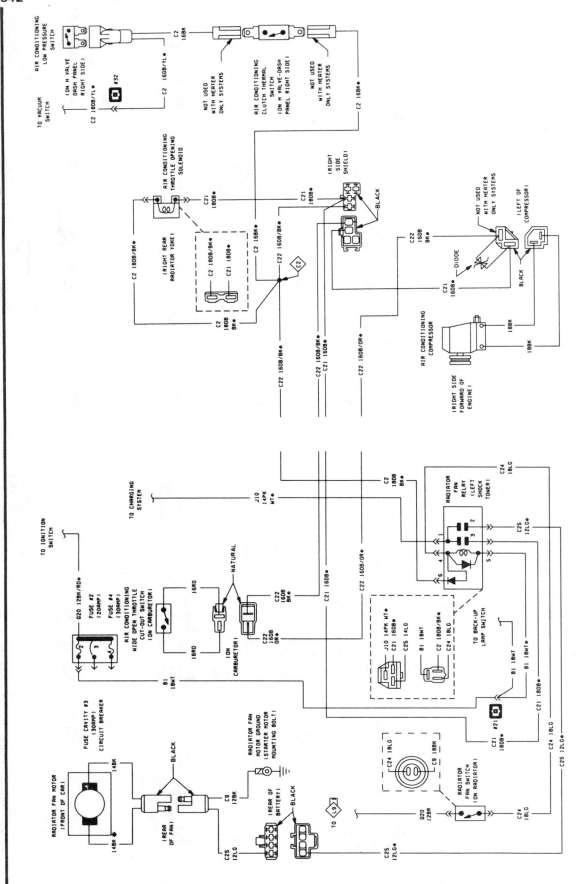

Fig. 13.61 Air conditioning and heater system (2.6L non-feedback) wiring diagram cont. (1985 models)

Fig. 13.60 Air conditioning and heater system (2.6L non-feedback) wiring diagram (1985 models)

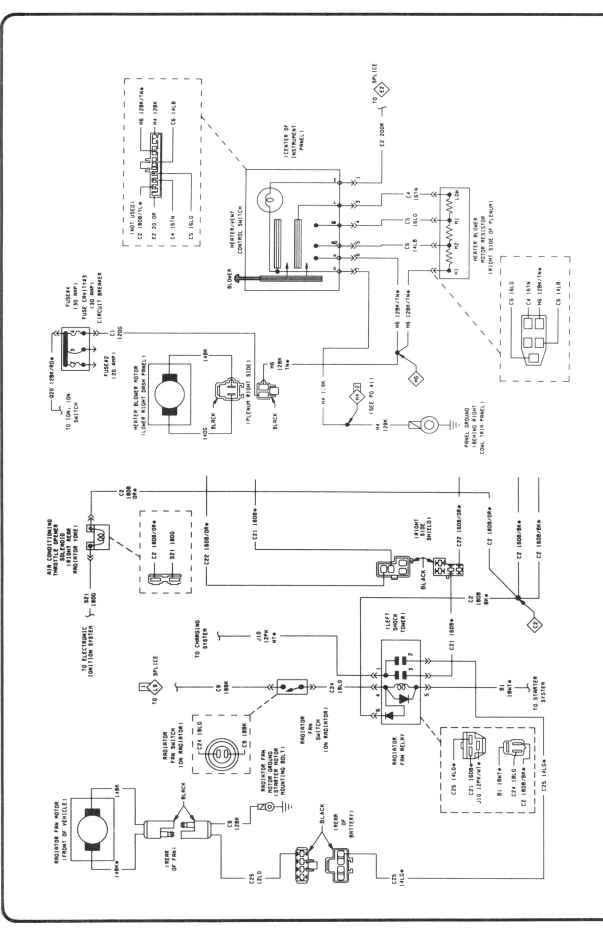

Fig. 13.63 Heater system wiring diagram (1985 models — 1986 on similar)

Fig. 13.62 Air conditioning and heater system (2.6L feedback) wiring diagram (1985 models)

13

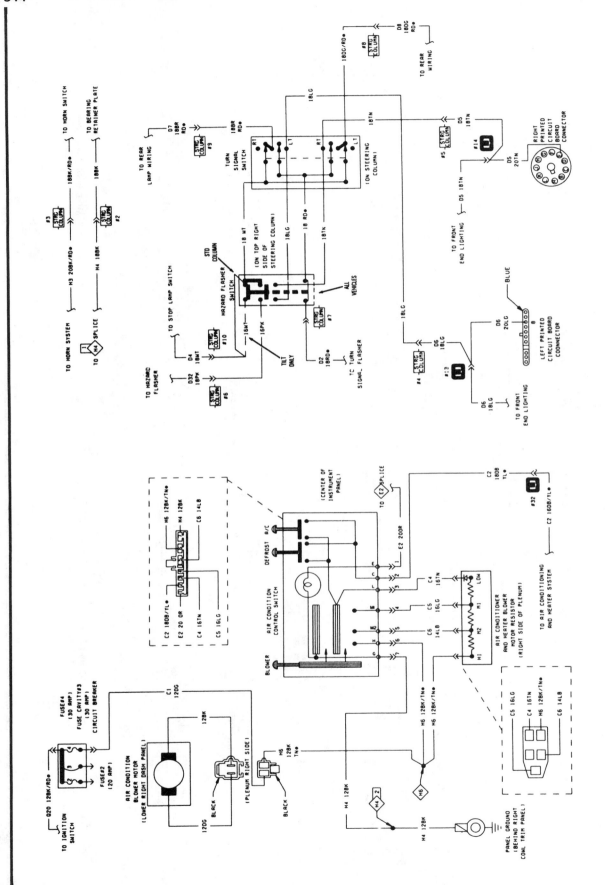

Fig. 13.65 Turn and hazard flasher system wiring diagram (1985 models)

Fig. 13.64 Air conditioning wiring diagram (1985 models)

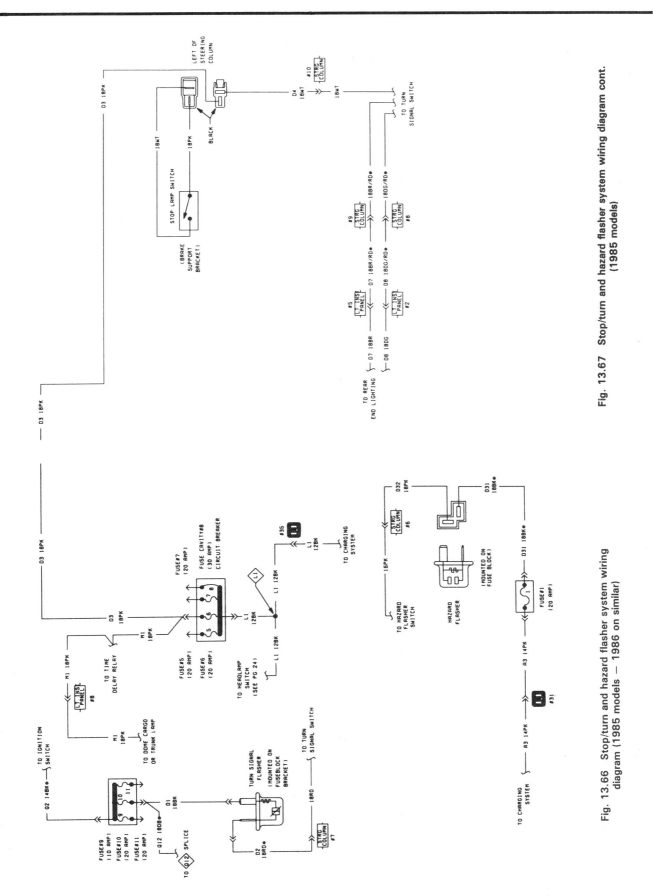

Fig. 13.67 Stop/turn and hazard flasher system wiring diagram cont. (1985 models)

Fig. 13.66 Stop/turn and hazard flasher system wiring diagram (1985 models — 1986 on similar)

13

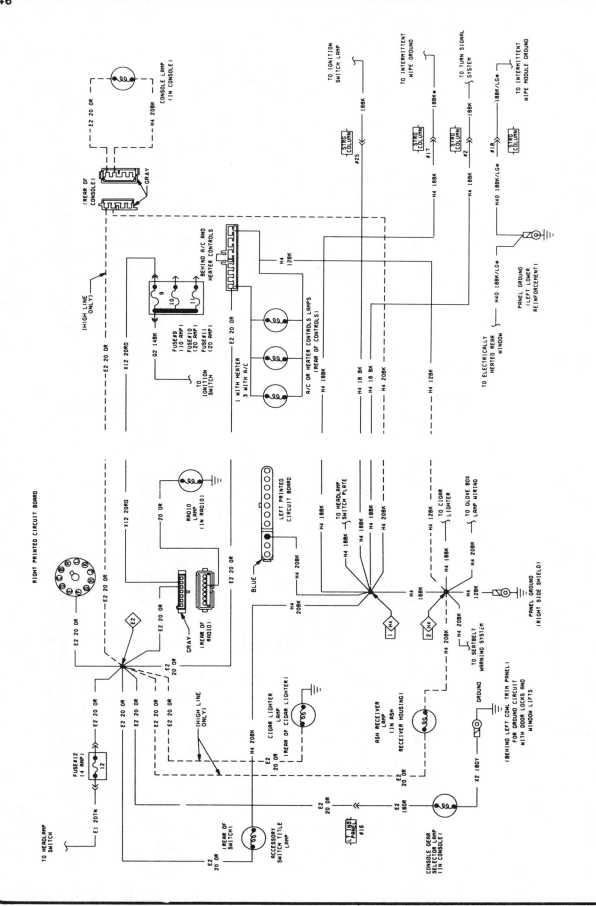

Fig. 13.69 Headlamp switch, controlled interior lighting
wiring diagram cont. (1985 models)

Fig. 13.68 Headlamp switch, controlled interior lighting
wiring diagram (1985 models — 1986 on similar)

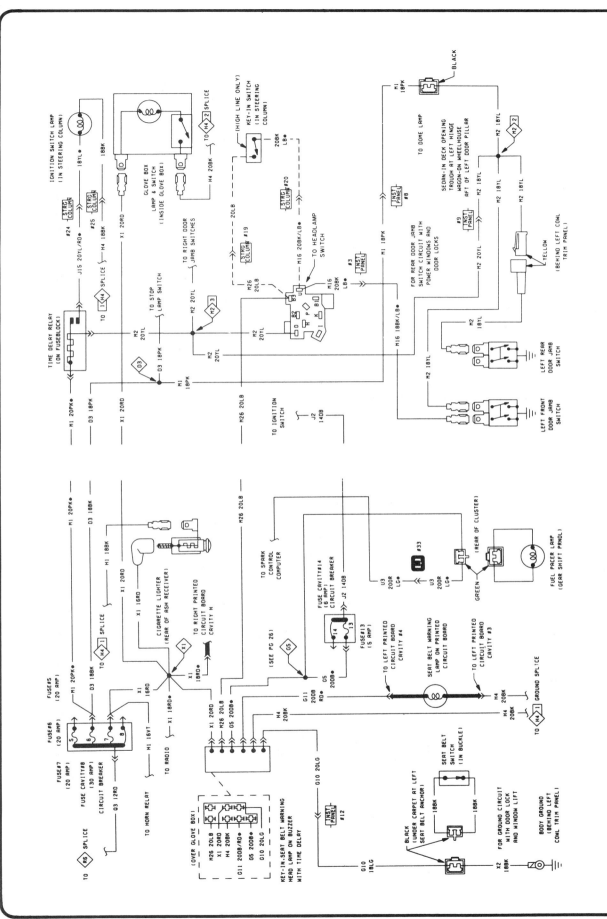

Fig. 13.71 Dome and courtesy lamp wiring diagram (1985 models — 1986 on similar)

Fig. 13.70 Seatbelt warning system wiring diagram (1985 models — 1986 on similar)

13

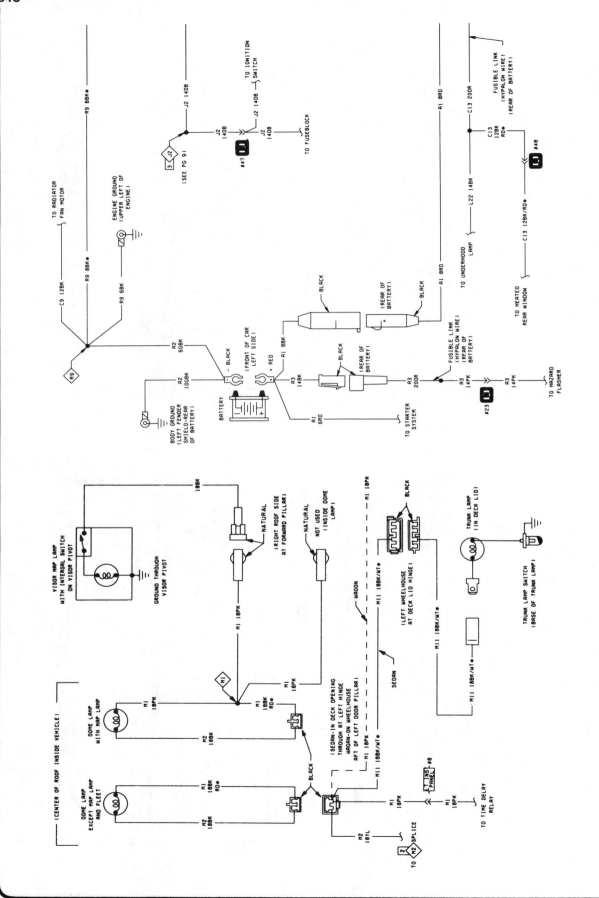

Fig. 13.73 Charging system electronic fuel injection wiring diagram (1986 and 1987 models — 1988 similar)

Fig. 13.72 Dome and courtesy lamp wiring diagram cont. (1985 models — 1986 on similar)

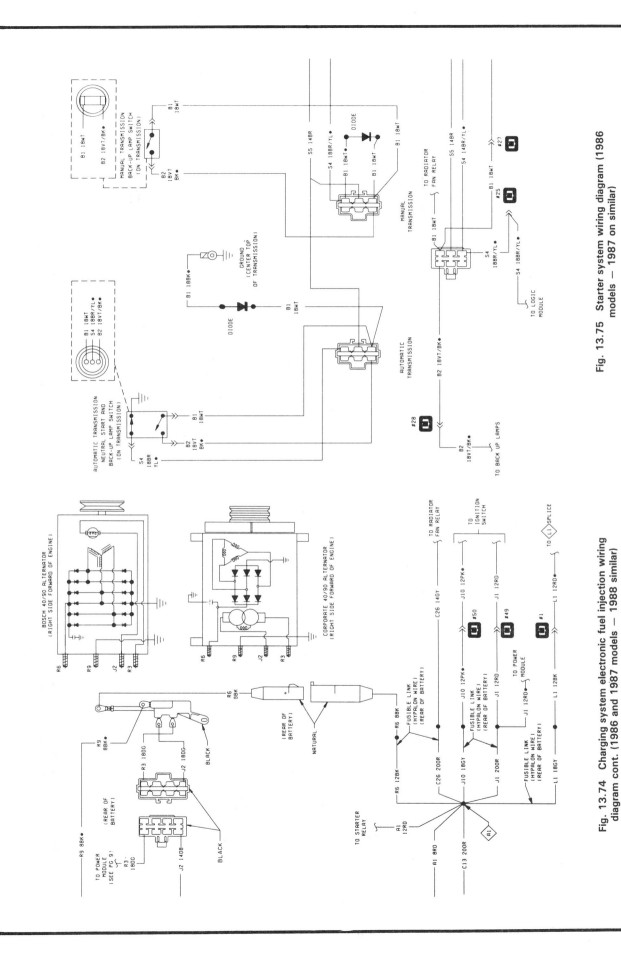

Fig. 13.75 Starter system wiring diagram (1986 models — 1987 on similar)

Fig. 13.74 Charging system electronic fuel injection wiring diagram cont. (1986 and 1987 models — 1988 similar)

13

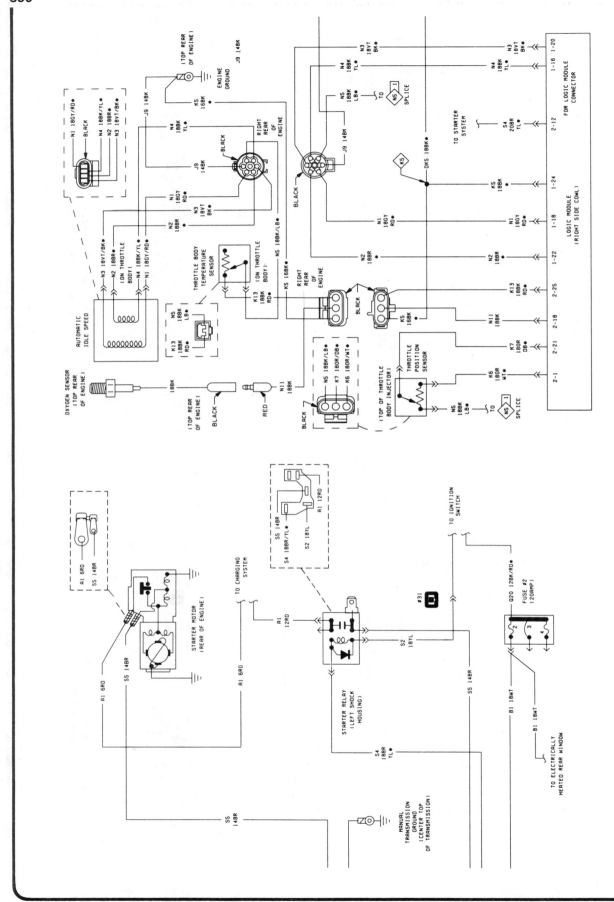

Fig. 13.77 Electronic Fuel Injection ignition system (1986 models – 1987 on similar)

Fig. 13.76 Starter system wiring diagram cont. (1986 models – 1987 on similar)

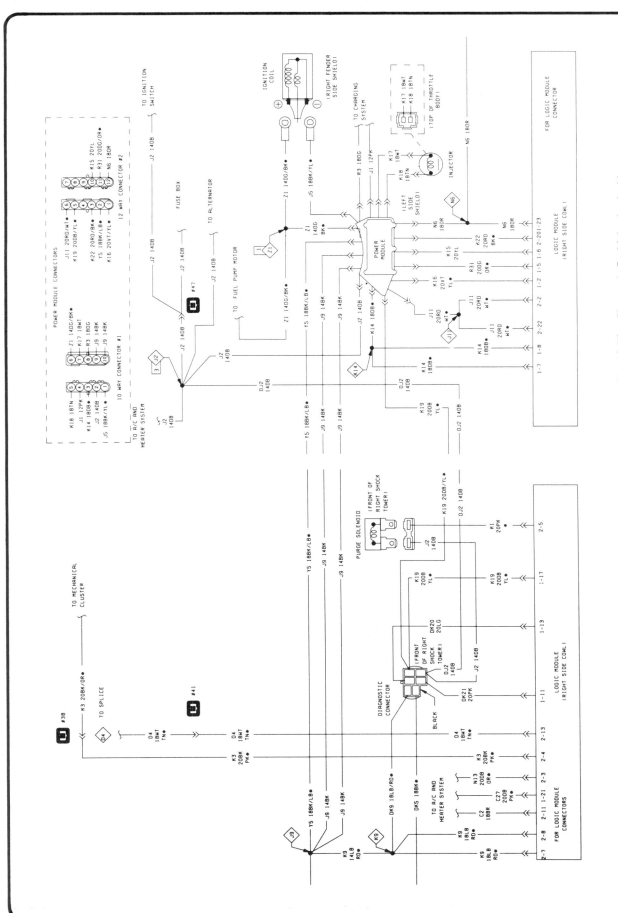

Fig. 13.79 Electronic Fuel Injection ignition system cont. (1986 models — 1987 on similar)

Fig. 13.78 Electronic Fuel Injection ignition system cont. (1986 models — 1987 on similar)

13

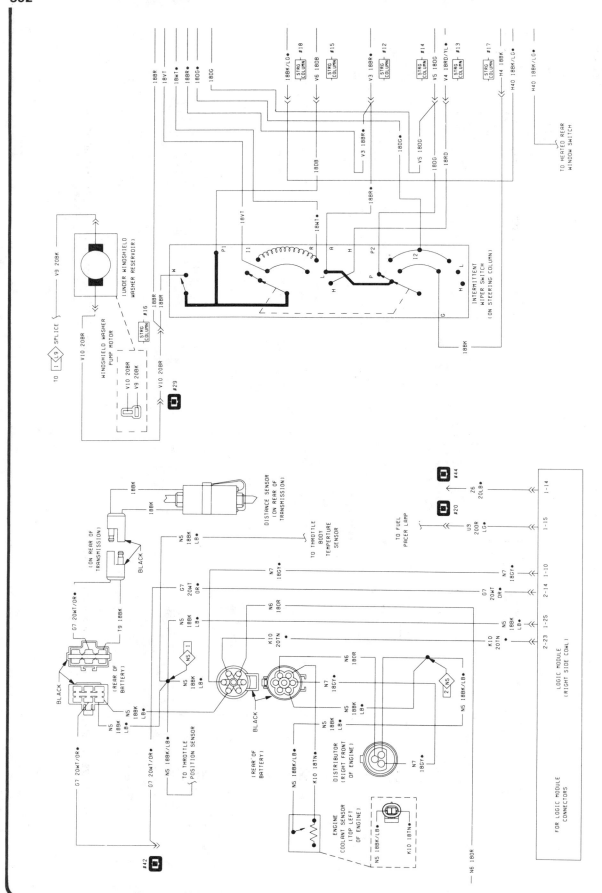

Fig. 13.81   Intermittent wiper system wiring diagram (1986 on)

Fig. 13.80   Electronic Fuel Injection ignition system cont. (1986 models – 1987 on similar)

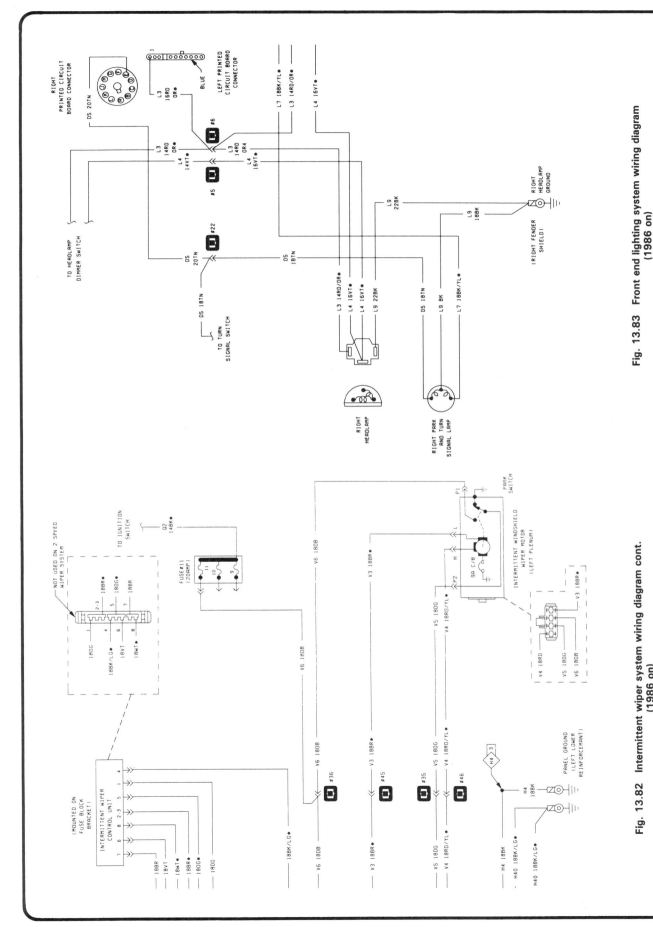

Fig. 13.83 Front end lighting system wiring diagram (1986 on)

Fig. 13.82 Intermittent wiper system wiring diagram cont. (1986 on)

13

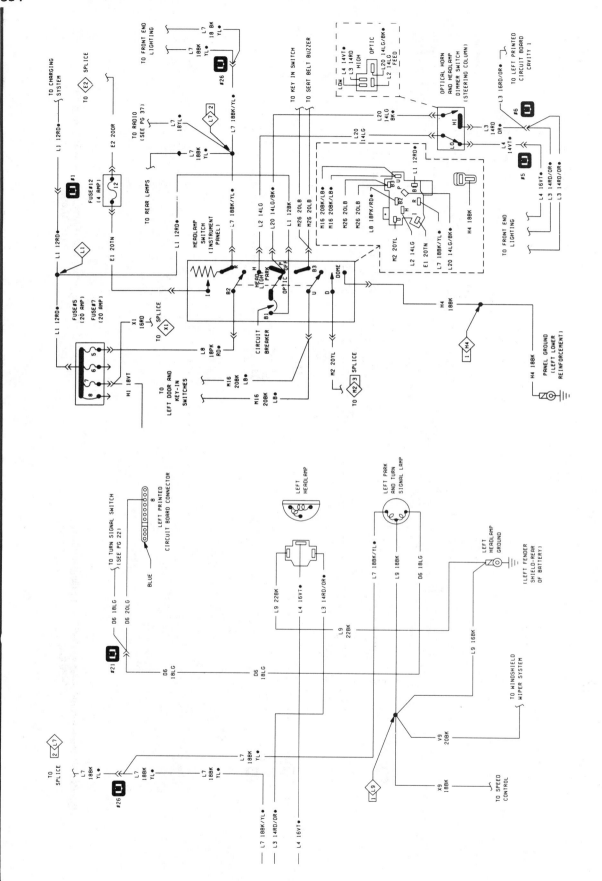

Fig. 13.85 Headlamp switch wiring diagram (1986 on)

Fig. 13.84 Front end lighting system wiring diagram cont. (1986 on)

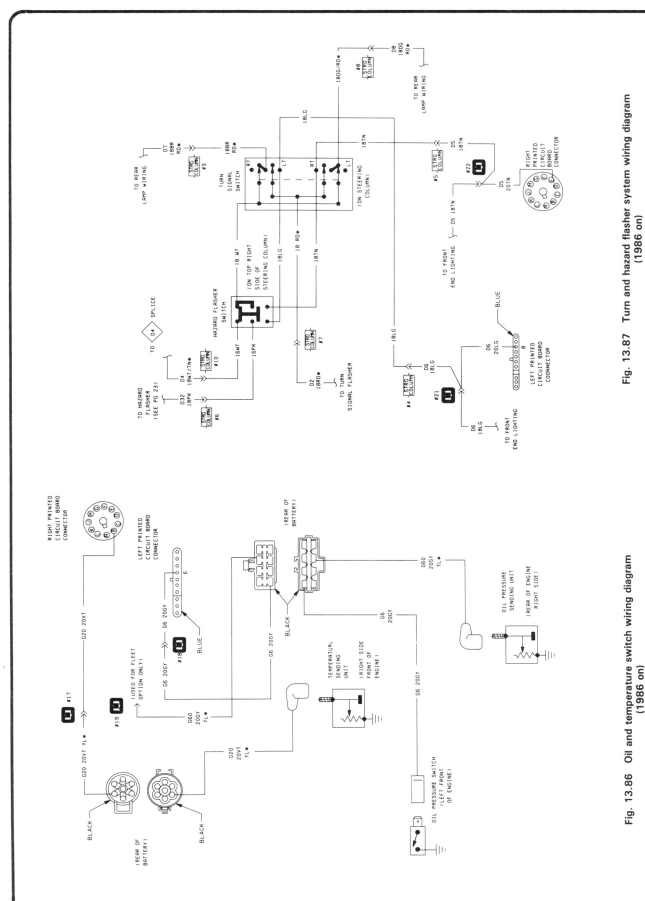

Fig. 13.87 Turn and hazard flasher system wiring diagram (1986 on)

Fig. 13.86 Oil and temperature switch wiring diagram (1986 on)

13

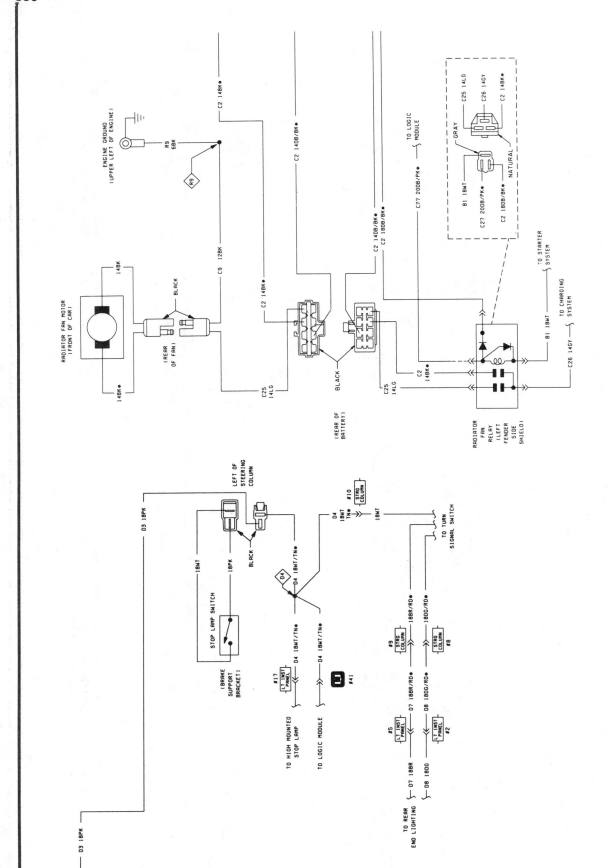

Fig. 13.89   Air conditioning and heater system wiring
diagram (1986 on)

Fig. 13.88   Stop, turn and hazard flasher system wiring
diagram cont. (1986 on)

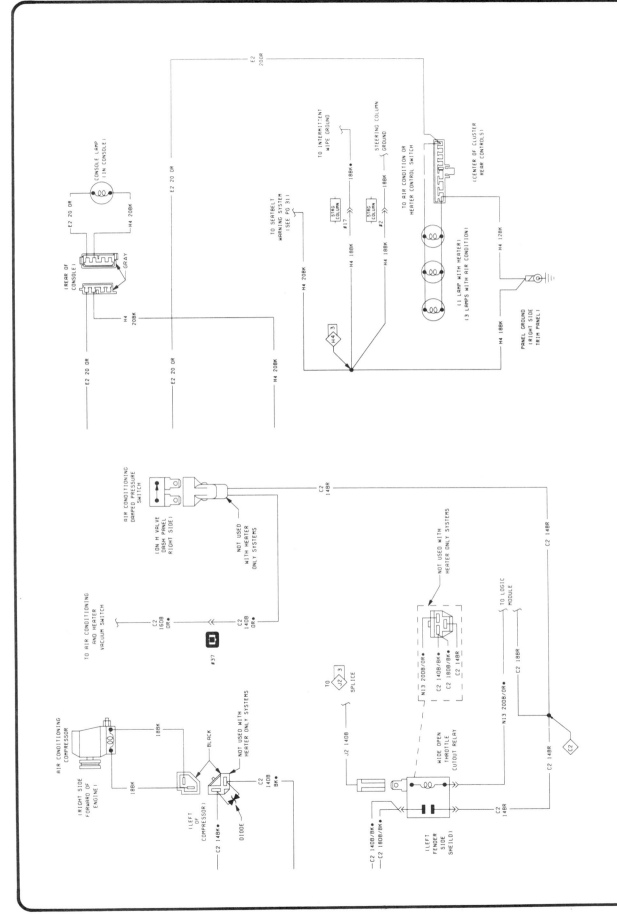

Fig. 13.91 Headlamp switch and controlled lighting wiring diagram cont. (1986 on)

Fig. 13.90 Air conditioning and heater system wiring diagram cont. (1986 on)

13

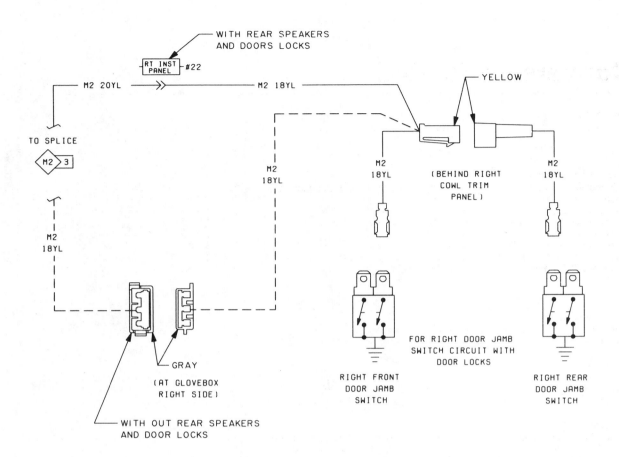

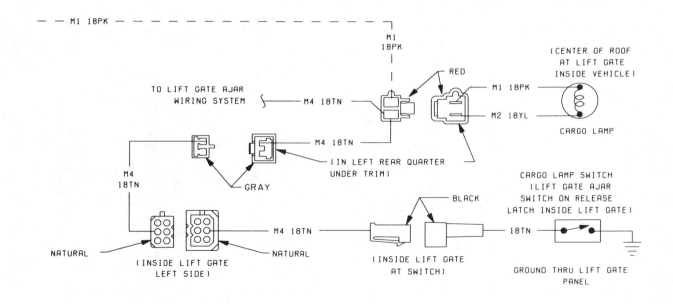

Fig. 13.92   Dome and courtesy lamp wiring diagram cont. (1986 on)

Conversion factors

Length (distance)

Inches (in)	X	25.4	= Millimetres (mm)	X 0.0394	= Inches (in)
Feet (ft)	X	0.305	= Metres (m)	X 3.281	= Feet (ft)
Miles	X	1.609	= Kilometres (km)	X 0.621	= Miles

Volume (capacity)

Cubic inches (cu in; in^3)	X	16.387	= Cubic centimetres (cc; cm^3)	X 0.061	= Cubic inches (cu in; in^3)
Imperial pints (Imp pt)	X	0.568	= Litres (l)	X 1.76	= Imperial pints (Imp pt)
Imperial quarts (Imp qt)	X	1.137	= Litres (l)	X 0.88	= Imperial quarts (Imp qt)
Imperial quarts (Imp qt)	X	1.201	= US quarts (US qt)	X 0.833	= Imperial quarts (Imp qt)
US quarts (US qt)	X	0.946	= Litres (l)	X 1.057	= US quarts (US qt)
Imperial gallons (Imp gal)	X	4.546	= Litres (l)	X 0.22	= Imperial gallons (Imp gal)
Imperial gallons (Imp gal)	X	1.201	= US gallons (US gal)	X 0.833	= Imperial gallons (Imp gal)
US gallons (US gal)	X	3.785	= Litres (l)	X 0.264	= US gallons (US gal)

Mass (weight)

Ounces (oz)	X	28.35	= Grams (g)	X 0.035	= Ounces (oz)
Pounds (lb)	X	0.454	= Kilograms (kg)	X 2.205	= Pounds (lb)

Force

Ounces-force (ozf; oz)	X	0.278	= Newtons (N)	X 3.6	= Ounces-force (ozf; oz)
Pounds-force (lbf; lb)	X	4.448	= Newtons (N)	X 0.225	= Pounds-force (lbf; lb)
Newtons (N)	X	0.1	= Kilograms-force (kgf; kg)	X 9.81	= Newtons (N)

Pressure

Pounds-force per square inch (psi; lbf/in^2; lb/in^2)	X	0.070	= Kilograms-force per square centimetre (kgf/cm^2; kg/cm^2)	X 14.223	= Pounds-force per square inch (psi; lbf/in^2; lb/in^2)
Pounds-force per square inch (psi; lbf/in^2; lb/in^2)	X	0.068	= Atmospheres (atm)	X 14.696	= Pounds-force per square inch (psi; lbf/in^2; lb/in^2)
Pounds-force per square inch (psi; lbf/in^2; lb/in^2)	X	0.069	= Bars	X 14.5	= Pounds-force per square inch (psi; lbf/in^2; lb/in^2)
Pounds-force per square inch (psi; lbf/in^2; lb/in^2)	X	6.895	= Kilopascals (kPa)	X 0.145	= Pounds-force per square inch (psi; lbf/in^2; lb/in^2)
Kilopascals (kPa)	X	0.01	= Kilograms-force per square centimetre (kgf/cm^2; kg/cm^2)	X 98.1	= Kilopascals (kPa)

Torque (moment of force)

Pounds-force inches (lbf in; lb in)	X	1.152	= Kilograms-force centimetre (kgf cm; kg cm)	X 0.868	= Pounds-force inches (lbf in; lb in)
Pounds-force inches (lbf in; lb in)	X	0.113	= Newton metres (Nm)	X 8.85	= Pounds-force inches (lbf in; lb in)
Pounds-force inches (lbf in; lb in)	X	0.083	= Pounds-force feet (lbf ft; lb ft)	X 12	= Pounds-force inches (lbf in; lb in)
Pounds-force feet (lbf ft; lb ft)	X	0.138	= Kilograms-force metres (kgf m; kg m)	X 7.233	= Pounds-force feet (lbf ft; lb ft)
Pounds-force feet (lbf ft; lb ft)	X	1.356	= Newton metres (Nm)	X 0.738	= Pounds-force feet (lbf ft; lb ft)
Newton metres (Nm)	X	0.102	= Kilograms-force metres (kgf m; kg m)	X 9.804	= Newton metres (Nm)

Power

Horsepower (hp)	X	745.7	= Watts (W)	X 0.0013	= Horsepower (hp)

Velocity (speed)

Miles per hour (miles/hr; mph)	X	1.609	= Kilometres per hour (km/hr; kph)	X 0.621	= Miles per hour (miles/hr; mph)

Fuel consumption*

Miles per gallon, Imperial (mpg)	X	0.354	= Kilometres per litre (km/l)	X 2.825	= Miles per gallon, Imperial (mpg)
Miles per gallon, US (mpg)	X	0.425	= Kilometres per litre (km/l)	X 2.352	= Miles per gallon, US (mpg)

Temperature

Degrees Fahrenheit = (°C x 1.8) + 32   Degrees Celsius (Degrees Centigrade; °C) = (°F - 32) x 0.56

*It is common practice to convert from miles per gallon (mpg) to litres/100 kilometres (l/100km), where mpg (Imperial) x l/100 km = 282 and mpg (US) x l/100 km = 235

Index

HAYNES AUTOMOTIVE MANUALS

NOTE: New manuals are added to this list on a periodic basis. If you do not see a listing for your vehicle, consult your local Haynes dealer for the latest product information.

ACURA
1776 **Integra & Legend** '86 thru '90

AMC
Jeep CJ – see JEEP (412)
694 **Mid-size models,** Concord, Hornet, Gremlin & Spirit '70 thru '83
934 **(Renault) Alliance & Encore** all models '83 thru '87

AUDI
615 **4000** all models '80 thru '87
428 **5000** all models '77 thru '83
1117 **5000** all models '84 thru '88

AUSTIN
Healey Sprite – see MG Midget Roadster (265)

BMW
276 **320i** all 4 cyl models '75 thru '83
632 **528i & 530i** all models '75 thru '80
240 **1500 thru 2002** all models except Turbo '59 thru '77
348 **2500, 2800, 3.0 & Bavaria** '69 thru '76

BUICK
Century (front wheel drive) – see GENERAL MOTORS A-Cars (829)
*1627 **Buick, Oldsmobile & Pontiac Full-size (Front wheel drive)** all models '85 thru '93
Buick Electra, LeSabre and Park Avenue; **Oldsmobile** Delta 88 Royale, Ninety Eight and Regency; **Pontiac** Bonneville
*1551 **Buick Oldsmobile & Pontiac Full-size (Rear wheel drive)**
Buick Electra '70 thru '84, Estate '70 thru '90, LeSabre '70 thru '79
Oldsmobile Custom Cruiser '70 thru '90, Delta 88 '70 thru '85, Ninety-eight '70 thru '84
Pontiac Bonneville '70 thru '81, Catalina '70 thru '81, Grandville '70 thru '75, Parisienne '83 thru '86
627 **Mid-size** all rear-drive **Regal & Century** models with V6, V8 and Turbo '74 thru '87
Regal – see GENERAL MOTORS (1671)
Skyhawk – see GENERAL MOTORS J-Cars (766)
552 **Skylark** all X-car models '80 thru '85

CADILLAC
*751 **Cadillac Rear Wheel Drive** all gasoline models '70 thru '90
Cimarron – see GENERAL MOTORS J-Cars (766)

CAPRI
296 **2000 MK I Coupe** all models '71 thru '75
205 **2600 & 2800** V6 Coupe '71 thru '75
375 **2800 Mk II** V6 Coupe '75 thru '78
Mercury Capri – see FORD Mustang (654)

CHEVROLET
*1477 **Astro & GMC Safari Mini-vans** all models '85 thru '91
554 **Camaro** V8 all models '70 thru '81
*866 **Camaro** all models '82 thru '92
Cavalier – see GENERAL MOTORS J-Cars (766)
Celebrity – see GENERAL MOTORS A-Cars (829)
625 **Chevelle, Malibu & El Camino** all V6 & V8 models '69 thru '87
449 **Chevette & Pontiac T1000** all models '76 thru '87
550 **Citation** all models '80 thru '85
*1628 **Corsica/Beretta** all models '87 thru '92
274 **Corvette** all V8 models '68 thru '82
*1336 **Corvette** all models '84 thru '91

704 **Full-size Sedans** Caprice, Impala, Biscayne, Bel Air & Wagons, all V6 & V8 models '69 thru '90
Lumina – see GENERAL MOTORS (1671)
Lumina APV – see GENERAL MOTORS (2035)
319 **Luv Pick-up** all 2WD & 4WD models '72 thru '82
626 **Monte Carlo** all V6, V8 & Turbo models '70 thru '88
241 **Nova** all V8 models '69 thru '79
*1642 **Nova and Geo Prizm** all front wheel drive models, '85 thru '90
*420 **Pick-ups '67 thru '87** – Chevrolet & GMC, all full-size models '67 thru '87; Suburban, Blazer & Jimmy '67 thru '91
*1664 **Pick-ups '88 thru '92** – Chevrolet & GMC all full-size (C and K) models, '88 thru '92
*1727 **Sprint & Geo Metro** '85 thru '91
*831 **S-10 & GMC S-15 Pick-ups** all models '82 thru '92
*345 **Vans** – Chevrolet & GMC, V8 & in-line 6 cyl models '68 thru '92

CHRYSLER
*1337 **Chrysler & Plymouth Mid-size** front wheel drive '82 thru '89
K-Cars – see DODGE Aries (723)
Laser – see DODGE Daytona (1140)

DATSUN
402 **200SX** all models '77 thru '79
647 **200SX** all models '80 thru '83
228 **B-210** all models '73 thru '78
525 **210** all models '78 thru '82
206 **240Z, 260Z & 280Z** Coupe & 2+2 '70 thru '78
563 **280ZX** Coupe & 2+2 '79 thru '83
300ZX – see NISSAN (1137)
679 **310** all models '78 thru '82
123 **510 & PL521 Pick-up** '68 thru '73
430 **510** all models '78 thru '81
372 **610** all models '72 thru '76
277 **620 Series Pick-up** all models '73 thru '79
720 Series Pick-up – see NISSAN Pick-ups (771)
376 **810/Maxima** all gasoline models '77 thru '84
124 **1200** all models '70 thru '73
368 **F10** all models '76 thru '79
Pulsar – see NISSAN (876)
Sentra – see NISSAN (982)
Stanza – see NISSAN (981)

DODGE
*723 **Aries & Plymouth Reliant** all models '81 thru '89
*1231 **Caravan & Plymouth Voyager Mini-Vans** all models '84 thru '91
699 **Challenger & Plymouth Saporro** all models '78 thru '83
236 **Colt** all models '71 thru '77
610 **Colt & Plymouth Champ (front wheel drive)** all models '78 thru '87
*556 **D50/Ram 50/Plymouth Arrow Pick-ups & Raider** '79 thru '91
*1668 **Dakota Pick-up** all models '87 thru '90
234 **Dart & Plymouth Valiant** all 6 cyl models '67 thru '76
*1140 **Daytona & Chrysler Laser** all models '84 thru '89
*545 **Omni & Plymouth Horizon** all models '78 thru '90
*912 **Pick-ups** all full-size models '74 thru '91
*1726 **Shadow & Plymouth Sundance** '87 thru '91
*1779 **Spirit & Plymouth Acclaim** '89 thru '92
*349 **Vans** – Dodge & Plymouth V8 & 6 cyl models '71 thru '91

FIAT
094 **124 Sport Coupe & Spider** '68 thru '78

479 **Strada** all models '79 thru '82
273 **X1/9** all models '74 thru '80

FORD
*1476 **Aerostar Mini-vans** all models '86 thru '92
788 **Bronco and Pick-ups** '73 thru '79
880 **Bronco and Pick-ups** '80 thru '91
268 **Courier Pick-up** all models '72 thru '82
789 **Escort & Mercury Lynx** all models '81 thru '90
*2046 **Escort & Mercury Tracer** all models '91 thru '93
*2021 **Explorer & Mazda Navajo** '91 thru '92
560 **Fairmont & Mercury Zephyr** all in-line & V8 models '78 thru '83
334 **Fiesta** all models '77 thru '80
754 **Ford & Mercury Full-size,** Ford LTD & Mercury Marquis ('75 thru '82); Ford Custom 500, Country Squire, Crown Victoria & Mercury Colony Park ('75 thru '87); Ford LTD Crown Victoria & Mercury Gran Marquis ('83 thru '87)
359 **Granada & Mercury Monarch** all in-line, 6 cyl & V8 models '75 thru '80
773 **Ford & Mercury Mid-size,** Ford Thunderbird & Mercury Cougar ('75 thru '82); Ford LTD & Mercury Marquis ('83 thru '86); Ford Torino, Gran Torino, Elite, Ranchero pick-up, LTD II, Mercury Montego, Comet, XR-7 & Lincoln Versailles ('75 thru '86)
*654 **Mustang & Mercury Capri** all models including Turbo '79 thru '92
357 **Mustang V8** all models '64-1/2 thru '73
231 **Mustang II** all 4 cyl, V6 & V8 models '74 thru '78
649 **Pinto & Mercury Bobcat** all models '75 thru '80
*1670 **Probe** all models '89 thru '92
*1026 **Ranger & Bronco II** all gasoline models '83 thru '92
*1421 **Taurus & Mercury Sable** '86 thru '92
*1418 **Tempo & Mercury Topaz** all gasoline models '84 thru '91
1338 **Thunderbird & Mercury Cougar/XR7** '83 thru '88
*1725 **Thunderbird & Mercury Cougar** '89 and '90
*344 **Vans** all V8 Econoline models '69 thru '91

GENERAL MOTORS
*829 **A-Cars** – Chevrolet Celebrity, Buick Century, Pontiac 6000 & Oldsmobile Cutlass Ciera all models '82 thru '90
*766 **J-Cars** – Chevrolet Cavalier, Pontiac J-2000, Oldsmobile Firenza, Buick Skyhawk & Cadillac Cimarron all models '82 thru '92
*1420 **N-Cars** – Buick Somerset '85 thru '87; Pontiac Grand Am and Oldsmobile Calais '85 thru '91; Buick Skylark '86 thru '91
*1671 **GM:** Buick Regal, **Chevrolet** Lumina, **Oldsmobile** Cutlass Supreme, **Pontiac** Grand Prix, all front wheel drive models '88 thru '90
*2035 **GM: Chevrolet Lumina APV, Oldsmobile Silhouette, Pontiac Trans Sport** '90 thru '92

GEO
Metro – see CHEVROLET Sprint (1727)
Prizm – see CHEVROLET Nova (1642)
Tracker – see SUZUKI Samurai (1626)

GMC
Safari – see CHEVROLET ASTRO (1477)
Vans & Pick-ups – see CHEVROLET (420, 831, 345, 1664)

(continued on next page)

---

* Listings shown with an asterisk (*) indicate model coverage as of this printing. These titles will be periodically updated to include later model years – consult your Haynes dealer for more information.

Haynes North America, Inc., 861 Lawrence Drive, Newbury Park, CA 91320 • (805) 498-6703

HAYNES AUTOMOTIVE MANUALS

(continued from previous page)

NOTE: *New manuals are added to this list on a periodic basis. If you do not see a listing for your vehicle, consult your local Haynes dealer for the latest product information.*

HONDA
- 351 **Accord CVCC** all models '76 thru '83
- *1221 **Accord** all models '84 thru '89
- 160 **Civic 1200** all models '73 thru '79
- 633 **Civic 1300 & 1500 CVCC** all models '80 thru '83
- 297 **Civic 1500 CVCC** all models '75 thru '79
- *1227 **Civic** all models '84 thru '91
- *601 **Prelude CVCC** all models '79 thru '89

HYUNDAI
- *1552 **Excel** all models '86 thru '91

ISUZU
- *1641 **Trooper & Pick-up**, all gasoline models '81 thru '91

JAGUAR
- *242 **XJ6** all 6 cyl models '68 thru '86
- *478 **XJ12 & XJS** all 12 cyl models '72 thru '85

JEEP
- *1553 **Cherokee, Comanche & Wagoneer Limited** all models '84 thru '91
- 412 **CJ** all models '49 thru '86
- *1777 **Wrangler** all models '87 thru '92

LADA
- *413 **1200, 1300. 1500 & 1600** all models including Riva '74 thru '86

MAZDA
- 648 **626** Sedan & Coupe (rear wheel drive) all models '79 thru '82
- 1082 **626 & MX-6 (front wheel drive)** all models '83 thru '91
- 370 **GLC Hatchback (rear wheel drive)** all models '77 thru '83
- 757 **GLC (front wheel drive)** all models '81 thru '86
- *2047 **MPV** '89 thru '93
  Navajo – *see FORD Explorer (2021)*
- *267 **Pick-ups** '72 thru '92
- 460 **RX-7** all models '79 thru '85
- *1419 **RX-7** all models '86 thru '91

MERCEDES-BENZ
- *1643 **190 Series** all four-cylinder gasoline models, '84 thru '88
- 346 **230, 250 & 280** Sedan, Coupe & Roadster all 6 cyl sohc models '68 thru '72
- 983 **280 123 Series** all gasoline models '77 thru '81
- 698 **350 & 450** Sedan, Coupe & Roadster all models '71 thru '80
- 697 **Diesel 123 Series** 200D, 220D, 240D, 240TD, 300D, 300CD, 300TD, 4- & 5-cyl incl. Turbo '76 thru '85

MERCURY
- *For all PLYMOUTH titles see FORD Listing*

MG
- 111 **MGB** Roadster & GT Coupe all models '62 thru '80
- 265 **MG Midget & Austin Healey Sprite** Roadster '58 thru '80

MITSUBISHI
- *1669 **Cordia, Tredia, Galant, Precis & Mirage** '83 thru '90
- *2022 **Pick-ups & Montero** '83 thru '91

MORRIS
- 074 **(Austin) Marina 1.8** all models '71 thru '80
- 024 **Minor 1000** sedan & wagon '56 thru '71

NISSAN
- 1137 **300ZX** all Turbo & non-Turbo models '84 thru '89
- *1341 **Maxima** all models '85 thru '91
- *771 **Pick-ups/Pathfinder** gas models '80 thru '91
- *876 **Pulsar** all models '83 thru '86
- *982 **Sentra** all models '82 thru '90
- *981 **Stanza** all models '82 thru '90

OLDSMOBILE
- **Custom Cruiser** – *see BUICK Full-size (1551)*
- 658 **Cutlass** all standard gasoline V6 & V8 models '74 thru '88
  Cutlass Ciera – *see GENERAL MOTORS A-Cars (829)*
  Cutlass Supreme – *see GENERAL MOTORS (1671)*
  Firenza – *see GENERAL MOTORS J-Cars (766)*
  Ninety-eight – *see BUICK Full-size (1551)*
  Omega – *see PONTIAC Phoenix & Omega (551)*
  Silhouette – *see GENERAL MOTORS (2035)*

PEUGEOT
- 663 **504** all diesel models '74 thru '83

PLYMOUTH
- ***For all PLYMOUTH titles, see DODGE listing.***

PONTIAC
- **T1000** – *see CHEVROLET Chevette (449)*
- **J-2000** – *see GENERAL MOTORS J-Cars (766)*
- **6000** – *see GENERAL MOTORS A-Cars (829)*
- 1232 **Fiero** all models '84 thru '88
- 555 **Firebird** all V8 models except Turbo '70 thru '81
- *867 **Firebird** all models '82 thru '91
  Full-size Rear Wheel Drive – *see Buick, Oldsmobile, Pontiac Full-size (1551)*
  Grand Prix – *see GENERAL MOTORS (1671)*
- 551 **Phoenix & Oldsmobile Omega** all X-car models '80 thru '84
  Trans Sport – *see GENERAL MOTORS (2035)*

PORSCHE
- *264 **911** all Coupe & Targa models except Turbo & Carrera 4 '65 thru '89
- 239 **914** all 4 cyl models '69 thru '76
- 397 **924** all models including Turbo '76 thru '82
- *1027 **944** all models including Turbo '83 thru '89

RENAULT
- 141 **5 Le Car** all models '76 thru '83
- 079 **8 & 10** all models with 58.4 cu in engines '62 thru '72
- 097 **12 Saloon & Estate** all models 1289 cc engines '70 thru '80
- 768 **15 & 17** all models '73 thru '79
- 081 **16** all models 89.7 cu in & 95.5 cu in engines '65 thru '72
  Alliance & Encore – *see AMC (934)*

SAAB
- 247 **99** all models including Turbo '69 thru '80
- *980 **900** all models including Turbo '79 thru '88

SUBARU
- 237 **1100, 1300, 1400 & 1600** all models '71 thru '79
- *681 **1600 & 1800** 2WD & 4WD all models '80 thru '89

SUZUKI
- *1626 **Samurai/Sidekick and Geo Tracker** all models '86 thru '91

TOYOTA
- *1023 **Camry** all models '83 thru '91
- 150 **Carina Sedan** all models '71 thru '74
- *2038 **Celica** Front Wheel Drive '86 thru '92
- 935 **Celica** Rear Wheel Drive '71 thru '85
- *1139 **Celica Supra** '79 thru '92
- 361 **Corolla** all models '75 thru '79
- 961 **Corolla** all models (rear wheel drive) '80 thru '87
- *1025 **Corolla** all models (front wheel drive) '84 thru '91
- *636 **Corolla Tercel** all models '80 thru '82
- 230 **Corona & MK II** all 4 cyl sohc models '69 thru '74
- 360 **Corona** all models '74 thru '82
- *532 **Cressida** all models '78 thru '82
- 313 **Land Cruiser** all models '68 thru '82
- 200 **MK II** all 6 cyl models '72 thru '76
- *1339 **MR2** all models '85 thru '87
- 304 **Pick-up** all models '69 thru '78
- *656 **Pick-up** all models '79 thru '92

TRIUMPH
- 112 **GT6 & Vitesse** all models '62 thru '74
- 113 **Spitfire** all models '62 thru '81
- 322 **TR7** all models '75 thru '81

VW
- 159 **Beetle & Karmann Ghia** all models '54 thru '79
- 238 **Dasher** all gasoline models '74 thru '81
- *884 **Rabbit, Jetta, Scirocco, & Pick-up** all gasoline models '74 thru '91 & **Convertible** '80 thru '91
- 451 **Rabbit, Jetta & Pick-up** all diesel models '77 thru '84
- 082 **Transporter 1600** all models '68 thru '79
- 226 **Transporter 1700, 1800 & 2000** all models '72 thru '79
- 084 **Type 3 1500 & 1600** all models '63 thru '73
- 1029 **Vanagon** all air-cooled models '80 thru '83

VOLVO
- 203 **120, 130 Series & 1800 Sports** '61 thru '73
- 129 **140 Series** all models '66 thru '74
- *270 **240 Series** all models '74 thru '90
- 400 **260 Series** all models '75 thru '82
- *1550 **740 & 760 Series** all models '82 thru '88

SPECIAL MANUALS
- 1479 **Automotive Body Repair & Painting Manual**
- 1654 **Automotive Electrical Manual**
- 1480 **Automotive Heating & Air Conditioning Manual**
- 1762 **Chevrolet Engine Overhaul Manual**
- 1736 **Diesel Engine Repair Manual**
- 1667 **Emission Control Manual**
- 1763 **Ford Engine Overhaul Manual**
- 482 **Fuel Injection Manual**
- 1666 **Small Engine Repair Manual**
- 299 **SU Carburetors** thru '88
- 393 **Weber Carburetors** thru '79
- 300 **Zenith/Stromberg CD Carburetors** thru '76

See your dealer for other available titles

---

* *Listings shown with an asterisk (*) indicate model coverage as of this printing. These titles will be periodically updated to include later model years – consult your Haynes dealer for more information.*

Over 100 Haynes motorcycle manuals also available

1-93

Haynes North America, Inc., 861 Lawrence Drive, Newbury Park, CA 91320 • (805) 498-6703